# The Rights of Roma in European Courts

# Endorsement Quotes

This essential volume shines a powerful new light on the potential—and limits—of litigation in achieving social change. With ground-breaking contributions on the decades-long struggle to combat Roma discrimination in the European courts, the book succeeds at two critical levels: offering an on-the-ground account of the strategic and doctrinal dimensions of Roma rights mobilization, while providing new theoretical insights on how courts shape movements for equality. In the end, it makes a compelling case that understanding how law treats the most marginalized among us holds profound lessons for the future of liberal democracy. It could not be more timely and urgent.

*Scott L Cummings, Robert Henigson Professor of Legal Ethics at the UCLA School of Law*

This book on Roma rights litigation is *necessary* not only for researchers, practitioners and human rights activists but also for all those who care about social justice. The various chapters eloquently highlight the most relevant example of systemic discrimination and socio-economic deprivation existing at the heart of Europe, and analyse in depth the role of transnational and domestic advocacy and the answers given by the European courts to the Roma's legal demands. The authors show how and why the strategic fight for the rights of the Roma populations, with its victories and shortcomings, is at the same time a fight for dismantling the 'European silence about race' and addressing extreme poverty, and social and political marginalization.

*Marzia Barbera, Emerita Professor of Labour Law and Antidiscrimination Law, University of Brescia*

Through comprehensive and fresh discussions on several issues regarding Roma rights and their defence, this volume reclaims judicial and semi-judicial mechanisms as essential avenues in the fight for Roma equality and inclusion. Interestingly, it also highlights how much Roma litigation has in the past decades itself advanced the evolution of several human rights standards. The volume offers a comprehensive snapshot of Roma rights in Europe, an explanation of different legal successes and challenges, and renewed faith in the law as a tool of materializing Roma rights. The Roma story is that of a persistently marginalized and discriminated group whose cultural distinctiveness is perceived as incompatible with the ways of life of the rest of the societies in which they live. Through an array of well-written, rigorously analysed and in-depth researched chapters, this volume proves that the celebration of cultural rights, namely Roma's rights to their way of life, can only be materialized if supported by the realization of other rights; and that such realization requires positive, continuing, and multi-layered action, also bringing the international to the local and regional level.

*Prof Alexandra Xanthaki, Professor of Law, Brunel Law School, Brunel University London*

This volume provides a new evaluation of Romani jurisprudence, pushing for a rethink of how critical Romani scholarship to date—particularly that by lawyers—has analysed and understood strategic litigation. It pushes the boundaries outwards of the scope of analysis and draws connections across the plane of Romani litigation that bring a fresh perspective. Neither wildly optimistic about the potential for human rights to address systemic discrimination and/or polarized societies, nor unduly pessimistic about the tools to hand, this is a sober account that suggests the possibility of other approaches, grounded in careful analysis of what has been achieved to date and the opportunities missed.

*Prof Morag Goodwin, Chair in Global Law and Development, Tilburg University*

# The Rights of Roma in European Courts

## *Strategic Litigation and the Boundaries of Human Rights*

*Edited by*

KRISTIN HENRARD AND LILLA FARKAS

OXFORD
UNIVERSITY PRESS

OXFORD
UNIVERSITY PRESS

Great Clarendon Street, Oxford, OX2 6DP,
United Kingdom

Oxford University Press is a department of the University of Oxford.
It furthers the University's objective of excellence in research, scholarship,
and education by publishing worldwide. Oxford is a registered trade mark of
Oxford University Press in the UK and in certain other countries.



Published in the United States of America by Oxford University Press
198 Madison Avenue, New York, NY 10016, United States of America.

British Library Cataloguing in Publication Data
Data available

Library of Congress Control Number: 2025931400

ISBN 978-0-19-891435-8

DOI: 10.1093/oso/9780198914358.001.0001

Printed and bound by
CPI Group (UK) Ltd., Croydon, CR0 4YY

MIX
Paper | Supporting
responsible forestry
FSC
www.fsc.org
FSC® C013604

The manufacturer's authorised representative in the EU for product safety is
Oxford University Press España S.A. of El Parque Empresarial San Fernando de Henares, Avenida de Castilla, 2 – 28830 Madrid (www.oup.es/en or
product.safety@oup.com). OUP España S.A. also acts as importer into Spain
of products made by the manufacturer.

# Foreword

For almost thirty years now, the question of how to advance the protection of human rights for Roma in Europe has become a question of major legal concern, but with no easy solution. Kristin Henrard and Lilla Farkas have brought together, in this book, a series of excellent studies revisiting the question of Roma rights protection in contemporary Europe. As announced in its title, this book contributes to three strands of the legal literature: to strategic litigation studies, to the study of the role of the European courts, and to the evolution of human rights law. The subject matter of all the chapters in the book is the protection of Roma rights in Europe, and all the chapters speak to at least one of the strands, while the vast majority speak to all three strands, albeit to different degrees.

Strategic litigation is the most consistently discussed theme in this book. The strategic litigation literature is now a central part of socio-legal studies in Europe, and no mean part of that literature has been built around the experience of international litigation for the advancement of Roma rights. Indeed, Roma rights cases before the European courts were almost invariably brought in the context of litigation strategies by domestic or transnational civil society organizations that were seeking to remedy structural disadvantages of the Romani population. Some chapters in this book revisit the general theory of strategic litigation in light of that long experience with Roma rights litigation, but we also find here very detailed studies of strategic litigation on specific high-profile cases, such as housing rights, the removal of Romani children from their families, and forcible sterilization of Romani women in Czechia and Slovakia. We get new insights not only on the emergence of strategic litigation but also on its impact on the ground once the European courts have spoken.

The role of those European courts is the second main theme of this book, with pride of place being taken by the activity of the European Court of Human Rights (ECtHR), including its dissenting judges, who form the object of a special chapter. As documented in various chapters, the ECtHR has occasionally been innovative and progressive, and on other occasions more cautious and deferential. The Court of Justice of the European Union has played a more modest role because, somewhat surprisingly, very few Roma rights cases have reached its docket. The book innovates by giving recognition to the role being played by a quasi-court, the European Committee of Social Rights, in advancing the formulation of social rights for Roma. That Committee is particularly welcoming for litigation brought by civil service organizations. Due attention is given to what happens after the European courts decide a case, since effective social change on the ground depends on what happens afterwards within the domestic legal systems. One chapter focuses on one new actor operating at the domestic level that can help to make the international human rights law a living reality, namely the equality body. The equality bodies in Central-Eastern European countries especially have been very actively engaged in trying to ensure Romani equality in all sorts of policy domains.

The third main theme is the way in which Roma rights litigation has actively influenced, over the years, scholarly thinking about human rights law. The most central human right, present in almost all cases discussed in this book, is the right to non-discrimination. The complex and deeply ingrained reality of anti-Roma discrimination has led, and is still leading, to the questioning and widening of traditional non-discrimination law, including in the reflection about the nature of systematic and intersectional discrimination that is present in several chapters of the book. But other human rights have also come to play major roles, not least among them the European Convention on Human Right's right to private and family life which, in its positive obligations mode, has become an additional source for the protection of the right to a home and to access water resources.

There is, therefore, so much food for thought in this book. It will be of interest, obviously, to all those who seek a comprehensive and up-to-date analysis of how Roma rights litigation has developed over the years at the European level, but the book will also appeal to scholars and students of human rights law, sociology of law and the role and impact of international courts. The stories told in this book offer many cautionary tales of how human rights achievements tend to be slow and tortuous, but they also feed the hope that justice can be achieved for those who continue to suffer poverty and discrimination in European societies.

Bruno De Witte
Professor Emeritus of European Law, Maastricht University

# Acknowledgements

We first of all want to express our gratitude towards our authors for their ongoing engagement and willingness to work with us, to fine tune the contours and the main development lines of this edited volume.

Secondly, we are most grateful to Robert Cavooris for his excellent guidance when we were developing our book proposal, and going through the various screening stages at Oxford University Press. A special mention should also go to Jacqueline Larabee for overseeing the production process of our book. Thirdly, we warmly appreciate the understanding of our colleagues at our respective institutions (Brussels School of Governance in Brussels, Belgium and ELTE University in Budapest, Hungary) during the numerous hours we spent working on this volume. Special thanks are also warranted to our student assistants for their help with the OSCOLA proofing of the respective chapters: Constantin Ritter (at the Brussels School of Governance, Brussels, Belgium) and Lapos Nóra and Ujvári Laura Olga (at ELTE University, Budapest, Hungary).

Kristin Henrard and Lilla Farkas

# Contents

## PART III STRATEGIC ROMA RIGHTS LITIGATION IN EUROPEAN COURTS



## PART IV SOCIO-LEGAL ANALYSIS OF STRATEGIC ROMA RIGHTS LITIGATION IN EUROPEAN COURTS

# Contributors

**Kristin Henrard**, Professor of International Law, Brussels School of Governance, Brussels, Belgium Migration, Diversity and Justice Research Centre Programme Director of the BA in International and European Law

**Lilla Farkas**, Associate Professor, ELTE Faculty of Social Science, Budapest, Hungary, Institute of Political and International Studies, Department of Human Rights and Politics

**Gwendolyn Albert**, Independent human rights activist, researcher and translator, journalist at Romea.cz, Czech Republic

**Serena D'Agostino**, Senior Researcher of Political Science at the Politics and Public Governance, University of Antwerp, Belgium, Senior Associate Researcher, Centre for Migration, Diversity and Justice, Brussels School of Governance, Brussels

**Dezideriu Gergely**, Doctoral candidate, University of Bucharest, Faculty of Political Science, Bucharest, Romania

**Kris Gledhill**, Professor of Law, Auckland University of Technology, Australia

**Aleksandra Gliszczyńska-Grabias**, Institute of Law Studies, Polish Academy of Sciences

**István Haller**, Lawyer, National Council Combating Discrimination, Romania

**Mária Herczog**, Chair and Programme Director, Family, Child, Youth Association, Budapest, Hungary

**Tamás Kádár**, Co-Director of Equinet, European Network of Equality Bodies, Brussels, Belgium

**Zsolt Körtvélyesi**, Maria Skłodowska-Curie postdoctoral fellow, Central European University, Vienna, Austria

**Tina Magazzini**, Senior Researcher, Department of Mobility and Migration, Institute of Ethnology, Czech Academy of Sciences

**Balázs Majtényi**, Head of the Department of Human Rights and Politics, UNESCO Chair in Human Rights and Peace, Eötvös Loránd University, Faculty of Social Sciences, Budapest, Hungary, Research Affiliate, CNR-ISGI, Rome

**Maroš Matiaško**, Human rights lawyer, Czech Republic

**Darren O'Donovan**, Senior Lecturer, La Trobe Law School, La Trobe University, Melbourne, Australia

**Helen O'Nions**, Vice-chair, Nottingham and Nottinghamshire Refugee Forum, Nottingham, UK

**Christopher M Roberts**, Associate Professor, Faculty of Law, The Chinese University of Hong Kong, Hong Kong, Centre for Comparative and Transnational Law

**Julija Sardelić**, Lecturer, Political Science and International Relations Programme, Victoria University of Wellington, Australia

**Anna Śledzińska-Simon**, Professor of Constitutional Law and Human Rights, Faculty of Law, Administration and Economics, University of Wrocław, Poland

**Eva-Esther Sobotka**, Head of sector, Fundamental Rights Agency of the European Union, Vienna, Austria

**Marek Szilvasi**, Manager for Climate Justice, Open Society Foundations, Bonn, Germany

**Peter Vermeersch**, Professor of Politics and Central and Eastern European studies, LINES, KU Leuven, Faculty of Social Sciences, Leuven, Belgium

# 1
# An Introduction

*Kristin Henrard and Lilla Farkas*

## 1. Introduction

Following an account of the overarching aim of, the methodologies used in, and the three-part structure of this edited volume, the respective chapters are briefly introduced, flagging each chapter's main contributions.

### 1.1. Overarching aim and frame

This edited volume aims to critically analyse Roma rights cases before European courts, exploring the extent to which strategic litigation can and does push the boundaries of human rights. In the process, the volume adopts a long-needed yet hitherto untested approach that situates Roma rights within the human rights edifice and identifies its key contributions.

Starting from a reflection on the notion of *human rights*, its counter-majoritarian core and the related special relevance of minorities' fundamental rights, the concept of 'boundaries of human rights', and the potential role of strategic litigation in pushing these boundaries, is explored in a context of systemic discrimination. Strategic litigation as a phenomenon confirms the dynamic nature of human rights and the crucial importance of interpretation, not only by national courts, but also ultimately by international courts. This type of litigation seeks to influence the way in which (international) courts take up their role, more particularly the interpretations that they develop, and the discretion they leave to states. In this respect the notions of 'boundaries of human rights' and of pushing or revealing these boundaries will be introduced and explained.

The Roma and their fundamental rights constitute a most appropriate case study since, as a particularly disadvantaged and vulnerable minority, the Roma have a history of sustained, systemic discrimination and relatedly of multiple human rights violations, which in turn have triggered robust strategic litigation before (international) courts.

While human rights are rights for every human being, at the same time, in line with their counter-majoritarian core, they are particularly important for persons

Kristin Henrard and Lilla Farkas, *An Introduction* In: *The Rights of Roma in European Courts*. Edited by: Kristin Henrard and Lilla Farkas, Oxford University Press. 
DOI: 10.1093/oso/9780198914358.003.0001

belonging to minorities. The way society treats its most vulnerable minorities is a litmus test of its true commitment to human rights. Indeed, persons belonging to minorities are often victims of discrimination; this tends to be systemic in nature, the underlying prejudice ingrained in societal structures and compounded by a host of other human rights violations, entailing a heightened vulnerability. The concept of 'minority rights' then refers to fundamental rights of minorities, encompassing not only general human rights but also minority-specific rights. 'Roma rights' similarly refer to all fundamental rights of Roma.

The systemic discrimination of Roma is visible in the multiple accounts of violations of various civil rights, socio-economic rights, and minority-specific rights. Civil rights violations result (inter alia) from (sometimes deadly) police violence, pogroms, hate speech, forced sterilizations, and forced removal of Roma children from their families. Various problems in terms of evictions, lack of equal access to education, and health care move from civil rights to more squarely social rights. The ensuing abundance of Roma rights cases before (international and) European courts and monitoring bodies demonstrates not only this minority's systemic disadvantage, but also its resilience and resolve to push the boundaries of human rights law, through strategic litigation.

The focus in this volume on strategic litigation before European courts, and its potential, goes hand in hand with a broad definition of courts to include supervisory bodies that do not generate legally binding judgments. At the same time, the focus on 'litigation' entails a focus on the outcome of complaints procedures. As will become clear in the subsequent overview of the respective chapters in this volume, the main focus is on the (quasi-)jurisprudence of three international courts situated in Europe, namely the European Court of Human Rights (ECtHR), the Court of Justice of the EU (CJEU), and the European Committee of Social Rights (ECSR). Some chapters also consider the supervisory practice of national courts and equality bodies of European states, and several chapters draw parallels with jurisdictions beyond Europe as well.

As is elaborated upon in the chapter by Gledhill (Chapter 4), *strategic litigation* may lack a generally accepted definition: in its baseline understanding it concerns conscious litigation seeking to achieve long-term and broader or systemic impact, looking beyond the interests of the individual applicant. Put differently, strategic litigation aims to obtain a change in the prevailing interpretation, in favour of victims of human rights violations.

Strategic litigation also confirms the dynamic nature of human rights, and the crucial importance of interpretation of human rights, and possible developments of the way in which international courts interpret these rights. Legal standards tend to use general terms, and the exact meaning and scope of rights and related state obligations is clarified through interpretation and application of these standards, ultimately by international courts. Strategic litigation before international courts aims to persuade courts to take up their role to co-determine international law and develop the interpretation in a way that enhances the effective protection of rights, while leaving no broad discretion to states.

The vulnerable position of Roma, and the ensuing multiplicity of human rights obligations they suffer, have resulted in a high number of cases before international courts. These cases, and their crucial nexus with (systemic) discrimination, provide these courts the opportunity to develop their jurisprudence and shift the boundaries not only of Roma rights but also of human rights in general.

The *boundaries of human rights* are determined, inter alia, by the scope of application of these rights, and the extent of the related negative and positive state obligations. For example, the question of whether living in a caravan is protected by the right to respect for privacy, family life, and home concerns the scope of application of the right. Limits on evictions would concern negative state obligations, while obligations to provide a certain number of well-serviced caravan sites concern the reach of states' positive state obligations.

As most fundamental rights are not absolute, and positive state obligations are never absolute, international courts have to apply the proportionality principle. When balancing the interests of the individual that their rights are respected with other public interests furthered by the state, international courts tend to give a certain discretion to states. An effective protection of fundamental rights is difficult to square with a broad discretion or margin of appreciation, since this would imply that the international court adopts a low level of scrutiny. Several chapters in this book analyse the extent to which international courts grant states discretion, and the underlying rationales at play, and thus contribute to that body of literature as well. Recurring factors are the European consensus (or lack thereof), and the extensive vulnerability of Roma, but a multifaceted picture emerges, with certain areas where the discretion is narrow, others a lot broader.

Another factor that is very important for the effective protection of fundamental rights is the *burden of proof*, its standard, and the allocation of the burden of proof between the parties. Given the known difficulties for victims to obtain proof of discrimination, a special allocation of the burden of proof, reducing the burden of the victim, has been devised. As is elaborated upon in one chapter in this volume (and visible in several others), unfortunately, this special allocation of the burden of proof is not yet fully taken up by international courts, and considerable uncertainty remains about its operation, particularly in cases set in a context of systemic discrimination. Cases concerning Roma have played a crucial role in the development of the relevant principles and are likely to continue to play a role in the related pushing of the boundaries of human rights.

Notwithstanding the focus of this volume on strategic litigation before European courts, some chapters have regard to trends that are visible in supervisory practice in the broader sense, namely also including the review of periodic state reporting, or even the supervisory practice of institutions that are not officially monitoring compliance with a particular rights instrument. Examples of the former would be the Advisory Committee (AC)'s country reviews under the Framework Convention for the Protection of National Minorities. The AC has various lines of interpretation concerning Roma, also discussing their systemic discrimination and ensuing vulnerability. It remains useful to discuss and compare these lines of interpretation with the jurisprudence of icourts, including the extent to which the AC's practice influences the jurisprudence of European courts. Similarly, some chapters have regard to thematic recommendations of the Organization for Security and Co-operation in Europe's High Commissioner on National Minorities, who has commissioned these recommendations from experts and uses them in practice. Also in this case, the focus is on the extent to which this can/could be used in complaints procedures by icourts, and what it could mean for strategic litigation. In some chapters there is even attention for a possible compliance pull on states of some of the Sustainable Development Goals, namely those on equality within states (SDG 10) and inclusive societies (SDG 16).

As already highlighted, strategic litigation often sets out to push the boundaries of human rights, particularly in relation to groups that suffer systemic discrimination, such as the Roma. However, this 'pushing' is not always successful. Various chapters in this book demonstrate that the jurisprudence of certain international courts rather reveals boundaries that these courts themselves erect because of legitimacy concerns, in the sense of concerns that the (contracting) states will not accept their findings. This is particularly visible in narrow interpretations of the scope of application of rights and the grant of a broad discretion for states. The European court where most 'revealing of boundaries' has been noted is the ECtHR: its traditional reluctance to establish discrimination, and the related preference to establish a procedural violation instead of a substantive violation, and the ongoing struggles in relation to the burden of proof, to mention just a few. At the same time it should be acknowledged that there are remarkable differences between policy fields in the Roma rights jurisprudence.[1] Fortunately, the baselines of the ECSR and the CJEU are more positive, resulting in different levels of engagement and a greater willingness to extend the boundaries of human rights. Nevertheless, also in relation to the latter European courts, there is room for improvement. Put differently, the specific characteristics and plight of the Roma invite further refinements of the human rights paradigm.

The case study of Roma rights also demonstrates that aiming for the effective protection of fundamental rights of a minority suffering systemic discrimination requires extending one's focus beyond the jurisprudence of international courts. On the one hand, the current era of global governance invites attention to the

[1] Compare Chapter 9 on education and Chapters 10 and 17 on housing in this edited volume.

role of international organizations and their attempts to influence policies, laws, and practice of their member states. On the other hand, the actual impact on the ground of promising decisions of international courts depends on domestic enforcement, involving not only national authorities, national courts, and equality bodies, but also sub-state authorities and administration. Hence, several chapters turn the attention to effective implementation and changes on the ground at the national and sub-national level.

## 1.2. Methodologies and structure

The challenging aims of this edited volume require the combination of various methodologies, thus going beyond legal doctrinal methods, and also including socio-legal and multidisciplinary legal methods. The latter acknowledges the relevance of other disciplines to assist filling in the legal framework, for example to determine what is reasonable, what is proportionate etc. As will become clear in the description below of the four parts of this edited volume, the use of these methodologies in the respective parts varies.

Throughout, there is extensive attention to case law or jurisprudence. Whereas the focus is on European courts, several chapters draw parallels with jurisdictions beyond Europe. The European courts covered here are mostly regional European courts, namely the ECtHR, the CJEU, and the ECSR. Some chapters also consider the jurisprudence of national courts and equality bodies in European countries.

The chapters are organized into four parts. The chapters in Part I are both descriptive and analytical, mapping the context of Roma rights in terms of the political commitment of nation-states to tackle systemic discrimination, as well as the role of international policy processes and strategic litigation in ensuring compliance. Vermeersch describes various understandings of the plight of Roma in Europe and describes the ways in which the Roma ethno-political movement taps into the human rights paradigm when framing claims about Roma rights violations in Europe. Majtényi highlights synergies and divergences across the various European international organizations that have developed policies and/or institutions to tackle the systemic disadvantages confronting Roma. In the end, both chapters underscore that Roma continue to suffer from systemic discrimination, notwithstanding the multiple initiatives adopted at European level, and the ensuing national action plans.

Part II sets out the legal building blocks for the analysis in Parts III and IV, while engaging with conceptual and legal doctrinal analysis. Gledhill introduces the notion of strategic litigation with specific attention for the way this has developed before the European Court of Human Rights. Henrard outlines in Chapter 5 the possibilities and constraints of international courts to extend the boundaries of human rights through their interpretation and adjudication. In Chapter 6 Henrard elaborates on the parallels and differences about the way in which European courts engage with the notion of systemic discrimination. Henrard and Roberts proceed with a discussion of the crucial importance of the burden of proof and more particularly the special allocation of the burden of proof, while comparing the practices of several European courts.

Each of the chapters in Part III zooms in on a particular recurring rights claim concerning Roma, set in a context of systemic racial discrimination, and discusses the relevant case law of a range of European courts, while highlighting the extent to which 'boundaries' of human rights are thus exposed and/or 'pushed'. Gliszczyńska-Grabias and Śledzińska-Simon critically analyse the anti-Roma hate speech cases before the ECtHR. Gergely outlines the limits and opportunities of litigation aiming at desegregated education for Roma children. O'Nions provides a comparative analysis of the case law of several European courts concerning the right to a home. Herczog and Körtvélyesi bring to the forefront a less well known practice of systemic discrimination against Roma, more particularly concerning the forced removal of children. D'Agostino and Magazzini turn to the problem of Roma women's forced sterilization, while inviting international courts to adopt an intersectional approach, acknowledging intersectional discrimination.

The chapters in Part IV provide a socio-legal take on issues discussed in Part III, assessing the major strands of Roma rights litigation, intersectional discrimination and Romani women's rights concerning forced sterilization, the right to housing and other social rights. These chapters explore the outcomes and impact of Roma rights litigation from the perspective of jurisprudence, policy, and actual social change, and highlight the role of non-governmental organizations that advocate and litigate strategically to push the boundaries of Roma rights. Farkas' chapter zooms in on factors that enable the emergence of Roma rights jurisprudence, such as the presence of a transnational advocacy network that facilitates cross-border borrowing of litigation strategies and legal framings of Roma rights claims.

Kadar and Haller catalogue the potential and actual activities of equality bodies in relation to Roma rights, and offer an in-depth case study of the Romanian equality body. Sardelić brings a relatively new approach to the socio-legal analysis of international courts, when she delves into a systematic assessment of dissenting opinions in the ECtHR's Roma rights rulings. Albert, Sobotka, and Farkas provide a detailed story line of NGO advocacy and strategic litigation on forced sterilizations, while demonstrating the interconnections between domestic, international, and European human rights advocacy and litigation. O'Donovan's case study of the Irish traveller movement highlights the advocacy and strategic litigation cycles in the fight for culture-specific housing, going back and forth between domestic and European levels. Finally, Matiaško and Szilvasi recount the activities of NGOs and activists in advocating and litigating the right to water, as related to housing.

## 1.3. The chapters

Part I of the edited volume sets the scene, by providing clear insights in the context of Roma rights, between politics and the law. Peter Vermeersch starts the discussion by an examination of the role of strategic litigation in the struggle for justice and human rights for the Roma in Europe. His chapter explores the historical context as well as the motivations, benefits, and challenges of using such legal action as a tool for social change in a context of systemic discrimination, and how strategic litigation interacts with the political, policy, and discursive environments that shape the Roma's predicament. It also aims to foster a dialogue between legal experts and Romani studies scholars by bringing the existing literature on strategic litigation for human rights into conversation with the literature on Roma.

In Chapter 3, Balázs Majtényi critically reflects on the attempts by three European international organizations to devise policies and strategies, more particularly to safeguard Roma rights. When a minority such as the Roma has no nation-state and is a victim of historical oppression, there is a greater need for international organizations to provide them with special protection, while naming and shaming the different forms of oppression. Majtényi points out that the Council of Europe, the Organization for Security and Co-operation in Europe, and the European Union have been involved over the past three decades in reporting on Roma rights violations, calling on states to address these violations, adopting comprehensive strategies to facilitate social change, and setting general standards for member states. Majtényi explores potential overlaps, gaps, synergies, and knowledge-sharing and cooperation, as well as the problems that may arise from their fragmentation and diverse toolkits.

Part II lays out the conceptual and legal frame that will be drawn upon in the subsequent parts of the edited volume. In Chapter 4 on 'The European Court of Human Rights and Strategic Litigation to Support Roma Peoples' Kris Gledhill outlines existing efforts to provide a working definition of 'strategic litigation', a phrase much used but without a commonly accepted meaning. He adds to these efforts by reviewing the use of 'strategic litigation' in the Roma rights context, namely by assessing the consistency of its use in this context with its more general use, but also by delving more deeply into various themes that go beyond the definitional. These include discussions of the risks of strategic litigation, and of special features that arise when it is used to advance the rights of Roma to non-discrimination in various contexts, most importantly accompanying strategies to deal with risks arising in litigation and to secure impact.

Kristin Henrard proceeds in Chapter 5 with a discussion of the critical role of international courts in the construction of international human rights law, through their interpretation of the human rights standards. This chapter considers not only the possibilities but also the constraints of European (regional) courts to push the boundaries of human rights through their interpretation and adjudication. The constraints become visible when international courts grant states a (generous) discretion in the proportionality analysis to manage their legitimacy concerns. The analysis of a range of landmark cases reveals roughly three trajectories. Some judgments combine very progressive statements of principles, with weak protection, hiding behind a broad discretion for states. Other judgments denote a gradual pushing of the boundaries of human rights in favour of minorities, while still others reveal 'frozen constraints' that seem to resist attempts to push the boundaries. The chapter concludes with a call for regional European courts to choose to optimize an effective enjoyment of human rights, also for persons belonging to minorities, by pushing the boundaries of human rights, at least gradually.

In Chapter 6, Henrard zooms in on the extent to which international courts address the critical problem for Roma of systemic discrimination, the context for numerous human rights violations that they face. Her chapter compares and contrasts the jurisprudence of the ECSR, the CJEU and the ECtHR, with regard to a) the extent to which they acknowledge the context of systemic discrimination, and b) the way in which this is reflected in the analysis of particular cases, including the level of scrutiny adopted, the allocation of the burden of proof, and the quantification of the damage, as related to the remedies and the range of positive state obligations that are identified. The comparative analysis demonstrates that when international courts are sufficiently probing, have regard to systemic discrimination and its related features, including possible hidden discrimination as well as knock-on effects of discrimination in one societal field for other fields, these courts are more likely to establish prima facie cases of discrimination (shifting the burden of proof) and properly quantify disadvantage, leading to the identification of appropriate positive state obligations. Cases concerning Roma and their fundamental rights thus invite international courts to factor in systemic discrimination, so as to provide more effective protection against discrimination and push the boundaries of human rights.

The last chapter of Part II focuses on a matter of vital importance when bringing a case to court, and that is the allocation of the burden of proof. In view of the difficulties for victims to produce sufficient proof of discrimination, a special allocation of the burden of proof has been devised, following which victims can suffice by proving facts that enable a court to establish a prima facie case of discrimination, after which the burden of proof shifts to the defendant. While several courts explicitly utilize the notions of prima facie case and rebuttal, there still is considerable uncertainty concerning the precise meaning and parameters of both.

Kristin Henrard and Christopher M Roberts analyse relevant case law of the ECtHR and the ECSR to explore to what extent a broader context of systemic discrimination, typical for Roma, has implications for the establishment of a prima facie case and its rebuttal. Notwithstanding differences in their complaints procedures (individual versus collective) and in their overall willingness to engage with discrimination complaints, striking similarities emerge in terms of both bodies' lack of explicit standards to operationalize the burden of proof and their greater reticence to establish a prima facie case of direct discrimination as opposed to indirect discrimination. The chapter concludes with recommendations for both icourts to develop clearer and more elaborate criteria in relation to the burden of proof, thus pushing the boundaries of human rights.

The chapters of Part III proceed with the analysis of various instances of strategic Roma rights litigation in European courts.

In Chapter 8, Gliszczyńska-Grabias and Śledzińska-Simon examine the approach of the ECtHR to hate speech and hate crimes against Roma. The chapter revisits the concept of vulnerability as a means to tackle structural inequality and broaden states' positive obligations. However, it is demonstrated that the application of this concept in Roma-related cases remains problematic. Specifically, the authors critically discuss how the ECtHR evaluates the hate speech component in anti-Roma cases, and determines victim status in cases of group-directed hate speech, while often overlooking Holocaust remembrance. Ultimately, the chapter questions whether the vulnerability framework effectively strengthens human rights protection in the case of Roma. It argues that the Court's inconsistent use of this concept may actually reflect underlying societal biases and limit the transformative potential of the human rights paradigm.

Dezideriu Gergely's chapter on the one hand takes stock of the desegregation litigation before the ECtHR, which has led to the standard-setting recognition of various forms of school segregation of Roma children as instances of racial discrimination and related positive state obligations to end school segregation, and on the other highlights the importance of the jurisprudence of national courts and equality bodies to the successful curbing of school segregation of Roma pupils. First, the chapter explores how the concept of racial segregation in international human rights law has been reflected in the Council of Europe acquis and jurisprudence at European level. Secondly, it analyses the way in which the ECtHR has progressively formulated more specific obligations for states, including instructions for the implementation of school segregation judgments. Third, it shows how the human rights paradigm developed by the ECtHR has been followed and implemented by national supreme courts through judicial review. Supreme courts and equality bodies have issued specific instructions based on the positive obligation paradigm established by the Strasbourg Court.

Helen O'Nions contrasts certain promising pronouncements of the Strasbourg Court, following which European states would have a positive obligation to 'facilitate the Gypsy way of life' and also to 'secure shelter to particularly vulnerable individuals' in exceptional cases, with the Court's grant of a wide margin of appreciation to states in areas of general policy. She notes that the space for Roma and Gypsy-Travellers to live securely and in accordance with their culture is shrinking across Europe. The right to enjoy a home and family life is undermined by planning restrictions, spatial segregation, forced eviction, and exposure to various hazards, significantly impacting on their dignity and undermining access to public amenities, health, and education. O'Nions' chapter compares case law before the ECtHR with the collective complaint mechanism of the European Social Charter, examining the opportunity for civil society to influence judgments and assist the Committee of Ministers with their supervision. Although the barriers to effective rights articulation and realization before the respective institutions are different, they are strikingly similar to those facing Roma, Gypsy, and traveller communities on a daily basis across Europe, namely a failure to appreciate and engage with the discriminatory nexus and a passive approach to enforcement that allows rights violations to continue without sanction.

In Chapter 11 Mária Herczog and Zsolt Körtvélyesi ponder ways of 'Addressing Discrimination in Removal of Romani Children from their Families'. Their starting point is that minority children are overrepresented in the alternative care of all developed countries, and this worrying trend also applies to Romani children in Europe. There is a virtual consensus on the need to systematically counter the ensuing human rights violations, but adequate action has not been taken and the history of pervasive discrimination, compounded by the detrimental outcome of the involvement of the authorities, raise concerns. The chapter first explores the debate on disproportionality and statistical data in the United States. It then presents the international human rights and equality standards, highlighting that in Europe anti-discrimination law covers socio-economic conditions and states have positive obligations to remedy structural discrimination as well. The chapter then assesses the case law of the ECtHR and analyses a Hungarian case to show how strategic litigation can address 'structural' removal of children from Roma families. Standing rules including representative standing, and the availability and proper analysis of statistics, unlock the law's potential to capture more complex forms of violations. The authors conclude that strategic litigation is particularly well-equipped to uncover the facts, identify the wrongdoing and engender effective remedies against the disproportionate removal of Romani children.

In Chapter 12 Serena D'Agostino and Tina Magazzini explore 'Pushing Human Rights Boundaries: Intersectional Discrimination and Reproductive (In)Justice for Romani Women'. The authors discuss the concept of intersectional discrimination and its potential for pushing the boundaries of human rights. They analyse reproductive injustice faced by Romani women, with a particular focus on involuntary sterilization procedures in Czechia and Slovakia. Despite the attempts of strategic litigation at pushing the current boundaries constructed by the jurisprudence, the failure of courts to recognize involuntary sterilization amounts to a structural intersectional discrimination practice which is highly problematic. This lack of recognition validates and reinforces traditional systems of subordination, infantilization and marginalization of Romani women, rooted in widespread and legitimized anti-Roma racism. The authors recommend that courts and policymakers adopt an intersectional approach to reverse this trend, push the boundaries of human rights and promote equality and social justice.

Part IV encompasses various chapters providing socio-legal analysis of strategic Roma rights litigation in European courts.

Lilla Farkas' chapter looks at factors that enable the emergence of Roma rights jurisprudence, such as the presence of a transnational advocacy network that facilitates cross-border borrowing of litigation strategies and legal framings of Roma rights claims. In the broader context of legal mobilization, Farkas assesses strategic litigation on Roma rights from its inception in the late 1990s and evaluates both the classic and critical scholarship pertaining to the subject. Taking a socio-legal approach, the chapter offers a fresh take on who does what and how, paying particular attention to master frames and legal framing innovations. It also reviews debates about a particular point of tension, namely the ethical concerns surrounding the legitimacy of international and non-Roma actors. The chapter draws a positive conclusion about the efficiency of litigation on Roma rights that uses international human rights law to overcome structural impediments at the national level.

In Chapter 14 Tamás Kádár and István Haller catalogue 'The contribution of equality bodies to countering discrimination against Roma in the EU'. They observe that the EU has created a strong, albeit not comprehensive, legal framework against discrimination, with the strongest protections against racial and ethnic discrimination, including for Roma. In parallel, equality bodies were created in all EU Member States (and beyond), to ensure the correct application and enforcement of this legislation and to increase access to justice. The authors study how this legal and institutional framework evolved, and the potential and practice of equality bodies to help prevent and tackle anti-Roma discrimination. The chapter provides a case study of the work of the Romanian equality body. It concludes by identifying some of the key obstacles to effective work by equality bodies and potential responses to these.

In Chapter 15 Julija Sardelić asks whether judges can be 'Pushing the boundaries of human rights through dissent: An analysis of ECtHR dissenting opinions on the rights of Romani minorities'. She offers a systematic socio-legal review of dissenting opinions in the ECtHR's Roma rights cases. She investigates how dissenting judges push the boundaries of human rights, especially where the ECtHR itself has been reluctant to take systemic racism as an underlying foundation for human rights violations against Romani minorities. Sardelić discusses how dissents challenge the boundaries of human rights, inter alia by highlighting the failure to take sufficiently into account how widespread structural racial discrimination is against the Roma, the broader scope of application of particular rights, and the need to reduce the state's margin of appreciation and expand positive state obligations. She concludes that dissents express strong criticism of the ECtHR's failure to acknowledge structural racial discrimination as a backbone of human rights violations against Roma and Travellers.

Gwendolyn Albert, Eva-Esther Sobotka, and Lilla Farkas discuss 'Seeking justice for forcibly sterilized Romani women in Czechia and Slovakia' as an example of a difficult and lengthy road to justice. They focus on the agency of Roma women in human rights field research and advocacy at the national and international levels and assess the advocacy impact of strategic litigation before the ECtHR and Czech as well as Slovak courts. They track differences in Czech and Slovak responses to forced sterilization claims and note that while the human rights paradigm has been indispensable, the direct causality between human rights litigation/advocacy and eventual policy changes is not straightforward, especially in the light of the time it has taken to remedy forced sterilization. Importantly, a notable failure by the ECtHR and national courts has been to recognize the discriminatory treatment of Romani women on racial and/or intersectional grounds.

Darren O'Donovan studies 'Strategic Litigation and Roma Housing Rights in Europe: The Complexities of Unlocking Change'. He provides a critical analysis of the dynamics which have shaped recent strategic litigation on behalf of the Roma facing inadequate housing conditions in Europe. He asks to what extent can strategic litigation catalyse change for those vulnerable to forced evictions, unfair social housing allocation, or lacking basic infrastructure and services? On the one hand, the ECSR and the United Nations human rights treaty bodies have provided persistent findings of rights violation and underscored the need for greater compliance. On the other, the ECtHR has struggled to address the violations of the right to housing and related discrimination. The absence of enforceable housing rights reflects a narrow civil and political rights paradigm which has failed to commit to achieving de facto equality. In the absence of such reform, communities will need to target litigation which reshapes relationships on the ground. O'Donovan also considers how future strategic litigation can be designed in a way that prompts greater domestic mobilization towards change.

Again from a bottom-up perspective, Matiaško and Szilvasi recount the activities of NGOs and activists in advocating and litigating for the right to drinking water. Their chapter examines one of the major manifestations of Roma rights and the right to water, namely the *Hudorovič and Others v Slovenia* case. The Roma from two neighbourhoods filed the first complaint to the ECtHR on the right to water, alleging ethnic discrimination. The Court unfortunately rejected the applicants' claims, despite recognizing their vulnerability, because it failed to take into account the inequities historically developed along racialized and ethnic lines through the uneven distribution of environmental burdens and benefits. Due to the problematic application of vulnerability, the outcome of strategic litigation in this particular case contributes to the reification of systemic discrimination against Roma, thus revealing the boundaries of human rights. To avoid it in the future, a possible reconceptualization of vulnerability is proposed, while inviting lawyers and civil society to bring new strategic cases to the Court or intervene as third parties relying on this redefined concept of vulnerability.

# PART I

# THE CONTEXT: ROMA RIGHTS BETWEEN POLITICS AND THE LAW

# 2

# Beyond the Courtroom

## Reflections on the Role of Strategic Litigation in the Broader Struggle for Justice and Human Rights for the Roma in Europe

*Peter Vermeersch*

## 1. Introduction

The plight of the Romani population in Europe has been an enduring concern that has drawn attention from researchers, activists, and legal experts alike. Over the years, the interlocking problems facing many members of this population have been extensively documented.[1] An overall picture of systemic discrimination resulting in severe socio-economic deprivation emerges, for example, from the latest report by the EU's Fundamental Rights Agency (FRA).[2] While anti-discrimination measures have been introduced, and campaigns to raise awareness have been tried, none of the countries surveyed by the FRA in recent years has met the EU target for reducing discrimination, and while discrimination in those countries has been clearly experienced as a problem by Roma, the level of reporting of cases of discrimination by Roma has remained low. Only 5 per cent of Romani victims of discrimination reported or complained about such incidents, the FRA concluded, showing that trust in institutions such as the police and legal systems has remained low among Roma compared to the general population.

[1] See eg Huub van Baar and Angéla Kóczé (eds), *The Roma and Their Struggle for Identity in Contemporary Europe* (Berghahn Books 2020); Jacqueline Bhabha, Andrzej Mirga, and Margareta Matache (eds), *Realizing Roma Rights* (University of Pennsylvania Press 2017); Anna Kende and others, 'The Last Acceptable Prejudice in Europe? Anti-Gypsyism as the Obstacle to Roma Inclusion' (2021) 24 Group Processes & Intergroup Relations 388; Ryan Powell and John Lever, 'Europe's Perennial "Outsiders": A Processual Approach to Roma Stigmatization and Ghettoization' (2017) 65 Current Sociology 680; Violetta Zentai, 'National Roma Inclusion Policies in Central and Eastern Europe: Diverging Learning Paths with Residual Outcomes' in A Batory, A Cartwright, and D Stone (eds), *Policy Experiments, Failures and Innovations: Beyond Accession in Central and Eastern Europe* (Edward Elgar 2018) 88.

[2] On page 5 the report says: 'The results of FRA's surveys in 2008, 2011, 2016 and 2019 show that the EU's and Member States' efforts result in limited and uneven progress. The surveys show the persisting impact of antigypsyism and the problems many Roma and Travellers face in enjoying their fundamental rights regarding employment, education, healthcare and housing.' European Union Agency for Fundamental Rights (FRA), *Roma in 10 European Countries. Main Results* (Publications Office of the European Union 2023).

Peter Vermeersch, *Beyond the Courtroom* In: *The Rights of Roma in European Courts*. Edited by: Kristin Henrard and Lilla Farkas, Oxford University Press. © Peter Vermeersch 2025.
DOI: 10.1093/oso/9780198914358.003.0002

Academic research focusing on the plight of the Roma has predominantly embraced a diagnostic approach, delving into the underlying causes of these challenges, relating them to, among others, failures of domestic and European policies.[3] There is also quite some work on developments in activism on Roma-related topics, scrutinizing its impact on socio-economic developments on the ground.[4] There exists only a relatively modest body of work, however, devoted to examining legal interventions aimed at alleviating the plight of the Roma.[5] This is a significant gap in the literature, since many of the fundamental problems that contribute to the overall systemic discrimination of Roma—such as lack of effective protection against violence, lack of political representation, lack of access to institution, the tenacity of socio-economic inequality, and so forth—could be, and have been, challenged by legal action. Moreover, many activists have indeed turned to courts, first national and later international, to advance the cause of the Roma, and several scholars have also advocated such an approach, as a way to seek redress for human rights violations against individual citizens and as a mechanism to instigate broader social, legal, and policy change. In other words, strategic litigation—which can be defined as legal action with the explicit intent of creating or facilitating a change that goes beyond the interest of the individual case[6]—has emerged as a pivotal facet within the 'Romani movement'.

The phenomenon of resorting to legal action and litigation to create societal change is, of course, not unique to Romani activism. It has been observed across diverse domains, including human rights protection more broadly, environmental protection, social rights, and gender equality. As Anagnostou has noted, courts are now often 'arenas where some of the most sharply contested societal issues today, concerning sexuality, migration, ethnic diversity and social integration, are debated and fought'.[7] Often strategic litigation complements other forms movement

[3] For example Huub van Baar, 'Europe's Romaphobia: Problematization, Securitization, Nomadization' (2011) 29(2) Environment and Planning D: Society & Space 203; Aidan McGarry, *Romaphobia: The Last Acceptable Form of Racism* (Bloomsbury Publishing 2017); Marton Rövid, 'One-size-fits-all Roma? On the normative dilemmas of the emerging European Roma policy' (2011) 21(1) Romani Studies 1.

[4] See Peter Vermeersch, *The Romani Movement: Minority Politics and Ethnic Mobilization in Contemporary Central Europe* (Berghahn Books 2006); Aidan McGarry, *Who Speaks for Roma? Political Representation of a Transnational Minority Community* (Continuum 2010).

[5] Some examples are Alphia Abdikeeva, Tamar Ezer, and Alina Covaci, 'Assessing Legal Advocacy to Advance Roma Health in Macedonia, Romania, and Serbia' (2013) 20 European Journal of Health Law 471; Tamar Ezer, Alphia Abdikeeva, and Martin McKee, 'Legal Advocacy as a Tool to Advance Roma Health' (2018) 13 Health Economics, Policy, and Law 92; James A Goldston and Mirna Adjami, 'The Opportunities and Challenges of Using Public Interest Litigation to Secure Access to Justice for Roma in Central and Eastern Europe' [2009] Marginalized Communities and Access to Justice 205; James A Golston, 'The Struggle for Roma Rights: Arguments That Have Worked' (2010) 32 Human Rights Quarterly 311; Dimitrina Petrova, 'Political and Legal Obstacles to the Development of Public Interest Law' (1996) 5 East European Constitutional Review 62.

[6] For a reflection on how to conceptualize strategic litigation, see Kris van der Pas, 'Conceptualising Strategic Litigation' (2021) 11 Oñati Socio-Legal Series 145.

[7] Dana Anagnostou, 'Law and Rights' Claiming on behalf of Minorities in the Multi-level European System' in Dana Anagnostou (ed), *Rights and Courts in Pursuit of Social Change: Legal Mobilisation in the Multi-Level European System* (Bloomsbury Publishing 2014) 2.

activity, such as public protests, strikes, and political mobilization within or outside the available channels of democratic participation and representation. In the case of the Roma, as with other minorities, the political opportunities for creating an effective movement within the usual channels of democratic participation and representation have turned out to be limited.[8] Because of systemic discrimination, Roma often face exclusion from these very channels, a problem which in turn also thwarts the emergence of their full engagement in politics and protest activities. Because protest activities have been so limited, or have had limited effect,[9] and more adequate political representation of Roma has been difficult to achieve, many Romani activists as well as those working on behalf of Roma have seen courts as important places to kick-start not only the legal but also broader policy reforms necessary to remedy structural disadvantage.

When it comes to strategic litigation for and on behalf of minority populations, questions need to be asked not only about the impact of legal action on those seeking redress, but also about the socio-political context relevant to the minority in question. What changes beyond the individual case does legal action hope to bring about, and what changes have already been achieved? If the legal route can indeed be a catalyst for policy change and social reform, it would be useful to see what empirical evidence there is to support this argument. It is also worth asking what the impact of legal action is on the broader societal and political context of minority/majority relations. For example, how do majorities view the claims of minorities following litigation initiated by or on behalf of those minorities? The answers must be nuanced. Particularly in the complicated and multifaceted case of the Roma, there is a need to examine more carefully how strategic litigation impacts on a range of dimensions related to the legal, socio-economic, and policy aspects of their struggle for justice and inclusion.

This work, however, does not have to start from scratch. There is already a wider debate about strategic human rights litigation as a means of securing the rights of minority populations facing socio-economic inequality or racism.[10] The discussion there revolves around the different perspectives on the effectiveness of strategic litigation, which seems to have several positive outcomes, certainly in cases of legal victories, but there are also potential drawbacks, such as the individualization

[8] For a broader discussion on this topic, see Huub van Baar and Peter Vermeersch, 'The Limits of Operational Representations: Ways of Seeing Roma beyond the Recognition-redistribution Paradigm' (2017) 3(4) East European Journal of Society and Politics 120.

[9] For a discussion on this topic, see Peter Vermeersch, 'The Romani Perspective: Experiences and Acts of Citizenship across Europe' in Engin Isin and Peter Nyers (eds), *The Routledge Handbook of Global Citizenship Studies* (Routledge 2014) 477–86.

[10] See eg Catherine Albiston, 'The Dark Side of Litigation as a Social Movement Strategy' (2011) 96 Iowa Law Review Bulletin 61. See also, for a broader discussion, Robin Stryker, 'Half Empty, Half Full, or Neither: Law, Inequality, and Social Change in Capitalist Democracies' (2007) 3(1) Annual Review of Law and Social Science 69.

of collective grievances. It is worth bringing this work into conversation with the existing literature on Roma.[11]

Can litigation improve the position of Roma in European societies? Do the positive outcomes outweigh the drawbacks? The research in this book helps to explore answers to such questions by examining specific court cases, ranging from issues such as the removal of Romani children from their families to anti-Roma hate speech and the forced sterilization of Romani women. There is a need for a comprehensive analysis of the legal frameworks and challenges associated with these critical issues.

As a prelude to these more detailed analyses, this chapter reflects on the socio-political context in which strategic litigation unfolds. It also reflects on the dynamics between legal efforts and the development of prevailing ideas regarding the causes and remedies of the problems facing the Roma. The aim is to examine the interplay between litigation, current political and policy contexts, and dominant discourses surrounding the Roma, and to foster a dialogue between legal scholars focused on the Roma and academics engaged in broader Romani studies.

The chapter has three main sections. After this introduction, section 2 explores why strategic litigation for Roma in Europe has become such a logical choice for many activists since the 1990s. This is partly related to the fact that the processes of European integration and EU enlargement have opened up important transnational legal avenues. In section 3, the chapter considers the burgeoning debate between optimistic and sceptical views on strategic litigation for Roma. What is at stake for Roma? What are the potential gains and challenges? And is there any empirically based assessment of the real-world impact so far? Section 4 reflects on how strategic litigation can be either hindered or facilitated by specific framings of the problems faced by Roma. This is particularly relevant when litigation is seen as part of an effort to enforce change beyond national borders.

Overall, these sections will show that while strategic litigation clearly has the potential to be a powerful tool for legal remedy and socio-political mobilization, its larger success of changing realities on the ground hinges to some extent on the more comprehensive strategies of activism it interacts with. These strategies would ideally encompass broader awareness-raising initiatives that seek to achieve attitudinal shifts towards the Roma within majority populations, counter prejudice and hostile stereotypes, diminish (political appeals to) racism and discrimination against the Roma, and increase participation of Romani citizens across diverse societal and political contexts. When these strategies are furthermore coupled with sustained efforts to educate European populations on the undiminished value of

[11] There are some studies that have attempted this, including Alphia Abdikeeva, Tamar Ezer, and Alina Covaci, 'Assessing Legal Advocacy to Advance Roma Health in Macedonia, Romania, and Serbia' (2013) 20(5) European Journal of Health Law 471; Raluca Rădescu, 'A Top-Down Approach to Roma Discrimination. International Litigation as a Solution for Human Rights Redress against Violations' (2012) 20 Sfera Politicii 63.

human rights norms and the importance of striving towards shared economic prosperity across ethnic groups, legal victories may indeed constitute an accelerator of socio-political transformation. The main point is not so much that the success of strategic litigation hinges upon the successes of the political mobilization of the Roma, but rather that the effectiveness of such litigation can only be maximized when it is accompanied by broader efforts to change attitudes towards Roma among majority populations. Less discriminatory majority attitudes towards the Roma should, in turn, also facilitate the political mobilization of Roma.

## 2. The Emergence of Strategic Litigation as a Form of Transnational Activism for the Roma: A History of New Opportunities and Abiding Limitations

Why did strategic litigation become such a logical choice for many activists concerned with the plight of the Roma in Europe? There are several reasons, all of which need to be seen in the context of the geopolitical developments in Europe since the early 1990s. As was the case with minority rights in general in that decade,[12] the rights of Roma became part of a discussion about transnational norms to be adopted in the wake of democratization efforts in post-communist Central and Eastern Europe, creating what some have a called a transnational 'European minority rights regime.'[13] This provided opportunities for activism for the Roma that so far had not been present. Although Roma had been the target of (sometimes highly problematic) policy-making before the 1990s,[14] and some limited local research on their position in communist societies was available,[15] the plight of the Roma first came under major international scrutiny only in the context of this emerging European minority rights regime.[16] This was caused not only by the fact that some former Eastern Bloc countries were home to large Romani communities, or by the concern of policy-makers in the West about growing labour migration from the East, but also by the large-scale economic and societal transformations that accompanied economic liberalization and brought the

[12] Timofey Agarin and Karl Cordell, *Minority Rights and Minority Protection in Europe* (Rowman & Littlefield 2016); Bernd Rechel (ed), *Minority Rights in Central and Eastern Europe* (Taylor & Francis 2010); Lynn M Tesser, 'The Geopolitics of Tolerance: Minority Rights Under EU Expansion in East-Central Europe' (2003) 17 Eastern European Politics and Societies 483.

[13] David J Galbreath and Joanne McEvoy, *The European Minority Rights Regime: Towards a Theory of Regime Effectiveness* (Springer 2011).

[14] For an overview see, eg, Huub van Baar, Ana Ivasiuc, and Regina Kreide, *The Securitization of the Roma in Europe* (Palgrave Macmillan 2019).

[15] See for Hungary, eg, Gábor Havas and Istvan Kemény, 'The Statistics of Deprivation' in Zsofia Zachar (ed), *Encounters: A Hungarian Quarterly Reader* (Balassi 1999) 361–70. For Czechoslovakia, Eva Davidová, *Romano Drom: Cesty Romů 1945–1990* (Vyd Univerzity Palackého 1995).

[16] More on this in, eg, Peter Vermeersch, 'The Plight of Eastern Europe's Roma' in Adam Fagan and Petr Kopecký (eds), *The Routledge Handbook of East European Politics* (Routledge 2017) 225.

marginalized position of many Romani citizens in that part of Europe into view. In those years, many European countries saw the rise of Romaphobia, or at least the indicators of it (hate speech, blatant discrimination, and other injustices) were more frequently documented and brought to the public eye. Growing media coverage and efforts by NGOs like Human Rights Watch, Amnesty International, Project on Ethnic Relations, and the European Roma Rights Centre and other activists engaged in efforts to document and raise awareness of Romaphobic hate crimes, which in turn helped to instigate the emergence of new initiatives within various international governmental bodies, within, for example, the OSCE and the Council of Europe, with a mandate to provide advice on issues pertaining to Roma.

Since the political, normative, as well as legal landscape in Europe had begun to shift, human rights and minority rights litigation became a more natural possible response to this development, especially in the former Eastern Bloc countries, even when it was also clear from the beginning that this was only one pathway for activism and could not be a panacea for all problems facing Roma. Nevertheless, the rise of legal efforts was clear. 'Under communism, the role of the courts was confined to the criminal sphere, the prosecutor had primacy in fulfilling the state's party-defined objectives by enforcing the law', Goldston and Adjami explain.[17] After 1989, however, the post-communist legal systems were in flux and 'law reforms transformed the role of the procuracy, restructured the judiciary, drafted new constitutions, created constitutional courts to interpret them and reorganised the legal profession'. Often taking inspiration from a tradition that had taken root in the US, various activists saw an unprecedented opportunity to explore the potential of public interest law to ameliorate the position of Roma. Even when it was not always supported by local Romani activists and representatives, strategic litigation, for example in the field of educational segregation,[18] became a potent tool for effect social change, used in conjunction with extra-legal activism.

This tendency was further advanced by another factor: Romani activism gained prominence, helped, for example, by international funding by private foundations and international governmental organizations that sought to support civil society development in Europe. International Romani activism had a longer history of course, for example in the form of the International Roma Union (IRU),[19] but new financial and practical support from international NGOs and governments in the 1990s led to increased collaboration between Romani activists across national borders, leading to what has been called the 'NGOization' of human rights.[20] This

17 Goldston and Adjami (n 5) 207.

18 James A Goldston, 'The Unfulfilled Promise of Educational Opportunity' in Jacqueline Babha, Andrzej Mirga, and Margareta Matache, *Realizing Roma Rights* (University of Pennsylvania Press 2017) 163–85.

19 Ilona Klímová-Alexander, *The Romani Voice in World Politics: The United Nationals and Non-State Actors* (Ashgate 2005).

20 Nidhi Trehan, 'The Romani Subaltern within Neoliberal European Civil Society: NGOization of Human Rights and Silent Voices' in Nando Sigona and Nidhi Trehan (eds), *Romani*

gave the claims of Romani activists, unlike those of national minorities who were usually active within the frame of a single state (or perhaps in relation to a kin-state), greater international resonance. As in the case of gender rights, it became somewhat easier to mobilize a network across national borders for Roma rights, which in turn made it in some ways more self-evident to collaborate across borders on legal matters and, for example, bring cases to European courts.[21]

Moreover, these transnationally connected civil society organizations and activists met a political context in which Europe-wide norms and regulations on human rights on minority protection were gaining further prevalence in the wake of other key developments within international governmental structures. Central and Eastern European countries were brought into the realm of international diplomacy around minorities as a result of their membership in the OSCE and the Council of Europe. Both the OSCE and the Council of Europe developed specific instruments to monitor the way in which their member states would deal with minority demands, and more specifically, both international structures developed a special interest in the situation of the Roma. In the context of the OSCE, at least two institutions gave special attention to the Roma. In 1994, a Contact Point for Roma and Sinti Issues was established at the Warsaw base of the OSCE's Office for Democratic Institutions and Human Rights. It continues to do monitoring research today and publishes regular fact sheets and 'Action Plan' reports. In the early 1990s, the Roma were, even if only for a limited period, the focus for reporting by the OSCE's High Commissioner on National Minorities.

At the end of the 1990s, the Council of Europe adopted two treaties that were of importance for minorities: the European Charter for Regional and Minority Languages and the Framework Convention for the Protection of National Minorities (FCNM). Neither of them created enforceable rights for minorities, and they related primarily to territorially and linguistically bound national minorities, and as such they were only of indirect importance to litigation for the Roma.[22] Nevertheless, they were key in reinforcing a soft law context in which

*Politics in Contemporary Europe: Poverty, Ethnic Mobilization, and the Neoliberal Order* (Palgrave Macmillan 2009).

[21] This 'transnational' path is, however, not always seen as an obvious route of action by Roma themselves, who may feel distant from international policy and legal contexts (see eg Mihai Surdu and Martin Kovats, 'Roma Identity as an Expert-Political Construction' (2015) 3 Social Inclusion 5.

[22] Linguistic and territorial claims are not prevalent in Romani activism, since Roma do not usually rely on an external homeland or kin state to claim some form of autonomy or self-governing power. Nevertheless, the issues of language and territoriality may be relevant here in other ways. For some, Romani minority language rights can become a way to achieve social mobility, as they are a symbol of protection of Romani culture. As regards territory, while no territorial rights are claimed in the conventional sense, some Roma, as McGarry has noted, 'have chosen to place themselves beyond the reach of the state and have sought to occupy de-territorialized zones of refuge where they are physically present on state territory but inhabit a different socio-political and cultural space'. In this kind of de-territorialized mode, Roma could, in principle, still be granted some form of autonomy by the state or acquire some kind of self-governing power.

norms of minority protection became important elements of legal as well as political action for the Roma.[23] Particularly in the framework of the FCNM, early on strong and sustained attention for Roma emerged. In the context of the charter on minority languages, Romani language protection received more attention than one would have assumed from the charter's apparent focus on 'regional' and 'territorial' language groups.[24] All of this added up to the growth of a multilevel European system of rights protection which, even outside the mentioned minority rights instruments, offered an increased legal opportunity structure for minority rights mobilization.[25] In addition, presumably as a result of increased awareness of human rights violations against Roma, there was a significant increase in the number of cases involving Roma in which the European Court of Human Rights issued a judgment.[26] Litigation levels for Roma were higher in the national context as well.[27]

This came in addition to legal possibilities for the Roma within the different domestic legal and institutional frameworks that had come into being. Because of rising norms on minority protection due to accession requirements for the EU, and the desire of post-communist countries to join the EU, Central Europe had become a laboratory for newly developed national legal arrangements and institutional landscapes that fit within the minority rights protection model.[28]

Moreover, following the desire of the countries of Central and Eastern Europe to join 'Europe', the European Union, too, began to scrutinize these countries' human rights records and minority protection mechanisms. The EU's 1993 Copenhagen European Council made the protection of ethnic and national minorities a precondition for the accession of new EU member states. Candidate countries realized that domestic policies, practices, and court decisions on minorities could have a profound impact on their bid for EU membership. Since then, minority rights and the adoption of anti-discrimination legislation, following the EU's Race Equality Directive, have become an integral part of the EU integration process and have been part of the membership conditionality associated with the EU's enlargement

[23] On the impact of the FCNM on minorities, see eg Rainer Hofmann, Tove H Malloy, and Detlev Rein, *The Framework Convention for the Protection of National Minorities: A Commentary* (Brill 2018); Gaetano Pentassuglia 'The EU and the Protection of Minorities: the Case of Eastern Europe' (2001) 12(1) European Journal of International Law 1.

[24] Robert Dunbar, *Comparative Study of the Working Methods and Conclusions of the Committee of Experts of the European Charter for Regional or Minority Languages and the Advisory Committee of the Framework Convention for the Protection of National Minorities* (Council of Europe 2005).

[25] Sophie Jacquot and Tommaso Vitale, 'Law as Weapon of the Weak? A Comparative Analysis of Legal Mobilization by Roma and Women's Groups at the European Level' (2014) 21 Journal of European Public Policy 587.

[26] Sandeep Chhabra, 'Rights at the Margin' [2011] World Outlook 60.

[27] See eg Adriána Zimová, *Strategic Litigation Impacts: Roma School Desegregation* (Open Society Justice Initiative 2016).

[28] Peter Vermeersch, *The Romani Movement: Minority Politics and Ethnic Mobilization in Contemporary Central Europe* (Berghahn Books 2006) 64–97.

strategy.[29] In addition, the EU itself has developed its own methods and tools to encourage national governments in member states to adopt new policies on Roma. These have become the focus of transnational Romani activism.[30] Transnational NGOs have written reports to shame governments about structural discrimination, and continue to do so.

Since its enlargement into Central Europe, the EU has continued to be an important context in which the struggle for better protection of the rights of the Roma takes place. In 2010, the EU's Communication on the economic and social integration of Roma in Europe stated that 'the EU and its Member States have a special responsibility towards the Roma'.[31] Many activists saw this as an avenue for advocacy, but it also raised a question about how transnational advocacy should use this path to the advantage of the Roma.

If the problems facing the Roma are similar across Europe, should this then mean that the European level ought to be primarily responsible for developing or encouraging better policies for Roma? And should the strategic litigation therefore also primarily be targeted at the EU level? While the EU's strategy, as exemplified by the European Commission's 2020 initiative in developing the EU Strategic Framework for Roma Equality, Inclusion and Participation,[32] did not primarily focus on elevating Roma to the legal status of a European transnational minority, it did start from the idea that there is a role for Europe-wide processes to incentivize individual member states to respect rights for Roma and develop new inclusion policies in order to facilitate the enforcement of those rights. The EU's 2020 Strategic Framework did not go so far as to demand that member states grant specific minority rights to Roma, but it called on national governments to step up their efforts to facilitate the position of Roma in society in the fields of material well-being, education, employment, housing, and healthcare, and to address persistent discrimination in all those domains. It also aimed to create a platform for dialogue, bringing together national governments, experts, and Roma activists. In other words, the EU's approach has sought to strengthen the voice of Roma both transnationally and within individual states, while facilitating cross-border cooperation to address common challenges and create new opportunities.

[29] Gwendolyn Sasse, 'National Minorities and the EU Enlargement: External or Domestic Incentives for Accommodation?' in John McGarry and Michael King (eds), *European Integration and the Nationalities Question* (Routledge 2006) 64.

[30] Peter Vermeersch, 'How Does the EU Matter for the Roma?' (2017) 64(5) Problems of Post-Communism 21.

[31] Communication from the Commission to the Council, the European Parliament, the European Economic and Social Committee and the Committee of the Regions, The social and economic integration of the Roma in Europe (2010) COM/2010/0133 final, <https://eur-lex.europa.eu/legal-content/EN/TXT/?qid=1444909812175&uri=CELEX:52010DC0133>.

[32] Communication from the Commission to the European Parliament and the Council, A Union of Equality: EU Roma Strategic Framework for Equality, Inclusion and Participation SWD (2020) 530 final.

Strategic litigation for Roma in this dynamic European context has proved to be important because of limitations regarding other avenues of social action for this population. The reasons for these limitations are varied. There are, for example, collective action issues that complicate the case of the Roma, such as the fact that Roma are not a homogeneous group whose collective interests are easy to define, which may in part be linked to the historical development of Romani communities, who have lived 'immersed within and dispersed among dominant (majority) populations'.[33] While many characteristics and socio-economic conditions are shared across communities, Roma remain a diverse group, not only in terms of self-identification but also in relation to living conditions, socio-economic status, and policy needs. Roma representatives may be selected by the state to ensure that Roma have a voice in policy-making discussions. In many countries, this is part of a wider landscape of legal arrangements and institutions designed to ensure a collective voice for minority populations in politics and policy-making. Without supporting minority representatives, a state cannot effectively ensure that the voice of that minority is heard. But different minority activists may have different views about who should be considered part of 'their' group and who should not. Moreover, there is no guarantee that by involving Romani voices in the debate, policy-makers will effectively seek to address the problems that Roma face. When confronted with problems related to the access of the political system, lack of resources for political mobilization, or other collective action problems, activists seeking to defend the interests of the group might rely on legal action as a movement tactic, such as has been the case, for example, in women's rights litigation.[34] Litigation might be one of the ways to avoid collective action problems or to circumvent the problems related to limitations of electoral politics or interest group representation for minority groups.[35]

## 3. Optimism and Scepticism Regarding Strategic Litigation for and on Behalf of Roma

There are both optimistic and sceptical views of strategic litigation for and on behalf of Roma. The optimistic view emphasizes the fact that strategic litigation can bring about transformative changes in policies and social practices. Legal victories, proponents argue, not only secure tangible rights but also play a crucial role in shaping social understandings. By attracting public attention and participation,

[33] Michael Stewart, 'Roma and Gypsy "Ethnicity" as a Subject of Anthropological Inquiry' (2013) 42 Annual Review of Anthropology 415.

[34] Susan M Olson, 'Comparing Women's Rights Litigation in the Netherlands and the United States' (1995) 28(2) Polity 141.

[35] Anagnostou (n 7) 9.

strategic litigation serves as a catalyst—some have called this kind of legal mobilization a form of 'counterpower'[36]—for the organization of social movements dedicated to advancing the human rights of minorities.

Has this happened in the case of the Roma? Clearly, strategic litigation has contributed to social and political movement formation for the Roma. The sustained activities of the European Roma Rights Centre, for example, illustrate that legal action can be accompanied by wider awareness-raising activities—through outreach, fact-finding, monitoring, and journalism[37]—and participation in policy debates, a combination which has inspired many Romani activists across Europe. Some of the research[38] seems to indicate that, when seen in relation to individual cases and small-scale change, Romani citizens are optimistic about the effect of successful legal advocacy.[39]

Litigation is only one of the elements of a broader set of tools that can be used in legal activism—others are legal awareness-raising, legal service provision, mediation services and dispute resolution, and law reform initiatives.[40] Szilvasi and Saitovic-Jovanovic have used the concept of 'legal empowerment'—which advances and facilitates a person's ability to 'use and shape the law in order to protect their rights',[41] and is therefore broader than strategic litigation—to examine the health situation of Roma in Romania and found that, despite serious challenges that remain,

> Roma-led accountability initiatives that embrace social accountability and legal empowerment approaches to advocate for equitable fulfilment of the right to health ... have led to the elimination of some harmful health practices (such as illegal cash bribes and violent and abusive treatment by medical professionals) and to improvements in health care, and some Roma communities have become driving forces for local and national health system reforms for advancing the fulfilment of health rights.[42]

[36] Jeff Handmaker and Sanne Taekema, 'O Lungo Drom: Legal Mobilization as Counterpower' (2023) 15(1) Journal of Human Rights Practice 6.

[37] As for example Stephanie Berry has argued, the monitoring of international human rights law may help to create more tolerant societies and protect vulnerable groups against human rights violations: Stephanie Berry, 'A Positive State Obligation to Counter Dehumanisation under International Human Rights Law' (2020) 3 Erasmus Law Review 5.

[38] See eg Zimová (n 27) in the field of education. On the issue of living conditions and culture see eg Leonie M Huijbers and Claire MS Loven, 'Pushing for Political and Legal Change: Protecting the Cultural Identity of Travellers in the Netherlands' (2019) 11(3) Journal of Human Rights Practice 508.

[39] For a broader discussion see Lilla Farkas, *Mobilising for Racial Equality in Europe: Roma Rights and Transnational Justice* (European University Institute 2020).

[40] Vivek Maru and Varun Gauri, *Community Paralegals and the Pursuit of Justice* (CUP 2018).

[41] ibid 3.

[42] Marek Szilvasi and Maja Saitovic-Jovanovic, 'Social Accountability and Legal Empowerment Initiatives: Improving the Health of Underserved Roma Communities in Eastern Europe' (2023) 25 Health and Human Rights 67.

One can understand this case as an example of how strategic litigation in an indirect manner—via the legal empowerment of citizens—may make a positive difference in the lives of Roma. Such legal empowerment is important in the context of giving Roma the opportunity to be the agents of their own lives instead of being passive victims.

Overall, however, the literature shows a mixed picture, with some findings supporting the usefulness of the legal approach for Romani activism, and others voicing frustration about the lack of impact of litigation on the level of social reform or social relations. This is where a more sceptical view of strategic litigation comes into play. For example, one report on legal and other forms of activism by and for Roma in Romania showed that while such activism could generate hope at the micro level, that is 'in the lives of individual people, and in hyperlocalized action', there was more disillusion when Roma were interviewed in connection to the potential of legal activism to address continued problems at the systemic level.[43]

While some small-scale changes are happening in response to legal action, it is also clear that large-scale change is still lacking. Moreover, there appears to be little trust in Roma from majority communities, a situation that is rooted in a longer history of structural discrimination and negative views on Roma and is likely to be perpetuated by current discourses and practices of Romaphobia and more general racism. Roma continue to be subjected to a homogenizing discourse, including in policy documents. Political and media representations mostly tend to ignore the cultural and socio-economic diversity of Roma and instead adhere to preconceived stereotypes that reinforce antiquated and misguided notions of Roma as perpetual outsiders or worse. Although many Roma are victims of exclusion and crime, in many public representations the Roma are portrayed as instigators of their own exclusion; their image is that of perpetrators of crime rather than of victims.[44] A purely legal approach may reinforce that image, rather than turning it around. As van Baar has demonstrated, the appearance of Roma in a legal context is widely associated with negative views on Roma: 'The argument goes that you are rightfully entitled to act against the Roma and treat them differently, because they cause inconvenience, indulge in criminal activity and can generally be expected to cause trouble. It is not "we", but "they" who violate rights and fail in their duties.'[45] Van Baar has called this phenomenon 'reasonable anti-Gypsyism' and explored its

[43] Adina Schneeweis, '"In Spite Of" and "Alongside": Disillusion and Success in Advocacy Communication for the Roma' (2019) 13 International Journal of Communication Systems 17. Obviously, any disillusion formulated regarding those who advocate for the rights of Roma should be seen against the background of much more important criticism that can be directed towards the politics and policies that fail to address structural discrimination of Roma, or even towards entire societies that do not respect the rights of Roma.

[44] Irene Daskalopoulou, Athanasia Karakitsiou, and Christina Malliou, 'Fear of Crime and Roma Integration' (2022) 44 Journal of Policy Modeling 344.

[45] Huub van Baar, 'The Emergence of a Reasonable Anti-Gypsyism in Europe' in Timofey Agarin (ed), *When Stereotype meets Prejudice: Antiziganism in European Societies* (Ibidem Verlag 2014) 31.

manifestations in politics and wider society. Policies specifically designed to integrate or improve the conditions of Roma often fail because they continue to be based on such problematic narratives about the target group, which in turn seem to legitimize the continuation of highly problematic attitudes and actions (including those by police and other official authorities).[46] The current landscape of regulatory practices aimed at addressing, or at least managing, that situation—which includes law and order policies, activation policies, reliance on NGOs for emergency assistance, housing programmes, settlement policies, border controls aimed at curbing Roma migration, and the establishment of European mechanisms to incentivize national policies for Roma inclusion—may therefore generate new ways of problematizing Roma. As van Baar and others have argued, certain policies may be targeted at 'assisting' the Roma and thereby making them a special category of citizens in need of help, but those same policies may fail to address poverty and structural discrimination.[47]

One could debate, of course, whether this 'failure' really points to an inadequacy of the legal action and the reliance on strategic litigation in a context of the lack of other political opportunities for defending the interests of the Roma. A better approach might be to argue that these are challenges that proponents of strategic litigation simply need to be aware of, even if such challenges cannot be directly addressed by litigation itself. This is where the sceptical view of strategic litigation may be useful: as a reminder of the challenges that need to be considered. Although the number of rights judgments related to Roma in the European Court of Human Rights is high, their broader social and political impact remains in some ways more modest, and there is still a significant gap between the grievances that have led to legal action and the more broad-scale challenges facing Roma. In other words, much work remains to be done, for example in the field of awareness-raising about the meaning of human rights judgments related to Roma. Legal victories should not be seen and reported as isolated cases, but as part of a broader social movement. Unless accompanied by other empowerment strategies and narratives, such individualization would risk diluting the impact of litigation on systemic issues affecting Romani populations. For this reason, the narratives surrounding litigation can be as important as the litigation itself, and this is a task that should be taken seriously by a whole range of actors, including those media outlets, journalists and politicians who are concerned with improving society.

Conveying the message that litigation involving Roma is part of a larger struggle for justice for Roma is also needed to avoid the legal route being used *against* the Roma.[48] There is research that shows how law and order policies, especially in a

[46] See eg Salomea Popoviciu and Cristian Tileagă, 'Subtle Forms of Racism in Strategy Documents Concerning Roma Inclusion' (2020) 30 Journal of Community & Applied Social Psychology 85.

[47] Van Baar, Ivasiuc, and Kreide (n 14).

[48] Anagnostou (n 7) 4.

media landscape that promotes stereotypical views of Roma as lawbreakers, can contribute to reinforcing stereotypical images of Roma as perpetrators rather than victims.[49] This can lead to increased permissiveness by authorities for 'reasonable anti-Gypsyism'.[50] In this way, legal victories can be undermined, for example, by powerful anti-Roma voices in politics and the media. It remains, therefore, imperative to promote the universal human rights ideology embedded in legal rulings that come with the promotion of legal empowerment. This is a task that lawyers might take up. They could venture outside the legal realm to challenge these Romaphobic interpretations.

A final point that the more sceptical view of strategic litigation may bring to the discussion relates to the limited impact of such litigation on inequality and poverty. Some have argued that the plight of the Roma should be addressed primarily through economic policy change and lobbying for redistribution.[51] There is a debate in the literature as to whether litigation can be a tool to address economic inequality.[52] While this question is certainly not an argument against strategic litigation for Roma, it is a call to be aware of its limitations in the field of social and economic rights.

## 4. Strategic Litigation and Questions Related to the 'Framing' of the Roma

Another aspect that is important to connect to the debate about strategic litigation for Roma concerns the narratives and frames that are used in relation to the problems facing the Roma. In this context, 'framing' relates to ways in which the stereotypical imaginaries surrounding the identity of Roma may reappear through litigation, and also may be counteracted by bringing into view new narratives of what it means to be Roma. The effectiveness of strategic litigation for a minority hinges on how (the plight of) the minority in question is publicly known. While successful litigation can force states or individuals to change their behaviour and encourage victims to seek legal remedy, it can also fail to produce change if it falls short of the mark. It can also fuel anti-minority movements if such litigation reinforces negative views of Roma or reinforces segregation and other types of rights violations. Proponents of strategic litigation should be aware of the possibility of such backlashes and try to counteract them. I'll discuss two forms of such backlash below.

[49] Anne C Kroon and others, 'Victims or Perpetrators? Explaining Media Framing of Roma across Europe' (2016) 31(4) European Journal of Communication 375.

[50] Van Baar (n 45).

[51] Van Baar and Vermeersch (n 8).

[52] Stryker (n 10).

### 4.1. The plight of the Roma and the introduction of cultural autonomy laws in a context of socio-economic deprivation and structural discrimination

One way in which legal arrangements may not be very effective for the Roma is when minority protection laws are focused merely on cultural recognition. In such cases, the common assumption is that Roma require legal protection of their language, culture and specific way of life. While this is a reasonable demand for protection on the part of the Roma, the legal structures put in place to achieve this do not necessarily lead to less discrimination or more socio-economic equality for the Roma.

Hungary, for example, has framed the issue of the Roma as one to be solved through some form of cultural autonomy, a frame that resonated well with EU accession criteria on minority protection. In practice, a system was introduced that ensured that Roma could elect their own representatives to form local self-governments, which in effect not only reinforced segregation but also functioned as poorly funded advisory bodies in the field of cultural activities, language promotion, monument protection, and folklore. At the national level, the self-governments could, in principle, act as partners with the parliament and the central government and provide input on proposed legislation and regulations affecting their own communities. Even though the Hungarian government had fully embraced that model of cultural rights protection for the Roma in the early 1990s—by designing these local and national cultural self-governments for Roma—it has so far not led to major advances in socio-economic justice or in the fight against discrimination. Reports show that it has not made much difference to the way Roma rights are protected or enforced on the ground. It appears, furthermore, to have done very little to improve Roma political participation and representation in mainstream government institutions.[53] In addition, reflecting on the current state of democracy in Hungary, it is important to ask what minority autonomy or protection systems may accomplish in terms of protecting the liberal democratic rights of minority citizens in cases where *all* citizens of the state can see those rights being weakened and violated.[54]

Variations of such minority rights protection systems have also been introduced in other countries in the region through the implementation of measures aimed at safeguarding minority languages and cultures. Part of the attractiveness of this

[53] Megan Volk Unangst, *The Hungarian Minority Self-Government System as a Means of Increasing Romani Political Participation* (National Democratic Institute 2006).

[54] Significantly, in 2022, the European Parliament questioned Hungary's status as a democracy through a broadly supported resolution, a significant stance against the government of Viktor Orbán. European Parliament, 'MEPs: Hungary Can No Longer Be Considered a Full Democracy' (Press Release, 15 September 2022) <https://www.europarl.europa.eu/news/en/press-room/20220909IPR40137/meps-hungary-can-no-longer-be-considered-a-full-democracy>.

minority rights model is undoubtedly related to the fact that it fits well with the practices and strategies of what has been called 'kin-state politics', so prominent in the region.[55] One could view the problems faced by Roma through the prism of their need for protection as an ethnic minority, which can lead to demands for policy efforts around ethnic minority protection; but such a view may also create a backlash. For example, some politicians, including some Romani politicians and activists, have invoked ethnic and cultural difference to argue in favour of segregated education. In some cases, special 'emergency' initiatives around Roma have been proposed that end up creating *more* exclusion. A well-known example is the way in which Roma asylum-seekers have been treated in some cases across Europe: not as 'regular' asylum-seekers, but as 'nomads without a home' who are placed in temporary camps that become permanent after a while. Their position of being 'in-between' (and thus belonging nowhere) is reinforced by a policy and legal framework that sets them apart, based on their ethnicity and culture, from any 'regular' group.[56]

Another example is the way language protection for Roma is organized in North Macedonia. In recent years, some legal initiatives have been taken to protect the use and teaching of minority languages, including the Romani language.[57] However, monitoring reports shows that discrimination remains widespread, including in education. According to a report by the Minority Rights Group,

> For those Roma children whose mother tongue is not Macedonian, it is even more difficult to follow lessons and integrate at school. Although the Law on Primary Education guarantees that Roma language and culture can be taught as an optional subject, in practice this provision is widely ignored and often this option is not available to Roma pupils.[58]

Creating a local or national legal framework that privileges cultural autonomy as a way of addressing the plight of the Roma constitutes a 'reframing' that may complicate the potential positive effects of strategic litigation. Do Roma need to be 'saved' only through the protection of specific group cultural rights? It is of course legitimate to view the problems of the Roma through the prism of their need for protection as a cultural group. Moreover, minority activists are often inclined to opt for the minority rights frame because it offers participation rights that no other frame does. But viewing the Roma primarily through this prism can also create

[55] Myra Waterbury, 'Kin-State Politics: Causes and Consequences' (2020) 48 Nationalities Papers 799.

[56] Nando Sigona, 'How Can a "Nomad" Be a "Refugee"? Kosovo Roma and Labelling Policy in Italy' (2003) 37 Sociology 69.

[57] European Commission for Democracy through Law (Venice Commission) North Macedonia: on the Law on the Use of Languages [2019] Opinion 946/2019.

[58] Andrea Spitálszky, *Roma in the Republic of Macedonia: Challenges and Inequalities in Housing, Education and Health* (Minority Rights Group International 2018) 5.

a backlash. Conversely, when litigation challenges ethnic segregation in education, it can be used by politicians as an argument not to introduce safeguards for Roma, thereby refusing to address barriers for Roma in mainstream colour-blind institutions.

## 4.2. The plight of the Roma as a 'European problem'

As mentioned earlier, the plight of the Roma gained prominence in the context of growing attention for minority rights in European governmental structures in the 1990s. Today, the Roma stand out as a minority group that has received significant attention from policy- and lawmakers at the European level, which in turn has created an unprecedented sense of cohesion among Roma across Europe.[59] The significance of the EU in all kinds of activism for Roma, including strategic litigation, owes much to the EU's enlargement process to Central and Eastern Europe. As explained earlier, during the late 1990s and early 2000s, the European Commission's progress reports played a pivotal role in evaluating Central European candidate countries against specific membership criteria, which included the safeguarding of various rights and protections, specifically in the field of minority protection and anti-discrimination. The EU's scrutiny placed considerable pressure on the candidate countries, and in response to this pressure, some candidate countries did indeed revise and strengthen their anti-discrimination and minority protection policies, laws, and regulations.[60] In the context of the ongoing enlargement process of the EU to the Western Balkans today, Romani activists still utilize membership requirements as a means of leverage. Governments, in turn, continue to make commitments to enhance the conditions of 'their' Romani communities as part of their efforts to advance their EU accession processes.[61]

However, the outcome of the enlargement process has not been uniformly favourable to Romani communities. Many of the national policy changes and legal reforms that resulted from the process were more symbolic and rhetorical than real—not only did they not adequately address minority rights, discrimination, and human rights challenges more broadly, they often also failed to translate rhetoric and regulations into effective changes on the ground. Even though anti-discrimination policies and laws have come into being as a result of conditionality, discrimination against Roma continues and often goes unnoticed. Moreover, in

[59] Neil Cruickshank, 'Perspectives on Europeanization: Roma and Integration' (2012) 364 L'Europe en Formation 401.

[60] Frank Schimmelfennig, 'European Regional Organizations, Political Conditionality, and Democratic Transformation in Eastern Europe' (2007) 21 Eastern European Politics and Societies 126.

[61] See eg the Poznań declaration, adopted in July 2019 at the Poznań Summit by the Western Balkans Prime Ministers. Regional Cooperation Council [2019] Declaration of Western Balkans Partners on Roma Integration within the EU Enlargement Process, https://www.rcc.int/docs/464/declaration-of-western-balkans-partners-on-roma-integration-within-the-eu-enlargement-process.

some cases the Roma themselves have been blamed for complicating the accession processes of candidate countries.[62]

Another negative effect of this development is that in some political narratives the plight of the Roma has come to be seen as a 'European problem', necessitating primarily intervention at the European level, not within the national state.[63] While Europe-wide incentives for the inclusion of Roma may still encourage the development of new policies in the national arenas of the individual member states, it has allowed certain politicians to 'reframe' the Roma as a 'European minority', making only legal action at the European level acceptable. In some cases, governments have tried to shirk their own responsibilities and remove the demands of Romani activists from the national political agenda, making it a matter for European institutions.[64]

Such 'Europeanization' has created opportunities for new forms of politicization of the plight of the Roma, in which the Roma themselves, irrespective of their impoverished or marginalized status, could be perceived and presented as 'beneficiaries' of the European integration process. This complicates all kinds of activism, including litigation, when it takes place, or is narratively related to, the European minority rights regime.

## 5. Conclusion

As the rest of this book demonstrates, strategic litigation for Roma is a complex phenomenon that has produced a range of outcomes, all of which merit careful analysis. The purpose of this chapter has been not only to reflect on the historical context in which activism through the law became an important way of addressing the plight of the Roma, but also to show that litigation alone may have some limitations. Its impact can be enhanced, however, when it is integrated into a comprehensive strategy for Roma that includes other types of advocacy and broader awareness-raising initiatives. Strategic litigation is more likely to be effective when it is accompanied by efforts to change public perceptions, to criticize and change government policies, to educate communities about human rights principles, and to promote public dialogue about the persistent and specific forms of discrimination that many Roma face.

Promoting the universal human rights norms that underpin legal decisions is essential to advancing the Roma's legal empowerment. Advocates of strategic litigation should therefore emphasize that the larger struggle for Roma justice must

[62] Peter Vermeersch, 'Ethnic Mobilisation and the Political Conditionality of European Union Accession: The Case of the Roma in Slovakia' (2002) 28 Journal of Ethnic and Migration Studies 83.

[63] Peter Vermeersch, 'Reframing the Roma: EU Initiatives and the Politics of Reinterpretation' (2012) 38 Journal of Ethnic and Migration Studies 1195.

[64] ibid.

address not only individual cases, but also the socio-economic processes that continue to marginalize Roma but are likely to remain beyond the scope of legal remedies—such as growing inequality and poverty. Strategic litigation alone is unlikely to transform the prospects of many Roma; new policies are also needed that actively transform social institutions and promote economic prosperity for all. The debate on strategic litigation for human rights in the protection of minorities highlights the need for a balanced and comprehensive approach. Legal victories can be transformative, but their impact is maximized when integrated into broader strategies that address societal perceptions and promote awareness. Activists, civil society organizations, journalists, educators, and politicians can all contribute to help accomplish this. Since explaining laws and legal victories can be part of such an awareness-raising effort, lawyers and legal scholars also have an important role to play. By addressing the complexities, the potential of strategic litigation to contribute to lasting change for minority populations is likely to increase. Arguably, it is the task of scholars to document and explain key developments, thereby inspiring new ways of using the law and legal systems to protect and advance the rights and interests of Roma in Europe.

# 3

# European Organizations and the Protection of Roma Rights

## Policy Priorities, Fragmentation, and Mutual Learning

*Balázs Majtényi*

### 1. Introduction

It is impossible to disagree with those who believe that in international relations, the language of human rights (HR) is the most powerful to claim the rights of those 'who have never had them'.[1] Excluded groups and civil rights activists must use this language as the most effective instrument in international law for limiting state sovereignty by reference to individual rights. Taking human rights seriously and referring to international documents as the basis of these rights are tools for empowering minority groups. Using international human rights is particularly important in the case of a minority such as the Roma, who have no nation-state and suffer from various forms of exclusion.

However, even if the language of human rights needs to be used to name and shame the different forms of oppression, it is not a realistic expectation that international organizations will solve the problems of excluded Roma through the development of effective human rights regimes and policies. As argued later, this is because the basic competencies required for this remain with the nation-states. Nevertheless, international mechanisms must take their work of implementing and interpreting fundamental rights seriously to maintain respect for them and to provide external constraints on nation-states.

Dealing with one minority group at the level of international and European law is interesting because it also touches on the question of the proper relationship between international human rights law and domestic constitutional law. Limiting state sovereignty always demands justification[2] because some ambitions of universalism 'can be criticized as illegitimate or, at least, ever inclined to overstep the

[1] Ratna Kapur, 'Human Rights in the 21st Century: Take a Walk on the Dark Side' (2006) 28(4) The Sydney Law Review 665.

[2] Tamás Győrfi, 'The Legitimacy of the European Human Rights Regime – A View from the United Kingdom' (2019) 8(1) Global Constitutionalism 128.

Balázs Majtényi, *European Organizations and the Protection of Roma Rights* In: *The Rights of Roma in European Courts*. Edited by: Kristin Henrard and Lilla Farkas, Oxford University Press. © Balázs Majtényi 2025.
DOI: 10.1093/oso/9780198914358.003.0003

boundaries of its legitimacy'.[3] There is also a need for justification if international law regulates something more specifically than is normally expected. Usually, international minority protection works via legal rules, which are generally applicable to all minorities or discriminated groups. The justification of the specific focus on Roma rights should be based on the following human rights arguments: the lack of a nation-state, which creates a disadvantaged position, the historical exclusion, systemic discrimination, and anti-Gypsyism. To underline the seriousness of the Roma issue, it is enough to mention the Porrajmos, the silent genocide of the Roma, that happened mainly on the territory of today's EU. Research on the *Porrajmos* only began in the 1970s and received more attention in the 1990s, partly as a result of the work of international organizations.

The effectiveness of international law itself raises questions, as reflected in the concept of relative normativity, which means that norms can be interpreted differently by actors with different interests (for example Roma-dense states and Roma rights NGOs). According to Neil Walker, there are more 'mock' compliances in international human rights law than in other areas of international law.[4] This is because the states are supposed to implement human rights treaties, and they are also the main perpetrators of human rights violations.

In international law, in the absence of a human rights court with general jurisdiction, there is generally no final authority that can provide a binding interpretation of human rights relating to Roma. Furthermore, most Roma live in Eastern, Central, and Southeastern European countries. Some of these countries have experienced a democratic backlash, and Hungary has become an autocracy again.[5] Dictatorships do not like the constitutionalization of international law, and it is less and less part of the identity of autocratizing states. In dictatorships and countries where there has been a democratic backlash, even the most effective international human rights instruments tend to have a more limited impact. For example, Hungary has failed to fully implement 76 per cent of the leading decisions[6] of the European Court of Human Rights (ECtHR).[7]

Another problem is the fragmentation of the treaty-based human rights system: different institutions, even in the European framework, do not always follow each other's jurisprudence. Not all provisions in a treaty framework apply to all parties, due to the non-ratification of protocols or other ways in which states can

[3] Neil Walker, 'Universalism and Particularism in Human Rights' in Cindy Holder and David Reidy (eds), *Human Rights: The Hard Questions* (Cambridge University Press 2013) 46.

[4] ibid 47.

[5] Gábor Attila Tóth, *Nemdemokrácia: Az alkotmányjogi patológia és terápia alapjai* (Oriold és Társai Kiadó 2024).

[6] These decisions 'require changes to laws or practices in order to prevent the same violation from happening again': European Implementation Network <https://www.einnetwork.org/countries-overview> accessed 2 December 2024.

[7] Hungary (European Implementation Network) <https://www.einnetwork.org/hungary-echr> accessed 2 December 2024.

avoid 'contracting in'. To take one important example: Protocol 12 of the European Convention on Human Rights (ECHR) expands the protection against discrimination to the enjoyment of any right, but many Roma-dense member states have not ratified the Protocol.[8]

European institutions necessarily seek to address Roma issues in areas where international and European law is weak or sometimes even non-existent, such as social and minority-specific rights. These rights, for example, are found only in the less effective human rights treaties of the Council of Europe (CoE). The European Charter for Regional or Minority Languages (Language Charter) and the Framework Convention on the Rights of National Minorities (FCNM) are not self-executing documents—they require implementation through domestic legislation and policies. Even the obligations under the European Social Charter (ESC) and in the case of the Language Charter (which reaches 'further into the public sphere' than the FCNM)[9] are based on decisions by member states. These documents have an 'à la carte' system, like in a restaurant, where member states can choose from the menu of different (strict and less strict) state obligations according to their preferences.[10] Their monitoring mechanisms are weak due to the lack of binding provisions.[11] Even if the outcome is not legally binding, the ESC's collective complaints mechanism[12] and the European Committee of Social Rights' decisions are important benchmarks for international human rights development: national courts cannot ignore them without justification.[13]

The ECHR, considered the most frequently used and effective human rights instrument, is mostly limited to civil and political rights. Moreover, the European protection system, based on a classical liberal approach to human rights, is more alien to social and group rights than its American counterpart.[14] There is no effective implementation mechanism at the European level either regarding social or minority-specific rights. However, specific minority rights advocates can

[8] Only 20 of the 46 member states have ratified the Protocol: the non-ratifiers include Bulgaria, the Czech Republic, Hungary, Poland, Slovakia, Italy, France, Germany, and the UK. <https://www.coe.int/en/web/ conventions/full-list?module=signatures-by-treaty&treatynum=177> accessed 2 October 2024.

[9] Patrick Macklem, 'Minority Rights in International Law' (2008) 6(3–4) International Journal of Constitutional Law 545.

[10] In the case of the Social Charter (1961) the selection method is set out in Part III, that of the revised Social Charter of 1996 is set out in Part III, Art A, and in the case of the Language Charter, Art 2.

[11] In the case of the Social Charter (1961), there are provisions on the monitoring mechanism in Art 25 of the Charter, in the 1991 Protocol amending the European Social Charter and in Part IV of the revised Charter (1991). Part IV of the Language Charter also sets out a monitoring mechanism.

[12] Urfan Khaliq and Robin Churchill, 'The European Committee of Social Rights' in Malcolm Langford (ed), *Social Rights Jurisprudence: Emerging Trends in International and Comparative Law* (Cambridge University Press 2009).

[13] Aoife Nolan, '"Aggravated Violations", Roma Housing Rights and Forced Expulsions in Italy: Recent Developments under the European Social Charter Collective Complaints System' (2011) 11(2) Human Rights Law Review 343.

[14] Thomas M Antkowiak, 'The Americas' in Daniel Moeckli and others (eds), *International Human Rights Law* (OUP 2017) 439.

effectively use the rights protected in the ECHR (Convention rights), such as freedom of religion, the right to family life, the prohibition of discrimination, and the right to free elections, to protect the interests of different minority communities. As Lilla Farkas underlines, even compliance with EU law, which is traditionally seen as a more efficient area of law than international law, could not solve the Roma problem 'because social and minority rights, which are particularly relevant to the group, are outside' this legal order.[15] At the level of the EU law, the problem is that while the EU has legislative competencies in areas such as equality, despite the existence of EU-level mechanisms, monitoring and enforcement are mostly left to the member states.

Despite the difficulties outlined above, international organizations have become important actors not only in the interpretation and implementation of international human rights to protect the Roma minority, but also in Roma policy-making and policy funding. This chapter focuses on the Roma policies of three European intergovernmental and supranational organizations: the Council of Europe (CoE), the Organization for Security and Co-operation in Europe (OSCE), and the European Union (EU). It seeks to contribute to the literature by mapping and analysing the implementation of Roma-related human rights and policy documents. It shows how the legal and policy framework has developed and what the main challenges are.

The first question is when and how international protection of the Roma minority began. Then, in the case of the three international organizations, the chapter tracks in chronological order the path that has been taken to establish the most recent policy mechanisms that deal specifically with the Roma minority. The aim is to address the principles and framework of each organization's Roma policy and its policy-making activities, focusing on institutions whose working mechanisms are based on representatives of states rather than on independent experts. The chapter presents the main non-political treaty-based and other mechanisms for the protection of Roma rights, too. It also examines whether there is coherence between the activities of the different mechanisms. Finally, it analyses the role and potential of European organizations in protecting Roma rights through binding human rights instruments and policy-making.

International courts make a major contribution to developing fundamental rights protection, and this activity also shapes European and national Roma policies. In addition to this judicial activity, since the early 2000s, European institutions have begun to develop policies to protect Roma rights even in the absence of strong international guarantees, thereby 'pushing the boundaries of human rights'. In addition to looking at the quality of the ECtHR's rulings, the chapter examines whether policy-making is broadly consistent with legislation and judicial activity

[15] Lilla Farkas, 'Mobilising for Racial Equality in Europe: Roma Rights and Transnational Justice' (2020) <https://cadmus.eui.eu/handle/1814/66916> accessed 2 December 2023.

at the European level. In the case of the ECtHR judgments, the chapter focuses only on these two aspects, as detailed descriptions of the judgments are given in other chapters in this volume.

The chapter also examines whether European policy-making is adapted to legal and political developments in the member states. It argues that international organizations have begun to push the boundaries because they have waited in vain for action at the national level and have therefore created policies directly at the European level. This approach contradicts the classic role of transnational policy-making: when a landmark judicial decision, for example on anti-segregation, 'fertilizes' legislative and judicial practice in the member states and leads to the adoption of national Roma policies. The occasional circumvention of national legislation and jurisprudence through the adoption of European-level policies is a route that does not create legal protection and may at times even contradict existing interpretation or provisions. Its feasibility is highly questionable in most policy areas, even though it has produced genuine results in some, for example recognition and research of the Roma holocaust.

## 2. The Beginning of the International Protection

Following the collapse of the Eastern Bloc–90 and the accession of Central and Eastern and Southeastern European countries (where most of the Roma live) to European organizations, the Roma began to be dealt with as a specifically European transnational community. This approach entailed the recognition of the European character of the Roma minority and its historical exclusion. This was exceptional, as international organizations are usually concerned with the situation of minorities in general, rather than with a specific minority group; the latter is primarily the task of nation-states.

Over time, the population considered by the majority to be Roma became the most populous ethnic minority, first within the CoE and later, after the accession of Central and Eastern and Southeastern European countries in 2004 and 2007, within the EU.[16] These organizations use the term 'Roma' or 'Roma and Sinti' as an umbrella concept for a population estimated by them to be between 10 and 12 million people.[17] The EU estimates that around six million Roma live on its

[16] EU accession negotiations with the first round of candidates began in the spring of 1998. Czechia, Estonia, Poland, Latvia, Lithuania, Hungary, Slovakia, and Slovenia, along with Cyprus and Malta, joined in 2004, and Bulgaria and Romania joined in 2007.

[17] See eg Council of Europe, Strategic Action Plan for Roma and Traveller Inclusion (2020–2025) 7 <https://rm.coe.int/coe-strategic-action-plan-for-roma-and-traveller-inclusion-en/16809fe0d0> accessed 2 December 2023, or EU, Roma Strategic Framework for Equality, Inclusion and Participation for 2020–2030 1 <https://commission.europa.eu/document/download/99cc0720-68c2-4300-854f-592bf21dceaf_en?filename=eu_roma_strategic_framework_for_equality_inclusion_and_participation_for_2020_-_2030.pdf> accessed 2 December 2024.

territory.[18] This estimate is based on data that includes not only those who identify themselves as Roma, but also those who are perceived as such by the majority. When these organizations focus on tackling poverty, prejudice, segregation, and exclusion, they can use estimated data. In other cases, the use of this data can be much more problematic, for example in the case of minority-specific rights, because a significant proportion of these people do not identify as Roma.[19] Minority-specific rights protect the religious, cultural, and linguistic elements of the identity if the members of the minority identify with them. The application of minority-specific rights is usually dependent on whether the minority group or those who belong to the group claim it or not. Given these conundrums, on behalf of the international organizations, a more nuanced approach regarding the number of Roma would be welcome.[20]

International documents use 'Roma' as an umbrella term for different groups, such as the Boyash, Sinti, and Travellers. In other words, they have made a strategic decision to use the data of people considered by the majority to be Roma and to treat all groups together as Roma in law and policy-making.[21] However, recognition of the Roma nation would not be jeopardized if policy documents in certain areas, such as housing, were to treat different Roma groups differently.

International institutions dealing with the Roma become part of the structures within which agencies of Roma politics operate in the transnational sphere. The question of whether Roma leaders could reach out to the wider Roma community was quickly raised as a result of the exclusion of the Roma and the lack of a Roma middle class. The recognition of Roma as a community has raised the unresolved question of who speaks for the Roma or the different Roma communities living in different countries[22]

The Roma intellectual elite is still small. According to Mirga and Gheorghe, the Roma leaders come from different backgrounds: there are traditional leaders and educated activists, but these are 'products of the majority education system'.[23] Sometimes, Roma intellectuals (for example, Andrzej Mirga or Miranda

[18] Roma equality, inclusion and participation in the EU. <https://commission.europa.eu/strategy-and-policy/policies/justice-and-fundamental-rights/combatting-discrimination/roma-eu/roma-equality-inclusion-and-participation-eu_en>, accessed 02 December 2024

[19] Balázs Majtényi and András Pap, 'Should Ethnic Data Be Standardized? Different Situations of Processing Ethnic Data' in Máté Dániel Szabó (ed), *Privacy protection and Minority Rights* (Eötvös Károly Institute 2009) 63.

[20] Ibid.

[21] A Union of Equality: EU Roma Strategic Framework for Equality, Inclusion and Participation 1 <https://commission.europa.eu/document/download/99cc0720-68c2-4300-854f-592bf21dceaf_en?filename=eu_roma_strategic_framework_for_equality_inclusion_and_participation_for_2020_-_2030.pdf> accessed 02 October 2024.

[22] Iulius Rostas, *A Task for Sisyphus: Why Europe's Roma Policies Fail* (CEU Press 2019).

[23] Nicolae Gheorghe and Andrzej Mirga, 'The Roma in the Twenty-First Century: A Policy Paper' (2001) Project on Ethnic Relations 2 <https://eriac.org/wp-content/uploads/2021/01/Mirga-Andrzej_Gheorghe-Nicolae_2001_The-Roma-in-the-Twenty_First-Century_A-Policy-Paper_Eurozine_12th-March.pdf> accessed 2 October 2024.

Vuolasranta) work for different international organizations and international NGOs, too, which helps the flow of information between different organizations. It is not always clear which NGOs or minority self-governments could represent Roma. Roma delegated by states to international organizations are sometimes not independent of nation-states and are not elected by Roma communities to represent the Roma in the international fora, so their participation in decision-making is not a real solution. The latter criticism is also true of the involvement of the educated Roma activists. Of course, it can be argued that including Roma in decision-making at least makes them visible. International organizations are trying to solve the lack of Roma representation by involving the existing independent Roma NGOs in the decision-making and monitoring process, but the Roma civil sector is also weak.[24]

In 2004, when most Central and Eastern European (CEE) countries joined the EU, the European Roma and Travellers Forum (ERTF), an international umbrella NGO, was established with the support of the CoE and Finland to become a negotiating partner that could represent Roma interests for European organizations. The way it was designed was similar to how the CoE works, for example the different organizations are represented by a consultative assembly (based on the representation of national forums and international Roma NGOs).[25] However, the democratic representation of Roma could not be resolved within an NGO framework and it was debated from the outset whether this organization could truly represent Roma interests.[26] As expected, the ERTF did not achieve its original goal of being the voice of the Roma at the CoE.[27]

Since 1989 international organizations' views of Roma groups have changed, too. Before 1989, the nomadic lifestyle, in addition to the excluded social situation, was presented in the documents of these organizations both as a manifestation of Roma social problems and often as an expression of Roma identity.[28] Later, because the majority of Eastern and Central and Southeastern European Roma are sedentary, the disadvantaged social situation of Roma communities[29] and claim for minority-specific rights (for example rights to cultural institutions, language

[24] Zoltan Barany, *The East European Gypsies: Regime Change, Marginality, and Ethnopolitics* (CUP 2001) 240; Farkas Lilla, 'Kis magyar jogvédelem-történet' (2009) 4 Fundamentum 161.

[25] Jud Nirenberg, 'Romani Political Mobilization from the First International Romani Union Congress to the European Roma, Sinti and Travellers Forum' in Nando Sigona and Nidhi Trehan (eds), *Romani Politics in Contemporary Europe. Poverty, Ethnic Mobilization and the Neoliberal Order* (Palgrave Macmillan 2009) 106.

[26] ibid 94–115.

[27] ibid 107.

[28] Recommendation 563 (1969), 'On the Situation of Gypsies and Other Travellers in Europe' <https://assembly.coe.int/nw/xml/XRef/Xref-XML2HTML-en.asp?fileid=14599&lang=en> accessed 2 October 2024.

[29] In Bulgaria, Hungary, Poland, Romania, and Ukraine the Roma are often represented in sociological research on the basis of their 'underclass' situation. Elena Marushiakova and Vesselin Popov, 'Between Exoticization and Marginalization. Current Problems of Gypsy Studies' (2011) 4(1) Behemoth 94.

rights) and representations gradually replaced the earlier nomadic image of the group in these documents. As Rövid states in international documents, the Roma developed from nomadic people into 'a true European minority'[30] and in the absence of the kin state, Roma leaders demanded recognition 'as a nation'.[31]

After 1990, the CoE, the OSCE, and the EU committed themselves to providing specific minority rights and combating discrimination and hatred against Roma through a series of non-binding policy documents.[32] These actions contributed to the recognition of Roma as a national/ethnic minority with access to minority rights, and to the fight against persecution and anti-Gypsyism in the member states. Policy documents in Europe that define Roma as a national minority themselves become part of the Roma nation-building process to which Roma communities can refer, both by confirming their minority status within their respective countries and by symbolizing transnational unity in the process of Roma identity-building. Past persecution, with its worst instance, the *Porrajmos*, became an important part of the common identity.[33]

## 3. Roma Policy and Some Landmark Human Rights Cases Within the Council of Europe

### 3.1. The institutional framework

This section summarizes the relevant institutional framework for Roma-related legislation, policy-making and case law within the CoE It focuses mainly on how the CoE institutions push the boundaries of human rights and how fragmentation creates problems.

The most important political mechanisms that shape the framework of CoE Roma policies are the Committee of Ministers and the Parliamentary Assembly (PACE). The Committee of Ministers is the decision-making body, that also reviews the functioning of human rights mechanisms, and the PACE is the main consultative body.

There are also non-political and non-treaty-based mechanisms dealing with Roma rights, with weaker monitoring than treaty-based mechanisms. Their advantage is that all member states of the CoE fall under their scrutiny, and their

[30] Márton Rövid, 'One-Size-Fits-All Roma? On the Normative Dilemmas of the Emerging European Roma Policy' (2011) 21(1) Romani Studies 3.

[31] Thomas Acton and Ilona Klímová, 'The International Romani Union: An East European Answer to a West European Question?' in Will Guy (ed), *Between Past and Future: The Roma of Central and Eastern Europe* (University of Hertfordshire Press 2001) 216.

[32] Balázs Majtényi and György Majtényi, 'A Transnational Nation: Roma National Identity in the Making' in Jenny Wüstenberg and Aline Sierp (eds), *Agency in Transnational Memory Politics* (Berghahn 2020) 298.

[33] ibid 295.

monitoring activity does not depend on the ratification of a treaty. One such Roma-related non-treaty body is the European Commission against Racism and Intolerance (ECRI), which operates in a similar fashion. It was established by the Committee of Ministers to combat 'racism, racial discrimination, xenophobia, anti-Semitism and intolerance'.[34] Another is the Commissioner for Human Rights, whose mandate is general, who influences the Roma policies. The Commissioner for Human Rights was created as an institution of the Committee of Ministers to 'promote education in, awareness of and respect for human rights' in all member states.[35] The Commissioner collects information from NGOs during country visits and also uses information from other international organizations, such as the OSCE field presences (gathered during country and crisis visits).

Additionally, there are mechanisms linked to various binding conventions whose scopes do not cover all human rights. The following treaty-based mechanisms often deal with the situation of Roma: the ECtHR of the ECHR, the ECSR of the ESC, the Advisory Committee of the FCNM, and the Committee of Experts of the Language Charter. The following analysis shows that the policies of the CoE institutions and the practice of the various monitoring mechanisms tend to converge, even if fragmentation causes problems.

Standard-setting by political mechanisms concerning Roma policy began in 1969, when the Consultative Assembly adopted Recommendation 563, 'On the Situation of Gypsies and Other Travellers in Europe', which dealt with appropriate stopping places for travellers' caravans, children's education, social security, and healthcare. In 1975, the Committee of Ministers adopted Resolution (75)13 'On the Social Situation of Nomads in Europe', which contains recommendations for improving the social situation of nomadic groups. The document called on governments to end discrimination, combat prejudice, improve camps and housing conditions, and take measures in the fields of education, health and social care, and social security. In 1983, the Committee of Ministers adopted Recommendation No R(83)1 'on stateless nomads and nomads of undetermined nationality' to protect the cultural heritage and identity of minorities. The Recommendation proposed measures for states to combat discrimination against stateless groups and to reduce the number of stateless persons. The significance of these documents is their recognition of Roma as a vulnerable group with special needs.

In 1991, the Secretary General, drawing a parallel between the European idea and the nomadic lifestyle, made the following remarkable statement in Strasbourg, referring to the growing Roma minority within the CoE: 'You are a truly European people as by definition and tradition Gypsies are nomads, travelling from country to country and without really recognizing frontiers in Europe.

[34] Resolution (2002)8 on the statute of the European Commission against Racism and Intolerance <https://rm.coe.int/CoERMPublicCommonSearchServices/DisplayDCTMContent?documentId=0900001680973356> accessed 2 December 2023.

[35] Resolution (99) 50 of the Committee of Ministers of the Council of Europe (7 May 1999) Art 1.

You are at home in the Council of Europe because for centuries you have already been Europeans.'[36] The significance of this statement is recognizing the European character of the minority because there has been, and still is, a tendency for European countries and the majority population to treat Roma as non-European foreigners. At the same time, a nomadic way of life was wrongly associated with the majority of Roma in Europe, as most Roma communities today no longer have a nomadic lifestyle, while the tradition of travelling is indeed part of the Roma memory.[37]

In the 1990s, two binding conventions on the protection of minorities were adopted: the above-mentioned Language Charter (1992) and the FCNM (1994). Despite vague provisions and weak monitoring mechanisms, they have become important reference points for Roma-specific minority rights and identity-building aspirations in the absence of more effective minority rights norms. The occasional lack of information on the Roma by international organizations is illustrated by the fact that Romani is mentioned in the non-binding explanatory report of the Language Charter as an example of a non-territorial language (lacking a territorial base) for whose protection state parties have almost no obligation.[38] This point of the explanatory report is based on a fundamental misunderstanding of the situation of the Roma, as most Roma communities have a territorial base. This misunderstanding may stem from the fact that Roma are often referred to as a non-territorial nation, not because of their itinerant lifestyle, but because they do not have a nation-state.[39]

Many states recognize Roma as a national minority and use specific minority rights to protect Roma rights.[40] However, the rights of national minorities enshrined in the two conventions mentioned above have a serious shortcoming. The FCNM leaves it up to states to decide how they apply the conventions, and many states tailor the concept of minorities to nationals, thus excluding migrant Roma communities. The Language Charter is limited to nationals, and mentions that regional or minority languages do not include the languages of migrants. So, according to Mirga and Gheorghe, 'it reinforces the fragmentation of the Romani population in a given state'; it divides, for instance, the Sinti and Roma migrants in Germany.[41] This European practice of excluding migrant minorities is contrary to

[36] Catherine Lalumière, at the hearing 'The Gypsy people and Europe' organized by the CLRAE, in Strasbourg in July 1991, quoted in Gypsies in Europe/Report/Doc 6733 11 January 1993 Point 20 <https://assembly.coe.int/nw/xml/XRef/X2H-Xref-ViewHTML.asp?FileID=6762> accessed 2 December 2023

[37] The Romani language song 'Gelem, gelem', originally composed by Jarko Jovanovič in 1969 to the melody of an old Romani folk song, contains references to the scattering, to the persecution, and to the *Porrajmos*. In Hungary, for example, a Hungarian-language song 'Zöld az erdő' ('The forest is green') is also used as a Roma anthem (there is a Boyash language version also) and refers to forced migration.

[38] Explanatory Report 5.XI.1992 to the European Charter for Regional or Minority Languages Strasbourg, Point 36. <https://rm.coe.int/16800cb5e5> accessed 2 December 2023.

[39] Gheorghe and Mirga (n 23) 13.

[40] ibid 17.

[41] ibid 15.

the spirit of international human rights law, which, in most cases, seeks to protect human rights regardless of citizenship.

### 3.2. Human rights adjudication and policy-making

After the Eastern enlargement, Recommendation 1203 (1993) of the Parliamentary Assembly'On Gypsies in Europe' was adopted. The Recommendation acknowledged the Roma minority and deemed it a 'true' European minority, albeit adding that they do 'not fit into the definitions of national or linguistic minorities'.[42] This was partly a reflection of the former policies that under state socialism, minority status generally was denied to the Roma.[43] Moreover, the Recommendation highlighted that Roma contribute greatly to European multiculturalism. The document added that since the accession of CEE countries into the CoE, the number of Roma within the organization had increased greatly. The PACE also recommended that the Committee of Ministers 'initiate, where appropriate by proposals to governments or the relevant local and regional authorities of member states'[44] various general or specific measures in the following areas: culture, education, provision of information, equal rights, and everyday life. In everyday life, member states should develop further programmes to improve housing, education, and employment opportunities. Overall, this document illustrates how the struggle against social disadvantage and exclusion of Roma appears as a common feature (similar to national culture) and thus becomes another important reference point—alongside the struggle for political recognition—in the demand for rights for Roma communities.

In 1995, the Committee of Ministers established the Group of Specialists on Roma/Gypsies (MG-S-ROM) as a new inter-governmentally organized committee (governments of member states designate their representatives) to oversee the situation of Roma; later, the Specialist Group made suggestions in the fields of, for instance, education, labour, and housing, for the improvement of national legislation, policies, and strategies. Over the years, the MG-S-ROM was renamed several times, in 2020 becoming the Committee of Experts on Roma and Travellers (ADI-ROM). ADI-ROM has a role in developing and implementing the CoE policy documents, but its efficiency is weak as ministry officials sitting there cannot be expected to monitor implementation effectively.

In 1996, the ECtHR in the *Buckley* case, in which the Roma applicant argued that the refusal to allow her to park her caravans on rural land which she owned was contrary to her right to private and family life under Article 8 ECHR and the

[42] Recommendation 1203 (1993) on Gypsies in Europe of the Parliamentary Assembly, Point 2.

[43] Balázs Majtényi and György Majtényi, *A Contemporary History of Exclusion: The Roma Issue in Hungary from 1945 to 2015* (CEU Press 2016) 63.

[44] Recommendation 1203 (1993) (n 42), Point 11.

prohibition of discrimination under Article 14, the ECtHR did not find a breach of the Convention. However, it recognized 'that Gypsics following a traditional way of life required special consideration'.[45] This was the first time that the Court had facilitated positive state obligations to protect Roma identity, even if the judgments used prejudiced and stereotypical language about Roma and their identity.[46] In paragraph 94 of *Chapman v the United Kingdom*, the Court[47] explicitly states that their special needs must be taken into account when laws are made and applied.

An interesting element of *Chapman v the United Kingdom* is that the Court received a third-party intervention from the European Roma Rights Centre. The ERRC argued that there is 'a growing consensus amongst international organizations about the need to take specific measures to address the position of Roma, inter alia, concerning accommodation and general living conditions'.[48] On this basis the Court examined the existing European framework for the protection of minorities and Roma-related European policy documents. The judgment refers to the policy documents of the CoE, OSCE, and the EU. It also refers to the FCNM, which was ratified by the UK on 15 January 1998. The main question was whether the FCNM reduced the margin of appreciation of states regarding the application of Article 8; the Court said that it did not, because the international protection of minorities did not create unambiguous applicable standards. 'The Framework Convention, for example, sets out general principles and goals but the signatory States were unable to agree on means of implementation.'[49]

In 2002, the PACE adopted Recommendation 1557 on the 'Legal situation of the Roma in Europe', urging member states to settle the legal status of Roma, who are socially disadvantaged as an ethnic or national minority group.[50] Despite these proposals, there are still members of the CoE, such as Turkey or France, that do not recognize the minority status of Roma.

In 2006, the Human Rights Commissioner published a major thematic report to draw the attention of PACE and the Committee of Ministers to the human rights situation of Roma, Sinti and Travellers in Europe, with a series of recommendations in the areas of housing, education, employment, health care, combating racist violence, and relations with law enforcement authorities.[51] Recommendations

[45] *Buckley v the United Kingdom* App no 20348/92 (ECtHR, 25 September 1996) para 71.
[46] Doris Farget, 'Defining Roma Identity' European Court of Human Rights' (2012) 3 International Journal on Minority and Group Rights 291–316.
[47] Kristin Henrard, 'The European Court of Human Rights, Ethnic and Religious Minorities and the Two Dimensions of the Right to Equal Treatment: Jurisprudence at Different Speeds?' (2016) 3 Nordic Journal of Human Rights 169.
[48] *Chapman v UK* App no 27238/95 (ECtHR, 18 January 2001) para 89.
[49] ibid para 96.
[50] Recommendation 1557, Legal situation of the Roma in Europe, Point 6. <https://pace.coe.int/en/files/16999/html> accessed 2 December 2023.
[51] Final Report on the 'Human Rights Situation of the Roma, Sinti and Travellers in Europe' (Commissioner's thematic report CommDH 2006) 1 <https://rm.coe.int/16806dab92> accessed 2 December 2023.

include regular human rights training for law enforcement officials and the recruitment of Roma into the police and judiciary.

In 2007, in *DH and Others v the Czech Republic*,[52] often labelled the 'European Brown case',[53] the ECtHR found there was racial or ethnic discrimination in education in special schools in Ostrava. The judgment raised the problem of the lack of an effective enforcement mechanism: there are still many cases of segregated and inferior education for Roma pupils today, showing that, many years after the *DH* case, not much has changed. Although some CEE Supreme Courts have implemented the ECtHR's standards on school segregation,[54] this has had no visible impact on the practice of national authorities to date. The parallel with US desegregation litigation is therefore misleading: the strong political will to enforce judgments that existed at the federal level in the US is barely present in the CEE states. In the US, for example, in the case of the Little Rock Nine in 1957, every possible tool, from legislation to sending military units, was used to desegregate schools.[55]

*DH* also highlights the inconsistent and divergent terminology used by international organizations, which came from the parallel operation of monitoring mechanisms. As Lilla Farkas states, *DH* highlighted contravention of UN treaties 'categorically prohibiting segregation' and recognized no possibility of justifying it objectively and reasonably. This is also the case for the ECRI, which defines 'segregation as de facto discrimination that can amount to direct or indirect discrimination'. Differently, the 1965 UN International Convention on the Elimination of All Forms of Racial Discrimination (ICERD) defines segregation as a separate form of discrimination and does not recognize the possibility of justifying it.[56] If the Court and ECRI do not seek to establish a higher level of protection, they should seek to interpret the Convention in line with the UN documents, to avoid increasing the fragmentation of international law through divergent interpretations.

In 2009, the Committee of Ministers issued a recommendation on Roma and Travellers education in Europe.[57] The recommendation deals with non-discriminatory access to education, proposes the development of policies to combat segregation and the transfer of Roma children to special schools, and recommends support for minority language education. The document also stressed

[52] *DH and Others v The Czech Republic* App no 57325/00 (ECtHR 7 February 2006).

[53] Farkas (n 15) 179.

[54] See Dezideriu Gergely's chapter (Chapter 9) and Dezideriu Gergely and Lilla Farkas, *Racial Discrimination in Education and EU Equality Law* (Publications Office of the European Union 2020) 17.

[55] Executive Order 10730 by President of the United States Providing Assistance for the Removal of an Obstruction of Justice Within the State of Arkansas.

[56] Farkas (n 15) 73.

[57] Recommendation on the education of Roma and Travellers (2009) 4 of the Committee of Ministers to member states, Council of Europe, Art 17. Roma history and culture should be appropriately reflected in the general curriculum, including teaching about the Roma extermination as part of the Holocaust/genocide of Roma, 17 June 2009.

the importance of Roma Holocaust education for promoting intercultural dialogue and the prevention of prejudice against Roma.[58]

In 2011, the ECtHR ruled in the case of *VC v Slovakia*, in which a Roma woman was sterilized without her informed consent during the delivery of her second child by caesarean section. The Court found that Slovakia had violated Article 3 (prohibition of inhuman and degrading treatment) and Article 8 (respect for private and family life) while failing to examine the violation of Article 14 (non-discrimination), despite invoking several monitoring reports (including CoE institutions, ECRI, and the Commissioner for Human Rights) on institutional discrimination and forced sterilization of Roma women.

In 2011, the ECRI adopted the 'General Policy Recommendation No 13 on combating anti-Gypsyism and discrimination against Roma' which defines anti-Gypsyism as 'a specific form of racism'.[59] It recommends that the member states ratify Protocol No 12 ECHR, as well as the FCNM. Point 8 deals with combating racist violence and crimes against Roma,[60] including effective investigations of racist crimes. Point 4 suggests measures in the field of education such as 'teaching on the Roma genocide ("Parraijmos") in school curricula'.[61] The document builds on previous ones issued by IOs on the fight against anti-Semitism.[62]

As we have seen above, except for ECRI and the Commissioner, European institutions were reluctant to declare Roma the victims of state-level discrimination. It was the European Committee of Social Rights which in 2012 established the existence of state-sponsored discrimination against Roma, condemning France for deporting around 1,000 Roma and the dismantling of 128 Roma camps.[63]

In 2016, the CoE adopted as an 'information' document the 'Thematic Action Plan on the Inclusion of Roma and Travellers (2016–2019)'. This document provided the framework for CoE action in the years 2016 to 2019 with the following priorities: tackling prejudice, discrimination, and 'anti-Gypsyism', offering innovative models for inclusive policies for the most vulnerable, and promoting models for local-level solutions.[64]

58 ibid 17.

59 European Commission Against Racism and Intolerance General Policy Recommendation no 13 on Combating Anti-Gypsyism and Discrimination against Roma (2011) 3, Strasbourg, <https://rm.coe.int/ecri-general-policy-recommendation-no-13-on-combating-anti-gypsyism-an/16808b5aeeon-combating-anti-gypsyism-an/16808b5aee> accessed 2 December 2023.

60 *Nachova and Others v Bulgaria* App nos 43577/98 and 43579/98 (ECtHR, 26 February 2004). The ECtHR in *Nachova* set a precedent for the investigation of racist crimes after the shooting of two Roma fugitives by military police.

61 ibid para 4.

62 Marius Taba, 'Antigypsyism in a time of neoliberalism: challenging the radical right through transformative change' in Andrew Ryder, Marius Taba, and Nidhi Trehan (eds), *Romani Communities and Transformative Change: A New Social Europe* (Policy Press 2020).

63 *European Roma and Travellers Forum v France* Complaint no 64/2011 (ECSR, 24 January 2012) para 66.

64 European Parliament resolution P8_TA (2015)0095 on the occasion of International Roma Day – anti-Gypsyism in Europe and EU recognition of the memorial day of the Roma genocide during World War II (15 April 2015), European Parliament document.

In 2017, based on the initiative of the Alliance for the European Roma Institute,[65] the Council of Europe, the Open Society Foundations and the German government established the European Roma Institute for Arts and Culture (ERIAC), the first European-level institution for the promotion of Roma arts and culture. The Institute aims to change the historical and cultural narratives about the Roma and to support Roma nation-building through the standardization of Roma language, culture, and art.

The 'Strategic Action Plan for Roma and Traveller Inclusion (2020–2025)' was adopted by the Committee of Ministers in 2020 to protect the human rights of Roma and Travellers, to combat anti-Gypsyism and discrimination, and to foster inclusion (for example in education) and enhance political participation and representation of the Roma. ADI-ROM helps the member states implement the strategic documents.

## 3.3. Fragmentation

Fragmentation can cause serious systemic problems, such as when the Court does not systematically review legislation, policies, and the practice of IOs. Exceptions also exist; for instance, the ECtHR did just this in the *Chapman* case, based on the request of the ERRC. The difficulties arising from fragmentation are illustrated here through the example of the parliamentary representation of the Roma. On 10 November 2022, in the case of *Bakirdzi and EC* the ECtHR ruled against Hungary, finding a violation of the ECHR regarding the Hungarian regulation of the Representation of Minorities in Parliament.[66] The judgment held that the rules governing the representation of national minorities in the Hungarian parliament violated the right to free elections (Article 3 of its First Protocol) in conjunction with the prohibition of discrimination (Article 14 of the Convention). In this judgment, the Court did not criticize the political system of the authoritarian state and ignored consideration of the domestic social context that, in this case, they were looking at the electoral rules of an electoral autocracy, where minority votes from beyond the borders and from Hungary itself were used to secure the parliamentary majority of the FIDESZ-KDNP party alliance.[67] It did not analyse how the post-2010 Hungarian authoritarian regime had forced minority self-governments, including Roma self-governments, into a strong dependency system.

The Court's argument that, in Hungary, the preferential parliamentary representation of national minorities would be contrary to the prohibition of

[65] The Alliance is founded by Romani organizations and individuals committed to the initiative of a European Roma Institute <https://www.facebook.com/AllianceforERI/> accessed 2 December 2023.

[66] *Bakirdzi and EC v Hungary* App nos 49636/14 and 65678/14 (ECtHR 10 November 2022).

[67] Balázs Majtényi, 'The Right Answer without a Reasonable Argument? The Shortcomings of *Bakirdzi and E.C. v Hungary*' (Strasbourg Observers blog, 19 January 2023) <https://strasbourgobservers.com/2023/01/19/the-right-answer-without-a-reasonable-argument-the-shortcomings-of-bakirdzi-and-e-c-v-hungary/> accessed 30 October 2024.

discrimination is particularly surprising, given that this institutional arrangement, which exists mainly in CEE, was introduced under pressure from European institutions, including the CoE, mostly to comply with international standards (such as Article 15 FCNM). Moreover, to see this, it would have been enough to read the opinions of the FCNM Advisory Committee concerning Hungary and the decisions of the Committee of Ministers. The latter's resolution adopted in 2011 recommends the establishment of the parliamentary representation of minorities.[68] The monitoring body of the Language Charter, the Committee of Experts' report on Hungary in 2019 stated that it considers 'the representation of regional or minority language speakers in the Hungarian Parliament is good practice in Europe'.[69]

Of course, preferential representation of minorities in parliament alone cannot solve the problems of minorities, and its justifiability is disputed; Vermeersch mentions that Roma have sometimes been given reserved seats in parliament or minority self-governments, yet they remain in a marginalized situation.[70] However international standards should be unambiguous in hard cases also.

To summarize the main findings of this section, it can be said that the various human rights mechanisms of the Council of Europe have developed together, ie monitoring, policy-making and the Court's human rights activism facilitated and strengthened each other. This is largely true, even if, as the *Bakirdzi* case shows, the fragmentation of the human rights system makes it difficult to ensure coherence between the work of different institutions. However, the problems are so obvious that, for example, the areas in which policy action should be taken (education, employment, housing, health care) seem self-evident. But we are no closer to implementation unless European policy-makers take into account the legal, political, and social differences between member states.

## 4. The Organization for Security and Co-operation in Europe: Gathering Information and Policy-making

### 4.1. The emergence of Roma rights protection within the organization

This section provides a chronological analysis of the relevant institutional framework for the OSCE's policy-making and information-gathering activities related

[68] Resolution CM/ResCMN(2011)13 on the Implementation of the Framework Convention for the Protection of National Minorities by Hungary (Adopted by the Committee of Ministers on 6 July 2011 at the 1118th meeting of the Ministers' Deputies) <https://www.coe.int/en/web/minorities/hungary> accessed 2 December 2023.

[69] European Charter for Regional or Minority Languages d. Seventh report of the Committee of Experts in respect of Hungary, Point 9.

[70] Peter Vermeersch, 'How Does the EU Matter for the Roma?' (2017) 5 Problems of Post-Communism 219.

to Roma. It highlights how the security policy approach has influenced the human rights protection of the minority.

The Helsinki Final Act established the OSCE's predecessor, the CSCE, to bridge the ideological divide between East and West while linking human rights and security interests. Founded as a regional security organization, the OSCE has become an important forum for political dialogue among participating states. Still, there are no binding conventions or related enforcement mechanisms within the organization's framework. The documents adopted by the representatives of the participating states at various conferences and summits are particularly important in terms of Roma policy-making. In the so-called 'executive' structure of the organization, the activities of two non-political mechanisms are analysed regarding Roma policy-making: the High Commissioner on National Minorities and the Office for Democratic Institutions and Human Rights (ODIHR), including its Contact Point for Roma and Sinti Issues.

Already in 1990, the Copenhagen Document mentioned that Roma face racial and ethnic hatred, xenophobia, and discrimination. The OSCE document 'The Challenges of Change', adopted in Helsinki on 10 July 1992, established the institution of the High Commissioner on National Minorities to monitor tensions involving national minorities.[71] The Commissioner provides—

> 'early warning' and, as appropriate, 'early action' at the earliest possible stage in regard to tensions involving national minority issues which have not yet developed beyond an early warning stage, but, in the judgement of the High Commissioner, have the potential to develop into a conflict within the CSCE area, affecting peace, stability or relations between participating States.[72]

The Commissioner discussed the Roma's situation in three comprehensive reports. The first report, adopted in 1993, justified the Commissioner's endeavours with the economic and social conditions of Roma; the subsequent report, adopted in 1999, found that the situation had continued to deteriorate, despite some notable efforts. Then, in 2000, an even more detailed report entitled 'Report on the situation of Roma and Sinti in the OSCE Area' described the Roma as a group left 'outside Europe's new security and prosperity'.[73] The focus of the report was to change the Roma's situation and to fight against racially motivated hatred and violence; to this end, specific recommendations were made against discrimination and racial violence in the fields of education, living conditions, and political participation.

[71] For more details, Kemp A Walter, *Quiet Diplomacy in Action: the OSCE High Commissioner on National Minorities* (Kluwer Law International 2001).

[72] CSCE Helsinki Document 1992 The Challenges of Change, II (3) <https://www.osce.org/files/f/documents/7/c/39530.pdf> accessed 2 December 2023.

[73] Report on the situation of Roma and Sinti in the OSCE Area, 3 <https://www.osce.org/files/f/documents/7/f/32350.pdf> accessed 2 December 2023.

Since the adoption of the 1999 report, the Roma have been dealt with more by the Contact Point than by the office of the High Commissioner (see details below).

The Commissioner's security policy approach is problematic because it sometimes leads the international community (also the EU) to focus on a particular minority when it, or hatred against this minority, is regarded as dangerous to international security, whereas no such attention is paid to other minorities in a similar situation.[74] However, the human rights approach provides special protection not because of security risks, but to compensate for the disadvantages resulting from the minority situation and to claim the legal protection of minorities based on the concept of the equal dignity of all persons. The granting of specific minority rights should not simply be a utilitarian distribution of rights, regardless of the moral equality of human beings. Within the framework of international human rights protection, it serves to protect the rights of persons belonging to national minorities who are in a disadvantaged position and to enable them to enjoy the human rights granted to all.[75]

## 4.2. The ODIHR and the policy-making of the OSCE

The Helsinki Document also defined the mandate of the ODIHR, which is based in Warsaw and observes elections, monitors human rights, conducts field assessment visits, and makes recommendations. In 1994, another OSCE document, 'Towards a Genuine Partnership in a New Era' was adopted in Budapest, Hungary; in which participating states decided 'to appoint within the ODIHR a Contact Point for Roma and Sinti issues'. The Contact Point is responsible for exchanging information on Roma and Sinti issues, monitoring discrimination, anti-Gypsyism and human rights violations, promoting contact between various international actors (IOs and NGOs in this field), and mediating between Roma and local authorities. Influential Roma intellectuals, such as Nicolae Gheorghe and Andrzej Mirga, have served as its chief. The Contact Point organizes the activities of the International Roma Contact Group (IRCG), which serves as a 'forum for discussion and reflection among Roma in elected office, Roma civil society representatives, activists, decision-makers and executive structures'.[76] Major INGOs (ERTF, the ERRC) and national Roma organizations (for example the Central Council

[74] However, this was done in the framework of international minority protection when the institution of the OSCE High Commissioner on National Minorities was established. It was established to identify and seek early resolution of ethnic tensions that might endanger peace, stability, or friendly relations between participating states. For more details, see Kemp (n 71).

[75] Balázs Majtényi, 'Utilitiarianism in Minority Protection? Status Laws and International Organisations' in Osamu Ieda and others (eds), *Beyond Sovereignty: From Status Law to Trans-national Citizenship?* (Slavic Research Center 2006) 3.

[76] International Roma Contact Group, 2021 <https://www.osce.org/odihr/481432> accessed 2 December 2023.

of German Sinti and Roma) participate in the work of the IRCG. The activities of the Contact Point are funded not only by the OSCE, but also by the European Commission and various participating states.[77]

In 2003, in Maastricht, as an annexe to the OSCE's Ministerial Council Decision No 3/03, 'The Action Plan on Improving the Situation of Roma and Sinti within the OSCE Area' was adopted 'to reinforce the efforts of the participating States and relevant OSCE institutions and structures aimed at ensuring that Roma and Sinti people are able to play a full and equal part in our societies, and at eradicating discrimination against them'.[78] This document serves as guidance for states on how to apply the Roma policies that have already been developed within the OSCE. References to specific minority rights are rather sporadic in the otherwise bulky Action Plan: for instance, the document calls for including Roma history and culture, as well as the Romani language, within the school curriculum, with a special focus on the suffering during the Holocaust of Roma and Sinti (Point 71, 72). The Contact Point helps the participating states in the implementation of the Action Plan.

In the case of the OSCE, in the absence of binding documents and monitoring mechanisms with strong competencies, it is difficult to say anything about its impact. It is important to note, however, that the organization itself, with the participation of Roma intellectuals, collects an enormous amount of information on the human rights situation in the participating states and makes recommendations based on this information. Other international organizations also use this information, in addition to other important sources, such as those coming from NGOs. Gathering information is an important activity because when it comes to Roma policy-making, international organizations face the same problem as in the case of many other oppressed groups: a lack of reliable data. (For example, we have very little data on Roma migration in Europe.)

## 5. The European Union: Focusing on Accession, Policy Tools and Gathering Information

This section maps the anti-discrimination legislation, case law, and policies regarding Roma rights in the EU. It argues that the EU has mainly focused on EU-level Roma and rarely used binding instruments, and that the latter activity has not pushed the boundaries of human rights.

[77] The ODIHR Contact Point for Roma and Sinti Issues: An Overview, 7 <https://www.osce.org/odihr/13996> accessed 2 December 2023.

[78] OSCE Ministerial Council, Decision No 3/03, 'Action Plan on Improving the Situation of Roma and Sinti within the OSCE Area', Maastricht, 1 and 2 December 2003, 31 <http://www.osce.org/odihr/17554> accessed 2 December 2023.

From the perspective of Roma rights and discrimination against Roma, it is significant to mention that the EU has had anti-discrimination provisions in its treaties from the beginning. However, it was not until the Treaty of Amsterdam (1997) that the fight against racism and ethnic discrimination was incorporated into the Treaties. Now, we can find the general principles of non-discrimination and equality in the Treaties and the Racial Equality Directive (2000/43 EC).[79] The Directive, which came into force in 2003, prohibits discrimination (direct and indirect, harassment, and victimization) in employment, education, housing, health, and services available to the public and requires member states to set up equality bodies. The Directive's scope includes not only public but also private actors, but it does not cover differences in treatment based on nationality and treatment with stateless persons, which limits its application in protecting third-country national and stateless Roma.

## 5.1. Anti-discrimination legislation and Roma policies before the accession of the CEE countries

The national courts, the Court of Justice of the EU and the European Commission have an important role in overseeing the implementation of the Directive. EU institutions build mainly on this anti-discrimination legislation when dealing with Roma rights and inclusion policies. Unlike anti-discrimination legislation, internal protection of minority and social rights is weak in the European Union. To review and evaluate EU policies in these areas, it is worth assessing what the EU has tried to do since the accession of the CEE states.

The European Union was committed to supporting the Roma communities during the accession of CEE countries. According to Ram, fear of migration was the prominent explanation for why the EU began to address the Roma issue.[80] Western countries and Eastern European leaders also often regard Roma as unwanted foreigners, so they wanted to prevent a major migration and refugee flow from the new member states.[81] In 2002, perhaps partly out of this fear, the Justice and Home Affairs Council of the EU issued a declaration 'which stated that the ten accession countries will, from the date of signature of the accession treaties, be considered "safe countries of origin"'.[82]

[79] Council Directive (EC) 2000/43 implementing the principle of equal treatment between persons irrespective of racial or ethnic origin [2000] OJ L180.

[80] Melanie H Ram, 'European Union Roma Policy: Under Construction' in Tove H Malloy and Balázs Vizi (eds), *Research Handbook on Minority Politics in the European Union* (Edward Elgar Publishing 2022) 251.

[81] ibid 252.

[82] Justice and Home Affairs Council of the EU, 'Collective Expulsions of Roma around Europe ... And again the European Court of Human Rights Rules the Practice Illegal' (7 November 2002) <http://

At the beginning of the accession process, in the 1997 country reports and the Agenda 2000, there were still very few references to Roma. However, with the ongoing process of enlargement and the realization of the gravity of the problem of social integration, the European Commission gradually devoted more attention to this issue.[83] Conducting accession negotiations and monitoring the preparedness of each candidate state were the responsibility of the European Commission. Regular reports, published annually by the Commission, assessed the fulfilment of the accession criteria (Copenhagen criteria), including minority protection policies. In the regular reports of the Commission, issues concerning Roma were not generally discussed within the framework of civil and political rights or economic, social, and cultural rights, but instead in a separate chapter on specific minority rights. Furthermore, the Commission recommended that candidate states comply with three binding international documents of minority protection in the case of Roma: the UN Covenant on Civil and Political Rights (particularly Article 27), the FCNM, and the Language Charter. In the last monitoring report from 2003, covering countries that joined in 2004, the situation of Roma was discussed as a social policy issue, which indicated a political shift.

During the accession process, too much emphasis was placed on the adoption of legislation, in the mistaken belief that compliance with the acquis was a guarantee of democratic transition, and less attention was paid to what was happening in practice, such as the rise of anti-Gypsyism. The other major problem with this policy was the double standards of demanding the protection of specific minority rights only from the candidate countries. This raises the question of why the protection of minorities is important in Bucharest but not in Paris.[84] The reason behind this policy could be that, as Macklem mentions, 'international law values minority protection not only for reasons of universal value but also because it mitigates' conflicts.[85]

Overall, it can be said that the enlargement criteria have not had a significant impact on the situation of the Roma; as Vermeersch underlines, 'policy responses and legal regulations often turned out to be more symbolic and rhetorical than substantive and effective'.[86] Because specific minority rights are not part of EU law, the EU has no sanctioning power after the accession.[87] However, to some extent,

www.errc.org/roma-rights-journal/collective-expulsions-of-roma-around-europe-and-again-the-european-court-of-human-rights-rules-the-practice-illegal> accessed 2 December 2023.

[83] Balázs Majtényi, 'Where Are They Headed? The Situation of the Roma Minority in Hungarian and International Law' [2004] REGIO 82.
[84] Macklem (n 9) 546.
[85] ibid 541.
[86] Vermeersch (n 70) 220.
[87] Rachel A Epstein and Ulrich Sedelmeier, 'Beyond Conditionality: International Institutions in Postcommunist Europe after Enlargement' (2004) 6 Journal of European Public Policy 798.

formal compliance continued after accession. Latvia, for example, ratified the CoE Framework Convention in 2007.[88]

EU funding for Roma integration in the CEE candidate countries has been available since the beginning of the accession process. CEE countries have eagerly taken up these funds but do not always spend them on Roma, or not in the way the donors have wanted. In some cases, there is a decades-long history of misuse of Roma inclusion funds, making it difficult to develop effective policy and monitoring mechanisms. To take just one example: in Hungary, the State Audit Office estimated that governments spent 120 billion HUF on Roma integration between 1996 and 2006. From 2002 these amounts spiked, thanks to EU funds. According to the Hungarian State Audit Office, the main state body for supervising financial and economic governance in Hungary, the proportion of funds that reached the intended beneficiaries could not be identified.[89] It therefore seems like window dressing that the European Roma strategy was adopted under the Hungarian EU presidency of the Council of the European Union in 2011. Not spending the money available for Roma projects is a problem in CEE, and the Commission seems to lack the tools or the will to monitor this. There have been a few exceptions, such as the refusal to transfer further EU funds to Nyíregyháza, a Hungarian city which had spent the first instalment on deepening housing segregation.[90]

## 5.2. Roma policies after the accession of the CEE countries

'The Decade of Roma Inclusion, 2005–2015' was a programme that strove to promote the social inclusion of Roma with the participation of Central and Eastern and Southeastern European countries. It was based on knowledge exchange across the IOs and global funders. Various organizations participated in the development and implementation of the programme: the Open Society Institute (OSI), the United Nations Development Programme (UNDP), the CoE, and EU institutions.[91] The Decade programme provided a framework for Roma inclusion programmes in the member states. The goals of the programme were twofold: ending discrimination against Roma and reducing inequalities between Roma and

[88] ibid 801.

[89] Dr Gyula Pulay and Dr János Benkő, 'A magyarországi cigányság helyzetének javítására és felemelkedésére a rendszerváltás óta fordított támogatások mértékéről és hatékonyságáról' [2008] Állami Számvevőszék Fejlesztési és Módszertani Intézet 23.

[90] Dóra Ónody-Molnár and László Glonczi, 'A magyar adózók pénzéből csináltak egy jó nagy cigánytelepet', 38 <https://jelen.media/kozelet/glonczi-laszlo-a-magyar-adozok-penzebol-csinaltak-egy-jo-nagy-ciganytelepet/> accessed 18 May 2024.

[91] Christian Brüggemann and Eben Friedman, 'The Decade of Roma Inclusion: Origins, Actors, and Legacies' (2017) 1 European Education 1.

majority society in a decade,[92] all by improving the employment, education, housing, and health conditions of the minority. The impact of the programme has been less than expected, illustrated by the following quote from the monitoring report: 'Government funding allocations have generally been insufficient, while the effects of EU funding on the situation of Roma are not well documented, and the documented effects are somewhat ambivalent.'[93]

In April 2011, the European Commission adopted the EU Roma Strategy ('EU Framework for National Roma Integration Strategies up to 2020').[94] The Strategy called for the adoption of inclusion strategies in four priority areas—employment, education, health care, and housing—to improve the situation of the Roma people. In addition to anti-discrimination measures, the document proposed positive measures in the four priority areas to further help Roma. The document required member states to adopt a government strategy by the end of 2011 or to introduce an integrated set of policies (for member states with small Romani populations) based on the principles of equal opportunity and equal treatment of EU citizens.[95] The Strategy was criticized heavily because the design of the national inclusion programme was dependent on the political will of the member states, and it lacked a proper implementation mechanism.[96] Because of these shortcomings and the lack of sufficient focus on Roma participation and the fight against structural racism, the strategy failed to narrow the gap between Roma and the majority society. The language of the programme indicated that in the transnational space, the Roma question is interpreted as a social and anti-discrimination issue, irrespective of the struggles of Roma self-determination.

EU member states have to transpose the Racial Equality Directive, but little can be expected from the transposition alone in the absence of strong state-level equality policies and without a strong commitment from states to implement these policies. The national courts, by referring cases to the CJEU and the Commission through infringement procedure, would have an important role in the implementation of the Directive, but only a few cases have been referred.[97] In 2015, *CHEZ* was the only case in which the Court dealt with the merits of a Roma-related case.[98]

[92] Marek Szilvasi, 'Roma and the Contradictions of European Inclusion Policies: Citizens Associated With European Societies' (Dissertation, University of Aberdeen 2015).

[93] Decade of Roma Inclusion: Progress Report, UNDP, 18 June 2015, 38 <https://www.undp.org/eurasia/publications/decade-roma-inclusion-progress-report> accessed 2 December 2023.

[94] Szilvási (n 92) 145–62; Peter Vermeersch, 'The European Union and the Roma: an Analysis of Recent Institutional and Policy Developments' (2013) 10 European Yearbook of Minority Issues 352.

[95] Roland Ferkovics, Andrew Ryder, and Marek Szilvasi, 'Mechanisms of Empowerment for the Roma in a New Social Europe' in Andrew Ryder and others (eds), *Romani Communities and Transformative Change: A New Social Europe* (Bristol University Press 2021) 35.

[96] ibid 39.

[97] Gráinne de Búrca, 'The Decline of the EU Anti-Discrimination Law?' 3 <https://www.law.nyu.edu/sites/default/files/upload_documents/The%20Decline%20of%20the%20EU%20Anti-Discrimination%20Law.pdf> accessed 2 December 2023.

[98] Case C-83/14, *CHEZ Razpredelenie Bulgaria AD v Komisia za zashtita ot diskriminatsia (Nikolova)* (CJEU 16 July 2015) para 82.

The Commission's inaction regarding the discrimination of the Roma is especially problematic because it has the strongest powers to tackle systemic discrimination through infringement actions. But in many cases, the Commission has not used its power, even in cases that have been problematized by the EU institutions. To take an example, in 2013 Viviane Reding, speaking as EU Justice Commissioner, listed the limitation of Roma rights in France, expulsion of the Roma, among three serious rule of law crises within the EU. The Commission also toyed with the idea of an infringement procedure, but there was no political will for it. As mentioned earlier, the ERTF then turned to the CoE's Committee of Social Rights, which has no competence to make binding decisions.

Both the Court and the Commission have been subjects of criticism for the lack of a stronger response to ethnic discrimination against Roma. As Búrca noted, prohibition of racial discrimination would require active measures, for example 'the dismantling of entrenched or long-term social disadvantage ... which the Court may be reluctant to address or require'.[99] The European Commission launched infringement proceedings against the Czech Republic in 2014, Slovakia in 2015, and Hungary in 2016 for failure to comply with the Racial Equality Directive, which also prohibits discrimination in education, without any significant results. The Commission has since brought infringement action against Slovakia on account of segregated education of the Roma but this is the only action in which it has challenged systemic discrimination against this minority.

In 2020, the Commission issued the 'EU Roma Strategic Framework for Equality, Inclusion and Participation', which promotes member states' actions to tackle anti-Gypsyism and intersectional approaches and to empower Roma.[100] The document set seven EU-level targets for 2030, but it is questionable how these will be achieved. There are three horizontal targets in the areas of equality, inclusion, and participation, and four sectoral targets in the fields of education, employment, housing, and health. There are also quantitative minimum targets, but their feasibility is ambiguous, and it is also unclear how they take into account the different political, legal, economic, and social contexts in the member states. To take just one example, how will Member States achieve the target of at least 60 per cent of Roma in paid employment? The labour markets and economic situations in member states are very different. Or how to achieve the target of reducing by a third the number of people in the majority population who are not happy to have a Roma neighbour? How to influence it in countries where government policy is essentially based on otherization and the constant search for enemies? The strategy is also applicable to non-member states from the Western Balkans,

[99] de Búrca (n 97) 25.

[100] Andrew Ryder, Marius Taba, and Nidhi Trehan, 'The Roma Movement at a Crossroads – Competing Visions of Roma Civil Society and their Implications for Sustainable Community Organizing' [2022] ELTE POL-IR Working Paper Series 2, 22.

which is problematic as they are not fully within the scope of EU law. They should have been covered by a separate strategy. However, as in the case of the previous Roma strategy, the national strategies adopted within this framework often still lack coordinated implementation,[101] even if the EU tries to involve Roma civil society in the monitoring process.[102] The national strategies often do not provide timeframes, financial transparency, or indicators for all programmes. For example, in Hungary, church organizations close to the government, rather than Roma NGOs, are involved in implementation of the strategy.[103]

The Fundamental Rights Agency (FRA) is the EU institution that collects information on the situation of the Roma in the member states and evaluates them in its reports. The FRA rarely confronts member states[104] even though it does not report much progress on the situation of the Roma either.[105]

In the accession process of Eastern and Southeastern European countries, the EU focused on ensuring specific minority rights alongside equality. Later, the focus shifted to equality and social policies based on anti-discrimination provisions. The EU Roma strategies address the issue of social rights in several areas, but at the same time, in the absence of social rights in EU law, this means only policy aspirations. Thus, the strategies offer and seek to implement social policies without protecting social rights in international or EU law. Inexplicably, the binding instruments available to promote equality in the member states have received less attention, and there is a painful lack of robust fundamental rights jurisprudence and the use of existing monitoring tools on the Roma and other racialized groups.

## 6. Conclusion

After the collapse of the Eastern Bloc, Roma policy took on a European and transnational character, partly due to the activity of international organizations. The discourse that developed at the European level, despite its inconsistencies and doctrinal weaknesses, underlined the historical exclusion of the Roma minority,

[101] A synthesis of civil society's reports on the quality of the national strategic frameworks for Roma equality, inclusion, and participation in the European Union, 9 <https://romacivilmonitoring.eu/wp-content/uploads/2023/09/RCM_2022_Synthesis-report.pdf> accessed 2 December 2023.

[102] Roma Civil Monitor 2021–2025 <https://romacivilmonitoring.eu> accessed 22 October 2024.

[103] Civil society monitoring report on the quality of the national strategic framework for Roma equality, inclusion, and participation in Hungary, 39 <https://romacivilmonitoring.eu/wp-content/uploads/2023/07/RCM2-2022-C1-Hungary-FINAL-PUBLISHED-CATALOGUE.pdf> accessed 2 December 2023.

[104] Balázs Majtényi, Júlia Mink, and Zsolt Körtvélyesi, 'Betrayal: The EU Fundamental Rights Agency's Unexpected Support for Authoritarianism in Hungary' VerfBlog (10 May 2023) 9 <https://verfassungsblog.de/betrayal/> accessed 2 December 2023.

[105] Fundamental Rights Report 2023, 5 'Roma Equality and Inclusion' 13 <https://fra.europa.eu/sites/default/files/fra_uploads/fra-2023-fundamental-rights-report-2023-opinions_en.pdf> accessed 22 February 2024.

supported a common identity and drew attention to several unresolved social rights and public policy issues regarding the socially disadvantaged situation of Roma.

The official documents adopted by international organizations on the one hand recognized the nation-building aspirations of the Roma civil rights movement and on the other, adopted the traditional instruments of European minority protection, referring to the Roma as 'a true European minority',[106] a 'special minority group',[107] 'the largest minority in Europe',[108] 'Europe's largest ethnic minority',[109] or simply as Roma and Sinti people.[110] As Rövid states, in international documents the Roma developed from nomadic people into 'a true European minority'.[111]

Since 1990, international organizations have shaped policy and discourse on the Roma as a single, unified European minority. This has been compounded by the case law of the European courts, which shows fragmentation and is not always taken as the basis of policy proposals. The focus of international organizations gradually shifted from nation-building and minority protection policies primarily to integration, inclusion, and social policies, given the persistent exclusion of Roma in various countries. This is due partly to the anti-discrimination focus of these organizations, partly to the inadequacy of state-level policies.

Vermeersch also points out that the effect of these documents is largely symbolic because of the vagueness of the requirements,[112] which, as this chapter shows, mainly originates from the lack of powers in the field of specific minority and social rights. Actions regarding social rights would be crucial, as segregation occurs in the first place in education, housing, health care, and employment. Vermeersch mentions another negative effect of the Europeanization of the Roma issue and the emergence of a European Roma policy, namely that it provides 'domestic governments an opportunity to evade their responsibility'.[113] Recognizing the European nature of the minority and the adoption of the European Roma policies does not mean that national governments do not have to do anything about Roma integration. At the same time, the states do not cooperate properly with the IOs in the implementation of European Roma policies. They refer to the existence of these

[106] See eg Recommendation 1203 (1993) of the Parliamentary Assembly on Gypsies in Europe, General Observation, Point 2.

[107] ibid Point 4.

[108] Resolution 1740 (2010) on the situation of Roma in Europe and relevant activities of the Council of Europe of the Parliamentary Assembly, Point 1; An EU Framework for National Roma Integration Strategies up to 2020, 1 Introduction.

[109] See eg Resolution P6_TA(2005)0151 on the situation of the Roma in the European Union of the European Parliament, 28 April 2005, Art A.

[110] See eg Action Plan on Improving the Situation of Roma and Sinti within the OSCE Area (MC.DEC/3/03).

[111] Rövid (n 30) 3.

[112] Vermeersch (n 70).

[113] Vermeersch (n 94) 357.

policies to avoid their responsibilities, which is a good example of the inertia of international organizations.

Although the minority's apparent transnational character could not achieve substantial change in either the treatment of Roma by national institutions or in dismantling structural discrimination, the unity of Roma living in different countries became an accepted idea supported by IOs. The concept of Roma unity in the transnational sphere is acknowledged by actors of European politics. Meanwhile, the Roma political movement is increasingly defined by equality and social rights demands within a human rights framework, rather than specific minority rights or ethno-political claims. It cannot happen otherwise, because to enjoy human rights, including specific minority rights, politics must first take a stand against racism and poverty. As Raz argues, for effective multicultural policy, the equality and the dignity of persons belonging to minorities should be ensured, and the recognition of national identity can come only after.

> It is crucial to break the link between poverty, under-education and ethnicity. So long as certain ethnic groups are so overwhelmingly overrepresented among the poor, ill-educated, unskilled and semiskilled workers the possibilities of cultivating respect for their cultural identity, even the possibility of members of the group being able to have self-respect and to feel pride in their cultures are greatly undermined.[114]

According to the well-known leftist Critical Legal Studies argument : law, even existing human rights law, favours the privileged and disadvantages the oppressed.[115] The Roma minority is a historically oppressed minority that has a different experience of the law, such as harassment by police officers and humiliation by existing social policies. To ensure real access to civil and political rights, as well as to specific minority rights, there is a need for social rights, effective social policies, and substantive equality. The key point is that this will not work without the involvement of nation-states; European regulation in itself cannot offer a route for social inclusion.

The practice of American-style anti-discrimination litigation is doomed to fail before European courts without supportive institutions. In the US, the federal state was a partner in the process also in the absence of social rights, with competencies and enforcement powers that European regional institutions are currently lacking. The ECtHR and CJEU judgments need similar support from the member states. The EU institutions, especially the European Commission, have failed to take stronger action against member states to promote equality for Roma under European anti-discrimination and equality law.

[114] Joseph Raz, 'Multiculturalism' (1998) 3 Ratio Juris 193.
[115] Lewis A Kornhauser, 'The Great Image of Authority' (1984) 1–2 Stanford Law Review 367.

International human rights and minority law are regulated at a very high level of abstraction and generally protect the rights of minorities. The nature of international law and the principle of state sovereignty make it difficult to deal with specific minorities at this level. Even if, due to their extreme marginalization, international and European law must deal with specific minorities and recommend specific policies, it cannot solve all the problems in national legal systems or policy processes. If regulation is uniform at the international level, specificities are lost. This is the case for example, if regulation seeks to cover the different situations of the British Travellers, the Roma in camps in Italy, and the municipal segregation of the Roma in Hungary.

To move towards more effective international regulation, it is necessary to discuss first the proper allocation of powers and responsibilities between nation-states and international actors. International organizations should hold nation-states accountable for unresolved issues and should not try, even with good intentions, to take on tasks for which they lack power. The lack of strong international commitments and monitoring mechanisms for social rights also makes it difficult for international organizations to develop effective social policies, Within the current legislative framework, more human rights activism on social rights would be needed from civil society and the European courts to strengthen the doctrinal basis of social policy. Still, even in this case, policy-making at the European level could not provide a real solution.

The chapter has highlighted two main reasons for the lack of results expected from law and European Roma policies. The first is the lack of strong competencies of the European institutions in the area of minority and social rights, which is inadequately compensated by CoE treaties and jurisprudence. Second, European organizations are keen to develop uniform policies on issues that should essentially be left to national actors. Still, international organizations have an important role in identifying human rights problems, keeping them on the agenda and naming and shaming states that persistently violate them. The effectiveness of international organizations can be greatly enhanced by the human rights activism of treaty-based bodies and EU institutions that can issue binding decisions on national governments. To push the boundaries of the minority and social rights of the Roma, they should focus on adopting, interpreting, and enforcing international human rights and EU fundamental rights law, and drop the illusion that by developing Roma policies at the European level they can avoid this responsibility.

# PART II
# THE CONCEPTUAL FRAME

# 4

# The European Court of Human Rights and Strategic Litigation to Support Roma Peoples

*Kris Gledhill*

## 1. Introduction—Explaining and Contextualizing Strategic Litigation

In *Strategic Human Rights Litigation: Understanding and Maximising Impact*,[1] Duffy explores various cases in which she was involved as a strategic litigator and provides an overview and taxonomy of impacts. She shows how litigation can have impacts at multiple levels. For victims who are parties to litigation, impacts can include positives, namely vindication, restoration, reparation, and the creation of activists;[2] negative impacts are risked, including repeated victimization.[3] Impacts can be more systemic, namely moving beyond the parties: for example, creating opportunities for other victims, changing laws, policies and practices that affect many others, and strengthening institutions and movements that lead to a better society.[4] The focus on impacts emphasizes how litigation can be both a remedy for the party bringing a case but also a vector for change that will help others: this will inevitably be a matter of interest where there are multiple victims. Systemic discrimination will be such a situation: hence a part of this chapter explores strategic litigation for Roma. First, we turn to matters of definition or conceptualization.

[1] Helen Duffy, *Strategic Human Rights Litigation: Understanding and Maximising Impact* (Hart Publishing 2018).

[2] ibid 50–59. At 75–76, she notes that parties who become activists may encourage other victims, a process of 'mobilisation and empowerment'.

[3] ibid 77–79.

[4] ibid. She refers to developing legal standards (at 59–63, including striking down national laws, prompting the enforcement of underused laws, developing normative standards (including transnational ones), or showing the need for reform and perhaps prompting it), changing or frustrating improper policies or practices (at 63–67), securing useful information and promoting more openness (at 76–77), strengthening institutions, including NGOs and the judiciary, involved in protecting rights, or more generally embedding the rule of law and democracy, including judicial review of government action (at 57–69, 76–77); there is also social or cultural impact from reframing issues and influencing attitudes in society, hopefully positively but with the risk of backlash (at 72–74, 77–79).

Kris Gledhill, *The European Court of Human Rights and Strategic Litigation to Support Roma Peoples*
In: *The Rights of Roma in European Courts*. Edited by: Kristin Henrard and Lilla Farkas, Oxford University Press.
 DOI: 10.1093/oso/9780198914358.003.0004

Despite the title of her book, Duffy not only eschews providing a definition of strategic litigation but comments that the 'hours of academic industry' this would entail are 'mostly a distraction' from the key focus on the impact of litigation.[5] Others have taken on the mantle of seeking to define strategic litigation or identify the components that cause organizations to self-identify as being involved in it. Accordingly, van der Pas sought to conceptualize strategic litigation in order to work towards a definition, noting that 'the exact definition … remains unclear'.[6] She concludes that for litigation (ie court proceedings) to be strategic, it has to involve the making of strategic choices within litigation but also using the litigation 'as a means to reach an overarching objective'.[7] The essential constituent is seeking broader change (ie not just securing the benefit to the individual client that is the focus of non-strategic—or 'regular'—litigation),[8] which desire to 'realise change' can be achieved in various ways.[9]

Van der Pas indexed and analysed the commonalities in results found by searching the term 'strategic litigation' on Google, Google Scholar and HeinOnline. Previously, Ramsden and I analysed entries from a Google search, which allowed us to suggest the four main features of how strategic litigation was being used.[10] The first was its extrinsic legacy component—seeking outcomes with a long-term impact, going beyond the origins of the claimant's complaint; this is consistent with the focus of Duffy and was part of what van der Pas considered central. The second was that it is a method of advocacy and so adaptable to a range of causes; this reflects the finding of van der Pas that has a focus on strategic litigation as a process rather than a cause in itself. The third feature was its multi-faced objectives, not limited to creating effects within the court system but extending to other mechanisms of securing social change. This arose from references such as its use in 'raising awareness; building political pressure; identifying gaps in the law; fostering public discussion and coalition building' and that 'change is not always aimed at the legal

[5] ibid 3. This is perhaps understandable for a litigator with practical concerns.

[6] Kris van der Pas, 'Conceptualising Strategic Litigation' (2021) 11(6(S)) Oñati Socio-Legal Series 116 <https://opo.iisj.net/index.php/osls/article/view/1315> accessed 18 March 2024. At 117, she notes 'it is unclear what elements and conditions are part of the concept'.

[7] ibid 124. At 130, she summarizes the first requirement as 'certain choices (or ploys)' being 'made within the process of strategic litigation' to secure the change.

[8] ibid 124–25; at 125 she states that 'The aim is to advance different interests and effect change', and at 130 that 'litigation is used as a means to reach certain objectives', namely 'creating change beyond the individual case or individual interest'.

[9] ibid 125: examples include vaguely phrased aims such as 'law and policy reform' or 'social change', to slightly more distinct but still broad aims of changing laws, practices, public opinion, or awareness, to more precise aims such as setting precedents or solving issues that are politically sensitive and so unresolved. She accepts that a case need not be strategic at the outset, but can become strategic at an appellate level: but it cannot become strategic afterwards, given the lack of a plan to secure change. Of course, since comments in any judgment may form the basis for further litigation, further lawyers can use any case in a strategic way.

[10] Michael Ramsden and Kris Gledhill, 'Defining Strategic Litigation' (2019) 4 Civil Justice Quarterly 407; van der Pas kindly indicates that this article was a catalyst for her work.

or policy-level, but sometimes at enforcement and practice or raising the visibility of an issue and changing attitudes'.[11]

The fourth feature was the broad understanding of 'litigation' to include tribunals and international mechanisms of redress. This means that bodies such as the European Court of Human Rights (ECtHR), with transnational coverage and hence potential impact, may be ideal for strategic litigation. The Strasbourg Court's function, set out in Article 19 of the European Convention on Human Rights 1950 (ECHR), is to 'ensure the observance undertaken by' the member states. Those include the general obligation in Article 1 to guarantee rights and that in Article 13 to provide remedies for any breach of rights.[12] The approach it has developed includes implying additional rights so that the ECHR regime is 'practical and effective' rather than 'theoretical and illusory',[13] and the 'living instrument' approach means that the content of rights can change over time.[14] A real dispute is required: as Article 34 requires a victim, the ECtHR will not accept an *actio popularis*.[15]

The ECHR is concerned with civil and political rights (including non-discrimination); the Council of Europe also has its European Social Charter (1961, revised in 1996). This is supervised by the European Committee of Social Rights, to which states report on implementation: the Committee comments on the propriety of this. Additionally, under a 1995 Additional Protocol, the Committee can hear collective complaints, including from approved non-governmental organizations, one of which is the European Roma Rights Centre. Consistently with the fourth main feature of strategic litigation, a willingness to look to processes such as these collective complaints is needed.

Understanding these accounts of strategic litigation is assisted by considering whether and if so how it differs from other phrases. Duffy suggests that strategic litigation is 'sometimes referred to as "public interest" or simply "impact" litigation'.[16]

[11] ibid 415.

[12] Art 2(2) of the International Covenant on Civil and Political Rights (adopted 16 December 1966, entered into force 23 March 1976) 999 UNTS 171 (ICCPR) is more directive, setting out that 'legislative or other measures' should be taken to secure rights not already in place; Art 2(3) requires remedies.

[13] *Airey v Ireland* App no 6289/73 (ECtHR, 9 October 1979) para 24: legal aid in civil proceedings might be required for fairness despite the Convention text referring expressly only to criminal legal aid. As the ECHR is phrased at a high level of principle or abstraction, implications are inevitable.

[14] The starting point is *Tyrer v UK* App no 5856/72 (ECtHR, 25 April 1978) para 31, where the Court noted that 'the Convention is a living instrument which ... must be interpreted in the light of present-day conditions'; it is a duty, it being noted in *Demir and Baykara v Turkey* [GC] App no 34503/97 (ECtHR, 12 November 2008) para 15 that 'a failure by the Court to maintain a dynamic and evolutive approach would risk rendering it a bar to reform or improvement'.

[15] See for example *Centre for Legal Resources on behalf of Valentin Câmpeanu v Romania* App no 47848/08 [GC] (ECtHR, 17 July 2014) para 101. In *Beizaras and Levickas v Lithuania* App no 41288/15 (ECtHR, 14 January 2020) para 80, it was noted that an NGO interested in conducting strategic litigation could represent applicants, even if it had a strategic litigation aim in doing so, so long as the applicants were genuine applicants, rather than raising an abstract claim).

[16] Duffy (n 1) 76–77; she also comments, ibid, that strategic litigation generally means 'litigation that pursues goals—or which concerns interests—that are broader than only those of the immediate

Similarly, the Open Society Justice Initiative indicated that its report 'Strategic Litigation Impacts: Roma School Desegregation' adds to the 'burgeoning field of strategic litigation, which is also referred to as public-interest or impact litigation'.[17]

In contrast, van der Pas suggests that, while there are overlaps, strategic litigation differs from public interest or impact litigation. She notes that whilst there is no settled definition of public interest litigation,[18] and although there is dispute about what amounts to the 'public interest',[19] certain criteria point towards litigation being with the concept. One is providing access to groups who do not have ready access to the courts or political fora, another is a motivation beyond merely seeking to win a case (and which can range from altruism to political commitment), and a third is the involvement of not-for-profit organizations.[20] Van der Pas suggests that strategic litigation differs in that, of these three pointers, access might be a goal of strategic litigation but is not a defining component, motivation to change could be relevant, but not-for-profit organizations are not necessary; and also that there is no political element, in that strategic litigation is a process and there is no regard to the political value of the change sought.[21]

Similarly, in relation to 'impact or test case litigation', van der Pas suggests there are clear overlaps with her working definition of strategic litigation in that 'A test case can have an overarching objective to create change (beyond the individual interest/case), but also a test case can be specifically designed, meaning that there is a specific strategy (multitude of ploys) used in the test case'.[22] On the definition offered by Ramsden and myself, strategic litigation can be part of raising the profile of an issue to build political momentum, which has a wider focus than an approach that is predicated on success within the court system, of establishing the point of law that will be used by others that is the component of impact or test case litigation.[23] Another phrase, 'cause lawyering', involves pursuing ends beyond just servicing a client and which have some form of political or moral commitment: van

parties' and in its human-rights based incarnation 'uses the courts to advance human rights in a way that reaches beyond the particular victims or applicants at the centre of the particular case'.

[17] Adriána Zimová, *Strategic Litigation Impacts: Roma School Desegregation* (Open Society Justice Initiative 2016) <https://www.justiceinitiative.org/publications/strategic-litigation-impacts-roma-school-desegregation> accessed 19 August 2024, 10: 'Strategic litigation, often also referred to as public interest litigation, impact litigation, or cause lawyering, can be many things'. See Ramsden and Gledhill (n 10) 418–20 for a discussion of other organizations that draw these equivalences.

[18] Van der Pas (n 6) 119: 'similar debates on the meaning of the U.S. counterpart of strategic litigation, public interest litigation, have been taking place for a longer period of time'.

[19] ibid 128.

[20] ibid 127–29. At 128, she notes that in India there is a more settled notion of litigation on behalf of under-represented people.

[21] ibid 128–29.

[22] ibid 130.

[23] It might be that litigation demonstrates that courts do not have the institutional capacity to effect the relevant change.

der Pas notes that, whilst the former aspect is part of strategic litigation, the latter commitment is not.[24]

Van der Pas places strategic litigation as 'part of the umbrella term "legal mobilisation"',[25] defined by Lehoucq and Taylor as 'the use of law in an explicit, self-conscious way through the invocation of a formal institutional mechanism'.[26] They point out that it can be used by social movements, but that this is not a necessary condition, as individuals and other groups could make use of the law in this regard. They also comment that litigation is not the only activity that counts: boycotts and letter-writing campaigns are given as other examples.[27]

Duffy's critique of taking time and effort to define strategic litigation is understandable: a practical focus on impact is key for a litigator. However, ongoing efforts to conceptualize and define strategic litigation, and place it in the context of other phrases, have value for two obvious reasons. First, not all lawyers are experienced and so these efforts help lawyers who wish to understand how to become strategic litigators. Secondly, strategic litigation requires clients and cases, and the efforts to provide a working definition and conceptualization show that the phrase is often used by civil society organizations who undertake or support the litigation: as non-lawyers may be involved, it helps that they know what makes litigation strategic. However, the efforts by Ramsden and myself and then van der Pas make clear that this is a work in progress. Hence, this chapter seeks to add further to this process by examining what has been written about strategic litigation in support of one cause, namely countering systemic discrimination against Roma.

## 2. Debating Strategic Litigation in the Roma Context

The original material in this chapter rests on an analysis of documents located by searching 'strategic litigation Roma' through Google, Google Scholar and Hein Online, with the expectation of locating both academic and popular materials.[28] Some materials appeared in more than one search; and academic

[24] Van der Pas (n 6) 129. See also Ramsden and Gledhill (n 10) 422–23.

[25] ibid 118. Ramsden and Gledhill (n 10) 408 noted that various scholars had used 'cause lawyering' as the overarching term: as our suggested definition of strategic litigation, based on how it was being used, extended beyond simply litigation, the use of 'legal mobilization' as the overarching term seems sensible.

[26] Emilio Lehoucq and Whitney K Taylor, 'Conceptualizing Legal Mobilization: How Should We Understand the Deployment of Legal Strategies?' (2020) 45 Law & Social Inquiry 166. At 186, they phrase it as 'the use of law in an explicit, self-conscious way through the invocation of a formal institutional mechanism', adding also definitions of '*legal consciousness* as the implicit, nonarticulated use of law to give meaning to an event, and *legal framing* as the explicit, self-conscious use of law to give meaning to an event'.

[27] ibid 173.

[28] This mirrors the approach of van der Pas, which builds on what Ramsden and I did. This rests on a snapshot of what the relevant search engines produce at the time of the search: it is a starting point for the collection of material to be analysed.

materials included reference to material from activists. There were, broadly, two categories: materials relating to strategic litigation more generally illustrated with references to Roma-linked strategic litigation as examples; and materials relating to strategic litigation that had a focus on Roma (sometimes exclusively and sometimes in the context of discrimination based on ethnic or national origin generally and with Roma as a centrally important group). The goals of the analysis were, first, to determine whether a focus on strategic litigation in one context assisted in clarifying the core elements of strategic litigation more generally; and, secondly, also to identify themes and disputes about strategic litigation as a tool to help Roma people.

## 2.1. Consistency with suggested definitions—particularly impact

The accounts in Part I note that strategic litigation can be used for various purposes. Naturally, strategic litigation for Roma people has one overarching purpose, namely a better future for Roma. Hence the indication given above that strategic litigation can be used for various purposes is not part of the discussion in this section. The key element of strategic litigation is the aim for a legacy beyond that of resolving the dispute brought by the parties. That is clearly central to those who take strategic litigation for Roma. Accordingly, the website of the European Roma Rights Centre (ERRC), clearly the most active strategic litigator for Roma, does not define strategic litigation but makes clear that there is an aim for impact.[29] Moreover, the impact should not merely be within the court system. Hence, there is reference to changing how 'police, ministers, judges, and others ... act'. Indeed, there was a plan of action designed to affect multiple actors, including those exercising important powers: 'We want the European Court to recognise the existence and scope of antigypsyism[30] and to push State officials and courts across Europe to respect Romani people's equality and dignity'. This involves a focus on systemic factors: references are made to the aim to 'expose and eliminate discriminatory structures', 'antigypsyism', and to secure respect for 'Romani people's equality and dignity'. Moreover, it extends across a wide geographical ambit, with references to cases across Europe.

In addition to this focus on impact, and reflecting the fourth element in the working definition offered by Ramsden and myself, there is an expressed

[29] European Roma Rights Centre <https://www.errc.org/what-we-do/strategic-litigation> accessed 19 August 2024. Its striking opening explanation is that it functions to 'take racists to court'.

[30] This first appears in an ECtHR judgment in *Vona v Hungary* App no 35943/10 (ECtHR, 9 July 2013), in which the ERRC was an intervener: concurring in the view that dissolving a nationalist and anti-Roma group did not breach Art 11, Judge Pinto de Albuquerque expressed the view that the Court should declare the need to criminalize the dissemination of racism. He cited multiple sources, including the Council of Europe Committee of Ministers' 'Declaration on the Rise of Anti-Gypsyism and Racist Violence against Roma in Europe', 1 February 2012.

willingness to seek national and transnational remedies, with reference made to domestic courts, the ECtHR, the European Committee of Social Rights and UN Treaty bodies. There is also reference to different ways of being involved in a case: bringing cases, supporting other lawyers, and intervening in cases.

Other relevant materials also have an emphasis on impact, setting it as an aim (and so supporting its position as a definitional component of strategic litigation); there is also material on how it can be secured.

### 2.1.1. The aim of having impact

Regular references to impacting problematic systemic features suggest this aim is an established central feature of strategic litigation for Roma. Accordingly, in 'Strategic Litigation Impacts: Roma School Desegregation', reference is made to 'strategic litigation as a social change agent', to its potential to generate 'social, political, and legal change', and its potential for 'breaking down longstanding injustices and opening new paths of human rights protection and enforcement'.[31] Sys has offered a definition that strategic litigation is 'designed to not only vindicate the rights of applicants, but to importantly contribute to a wider package of activism in an attempt to redress widespread abuses and create social impact'.[32] Goldston comments that it 'can ... lead to pathbreaking declarations of fundamental principle, and shine a spotlight on injustices in a manner that commands attention' and 'can improve laws, institutions and lives'.[33]

Similarly, authors from the Centre for Legal Resources in Romania note that strategic litigation is taken to win both 'cases' and 'also human rights causes',[34]

[31] Zimová (n 17) 10: it is noted that strategic litigation is 'bringing a case before a court with the explicit aim of positively impacting persons other than the individual complainants before the court'. The impacts studied are 'changes in policy, practice, and mobilization', and there is reference to 'quantitative indicators', including changes in numbers in segregation and numbers of segregated schools.

[32] Filip Sys, 'DH v Czech Republic: Roma Educational Equality and the Vulnerability of Strategic Litigation' (2020) 20(1) Acta Universitatis Carolinae Studia Territorialia 71, 72 <https://www.researchgate.net/publication/347299705_DH_v_Czech_Republic_Roma_Educational_Equality_and_the_Vulnerability_of_Strategic_Litigation>, accessed 19 August 2024. At 87, the aim is noted to be to 'vindicate applicants' rights but, more profoundly, to also impact victimised communities'; and its attraction is the opportunity for 'reshaping jurisprudential and legal landscapes' (albeit that, as is noted at 75, this entails enforcing obligations undertaken by states). He uses the example of the *DH* litigation, commenting at 73 that its 'wider effect ... was to vicariously represent the denied rights of a historically marginalised community, systemically reform national education policy and attempt to break the generational abuse of' exclusion from society, commencing in childhood; and at 75 he comments that changes were unlikely without strategic litigation.

[33] James A Goldston 'Challenges in Executing Judgments of the European Court of Human Rights: the case of the Roma' EJIL: Talk! (8 December 2023) <https://www.ejiltalk.org/challenges-in-executing-judgments-of-the-european-court-of-human-rights-the-case-of-the-roma/> accessed 19 August 2024. He uses the *DH* litigation as an example: it represented a 'giant jurisprudential leap forward', by showing that Art 14 could be breached by indirect discrimination, but also changed public debate by precluding arguments based on justifying segregation as the way things were or even as being in the interests of Roma, led to 'better data collection ... better informed consent, better cultural validity to diagnostic tests and regular re-tests, and law that those without disability not follow curricula for those with disability'.

[34] Ágnes Csonta and Delia-Luiza Niţă, *Human Rights Litigation on Behalf of The Roma. A Guide for Lawyers* (Centre for Legal Resources, Romania 2014) <https://ec.europa.eu/justice/discrimination/

and its 'aim to persuade policy makers and legislators that a different approach is needed'.[35] The contention is that the title 'strategic' is applicable when a case is 'representative for a broader number of people, or for a specific rights breach which happens with frequency, or for a problematic legal provision in need of change, or for a particular practice which must be changed'.[36]

In its handbook, *Strategic Litigation*, Equinet, the European Network of Equality Bodies, notes the intention of strategic litigation proceedings to 'have a positive broader impact on law and policy development as well as setting a precedent for the outcome in similar cases'.[37] Equinet also provides a useful categorization of the types of impact sought, noting that they can be 'intra-legal and extra-legal', namely those aimed at the content or coverage of the law, and those that are not.[38] The former type includes establishing good precedents (eg clarity that something is discrimination) or overturning bad ones, the latter type includes highlighting a situation as part of a campaign.

### 2.1.2. The mechanisms of impact

Reflecting the suggestion by Duffy, noted in section 1, that impact can be in various forms, materials relating to strategic litigation for Roma note that impact can occur in several ways. Litigation may lead to directions given in a successful court judgment, including declarations of how a law is to be interpreted and whether a purported law is constitutionally valid, or injunctions to prevent things happening or recurring. Judgments of some courts, including international bodies, may have particularly wide-ranging effects, which is one reason for their use. Rulings of the ECtHR may be directly relevant to the constitutional provisions in a state or may have statutory impact through legislation such as the UK's Human Rights Act 1998 or Ireland's European Convention on Human Rights Act 2003. As such, doctrines developed by the ECtHR, such as the obligations to take steps to prevent private actors breaching rights or more generally to require positive steps to protect rights, can have significant impact in multiple jurisdictions.

However, courts have institutional limitations. For example, they can critique legislation, pointing out its flaws, but cannot draft the proper replacement.

files/roma_lawyers_guide_en.pdf> accessed 19 August 2024, 6; at 13, there is reference to how more cases against discrimination 'would help to effectively dismantle these barriers'.

[35] ibid 16.

[36] ibid 15.

[37] Equinet, *Strategic Litigation*, 2017 <https://equineteurope.org/wp-content/uploads/2018/05/equinet-handbook_strategic-litigation_def_web-1.pdf> accessed 19 August 2024, 10: the potential for 'widespread benefits for society in general in addition to those involved in the specific case' is noted (possible outcomes being 'changes in legislation and government policy', higher 'public awareness' or 'support for a particular issue'; at 40, the importance of follow-up is noted, given the aim 'to have a wider impact on law and society beyond those involved in an individual case', which should be 'meaningful and effective'.

[38] ibid 9.

In addition, implementation is usually not for the court, particularly if it is an international court which has to rely on the duty of states to comply with judgments: enforcing international law is often a matter of politics. For example, Article 41 of the ECHR puts the Council of Ministers in charge of implementing judgments of the ECtHR. (Further material on difficulties of implementation is discussed below.)

As such, there may be a disconnect between the aim of a broad impact beyond the dispute between the parties and what can realistically come directly from a court judgment. But this is why strategic litigation is packaged together with other forms of advocacy as an element in a broader campaign. Abdikeeva, Ezer, and Covaci, writing in the context of health law, have suggested features that can be used to assess effectiveness: their criteria also speak to the sorts of things that could be included in a plan to build on a positive judgment in the context of a wider campaign. They refer to assessing effectiveness through examining—

> changes … including (i) changes resulting from novel jurisprudence; (ii) the increased effectiveness of under-utilised legal procedures; (iii) amendments to health rights legislation; (iv) improvements in the capacity of NGOs to carry out strategic litigation; and (v) increased legal awareness among Roma communities.[39]

Indeed, the process of change may not necessarily arise from a judgment but from the proceedings. Hence, the Centre for Legal Resources in Romania notes the prospect that a case might 'raise general awareness on the law, but also change people's notion of what is permissible and what is not',[40] which may change the approach of policy-makers and legislators through the case itself and 'the ensuing public debate around the problem'.[41] They also raise the possibility that policy-makers might make the necessary changes before a case is finished.[42] As such, a strategic litigation case may be taken without a primary aim of winning it. Hence, the Centre's authors note that—

> Some cases can be strategic simply because they provide the opportunity to bring important problems which need to be debated into the public arena, and they

[39] Alphia Abdikeeva, Tamar Ezer, and Alina Covaci, 'Assessing Legal Advocacy to Advance Roma Health in Macedonia, Romania, and Serbia' (2013) 20 European Journal of Health Law 471, 485 <https://brill.com/view/journals/ejhl/20/5/article-p471_3.xml> accessed 19 August 2024. The authors are part of the Open Society Foundations. They note that more legal challenges leading to findings of civil or criminal responsibility should change medical practices, adding that parallel aspects of the wider campaign, such as 'media advocacy and stakeholder dialogue' should lead healthcare professionals to act 'not simply on the fear of lawsuits but also on a genuine change in attitudes resulting from a better understanding of the Roma's situation'.

[40] Csonta and Niţă (n 34) 13.

[41] ibid 16. See also at 13, where there is reference to changing notions of what is permissible.

[42] ibid 16.

may be worthwhile pursuing for this reason alone, even if victory is not necessarily very likely.[43]

Likewise, the Equinet handbook notes that 'losing a case in court can entail progress towards achieving a strategic objective' by 'demonstrating that a change in the law is necessary'.[44] Whilst this is a potentially risky approach, as is discussed below, it makes the point that litigation is not to be viewed as standing alone.

### 2.1.3. Impact through empowerment

The fifth measure suggested by Abdikeeva and others, noted above, is the extent of increased knowledge of rights amongst Roma. This knowledge, important in itself, is also a mechanism for impact through empowerment. The ERRC website also referenced the important and empowering function of the rule of law: one aspect of this was the point that discrimination by states involves them 'breaking the laws they agreed to respect', such that strategic litigation was using the power of the law to secure respect for the law. A further aspect was the aim to build the confidence of Roma to use the law to counter discrimination against them.

This important form of impact is reflected in other materials. Accordingly, an entry on the ERRC website from 2015 notes that cases have to be 'part of their emancipation story, so that litigation becomes part of the movement'.[45] The guide from the Centre for Legal Resources in Romania refers to the fact that successful cases 'also help empower Roma as they would become aware that it is actually possible to win'.[46] Further, Sys refers to emancipation stories from Roma being believed, allowing case victories 'to provide an emotional cornerstone on which victims, NGOs and other stakeholders can rely and build'.[47]

### 2.1.4. Coordination for impact

The institutional limitations on courts, noted above, including their inability to enforce and draft suitable laws, is one reason why strategic litigation should be used in conjunction with other tools.[48] Accordingly, the Open Society Justice Initiative

[43] ibid 15–16.

[44] Equinet (n 37) 39: it is noted that suitable publicity, particularly of sympathetic facts, 'may serve to increase public awareness of a legal problem, or garner support for a change in the law'.

[45] Adam Weiss, 'What Is Strategic Litigation' 1 June 2015 <https://www.errc.org/news/what-is-strategic-litigation> accessed 19 August 2024.

[46] Csonta and Niţă (n 34) 13.

[47] Sys (n 32) 87–90: he records how the *DH* litigation had practical impacts, including community consciousness of rights and using rights to secure better education opportunities for Roma children, and he cites an interview with James A Goldston in which the latter made the point that Roma came to understand that the law, which hitherto had been used to counter their rights, came to be seen as something that could be used to secure justice, empowering people to become activists against the status quo, translating the legal victory from the courtroom to the community.

[48] Ramsden and I noted that some NGOs included 'nonlegal tools within the armour of a strategic litigator', though we suggested that 'these tools fall within the much broader field of cause advocacy': Ramsden and Gledhill (n 10) 425. The suggestion of van der Pas, noted in Part I above, that

refers to strategic litigation as 'one tool among many' that can secure change 'in combination with other efforts';[49] the Centre for Legal Resources in Romania notes that 'strategic litigation for Roma is generally part of larger advocacy campaigns'.[50] Sys links this directly to the limitations on litigation: 'legal strategies alone are vulnerable to various obstacles and, consequently, extra-legal activism must play a pivotal role in implementation efforts'.[51] Indeed, this illustrates the need for a different approach by strategic litigators: securing a legacy involving social change, ie going beyond the court system, requires a focus beyond the judgment, namely ensuring that the judgment makes a difference for those other than the parties. This additional focus supports the need for coordination before, during and after litigation.

### (a) *Coordination prior to and during litigation*

Change may be of interest to more than one organization or group of people: whilst different groups may take different approaches, communication and coordination may help, or at least reduce the risks of efforts being undermined. The Centre for Legal Resources in Romania notes that national or international 'NGOs or networks' might assist through *amicus curiae* interventions or 'gathering statistical data' that might be presented.[52] Collaboration may also lead to suitable clients being identified so that a case can be taken. Hence, the Equinet handbook records that: 'strategic cases often reach the [equality] body through nongovernmental organizations, lawyers, media, other public and private entities, as well as complaints directly from individuals'.[53]

there has to be a strategy within the litigation and about the litigation supports the centrality of these 'nonlegal tools' as part of the process of securing social change. It may be that the lawyer carrying out the litigation does not have a focus on these wider tools: but the designation of litigation as strategic rather than client-centred suggests that someone has this focus.

[49] Open Society Justice Initiative, introducing Zimová's report (n 17) <https://www.justiceinitiative.org/publications/strategic-litigation-impacts-roma-school-desegregation> accessed 19 August 2024; see also Abdikeeva, Ezer, and Covaci (n 39) suggesting that court cases combined with parallel advocacy will lead to changes in attitudes rather that defensive practices designed to avoid lawsuits; and Goldston (n 33), writing about executing judgments, makes the point that strategic litigation 'is neither a panacea nor an invitation to disaster. Rather, it is one tool among many, a tactic that—under the right circumstances and in combination with other efforts—can improve laws, institutions and lives'.

[50] Csonta and Niţă (n 34) 15.

[51] Sys (n 32) 75. His article calls for the combination of legal proceedings with activism: at 78, he records that 'extra-legal activism' was 'essential in keeping the spotlight on respondent states' in relation to education, and at 89 he notes that ensuring rights-consciousness amongst Roma parents to ensure they insisted on the rights for their children made them 'everyday activists', ensuring that 'the fight for emancipation' represented by *DH* did not 'cease in the courtroom'.

[52] Csonta and Niţă (n 34) 16.

[53] Equinet (n 37) 36. These routes are then discussed in turn. The focus of the quotation is ensuring that suitable cases reach domestic equality bodies: there seems no obvious reason why clients for strategic litigation before a transnational body cannot be identified in a similar way.

*(b) Coordination with those arguing cases*

Lawyers who argue a case will not necessarily work in-house with an organization that has a strategic aim, and in any event have ethical duties towards clients and courts that precludes them simply being the voice of their employer. Accordingly, there should be coordination between litigators and those involved in wider advocacy. The Centre for Legal Resources in Romania sets out joint and individual roles, noting that NGOs 'generally ... identify and document the cases which lawyers represent legally', 'supports the victim throughout the process', 'usually manage the relationship with the media and eventual partnerships'; NGOs and lawyers together 'decide on the best legal strategy for the case and assess their success prospects, as well as the risks', 'explain to the general public the stakes at play in the case, why these stakes matter, and ... work with the media to send the messages to the public'; and lawyers will advise on coordination with other NGOs as to interventions and statistical evidence.[54]

*(c) Coordination for implementation*

There is also a need for coordination to ensure that any court ruling secures change. The Centre for Legal Resources in Romania notes that, with exceptions,

> policy and legislation change with great difficulty even when the case is won. It often takes more legal cases to determine change, and it is therefore important that victory is capitalized upon, that the case results are further advertised and introduced in legal training curricula, that monitoring of implementation happens and that the NGO which supported the case further foresees resources to ensure implementation.[55]

The Equinet handbook refers to the value of a 'communication plan' and also follow-up work to consolidate impact.[56] Similarly, Sys refers to the need for 'extra-legal activism', namely 'measures which are beyond litigation and post-judgment legislative reforms' as 'an essential partner to strategic litigation', examples being 'collecting ethnically disaggregated data of Roma children in special education, creating victim empowerment projects, raising public awareness or giving agency to Roma communities'.[57]

[54] Csonta and Niţă (n 34) 15–16.

[55] ibid 16.

[56] Equinet (n 37) 38–40. The communication plan can include seeking to counter what a state might say to try to minimize a case it has lost, or to garner support for a change in the law if the claimant has lost.

[57] Sys (n 32) 75: he notes that 'a historically hostile socio-political environment' has to be taken into account; and at 76 he comments that 'simply relying on strategic litigation to independently reform hostile environments is futile and requires extra-legal activism to confront underlying discriminatory attitudes and inequalities'.

The value of impact is self-evident in the context of rights not being respected. The need for supporting actions, including coordination, suggests that securing impact may have complexities and cannot be guaranteed. This points to a wider issue, namely the need to assess risks and challenges.

## 2.2. Risks and challenges to balance against benefits

Public interest litigation, which as noted above has some overlaps with strategic litigation, has been subject to significant analysis, including as to its value. For example, Cummings and Rhode have noted that 'the vision of court-centered social change' that emerged as the public interest law movement in the USA in the 1960s and 1970s was successful because of a 'receptive' judiciary and outcomes that could be achieved 'through impact lawsuits'.[58] But this led to changes that undermined its potential—the appointment of 'less hospitable' judges, changed structures of government that were less amenable to such lawsuits and 'procedural and financial constraints' on strategic litigators.[59] Moreover, there were strands of 'scholarly critique', including research that questioned how law reform could have a significant effect, that it diverted from the need to secure real change through political movements, and that it did not properly reflect the wishes of affected communities.[60]

This leads to questions about whether the aim of impact is better secured through actions other than litigation.[61] Not surprisingly, there is similar discussion in the context of strategic litigation.

### 2.2.1. Challenges

The challenges of implementation might be one reason to consider whether resources—financial, expertise and time—expended on strategic litigation might better be used elsewhere. Goldston has commented that strategic litigation is 'complex, time-consuming, and uncertain', and difficult to enforce.[62] Similarly, Sys comments on the 'perilous litigation journey' that can arise from 'obstacles such as hostile socio-political environments, selecting the most effective case or overall strategy and the risk of impotent judicial remedies'.[63] The Open Society Justice

[58] Scott L Cummings and Deborah L Rhode, 'Public Interest Litigation: Insights from Theory and Practice' (2009) 36 Fordham Urb LJ 603, 606–07: they point to "centralized administrative agencies susceptible to reform" and "a system of welfare entitlements open to enforcement and expansion".

[59] ibid 607.

[60] ibid 607–08.

[61] The alternative, naturally, is to modify how public interest or strategic litigation operates: that is the focus of the Cummings and Rhode article.

[62] Goldston (n 33): the *DH* litigation, he notes, took more than eight years, such that the children affected had left school by the time of the final outcome, receiving 'exceptionally modest awards of just satisfaction—4,000 Euros each in non-pecuniary damages—that could not come close to compensate them for the irrevocable damage done to their personal, educational and professional lives'.

[63] Sys (n 32) 73.

Initiative commented in the education context that 'strategic litigation can be complex, time-consuming, expensive, and risky'.[64] They were even more sanguine in the context of health rights:

> Very few legal challenges actually come to fruition, as a result of inadequate legislation, deficient mechanisms for redress, inexperienced lawyers, lengthy and complex proceedings, and the prohibitive costs of litigation. A lack of legal challenges means a lack of justice against perpetrators, which in turn results in a failure to deter future rights violations and a lack of pressure to review current practices.[65]

### 2.2.2. Risks

References to risks feature regularly. The Centre for Legal Resources in Romania notes that, whilst strategic litigation need not necessarily be successful, because of other ways that litigation can be used to further a cause, it will rarely be sensible to lose a case about Roma: this is because losing will 'send a strong message to the majority of society which holds discriminatory beliefs that they are right in so doing, potentially reinforcing situations of discrimination and providing new impetus to those who want to keep things as they are', the context being the high level of discrimination in place.[66]

Indeed, the Open Society Justice Initiative notes that winning a case may 'engender a powerful backlash against the very values and protections it seeks to enshrine in law' and that ongoing discrimination has 'led to disillusionment with the courts and new manifestations of discrimination' and 'unintended consequences', which means it is not a 'panacea'.[67]

The Equinet handbook lists various risks, that can be categorized as: (i) risks in the litigation, (ii) risks relating to the fact of litigation, and (iii) risks arising from the outcome of the litigation. Risks in the litigation are of disagreements between parties and interveners, low levels of understanding by lawyers or judges of the relevant laws, and also of litigation settling in a way that reduces its impact.[68] Risks from the fact of litigation include political and media backlash, and, where conflicting rights are engaged, of undermining the rights of others.[69] Risks from the

[64] Open Society Justice Initiative (n 49).

[65] Extract from Open Society Foundations Initiative on Legal Advocacy for Roma Health Rights, 'Roma Health Rights in Macedonia, Romania and Serbia: A Baseline for Legal Advocacy' <[https://www.jstor.org/stable/pdf/resrep27136.7.pdf> accessed 19 August 2024, 32.

[66] Csonta and Niţă (n 34) 14: they record that litigation, as opposed to other forms of advocacy, may be a last resort in light of its confrontational nature.

[67] Open Society Justice Initiative (n 49). The extract referenced at n 65 noted that 'strategic litigation may not be the most appropriate tool to secure change—and that in certain contexts it may even be counter-productive'.

[68] Equinet (n 37) 32.

[69] ibid 31–32.

outcome are not achieving the aim sought, indeed setting a bad precedent, and/or having to pay costs.[70]

### 2.2.3. Responding to risks

Some, if not most, of these risks arise from a high level of discrimination. This suggests that political solutions are unlikely to succeed, which may leave litigation as the only realistic tool. This means not ignoring the risks of strategic litigation, but being prepared to counter or minimize them.

#### *(a) Strategic litigation should not stand alone*

Accordingly, Sys has noted that backlash may be a particular problem, with the development of 'populist' political parties. But he adds that a 'fear-induced pushback is exactly why legal strategies are vulnerable and cannot be solely relied upon to effectively implement long-lasting societal change': rather, 'extra-legal activism is vital in giving confidence to the Roma community and instilling a strong sense of personal identity to counter widespread discrimination'.[71] In short, the risk has to be recognized and countered by activism of other sorts—which is how strategic litigation should work in any event, as part of a wider advocacy campaign.

#### *(b) Case selection strategies*

The centrality of impact beyond the facts of the case may lead to discussions about such matters as the remedy and the forum, but also the suitability of the particular facts for the additional steps that should be taken in strategic litigation. Hence, the Equinet handbook, in a chapter on 'Principles of Case Selection', suggests developing criteria to identify strategic possibilities. The essence is that, in contrast to client-based litigation, the case can serve the wider aims already noted, namely 'to clarify or strengthen the law ... to increase compliance with the law ... to shed light on a particular problem' or involves 'a serious' or 'widespread infringement of the law'.[72]

This is largely premised on litigation being successful, save that light could also be shed on a problem by simply bringing a case. This leads to the question of whether it is possible to select cases that are more likely to win and so play a role in securing a step forward. Such case selection is consistent with van der Pas's contention that strategic litigation involves being strategic in the case and strategic about the case. However, prescience about determining what the relevant forum will do is debated. Ramsden and I commented that some litigators were clear that their expert judgment allowed them to select cases that were likely to succeed and have

[70] ibid 32: it is also noted that public bodies such as equality commissions may be under pressure to be involved in a case and might be criticized for not doing so.

[71] Sys (n 32) 90–91. He also records examples of Roma groups countering negative presentations.

[72] Equinet (n 37) 17. They also address the question of the proportionality of taking action, including in light of the costs of litigation and the risk of additional costs on losing.

an impact, but also that there was dissent—that there was too much unpredictability for this claimed expertise.[73] The dissent was sourced from a 2015 post on the ERRC website by Adam Weiss, who contended that strategic litigation is not a matter of expertise but more of clever gambling—trying to secure a 'big unpredictable judgment' whilst 'reducing the risk to individual clients'.[74]

The Equinet handbook makes various suggestions, including (i) avoiding disputed facts if the aim is to change the law, so that the court can focus on that aim and not be distracted by the facts; and (ii) ensuring a 'strong moral dimension' if the aim is to push for a change in the status quo, so that the court (or media opinion) 'will find it reasonable to condemn the perpetrator of discrimination and find for the victim'.[75] Also required is clarity about the facts, the breach of rights and the relevant policy considerations (in relation to which their focus is the right to non-discrimination).[76] Accordingly, the 'facts and circumstances … should favour the policy outcome sought', which requires a 'policy case' that is 'strong' so as to allow '"selling" a particular outcome as attractive to the court' (or at the very least ensuring that 'the individual circumstances should not work against the desirable outcome'.[77] However, the Centre for Legal Resources in Romania notes that: 'the most vulnerable clients usually have complicated histories behind them and are never "ideal"'.[78]

*(c) Risk reduction processes*

Whether or not it is possible to select only ideal claimants, as the costs and uncertainties of litigation mean that it is rarely the first choice, other options will be considered first;[79] and it is sensible to have a checklist in light of 'the difficulties and the

[73] Ramsden and Gledhill (n 10) 415–16.

[74] Weiss (n 45). He uses the well-known *DH* litigation as the example: the Chamber judgment, in which the ECtHR supported the government, represented a traditional approach, and the reversal of this by the Grand Chamber, a significant victory for Roma, was something that caught most people by surprise—a Black Swan moment (by analogy to Nassim Nicholas Taleb's work on unpredictable but highly influential events, in his book *The Black Swan* (2007). This account is supported in the asylum context by Jeff Walsh, 'Strategic Litigation at a European Level, European Database of Asylum Law' (14 February 2017) <https://www.asylumlawdatabase.eu/en/journal/strategic-litigation-european-level> accessed 19 August 2024.

[75] Equinet (n 37) 18.

[76] ibid 18–20.

[77] ibid. Their focus is on the circumstances being discriminatory and so breaching the right against discrimination.

[78] Csonta and Niţă (n 34) 18. This, it is worth noting, involves a reply to a book, European Roma Rights Centre, Interights, Migration Policy Group, *Strategic Litigation of Race Discrimination in Europe: From Principles to Practice* (Russell Press Limited, 2004) (available at <https://www.errc.org/training-materials/strategic-litigation-of-race-directive-in-europe-from-principles-to-practice>, accessed 19 August 2024) in which there is reference at 56 to the need for the client to have 'personal characteristics' that will 'find favour of the court … and facilitate successful litigation'; similarly, at 43, there is reference to the need for the '"right" client', though with the acceptance that 'Ideal clients are not easily found in the real world'.

[79] There are exceptions: litigious people with deep pockets use litigation or the threat of litigation for various purposes. This defensive use of the law may involve strategic lawsuits against public participation

potential negative impact of losing strategic cases'.[80] The Equinet handbook notes that risks may mean that litigation is not proceeded with,[81] for example, if alternative approaches are less risky when a bad precedent or political backlash might be the outcome. Similarly, it might be better not to intervene in a case when there might be differences of view with the lawyers for the applicant. Other risks might be countered or reduced. For example, risks of negative publicity might be managed through press briefings, perhaps jointly with the other side to the litigation; and risks of alienating other groups whose rights might be in conflict might be managed by appropriate use of language in pleadings and press briefings. Similarly, risks that a case might settle and not achieve its full potential might be countered by initial publicity to stimulate debate and create support, and exploring publicity as part of the settlement agreement.[82] Risks from the outcome of a case include incurring or not recovering costs: one option here might be to partner with other organizations to spread the risk.

Sys has noted that the choices to be made, including whether to litigate, to join as amicus or use other methods of advocacy, has to be linked to the need to be inclusive. He notes that the 'right strategy' has to be selected, given 'the hostility of some environments and the emotional weight of strategic litigation'—the key factor being to avoid alienating those affected, or leaving them thinking that justice is dependent on others.[83] He also makes the important point that cases 'are often part of lengthy, sequential plans to effect reform', reflecting 'an incremental process to emancipation'—often not assisted by judgments that 'do not provide an adequate deterrent' or do not adequately 'express urgency', such that 'sustained extra-legal pressure is vital'.[84] The affected community is the one most likely to sustain such ongoing pressure. This leads, naturally, to the particular features of the affected community.

(SLAPPs): the EU is proposing to take action to curtail these (see Rafal Manko, European Parliamentary Research Service, 'Strategic Lawsuits Against Public Participation (SLAPPs)', February 2024 Briefing Paper <https://www.europarl.europa.eu/RegData/etudes/BRIE/2022/733668/EPRS_BRI(2022)733668_EN.pdf> accessed 19 August 2024).

[80] Equinet (n 37) 18.

[81] Equinet (n 37) 31–32.

[82] It might, however, be the case that publicity at the outset raises stakes and makes a settlement less likely: given a lawyer's duty to their clients, a suitable settlement is often a good outcome, such that publicity may require careful thought.

[83] Sys (n 32) 77. This is reminiscent of the powerful insistence of the disability community on being engaged in policy development relating to their needs and aspirations: 'nothing about us without us': naturally, those most expert in understanding the problems caused and best placed to identify solutions are those most directly affected by a rights-breaching situation. Sys notes that steps such as 'legal teams updating community representatives or hosting presentations on case developments' may lead to finding 'a more lasting and inclusive solution'.

[84] ibid 77–78.

## 2.3. Special features of strategic litigation aimed at Roma interests

Various comments have been made about the special features affecting Roma in the context of strategic litigation, including factors that point to: (i) the particular need for strategic litigation, (ii) the difficulties in organizing strategic litigation, and (iii) the problems of securing real life impact for Roma through strategic litigation.[85]

### 2.3.1. Background/structural factors

A feature noted by the Centre for Legal Resources in Romania is that NGOs for Roma 'often lack financial and human resources', the latter including an absence of lawyers because of the lack of a pro bono tradition in countries where Roma are prominent.[86] Goldston has reinforced this, noting both background and practical problems. The former include distrust of public institutions, including the judiciary, and the bias against Roma within the judiciary and legal profession; the practical problems include the cost and length of proceedings, limitations on legal aid, lack of class actions, and unwillingness of courts to consider empirical evidence.[87]

Separately, Goldston has commented that the power of anti-Roma prejudice has undermined the ability of strategic litigation to succeed, citing features that undermine the power of the law. These include ideas that law and politics are separate, that politicians tend to refuse to accept the pervasiveness of racism, and that judges may be reluctant to intervene in discrimination because it is sensitive and so defer to those politicians, and court costs.[88] This particular feature has been noted by the Open Society Justice Initiative (with which Goldston is involved), which has commented that judging the impact of litigation might also be affected by 'the pervasiveness and severity of anti-Roma discrimination', leading to some Roma not registering themselves under that ethnicity, and so skewing data.[89] The obvious point to note here is that the problem of systemic discrimination against Roma that

[85] Indeed, as strategic litigation may involve several layers of domestic courts and then international tribunals, the time delay may mean that the litigants have no practical remedy for their own situation due to the passage of time, such that benefiting others now in a similar position is the only remedy in play.

[86] Csonta and Niţă (n 34) 8.

[87] James A Goldston, 'The Struggle for Roma Rights: Arguments That Have Worked' (2010) 32 Hum Rts Q 311, 317. He adds the point that racism and discrimination continue to exist in other settings where the structures may be different, including the US, where litigation is an established tool to secure change.

[88] Goldston (n 33), using the *DH* litigation as an example: it represented a 'giant jurisprudential leap forward' by showing that Art 14 could be breached by indirect discrimination, but also changed public debate by precluding arguments based on justifying segregation as the way things were, or even in the interests of Roma, led to 'better data collection ... better informed consent, better cultural validity to diagnostic tests and regular re-tests, and law that those without disability not follow curricula for those with disability'.

[89] Zimová (n 17) 11; it is also noted that Greece does not keep data on minority enrolment in schools.

produces the need for strategic litigation is itself a feature that needs to be overcome in that litigation.

### 2.3.2. Strategies needed

Given these risks of inflaming existing discrimination, the Centre for Legal Resources in Romania notes that strategic litigation for Roma needs to be undertaken with eyes open to the risk of backlash against the community and the cause, victimization of parties (which requires a strategy to deal with it), and the risk of costs awards (which require adequate funding); note is also made that the litigator, if not local, needs to work with local lawyers so as to understand the local 'legal culture and rights awareness among judges' and other relevant features.[90]

### 2.3.3. Potential benefits

These risks—reduced by counter-actions—are balanced against the potential upsides, which has led various groups to take action. Part of this was timing. As Goldston has noted, the lack of a tradition of strategic litigation in states in Central and Eastern Europe was met with the opportunity to develop it when they joined the Council of Europe and the ECHR: matters were reframed as discriminatory breaches of legal rights.[91] This occurred just as anti-discrimination law was being strengthened.[92] As systemic discrimination against Roma would be reflected in a lack of political influence, this reframing of the situation as justiciable breaches of rights would naturally feed into the idea of progress through litigation being a viable strategy, perhaps the most viable one.

### 2.3.4. The job is not yet complete

And yet, these upsides have only been partially delivered. Goldston has noted the 'pathbreaking declarations of fundamental principle', but also that a declaration and its implementation are different matters.[93] Hence, for all the plaudits flowing from the *DH* litigation, 'a staggering disproportion of Roma remain mired in second-class, often separate education or are otherwise denied equal educational

[90] Csonta and Niţă (n 34) 19.

[91] Goldston (n 87) 315–16. Similar points are made in James A Goldston and Mirna Adjami, 'The Opportunities and Challenges of Using Public Interest Litigation to Secure Access to Justice for Roma in Central and Eastern Europe' in Yash Ghai and Jill Cottrell (eds) *Marginalized Communities and Access to Justice* (Routledge 2009): in addition to the legal framework to challenge discrimination, reference is also made to the development of bodies and funders willing to support litigation, promote education on rights and engage in political processes. They comment that support for Roma rights was the exemplar of public interest litigation.

[92] Goldston (n 87) 316, citing Protocol 12 ECHR (ETS No 177, opened for signature 4 November 2000, entered into force 1 April 2005), adding the free-standing right not to be discriminated against, and the EU Council Directive 2000/43/EC implementing the principle of equal treatment between persons irrespective of racial or ethnic origin (RED) [2000] OJ L180.

[93] Goldston (n 33).

opportunity'.[94] He points to structural problems: the ECtHR has no 'enforcement powers' of its own, but also has 'declined to issue any specific orders' other than compensation, and the Committee of Ministers that supervises implementation of Court judgments has been unable to require states 'to address issues of structural discrimination'.[95] Hence the question of whether it is better to continue to use the law or to 'turn primarily to political action—mobilization, registration, voting and running for elective office—to secure equal rights?'.[96]

Previously, Goldston noted the value of two foci in strategic litigation: (i) process-based arguments (for example finding ancillary obligations, such as a duty to investigate allegations of breaches of rights, or shifting burdens of proof to the government)[97] and (ii) providing evidence of systemic problems, including by documenting the evidence.[98] To these, he added a third lesson: persistence may be necessary to persuade a court that the evidence reveals discriminatory motivations.[99]

His later reflection was that political action was important, but that 'legal pathways remain essential complements' because Roma cannot depend 'only on political majorities' but require 'the protection of law and courts for the enjoyment of their fundamental rights', which rights 'liberty, equality and the right to life itself—are so central to European values that they must not vary with the political winds, but rather must stand securely on legal foundations regardless of the results of partisan elections'.[100]

## 3. Concluding Comments

Efforts are being made to secure an understanding of the meaning of 'strategic litigation'. This chapter seeks to add to those efforts by analysing themes in comments about strategic litigation in the context of supporting Roma. In section 1,

[94] ibid. He notes that recent surveys show that 'Roma in the Czech Republic continue to account for well over a quarter of pupils educated in segregated settings'. He accepts that change in education is complex, involving many institutions and officials (from teachers to legislators), and discrimination can be shown in many ways, 'from overtly hostile statements to subtle, even implicit or unconscious forms of bias affecting what are often misunderstood to be neutral customs' (examples being 'the use of special classes, misdiagnosis, discrimination in the enrollment process, the choice of tests and how they are normed for different populations, the bullying of Roma children in mainstream schools, pressure on parents to transfer to mainstream schools, and the design of school catchment areas').

[95] ibid. Nor have there been many domestic cases, even in Hungary, which allows *actio popularis* litigation.

[96] ibid.

[97] Goldston (n 87) 317–21.

[98] ibid 323–25.

[99] ibid 321–23. In a blogpost about the need for judgments to be enforced, he references the steadfastness required, commenting that 'For close to three decades, a small but determined group of activists and practitioners has worked with courageous members of Roma communities' on relevant litigation: Goldston (n 33).

[100] Goldston (n 33).

a summary of existing writing was given, suggesting that strategic litigation (i) involves being strategic within litigation but also about whether to use litigation, (ii) has a focus on impact beyond the outcome for the litigants, in the form of wider social change, (iii) is a method of advocacy that can be used for various causes, and (iv) considers using various mechanisms, both domestic and international.

Material relating to the use of strategic litigation for a particular cause, namely countering structural discrimination against Roma was analysed in section 2. It helps to confirm some aspects of this broader material. First, it confirms the centrality of impact, and also, secondly, that this impact can be intra-legal (such as creating new jurisprudence) or extra-legal (including such outcomes as empowering people to take additional steps. Thirdly, it makes clear that securing impact requires a broader advocacy regime—not just court-room advocacy—to translate useful court outcomes into practical change.

The material in section 2 also amplifies an important factor arising from the risks of litigation: strategies are required to deal with the risks that arise from losing, because this may entrench a problem. But there are also risks, including of backlash, from taking or winning litigation. This reiterates the need for a strategy around the litigation, recognizing that litigation is a mechanism within the cause that should not stand alone.

This is particularly important for groups such as Roma, who have a history of marginalization that means discrimination against them is systemic and who may be vulnerable to the rise of populism in politics. Of course, this history reflects the failure of the political process to implement human rights standards to which politicians have agreed. This adds to the importance of considering litigation, which may be the only realistic option, even with its risks. This in turn means, as Goldston has recommended, that more needs to be done in terms of 'support for more lawyers and claimants to bring many more well-documented and well-argued cases', more of a focus on 'systemic discrimination and structural remedies', and advocacy for 'more effective execution'.[101] These are factors that should secure the impact that is the central aim of strategic litigation.

Finally, I should reiterate the need for ongoing research, both on strategic litigation generally and in the context of Roma. The fresh analysis in this chapter reflects a snapshot of the material currently prominent on search engines. A historical review would elucidate what has developed in terms of understandings of strategic litigation for Roma.

[101] ibid. He notes, inter alia, that cases will have to commence before national courts but may have to proceed to the ECtHR or EU courts, and that more effective execution can come from individual states but also through the Committee of Ministers and the EU.

# 5

# International Courts and the Interpretation of Human Rights

## About Possibilities and Constraints to Push the Boundaries of Human Rights

*Kristin Henrard*

### 1. Introduction

One of the first things law students learn is that 'knowing the law' implies more than just knowing the relevant legal texts. It is just as important to know how these texts are interpreted and applied by (international) courts. Indeed, law tends to consist of norms of a general character, often using concepts that entail a certain vagueness. When these norms need to be applied to particular cases, this invariably requires an act of interpretation.[1] Human rights conventions tend to put in place supervisory bodies with an official mandate to supervise compliance by state parties,[2] implying that these supervisory bodies, coined 'international courts' or 'icourts',[3] have officially the last word about the interpretation of the conventions. This official status and related power of icourts implies a certain initial legitimacy for its judgments and reasoning and a certain power of co-determination, and thus also the power to push the boundaries of human rights.[4] This power of international courts is to some extent constrained in terms of acceptable interpretation principles, and to a greater extent by the limited enforcement possibilities against sovereign states and related legitimacy concerns.

[1] See inter alia Duncan B Hollis, 'The Existential Function of Interpretation in International Law' in Andrea Bianchi, Daniel Peat, and Matthew Windsor (eds), *Interpretation in International Law* (Oxford University Press 2015; online edn) accessed 17 October 2024.

[2] For example the European Court of Human Rights for the ECHR, the European Committee on Social Rights for the European Social Charter, and the Human Rights Committee for the ICCPR.

[3] In this chapter a broad understanding of international courts is used as referring to supervisory bodies with an official mandate to supervise state compliance with international standards, also when their findings are not legally binding, and also outside complaints procedures (eg periodic state reporting). See also for the position of icourts, the Danish Centre of Excellence for International Courts: <https://jura.ku.dk/icourts/research/>.

[4] See also Yuval Shany, 'No Longer a Weak Department of Power? Reflections on the Emergence of a New International Judiciary' (2009) 20 European Journal of International Law 73.

Kristin Henrard, *International Courts and the Interpretation of Human Rights* In: *The Rights of Roma in European Courts*. Edited by: Kristin Henrard and Lilla Farkas, Oxford University Press. © Kristin Henrard 2025.
DOI: 10.1093/oso/9780198914358.003.0005

Over time, certain rules governing interpretation have been devised, as is visible in the Vienna Convention on the Law of Treaties (VCLT). International human rights law has further developed these interpretation principles, while adding a few that are specific to human rights.[5] The official status of international courts does not guarantee that states will not criticize their decisions, let alone actually comply with them. What is more, general international law does not provide many tools to enhance state compliance with international courts' judgments.[6] Hence, international courts are concerned about undermining their own legitimacy if they provoke severe criticism or serious non-compliance.[7] To manage this minefield, international courts have adopted strategies to step back when faced with controversial questions. These legitimacy concerns thus translate into (perceived) constraints on the adjudicatory power of international courts and as such rather reveal the boundaries of human rights.[8]

This chapter starts with a general account of interpretation by international courts and provides some insights into the range of interpretation principles that have been devised in international human rights law and steer international courts. The second section delves further into this theory on courts co-determining the law; the courts actively taking part in the development of the law. Various examples are provided, some pertaining to general human rights law, others focusing on particular vulnerable groups and minorities. The third section examines the (perceived) legitimacy constraints of international courts, and the ways and extent to which these courts may prefer to step back, inter alia by providing ample state discretion. These arguments are further supported by the analysis of several landmark judgments of a variety of European courts in relation to Roma and other vulnerable minorities. The list of judgments included is by no means exhaustive, but rather exemplary. The analysis reveals roughly three trajectories. A first trajectory concerns cases in which the respective courts start with bold pronouncements on the scope of application of rights and/or the related state obligation, thus pushing the boundaries of human rights, but then stop short of providing protection, and ultimately step back. The second trajectory encompasses cases that reveal that in some of these controversial areas, there has been (some) room for a gradual, incremental development. The third trajectory reflects 'frozen constraints' and shows

[5] Inter alia Sandra Fredman's chapter on 'Interpreting Human Rights Law' in her book, *Comparative Human Rights Law* (Oxford 2018; online edn) accessed 17 October 2024.

[6] States' sovereignty ultimately implies that even if violations are found by international courts, and remedies are identified, there are scant possibilities to really enforce these remedies.

[7] See also Mikael Rask Madsen, Pola Cebulak, and Micha Wiebusch, 'Backlash against International Courts: Explaining the Forms and Patterns of Resistance to International Courts' (2018) 14 International Journal of Law in Context 197.

[8] See also Konstantin Dzehtsiariou, *European Consensus and the Legitimacy of the European Court of Human Rights* (CUP 2015); Nick Huls, Maurice Adams, and Jako Bomhoff (eds), *The Legitimacy of the Highest Courts' Rulings. Judicial Deliberations and Beyond* (Asser Press 2009).

that ultimately, international courts remain cautious in several areas that are considered too complex or too controversial.

The chapter concludes with a call to regional European courts to optimize an effective enjoyment of human rights, including for persons belonging to minorities, by pushing the boundaries of human rights, at least gradually.

## 2. Law and Interpretation

Due to the general nature of the concepts used, the importance of interpretation of legal standards, inter alia in order to apply them to particular cases, has long been recognized. Human rights standards often use general concepts that have indeterminate meanings.[9] Consider for instance the notion of 'home': can this apply to a 'caravan' or a make-shift construction? Or the notion of 'privacy': does this also apply to conversations in the public space? When various meanings could be possible, how does an international court decide which meaning the concept will have in the frame of a particular convention?[10] Similarly, if the meaning of the right is indeterminate, so are the related state obligations. The latter is particularly so for positive state obligations and the determination of what can reasonably be expected from a state.

Over time, certain interpretation principles have been developed, several of which have been enshrined in the VCLT. Article 31, 1 VCLT refers to both the textual interpretation (following the ordinary meaning of the text) and the teleological interpretation (having regard to context and object/purpose). International human rights courts tend to recognize the relevance of the VCLT interpretation principles, while elaborating them further. For human rights treaties the teleological interpretation is vital, with telos concerning both the telos of the category of human rights, namely human dignity, and the telos of the particular fundamental right.

The fundamental nature of human rights, and the overarching telos of human rights, as rights required for human dignity, point to the paramount importance of the effective enjoyment of these rights. Several icourts make ample use of the effectiveness principle to guide its interpretation and assessment, aiming for rights to be 'practical and effective, not theoretical or illusory'.[11] The effective enjoyment of human rights presupposes on the one hand a broad or generous interpretation

[9] Illan rua Wall, 'The Indeterminacy of Human Rights: A Response to O'Connell' <https://criticallegalthinking.com/2015/06/22/the-indeterminacy-of-human-rights-a-response-to-oconnell/> accessed 3 July 2024.

[10] See also below (text to fn 15) on the principle of autonomous interpretation in terms of international human rights law.

[11] This expression is often used by the ECtHR inter alia in *Chassagnou and Others v France* App no 25088/94 (ECtHR, 29 April 1999) para 100.

of the scope of application of a fundamental right, and on the other a narrow or restrictive interpretation of (acceptable) limitations.[12] The latter would imply that courts adopt a meaningful level of scrutiny, as opposed to granting states a high degree of discretion.[13]

Related to the teleological interpretation is also the dynamic or evolutive interpretation: what is required for human dignity and a dignified life is not static but develops over time, in line with changes within society.[14] Finally, the autonomous interpretation principle is an important stepping stone for a bold interpretation by international courts, since it implies that the international court decides authoritatively on the meaning of concepts used in the convention it is supervising, and that this meaning can be different from the meaning of similar concepts in the respective national legal systems.[15]

Clearly, the above principles do not point to a 'set' solution: courts will still have to make choices and the underlying value judgments. In other words, by adopting particular interpretative stances, international courts can choose to push the boundaries of human rights, by progressively extending the scope of application of particular rights and make state obligations more stringent, as well as more demanding.

A very important line of jurisprudence that implied a considerable push of the boundaries in human rights, concerns the recognition of positive state obligations, also in relation to civil and political rights.[16] The European Court of Human Rights (ECtHR) has an extensive jurisprudence recognizing that in addition to the negative state obligations of non-interference with civil and political rights, the effective enjoyment of these rights may require the recognition of positive state obligations.[17] Over time, the range and detail of these positive obligations has steadily expanded.[18] Some of these are especially relevant for Roma and other ethnic and

[12] Nihal Jayawickrama, *The Judicial Application of Human Rights Law: National, Regional and International Jurisprudence* (CUP 2002) 184.

[13] The level of scrutiny adopted by an international court is inversely related to the margin of appreciation or discretion left to states. The case law of the ECtHR is very explicit about this, emphasizing that a narrow margin of appreciation goes hand in hand with a heightened scrutiny, inter alia in case of differentiations on suspect grounds: 'where a difference in treatment is based on race or ethnicity, the notion of objective and reasonable justification must be interpreted as strictly as possible' (*Sejdic and Finci* App nos 27996/06 and 34836/06) (ECtHR, 22 December 2009) para 44).

[14] See inter alia the discussion in ch 6, 'The Interpretative Methods of International Law: What are they and Why use them?' in Odile Ammann, *Domestic Courts and the Interpretation of International Law* (Brill 2020).

[15] The ECtHR adopts this autonomous interpretation, for example in relation to the concepts of 'law' (in limitation analysis), 'home', and 'privacy' in Art 8: *Marckx v Belgium* App no 6833/74 (ECtHR, 13 June 1979) paras 44–45.

[16] Gunar Beck, 'Human Rights Adjudication under ECHR Between Value Pluralism and Essential Contestability' (2008) EHRLR 214, 229, emphasizing that these positive state obligations constitute a judicial construct that strengthens human rights protection.

[17] Inter alia *Van Kück v Germany* App no 35968/97 (ECtHR, 12 September 2003) para 69; *Plattform 'Ärzte für das Leben' v Austria* App no 10126/82 (ECtHR, 25 May 1988) para 34.

[18] See also Vladislava Stoyanova, 'Framing Positive Obligations under the ECHR Law: Mediating between the Abstract and the Concrete' (2023) 23 Human Rights Law Review 1–34.

religious minorities, especially as they have to face considerable societal prejudice and related discrimination. Examples of the latter include the recognition that states have a special obligation to unveil discriminatory motives of violence or other crimes,[19] and state duties to ensure that human rights are respected, also between private parties.[20] In terms of the freedom of religion, the ECtHR has a steady line of jurisprudence requiring states, in case of tensions between religious groups, not to favour one over the other, but rather to ensure that the groups tolerate each other.[21] In *Chapman v UK* the ECtHR established that states have a positive obligation to facilitate the gypsy way of life,[22] undoubtedly one of the most memorable findings in relation to Roma. Furthermore, the 'gypsy way of life' was for the first time accepted as part of the scope of application of Article 8 ECHR in that judgment.[23]

The European Committee of Social Rights (ECSR), supervising the (Revised) European Social Charter, has adopted several bold interpretations, also in relation to positive state obligations. One of the most striking decisions contained a *contra legem* interpretation of the Charter, extending a basic level of protection of social rights to illegal migrants, because of the underlying value of human dignity.[24] The Committee opted for a teleological interpretation, taking into account the underlying central value of human dignity of the Charter, to read down the Charter's explicit exclusion of illegal migrants from its personal scope of application.[25]

This may not concern traditional minorities, but this interpretative leap of the Committee clearly pushed the boundaries of the human rights paradigm significantly.[26] Throughout its jurisprudence the ECSR has also been generous in its identification of positive state obligations in relation to Roma and does not shy away from finding instances of prohibited discrimination. For example, already in 2005 the Committee found in *European Roma Rights Centre v Italy* a violation of the right to housing in combination with the prohibition of discrimination, since Italy had not done enough to secure sufficient camp sites offering acceptable living

19 State authorities are required by the ECtHR to conduct an effective and adequate investigation to ascertain whether there were discriminatory motives and whether feelings of hatred or prejudice based on an individual's personal characteristic played a role in the events (*Abdu v Bulgaria* App no 26827/08) (ECtHR, 11 March 2014) para 44.

20 A typical example here would concern questions of domestic violence, or a journalist writing about intimate issues of the private life of famous persons.

21 *Mehmet Agga v Greece* App nos 50776/99, 52912/99 (ECtHR, 17 October 2002) para 60.

22 *Chapman v the United Kingdom* App no 27238/95 (ECtHR, 18 January 2001) para 96.

23 See inter alia Julie Ringelheim,'Chapman Redux: The European Court of Human Rights and Roma Traditional Lifestyle' in E Brems (ed), *Diversity and European Human Rights: Rewriting Judgments of the ECtHR* (CUP 2013) 430.

24 *Defence for Children International (DCI) v The Netherlands* Comm no 47/2008 (ECSR, 20 October 2009).

25 ibid paras 28–37.

26 See inter alia Marie-Francoise Valette, 'Protection and Promotion of Migrants' Social Rights by the European Committee of Social Rights' (2016) 32 Revue Europeenne des Migrations Internationales.

conditions for Roma.[27] Similarly, Bulgaria's failure to take proactive steps to address the particular vulnerabilities and related needs of Roma women in relation to effective access to health care, amounted to a failure to comply with its positive state obligations, and constituted a violation of the rights to health and non-discrimination under the Revised European Social Charter.[28] In its evaluation, the Committee explicitly factors in the background of systemic discrimination suffered by Roma, and their extensive degree of exclusion, which further heightens the state obligation to act proactively.[29]

The Court of Justice of the EU (CJEU) in several of its cases, which are of relevance to human rights and the prohibition of discrimination, has adopted bold interpretations that contributed to pushing the boundaries of human rights. The *Feryn* case, for example, established that mere speech, irrespective of any actual practice, could amount to a prohibited instance of racial discrimination.[30] The CJEU thus acknowledged that an announcement by an employer that he would not hire members of a particular group, does inhibit members of that group to apply. Not prohibiting the speech as such would thus imply playing down the discriminatory effects of such statements.[31] Similarly, in *CHEZ* the Court accepted the notion of a 'victim by way of collateral damage', allowing a non-Roma to complain about a racially discriminatory practice in a city district predominantly inhabited by Roma, because she was similarly affected by the practice.[32] In addition, the CJEU was particularly detailed and specific about its guidance why this practice could amount to an instance of discrimination, identifying underlying prejudice, emphasizing inter alia the lack of actual proof of allegations against Roma.[33]

The above cases clearly show how applying the law goes beyond the mechanical application and requires interpretations of the law that clarify the meaning of the law, while further developing that meaning and thus the reach of the law. Hence, international courts can be seen to take actively part in law making, and these interpretations adopted by the European courts can be seen to push the boundaries of human rights. To properly gauge the power of international courts in this respect, contemporary theories of international law making should be considered.

[27] *European Roma Rights Centre (ERRC) v Italy* Comm no 27/2004 (ECSR, 7 December 2005) paras 36–37.

[28] *European Roma Rights Centre (ERRC) v Bulgaria* Comm no 151/2017 (ECSR, 5 December 2018) paras 81–85.

[29] ibid paras 84–85.

[30] Case C-54/07 *Centrum voor gelijkheid van kansen en voor racismebestrijding v Firma Feryn NV* (CJEU, 10 July 2008) para 28.

[31] ibid para 25.

[32] Case C-83/14 *CHEZ Razpredelenie Bulgaria AD v Komisia za zashtita ot diskriminatsia* (CJEU, 16 July 2015) para 60.

[33] ibid paras 81–84 and 106–08.

## 3. International Courts and Contemporary Theories of International Lawmaking

International conventions with human rights provisions tend to establish a system to supervise whether states comply with the legal obligations they accepted when ratifying the convention.

The conventions also establish and identify supervisory bodies (international courts) that have the official authority to establish whether the contracting states have complied with their obligations. This in turn means that these bodies' interpretations of the content of these state obligations and their assessment have official authority.[34]

Not all human rights conventions have the same type of supervisory mechanism. Broadly two categories can be distinguished: periodic state reporting and complaints procedures. Some conventions make use of periodic state reporting, which requires contracting states to submit every few years a general report of the way in which they are fulfilling their state obligations under the convention. The icourts will review these reports, take into account shadow reports from NGOs and possibly undertake visits to the state concerned, in order to talk to all relevant stakeholders. While the outcome of such general performance reviews allows for the identification of certain supervisory 'lines', the focus in this chapter will be on complaints procedures, encompassing individual complaints, inter-state complaints and collective complaints by NGOs.

As the introduction has outlined, this edited volume focuses on European courts established at the regional level, and zooms in on the outcome of complaints procedures. The jurisprudence of the ECtHR will receive the most attention, as it covers most ground and predominantly adjudicates individual complaints. Meanwhile, the European Committee of Social Rights only considers collective complaints, which per definition invite a broader, systemic perspective.[35] The CJEU is a special (supranational) court and the bulk of its jurisprudence is comprised of an additional type of procedure, namely the preliminary ruling procedure. The latter concerns questions by national courts that are faced with doubts about the proper interpretation of EU law and enables the CJEU to ensure the uniform interpretation and application of EU law throughout the member states. The judgments of the CJEU are legally binding.[36] In addition to what will be said below in terms of modern theories of international law making, the Court's preliminary

[34] See also Art 12 of the Optional Protocol to the European Social Charter Providing for a System of Collective Complaints (ETS no 158), linking the legal obligaitons under the convention to the supervision. See below on the modern theories of international law making.

[35] The collective complaints mechanism was established by an Optional Protocol of 1995 to the European Social Charter, but is now incorporated in Art D of the Revised Social Charter. The review of the periodic state reports will not be included in the analysis here.

[36] Art 19.1 TEU and Art 280 TFEU.

rulings are *in se* meant to have broader ramifications than just providing a binding clarification of EU law for the national courts in the cases before it. In addition, the Court's judgment binds other national courts before which the same problem is raised.[37]

The judgments of traditional courts are legally binding for the state against which they are pronounced.[38] The decisions of other international courts, such as those of the European Committee of Social Rights, may not be legally binding on the state, but their pronouncements are still authoritative, given the courts' status as official supervisors of the legal instruments concerned. Both types of decisions go hand in hand with a certain power of international courts to take part in international lawmaking, providing opportunities to push the boundaries of human rights, as well as certain constraints related to their legitimacy. The latter will be further explored in section 4 of this chapter; the former makes up the remainder of this section.

### 3.1. International courts taking part in international lawmaking

Discussing (theories of) international lawmaking, inevitably brings one to discussions on the sources of international law, the rules of pedigree, and the related doctrine on subjects of international law, since by definition subjects of international law take part in the making and development of international law.[39] In line with the traditional understanding of international law as law made by states for states, governing their interactions, states are the primary subjects of international law and have a central role in the making thereof.[40] This is also visible in the formulation of the sources of international law that are to be considered by the International Court of Justice when deciding cases. Whereas treaties and customary international law are formal sources of law, judicial decisions are merely 'subsidiary means for the determination of international law'.[41] The minimal impact of judicial decisions is corroborated by the understanding expressed in Article 59 of the ICJ statute, that a judgment of the ICJ is only binding on the state concerned, and only in the case at hand. However, the presumed lack of *stare decisis* stands in stark contrast to the way in which the ICJ itself relies on its previous case law in its judgments,[42] as do

[37] CJEU Presentation < https://curia.europa.eu/jcms/jcms/Jo2_7024/en> accessed 14 August 2024.
[38] See Art 59 ICJ Statute, Art 46 ECHR, Art 19.1 TEU, Art 280 TFEU, and Art 12 Additional Protocol to the European Social Charter on a Collective Complaints mechanism.
[39] James Crawford, *Brownlies Principles of Public International Law* (OUP 2019) 105–08.
[40] Malcom Shaw, 'International Law', *Encyclopedia Britannica* <https://www.britannica.com/topic/international-law> accessed 17 October 2024.
[41] Art 38.1(d) ICJ Statute.
[42] For a very in-depth and nuanced discussion of the possible role of precedents in international law, see Mark Jacob, 'Precedents: Law-making through International Adjudication' (2011) German Law Journal (special issue: Beyond Dispute: International Judicial Institutions as Lawmakers) 1005.

parties before international courts in their argumentation.[43] Similarly, the case law of international courts tends to take a central role in explaining the evolving doctrines of international law in textbooks. With regard thereto it is telling that even today some old judgments are still considered landmark judgments.[44] Other judgments featured in textbooks or academic articles mark the development of international law.[45] In short, most fields of international law cannot be explained or fully understood without making reference to previous case law of international courts.

It is important to keep in mind that legal norms often encapsulate general concepts and that their exact meaning only becomes clear through application in concrete cases. Put differently, it is the interpretation and application of these norms that gives more substance to the norms concerned and ultimately further refines and thus develops them. Indeed, interpreting and applying the law is not a purely mechanical, mathematic process.[46] Rather the courts' reasoning in particular cases impacts the general legal normativity,[47] alters the understanding of the law,[48] and hence develops the law.[49] In this regard the understanding grew that applying the law equals taking part in the development of the law and thus taking part in law-making. Admittedly, this judicial process of law making works differently than the 'broad brush strokes' of a legislative process,[50] and is typically an incremental process.[51] Still, judicial lawmaking's incrementality does not alter the fact that judicial decisions take part in the development of international law.

The above characterization of international law norms as vague and indeterminate is equally if not more applicable to international human rights law. Indeed, the vagueness of the concepts used in human rights norms makes a variety of interpretations plausible.[52] Nevertheless, even critical legal studies tend to acknowledge that while fundamental rights are normatively indeterminate, the jurisprudence of

[43] See also Yuval Shany, 'No Longer a Weak Department of Power? Reflections on the Emergence of a New International Judiciary' (2009) EJIL 73, in which she develops the argument that the international judiciary is clearly moving beyond dispute settlement to more outright international norm-advancement.

[44] For example *Military and Paramilitary Activities in and against Nicaragua (Nicaragua v United States of America)* (ICJ, 26 November 1984) is used in all textbooks on public international law.

[45] An example in the field of international human rights law, would concern cases that extend the scope of application of the right to respect for privacy also to the work sphere, such as *Niemietz v Germany* App no. 13710/88 (ECtHR, 16 December 1992).

[46] Joseph Dainow, 'The Civil Law and the Common Law: Some Points of Comparison' (1966–67) 15 American Journal of Comparative Law 426–27.

[47] See also Allan Boyle and Christine Chinkin, *The Making of International Law* (OUP 2007) 2.

[48] See also Andrew Guzman, 'The Consent Problem in International Law' (2011) <https://escholarship.org/uc/item/04x8x174> accessed 4 October 2024, 55.

[49] Armin Van Bogdandy and Ingo Venzke, 'On the Functions of International Courts: An Appraisal in Light of their Burgeoning Public Authority' (2012) ACIL Research Paper 2012-10, 9; Thomas Buergenthal, 'Lawmaking by the ICJ and other International Courts' (2009) ASIL Annual Meeting Proceedings 403.

[50] ibid.

[51] Van Bogdandy and Venzke 2012 (n 49) 10–11, 22, 25; Buergenthal 2009 (n 49) 403.

[52] Michael K Addo, *The Legal Nature of International Human Rights* (Brill 2010) 19–22.

international courts 'attempts to suture this normative indeterminacy'.[53] Through their developing jurisprudence, international human rights courts delimit the contours of the concepts and clarify the range of state obligations, at least to some extent.[54] In this regard, human rights textbooks and academic articles reveal several lines of jurisprudence that international human rights courts have developed. These courts themselves refer to older case law in their reasoning, thus revealing how they construct and develop the law over time.[55] The vagueness of the concepts and norms facilitates or even invites teleological and evolutive interpretation, as is nicely captured in the living instrument doctrine of the ECtHR.[56] As societies change, the meaning and reach of human rights must evolve to ensure an effective enjoyment of fundamental rights. International human rights courts can thus push the boundaries of human rights through their interpretative choices and the lines of jurisprudence that they develop.

As will be further developed in the next section, exactly because of this inherent indeterminacy, international courts may choose to leave the contracting states a certain discretion in the way they determine their human rights obligations. The indeterminacy of human rights is 'exposed' when human rights courts adopt diverging lines of jurisprudence, as has been the case for the HRC and the ECtHR in relation to religious minorities. The HRC does not follow the ECtHR's grant of a broad margin of appreciation to states regarding the way in which they regulate relations between state and religion, which results in a stronger protection of minorities' fundamental rights.[57] These differences in the case law on religious minorities and the related controversies have been visible for more than twenty years and do not seem to abate.

Nevertheless, in many other fields, one can denote 'transnational judicial dialogue' and the related mutually reinforcing lines of jurisprudence. The impact of international courts' jurisprudence on international lawmaking arguably increases when the jurisprudence becomes transnational as a consequence of the phenomenon of transnational judicial dialogue. First introduced and traced by Anne-Marie Slaughter, in the present-day globalized legal context courts in

[53] Illan rua Wall, 'The Indeterminacy of Human Rights: A Response to O'Connell' <https://criticallegalthinking.com/2015/06/22/the-indeterminacy-of-human-rights-a-response-to-oconnell/> accessed 3 July 2024.

[54] ibid.

[55] See Section 2 the example of positive state obligations.

[56] The ECtHR is known for its living instrument doctrine, following which the Convention is a 'living instrument, which must be interpreted in the light of present day conditions'. This line of thinking was taken over by the Inter-American Court of Human Rights in *Mayagna (Sumo) Awas Tingni Community v Nicaragua*: 'human rights treaties are living instruments, the interpretation of which must evolve over time in view of existing circumstances'.

[57] See inter alia Stephanie Berry, 'A "Good Faith" Interpretation of the Right to Manifest Religion? the Diverging Approaches of the European Court of Human Rights and the UN Human Rights Committee' (2017) 37 Legal Studies 672. See also Fabienne Bretscher, *Protecting the Religious Freedom of New Minorities under International Law* (Routledge 2019).

different jurisdictions increasingly take note of their respective jurisprudence and interact with each other, leading to cross-fertilizing lines of jurisprudence,[58] ultimately captured in the expressions 'transnational judicial dialogue' or 'judicial globalization'.[59] The lines of jurisprudence that emerge therefrom, when dealing with roughly comparable questions under roughly comparable legal standards at different courts, arguably carry even more weight than judgments from one particular international court, as the former benefit from a so-called multiplication or accelerating effect. Indeed, the recognition of a norm throughout the international judiciary can be argued to seal and consolidate its status.

A good example of transnational judicial dialogue of particular relevance to minorities is the recognition that the prohibition of discrimination rules out not only direct discrimination but also indirect discrimination. The latter concerns seemingly neutral measures having a disproportionate and unjustifiable negative impact on a particular group.[60] As indirect discrimination allows less obvious instances of discrimination to be captured without an explicit causal link between the disadvantageous treatment and a particular ground of prohibited discrimination, it is welcomed.[61] The latter broad interpretation of the prohibition of discrimination is particularly relevant for persons belonging to minorities, since seemingly neutral measures tend to reflect the dominant norm, and thus will produce disproportionate negative effects on persons belonging to minorities.[62]

Indirect discrimination started off as a judicial construct, and hence was built through interpretative choices of (international) courts. In Europe, it was the CJEU that took the lead early on in its developing non-discrimination jurisprudence.[63]

[58] Examples of such influence between international courts is particularly visible in the domain of human rights, where the jurisprudence of the ECtHR and interpretations adopted by that Court has influenced the jurisprudence of the Inter-American Court of Human Rights and the UN Human Rights Committee, eg regarding the right to privacy and homosexual conduct between consenting adults (compare *Toonen v Australia,* No 488/1992 (Human Rights Committee, 31 March 1994) with *Modinos v Cyprus* App no. 15070/89 (ECtHR, 22 April 1993)).

[59] In her article on judicial globalization Anne Marie Slaughter distinguishes five categories of judicial interaction, referring to judicial interaction across, above and below borders, encompassing horizontal, vertical, and mixed horizontal-vertical judicial dialogue (Anne Marie Slaughter, 'Judicial Globalization' (2000) 40 Virginia Journal of International Law 1103. Anne Marie Slaughter further devised a typology for this so-called 'transnational judicial communication', encompassing a horizontal, vertical, or mixed horizontal-vertical communication Anne Marie Slaughter, 'A Typology of Transjudicial Communication' (1994) 29 University of Richmond Law Review 99.

[60] Titia Loenen, 'Indirect discrimination as a vehicle for change' (2000) 6 Australian Journal of Human Rights 77.

[61] As awareness grows about the unacceptability of direct discrimination, indirect discrimination at times veils hidden direct discrimination. A good example, where the court itself hints at this possibility, is *Horvath and Kiss* App no 1146/11(ECtHR, 29 January 2013).

[62] See also John Wrench, 'Raising Awareness of the Problem of Discrimination Against Migrants and Minorities in Employment' <https://www.globalmigrationpolicy.org/articles/Events/WrenchGenevaAug2015.pdf> (accessed 31 July 2024), paper presented to Committee on the Elimination of Racial Discrimination, Geneva, 14 August 2015.

[63] For a detailed analysis of the CJEU's development of the notion of indirect discrimination for EU law, see Christa Tobler, *Indirect Discrimination: A Case Study into the Development of the Legal Concept of Indirect Discrimination under EC Law* (Intersentia 2005) 100ff.

Whereas the European Committee of Social Rights smoothly incorporated indirect discrimination in its jurisprudence,[64] the path was bumpier for the ECtHR. After multiple cases in which the notion of indirect discrimination was kept at bay, it was only in 2007 that the Grand Chamber judgment of *DH et al v Czech Republic* fully accepted the notion in a case on Roma children being sidelined to inferior education for the mentally disabled.[65] Subsequently, it took another decade before the ECtHR was ready to extend the notion beyond education.[66] This example of the slow development of particular lines of jurisprudence provides for a suitable transition to the next section, which emphasizes the constraints faced by international courts in pushing the boundaries of human rights through their jurisprudence.

## 4. When International Courts do not Push the Boundaries of Human Rights but Rather Step Back due to (Perceived) Legitimacy Constraints

International courts, as officially mandated to supervise state parties' compliance, have a so-called initial legitimacy.[67] The initial legitimacy of their pronouncements is further enhanced due to them being composed of independent experts.[68] Possible legitimacy constraints of icourts need to be understood in light of the circumstance that ultimately icourts cannot take state compliance as given: states cannot be forced to comply, as a result of the interrelated effect of state sovereignty and limited enforcement possibilities against states. This implies that states need to be persuaded to comply. Hence, icourts may be concerned that if they adopt a progressive interpretation of the scope of application of rights and the related state obligations in controversial matters and thereby question the status quo,

[64] See inter alia *International Association Autism Europe v France* Comm no 13/2002 (ECSR, 29 September 2003) para 52; *European Roma Rights Centre (ERRC) v Bulgaria* Comm no 31/2005 (ECSR, 18 October 2006) para 40.

[65] *DH et al v Czech Republic* App no 57325/00 (ECtHR, 13 November 2007).

[66] See also Mathias Möschel, 'The Strasbourg Court and Indirect Race Discrimination: Going Beyond the Education Domain'(2017) 80 The Modern Law Review 121.

[67] See also Kanstantsin Dzehtsiarou, *European Consensus and the Legitimacy of the European Court of Human Rights* (CUP 2015) 143.

[68] In case of a two-prong supervisory mechanism, where the bulk of supervisory work is done by an expert body, but the final assessment by a body of state representatives, it is particularly important that the political body follows the interpretation lines set out by the independent expert body. The supervisory mechanism of the European Social Charter is laid out in Part IV of the Charter. The periodic state reporting is set out in Art 21, while Art 24 entrusts the examination of these reports to a committee of experts (the European Committee of Social Rights). Art 29 recognizes the competence of the Committee of Ministers to pronounce recommendations. The FCNM system is explained in Arts 24(1) and 26(1) respectively. At this level it is merely provided that the Committee of Ministers is assisted by an Advisory Committee (AC), consisting of experts. Further details about the way in which the members of the AC are selected and the way in which the AC assists the Committee of Ministers had to be determined by the latter within one year after the coming into force of the FCNM. Fortunately, the Committee of Ministers' recommendations have de facto tended to follow the opinions of the respective expert bodies.

states might react critically and even reject court decisions.[69] Depending on the number and strength of states concerned, icourts' legitimacy could be undermined by this criticism, which would constrain their powers of persuasion more generally and consequently undermine their supervisory function, as well as their role as a guardian and protector/promotor of the effective protection of fundamental rights.[70] A striking example of an icourt's decision undoubtedly infused by legitimacy concerns is the Grand Chamber's reversal of the Chamber judgment in the *Lautsi* case. The Chamber's conclusion that the requirement to have crucifixes in all classrooms of public schools violated the ECHR had elicited vehement criticism by many states. The Grand Chamber arrived at the opposite conclusion, since states ought to have a wide margin of appreciation in the matter.[71] The ten intervening states clearly did not accept the icourt's interference in their national constitutional identity, and the Grand Chamber 'went along'.[72]

Icourts have developed a range of techniques that allow them to step back whenever they are confronted with controversial or highly complex matters. To some extent[73] a high level of proof and the way in which the court allocates the burden of proof between the parties allows courts to avoid dealing with the merits of a case. The scope of application of rights can also be narrowly construed, as is often visible in relation to the linguistic dimension of particular fundamental rights.[74] The most prevalent technique of icourts to avoid pronouncing on the merits is the discretion (or margin of appreciation) they grant states, when assessing the proportionality of interferences or positive state obligations.

[69] Let's not forget that individual complaints procedures against states for most icourts still require additional acceptance of their contentious jurisdiction, next to the ratification of the human rights convention: see inter alia the (additional protocols to) UN conventions, the African and Inter-American human rights courts.

[70] Neus Torbisco-Casals, 'The Legimacy of International Courts: The Challenge of Diversity' (2021) 52 J Soc Philos 491, 494–95. See also Lucas Gruszczynski and Wouter Werner, 'Introduction' in Lucas Gruszczynski and Wouter Werner (eds), *Deference in International Courts and Tribunals* (OUP 2014).

[71] For a nice analysis, see Lorenzo Zucca, 'Lautsi: A Commentary on a Decision by the ECtHR Grand Chamber' (2013) 11 IJCL 218.

[72] For a critical note about the ECtHR leaving too much discretion to states to safeguard their national constitutional identity, see Daniel Augenstein, 'Religious Pluralism and National Constitutional Traditions in Europe', in L Zucca and C Ungureanu (eds) *Law, State and Religion in the New Europe: Debates and Dilemmas* (CUP 2012) 261.

[73] Stepping back to avoid controversies could also be realized at the admissibility stage, by using the argument that the case is manifestly ill-founded without much reasoning (see inter alia Helen Keller, Andreas Fischer, and Daniela Kühne, 'Debating the Future of the European Court of Human Rights after the Interlaken Conference: Two Innovative Proposals'(2010) 21 European Journal of International Law 1025). The additional admissibility requirement of 'no significant disadvantage' (added with Additional Protocal 14, to manage the flow of cases) could also be used in this respect. The analysis here will focus on 'stepping back' at the merit stage, and especially the proportionality analysis.

[74] The ECtHR has several cases in which it specified that the freedom of expression would not imply the choice of language in which to communicate in courts or with administrative authorities: *Isop v Austria* App no 808/60 (ECtHR, 8 March 1962), *Inhabitants of Leeuw-St Pierr v Belgium* App no 2333/64 (ECommHR, 15 July 1965).

The ECtHR is undoubtedly the icourt that has used this technique the most, through its margin of appreciation doctrine.[75] Granting states a certain margin of appreciation is justified because national authorities are 'better placed' to make proportionality evaluations, and because the international supervision always is subsidiary to the primary responsibility of states.[76] Throughout ECtHR case law, various factors emerge that are used by the Court to determine the width of the margin of appreciation in a particular case: European consensus, general policy decision, the kind of legitimate aim, the nature of the right, and conflicting rights.[77] General policy decisions, conflicting rights, and the lack of European consensus point to a broad margin, as do particular legitimate aims such as morals and national security. The lack of further clear criteria and parameters allows the Court to 'mould' the width of the margin of appreciation by emphasizing those criteria that allow it to conclude to a broad margin when faced by controversial or highly complex issues.[78]

Nevertheless, as will be discussed below, even in areas where the ECtHR started off with a broad margin of appreciation for states, over time, incremental steps towards higher scrutiny have proven possible. In this respect, it has been noted that over time, European consensus can be created,[79] while the boundaries of human rights are pushed incrementally.

The following analysis of various landmark judgments reveals broadly three trajectories. A first trajectory (4.1) concerns cases in which the respective courts start with bold pronouncements on the scope of application of rights and the related state obligation, whereby they initially push the boundaries of human rights but stop short of providing 'full' protection. Instead, the icourts ultimately step back, presumably to avoid overstepping and going counter to sovereign state choices. The second trajectory (4.2) reveals that in certain of these controversial areas, there has been (some) room for a gradual, incremental development by icourts, whereas the third trajectory (4.3) demonstrates that there are some issues that are so complex and controversial that they seemingly become 'frozen constraints' for icourts.

[75] The 15th Additional Protocol amended the ECHR accordingly.

[76] For an extensive discussion of the principle of subsidiarity and the way in which it is used in the jurisprudence of the ECtHR, see Jonas Christoffersen, *Fair Balance: Proportinality, Subsidiarity and Primarity in the ECtHR* (Martinus Nijhoff 2009) 227ff.

[77] See also Thomas A O'Donnell, 'The Margin of Appreciation Doctrine: Standards in the Jurisprudence of the European Court of Human Rights' (1982) 4 Human Rights Quarterly 474.

[78] For a deeper analysis, see Kristin Henrard, 'How the ECtHR's Use of European Consensus Modulates the Effective Protection of Fundamental Rights: Balancing Mandate, Legitimacy Concerns and Epistemological Uncertainty' in Panos Kapotas and Vassilis Tsevelekos (eds), *Building Consensus on European Consensus* (CUP 2019) 141.

[79] See also Shai Dothan, 'Judicial Deference Allows European Consensus to Emerge' (2018) 18 Chicago Journal of International Law 393.

## 4.1. One step forward, two steps back?

This section will discuss cases in which the icourt makes an important step forward at the level of principles, recognizing minorities' fundamental rights and reducing state discretion, but where in the application to the facts of the case the icourt actually takes two steps back, ultimately providing scant protection.

This phenomenon can be detected in several cases concerning Roma and religious minorities. The landmark case *Chapman* is a very telling example concerning the housing of Roma, where land planning regulations prevented a Roma woman from stationing her caravan on her own plot of land.[80] This judgment is very important in at least three interrelated respects. It was the first judgment in which the ECtHR recognizes that leading a traditional way of life is within the scope of application of Article 8 ECHR, when combining the right to respect for privacy, family life, and home.[81] Furthermore, the Court recognized positive state obligations to facilitate the Gypsy way of life, and opined that 'the vulnerable position of Gypsies as a minority means that some special consideration should be given to their needs and their different lifestyle both in the relevant regulatory planning framework and in reaching decisions in particular cases'.[82] These interpretative findings, and even hints at the need to adopt Roma-specific measures, are informed by the Framework Convention for the Protection of National Minorities (FCNM). According to the Court, the FCNM reflects 'an emerging international consensus amongst the Contracting States of the Council of Europe recognising the special needs of minorities and an obligation to protect their security, identity and lifestyle'.[83] However, the Court immediately tones down this consensus, as not being sufficiently concrete to interpret Article 8 as implying a far-reaching positive state obligation of general social policy. More particularly, the states would not be obliged 'to make available to the Gypsy community an adequate number of suitably equipped sites'.[84] After all, the framework nature of the FCNM with its general principles 'reinforces the Court's view that the complexity and sensitivity of the issues involved in policies balancing the interests of the general population, in particular with regard to environmental protection, and the interests of a minority with possibly conflicting requirements, renders the Court's role a strictly supervisory one'.[85] In other words, ultimately the Court granted the UK a broad margin of appreciation, and concluded that Article 8 ECHR was not violated.[86]

80 *Chapman v the United Kingdom* App no 27238/95 (ECtHR, 18 January 2001).
81 ibid paras 73–74.
82 ibid para 96.
83 ibid para 93.
84 ibid para 98.
85 ibid para 94.
86 ibid para 116.

In *Muños Diaz*,[87] a case concerning a double discrimination complaint related to the lack of recognition of a Roma marriage, as the marriage had been concluded following Roma rites, the ECtHR relied and built on the reasoning in *Chapman*. The first complaint concerned the denial of a survivors' pension to the Roma widow, as her marriage was not recognized as having been 'one in good faith'. The second complaint focused on the lack of official recognition of a marriage conducted in accordance with Roma traditions. In both respects, the claimant argued a differential treatment of comparable marriages without reasonable and objective justification. The ECtHR adopted a radically different approach to the two discrimination complaints: with regard to the more 'neutral' socio-economic issue, it fully engaged with the discrimination analysis and questions of comparability, but the Court ducked the question, which is more controversial for states, about what marriages they should officially recognize in addition to civil marriages.[88]

In relation to the former complaint, the Court closely investigated Spanish law and jurisprudence, noting that the latter had recognized survivors' pensions for marriages in good faith.[89] The ECtHR then critically scrutinized the Spanish courts' refusal to recognize the marriage as good faith. On the one hand, it underscored that the Spanish authorities had issued the claimant a number of official documents certifying her status as the spouse of the deceased.[90] On the other, the Court argued that the Spanish authorities should have attached sufficient weight to the 'collective beliefs of a community that is well defined culturally' in relation to the validity of a marriage.[91] In connection with the first complaint, the ECtHR used the *Chapman* ruling's emphasis on positive state obligations to protect the identity and lifestyle of minorities and thus to take their special needs into account when applying the law.[92] The Court found a violation of Article 14 junctio 8 in this respect.[93]

The other discrimination complaint challenged the differential treatment between other (religious) marriages that are officially recognized and a marriage according to Roma rites, because the Roma marriage was not only deeply rooted in the culture of her community but it also had been part of Spanish history over

[87] *Muñoz Díaz v Spain* App no 49151/07 (ECtHR, 8 December 2009).

[88] This special sensitivity about the official recognition of marriages and the related absence of European consensus regarding LGBT marriages is visible in the landmark judgment of *Schalk and Kopf v Austria* (App no 30141/04 (ECtHR, 24 June 2010), and the following jurisprudence. While later jurisprudence has obliged states to have and strengthen a legal status for LGBT persons in a stable relationships, the Court has not wavered in granting states a wide margin of appreciation to decide whether or not to allow the institution of marriage for persons of the same sex. See also Geoffrey Willems, 'Same-Sex Marriage as a Human Right: How the Strasbourg Court Could Draw Inspiration from the US Supreme Court and the Inter-American Court of Human Rights to Affirm Marriage Equality' (2024) 14 Oñati Socio-Legal Series 176.

[89] *Muñoz Díaz v Spain* App no 49151/07 (ECtHR, 8 December 2009) para 53.

[90] ibid para 61.

[91] ibid para 59.

[92] ibid para 60.

[93] ibid para 71.

five hundred years. The Court summarily dismissed this discrimination complaint because the other marriages were religious marriages, which would not be comparable to Roma marriages.[94] In the process, the Court adopted a formal equality approach, and pointed to civil marriages being open to everyone without distinction.[95] The Court thus not only avoided the challenge of identifying the relevant criteria to assess comparability of marriages in relation to official recognition, but also the underlying complex questions about substantive equality.

A similar mix of very promising statements pointing to high levels of scrutiny, but ultimately a broad margin of appreciation because of lacking European consensus and the related complexity/controversiality, is visible with religious minorities. The ECtHR has often underscored the importance of the freedom of religion as one of the cornerstones of democratic societies, also because religion is one of the essential elements of one's identity.[96] Relatedly, the state has positive obligations of neutrality and impartiality towards the distinct religions within its territory.[97] Nevertheless, when determining the width of the margin of appreciation under Article 9 the starting point seems to be that the margin is rather wide, particularly whenever there is no European consensus on a particular matter, such as the particular choice of relations between the state and religious denominations, or in the case of conflicting Convention rights.[98] A particularly striking case, in which the Court combined some promising statements (implying developments in the case law in favour of religious minorities) with highly problematic majoritarian reasoning and ultimately a lack of protection for religious minorities is *SAS v France*. This infamous case concerned the French law criminalizing the wearing of face-covering garments. When reviewing the legitimate aims of this interference (with the freedom to manifest one's religion) the Court did not accept 'gender equality' as an argument 'to ban a practice that is defended by women'.[99] Similarly, it did not accept the human dignity argument either, since wearing the full-face veil in public space 'is an expression of a cultural identity which contributes to the pluralism that is inherent in democracy'.[100] The Court took 'two steps back' when it accepted the notion that the requirements of living together amounted to the 'rights of others' as a legitimate aim for the interference.[101] Since the 'others' here pointed to the majority, the Court built its case on a majoritarian argument,

[94] ibid paras 76–80.
[95] ibid paras 79–80.
[96] Inter alia *Kokkinakis v Greece* App no 14307/88 (ECtHR, 25 May 1993) para 31.
[97] Inter alia *Eweida et al v the United Kingdom* App nos 48420/10; 59842/10; 51671/10; 36516/10 (ECtHR, 15 January 2013) para 81.
[98] *Tonchev et al v Bulgaria* App no 56862/15 (ECtHR, 13 December 2022) para 49. See also for a more detaiiled coverage, Registry of the ECtHR, 'Guide to Article 9 of the European Convention on Human Rights' <https://ks.echr.coe.int/documents/d/echr-ks/guide_art_9_eng> (updated until 29 February 2024) accessed on 22 August 2024 20–21.
[99] *SAS v France* App no 43835/11 (ECtHR, 1 July 2014) para 119.
[100] ibid para 120.
[101] ibid para 121.

whereas human rights are supposed to provide counter-majoritarian protection. The Court advanced a step forward when it acknowledged the inherent flexibility of the notion of living together and the related risk of abuse, which called for a careful examination of the necessity of the measure concerned.[102] Again taking two steps back, the Court proceeded with an awkward line of argumentation to identify a lack of European consensus, in order to be able the grant a wide margin of appreciation to France,[103] and concluded that the ECHR was not violated.

The strong emphasis on a lack of European consensus to justify a broad margin of appreciation for states appears to confirm the underlying legitimacy concerns of the ECtHR: when the Court senses that particular matters are highly sensitive for member states, it prefers to step back, not take a position, and thus avoid possible pushback from the states. Interestingly, the CJEU had signalled in its early post-2000 judgments of Article 17 TFEU that it would not adopt the ECtHR's broad margin of appreciation as a baseline for religious matters.[104] Unfortunately, however, when the CJEU was confronted with a range of cases concerning often controversial manifestations of religion by members of the Muslim minority in European states, more particularly ritual methods of slaughter and the wearing of headscarves at work, it has chosen to embrace explicitly the ECtHR's broad margin of appreciation.[105]

### 4.2. Incrementalism and gradual pushing of the boundaries

The second trajectory concerns cases in which international courts have developed case law incrementally, pushing the boundaries of human rights gradually, notwithstanding the controversial and complex nature of particular topics and the related legitimacy concerns of international courts. This development confirms not only the dynamic, evolutive nature of human rights, but also the de facto power of international courts to forge, or at least steer, particular developments of the law.

At times, international courts must come to terms with a complex concept itself, such as indirect discrimination, before feeling confident to apply it in cases against states. In some cases, such as positive state obligations to adapt official registers to new post-operative gender, the international court sends signals about possible

[102] ibid para 121.

[103] ibid paras 153–55: France being in a minority position at the time in adopting this ban, while other states did not have clear positions, seems the perfect opportunity for the Court to have provided guidance and to steer the states in a certain direction (albeit not a uniform solution).

[104] Case C-68/17 *IR v JQ* (CJEU, 11 September 2018) para 48; Case C-414/16 *Vera Egenberger v Evangelisches Werk für Diakonie und Entwicklung e.V.* (CJEU, 17 April 2018) paras 56–58.

[105] See below under sections 4.2 and 4.3 for the names and references of these cases concerned. The analysis there will show that the CJEU seems to have moved towards stricter scrutiny in relation to private companies, while in relation to public authorities as employer the broad margin of appreciation seems to stand.

changes in the case law, thus preparing the hearts and minds of states. Once the international court perceives enough positive signs, it will push the boundaries of human rights.[106] In other cases, such as that of conflicting rights, the case law starts with the general 'rule' that in case of conflicting rights states have a broad margin of appreciation, but then over time, and after several cases on similar conflicting rights, the icourt develops ever more detailed criteria.[107] Put differently, gradually state discretion is reduced in tandem with the developing (European) consensus, while icourts take an active part in the norm articulation and thereby push the boundaries of human rights. In relation to minorities, it is also possible to denote a gradual norm building on particular topics, which goes hand in hand with an emerging European consensus on that particular topic.[108] The latter consensus provides icourts the necessary confidence to limit state discretion and formulate firmer state obligations about the topics concerned. In other words, in relation to minorities, and certainly religious minorities and Roma, not only a gradual but also a very piecemeal development can be observed.[109]

The long journey before the ECtHR incorporated 'indirect discrimination' as one of the dimensions of the prohibition of discrimination under the ECHR has been portrayed numerous times.[110] The Court grappled with the special nature of indirect discrimination (and related challenges of proof) as seemingly neutral measures where the 'problem' was not so much the intent to discriminate, but rather an (unjustified) disproportionate effect on members of a particular group. Tellingly, the landmark case in which the Court finally embraced and started to develop its case law on the prohibition of indirect discrimination is a Roma case, more particularly concerning the disproportionate sidelining of Roma children to inferior education for the mentally disabled.[111]

The importance of strategic litigation can already be flagged here, given that cases which invite the Court to develop its reasoning require carefully crafted arguments.[112]

[106] See for example the reasoning deployed in *Christine Goodwin v the United Kingdom* App no 28957/95 (ECtHR, 11 July 2002) discussed below (and blogs).

[107] See inter alia the ECtHR case law on conflicting rights between the right to respect for privacy of famous persons on the one hand, and the freedom of expression of journalists on the other: see the range of cases following the Grand Chamber judgment in *Von Hannover v Germany* App nos 40660/08 and 60641/08 (ECtHR, 7 February 2021). See also *Couderc and Hachette Filipacchi Associés v France* App no 40454/07 (ECtHR, 10 November 2015).

[108] See the following discussion denoting differences between minority groups and between topics for the same minority group: eg for Roma the ECtHR is willing to enhance positive state obligations in relation to education and forced evictions, but not really in relation to the right to identity and housing.

[109] See also below under section 4.3 for the seemingly more 'frozen' topics. See also Chapter 7 in this volume on the burden of proof.

[110] This picture has been painted in different levels of detail in blogs and case notes, drawing out the developments in case law, particularly since *Thlimmenos* App no 34369/97 (ECtHR, 6 April 2000) and *Hoogendijk* App no 58641/00 (ECtHR, 6 January 2005), in articles and in book. See inter alia Corinna Ferguson, 'Running Ahead of Strasbourg: Indirect Discrimination and Article 14 ECHR' (2008) 13 Judicial Review 71.

[111] *DH et al v the Czech Republic* App no 57325/00 (ECtHR, 13 November 2007).

[112] See also the chapters of Kris Gledhill and Lilla Farkas in this volume.

The way in which an ongoing stream of cases is important in order to give the Court 'new' chances to develop its case law, applying teleological and evolutive interpretation methods, is equally visible in the line of cases running up to the Grand Chamber decision in *Christine Goodwin*. With regard to the specifics of the public registry system in the UK, for a long time the Court had maintained that Article 8 would not encompass far-reaching positive state obligations to adapt their official registries to the new reality of post-operative transsexuals. However, the Court did flag in these judgments that at some point this balancing exercise might tip in favour of the transsexuals, in view of ongoing developments in society.[113] In *Christine Goodwin* the Court acknowledged that in view of the new data and related understanding of the hardship of transgender persons, their concerns to have their new gender officially recognized outweighed administrative concerns of public authorities, accordingly shrinking the state's margin of appreciation, notwithstanding the UK's opposition.[114] The ECtHR clearly felt strengthened in its decision to reverse its line of jurisprudence in view of the European consensus that had emerged on the matter.

The ECtHR goes beyond 'warming hearts and minds' in relation to conflicting rights. The baseline position in this regard is that when equal fundamental rights conflict with one another there is no clear rule on which takes precedence; states have a broad margin of appreciation to take into consideration local conditions. In some respects the ECtHR remains reluctant to steer, for instance when religious convictions conflict with the prohibition of discrimination on grounds of sexual orientation.[115] In other respects, the Court has chosen to provide guidance to states about relevant parameters and how these should be considered when balancing the two rights, thus forging European consensus. Over the years the Court then feels able to gradually add further detail and specifications. This development is clearly visible in relation to conflicting rights between journalists' freedom of expression and the right to respect for privacy of public figures.[116]

The ECtHR has a long line of jurisprudence on states having a broad margin of appreciation with regard to relations between state and religion, a notion which it has defined very broadly. Nevertheless, over time the Court did heighten its scrutiny in certain matters pertaining to religious regulation.[117] One of the examples where this tightening of the review and the related 'steering', the pushing

[113] See also Henriette Jakobien Liesker,'Caught in a Balancing Act: The ECtHR and the Road to Recognition for Sexual Minorities' (2017) 4 Oslo Law Review 172.

[114] *Christine Goodwin v the United Kingdom* (n 106) paras 92–93.

[115] See inter alia *Eweida et al v the United Kingdom* App nos 48420/10; 59842/10; 51671/10; 36516/10 (ECtHR, 15 January 2013) and the cases of *Ladele and McFarlane v the United Kingdom* App nos 51671/10; 36516/10 (ECtHR, 12 April 2011).

[116] See also n 107.

[117] For a more detailed analysis, see inter alia Kristin Henrard, 'How the European Court of Human Rights' Concern Regarding European Consensus Tempers the Effective Protection of Freedom of Religion' (2015) 4 Oxford Journal of Law and Religion 398.

of the boundaries of human rights, by the ECtHR is visible, concerns religion/state models: the Court identifies increasingly precise demands about objective criteria and transparent procedures for such models.[118]

The CJEU's first judgments regarding company rules that amounted to prohibitions of the headscarf in the work environment triggered considerable criticism, as the Court was not very critical about alleged neutrality policies of companies, also when these 'appeared' in response to concrete requests to wear a headscarf at work.[119] In the three subsequent cases regarding companies,[120] the CJEU does de facto increase the scrutiny, as it requires the companies involved to be able to prove a genuine need to have a neutrality policy,[121] in the form of a sufficiently specific risk of its business activities being undermined without a neutrality policy.[122] Put differently, the CJEU over time developed its jurisprudence to provide stronger protection against discrimination on grounds of religion in the private work environment.[123]

A nice example of the ECtHR gradually pushing the boundaries of human rights in relation to Roma concerns their equal access to quality education. It was highlighted earlier that it was in exactly this area that the Court embraced the notion and developed the first steps of its jurisprudence on indirect discrimination. Gradually, the Court has added a range of positive state obligations to prohibit states from engaging in the disproportionate sidelining of Roma to inferior education. The Court has recognized that decades of discrimination in the educational field has lingering effects, which triggers positive state obligations to adopt affirmative action measures to redress this past discrimination.[124] Gradually the Court has also identified positive state obligations to counter segregation, implying that the mere fact of having a school with almost exclusively Roma children is problematic and the authorities need to counter this as soon as possible.[125]

Again, the gradual building of lines of jurisprudence points to the importance of having a steady stream of strategically chosen cases inviting icourts to develop their reasoning and their jurisprudence.

118 A recent example concerns *Anderlecht Christian Assembly of Jehovah's Witnesses and others v Belgium* App no 20165/20 (ECtHR, 5 April 2022).

119 Case C-157/15 *Samira Achbita and Centrum voor gelijkheid van kansen en voor racismebestrijding v G4S Secure Solutions NV* (CJEU, 14 March 2017) and Case C-188/15 *Asma Bougnaoui and Association de défense des droits de l'homme (ADDH) v Micropole SA* (CJEU, 13 July 2016).

120 Case C-804/18; 341/19 *IX v WABE eV and MH Müller Handels GmbH v MJ* (CJEU, 15 July 2021).

121 ibid paras 64 and 67.

122 ibid paras 76 and 85.

123 Unfortunately, the CJEU returned to granting states a de facto broad margin of discretion in relation to employment in the public sector, allowing public authorities to adopt a principle of exclusive neutrality: Case C-148/22 *Commune d'Ans* (CJEU, 28 November 2023) para 33.

124 *Horváth and Kiss v Hungary* App no 11146/11 (ECtHR, 29 January 2013) para 116.

125 *Szolcsán v Hungary* App no 24408/16 (ECtHR, 30 June 2023).

### 4.3. Frozen constraints?

Notwithstanding developments in the case law that show that icourts are willing and able to reduce state discretion in relation to minorities,[126] the case law also reveals that there are certain fields of law, certain topics where icourts appear to identify 'frozen' constraints on their powers of interpretation and adjudication, and related 'lawmaking' function. These topics appear to be either too complex or too controversial for icourts to step in and steer states in a particular direction, thus pushing the boundaries of human rights. Courts seem to be concerned that states' criticisms and rejection in response thereto could undermine their own legitimacy.

These 'frozen' constraints are also visible in relation to other 'minorities' than the Roma. The ECtHR may have strengthened the rights of LGBT people to a recognized status of their relationship and related rights; however, it so far has refused to interpret Article 12 ECHR as enshrining a right to marriage for same-sex couples.[127] While the CJEU had to somewhat impose a duty on member states to recognize gay marriages that were officially contracted in other member states, in order not to inhibit free movement rights, it was careful to underscore that EU states do not have to permit persons to contract gay marriages in their own state.[128] As acknowledged above in relation to religious minorities, both the ECtHR and CJEU have several lines of jurisprudence that over time, in line with an emerging European consensus on the matter, have provided protection and restrict state discretion. However, in relation to questions of headscarves in employment and the public space, as well as ritual slaughter, the underlying controversies and lack of European consensus have resulted in both European transnational courts preferring to step back and grant states a broad margin of appreciation.[129]

As the analysis in the chapters of Parts II and III will further clarify, there are clear differences in the extent to which the ECtHR has been willing to push the boundaries of human rights concerning fundamental rights for Roma. In relation

[126] For an account of such developments in relation to linguistic minorities, and language rights of ethnic minorities, see inter alia Kristin Henrard, 'Accountability challenges for minorities' (equal enjoyment of) fundamental rights: vague norms, states' sovereignty and legitimacy concerns of international courts' in Kristin Henrard and Michelle Duin (eds) *Research Handbook on Accountability for Human Rights Violations* (Edward Elgar forthcoming in 2024–25).

[127] See also n 88.

[128] Case C-673/16 *Relu Adrian Coman and Others v Inspectoratul General pentru Imigrări and Ministerul Afacerilor Interne* (CJEU, 5 June 2018). See also Case C-490/20 *VMA v Stolichna obshtina, rayon 'Pancharevo'* (CJEU, 14 December 2021) regarding recognition of the parenthood of a same-sex couple in the child's birth certificate.

[129] Admittedly, in relation to neutrality policies of companies, the CJEU had become more demanding, requesting companies to demonstrate a real need for such policies. Nevertheless, it sends a most worrying signal when the CJEU is even willing to sacrifice one of the four freedoms central to the EU's interna market in favour of the broad margin of appreciation for states in religion-state affairs: see Case C-372/21 *Freikirche der Siebenten-Tags-Adventisten in Deutschland KdöR v Bildungsdirektion für Vorarlberg* (CJEU, 2 February 2023) paras 30–32, 41–43.

to hate speech, Gliszczynska and Sledzinska demonstrate that the level of protection provided is in several respects disappointing, compared with the much stronger protection that the Court gives against hate speech affecting Jews.

In relation to the burden of proof, Chapter 7 by Henrard and Roberts highlights that a distinction needs to be made between indirect and direct discrimination complaints. In relation to the former, the ECtHR's jurisprudence also pertaining to Roma and equal access to education has definitely had a part in pushing the boundaries of human rights. However, a different picture emerges in relation to proof for allegedly discriminatory violence, where several recent cases demonstrate that the Court sets the bar too high for a prima facie case of discrimination and thus a meaningful allocation of the burden of proof between the alleged victim and a state.[130] The Court seems more concerned about not imposing an unreasonable burden on the state than providing the victim with effective protection against discriminatory violence. In connection herewith, the case law on Roma reveals the more generally visible boundaries of the human rights paradigm. Nevertheless, the promising developments that have been introduced by *WA Baile v Switzerland*[131] for the allocation of the burden of proof in cases of 'ethnic profiling' undoubtedly hold promise for a pushing of the boundaries concerning discriminatory violence.

Both the ECtHR and the European Committee of Social Rights have heard several cases on Roma and access to housing. Chapter 10 by O'Nions in this handbook reveals that the ECtHR jurisprudence has over time provided stronger protection against particular modalities of eviction, while also becoming more demanding about the alternative housing that is provided by the state. The pushing of the boundaries in this respect has gone hand in hand with a revealing of the ongoing boundary of human rights in the form of a lack of protection of Roma's traditional way of life. The ECtHR has so far not been willing to identify (far-reaching) state obligations to provide sufficient stopping places for Roma, keeping in mind the social rights dimension thereof, whereas the ECHR is a civil and political rights instrument. The ECSR, on the other hand, has used its stronger mandate regarding social rights to identify positive state obligations to ensure adequate stopping places for caravans, while adding suitability dimensions in terms of size, location, and cultural factors concerning the extended family.[132] O'Nions also underscored that, unlike the ECtHR, the ECSR has been willing to explore the discriminatory nexus, which is the background of systemic discrimination that informs the policies and practices concerning Roma.[133]

[130] See inter alia *PH v Slovakia* App no 37574/19 (ECtHR, 8 December 2022).

[131] *Wa Baile v Switzerland* App no 43868/18; 25883/21 (ECtHR, 20 February 2024).

[132] *European Roma Rights Centre (ERRC) v France* Comm no 51/2008 (ECSR, 19 October 2009); *European Roma Rights Centre (ERRC) v Portugal* Comm no 61/2010 (ECSR, 30 June 2011) paras 49–50.

[133] Inter alia *International Centre for the Legal Protection of Human Rights (Interights) v Greece* Comm no 49/2008 (ECSR, 11 December 2009); *European Roma and Travellers (ERTF) v France* Comm no 119/2015 (ECSR, 5 December 2017) paras 114, 126, 129.

The following chapter will develop the extent to which international courts do (or do not) factor in a background of systemic discrimination, which tends to determine the outcome of a case. The ECtHR has proven to be rather weak in this respect, which also becomes visible in the cases on environmental justice and intersectional discrimination. The actual progress that has been achieved by the ECtHR regarding the identification of positive state obligations concerning access to equal education for Roma children demonstrates that there is potential for actual progress after all.

## 5. Conclusion

International courts have an important role to play in the 'pushing of the boundaries of human rights', more particularly through the adoption of broad, teleological, and dynamic interpretations not only of the scope of application of rights but also in the reach of state obligations. Relatedly, Icourts need to adopt a high level of scrutiny towards justifications put forward by states, to steer states sufficiently. Through their interpretations and applications of human rights, icourts have the power to develop international human rights law, while pushing its boundaries. At the same time, icourts may feel constrained in adopting interpretations—and levels of scrutiny—that states would consider to be encroaching too much on their sovereignty, particularly when there is no (European) consensus on a particular matter.

Nevertheless, this chapter concludes with a call on regional European courts to choose to optimize an effective enjoyment of human rights, for persons belonging to minorities more generally and Roma in particular. This would entail adopting an interpretation that would realize a broad scope of application of fundamental rights and would adopt an appropriate level of scrutiny when assessing state compliance with human rights obligations; also in relation to positive state obligations. In the face of sovereign states and controversial or complex issues, international human rights courts should strive for a gradually advancing of the boundaries of human rights, especially for the seemingly 'frozen' constraints. The remarkable development of the field of equal access to education by the ECtHR reveals the power of a gradual, incremental approach. Bolder stances of other international courts, and the power of transnational judicial dialogue more generally, can be relied upon by other courts to strengthen their own gradual raising of the bar, also in the face of recalcitrant states.

# 6

# The European Courts' Engagement with Systemic Discrimination against Roma

## Different Shades of Acknowledgement and Implications for Review

*Kristin Henrard*

### 1. Introduction

This chapter analyses the way and the extent to which regional European courts address systemic discrimination. The related comparison will reveal ongoing challenges in this respect, while corroborating relevant variables and thus possible pathways for international courts to improve the protection they provide against systemic discrimination.

The chapter builds on the importance of interpretation by (international) courts, as both the interpretation and application of the law play a critical role in defining the content of legal standards and the concomitant obligations of the duty-bearers. It has long been acknowledged that the right to equal treatment, including the prohibition of discrimination, is particularly important for minorities, as it paves the way for their inclusion while retaining their distinct identity.

The previous chapter highlighted how the recognition of indirect discrimination is particularly relevant for persons belonging to minorities, since the underlying neutral measures will reflect the dominant norm and are thus more likely to have a disproportionate effect on them. This chapter looks at the phenomenon of systemic discrimination as a particular type of ingrained discrimination, societal prejudice, and related exclusionary implications throughout society.[1] This first conceptual brush already shows the deeply problematic nature of this type of discrimination and reveals that it will typically affect individuals belonging to minorities. In Europe, the Roma are generally recognized, including by the Council of Europe,[2] the

[1] See the multiple references in section 2.

[2] The Council of Europe has a 'Roma and Travellers Division' dedicated to assist member states in the development of laws and policies, inter alia, to combat discrimination and anti-Gypsyism: https://www.coe.int/en/web/roma-and-travellers/about-us. The Council of Europe also has a Strategic Action Plan for Roma and Traveller Inclusion 2020–25, which is overseen by an intergovernmental Committee of Experts on Roma and Traveller Issues (ADI-ROM).

Kristin Henrard, *The European Courts' Engagement with Systemic Discrimination against Roma*
In: *The Rights of Roma in European Courts*. Edited by: Kristin Henrard and Lilla Farkas, Oxford University Press.
 DOI: 10.1093/oso/9780198914358.003.0006

EU,[3] and the OSCE,[4] as a paradigmatic case of systemic discrimination.[5] Relatedly, Equinet, the European Network of Equality Bodies, identifies as one of its areas of attention the widespread discrimination against, and stereotyping of Roma and Traveller communities.[6]

The pervasive, deeply ingrained and society-wide nature of systemic discrimination implies that it has multiple knock-on effects. Unequal access to education will result in lower qualifications, thus limited employment possibilities, a higher likelihood of poverty, and less resources to access good accommodation, health care, goods and services and education. Systemic discrimination thus creates and perpetuates vicious circles of unjustified disadvantage, and necessitates an appropriate response, ultimately by international courts.

This chapter starts with a conceptual discussion of 'systemic discrimination' which is translated to (possible) points of attention for international courts in their analysis. Subsequently, the supervisory practice of the three regional European courts is analysed, with regard to the extent to which they acknowledge systemic discrimination, and the ways in which systemic discrimination influences their analysis and evaluation. The supervisory practice of these three icourts is discussed in turn, in order to do full justice to the way in which the jurisprudence on systemic discrimination relates to the specific characteristics of the supervisory mechanism and the overall jurisprudence. The latter characteristics determine the order in which these courts are analysed. The analysis starts by looking into the supervisory practice of the European Committee of Social Rights (ECSR), to then proceed to the CJEU, and thirdly turn to the European Court of Human Rights (ECtHR). In the concluding observations a link is made to states' political commitment to Sustainable Development Goals as something that could be drawn upon by icourts to strengthen the pull of their reasoning.

## 2. Systemic Discrimination: From Conceptual Clarification to Points of Attention for International Courts' Interpretation

A legally enshrined definition of systemic discrimination does not yet exist. The increasing attention to this phenomenon by academics from various disciplines

3 The 2020–30 EU Roma strategic framework for equality inclusion and participation similarly requires member states to develop and implement National Roma Strategies.

4 The OSCE Contact Point for Roma and Sinti Issues also aims at countering the widespread racism and discrimination faced by Roma.

5 Comparisons with African Americans in the US have been made. For an article considering racial discrimination in the US and Europe, see Ioanna Toukochoriti, '"Disparate Impact" and "Indirect discrimination": Assessing Responses to Systemic Discrimination in the US and the EU' (2015) European Journal of Human Rights 207, who claims that Europe does not experience racial discrimination to the same extent as the US, while giving prominence to the fight against racial discrimination affecting Roma, at 298.

6 See inter alia <https://equineteurope.org/8-april-international-roma-day>.

(social sciences, political sciences, and law), international organizations, and institutions does reveal a common core understanding, which is captured in the following discussion. Furthermore, the respective writing often uses 'systemic discrimination' interchangeably with 'endemic', 'institutional', 'societal', or 'structural' discrimination.[7] Systemic discrimination is often related to pervasive discrimination, which pervades all spheres of life, is persistent, and is 'entrenched in social behaviour and organization'.[8] This type of pervasive discrimination operates almost per definition at the intersection of civil, political and economic, social and cultural rights, and thus requires a comprehensive, multi-pronged response.[9] When discrimination is ingrained in the way society is organized, it will often be unconscious, and thus not intentional. In this regard, systemic discrimination can be related to implicit bias.[10]

When discrimination is entrenched in society and societal organization it is bound to concern, or at least encompass, indirect discrimination. The preceding description of systemic discrimination—more particularly, the irrelevance of intent and focus on the effect on 'historically oppressed social groups'[11]—clearly reveals a close connection with the notion of indirect discrimination. Both systemic and indirect discrimination have an implicit group focus, in the sense that both signal disadvantage at the group level. Systemic discrimination has also been defined as the 'combination of direct and indirect discrimination, linked to ... pervasive practices that have the combined effect of systematically disadvantaging ... protected groups'.[12] The latter definition maintains the typical group focus while being more comprehensive in coverage by not confining 'systemic discrimination' to indirect discrimination but also as encompassing direct discrimination against the vulnerable groups concerned. In this regard, it is important to point to the phenomenon of hidden direct discrimination. The growing societal understanding about the prohibition of discrimination and the unacceptability of differentiations on protected grounds entails a transformation towards more covert forms of direct discrimination, that may be more subtle but still (aim to) exclude and disadvantage particular protected groups.[13]

[7] See also Marie Mercat-Bruns, 'Systemic Discrimination: Rethinking the Tools of Gender Equality' (2018) European Equality Review 1: the subtitle focuses on 'how it is different', but the explanation rather confirms that the respect concepts cover the same or highly similar ground (maybe approached from a different perspective).

[8] CESCR/C, General Comment no 20: Non-Discrimination in Economic, Social and Cultural Rights, E/C.12/GC/20, para 12.

[9] See also below regarding remedies.

[10] Elizabeth Sarine, 'Regulating the Social Pollution of Systemic Discrimination Caused by Implicit Bias' (2012) 5 California Law Review 1359.

[11] Tourkochoriti (n 5) 299.

[12] Mercat-Bruns (n 7).

[13] See inter alia Conrad Lashley, 'Hidden in Plain Sight? Covert Prejudice and Subtle Discrimination', in Conrad Lashley (ed) *Prejudice and Discrimination in Hotels, Restaurants and Bars* (Routledge 2022); Jared Strohl, 'The Transformation of Exclusion from an Overt to a Covert Process' in Robert Adelman and Christopher Mele (eds) *Race, Space and Exclusion* (Routledge 2014).

Addressing systemic discrimination and the 'deep rooted structural barriers to equal opportunity'[14] and the thereto related, 'demonstrable pattern of group-based inequality, notable over historical time, and across institutions',[15] is clearly of particular relevance for groups with a history of subordination,[16] and thus ethnic (religious or linguistic) minorities.[17] The introduction has emphasized that Roma have been widely acknowledged to be victims of systemic discrimination in Europe.[18] The aforementioned intrinsic characteristics and far-reaching consequences of systemic discrimination corroborate the need for liberal democracies to address and counter systemic discrimination.

## 2.1. Points of attention for international courts, translating into points of analysis for the jurisprudence

When a specific, individual case is brought before the Court, it is that specific complaint that needs to be decided. Admittedly, even if there is considerable discrimination against a particular group, this does not entail that each person from that group is discriminated against. Nevertheless, it remains important to be extra vigilant about a context of sustained prejudice against a group when evaluating individual cases. The following paragraphs will discuss related attention points for international courts in terms of the level of scrutiny they adopt (1), also in relation to the distinction between indirect and direct discrimination (2), the allocation of the burden of proof (3), and the quantification of the damage, as related to the remedies and the range of positive state obligations that are identified (4). Finally, a reflection is provided on the way in which international courts can draw on states' political commitments in terms of the Sustainable Development Goals (SDGs) for cases concerning minorities that are set against a background of systemic discrimination (5).

A first, overarching point concerns the pervasive, ingrained, and mostly unconscious character of systemic discrimination, which implies that it is difficult to identify, and even more so to counter. International courts thus need to be sufficiently probing, adopting elevated levels of scrutiny, and be willing to probe second-guess explanations and justifications put forward by governments. The latter is particularly called for in the context of sustained discrimination against a

14 Mercat-Bruns (n 7).

15 Mercat-Bruns (n 7) 3. See also Allison Harell and Dietlind Stoll, 'Diversity and Democratic Politics: An Introduction' (2010) 43 Canadian Journal of Political Science 235.

16 Tourkochiriti (n 5) 307.

17 EQUINET refers to 'a society structure that maintains an oppressive system that privileges some and oppresses minority groups in society', and anti-minority bias ingrained in laws and their application: ... See also ECRI General Policy Recommendation no 2, Equality Bodies to Combat Racism and Intolerance at National Level (7 December 2017).

18 See nn 1, 2, and 3 above.

particularly disadvantaged and thus vulnerable group.[19] The underlying systemic prejudice needs to be recognized and made explicit.

A related, second point delves into the murky dividing line between direct and indirect discrimination, and implies the need for international courts to be aware of the possibility of hidden direct discrimination, or direct discrimination veiled as indirect discrimination. To be sure, acknowledging and identifying cases of indirect discrimination is important, as it reveals a willingness and ability to look below the surface. Indeed, whereas direct discrimination requires a direct link between the disadvantage and the prohibited ground, for indirect discrimination a more indirect link suffices. The definition of indirect discrimination focuses on neutral measures that disproportionately disadvantage particular groups,[20] without the need to prove 'intent'.[21] Interestingly, the definition of discrimination in UN conventions, the references to distinctions with the 'purpose or effect' of disadvantaging persons on particular grounds,[22] appears to link 'purpose' (intent) to direct discrimination and 'effect' to indirect discrimination. Put differently, whilst direct discrimination concerns conscious differentiations on particular grounds, indirect discrimination are 'side-effects' of neutral measures.[23]

In European anti-discrimination law it is not necessary to prove intent to discriminate to find direct discrimination.[24] Nevertheless, when one could prove such intent, it would surely demonstrate a direct link.[25] More generally, it has been noted that contrary to adjudicators' explicit rejection of the intent requirement for direct discrimination, implicitly they do rely on this requirement, thus confirming that 'intent—effect' matches 'direct—indirect discrimination'.[26] The issue seems to be differences of opinion on what exactly amounts to 'intent' or 'targeting'.[27] Either way, the prohibition of indirect discrimination is a very important tool with which to address systemic discrimination, particularly the ingrained, unconscious

[19] The ECtHR has recognized several times that for cases concerning persons belonging to a vulnerable group, a more elevated level of scrutiny is called for on its part.

[20] Compare in this respect the 'disparate impact doctrine' in the US with the reference to neutral measures that particularly disadvantage groups defined by protected grounds in EU directives: see inter alia Tourkochoriti (n 5).

[21] Inter alia *DH and Others v the Czech Republic* App no 57325/00 (ECtHR [GC], 13 November 2007) para 184.

[22] See inter alia Art 1.1 CERD and Art 1 CEDAW.

[23] But note the discussion about possible hidden direct discrimination: these neutral measures could use proxies of protected grounds.

[24] Inter alia Case C-177/88 *Elisabeth Johanna Pacifica Dekker v Stichting Vormingscentrum voor Jong Volwassenen (VJV-Centrum) Plus* (CJEU, 8 November 1990) para 24.

[25] Raphaele Xenidis, 'The Concept of Direct Discrimination in European Anti-Discrimination Law: Theory, Practice and Limits' (Icourts Working Paper series no 285/2022) 8.

[26] See also Andy Yu, 'Direct Discrimination and Indirect Discrimination: A Distinction with a Difference' (2019) 9 W J Legal Stud 1, 2.

[27] A good example here would be the ECtHR judgement in *Aksu v Turkey*, concerning the use of derogatory stereotyping of the Roma community in books used in schools. According to the Court there would be no violation of Art 14 because the author would have 'no intention to insult the Roma community': *Aksu v Turkey* App nos 4149/04 and 41029/04 (ECtHR, 27 July 2010) para 56.

component thereof. Both types of discrimination share a group focus, and have a disproportionate impact on a group, that further enhances that group's vulnerability.

When direct and indirect discrimination are equally prohibited, why would it matter whether it is qualified one way or the other? Admittedly, the distinction between direct and indirect discrimination matters, particularly for jurisdictions with very different justification mechanisms for the two types of discrimination.[28] Nevertheless, even in jurisdictions that use the same justification formula for both, possible justifications for direct discrimination (actually preventing direct differentiations from amounting to direct discrimination) will be fewer than for indirect discrimination.[29] This difference in possible justifications confirms the intuition that while both direct and indirect discrimination are morally wrong,[30] direct discrimination is even more problematic than indirect discrimination.[31] This also explains why one would try to veil direct discrimination as indirect discrimination, while justifying it in seemingly 'neutral' terms.

The underlying reality of ingrained prejudice implies that in the case of systemic discrimination there is bound to be direct discrimination as well. Given the different nature and moral load of direct discrimination, international courts should remain vigilant in identifying cases of hidden direct discrimination. The latter would be the case when seemingly neutral rules with a disproportionate negative impact on a particular group are conscientiously adopted or maintained. An example of this is the continuous use of a particular measure, when its disproportionate effects should be known and could thus be avoided. Clearly, in such circumstances, the disproportionate impact would no longer be an unintended side-effect of the way society is structured, but rather the intended result of a targeted action.[32] Continuing to use these measures, or starting to use similar measures again, would amount to (hidden) direct discrimination.[33]

[28] See below section 4, in the part that zooms in on EU non-discrimination law.

[29] The fact that some jurisdictions go as far as making direct differentiations in principle not allowed, whereas for indirect differentiations they are engaging with the reasonable and objective justification formula, clearly signals that the former is considered, by way of principle, more problematic than the latter.

[30] See inter alia Frej Klem Thomsen, 'Discrimination', *Oxford Research Encyclopedia of Politics* <https://oxfordre.com/politics/view/10.1093/acrefore/9780190228637.001.0001/acrefore-9780190228637-e-202> (accessed 5 September 2024).

[31] Contra Sophia Moreau, 'Indirect Discrimination', *Faces of Inequality: A Theory of Wrongful Discrimination* (online edn, Oxford Academic 2020) accessed 16 September 2024.

[32] In such instances, it is possible to infer an intent to discriminate.

[33] See Opinion of AG Sharpston in Case C-188/15 *Asma Bougnaoui and Association de défense des droits de l'homme (ADDH) v Micropole SA* (CJEU, 13 July 2016) para 74 and AG Sharpston, shadow opinion in Joined Cases C-804/18; 341/19 *IX v WABE eV and MH Müller Handels GmbH v MJ* (CJEU, 15 July 2021) para 122. See also the ECtHR's reference to 'discriminative practices *disguised* in allegedly neutral tests' (emphasis added) in *Horváth and Kiss v Hungary* App no 11146/11 (ECtHR, 29 January 2013) para 116.

Thirdly, the all-encompassing nature of systemic discrimination, and the extent to which it per definition permeates public bodies and institutions, should have implications for the allocation of the burden of proof.[34] The difficulties in proving discrimination have been widely acknowledged, and certainly when it concerns indirect discrimination and hidden forms of direct discrimination.[35] This recognition inspired the development of the so-called special allocation of the burden of proof. Instead of requiring 'full proof' of a differential treatment based on a protected ground, it is sufficient that the claimant can prove facts on the basis of which the court can establish a prima facie case of discrimination. Subsequently, it is the defendant who carries the burden of proof to rebut this presumption by proving that no discrimination took place.[36] These principles are promising to alleviate the burden of proof of the claimant. Nevertheless, there is still a substantial lack of clarity about the relevant parameters to establish a prima facie case,[37] with the risk that courts will put the bar too high. In a context of systemic discrimination against a particular group, it is appropriate to lower the threshold to establish a prima facie case, exactly because of this context of deep-seated prejudice. The latter seems particularly appropriate when reports by international and national NGOs establish widespread targeting of or sustained lack of attention for the special (protection) needs of the group concerned.[38] Since this matter is the subject of a separate chapter in this volume, the further analysis of the case law here will not focus on it.

Fourthly, in relation to systemic discrimination, a proper quantification of the damage resulting from the discrimination necessitates the recognition of knock-on effects of discrimination on other societal fields.[39] For example, being evicted from one's house and/or related inhuman living conditions have obvious implications for one's effective access to education, and healthcare, which in turn impacts educational achievements, related possibilities in terms of employment, and broader participation in national society. Relatedly, when a context of systemic discrimination and exclusion leads to a disproportionate exposure to environmental hazards, this similarly has broad knock-on effects.

[34] Inter alia Mercat-Bruns (n 7) 16 who recalls the importance of a 'plaintif-friendly evidentiary standard in antidiscrimination law' to uncover and address systemic discrimination. See also for US case law on systemic discrimination: Christine Tang, 'Uncovering Systemic Discrimination: Allowing Individual Challenges to a "Pattern or Practice"' (2013–14) 32 Yale Law & Policy Review 319, 320–21. See also Chapter 7 on the burden of proof in this volume.

[35] See also Sarine (n 10) 1359.

[36] The CJEU took the lead in Europe to develop the special allocation of the burden of proof, the principles of which were subsequently enshrined in EU's Equality Directives, eg Art 8(1) of Directive 2000/43 EC (Race Equality Directive).

[37] This is certainly visible when considering the range of preliminary questions on these questions that reach the CJEU.

[38] See also the ECtHR's reasoning in a domestic violence case: *Eremia et al v Moldavia* App no 3564/11 (ECtHR, 28 May 2013) para 89.

[39] Inter alia <https://equineteurope.org/the-other-pandemic-systemic-racism-and-its-consequences/> (accessed 5 September 2024).

Acknowledging a context of systemic discrimination implies the need for far-reaching remedies to compensate the deep-rooted inequalities. In this regard it has been suggested that systemic discrimination requires more targeted positive action,[40] or at least the identification of a 'concrete' level of positive state obligations.[41] The recognition of a history of sustained discrimination and the related persistent inequality calls for the adoption of affirmative action measures, aimed at redressing the disadvantages suffered and its lingering effects.[42] In such instances, international courts should follow an asymmetrical approach to the prohibition of discrimination, in the sense of not adopting a high level of scrutiny for affirmative action measures, in view of their primary positive aim.[43]

Fifthly, when identifying positive state obligations to address systemic discrimination, international courts could strengthen their argumentation by linking these obligations to the political commitments of states towards realization of the Sustainable Development Goals (SDGs).[44] Sustainable Development Goal 10, 'Reducing inequality within … countries', has two indicators that explicitly or implicitly confirm the importance of rooting out discrimination. Indicator 10.2 flags state obligations to promote inclusion of all, 'irrespective of … race, ethnicity, origin, religion', whereas indicator 10.3 goes one step further and calls for equal opportunities and reducing inequality of outcome. States are not only supposed to eliminate discriminatory laws, policies, and practices, but are also expected to actively work towards reducing the number of persons that feel discriminated. In other words, SDG 10 calls on states to make serious efforts to counter systemic discrimination, including change 'on the ground'. SDG 16 further confirms the importance of protecting fundamental rights and the development of inclusive institutions towards the realization of inclusive societies.[45] In other words, when states are respecting their human rights obligations, they are similarly living up to their political commitments in terms of SDGs. Conversely, the pull of SDG political commitments could contribute to state compliance with the related human rights obligations.

40 Mercat-Bruns (n 7) 7 and 16–17.

41 See also Vladislava Stoyanova, 'Framing Positive Obligations under the European Convention on Human Rights Law: Mediating between the Abstract and the Concrete' (2023) 23 *Human Rights Law Review* 1.

42 Lizzie Barms, 'Equality Law and Experimentation: the Positive Action Challenge' (2009) Cambridge Law Journal 623, 627.

43 ibid 627–30.

44 In this regard, human rights and Sustainable Development Goals (SDG) may seem two sides of the same coin: <https://www.undp.org/blog/human-rights-and-sdgs-two-sides-same-coin>. See also the Danish Institute for Human Rights, 'Sustainable Development' <https://defend.humanrights.dk/connecting-the-dots-0/sustainable-development> underscoring that 'Sustainable Development Goals (SDGs) have a symbiotic and mutually enforcing relationship with human rights'.

45 See particularly indicators 16.6, 16.7, and 16.10: Global indicator framework for the Sustainable Development Goals and targets of the 2030 Agenda for Sustainable Development <https://unstats.un.org/sdgs/indicators/Global%20Indicator%20Framework%20after%202022%20refinement_Eng.pdf>.

The preceding discussion of points of attention for international courts when dealing with cases concerning minorities facing systemic discrimination corresponds to similar points of analysis when reviewing the jurisprudence of icourts. The following analysis of the jurisprudence of the European Committee of Social Rights (ECSR), the Court of Justice of the European Union (CJEU), and the European Court of Human Rights (ECtHR) respectively, starts each time with the specific characteristics of the supervisory mechanism concerned, the ensuing appropriateness to tackle systemic discrimination, and the icourt's baseline in relation to allegations of discrimination (1). The analysis then proceeds with a discussion of landmark cases concerning Roma, having regard to, on the one hand, the extent to which the icourt actually recognizes systemic discrimination (2), and on the other, to what extent a background of systemic discrimination affects its analysis (3). The latter evaluation considers, in so far as relevant, various factors, including the level of scrutiny adopted, the correct delineation between direct and indirect discrimination, and the identification of concrete positive state obligations (to move beyond and counter systemic discrimination). The discussion of each icourt's jurisprudence ends with an overall assessment (4).

## 3. The ECSR and Systemic Discrimination

### 3.1.

The ECSR combines a periodic reporting procedure, with a system of collective complaints, whereby complaints cannot be brought by individuals but by NGOs holding consultative status with the Council of Europe and employee/employer organizations. In relation to the Roma's fundamental rights, various cases have been submitted to the ECSR. The Roma-related cases before the Committee span a range of issues,[46] but the most prevalent ones are access to health care and matters related to housing. The latter concern evictions and problems of substandard housing (lack of access to social housing), lack of sites for caravans, and segregation.

Obviously, collective complaints per definition go beyond the confines of one individual case and represent a broader picture, thus allowing for arguments concerning more structural problems and failures of states to respect their human rights obligations.[47] In line with the underlying group focus of collective

[46] For an article focusing on forced expulsions, see Aoife Nolan, 'Aggravated Violations', Roma Housing Rights and Forced Expulsions in Italy: Recent Developments under the European Social Charter Collective Complaints System (2011) 11 Human Rights Law Review 343.

[47] See also Katelyn Sheehan and Rebecca Cook, 'Collective Dimensions of Complaints and Remedies' (2022) 19 JL & Equal 50, 52.

complaints, the Committee relies heavily on reports of NGOs, views and concluding observations of UN treaty bodies, the Council of Europe Commissioner of Human Rights, and its own previous decisions on merits and periodic reviews of the state concerned.[48] Furthermore, the Charter's focus on socio-economic rights will reveal the various knock-on effects of systemic discrimination, while having a strong focus on positive state obligations. More generally, as will become clear throughout the analysis of several of the ECSR's decisions on the merits phase, the ECSR is neither reluctant nor hesitant to engage in discrimination analysis. From its early case law onwards, the ECSR did not shy away from addressing complaints about discrimination or from recognizing a discriminatory dimension to a violation of social rights. What is more, the Committee has embraced substantive equality, recognizing that the prohibition of discrimination also encompasses a prohibition of indirect discrimination as well as duties of differential treatment, when persons are differently situated and have specific needs.

This setting of collective complaints, and the ECSR's baseline readiness to address discrimination complaints, thus promises a rather proactive approach of the Committee, both in terms of the recognition of a context of systemic discrimination, and in terms of implications for the evaluation of cases.

## 3.2.

Throughout the Committee's case law, a pronounced awareness of the background of systemic discrimination of Roma and their resulting vulnerable position is visible. For example, in *ERRC v Bulgaria* (46/2007) the Committee recognizes the specific needs of Roma in relation to their unhealthy living conditions, as informed by the systemic discrimination they face in Bulgaria.[49] Importantly, the ECSR builds in its later collective complaints about similar problems against the same state, on the principles developed in earlier cases. The Committee remains vigilant about the background of systemic discrimination that Roma suffer and the related vulnerability of the Roma.[50] It is particularly critical of the fact that the problems in accessing health care for Roma have not been redressed by the state throughout a ten-year period. Roma's ongoing disproportionate exclusion and the lack of action by the state to ensure effective and equal access to health care translate into a prohibited indirect discrimination, violating Article E junction Article 11 para 1 of the Charter.[51]

[48] See examples in notes 49, 55, and 57.

[49] *European Roma Rights Centre (ERRC) v Bulgaria* Comm no 46/2007 (ECSR, 3 December 2008), paras 45–51.

[50] *European Roma Rights Centre (ERRC) v Bulgaria* Comm no 151/2017 (ECSR, 5 December 2018), paras 36, 81.

[51] ibid paras 84–85.

## 3.3.

Several cases reveal both the extent to which the ECSR recognizes the context of systemic discrimination and the related high scrutiny it adopts when assessing governments' justification attempts. *ERTF v France*[52] is a very interesting case in which the ECSR showed the extent to which it recognized the knock-on effects of problems related to housing for other domains of economic participation, and more particularly education and employment. The Committee acknowledged how threats of eviction, the resulting instability, and problematic living conditions jeopardized Roma children's access to education.[53] Similarly, the ECSR considered not only the substance of the measures that had been taken, but also their actual impact on the ground, and was critical about the limited actual change. In this regard the Committee criticized the high level of discretion left to local authorities, as this created the risk of discretion being used in a discriminatory fashion. This in turn engendered 'discrimination through social rejection [with] the effect or consequence of impeding access to schooling for the children concerned or impeding or preventing access by young adults to vocational training and depriving them of support in access to employment or employment policy measures, thereby placing them in a less favourable position than non-Roma persons'.[54] The Committee thus elegantly exposed the ways in which discrimination in the vertical and horizontal spheres was reinforced, leading to systemic discrimination.

The high level of scrutiny is also nicely visible in several cases before the ECSR that touch on the problem of segregation of Roma in camps, settlements, and at times walled-off settlements. In *ERRC v Portugal*,[55] a very blatant case of outright targeting of the Roma community, the Committee noted that Roma disproportionately were rehoused in a manner that led to segregation. Furthermore, the Committee denounced that in these segregated settlements, Roma faced discriminatory lack of access to services, while the public authorities did not take the necessary measures to counter deteriorating residential conditions. The Committee concluded that this amounted to prohibited discrimination, because the discriminatory policies of the local authorities were not redressed by the central authorities.[56]

Similarly, Italy has had numerous collective complaints filed against it in relation to discrimination against Roma. In *Amnesty International v Italy*[57] the Committee criticized the lack of progress Italy has made to counter segregated and substandard housing of Roma, particularly with regard to the vulnerability of Roma.[58] What is

[52] *European Roma and Travellers (ERTF) v France* Comm no 119/2015 (ECSR, 5 December 2017).
[53] ibid paras 67–76.
[54] ibid paras 112–13.
[55] *European Roma Rights Centre (ERRC) v Portugal* Comm no 61/2010 (ECSR, 30 June 2011).
[56] ibid paras 48 and 71.
[57] *Amnesty International v Italy* Comm no 178/2019 (ECSR, 18 October 2023).
[58] ibid paras 69 and 75.

more, the living conditions in the Roma camps and settlements are inadequate.[59] The Committee highlighted as problematic that, notwithstanding the debate about the segregation of Roma, there has not been any serious recognition of the fact that segregation as such amounts to discrimination.[60] Social rights may concern progressive obligations, but *in casu* the lack of a coherent and coordinated national approach towards inclusion has entailed the failure to realize meaningful change. The Committee concluded by finding a prohibited discrimination, as many Roma families still live in substandard and segregated housing in Italy.[61]

The Committee's ensuing concern to ensure effective access to rights for the Roma engenders an extensive engagement with positive state obligations, while being keen to tailor these to the Roma's specific needs.[62] The ECSR's ease with the identification of positive state obligations is also visible in its extensive use of the duties of differential treatment, as a distinct dimension of the right to equal treatment. Throughout its decision in *ERTF v France* the Committee underscored how the right to equal treatment implies duties of differential treatment, aimed at the effective enjoyment of fundamental rights.[63] Similarly, in the case regarding access to health care in Bulgaria, the ECSR deduced from the specific needs and circumstances of Roma positive state obligations to take the necessary measures 'to address the exclusion, marginalisation and environmental hazards which Romani communities are exposed to in Bulgaria'. When a state fails to do so, and also fails to address the problems Roma face in accessing health care services, a prohibited discrimination in relation to access to health care is present.[64]

The ECSR's generous engagement with positive state obligations can also be related to its adoption of a holistic approach, not only in terms of the recognition of the context of systemic discrimination, but also in terms of the recognition of knock-on effects of problems. For example, problems in terms of evictions, secure housing, and sanitation, result in problematic living conditions, while the related stigmatization has implications for effective access to education and to employment. The ECSR's decision on the merits in *ERTF v France*, a case on forced evictions of Roma, underscored that measures which imply an exacerbation of the Roma's situation of poverty and social exclusion, and which furthermore deprive them of the enjoyment of the right to education and hamper their access to services,

[59] ibid para 98.
[60] ibid para 99.
[61] ibid para 101.
[62] See, inter alia, *ERRC v Belgium* Comm no 185/2019 (ECSR, 8 December 2022) paras 83–84; *European Roma Rights Centre (ERRC) v Bulgaria* Comm no 151/2017 (ECSR, 5 December 2018) paras 84–86.
[63] *European Roma and Travellers (ERTF) v France* Comm no 119/2015 (ECSR, 5 December 2017) paras 67,108.
[64] *European Roma Rights Centre (ERRC) v Bulgaria* Comm no 31/2005 (ECSR, 18 October 2006) paras 49–51.

amount to a violation of the prohibition of discrimination.[65] The Committee often identifies far-reaching positive state obligations to adopt a proactive approach, requiring states to adopt measures aimed at preventing and removing obstacles to access to fundamental social rights.[66] A similar proactive approach is also required in relation to ensuring access to remedies. Having legal avenues available is not sufficient in the case of vulnerable groups like the Roma 'whose degree of exclusion, past experience and social status places them in a situation where they may not have the means for seeking such remedies'.[67]

The Committee's attention for the particular vulnerability of the Roma also translates into the recognition of positive state obligations aimed at respect for their right to a distinct identity, including a distinct lifestyle. The latter lifestyle should allow for their effective socio-economic participation, which in turn would require the adoption of special measures, tailored to their specific needs:

> The Committee emphasises that States Parties are required to do their utmost to foster acceptance of the different lifestyle of Travellers. One of the consequences of this is that because Traveller families fall into an especially vulnerable category, States must protect them against the threats of eviction to which they are exposed, promote the provision of an adequate supply of housing for families and take the needs of families into account in housing policies.[68]

In other words, the ECSR understands and signals to states that equal and effective access to socio-economic rights for Roma requires public authorities to adopt tailored measures so as to respect Roma's right to a distinct identity.

## 3.4.

Overall, the European Committee of Social Rights has been eager to engage with discrimination complaints and has not been slow in identifying a discriminatory nexus to a state failure to comply with its obligations under the European Social Charter in relation to a particular group. Furthermore, the Committee has been attentive to the background of systemic discrimination that Roma face. The collective complaints mechanism has the benefit of emphasizing the group=related phenomena inherent in systemic discrimination. This also becomes visible in relation to the burden of proof, where the ECSR is comfortable to rely heavily on reports by international NGOs as well as UN treaty bodies and other Council of

65 *European Roma and Travellers (ERTF) v France* Comm no 119/2015 (ECSR, 5 December 2017) para 127.

66 *European Roma Rights Centre (ERRC) v Bulgaria* Comm no 151/2017 (ECSR, 5 December 2018).

67 ibid para 84.

68 ibid.

Europe bodies. The overall high level of scrutiny adopted by the ECSR also encompasses the critical assessments of states' positive obligations. The recognition of knock-on effects (from problems in housing, to the spheres of education and employment), goes hand in hand with the identification of far reaching positive obligations to counter systemic discrimination. Finally, the early recognition of segregation as amounting per se to prohibited discrimination is particularly relevant for the Roma.[69]

## 4. The CJEU and Systemic Discrimination

### 4.1.

As the effective prohibition of discrimination on grounds of nationality (of one of the EU member states) and gender is essential toward the realization of the EU internal market and the related free movement rights, the CJEU has been keen to develop its non-discrimination jurisprudence. Hence, the latter jurisprudence is considered firm, well developed and theoretically fleshed out.[70] Throughout its elaborate case law on gender discrimination, the CJEU has provided vigorous protection against gender discrimination, also to counter the more subtle mechanisms of discrimination that blocked women's equal participation. In the process, the CJEU has developed a sophisticated understanding of discrimination, de facto acknowledging systemic discrimination and seeking to address it.[71]

Even though the CJEU may not have formally referred to systemic discrimination, it is widely understood that CJEU case law (in relation to gender equality) 'adhered to its logic and provided tools of interpretation to flesh out group disadvantage'.[72] Admittedly, there have been critical assessments of the CJEU's case law on the wearing of headscarves at work and the regulation of ritual slaughter, as insufficiently taking into account Islamophobia and its implications for the qualification of direct, rather than indirect discrimination.[73] On other grounds, such as

[69] Compare in section 5 the ECtHR's slow journey towards a strong position against segregation. See also M Goodwin, 'Taking on Racial Segregation: the European Court of Human Rights at a Brown v Board of Education moment?' (2009) 170 Rechtsgeleerd Magazijn Themis 93.

[70] Evelyn Ellis and Paul Watson, EU Anti-Discrimination Law (OUP 2012) 498. See also Sasha Prechal, 'Competence Creep and General Principles of Law' (2010) 3 Review of European Administrative Law 20.

[71] Case-C 43/75 *Gabrielle Defrenne v Societe Anonyme Belge de Navigation Aérienne Sabena* (CJEU, 8 April 1976).

[72] Mercat-Bruns (n 7) 13.

[73] See Opinion of AG Sharpston in Case C-188/15 *Asma Bougnaoui and Association de Défense des Droits de l'Homme (ADDH) v Micropole SA* (CJEU, 13 July 2016) para 74. See also Erica Howard, 'Islamic Headscarves and the CJEU: Achbita and Bougnaoui' (2017) 23 Maassricht Journal of European and Comparative Law 348; Titia Loenen, 'In Search of an EU Approach to Headscarf Bans: Where to go after Achbita and Bougnaoui?' (2017) 10 Review of European Administrative Law 47; Lena Hehemann, 'Religious Slaughtering, a Stunning Matter: Centraal Israëlitisch Consistorie van België and Others' (2021) 6 European Papers 111.

sexual orientation and age, the CJEU anti-discrimination jurisprudence has continued on its firm path providing 'one of the highest ceilings of protection in comparative anti-discrimination law'.[74]

Regarding the ground of race, the evaluation has been more nuanced. Some cases have demonstrated that the CJEU either interprets this ground narrowly, as only referring to a person of a particular ethnic origin,[75] or gives a broad reading to the exception in Article 3 Race Equality Directive (Directive 2000/43/EC), excluding the treatment which arises from the legal status of third country nationals.[76] Still, the few cases in which the Court actually engages with the discrimination complaint, have confirmed the Court's eagerness to provide a solid protection against racial discrimination.[77]

The *CHEZ* case[78] concerned a non-Roma who owned a shop in a city district that was inhabited predominantly by Roma. She complained about the inaccessible height at which electricity meters were installed in the district concerned, namely at 6 to 7 metres instead of the usual 1.6 metres. She claimed before the national courts that this differential practice amounted to a prohibited discrimination on grounds of race. The case engendered the first judgment on the merits by the CJEU concerning Roma and the systemic discrimination they face.

## 4.2.

The preliminary ruling reveals in several respects that the CJEU seeks to provide optimal protection against systemic racial discrimination and is keenly aware of the context of systemic discrimination against Roma. This attitude is visible in the CJEU's adoption of a broad reading of the standing requirements to bring a complaint about racial discrimination and in its very detailed guidance to the member states (see also under section 4.3).

To be sure, a broad interpretation of the standing requirements is particularly apt in cases of systemic discrimination. The CJEU took the opportunity to further build its non-discrimination jurisprudence by accepting the standing of Ms

[74] Uladzsilau Belavusau and Kristin Henrard, 'The Impact of the 2000 Equality Directives on EU- Antidiscrimination Law: Achievements and Pitfalls', in Belavusau and Henrard (eds) *EU Anti-Discrimination Law Beyond Gender* (Hart 2018) 37.

[75] C-668/15 *Jyske Finans* (CJEU, 8 December 2005). See also the narrow reading adopted in C-391/09 *Runevic-Vardyn* (CJEU, 12 May 2011).

[76] C-571/10 Kamberaj (CJEU, 24 April 2012).

[77] Inter alia Mathias Möschel, 'Eighteen Years of Race Equality Directive: A Mitigated Balance' in Ulad Belavusau and Kristin Henrard (eds), *EU Anti-Discrimination Law Beyond Gender* (Hart 2019) 144–46.

[78] Case C-83/14 *CHEZ Razpredelenie Bulgaria AD v Komisia za zashtita ot diskriminatsia* (CJEU, 16 July 2015). At times this case is referred to as 'Nikolova', the name of the alleged victim in the national case.

Nikolova as a non-Roma to complain about the racially discriminatory nature of the measure. The CJEU underscored that Ms Nikolova suffered the less favourable treatment in the same way as Roma did living in that city district, and that she had a plausible claim that race was a factor on the basis of which the differential treatment had been adopted.[79] The Court thus adopted a teleological interpretation and acknowledged discrimination by way of collateral damage, discrimination by way of association, which the Court had already established in the *Coleman* case.[80] The fact that Ms Nikolova suffered in the same way as Roma living in the district confirmed the sweeping character of the measure, affecting all the inhabitants of a district predominantly inhabited by Roma. That the measures also affected non-Roma confirmed that they were insufficiently tailored to affect only persons that were actually involved in damaging or tampering with the meters, but were grounded on group-based prejudice.[81]

## 4.3.

Accepting that 'discrimination by way of collateral damage' is also prohibited by the Race Equality Directive confirms the CJEU's resolve to tackle systemic discrimination. It implies concomitant obligations on member states to accept this reading, and to broaden—if need be—their national standing requirements.

Establishing a more general *heightened level of scrutiny* in a preliminary ruling has distinct parameters due to the specific features of a preliminary ruling, in response to a preliminary question coming from a national court. In principle, the CJEU only provides the correct interpretation of EU law, after which the actual application to the facts of the national case is done by the national court, following this interpretation of the CJEU. However, when the CJEU gives very detailed and concrete guidance to the national court, the CJEU is de facto more or less deciding the national case.[82] Such detailed guidance thus implies that the CJEU is pulling the national case towards it, and indicates that it wants to retain control of the application of EU law. Such detailed and concrete guidance can thus be likened to 'a high level of scrutiny'.

Obviously, in a context of systemic discrimination and underlying deep-seated prejudice against a particular group, it may not be straightforward to distinguish between instances of 'true' indirect discrimination and those of hidden direct

[79] ibid.

[80] Case C-303/06 *S Coleman v Attridge Law and Steve Law* (CJEU, 17 July 2008).

[81] Case C-83/14 *CHEZ* (n 78).

[82] Koen Lenaerts, 'The Unity of European Law and the Overload of the CJEU – The System of Preliminary Rulings Revisited' in I Pernice, J Kokott, and C Saunders (eds), *The Future of the European Judicial System in a Comparative Perspective* (Nomos 2006) 217. See also Rasmussen, 'Remedying the Crumbling EC Judicial System' (2000) Common Market Law Review 1101.

discrimination, in which seemingly neutral rules target a particular group[83] with the intention of affecting the group disproportionately. Put differently, when there is a history of discrimination against a group, and society is riddled with prejudice against that group, measures based on prejudiced assumptions about that group may be presented as 'neutral'. Obviously, it is essential then to closely scrutinize the alleged justification by the defendant, and where necessary to identify the prejudice, and thus the more direct link between the ground and the disadvantage.

In EU law the requalification of an at first sight indirect discrimination as direct discrimination is accompanied by important consequences. As is nicely visible in the EU's Equality Directives, the definitions of direct and indirect discrimination clarify that the former is in principle prohibited unless an explicit exception is provided in law, whereas the latter has a broader possibility of 'reasonable and objective justification'.[84] Put differently, once something is requalified as direct discrimination, it is almost certainly prohibited. The latter is particularly the case for racial discrimination, as Directive 2000/43/EC includes very few exceptions for direct differentiation on grounds of race.[85]

The blurry dividing line between direct and indirect discrimination in a context of systemic discrimination is nicely exemplified by the numerous questions of the national court to the CJEU about the appropriate qualification. In *CHEZ*, the CJEU provided an elaborate answer to the national court, which also confirmed that it was indeed possible to conceive the case as an instance of direct or indirect racial discrimination. Throughout its reasoning the CJEU exhibited a keen willingness to look beyond explicit frames, revealing possible underlying prejudice against Roma and considering the impact on the ground. Whilst the CJEU ultimately left the choice in the national case to the national court, following the preliminary ruling procedure, it sent a clear signal that it considered the prohibition of discrimination as violated. Furthermore, the Court identifies no fewer than four factors that suggested that the practice was based on ethnic stereotypes and prejudice against Roma, thus establishing a prima facie case of direct racial discrimination:[86] (1) these high electricity meters were only found in urban districts where the majority of the inhabitants were Roma; (2) relying on assumptions about Roma causing damage and doing unlawful things; and (3) maintaining this district-wide practice without any actual and individualized proof thereof. While the CJEU indicated that prima facie racial discrimination would shift the burden

[83] In *CHEZ*, the CJEU identified direct discrimination when the measure was imposed 'in view of the Roma ethnic origin shared by most of the districts' inhabitants', or 'if ethnic origin determined the decision to impose the measure' (*CHEZ* (n 78) paras 75–76).

[84] See inter alia Art 2 of Directives 2000/43/EC and 2000/78/EC.

[85] Directive 2000/43/EC only has one exception (in addition to the circumscribed exception for positive action) and that is 'genuine and determining occupational requirements': Art 4.

[86] Case C-83/14 *CHEZ* (n 78) paras 81–84.

of proof to the electricity company to prove that the practice was not based on the ethnic origin of the majority of the inhabitants of the district,[87] and that the referring court needs to determine this,[88] the CJEU's preceding reasoning undeniably favoured a finding of direct racial discrimination.

The CJEU then answered the preliminary questions concerning a possible case of indirect racial discrimination. The CJEU acknowledged that the practice could have been based on an apparently neutral measure, in so far as the district had had numerous problems of tampering,[89] establishing the common understanding that Roma face a particular disadvantage.[90] In this regard, it is important that the CJEU also emphasized the 'offensive and stigmatising nature of the practice at issue'.[91] The CJEU proceeded to clarify the possible justification for such a prima facie case of indirect racial discrimination. The CJEU was willing to countenance that the practice had a legitimate aim of countering tampering with the electricity meters,[92] but it was highly critical of the lack of objective proof of such tampering, while the practice had been ongoing for 25 years. The CJEU's guidance concerning the proportionality review emphasized the harm caused by the stigmatization as well as the practical problems related to the practice.[93] Furthermore, the widespread and lasting nature of the practice weighed negatively in this respect. The CJEU's guidance thus clearly steered the national court towards the finding of a prohibited indirect discrimination.

## 4.4.

*CHEZ* shows that in regard to racial discrimination against Roma the CJEU continues on its path of providing an elevated level of protection against discrimination, while simultaneously fully engaging with the context of systemic discrimination. Its recognition of a victim by way of collateral damage is particularly useful in capturing and addressing the related ingrained forms of discrimination. Furthermore, the detailed and fact-specific guidance the CJEU provided to the national court strongly invited that court to find a prohibited instance of discrimination. The recognition of ingrained prejudice against Roma and actions infused by that prejudice are best qualified as hidden direct discrimination. Put differently, a context of systemic discrimination reveals that 'neutral rules with a disproportionate effect' are not really neutral, but rather concern measures that target the

87 ibid para 85.
88 ibid para 91.
89 ibid para 106.
90 ibid para 107.
91 ibid para 108.
92 ibid para 114.
93 ibid paras 124 and 126.

group concerned. The CJEU's critical awareness of the deep-seated nature of prejudice against Roma informs its reasoning throughout.

## 5. The ECtHR and Systemic Discrimination

### 5.1.

The initial reluctance of the ECtHR to explicitly evaluate complaints of discrimination has been widely documented.[94] Fortunately, particularly over the past decade the ECtHR has been engaging more actively with discrimination claims, especially those regarding invidious discrimination.[95] The recognition of certain grounds of differentiation as suspect, triggering heightened scrutiny, certainly plays an important role.[96] At the same time, the Court's understanding that the prohibition of discrimination also encompasses duties of differential treatment when persons find themselves in distinct positions has been much less developed, particularly when the differential treatment implied a group dimension related to a distinct identity.[97] The Court's unease with such a group dimension and broader contextual information flows from its focus on the individual case before it, and the specific circumstances of that case, with the Court tailoring its reasoning to these specifics. The Court's long journey towards the acceptance of the notion of indirect discrimination was also informed (at least partially) by the group dimension of indirect discrimination. In the meantime, the ECtHR has fully embraced and incorporated indirect discrimination in its jurisprudence, but the Court's non-discrimination jurisprudence[98] still reveals some gaps and inconsistencies.[99]

[94] See, inter alia, Samantha Besson, 'Evolutions in Non-Discrimination Law within the ECHR and the ESC Systems: It Takes Two to Tango in the Council of Europe' (2012) 60 American Journal of Comparative Law 147.

[95] See also Carmelo Danisi, 'How far can the European Court of Human Rights go in the Fight Against Discrimination? Defining New Standards in its Nondiscrimination Jurisprudence' (2011) 9 ICON 793.

[96] Rory O'Connell, 'Cinderella Comes to the Ball: Article 14 and the Right to Non-discrimination in the. ECHR' (2009) Legal Studies 211, 225.

[97] See also Kristin Henrard, 'The European Court of Human Rights, Ethnic and Religious Minorities and the Two Dimensions of the Right to Equal Treatment: Jurisprudence at Different Speeds?' (2016) 34 Nordic Journal of Human Rights 157.

[98] Inter alia Elif Askin, 'Guidance for Assessing Discrimination under Article 14 ECHR: Advisory Opinion on the Difference in Treatment between Landowners' Associations "having a recognised existence on the date of the creation of an approved Municipal Hunters' Association" and Landowners' Associations set up after that Date' (Strasbourgobservers, 31 January 2023) < https://strasbourgobservers.com/2023/01/31> accessed 10 September 2024.

[99] See also Oddný Mjöll Arnardóttir, 'The Differences that Make a Difference: Recent Developments on the Discrimination Grounds and the Margin of Appreciation under Article 14 of the European Convention on Human Rights' (2014) 14 Human Rights Law Review 647.

## 5.2.

In line with the focus of this chapter, the analysis here zooms in on the extent to which the ECtHR identifies and seeks to address systemic discrimination. Clearly, there is no principled stance against recognizing and addressing systemic discrimination. In some fields, the ECtHR has been willing to identify the systemic nature of a problem, and to identify far-reaching positive state obligations to counter this. Relevant landmark cases concern domestic violence[100] and the treatment of persons with mental disabilities.[101] However, the Court has not been so forthcoming in cases that centre on complaints about allegedly neutral measures having a disproportionate impact on Muslim women, notwithstanding signs of an Islamophobic undercurrent.[102] The ECtHR's inconsistent approach to instances of systemic discrimination, the recognition of such a background, and implications of this recognition for the assessment of a discrimination complaint, is similarly visible in relation to Roma. On the one hand, the case law reveals a Court that acknowledges a context of systemic discrimination and is eager to establish increasing positive state obligations for Roma's equal and effective access to quality education and adequate protection against forced evictions. On the other hand, the Court's case law regarding lack of access to appropriate sites for caravans, and lack of access to housing sanitation is criticized for insufficiently acknowledging and taking into account the context of sustained disadvantage of and prejudice against Roma. The latter assessment can also be made in relation to discriminatory violence,[103] forced sterilization, child removal and hate speech. The scope of this chapter does not allow for an in-depth discussion of all these topics, but reference can be made to other chapters of this edited volume for further information and analysis, which will at least implicitly corroborate the point made here concerning systemic discrimination.

The domain of equal and effective access to education was mentioned earlier as providing fertile ground for the initial elaboration and inclusion of the prohibition of indirect discrimination in ECtHR case law, and the related identification of group disadvantage and underlying prejudice. Over time, the Court became more robust in its acknowledgement of the systemic nature of the related discrimination. In its initial case law the Court emphasized the problem of the inferior education

[100] *Opuz v Turkey* App no 33401/02 (ECtHR, 9 June 2009); *Eremia et al v Moldavia* App no 3564/11 (ECtHR, 28 May 2013); and *Kurt v Austria* App no 62903/15 (ECtHR, 15 June 2015) paras 168, 174–76.

[101] *V.I. v the Republic of Moldova* App no 38963/18 (ECtHR, 26 June 2024), paras 168, 172–75.

[102] Kristin Henrard, 'Majoritarian Reasoning at the ECtHR: A Flawed Response to Rising Islamophobia and Intolerance against Muslims', in Ida Caracciolo (ed), *Protection of Cultural and Religious Minorities. Leadership for International Peace and Security* (Giappichelli 2020) 29–57.

[103] The case law on discriminatory violence is covered in Chapter 7 on the burden of proof in this volume.

that was provided in classes/schools for the mentally disabled, where Roma were overrepresented, and did not strongly pronounce the problematic nature of segregation as such.[104] In subsequent cases the Court has become more vocal about the inherent discriminatory nature of segregation as a consequence of overrepresentation of Roma in particular schools.

## 5.3.

The latter understanding translated into the identification of very concrete positive state obligations to implement swift and comprehensive desegregation measures, also countering opposition of non-Roma parents.[105] The strong opposition of non-Roma parents clearly confirms the societal prejudice and related background of systemic discrimination. The Court's emphasis on state obligations to pursue desegregation measures notwithstanding, this opposition sends an important signal that states cannot simply stand by whenever de facto segregation is present. Furthermore, as is also highlighted in Chapter 9 on the right to education in this volume, the Court's identification in *Szolcsan* of an obligation to adopt a country-wide policy to eliminate segregation in education shows the culmination of ever-more concrete positive state obligations.

The increasingly overt positive state obligations to counter segregation in education implies a heightening by the Court of the level of scrutiny.[106] The Court has also more generally recognized that when 'a restriction on fundamental rights applies to a particularly vulnerable group in society, who have suffered considerable discrimination in the past … then the State's margin of appreciation is substantially narrower'.[107] In line with this narrower margin of appreciation, and thus increasing the 'steering' conducted by the ECtHR, the Court has identified duties of positive action of states 'to undo a history of racial segregation',[108] thus recognizing states' obligations to address structural disadvantages caused by past discrimination.[109] In the same case, the Court even hinted at the requalification of a case of indirect discrimination to one of hidden direct discrimination, where it flags 'discriminatory practices disguised in allegedly neutral tests'.[110]

[104] See also Chapter 9 by Gergely in this edited volume, and the case law that he cites.
[105] *X et al v Albania* App nos 73548/17 and 45521/19 (ECtHR, 31 August 2022); *Elmazova et al v North Macedonia* App nos 11811/20; 13550/20 (ECtHR, 13 December 2022); *Szolcsán v Hungary* App no 24408/16 (ECtHR, 30 June 2023).
[106] Vladislava Stoyanova, 'Framing Positive Obligations under the ECHR Law: Mediating between the Abstract and the Concrete' (2023) 23 Human Rights Law Review 1.
[107] *Horvath and Kiss* (n 33) para 128.
[108] ibid para 127.
[109] See also ibid para 116.
[110] ibid.

O'Nions nicely shows in Chapter 10 in this volume a similar development of increasing attention by the ECtHR, and related heightened scrutiny, for sufficient procedural safeguards in cases of evictions, accompanied by very concrete positive state obligations with regard to alternative accommodation.[111] However, both O'Nions and O'Donovan[112] in their respective chapters in this volume reveal a very different picture in relation to sufficient (legal) stopping places for caravans with adequate amenities. In connection therewith, the ECtHR has so far avoided an actual evaluation of possible challenges of (indirect) discrimination, in light of the context of sustained disadvantage of and prejudice (systemic discrimination) against Roma.

Another important and striking example of a case that at its heart has a context of systemic discrimination of Roma is the *Hudorovic* case,[113] regarding a decade-long lack of access to water, sanitation, sewerage, and electricity. This case is discussed in detail in the last chapter of this edited volume, but merits some attention here as well. The extremely poor living conditions of the Roma in the settlement concerned and the related stigmatization also affected the children and their effective access to schooling. As the complaints concerned a discriminatory lack of effective enjoyment of a range of social rights, to some extent the conclusions of the ECtHR can be explained by the ECHR being a civil and political rights instrument. However, the judgment also revealed a glaring lack of attention for the overall context of systemic discrimination of Roma and its knock-on effects. The Court acknowledged that Roma face greater obstacles in accessing basic utilities,[114] and also that the standards used could produce disproportionate effects on Roma in illegal settlements.[115] Nevertheless, the Court did not conclude in finding a prohibited instance of indirect discrimination because of the low level of scrutiny it adopted: the state was granted a broad margin of appreciation in relation to general policy choices concerning the use of limited resources, while special measures had been taken in favour of Roma to offset these disadvantages.[116] Unfortunately, the Court did not properly take into account the context of systemic discrimination to establish an underlying prejudice against Roma: the fact that these Roma settlements were informal/illegitimate may itself be the consequence of systemic discrimination in the past. When the government through its policies and laws contributes to the illegality of settlements and then utilizes this illegality as a ground for not to providing drinking water, knowing the disproportionate impact thereof, would this not rather qualify as a case of direct discrimination?

111 See Chapter 10 by O'Nions in this edited volume.
112 See Chapter 17 by O'Donovan in this edited volume.
113 *Hudorovič et al v Slovenia* App no 24816/14 (ECtHR, 10 March 2020).
114 ibid para 143.
115 ibid para 147.
116 ibid para 156.

### 5.4.

Notwithstanding several improvements in the ECtHR's jurisprudence on discrimination, its case law still reveals some of its traditional reluctance to engage with discrimination complaints. Furthermore, the Court's focus on the specific circumstances of the case before it informed its struggle with a group dimension of a complaint, and with taking into account information about systemic discrimination. In the meantime, the Court is more willing to address complaints with an underlying group dimension, and to acknowledge and factor in a context of systemic discrimination. While the latter attitude is not (yet) visible throughout its jurisprudence, it can be witnessed in relation to some of the recurring rights complaints of Roma.[117]

## 6. Conclusion

Systemic, deeply ingrained discrimination against a particular group, and the related entrenched disadvantageous position of this group, is difficult to reconcile with the foundational principles of liberal democracies, holding human rights and rule of law in high regard. At the same time, when a society is riddled by systemic discrimination, the underlying prejudice will also have seeped into its institutional structures. Hence, international courts have an important role to play in breaking the vicious circle.

This chapter examined the way and extent to which three regional European icourts have engaged with the context of systemic discrimination in which Roma cases are set. The preceding analysis reveals how differences in 'baseline' approach towards discrimination complaints, and the typical characteristics of the respective (quasi-) judicial mechanisms, result in striking differences between the three icourts. The ECSR surely has the strongest record, due to its combination of a firm approach to the prohibition of discrimination, also embracing the prohibition of indirect discrimination and duties of differential treatment, with a collective complaints procedure. Due to the social rights content of the Charter, the Committee furthermore has a strong mandate to identify positive state obligations. The collective complaints' inherent group dimension enables the Committee to rely extensively on general reports from NGOs and evaluations from UN treaty bodies and other Council of Europe institutions, and pictures of systemic discrimination painted in these reports.

Secondly, the Court of Justice has since its early non-discrimination jurisprudence been keen to identify and counter systemic forms of discrimination. The

[117] See below Chapters 9 by Gergely on education and 10 by O'Nions on evictions.

*CHEZ* case nicely demonstrates the CJEU's willingness to extend its gender discrimination approach to racial discrimination, and towards Roma in particular.

The ECtHR has the weakest cards, considering the ongoing visibility of its traditional reluctance to engage with discrimination complaints, and its focus on the circumstances of the individual complaint before it, which makes it less willing to factor in broader contextual information. Interesting here is that in the meantime several lines of jurisprudence have been developed by the ECtHR in which it does show a willingness to engage and address systemic discrimination. More important even is the fact that while several of these lines of jurisprudence concern other grounds, such as gender (domestic violence), some do concern Roma and their effective enjoyment of rights.[118]

The comparative analysis demonstrated that when international courts are sufficiently probing, have regard to systemic discrimination and its related features, including historical discrimination, possible hidden discrimination as well as knock-on effects of discrimination on other societal domains, these courts are more likely to properly quantify disadvantage, leading to the identification of appropriate positive state obligations. Cases concerning Roma and their fundamental rights thus invite international courts to factor in systemic discrimination, so as to provide more effective protection against discrimination and push the boundaries of human rights.

In so far as icourts are reticent not to impose too far-reaching obligations on states, it might be useful for them to rely on the political commitments states have accepted in terms of the Sustainable Development Goals, in so far as SDG 10 calls on states to make serious efforts to counter systemic discrimination, including change 'on the ground'. Icourts could thus seek to enhance the pull of these political commitments towards state compliance with their underlying human rights obligations.

[118] See below Chapter 9 by Gergely on education and Chapter 10 by O'Nions on evictions.

# 7

# The Burden of Proof in Discrimination Cases involving Roma before the European Court of Human Rights and the European Committee of Social Rights

*Kristin Henrard and Christopher M Roberts*

## 1. Introduction (Including Theories on the Burden of Proof)

When bringing a case to court, questions of proof are of vital importance, including questions concerning to what extent claims need to be proven (the standard of proof) and the allocation of the burden of proof between the parties, indicating which party must convince the court on each relevant issue. Since these rules determine the opportunities claimants have to bring a successful case, they are essential for effective protection against human rights violations.[1] Difficulties faced by the victims of human rights violations in producing sufficient proof, and in particular in relation to the right to be free from discrimination, have entailed the development of a special allocation of the burden of proof, which implies a reduction of the burden of proof to be carried by the claimant.

The following analysis will reveal that several landmark cases regarding the burden of proof concern Roma. As is discussed in the introduction of this volume, Roma are widely acknowledged to have suffered systemic discrimination, which has caused serious and ongoing disadvantages and related human rights violations. Cases concerning Roma thus tend to involve questions of proof in a context of sustained prejudice that has often seeped into official institutions and structures. Particularly relevant for this volume is the extent to which a broader context of systemic discrimination, typical for Roma, has implications for the establishment of a prima facie case and its rebuttal. In this context, the experiences of Roma have challenged the boundaries of the human rights paradigm and have invited further

[1] Tobias Thienel, 'The Burden and Standard of Proof in the European Court of Human Rights' (2007) 50 German Yearbook of International Law 579; Oddny Mjoll Arnardottir, 'Non-Discrimination under Article 14 ECHR: The Burden of Proof' (2007) 51 Scandinavian Studies in Law 13, 16.

Kristin Henrard and Christopher M Roberts, *The Burden of Proof in Discrimination Cases involving Roma before the European Court of Human Rights and the European Committee of Social Rights* In: *The Rights of Roma in European Courts*. Edited by: Kristin Henrard and Lilla Farkas, Oxford University Press. © Kristin Henrard and Christopher M Roberts 2025. DOI: 10.1093/oso/9780198914358.003.0007

clarifications and developments. This mirrors the manner in which some clarifications and refinements regarding the burden of proof have been developed in cases of alleged discrimination that do not concern the ground of 'race'.

This introductory section discusses the relevant concepts and their meanings, while elaborating on the different steps of the special allocation of the burden of proof and how they relate to each another. Human rights treaties do not specify rules on the burden of proof, the standard of proof, or the allocation of the burden of proof.[2] Consequently, these rules are forged through the jurisprudence of icourts. Most significant in this context is whether or not a special allocation of the burden of proof is adopted, which accordingly is the central focus of this analysis. While a special approach to the burden of proof in cases involving alleged discrimination has been widely accepted, there is still ample uncertainty and confusion about what exactly it entails and how it operates.[3]

Hence, a further exploration of the special allocation of the burden of proof is warranted.[4] Following the rule '*actori incumbit probatio*', a party bringing a claim needs to prove it. For discrimination cases this means the claimant needs to prove 'differential treatment on grounds of [race]' (phase 1), after which the government will need to prove that no discrimination took place (phase 2), in order to prevail in the case. This burden on the government in phase 2 constitutes one form of reversal of the burden of proof.

Proving a causal link between disadvantageous treatment and the ground of discrimination is often extremely difficult for alleged victims. Consequently, the special allocation of the burden of proof only requires that the claimant showcase facts that enable the court to establish a prima facie case of 'differential treatment on grounds of [race]'. This requires proof of a disadvantageous treatment and some indications that this is on grounds of race (or some other prohibited ground). After the claimant has met the lower standard of proof required for the establishment of a prima facie case, the government can try to rebut the presumption by negating the causal link. For each of the two steps within phase 1 the burden of proof is with a different party: for the prima facie case with the claimant, and for the rebuttal with the respondent state.

If the government succeeds in rebutting the presumption, the claimant loses. If the government does not succeed in rebutting the presumption it is established that there is 'differential treatment on grounds of race'. This in turn triggers the second phase, the justification phase, which allows the government to 'justify' this differential

[2] Unlike the UN Equality Directives, eg Directive 97/80/EC on the burden of proof in cases of discrimination based on sex; Art 19 Directive 2006/54/EC on the implementation of the principle of equal opportunities and equal treatment of men and women in matters of employment and occupation (recast); Art 8 Directive 2000/43 and Art 8 Directive 2000/78.

[3] See also the ongoing preliminary questions from national courts about the special allocation of the burden of proof in relation to the EU Equality Directives.

[4] See also the chapter by Robert Thienel in *Research Handbook on Accountability for Human Rights Violations* (Edward Elgar forthcoming).

treatment by showing a legitimate aim and proportionality. However, establishing justification is notoriously difficult where there has been differential treatment on suspect grounds. Put differently, when the special allocation of the burden of proof is employed, the critical shift of the burden of proof is situated within phase 1.

Several icourts adopt the special allocation of the burden of proof and use the terms 'prima facie case' and 'rebuttal'. Nevertheless, it is far from clear how much evidence is exactly required to establish a prima facie case, and how much to rebut the presumption. In relation to Roma and this edited volume, what is particularly relevant is the extent to which a broader context of systemic discrimination has implications for establishing a prima facie case and its rebuttal.[5]

This chapter focuses on the case law of two European supervisory bodies that can be deemed to be international courts (icourts). Following the definition developed in Chapter 3, icourts are supervisory bodies with an official mandate to supervise compliance by state parties, thus having the last word in the interpretation of the human rights conventions concerned.[6] One of these icourts deals with individual complaints and the other with collective complaints. These different 'settings' already explain to some extent the different starting positions of the respective icourts as regards the recognition of the structural and group dimensions of human rights problems. The latter difference strengthens their different starting points in terms of their willingness to address complaints of discrimination. Whilst one is rather reticent, the other is more 'eager' to do so. Notwithstanding these different starting positions, similarities are visible in the approaches both icourts' take in relation to the allocation of the burden of proof between the parties. First, the relevant jurisprudence of each of the two European icourts selected is discussed (in sections 2 and 3 respectively). The chapter then proceeds with a comparative and normative analysis of possible routes for the further development of criteria for the special allocation of the burden of proof (section 4), with specific regard for contexts of systemic discrimination, of which the situation of Roma in Europe constitutes a prime example. The chapter closes with overarching conclusions and recommendations (section 5).

## 2. The European Court of Human Rights, Discrimination and Burden of Proof

The European Convention on Human Rights (ECHR) allows for both individual and interstate complaints.[7] The overwhelming majority of the cases brought before the European Court of Human Rights (ECtHR) are individual complaints.

[5] For more, see the preceding chapter.
[6] See also Chapter 5 by Kristin Henrard in this edited volume.
[7] Arts 33–35 ECHR.

The ECtHR has traditionally emphasized that its task is not to consider the validity of laws or policies but rather to evaluate the case before it, and in particular to evaluate states' compliance with their human rights obligations in relation to the specific facts of a case. Consequently, the Court has been reluctant to give broader contextual information, included statistics, much weight.[8] In cases that centred around prejudice or stigmatization of a particular group, this leads to positions that are difficult to reconcile. On the one hand, the Court often acknowledges that a particular group is vulnerable due to a history of systemic discrimination, inviting closer scrutiny.[9] On the other hand, the Court tends to be reluctant to rely too heavily on general reports about discrimination against a group when deciding a particular case of alleged discrimination.[10]

The latter needs to be understood in light of the ECtHR's past tendency to avoid engaging in detailed analysis of the non-discrimination obligation.[11] The Court at times still holds that when it has found a violation of a substantive right, it is no longer necessary to consider claims of discrimination.[12] Furthermore, in the past when the Court evaluated discrimination complaints it often granted states a broad margin of appreciation.[13] Fortunately, the latter has changed over time, and the Court has come to recognize that certain grounds are (highly) suspect, demanding 'very weighty reasons' to justify differential treatment.[14] Notwithstanding earlier signals,[15] the ECtHR recognized only rather late that 'race' and 'ethnic origin' were suspect grounds.[16]

As it happens, there is a long line of ECtHR case law in which it recognizes that '[a]s a result of their turbulent history and constant uprooting the Roma have become a specific type of disadvantaged and vulnerable minority', hence 'they therefore require special protection'.[17] In other words, the Court acknowledges a context

[8] Inter alia *Nachova et al v Bulgaria* App nos 43577/98 and 43579/98 (ECtHR, 6 July 2005) para 155; *Terna v Italy* App no 21052/18 (ECtHR, 14 January 2021) para 98; *MB and others v Slovakia* App no 45322/17 (ECtHR, 1 July 2021) para 106.

[9] See inter alia Lourdes Peroni and Alexandra Timmer, 'Vulnerable Groups: The Promise of an Emerging Concept in European Human Rights Convention Law' (2013) 11 International Journal of Constitutional Law 1056.

[10] See case law discussed below.

[11] See also Oddny Ornadottir, 'Non-discrimination in International and European Law: Towards Substantive Models' (2008) 25 Nordic Journal of Human Rights 140.

[12] Inter alia *VC v Slovakia* and *IG and others v Slovakia* (App no 18968/07 (ECtHR, 8 February 2012) para 167 regarding forced sterilization of Roma women; and *Hudorovic and others v Slovenia* App nos 24816/14 and 25140/14 (ECtHR, 10 March 2020) para 162.

[13] See also Olivier de Schutter, 'Observations. Le Droit au Mode de Vie Tsigane devant la Cour Europeenne des Droits de l'Homme' (1997) Rev Trim Dr H 64, 89–90.

[14] See inter alia for 'gender' *Abdulaziz, Cabales and Balkandali and others v UK* App no 9214/80 (ECtHR, 28 May 1985); for 'nationality' *Gaygusuz v Austria* App no 17371/90 (ECtHR, 28 May 1985); and for sexual orientation *Salgueiro da Silva Mouta v Portugal* App no 33290/96 (ECtHR, 13 June 1979).

[15] Inter alia *Nachova* (n 8) para 145 referring to racist violence as a particular affront to human dignity, that required special vigilance and a vigorous reaction from the authorities.

[16] *Timishev v Russia* App nos 55762/00 and 55974/00 (ECtHR, 13 December 2005) para 58.

[17] *DH and others v the Czech Republic* App No 57325/00 (ECtHR, 13 November 2007) para 182. This quote has featured in many subsequent cases.

of systemic discrimination against Roma, which arguably calls for careful scrutiny of individual cases of disadvantageous treatment of Roma. Furthermore, given that the ECtHR requires special vigilance and a vigorous reaction from authorities in relation to racist discrimination, and particularly racist violence, it stands to reason that similar special vigilance should be deployed by the ECtHR, including in the form of heightened scrutiny. Nevertheless, as the following analysis will demonstrate, even in cases involving systemic discrimination and racist violence, the Court has dismissed Article 14 complaints, either summarily for the same reasons that it concluded there was no violation of a substantive right, or because it concluded it was no longer necessary to consider it, after having found a violation of a substantive right.[18]

The following analysis will reveal different lines of development for the ECtHR's use of the special allocation of the burden of proof in cases of indirect racial discrimination on the one hand and direct racial discrimination on the other. While the dividing line between direct and indirect discrimination is not sharp,[19] the difference of degree with which the ECtHR embraces the special allocation of the burden of proof is remarkable. For indirect discrimination the special allocation of the burden of proof is mostly 'set' now, while for cases of direct discrimination, particularly when national criminal law is involved, there is a striking lack of clarity about relevant parameters and thus seemingly inconsistent practice.

The different approach to the special allocation of the burden of proof invites some further thoughts as to whether the respective nature of direct versus indirect discrimination can explain this difference. The terms 'direct' and 'indirect' discrimination refer to the difference in directness of the causal link between the disadvantageous treatment and the grounds of differentiation.[20] Direct discrimination concerns disadvantageous treatment of an individual in comparison with one or more other individuals 'on grounds of', ie because of a particular ground. Indirect discrimination in contrast involve at first sight neutral measures that have a disproportionate negative impact on members of a particular group, but which however do not appear to target the group in particular. In this regard, one can explain the use of the expression 'intent or effect' in definitions of 'discrimination' in UN human rights conventions: whereas 'effect' points to indirect discrimination, 'intent' links to direct discrimination. Each of these types of discrimination has its own evidentiary challenges. European non-discrimination law acknowledges that proving intent is extremely demanding and does not require

[18] Inter alia *Evans v the United Kingdom* [GC] App no 6339/05 (ECtHR, 10 April 2007) para 95; *VC v Slovakia* App no 18968/07 (ECtHR, 8 November 2011) paras 179–80.

[19] See section 2.2 below for a discussion of cases of direct discrimination as dressed up (hidden) as indirect discrimination.

[20] See the definitions in the EU's equality directives, eg Art 2(2)(a) and (b) of the Race Equality Directive 2000/43/EC.

proof of discriminatory intent.[21] Nevertheless, proving a direct causal link and thus 'direct causation' tends to concern questions of motivation or bias.[22] Indirect discrimination requires the court to consider the effects of a measure on members belonging to a particular group, and thus has an inherent group dimension. This group dimension is challenging in at least two respects: establishing that a measure is discriminatory because of its effects even without discriminatory intent, and establishing that someone is indirectly discriminated against because of his/her membership of a group. Taking into account effects on a group requires the court to go beyond the confines of the individual claimant and to consider the broader context. The latter is particularly demanding for courts that primarily consider individual complaints.

### 2.1. The ECtHR—indirect (racial) discrimination and the distribution of the burden of proof

The ECtHR struggled with the notion of indirect discrimination for a long time, and in particular with the role of 'intent' and the group dimension that was introduced by giving attention to disproportionate impacts on groups.[23] The Court's case law is casuistic, since it relates its reasoning to the specific circumstances of each case: 'it has to confine itself as far as possible to the examination of the concrete case before it .... It is not its task to assess the overall social context'.[24] This focus on the specific cases before it helped to lead the Court into ignoring broader patterns of oppression and vulnerability, and thus also more subtle or covert forms of discrimination.[25]

By 2000–01, the Court had gradually[26] come to terms with the idea that discrimination could occur because general laws and norms impact groups differently, affecting some groups disproportionately, even when the groups concerned are not targeted directly.[27] Nevertheless, the Court was unsure what evidence was sufficient to establish a prima facie case of indirect discrimination and at first

[21] Inter alia *Case 'relating to certain aspects of the laws on the use of languages in Education in Belgium'* App no 1474/62 (ECtHR, 23 July 1968) para 10.

[22] It is noted that prejudice may even be unconscious: see inter alia Kasper Lippert Rasmussen, *Born Free and Equal?* (Oxford University Press 2014) 59–60; Amy Wax, 'The Discriminating Mind: Define it, Prove it' ( 2008) 40 Connecticut Law Review 979, 983.

[23] Christa Tobler, 'Equality and Non-Discrimination under the ECHR and EU Law: A Comparison Focusing on Discrimination against LGBTI Persons' (2014) 74 ZaöRV 521, 523–33. See also Ruth Rubio-Marín and Mathias Möschel, 'Anti-Discrimination Exceptionalism: Racist Violence before the ECtHR and the Holocaust Prism' (2015) 26 European Journal of International Law 881.

[24] *RR and RD v Slovakia* App no 20649/18 (ECtHR, 1 September 2020) para 124.

[25] See also Olivier de Schutter (n 13).

[26] Some of the cases concern Roma/race, but several others concern religion and gender. In this chapter only the cases on Roma will be mentioned.

[27] Inter alia *Hugh Jordan v UK* App no 2474/94 (ECtHR, 4 May 2001) para 154.

considered 'mere' statistics 'in themselves' not to be enough.[28] It took the Court another four years before it found a way to allow for 'statistics' to establish a prima facie case of discrimination, in which context it came to insist on certain standards, namely the statistics needed to be 'official' and 'convincing'.[29]

A slightly later judgment, *DH and others v Czech Republic*, is considered to be the landmark case in this context, firmly enshrining the notion of indirect discrimination in the ECtHR's non-discrimination jurisprudence. *DH* concerned the disproportionate enrolment of Roma students in education programmes for students with mental disabilities. The 2006 Chamber judgment in the case ignored the Court's progress since 2000/01.[30] Fortunately, the 2007 Grand Chamber judgment in *DH*[31] reversed the Chamber's judgment and confirmed the Court's recognition of and approach to indirect discrimination, as well as its quality demands for statistics relied on to establish a prima facie case of indirect discrimination.[32] The Grand Chamber justified the reversal of the burden of proof in such cases on the ground that otherwise 'it would be extremely difficult in practice for applicants to prove indirect discrimination'.[33]

One can argue that the ECtHR's slow coming to terms with the notion of indirect discrimination ultimately hinged on it finding a 'fair' distribution of the burden of proof between the parties, specifically one that is not too demanding on the victim, while being sufficiently demanding so as not to shift the burden too quickly onto the government.[34] While the Grand Chamber went on to consider the government's arguments that the children in question were placed in special schools as a result of their needs and that there had been parental consent, it rejected this attempt by the state to suggest non-discriminatory justifications for the actions in question.[35] The Court subsequently found Article 14 was violated.[36] In *Horváth*, which also involved claims of discrimination against Roma in the context of education, the Court found that 'a general policy or measure exerted a disproportionately prejudicial effect on the Roma, a particularly vulnerable group' and that as a result 'a *prima facie* case of indirect discrimination' had been established.[37] While the Court didn't explicitly indicate it was reversing the burden of

[28] ibid.

[29] *Hoogendijk v the Netherlands* App no 58641/00 (ECtHR, 6 January 2005).

[30] For another example of the way in which the Court was still wavering in relation to indirect discrimination prior to 2007, is *Zarb Adami v Malta* App 17209/02 (ECtHR, 20 June 2006) paras 77–78, where the Court did not worry at all about quality standards for statistics.

[31] *DH and others v Czech Republic* App no 57325/00 (ECtHR, 13 November 2007).

[32] The Grand Chamber in *DH* highlighted 'the undisputed official' nature of the statistics as 'statistics which appear on critical examination to be reliable and significant': ibid paras 187–88.

[33] *DH* (n 31) para 189.

[34] ibid para 189.

[35] These arguments were rejected on the grounds the tests in question were themselves quite possibly biased and that the consent in question had not been adequately informed. See *DH* (n 31) paras 196–204.

[36] See ibid holding para 2.

[37] *Horváth and Kiss v Hungary* App no 11146/11 (ECtHR, 29 April 2013) paras 110–11.

proof, its suggestion that 'a *prima facie* case of indirect discrimination' had been found suggested exactly that. The Court went on to reason in a manner highly similar to *DH* relative to the government's attempted justifications for the situation in question and ultimately again found a violation of Article 14, read in conjunction with Article 2 of Protocol 1.[38]

Since the Grand Chamber judgment in *DH* the Court has further fine-tuned its special allocation of the burden of proof in cases of indirect discrimination. In *Orsus et al v Croatia*, a case also concerning Roma children being allocated disproportionately to separate and inferior schooling, the Grand Chamber found that the statistics put forward did not disclose a clear discrepancy and as such did not suffice to establish a prima facie case. Nevertheless, the Court chose to rely in addition on reports of ECRI, the Council of Europe's Commissioner for Human Rights, and of other similar expert bodies to conclude a prima facie case had been established.[39] In a later case concerning persons of 'foreign ethnic origin', the Court clarified that the absence of available statistics does not prevent it from finding a prima facie case of indirect discrimination being established.[40] This suggests that the ECtHR is becoming more confident in recognizing situations of indirect discrimination, also on the basis of assumptions and inferences.[41]

## 2.2. The ECtHR—direct (racial) discrimination and distribution of the burden of proof

The ECtHR has struggled to operate the special allocation of the burden of proof in cases on alleged direct discrimination. The following analysis will advance several critiques concerning the extent to which and the way in which the ECtHR has operated the special allocation of the burden of proof in cases of direct racial discrimination. First, while the Court has identified a few relevant parameters for the determination of a prima facie case of direct racial discrimination, it does not really apply them *in concreto* in cases before it. Second, the Court applies too high a standard for finding a prima facie case of direct racial discrimination, as in the few instances where it has established such a case, it had sufficient proof to find actual prohibited differential treatment on grounds of race. Third, and of particular relevance for groups like the Roma, the Court has failed to take into account contexts of systemic discrimination when evaluating whether a prima facie case of direct discrimination has been made. Fourth, the Court's identification of a procedural

[38] See ibid paras 113–29, holding para 2.

[39] *Orsus et al v Croatia* App no 15766/03 (ECtHR, 16 March 2010) paras 152–55.

[40] *Biao v Denmark* App no 38590/10 (ECtHR, 24 May 2016) paras 112–13.

[41] In the *Biao* case the ECtHR considered that 'it can reasonably be assumed that ... persons acquiring Danish citizenship at a later point in their life .... would generally be of foreign ethnic origin' (paras 112–13).

dimension of the prohibition of discrimination, in addition to the traditional substantive dimension, is welcomed, as it allows for flawed investigations into possibly discriminatory violence to be condemned as prohibited discrimination. Nevertheless, the Court's refusal to draw inferences from flaws in investigations, for a prima facie case of substantive discrimination, needs to be revisited to some extent, particularly in the context of systemic discrimination.

Few cases involve allegations of overt racial discrimination. Clear proof of it would require, for example, official documents that call for differential treatment on ethnic grounds, or that reveal prejudice as informing a particular police raid. Such documents would amount to proof of 'differential treatment on racial grounds' that states can no longer negate, yet may try to explain in terms of a reasonable and objective justification. The *Timishev* case[42] is a textbook example, in which the Court noted that the official order to the police at the administrative border between the Russian regions of Ingushetia and Kabardino-Balkaria to not allow Chechens to pass is, correctly found, not a prima facie case, but rather 'a clear inequality of treatment in the enjoyment of the right of movement on account of one's ethnic origin'.[43] The Court then moved to the second or justification phase, enabling the government to 'show that the difference in treatment could be justified'.[44]

Broad awareness of the unacceptability of direct racial discrimination entails that most direct racial discrimination will occur in a covert manner. In such cases, it is very challenging for a claimant to put forward proof of a direct causal link between disadvantageous treatment they suffer and their race or ethnic origin. While in theory it is not necessary to prove intent on the part of the alleged perpetrator to establish direct differential treatment,[45] de facto establishing a direct causal link in cases of covert direct discrimination comes very close to demonstrating discriminatory intent.

When discriminatory intent is an element of an alleged crime in national criminal law, requiring only a prima facie showing to establish a presumption of discrimination would raise serious questions, as such a rule would run contrary to the presumption of innocence, a cardinal principle of criminal law and a human rights obligation. As the following analysis will show, the ECtHR's case law suggests that the Court is overly concerned with not imposing an unreasonable demand on states relative to the manner in which they address covert direct racial discrimination in their criminal law. This concern manifests itself in a lack of guidance that could clarify and thus enable national courts to establish prima facie cases of direct racial discrimination, and with a de facto too high threshold to establish a 'prima

42 *Timishev v Russia* App nos 55762/00 and 55974/00 (ECtHR, 13 December 2005).
43 ibid para 54.
44 ibid para 57.
45 See, inter alia, *Case 'relating to certain aspects of the laws on the use of languages in Education in Belgium'* App no 1474/62 (ECtHR, 23 July 1968) para 10.

facie' case. Both of these manifestations work to the detriment of victims, who do not benefit from a reduced standard of proof.

The landmark case on covert racial direct discrimination in which the ECtHR has developed the principles regarding the allocation of the burden of proof that it still relies on is *Nachova and others v Bulgaria*.[46] The case concerned the shooting of two Roma men by the Bulgarian police. The case resulted in two judgments, with sharply different outcomes, due to different approaches to the special allocation of the burden of proof. Despite the differences and having regard to the rules on the burden of proof enshrined in EU Equality Directives and the Racial Equality Directive in particular, not only the Chamber but also the Grand Chamber acknowledged that a special allocation of the burden of proof may be called for.[47]

The Chamber identified a prima facie case of direct racial discrimination because of severe flaws in the investigations conducted by the Bulgarian authorities and particularly the blatant disregard of evidence pointing to possible discriminatory motives of the police officers.[48] Following a critical evaluation of the government's justifications, the Chamber opined that Bulgaria was unable to rebut the presumption, thus concluding direct racial discrimination had taken place.[49] The Bulgarian authorities requested a referral to the Grand Chamber, which was accepted because of the importance to the ECtHR's jurisprudence of the question of how the burden of proof should be approached.

The Grand Chamber's judgment in this case remains a leading case in several respects, but has also triggered criticisms, thus inviting further developments. The Grand Chamber confirmed that a special allocation of the burden of proof might be utilized in some instances, observing that it could not exclude the possibility that in certain cases a prima facie case of racial discriminatory violence could be established, after which the government would be called on to rebut the presumption.[50] However, the Grand Chamber constrained the extent to which such a prima facie case could be established, due to its concern that reversing the burden onto the government would require the government to prove a negative (the absence of racial animus), which it considered impossible.[51] Furthermore, the Grand Chamber suggested that flaws in police investigation could not lead to inferences concerning substantive discrimination by the police.[52] On the positive side, the Grand Chamber did identify criteria that should inform the decision to establish a prima facie case of direct racial discrimination, namely 'the specificity of the facts',

[46] *Nachova and Others v Bulgaria* App nos 43577/98 and 43579/98 has two judgments, one from a Chamber on 26 February 2004 and one from the Grand Chamber on 6 July 2005.

[47] See, inter alia, *Nachova* 2004 (n 46) para 168 and *Nachova* 2005 (n 46) para 128.

[48] *Nachova* 2004 (n 46) para 169.

[49] ibid para 170.

[50] *Nachova* 2005 (n 46) para 157.

[51] ibid.

[52] But see the following paragraphs on the identification of a distinct, procedural dimension of the prohibition of discrimination.

'the nature of the allegations made', and 'the convention right at stake'.[53] However, the Court did not operationalize these criteria by applying them to the specific facts of the case.

In addition, while as noted the Court did not allow inferences from procedural investigatory flaws towards findings of substantive discrimination, it did add a procedural dimension to the prohibition of discrimination, namely a special investigatory 'duty … to take all possible steps to investigate whether or not discrimination may have played a role in the events'.[54] The Court thus found a new way in which to conclude that a violation of the Convention's prohibition of discrimination had taken place. While the Court narrowed claimants' ability to establish a prima facie case of direct racial discrimination, paving the way to a finding of substantive discrimination, it enabled a failure in regard to states' investigatory duties to lead to a finding of discrimination in the procedural dimension.[55]

Subsequent ECtHR case law on cases of hidden racial discrimination (often involving discriminatory violence) against Roma confirmed both the Court's failure to indicate when and how the *Nachova* criteria pertaining to the establishment of a prima facie case might be met, and its enduring reluctance to establish substantive direct racial discrimination.[56] The Court continues to distinguish between the procedural and the substantive dimension of discrimination. To some extent, the procedural dimension of discrimination can be seen to entail an important second layer of protection against discrimination, allowing for findings of procedural discrimination even when the Court does not consider substantive discrimination established. At the same time, the Court's reluctance to allow for inferences based on serious flaws in investigations into possible discriminatory motivations suggests that the ECtHR's traditional reluctance to establish direct racial discrimination persists.[57]

### 2.2.1. Criteria for a prima facie case: a call for additional guidance

Unfortunately, the ECtHR's case law has not yet clarified how the 'prima facie case' criteria laid out in *Nachova*—'the specificity of the facts', 'the nature of the allegations', and 'the convention right at stake' – might be operationalized. In some cases the Court does not mention the criteria explicitly, or only refers to one particular criterion without identifying it as such and without providing further guidance on the relative weight of the three criteria.[58] Rather, the Court seems to prefer to remain vague and ambiguous about the operationalization of the *Nachova* criteria.[59]

[53] *Nachova* 2005 (n 46) para 147.
[54] ibid para 168.
[55] ibid paras 159 and 168.
[56] See the discussion of subsequent case law below.
[57] See also the cases discussed immediately below.
[58] See inter alia *RR and RD v Slovakia* (n 22) para 216.
[59] See the immediately following paragraphs, where some normative suggestions will be made about the way in which these criteria could operate.

This invites further consideration of how these criteria could be applied in general and in particular in contexts of systemic discrimination.[60] The criterion on the 'specificity of the facts' seems appropriate in the sense that when the facts are very detailed and specific, this speaks in favour of finding a prima facie case. The criterion on 'the nature of the allegations' enables a court to be more demanding about the establishment of a prima facie case in the sense that the evidence needs to be more compelling when the allegations are more serious. This line of thought is followed in several jurisdictions.[61]

The third criterion, 'the convention right at stake', seems to hint at some human rights being more important or more fundamental than others, thus reflecting a hierarchy among fundamental rights. At a principled level, a hierarchy of human rights is rejected.[62] Nevertheless, certain features of international human rights law suggest an inbuilt hierarchy, including that some rights do not have limitation clauses and are even considered non-derogable during states of emergency.[63] This suggests such rights may have greater hierarchical value. In this context, the ECtHR has held that some instances of racial discrimination qualify as inhuman or degrading treatment, and as such are absolutely prohibited.[64] In addition, and as already highlighted, the Court has identified several grounds as particularly suspect, justifying very strict scrutiny and at times even indicating that differentiations on such grounds are absolutely unacceptable.[65]This rationale can be considered to support a fair, not too demanding burden of proof for the alleged victim to establish a prima facie case of discrimination. This reasoning would a fortiori apply in the context of racial discrimination, as the ECtHR has often underscored how particularly invidious racial discrimination is, and has opined that 'no difference in treatment which is based exclusively or to a decisive extent on a person's ethnic origin is capable of being objectively justified in a contemporary democratic society built on the principles of pluralism and respect for different cultures'.[66] The latter wording can be understood as indicating that race is suspect par excellence.

[60] This is based on Henrard's argument in her article in Dembour's special issue on the burden of proof before the ECtHR: 'The European Court of Human Rights and the "Special" Distribution of the Burden of Proof in Racial Discrimination Cases: The Search for Fairness Continues' (2023) 4 European Convention on Human Rights Law Review 426.

[61] Thienel (n 1) 573.

[62] T Koji, 'Emerging Hierarchy in International Human Rights and Beyond: From the Perspective of Non-Derogable Rights' (2001) 12 European Journal of International Law 917.

[63] See eg Art 15, para 2 ECHR. In addition, the ECtHR's case law highlights the crucial importance of particular rights for democratic societies, such as the freedom of expression. See, inter alia, *Lingens v Austria* App no 9815/82 (ECtHR, 8 July 1986). This hints that the right to freedom of expression enjoys a somewhat elevated status, at least from the ECtHR's point of view.

[64] Inter alia *Moldovan and others v Romania (no 2)* App nos 42238/98 and 64320/01 (ECtHR, 12 July 2005); *Burlya and others v Ukraine* App no 3289/10 (ECtHR, 6 November 2018) paras 121 and 124.

[65] See also Elizabeth Holzleithner, 'Mainstreaming Equality: Disentangling Grounds of Discrimination' (2005) 14 Transnational Law and Contemporary Problems 927, 953.

[66] Inter alia *DH* (n 31) para 176; *Sejdic and Finci v Bosnia Herzegovina* App nos 27996/06 and 34836/06 (ECtHR, 22 December 2009) para 44.

While attention to the second criterion tends to work in favour of the respondent state, the third tends to operate in favour of the alleged victim. The first criterion is dependent on the specific circumstances of the case and should assist in striking an appropriate balance overall, ensuring that the burden of proof is not unreasonably high for either the respondent state or the claimant. It should be kept in mind however that the special allocation of the burden of proof is foremost meant to alleviate the burden of the alleged victim of discrimination and that it developed in recognition of the hurdles faced by the claimants in gathering proof often being insurmountable. Overall, therefore, the threshold to establish a prima facie case of racial discrimination should not be unreasonably high.

In addition to the preceding arguments, the existence of a context of systemic discrimination calls for various reasons for a lowering of the threshold to establish a prima facie case. First and most simply, awareness of any context of systemic violation leads to different sorts of probabilistic conclusions as to the likelihood of a violation in any particular case, such that a reversal of the burden may be understood as factually or logically justified. Furthermore, the allocation of the burden of proof is always in part a determination of the balance of the risk of error. In this context, reversing the burden of proof is appropriate in connection with systemic violations insofar as there is less to be lost should an erroneous finding be reached in the claimant's favour than in the respondent's favour. Should a state erroneously be found not to be committing a violation, an individual's rights will go unremedied, while no pressure is brought to end the situation of systemic violations in question. Should a finding against the state be made in error, the case will still exert positive pressure to end the discriminatory situation in question. Reversal is in particular justified in the context of systemic discrimination due to the fact that states are likely to have far greater access to the information necessary to cast a clearer light on the overall picture than individual applicants from discriminated against groups. When prejudice and discrimination is deeply ingrained it will tend to be extra difficult to proof. In addition, states will only feel obliged to share information more broadly if compelled to do so.

### 2.2.2. The ECtHR adopts a threshold for a prima facie case that is too high

In addition to the lack of guidance about the three criteria the Court refers to for the determination of a prima facie case, the Court appears to apply a very high threshold for establishing a prima facie case. Often, when the Court recognizes that a prima facie case of racial discrimination has been made, there is enough proof to establish an instance of actual differential treatment on the ground of race or ethnic origin (ending phase 1). For example, in *Antayev and others v Russia*[67] the Court had proof of internal police instructions that targeted Chechens for

[67] *Antayev and others v Russia* App no 37966/07 (ECtHR, 3 July 2014). See also *Makuchyan and Minasyan v Azerbaijan and Hungary* App no 17247/13 (ECtHR, 26 May 2020).

disadvantageous treatment, as well as detailed allegations of racist abuse by specific police offenders. This would appear to suffice to establish differential treatment on racial grounds, shifting the burden of proof of justification to the government. Instead, the Court established a prima facie case of discrimination.[68] In the end, the Court did conclude that prohibited racial discrimination had taken place.[69] Nevertheless, identifying a prima facie case of discrimination when there was extensive proof of the differential treatment on grounds of race makes clear that the Court is imposing too high of a standard relative to the establishment of a prima facie case, and thus requiring too much from applicants.

### 2.2.3. A prima facie case of discrimination in a context of systemic discrimination

A situation of systemic discrimination is one in which prejudice is ingrained in society and hence presumably widespread among private individuals as well as official institutional structures.[70] In such contexts, the threshold to establish a prima facie case should be reduced. In this regard it is useful to recall the strong dissent six judges issued in the Grand Chamber's *Nachova* case, reflecting a concern both that the majority had set the threshold to establish a prima facie case too high and that it had not sufficiently taken into account the background of systemic discrimination against Roma.

The joint dissent in *Nachova* argued that procedural shortcomings should be central to the allocation of the burden of proof and suggested that sufficiently grave procedural shortcomings to investigate discriminatory motives might in themselves suffice to establish a prima facie case.[71] The dissent also considered the distinction between procedural and substantive dimensions of discrimination unhelpful because the factual evidence of the case as a whole generated sufficiently strong, clear, and concordant evidence to justify certain presumptions of racial discrimination.[72] In this regard, it is noteworthy that several of the factual elements identified by the dissent as pointing towards discrimination related to the existence of systemic prejudice and discrimination against Roma. These included published records of hostility against Roma, anti-Roma slurs uttered by the police after the shooting and cases before the ECtHR concerning police violence against Roma in Bulgaria.[73] Put differently, the dissenting judges favoured adopting a lower threshold to establish a prima facie case of discrimination in a context of systemic discrimination. Judge Bratza in his concurring opinion further developed this line

[68] *Antayev* (n 67) para 128.
[69] ibid paras 128–29.
[70] *RB v Hungary* App no 64602/12 (ECtHR, 12 September 2016), paras 84, 88.
[71] *Nachova* 2005 (n 46) joint partly dissenting opinion of Judges Casadevall, Hedigan, Mularoni, Fura-Sandström, Gyulumyan, and Spielmann para 6.
[72] ibid paras 2–3 and 7.
[73] ibid para 5.

of reasoning, arguing that a shift in the burden of proof is appropriate where 'the evidence showed that attempts to arrest persons of a particular ethnic group had invariably or consistently resulted in the deaths of the persons concerned, while the arrests of persons of other ethnic origin had seldom if ever resulted in the loss of life', or 'where the evidence showed that in the planning of an arrest operation it was only where persons of a particular ethnic origin were involved that the arrest team was provided with, or authorised to use, firearms'.[74]

Unfortunately, so far the Court has not followed this line of argumentation. On multiple occasions, the Court has recognized systemic discrimination to one degree or another: it has acknowledged a 'background of international reports describing a pattern of persistent anti-Roma prejudice, in particular on the part of certain law-enforcement officers';[75] it has recognized that 'the Roma communities are often confronted with institutionalised racism and are prone to excessive use of force by the law-enforcement authorities';[76] it has identified 'patterns of violence and intolerance against an ethnic minority', 'the general hostile attitude against the Roma community',[77] and 'large-scale, coordinated intimidation' due to 'marches involving large groups and targeting the Roma minority';[78] and it has noted more generally the 'disadvantageous and vulnerable position of Roma and the need for their special protection'.[79]

These recognitions by the Court of systemic discrimination against Roma are important in their own right. However, the Court has not connected its observations with regard to its approach to the allocation of the burden of proof. At times, this has not affected the outcomes of cases, as there is sufficient detailed and clear proof, such as racist police intervention plans,[80] to ground a potential finding of discrimination even without shifting the burden of proof to the government.[81] Nevertheless, the Court's argument in *Lingurar* that, 'where there is evidence of patterns of violence and intolerance against an ethnic minority, the positive obligations incumbent on member States require a higher standard of response to alleged bias-motivated incidents'[82] does seem to entail that in case of systemic discrimination the ECtHR should scrutinize more strictly and be more demanding

[74] *Nachova* 2005 (n 46), Judge Bratza concurring. Judge Bratza actually confirmed the strong dissent of Judge Bonello in *Anguelova v Bulgaria*, a similar case of police violence against Roma, in which Bonello had called out the ECtHR's lack of Art 14 jurisprudence and had highlighted the need for the burden of proof to be shifted in such cases: see *Anguelova v Bulgaria* App no 38361/97 (ECtHR, 13 September 2002), Bonello dissenting.

[75] *Burlya and Others v Ukraine* App no 3289/10 (ECtHR, 6 February 2019), paras 145 and 169.

[76] *Lingurar v Romania* App no 48474/14 (ECtHR 16 Apr 2019), para 80.

[77] *RB v Hungary* App no 64602/12 (ECtHR, 12 September 2016), paras 84, 88.

[78] *Király and Dömötör v Hungary* App no 10851/13 (ECtHR, 17 April 2017) para 77.

[79] ibid para 161. See also *Budinova and Chaprazov v Bulgaria* App no 12567/13 (ECtHR, 16 May 2021), para 64.

[80] ibid paras 79, 81, holding paras 2–3.

[81] See *Burlya* (n 75) paras 145, 169. See also *Paketova and Others v Bulgaria* App nos 17808/19 and 36972/19 (ECtHR, 4 January 2023).

[82] *Lingurar* (n 76) para 80.

on states. This line of reasoning supports the argument that in contexts of systemic discrimination a reversal of the burden of proof onto the state, to negate or justify, should occur 'faster'.

The ECtHR has been unwilling to take this step though, regardless of how extensive the evidence advanced by claimants or third-party interveners concerning systemic discrimination against Roma in society and within public authorities is. The Court has maintained its reluctance, even when case submissions have been accompanied by the explicit argument of systemic discrimination, which should affect the Court's approach to the burden of proof.[83] In *MB and others v Slovakia*,[84] a case concerning ill-treatment of Roma minors by the police in a context of systemic racism in policing in Slovakia, the Court not only expressed awareness of the 'generally sensitive nature of the situation related to Roma at the relevant time'[85] but also noted in its assessment of Article 3 that the Slovakian authorities had established that racism had played a role in relation to a related incident between the same Roma and police officer.[86] Nevertheless, the Court did not consider that a prima facie case of racial discrimination had been established, either in connection with the related incident (substantive discrimination) or because of the lack of an investigation into the racist motives of the incident (procedural discrimination).[87]

The Court's failure to take systemic discrimination into account in relation to the burden of proof is also visible in other cases, such as *Terna v Italy*, which concerned child removal and related visiting rights.[88] The Roma grandmother in the case claimed direct discrimination, both regarding the decision to take her granddaughter away from her and place her in foster care, and regarding her lack of visiting rights. In the latter respect, she claimed that the decisions of the specially appointed guardian were clearly based on prejudice against Roma.[89] The ERRC, as a third party, underscored anti-Roma stereotypes and institutional racism in Italy's child care system, which it suggested were linked to the gross overrepresentation of Roma children in public care as well as the state's failure to guarantee visiting rights of Roma parents and grandparents.[90] The Court however suggested that it needed to confine itself, as far as possible, to an examination of the specific case before it. In that context, the Court chose to focus on the absence of explicit or apparent racist motivation on the part of the national courts, which had considered the case, and glossed over evidence of the prejudice of the guardian that had set the entire process in motion, as well as the lack of enforcement of the judicially determined

[83] See inter alia *MB and others v Slovakia* App no 45322 (ECtHR, 1 July 2021) para 100.
[84] ibid.
[85] ibid para 106.
[86] ibid para 87.
[87] ibid paras 105–06.
[88] *Terna v Italy* App no 21052/18 (ECtHR, 14 January 2021).
[89] ibid paras 98–99.
[90] See ibid para 90.

visiting rights.[91] Without any detailed consideration of whether or not a special allocation of the burden of proof might apply, the Court concluded that no discrimination had occurred.[92]

### 2.2.4. Failure to consider inferences between the procedural and substantive prohibition of discrimination

As was noted above, identifying the procedural dimension to the prohibition of discrimination in the form of a special investigatory 'duty … to take all possible steps to investigate whether or not discrimination may have played a role in the events'[93] is beneficial insofar as it enables the Court to conclude procedural discrimination has taken place in instances in which the Court considers there is insufficient proof to conclude substantive discrimination was present. Furthermore, requiring national public authorities to conduct special investigations will hopefully help uncover some of the evidence victims of substantive discrimination often need to proceed with their cases, and thus contribute to the realization of suitable remedies at the national level.[94] More generally, increasingly critical review by the ECtHR of the special investigatory duty to unveil possible discriminatory motives could improve public authorities' awareness and performance in undertaking such investigations.

At the same time, as has been underscored by the dissenting opinions in *Nachova*, distinguishing between the two dimensions may make it easier for the Court to fail to take the full picture of the underlying prejudice and discriminatory motivation into account when reaching its judgment on substantive discrimination. It is important to keep in mind that in circumstances of systemic discrimination, prejudice against a group may also inform lack of fulfilment of the special investigatory duty. Put differently, the procedural and substantive dimension of the prohibition of discrimination are interconnected. The Court has recognized this connectedness to some extent in judgments where its evaluation of both dimensions of discrimination are integrated to a great extent, in which problems in relation to both are identified and then one overall violation of the prohibition of discrimination is identified.[95] In some cases the ECtHR has been open to drawing inferences from flawed investigations into discriminatory motives to conclude a prima facie case of substantive discrimination has been established.[96] In others, it has suggested that a failure to comply with the special investigatory duty to

[91] ibid para 98.

[92] See ibid para 100. The Court did find Art 8 had been violated, however. See ibid para 77, holding para 2.

[93] ibid para 168.

[94] See inter alia, *Boaca and others v Romania* App no 40355/11 (ECtHR, 12 January 2016).

[95] *Adzhigitova and others v Russia* App no 40165/07 (ECtHR, 22 June 2021) concerning the unlawful detention and ill-treatment of a group of Avars (paras 273–74 and 278).

[96] See, inter alia, *Antayev and others v Russia* (n 67).

investigate discriminatory motives reveals the indifference of the government and possibly even 'official acquiescence to or even connivance with hate crimes'.[97]

## 3. Revealing the Specific Struggles of the European Committee on Social Rights

The introduction of this chapter highlighted that the European Committee on Social Rights (ECSR) does not hear individual complaints but only collective complaints, either from employee/employer organizations or from NGOs with consultative status to the Council of Europe. Several cases before the ECSR have concerned Roma, all of which were brought by NGOs. Collective complaints per se concern problems that stretch beyond an individual person and that often affect particular groups. By nature, these complaints are particularly likely to implicate legislative and institutional frameworks and their working in practice.[98] Several of the cases brought relating to Roma have concerned housing issues, including segregation, lack of access to social housing, and evictions. A range of other issues have also been raised,[99] including complaints about access to health care and segregated maternity wards, family allowances for children, and child removal from parents and placement in public care.

From the start, and unlike the ECtHR, the ECSR has been willing to address discrimination complaints, to identify a discrimination nexus, and to conclude that states have engaged in prohibited discrimination.[100] The Committee typically starts its analysis by recalling the reasonable and objective justification formula of discrimination. Its subsequent analysis has a strong emphasis on the prohibition of indirect discrimination and duties of differential treatment, aimed at ensuring the effective enjoyment of social rights, also by the most vulnerable.[101] Thereafter, the Committee does not really return to this formula, nor does it reflect in detail on the differences between indirect and direct discrimination, or on the level of scrutiny it should employ. Nevertheless, it is obvious that the ECSR reviews state justifications critically. Arguments that no differentiations on the basis of race have been made are met by a critical reminder that mere formal equal treatment is not sufficient, and that vulnerable persons require special measures that are tailored to

[97] *MC and AC v Romania* App no 12060/12 (ECtHR, 12 April 2016) para 124. See also *Turkan Cakir v Belgium* App no 44256/06 (ECtHR, 10 March 2009) para 72.

[98] Katelyn Sheehan and Rebecca Cook, 'Collective Dimensions of Complaints and Remedies' (2022) 19 JL & Equal 50, 52.

[99] See also Aoife Nolan, '"Aggravated Violations", Roma Housing Rights and Forced Expulsions in Italy: Recent Developments under the European Social Charter Collective Complaints System' (2011) 11 Human Rights Law Review 343.

[100] For a more detailed evaluation also in terms of the de facto high level of scrutiny adopted, see the preceding chapter in this book on systemic discrimination.

[101] For example, *Amnesty International v Italy* Comm 178/2019 (ECSR, 18 October 2023) para 68.

ensure their effective enjoyment of fundamental rights.[102] In this context, merely spending a lot of resources is still considered insufficient when the effect on the ground is simply non-existent (eg in terms of living conditions), due to the lack of a coherent and coordinated national approach.[103]

The ECSR has not developed clear rules or parameters relative to either the standard of proof or the proper allocation of the burden of proof. In addition, the final evaluations of the ECSR tend to identify violations of the prohibition of discrimination without distinguishing between direct and indirect discrimination. In the case law on Roma, the ECSR seems most at ease when dealing with complaints in the frame of indirect discrimination, and by emphasizing related duties of differential treatment.[104] This preference is understandable, as a collective complaint procedure naturally enables critical review of the disproportionate impacts of a measure or practice. In line with the collective nature of the complaints before it, the Committee relies heavily on reports of UN treaty bodies such as the UN Committee on Economic, Social and Cultural Rights and bodies of the EU and the Council of Europe, like the ECRI, the Advisory Committee of the Framework Convention for the protection of National Minorities (FCNM), the EU's Fundamental Rights Agency, other EU bodies, and international NGOs.[105] The ECSR also has regard to its own decisions on collective complaints against the same state.[106] In cases that fit the indirect discrimination frame, the Committee proceeds to discuss counter-arguments of the government, whereby it acknowledges at least implicitly that general reports are sufficient to shift the burden of proof to the state.

The ECSR's reluctance to address direct discrimination is visible in some cases. In *ERT v Bulgaria*, for instance, the Committee explicitly states that 'legislative measures ... targeted the Roma population, as during the debates preceding the adoption of the reform the situation of Roma minors ... was explicitly taken into account'.[107] This recognition of potential evidence of direct discrimination is not further developed in the case, however, as the ECSR instead proceeds with its typical focus on indirect discrimination and duties of differential treatment.[108]

The Committee decisively condemns prohibited direct discrimination in so far as this is visible in public documents, such as policies that explicitly target Roma,

[102] *Equal Rights Trust v Bulgaria* Comm 121/2016 (ECSR, 16 October 2018) para 94.

[103] *Amnesty International v Italy* (n 101) paras 98–99.

[104] *ERT v Bulgaria* Comm 121/2016 (ECSR, 16 October 2015) para 80; *ERRC v Bulgaria* Comm 151/2017 (ECSR, 5 December 2018) paras 82.

[105] See inter alia *ERT v Bulgaria* Comm 121/2016 (ECSR, 16 October 2015) paras 90–91, which relies on statistics of the FRA, the European Parliament and Council of Europe reports, and *ERTF v Czech Republic* Comm 104/2014 (ECSR, 17 May 2016) paras 76–77, 123, which relies on reports from the ECRI and the UN Committee on Economic, Social and Cultural Rights.

[106] See inter alia *ERRC v Bulgaria* Comm 151/2017 (ECSR, 5 December 2018) para 85 referring to *ERRC v Bulgaria* Comm 46/2007 (ECSR, 3 December 2008); *ERT v Bulgaria* Comm 121/2016 (ECSR, 16 October 2018) para 89.

[107] *ERT v Bulgaria* Comm 121/2016 (ECSR, 16 October 2018) para 86.

[108] ibid paras 80, 87.

or having police units focused on Roma.[109] In other cases, without explicit differentiations on the basis of race, the ECSR appears to struggle to find an appropriate approach. Collective complaints imply less need for individualized proof, but the Committee still requires 'sufficient proof' at the group level. In this regard the ECSR has opined that a few individual cases would not necessarily reach the level of proof required on the 'group level'.[110] Due to the lack of explicit reasoning in this respect, no further parameters are provided.

*ERRC and MDAC v Czech Republic*,[111] a case on the disproportionate placement of Roma children into public care, emphasized one important positive obligation, but also demonstrated reluctance on the part of the ECSR to find discrimination even in the face of significant evidence. The complaint referred to official statistics that clearly revealed that Roma children were overrepresented in public care in the Czech Republic. The Committee considered that the data on ethnic distribution of children in schools was insufficient, while acknowledging that there were significant indications of a particularly high number of Roma children being in public care.[112] Positively, the Committee identified a state duty to collect data when there is a generally acknowledged risk of a disparate impact on a particular group.[113] Unfortunately, the ECSR reached no inferences from the lack of such official ethnic specific data, finding neither direct nor indirect discrimination[114]—though the Committee did find a violation of the substantive right concerned.[115]

## 4. Emerging Lines of Jurisprudence on the Burden of Proof: Comparative Notes on the ECtHR and the ECSR

The lack of explicit treaty standards on the burden of proof obliges us to look for standards in the jurisprudence of icourts. The preceding paragraphs have discussed the jurisprudence of two European courts with ample jurisprudence on Roma, the prototypical example of a group suffering systemic discrimination in European states, entailing a variety of cases all set against a background of systemic discrimination. Here, some comparative notes are made about the respective jurisprudential lines that have developed so far.

The two European courts have fundamentally different complaints procedures, which implies different challenges in terms of the burden of proof. The ECtHR emphasizes the importance of focusing on the circumstances of the specific case

109 *Amnesty International v Italy* (n 101) paras 74–76.
110 *ERRC v Bulgaria* Comm 151/2017 (ECSR, 5 December 2018) para 50.
111 *ERRC and MDAC v Czech Republic* Comm 151/2017 (ECSR, 5 December 2018).
112 ibid paras 172–73.
113 ibid para 172.
114 ibid para 175.
115 *In casu* Art 17 on social protection of children.

before it and is reticent about drawing inferences from general reports, even when these concern trends of discrimination against the group concerned. The ECSR's focus on collective complaints at times make it hesitant to establish a collective violation on the basis of information about a range of individual cases. In addition, the two icourts have different basic approaches to reviewing discrimination complaints. Whereas the ECtHR was traditionally very reluctant to even evaluate discrimination complaints, let alone conclude that a prohibited violation had taken place, the ECSR has been alert to problems of systemic discrimination suffered by the Roma and has not been hesitant to identify a discriminatory nexus to social rights violations.

The ECtHR has consistently indicated that it requires violations to be proven 'beyond reasonable doubt'. The standard of proof required is ambiguous, however, as the Court has also emphasized that it does not intend to suggest that it requires the same demanding standard of proof the term connotes in a national criminal law context. Nonetheless, the Court still seems to require that violations be proven to a high standard. In this context, the special allocation of the burden of proof that has been used in discrimination cases does imply an alleviation of the burden of proof for victims. The ECSR has not been explicit about what standard of proof it employs. Nevertheless, it is obvious that the Committee is less reticent to conclude that prohibited discrimination has taken place and thus, seems to operate with a de facto lower standard of proof.

The ECtHR has very distinct lines of development regarding the special allocation of the burden of proof for direct discrimination on the one hand and indirect discrimination on the other. The ECtHR had difficulties in coming to terms with the notion of indirect discrimination, and in finding a suitable allocation of the burden of proof in cases involving evidence of discrimination against groups. Here it is important to return to the distinct steps of the special allocation of the burden of proof. One of the reasons the Court struggled with allowing statistics to establish a prima facie case of indirect differentiation on racial ground could very well be that the indirect causal link would then be impossible to negate. Because for indirect differentiation on racial ground there is the possibility of justification by the government, the ECtHR in 2007 'came around'. Since then, the special allocation of the burden of proof for indirect discrimination was accepted and the criteria have been fine-tuned. For direct discrimination, and more particularly hidden direct discrimination, the ECtHR remains reticent to adopt the special allocation of the burden of proof. This reticence can be explained by the scant possibilities the government would have to negate or justify differential treatment once a prima facie case of direct discrimination was established. The reticence is visible in the lack of guidance concerning the *Nachova* criteria, while the ECtHR has de facto set too high a threshold for a *prima facie* case to be established, even in the context of systemic discrimination.

In this 'setting' of limited reduction of the burden of proof on claimants in cases of direct discrimination, the ECtHR has identified a distinct procedural dimension of the prohibition of discrimination. This allows the Court to sanction the failure to investigate possible discriminatory motives of misdeeds. While this additional dimension allows for findings of prohibited discrimination in instances where there is not sufficient proof for the ECtHR to establish direct discrimination and may push public authorities to conduct investigations, it avoids recognizing that both dimensions may be intertwined. Put differently, the Court has so far not addressed the manner in which (grave) investigatory flaws should be taken as supporting the establishment of a prima facie case of substantive discrimination.

The ECSR is less elaborate in its reasoning and does not explicitly discuss the allocation of the burden of proof. The Committee's overall readiness to evaluate discrimination complaints and recognize discrimination implies it also applies a de facto lower threshold to shift the burden of justification to the government. The group dimension implicit in collective complaints helps the Committee to rely on general reports from other supervisory bodies and consider these sufficient to shift the burden. These general reports are particularly useful in establishing indirect discrimination, which seems the preferred 'route' for the ECSR. The Committee is also explicit about the context of systemic discrimination towards Roma. For direct discrimination, the Committee requires more specificity and has been reluctant to move from individual instances to findings of systemic violation. The Committee has provided no further guidance on what would be required to bridge this gap. The ECSR has also identified and underscored states' duty to undertake proper ethnic data collection, in order to measure the disproportionate impact of particular laws and policies. Nevertheless, when a state has failed to do so, the Committee has been unwilling to conclude on the basis of the absence of official data, and the presence of other information suggesting disproportionate impact, that discrimination had taken place.[116]

While the two European courts have distinct *modi operandi* in relation to discrimination complaints, both need to provide further guidance in relation to the burden of proof and its allocation between the parties, particularly relative to direct discrimination. Furthermore, both bodies have demonstrated reticence in drawing inferences, including from failures in investigatory duties and from failures to engage in ethnic data collection. In this respect, further elaboration of the relevant standards would be welcomed.

## 5. Conclusion

Both the standard of proof and the allocation of the burden of proof are of critical importance to the effective protection against human rights violations. Irrespective

[116] See the analysis in section 3 above on *ERRC and MDAC v Czech Republic* (n 111).

thereof, human rights treaties have not specified detailed rules on the standard and burden of proof.[117] Hence, the rules about the burden of proof need to be and have been made jurisprudentially, through lines of jurisprudence developed by icourts. A special allocation of the burden of proof in cases of alleged discrimination seems to be widely accepted, but there is still considerable uncertainty among national courts about the parameters for establishing a prima facie case and its rebuttal. As the preceding analysis has clarified, landmark cases for the burden of proof and the prohibition of discrimination have often concerned Roma. This reflects their vulnerability to human rights violations, which in turn is related to the systemic discrimination they suffer and underlying ingrained prejudice. The fight for Roma rights has thus pushed forward the boundaries of human rights, including relative to the burden of proof.

This chapter focused on the jurisprudence of two European courts, considering a substantial number of cases regarding Roma and an analysis of developing lines of jurisprudence on the allocation of the burden of proof between the parties. The special allocation of the burden of proof implies a reduction of the burden of proof on the claimant, in that the claimant does not have to establish differential treatment on racial grounds, but can suffice by presenting evidence that allows a court to establish a prima facie case thereof. The burden of proof then shifts to the government, which can try to negate the causal link. If this negation is successful then there is nothing that needs justification and the case has come to an end. If the government cannot negate the prima facie case, it is established that there is a 'differential treatment on grounds of race', which still leaves the possibility for the government to 'justify' this differential treatment. This chapter paid particular attention to the question of whether a context of systemic discrimination should have implications for the burden of proof and more particularly the threshold for establishing a prima facie case.

The preceding analysis has demonstrated that in the end both the ECtHR and the ECSR are ready to (de facto) identify prima facie case of indirect discrimination on the basis of general reports of supervisory bodies and NGOs, while there has been more reticence in relation to prima facie cases of hidden direct discrimination.[118] The ECSR has been more willing to engage with discrimination complaints and often more ready to acknowledge the discriminatory nexus than the ECtHR. The ECSR's collective complaints consider broader contextual information per se, and the ECSR also readily acknowledges the systemic discrimination

[117] Some EU equality directives have gone further in this area. These include Directive 97/80/EC on the burden of proof in cases of discrimination based on sex; Art 19 Directive 2006/54/EC on the implementation of the principle of equal opportunities and equal treatment of men and women in matters of employment and occupation (recast); Art 8 Directive 2000/43; and Art 8 Directive 2000/78.

[118] See also Samantha Besson, 'Evolutions in Non-Discrimination Law within the ECHR and the ESC Systems: It Takes Two to Tango in the Council of Europe' (2012) 60 American Journal of Comparative Law 147.

faced by Roma. However, the ECSR has not explicitly laid out its approach to the standard of proof and the allocation of the burden of proof, which entails a lack of guidance to national authorities. Having clear standards on these subjects would not only be preferable from a rule of law perspective, but could also strengthen the Committee's reasoning in support of findings of prohibited indirect and direct discrimination.

The ECtHR has developed more explicit standards and jurisprudence in relation to the special allocation of the burden of proof for indirect discrimination. The Court is invited to implement the *Nachova* criteria informing the allocation of the burden of proof for cases of hidden direct racial discrimination, while not setting too high the threshold to establish a prima facie case.

Furthermore, in cases of systemic discrimination, as in the case of Roma, flaws in the police investigation of suspicious killings and beatings on the one hand and substantive discrimination on the other are clearly correlated in practice. In such contexts of ingrained prejudice it is likely that the lack of proper investigations is informed by prejudice. However, the ECtHR has so far not drawn such related inferences from procedural flaws in investigations in such contexts. The ECtHR is called upon to reconsider possible inferences between procedural flaws and findings of substantive discrimination.

Icourts' mandate to monitor state compliance ultimately aims at optimizing the effective protection of human rights. This can only be done through the adoption of clear, effective procedural and evidential standards. Accordingly, this chapter calls on the ECtHR and the ECSR to adopt clearer, more elaborate guidance on the allocation of the burden of proof in cases of discrimination, and particularly hidden direct discrimination. Among other things, this chapter has formulated some suggestions on the ways in which the *Nachova* criteria could be elaborated upon; has emphasized that contexts of systemic discrimination should be centrally taken into account; and has invited the ECtHR to reconsider drawing inferences from procedural flaws relative to substantive discrimination.

The multiple human rights violations suffered by Roma have generated a multitude of cases, several of which have become landmark judgments as regards the allocation of the burden of proof. European courts are invited to further develop clear standards of assessment concerning the burden of proof, which will enable them to play a leading role in this area in the future, advancing the protection of human rights.

# PART III

# STRATEGIC ROMA RIGHTS LITIGATION IN EUROPEAN COURTS

# 8

# Anti-Roma Hate Speech Before the European Court of Human Rights

## Revisiting the Concept of Vulnerability in the Human Rights Paradigm

*Aleksandra Gliszczyńska-Grabias* and Anna Śledzińska-Simon***

## 1. Introduction

Hostility towards Roma,[1] also known as 'anti-Gypsyism',[2] is one of the most glaring examples of hatred and violence based on race and ethnicity.[3] In Europe, anti-Gypsyism is recognized as 'a specific form of racism, an ideology founded on racial superiority, a form of dehumanisation and institutional racism nurtured by historical discrimination, which is expressed, among others, by violence, hate speech, exploitation, stigmatisation and the most blatant kind of discrimination.'[4]

* The research presented in this chapter by Aleksandra Gliszczyńska-Grabias was conducted within research project no UMO-2019/33/B/HS5/01634 (contract number), financed by the National Science Centre.

** The research presented in this chapter by Anna Śledzińska-Simon was conducted within research project no UMO-2021/41/B/HS5/01421 (contract number) financed by the National Science Centre.

[1] In our analysis, we use the word 'Roma' as an umbrella term which includes different related groups, whether sedentary or not, such as Roma, Travellers, Gens du voyage, Resandefolket/De resande, Sinti, Camminanti, Manouches, Kalés, Romanichels, Boyash/Rudari, Ashkalis, Égyptiens, Yéniches, Doms, Loms, and Abdal that may be diverse in culture and lifestyles. We note that the use of terms corresponding to the postulates of the vulnerable groups affected should be perceived as a positive development within human rights discourse.

[2] In this chapter, we use the term 'anti-Roma' to denote anti-Gypsyism and Roma discrimination as forms of racism. See more at <https://holocaustremembrance.com/resources/working-definition-antigypsyism-anti-roma-discrimination> accessed 10 June 2024.

[3] See Ad hoc Committee of Experts on Roma and Traveller Issues (CAHROM), 'The thematic group on combating anti-Gypsyism, hate speech and hate crime against Roma' (December 2013) <https://rm.coe.int/native/16800890fb> accessed 10 June 2024; Zoë James, 'Hate Crimes Against Gypsies, Travellers and Roma in Europe' in Nathan Hall, Abbee Corb, Paul Giannasi, and John GD Grieve (eds), *The International Handbook of Hate Crime* (Routledge 2015); Ismael Cortés Gómez and Markus End (eds), *Dimensions of Antigypsyism in Europe* (European Network Against Racism (ENAR) and the Central Council of German Sinti and Roma 2019).

[4] ECRI, General Policy Recommendation No 13 'On combating anti-Gypsyism and discrimination against Roma' (2020) 3 <https://rm.coe.int/ecrigeneral-policy-recommendation-no-13-on-combating-antigypsyism-an/16808b5aee > accessed 10 June 2024.

Aleksandra Gliszczyńska-Grabias and Anna Śledzińska-Simon, *Anti-Roma Hate Speech Before the European Court of Human Rights* In: *The Rights of Roma in European Courts.* Edited by: Kristin Henrard and Lilla Farkas, Oxford University Press. © Aleksandra Gliszczyńska-Grabias and Anna Śledzińska-Simon 2025.
DOI: 10.1093/oso/9780198914358.003.0008

Severe human rights violations against Roma are deeply intertwined with social issues, as centuries-old prejudices and stereotypes remain deeply ingrained in the public perception of Roma across Europe today.[5] Hate-motivated physical and verbal violence, police brutality, forced expulsions, segregation of Roma children in schools, discrimination in access to healthcare, and the forced sterilization of Roma women are among the most pervasive abuses they face. Despite efforts to combat these injustices, hateful attitudes and violent attacks against the Roma community have not diminished but rather increased in recent decades.[6]

The history of the persecution of the Roma, along with their current disadvantaged position, renders them a vulnerable group. The European Court of Human Rights (ECtHR/Strasbourg Court) first addressed the significance of this vulnerability in *Chapman v United Kingdom*.[7] The Court ruled that the vulnerable status of Gypsies as a minority necessitates special consideration of their needs and way of life, forming part of the state's positive obligations under the European Convention of Human Rights (ECHR). Later, it reaffirmed this position, stating that 'as a result of their turbulent history and constant uprooting, the Roma have become a specific type of disadvantaged and vulnerable minority' in need of special protection.[8] We adopt this position as a starting point for our further analysis, which assumes that the Roma are a vulnerable group.

The concept of vulnerability has gained increasing popularity not only in public discussions of the social dimensions of discrimination, but also in legal science. It is seen as a powerful tool for dealing with structural inequalities, demanding both a higher level of judicial scrutiny and broadening the scope of positive obligations for states.[9] As Peroni and Timmer point out, the concept of group vulnerability helps achieve substantive equality.[10] As it turns out, however, this model does not extend equally to the Roma. Put differently, their achievement of substantive equality in the protection of rights is a very arduous and slow process.[11]

[5] Anna Kende, Márton Hadarics, and Barbara Lášticová, 'Anti-Roma attitudes as expressions of dominant social norms in Eastern Europe' (2017) 60 International Journal of Intercultural Relations 12.

[6] See eg Commissioner for Human Rights, *Human Rights of Roma and Travellers in Europe* (Council of Europe Publishing 2012).

[7] In this case, the Court found that national authorities have a positive obligation resulting from Art 8 of the Convention to facilitate the Gypsy way of life. *Chapman v United Kingdom* App no 27238/95 (ECtHR, 18 January 2001) para 96; see also *Buckley v United Kingdom* App no 20348/92 (ECtHR, 29 September 1996).

[8] *Horvath and Kiss v Hungary* App no 11146/11 (ECtHR, 29 January 2013) para 102.

[9] Andrea Broderick, 'A Reflection on Substantive Equality Jurisprudence: The Standard of Scrutiny at the ECtHR for Differential Treatment of Roma and Persons with Disabilities' (2014) 15(1-2) International Journal of Discrimination and the Law 1. See also Ingrid Nifosi-Sutton, 'The Vulnerability Paradigm of the European Court of Human Rights' in Ingrid Nifosi-Sutton, *The Protection of Vulnerable Groups under International Human Rights Law* (Routledge 2017).

[10] Lourdes Peroni and Alexandra Timmer, 'Vulnerable Groups: The Promise of an Emerging Concept in European Human Rights Convention Law' (2013) 11(4) International Journal of Constitutional Law 1065, 1074.

[11] See Kristin Henrard, 'The European Court of Human Rights, Ethnic and Religious Minorities and the Two Dimensions of the Right to Equal Treatment: Jurisprudence at Different Speeds?' (2016) 34(3) Nordic Journal of Human Rights 157.

This chapter aims to explore the scope and degree of protection provided to members of vulnerable groups who fall victim to hate speech and hate crime. We focus specifically on whether the ECtHR's approach to anti-Roma hatred may itself reflect structural discrimination, as it potentially mirrors the widespread societal hostility towards Roma communities across Europe. While we concur with Waldron's assertion that '[a]ll victims of hate speech become vulnerable, because hate hurts, humiliates, and intimidates,'[12] we question whether the ECtHR's jurisprudence sufficiently counters or instead inadvertently perpetuates this vulnerability. In essence, in this chapter we aim to evaluate whether the concept of vulnerability operates as a tool for pushing or limiting the boundaries of the human rights paradigm in cases concerning Roma victims of hate.

The chapter proceeds as follows: section 2 explores the significance of vulnerability in developing human rights protection systems and difficulties in implementing this concept to safeguard Roma rights. Section 3 discusses the evolution of positive state obligations, particularly in determining the scope of human rights protection for Roma victims of hate speech and hate crimes. Sections 4 and 5 delve deeper into the inconsistencies and variations in the Court's reasoning when addressing hate speech and cases related to the Holocaust across different groups. The discussion advances to section 6, which tackles the issue of victim status—a particularly troubling aspect of this chapter's focus. Section 7 provides the conclusion.[13]

## 2. The Concept of Vulnerability and its Application to the Protection of Roma Rights

Historically, human rights have been conceived as the rights of minorities, with successive international human rights treaties addressing the specific collective and individual needs of members of minority groups.[14] The core human rights treaties do not explicitly mention the concept of vulnerability.[15] However, the adoption of distinct international treaties tailored to specific groups implicitly acknowledges their unique vulnerabilities and marginalized status within society—often stemming from a history of persecution, systemic injustice, or social exclusion. This recognition highlights the need for targeted legal frameworks

[12] Jeremy Waldron, *The Harm in Hate Speech* (Harvard University Press 2012).

[13] The present chapter was prepared as part of the research project on vulnerability, funded by the Polish National Science Centre (Research Grant OPUS 2019/33/B/HS5/01634).

[14] Wiktor Osiatyński, *Human Rights and Their Limits* (CUP 2009).

[15] Athanasia Spiliopoulou Åkermark, *Justifications of Minority Protection in International Law* (Martinus Nijhoff Publishers 1997).

to address the entrenched inequalities these groups face and to provide them with enhanced protections under international law.[16]

The universal and regional special 'sub-systems of human rights protection' created on this basis (for racial, ethnic, and national minorities, women, children, persons with disabilities, etc) expressly confirm their rights, and thus the need to remedy their disadvantaged position. These groups have been persecuted or excluded from legal protection in the past and continue to be under- or disproportionately represented in legislative and decision-making processes. Without human rights, and especially without international human rights protection mechanisms, those in power (ruling majorities) are inclined to disregard minority rights or not take them seriously. However, this counter-majoritarian understanding of human rights is subject to criticism and revision, and it is one of the main causes of populist backlash.[17] Moreover, in many parts of the world, we are witnessing the misappropriation of the very concept of human rights, seized to serve majority interests.[18]

The concept of vulnerability in the human rights paradigm may be used in two distinct contexts.[19] The first one, where vulnerability is related to personal constraints: here some groups are identified as vulnerable due to their fragile physical or mental condition. This kind of vulnerability is closely connected to the physical fragility of the persons belonging to these groups, but also because of the social perception of such persons as weaker, more prone to becoming victims of human rights violations, as not being able to protect themselves from various forms of abuse. Secondly, there is also a reading of vulnerability as related to social positions: in this context some groups are identified as vulnerable due to structural discrimination or disadvantage they experience, or critical situations they face. While in the first above-mentioned context the vulnerability of the groups can lead to the advancement of the protection offered, in the case of vulnerability related to social position, the challenges appear to be of a more complex nature. The latter challenges are closely related to prejudice and often hostile attitudes towards the members of the groups so defined. It should also be noted that structural discrimination that both results from and causes further vulnerability is much more challenging. At the same time, there can be no doubt that race and ethnicity are

[16] Audrey R Chapman and Benjamin Carbonetti, 'Human Rights Protections for Vulnerable and Disadvantaged Groups: The Contributions of the UN Committee on Economic, Social and Cultural Rights' (2011) 33(3) Human Rights Quarterly 682–732.

[17] Anna Śledzińska-Simon, 'Learning Lessons from the Populist Defeats: From Negative to Positive Constitutionalism' (2023) 32(6) Social and Legal Studies 893.

[18] Gráinne de Búrca, Katharine G Young, 'The (Mis)Appropriation of Human Rights by the New Global Right: An Introduction to the Symposium' (2023) 21(1) International Journal of Constitutional Law 205–23.

[19] Joana Abrisketa and others, 'Human Rights Priorities in the European Union's External and Internal Policies: An Assessment of Consistency with a Special Focus on Vulnerable Groups' (FP7-FRAME, 2016) <https://www.fp7-frame.eu/wp-content/uploads/2016/08/24-Deliverable-12.2.pdf> accessed 10 June 2024.

factors that increase the risk of vulnerability, regardless of the exact definition or context. And thus, among vulnerable groups, some can find themselves in a particularly critical position due to multiple factors that expose them to human rights violations.[20]

Given these two contexts, Roma are undoubtedly a special category of 'vulnerable' group. On the one hand, they are perceived as socially vulnerable, mainly due to their lack of social resources or access to them, including knowledge of the official language, the legal system or their rights. On the other hand, violations of their rights are largely 'normalized' as a result of exclusions (from the education system, health care, social housing, vocational training) which are rationalized as a voluntary 'opt-out' from the legal protection of human rights, ie due to lifestyles and other life choices often linked to Roma culture and traditions. Consequently, violations of Roma rights do not arouse as much public outrage as they do for other groups.[21]

Roma vulnerability is particularly visible in the context of verbal attacks, insults, and incitement to hatred they experience. Such manifestations of hatred are nowadays labelled as 'hate speech'.[22] Although there is no binding legal definition of hate speech in human rights treaties so far, the most visible convergence in the legal approaches towards hate speech exists among the European states. On this basis, the CoE Committee of Ministers recognized as hate speech '[a]ll forms of expression which spread, incite, promote or justify racial hatred, xenophobia, antisemitism or other forms of hatred based on intolerance, including: intolerance expressed by aggressive nationalism and ethnocentrism, discrimination and hostility against minorities, migrants and people of immigrant origin'.[23] The very idea of introducing a legal category of hate speech was triggered by an emerging need to indicate limits to freedom of expression in multinational, multicultural, and multireligious societies, with its roots in the aftermath of the Holocaust, and the horrific effects of Nazi propaganda of hatred towards Jews and Roma.[24]

[20] Eg Audrey R Chapman and Benjamin Carbonetti, 'Human Rights Protections for Vulnerable and Disadvantaged Groups: The Contributions of the UN Committee on Economic, Social and Cultural Rights' (2011) 33(3) Human Rights Quarterly 682; Dorothy Estrada-Tanck, *Human Security and Human Rights under International Law: The Protections Offered to Persons Confronting Structural Vulnerability* (Hart Publishing 2016); Oddný Mjöll Arnardóttir, 'Vulnerability under Article 14 of the European Convention on Human Rights. Innovation or Business as Usual?' (2017) 4(3) Oslo Law Review 150; Corina Heri, *Responsive Human Rights Vulnerability, Ill-treatment and the ECtHR* (Hart Publishing 2021).

[21] Jacqueline Bhabha, Andrzej Mirga, and Margareta Matache (eds), *Realizing Roma rights* (University of Pennsylvania Press 2017).

[22] See Bartosz Hordecki, 'What and Why is Missing in Theoretical and Practical Discourses on the So-Called "Hate Speech" Against the Roma Communities?' (2017) 32(4) Journal of Media Ethics 242.

[23] Committee of Ministers of the Council of Europe, Recommendation No R (97) 20 to member states on 'hate speech' (30 October 1997). < https://rm.coe.int/CoERMPublicCommonSearchServices/DisplayDCTMContent?documentId=0900001680645b44> accessed 10 June 2024.

[24] Jeffrey Herf, *The Jewish Enemy: Nazi Propaganda during World War II and the Holocaust* (Harvard University Press 2008).

However, Roma have been labelled the 'forgotten victims' of the Holocaust, remaining to this day outside the mainstream of Holocaust memory. This historical marginalization reflects broader social neglect and underscores the continuing challenges Roma communities face in seeking recognition and justice. Despite the atrocities committed against Roma during the Holocaust and the enormity of their suffering, Roma have often been excluded from the collective memory and narratives that shape post-Holocaust remembrance. This exclusion not only perpetuates their invisibility, but also underscores the critical need for a more inclusive and comprehensive approach to historical justice and contemporary human rights protection. As movingly stated in the opening part of the recent book by Ari Joskowicz:

> Across Europe, Jews and Roma died together at the hands of the same murderers, in the very same places. Yet the world did not register and acknowledge their destruction equally. In the years and decades that followed, Jews managed to have their accounts of persecution heard and documented. Roma, by contrast, struggled to gain recognition of everything they had suffered and lost.[25]

Today, hatred against Roma does not seem to provoke the same level of public protest, emotion, and rejection as racism against other groups. Often, drastic Nazi-style manifestations of hatred against Roma go unaddressed by the media or the public. Such events were the backdrop of the case *Király and Dömötör v Hungary*,[26] which concerned the failure of local authorities to respond to public speeches containing racist threats against Roma by demonstrators armed with sticks, stones, whips, and metal pipes. Furthermore, as stated in the submission to the Court, 'two of the demonstrators leading the march had a list and had pointed out to the crowd the houses that were inhabited by Roma people'.[27]

In conclusion, vulnerability and hate speech are closely linked, as vulnerable groups tend to be more prone to hate speech. Verbal hatred can be not only offensive or demeaning to the person at whom it is directed, but also reflects on the group as a whole, contributing to its further marginalization and exclusion. Moreover, group hatred present in public spaces is one of the 'early warning' signals that a group is one of those in need of special legal protection. It is for these reasons that the drastic and systemic nature of hatred and prejudice against Roma requires an effective legal response. However, public reactions to hatred against Roma appear to be much more ambivalent than in the case of hatred directed against other 'others'. The question remains whether the legal responses to anti-Roma hate speech, including ECtHR's case law, are equally ambivalent.

[25] Ari Joskowicz, *Rain of Ash: Roma, Jews, and the Holocaust* (Princeton University Press 2023) 2.
[26] *Király and Dömötör v Hungary* App no 10851/13 (ECtHR, 17 January 2017).
[27] ibid para 13.

## 3. Positive State Obligations in the Context of Anti-Roma Hate Crime and Hate Speech

This section examines the evolution of the concept of positive obligations in addressing the challenges of providing effective human rights protection for Roma victims. Our argument is structured as follows: first, we trace the evolution of the scope and nature of positive state obligations. Next, we analyse how the development of this concept has facilitated the identification of human rights violations in cases involving Roma victims that were previously neglected. Finally, we investigate how this concept has contributed to more effective protection against hate speech.

The ECtHR devised the doctrine of positive state obligations to secure and guarantee effective human rights protection.[28] The Court's dictum in the *Belgian Linguistic case*[29] marks the beginning of a growing recognition that virtually all the provisions of the Convention imply not only negative but also positive state obligations. This expansion of positive state obligations can definitely be welcomed as broadening the boundaries of human rights protection. As rightly noted by Mowbray, the Court's expansive approach to the concept of positive obligations approach serves as a tool of 'dynamic interpretation of the convention in the light of changing social and moral assumptions'.[30]

The concept of negative obligations of states, particularly in relation to civil and political rights such as those enshrined in the European Convention on Human Rights, is more straightforward: states are required to refrain from arbitrarily interfering with the rights and freedoms guaranteed. Specifically, within the context of freedom of speech, this translates into the state's obligation to avoid interference in the free expression of views, ideas, or any other speech-related content. Conversely, positive state obligations require national authorities to take necessary measures to safeguard a right.[31] This entails adopting reasonable and suitable measures to protect such right, including shielding individuals from interferences by private parties. In essence, while negative obligations focus on non-interference, positive obligations emphasize proactive protection and promotion of rights.[32] The latter difference, may explain why, in general, states enjoy per definition a wide margin of discretion in the manner in which they implement positive obligations.

[28] On some aspects of the doctrone see Vladislava Stoyanova, 'Fault, Knowledge and Risk within the Framework of Positive Obligations under the European Convention on Human Rights' (2020) 33 Leiden Journal of International Law 601. See also Lilla Farkas and Theodoros Alexandridis, 'The Potential of Positive Obligations Against Romaphobic Attitudes and in the Development of "Roma Pride"' (2020) 13(3) Erasmus Law Review 65.

[29] *Case 'relating to certain aspects of the laws on the use of languages in education in Belgium' v Belgium (merits)* App nos 1474/62, 1677/62, 1691/62, 1769/63, 1994/63 and 2126/64 (ECtHR, 23 July 1968).

[30] Alastair R Mowbray, *The Development of Positive Obligations under the European Convention on Human Rights by the European Court of Human Rights* (Hart Publishing 2004) 5.

[31] *Hokkanen v Finland* App no 19823/92 (ECtHR, 24 August 1994).

[32] *López-Ostra v Spain* App no 16798/90 (ECtHR, 9 December 1994).

At the same time, it is important to emphasize that the Court, in its rulings, identifies actions that states have failed to take in order to effectively fulfil their positive obligations. In other words, while states generally have greater discretion in fulfilling their positive obligations compared to their negative obligations under the Convention, the Court provides guidance on which failures by state authorities have led to human right violations. Therefore, we cannot speak of a general or closed list of positive obligations. However, some of the most typical examples of such obligations include ensuring effective procedures for, for example, investigation or prosecution, enforcement of judicial sanctions, as well as preventing and responding to human rights violations by third parties. Furthermore, the concept of positive obligations is extremely helpful in combating violations resulting from the actions of third parties, for example in the area of racially motivated violence, or hate speech.[33] In this way, the concept of positive state obligations enables the provision of genuine and effective protection of human rights in horizontal relations.

The evolution of the concept of positive obligations is characterized by several key trends. First, these obligations complement negative obligations, thereby broadening the scope of protection in situations where mere inaction by the state is insufficient to effectively safeguard rights or freedoms. Second, over the years, the Court has expanded its jurisprudence to encompass freedom-oriented rights, such as the right to respect for private and family life, freedom of expression, and the rights to association and assembly. Third, as this concept has evolved, there has been a noticeable reduction in the state's margin of discretion regarding actions necessary to fulfil its positive obligations.

This evolution is evident in the Court's case law concerning homophobic speech. In *Identoba and Others v Georgia*,[34] the Court found that the national authorities had violated their positive obligations under Article 11, read in conjunction with Article 14, by failing to provide effective protection to the applicants, who had participated in the gay pride event, against homophobic and violent attacks by counter-demonstrators. In a similar case of a homophobic attack, but on the internet, the Court found 'the failure on the part of the relevant public authorities to discharge their positive obligation to investigate in an effective manner whether the comments regarding the applicants' sexual orientation constituted incitement to hatred and violence.'[35] It held that 'by downplaying the seriousness of the comments, the authorities at the very least tolerated them'.[36] In this case, the Court stressed that the choice of means to ensure compliance with Article 8 regarding protection against acts by individuals generally falls within the state's

[33] Tuğba Sarıkaya Güler, '"Positive Obligations" Doctrine of the European Court of Human Rights: Is it Cogent or Obscure?' (2017) 2(6) European Journal of Multidisciplinary Studies 359.

[34] *Identoba and Others v Georgia* App no 73235/12 (ECtHR, 12 May 2015).

[35] *Beizaras and Levickas v Lithuania* App no 41288/15 (ECtHR, 14 January 2020) para 129.

[36] ibid para 129.

margin of appreciation, but effective deterrence against serious acts affecting essential aspects of private life necessitates efficient criminal law provisions.[37]

Relying on the concept of positive obligations, Roma rights advocates have successfully advanced procedural state obligations. Initially, the Court only recognized the state's duty to conduct an effective investigation into the circumstances of deaths or acts amounting to torture or cruel, inhuman, or degrading treatment within the procedural prongs of Articles 2 and 3 of the Convention. Notably, the adoption of this rigorous standard developed gradually over the years, similar to the recognition of the state's positive obligation to investigate racist motives in crimes. Nevertheless, as rightly observed by Goldstone, '[t]e fact that, in such a short space of time, some arguments have carried the day in Europe's highest merits examination, if not celebration'.[38]

In the landmark judgment *Nachova and Others v Bulgaria*,[39] the Grand Chamber recognized that the positive obligation arising from Article 14 of the Convention, in conjunction with Article 2, necessitates that the state investigates the racist motives behind violent actions. Following the *Nachova* case, the Court's interpretation of positive obligations under Articles 2 and 3 of the Convention mandates a prompt, impartial, and effective investigation into the racist motives behind crimes targeting Roma.[40] In this way, the concept of positive obligations paved the way for establishing a procedural dimension to the prohibition of discrimination, which applies throughout the Convention, including to Article 8 in cases of violence that fall below the Article 3 threshold.

In a number of judgments concerning positive obligations under Articles 8 and 14 of the Convention, the Court has qualified 'threats to cause a well-founded fear of violence', 'verbal assault and physical threats', 'harassment motivated by racism', or 'intentional intimidation' as unacceptable manifestations of racism against Roma. Furthermore, the Court found that the national authorities had not offered effective remedies in these cases. The lack of remedies for acts of racism was in itself a violation of Article 8 of the Convention, as it also covers the 'physical and mental integrity of the person'[41] and the 'ethnic identity of the individual'.[42]

More recently, the Court has identified new elements of positive state obligations in relation to hate speech in *Budinova and Chaprazov v Bulgaria*.[43] In this case, the

[37] ibid para 110.

[38] James A Goldston, 'The Struggle for Roma Rights: Arguments that Have Worked' (2010) 32(2) Human Rights Quarterly 311, 312.

[39] *Nachova and Others v Bulgaria* App nos 43577/98 and 43579/98 (ECtHR, 5 July 2005).

[40] *Burlya and Others v Ukraine* App no 3289/10 (ECtHR, 6 November 2018).

[41] *Beizaras and Levickas v Lithuania* (n 35) para 109.

[42] *Aksu v Turkey* App nos 4149/04, 41029/04 (ECtHR, 14 March 2012) para 58.

[43] *Budinova and Chaprazov v Bulgaria* App no 12567/13 (ECtHR, 16 February 2021). This judgment was accompanied by a second, almost identical one, issued in response to an application by Bulgarian nationals of Jewish ethnic origin, complaining about the lack of action taken by the Bulgarian authorities against a series of antisemitic statements. See *Behar and Gutman v Bulgaria* App no 29335/13 (ECtHR, 16 February 2021).

applicants claimed that various statements made by a Mr Siderov, the leader of Ataka, a xenophobic party, in his television programme, interviews, speeches, and a book constituted harassment and incitement to discrimination against Roma people. The applicants sought a court order requiring Mr Siderov to cease his discriminatory statements and restore the status quo ante by publicly apologizing for his remarks. In its landmark decision, the Court ruled that by failing to provide adequate redress for Mr Siderov's statements, the national authorities had failed in their positive duty to adequately address the applicants' ethnic discrimination. In particular, it held that the inadequate response to the racially discriminatory statements violated the applicants' right to respect for their private life. As a result, the Court found a violation of Article 8 in conjunction with Article 14 of the Convention.

In the following analysis, we will discuss how the ECtHR assesses the hate speech component in the Roma cases, omits references to Holocaust remembrance, and establishes victim status in hate speech cases directed against a group, with a challenging aspect of navigating between avoiding *actio popularis* and acknowledging the fact that group hatred rarely targets specific, named individuals. In each of the sections, we seek to determine whether the Court's approach pushes the boundaries of human rights protection, or rather reveals them.

## 4. Assessing the Hate Speech Component

Strasbourg case law reflects the ECtHR's awareness of the violent potential inherent in speech directed against vulnerable groups. However, the Court's prevailing approach often confines the recognition of hate speech to instances where it accompanies physical threats, and even then, it tends to identify race-related violence rather than address the broader scope of verbal aggression. The ECtHR judgment in *Koky and Others v Slovakia* offers a striking example of this tendency.[44]

In February 2002, several men, armed with baseball bats and iron rods and shouting racist threats, launched a violent assault on a Roma settlement. The ten applicants were brutally beaten during the attack, which followed an incident in a bar where a non-Roma waitress had refused to serve a Roma man. The applicants contended that Slovak authorities had failed to carry out a prompt, impartial, and effective investigation into the attack, attributing this failure to the likely racist motives behind the negligence. The ECtHR upheld the applicants' arguments, ruling that the investigation and the authorities' handling of the racially motivated attack were ineffective, amounting to a violation of Article 3 of the Convention (prohibition of torture or inhuman or degrading treatment).[45] This judgment underscores

[44] *Koky and others v Slovakia* App no 13624/03 (ECtHR, 12 June 2012).

[45] See also *Burlya and Others v Ukraine* (n 40); *Moldovan and Others v Romania (No 2)* App nos 41138/98 and 64320/01 (ECtHR, 12 July 2005).

the Court's recognition of the intersection between verbal racist threats and physical violence. Yet, it also highlights the Court's tendency to focus on the physical manifestation of violence, leaving the hateful, verbal incitement less fully examined in terms of its broader implications for state responsibility in preventing and addressing racist aggression.

In a similar vein, in the three cases against Hungary—*RB*,[46] *Király and Dömötör*,[47] and *Vona*,[48] the anti-Roma hate speech was not adequately identified or assessed. The first two cases, *RB* and *Király and Dömötör*, involved the failure of national authorities to properly investigate and prosecute incidents that took place during anti-Roma marches organized by right-wing political parties and their paramilitary supporters. In *RB*, the applicant was subjected to racist verbal abuse, including threats such as 'Go inside, you damned dirty gypsies' and 'We will build a house out of Roma blood', and faced an attempted assault while in the presence of her child.[49] In *Király and Dömötör*, masked demonstrators wielding sticks and whips chanted slogans like 'Roma, you will die' and 'We will burn your house down and you will die inside.'[50] While the ECtHR noted the racist nature of these slogans, it failed to sufficiently explore the extent of the state's responsibility to combat the most extreme racist content in the public sphere, particularly when directed against such a vulnerable minority. Although the physical threats posed during these events were severe, the hateful and genocidal rhetoric accompanying them carried an equally, if not more, profound potential for inciting violence. Therefore, special attention should be given to the genocidal undertones of these statements, as they constituted direct calls for violence against the Roma community.

The same concerns were raised in *Vona*, which was brought to Strasbourg by a hate-spreading organization involved in anti-Roma rallies. The case concerned the dissolution of an association because of its involvement in spreading open hatred against Roma. The association had also founded the Magyar Gárda Mozgalom (Hungarian Guard Movement—'the Movement'), whose aim was defined as 'defending Hungarians deprived of physical, spiritual and intellectual protection'.[51] Yet, this 'defence' mainly took the form of attacking Roma. The Court found that the dissolution of the organization did not amount to an infringement of freedom of association. The Court recalled that, as in the case of political parties, in this case too, the state was entitled to take preventive measures to defend democracy against organizations that undermine democratic values through direct violations of the rights of others.[52] In this case, a movement formed by the association had

[46] *RB v Hungary* App no 64602/12 (ECtHR, 12 April 2016).
[47] *Király and Dömötör v Hungary* App no 10851/13 (ECtHR, 17 January 2017).
[48] *Vona v Hungary* App no 35943/10 (ECtHR, 9 July 2013).
[49] *RB* (n 46) para 10.
[50] *Király and Dömötör* (n 47) para 11.
[51] *Vona* (n 48) para 8.
[52] ibid paras 102–03.

organized demonstrations where racial and ethnic hatred was openly and directly spread, in a manner reminiscent of the Hungarian Nazi movement (the Arrow Cross Party) and aimed at intimidating and humiliating the Roma minority. Here, the Court rightly stressed that violence should be a premise for the dissolution of an organization, while noting that violence here is not limited to the physical dimension and can occur in the form of intimidation and verbal assaults.[53] At the same time, the correct approach in this case would be to consider the application as an abuse of rights under Article 17. The Court used this argument in the case of *W.P. and others v Poland*, in which it declared the application inadmissible. In this way, it declined to even evaluate the decision of the Polish authorities refusing to register the association on the basis of a statute containing anti-Semitic content.[54] In contrast, in *Vona*, the Court missed an opportunity to send a clear signal that anti-Roma hatred falls outside the protection scope of the Convention.[55]

A similar assessment applies to the Court's approach to anti-Roma speech in *Aksu v Turkey*.[56] The Grand Chamber assessed the use of offensive stereotypical images of Roma in a government-sponsored publication. There, the Court found that certain expressions are 'capable of impacting on [a] group's sense of identity and the feelings of self-worth and self-confidence of members of the group'[57] and if they meet a certain level of seriousness, they can be classified as affecting an individual's private life. The Court failed to explain (or perhaps underestimated) the impact of statements demeaning the group on those who belonged to it, deeming anti-Roma statements in the case insufficiently harmful to the applicant. In contrast to this majority opinion, Judge Gyulumyan's dissent in this case is worth quoting at length:

> In my opinion, Turkey stands in violation of at least Article 8 of the Convention for supporting and not prohibiting the distribution of the books in question. There is no conflict with Article 10 inasmuch as the latter, in paragraph 2, refers to duties and responsibilities associated with freedom of expression and to the protection of the reputation and rights of others. It is of crucial importance that freedom of expression not only confers the right to hold opinions, but also imposes duties and responsibilities. It cannot therefore be interpreted as allowing

[53] ibid paras 63–64.

[54] *WP and Others v Poland* App no 42264/98 (ECtHR, 2 September 2004) paras 10–11.

[55] It should be noted that the Court did not refrain from invoking Art 17, not only in cases concerning anti-Semitic speech but also those concerning homophobic speech. In the admissibility decision in *Lenis v Greece* App no 47833/20 (ECtHR, 31 August 2023), the Court found that the applicant had attempted to deflect Art 10 from its real purpose by using it for ends which were clearly contrary to the values which the Convention sought to promote. Notably, at the time of events, the applicant was the Metropolitan of the Greek Orthodox Church for Kalavryta and Aigialeia, who called homosexuality a 'social felony' and a 'sin', and homosexuals 'the scum of society', 'defective', 'mentally ill', and invited people to spit on them.

[56] *Aksu v Turkey* (n 42) para 58.

[57] ibid para 58.

the promotion or dissemination of the ideas of ethnic hatred and the superiority of one nation *vis a vis* other ethnic groups.[58]

Belavusau correctly notes that in *Aksu*, the Court used the margin of appreciation clause under Article 8 to avoid considering anti-Roma stereotypes as hate speech. It thus refused to follow the judicial standard applied in other cases (against other groups) in which hate speech was treated more rigorously.[59] The Court also referred to expert opinions presented in the domestic proceedings, in which the preaching of prejudice against Roma was presented as part of academic freedom.[60]

Thus, it should be emphasized that hate cases against Roma include both hate speech and hate crime components. However, the ECtHR's analysis focuses not only on anti-Roma hate speech as a separate issue. As a result, one would expect the Court to address the hate speech component of anti-Roma hatred, regardless of the substantive scope of the application. For the time being, as Ilieva noted, one gets the impression that in hate cases against Roma, the Court manifests an 'anti-victim bias', reluctantly treating complaints brought by the Roma victims.[61] At the same time, when the application comes from a racist, anti-Roma organization outlawed at the national level, as in *Vona*, the Court does not invoke Article 17 of the Convention to place such expressions of hatred in line with other cases deemed inadmissible by the Court due to the abuse of rights. This approach reveals the double standards within the human rights paradigm due to inherent limitations in understanding the social standing of all protected groups, especially the vulnerable. These limitations may arise from prejudice or unconscious biases, even within the ECtHR itself.

## 5. The Missing Holocaust Context

The ECtHR's approach to anti-Roma hate speech can also be seen as overlooking the memory of the Holocaust, in which Roma were also victims. In this respect, Strasbourg case law highlights the boundaries of the human rights paradigm, where only specific vulnerable groups are treated as deserving enhanced protection. One example is the Court's special treatment of Holocaust-related cases,

58 ibid para 10 of the dissenting opinion.

59 Uladzislau Belavusau, 'Experts in Hate Speech Cases: Towards a Higher Standard of Proof in Strasbourg?' in Łukasz Gruszczynski and Wouter Werner (eds), *Deference in International Courts and Tribunals: Standard of Review and Margin of Appreciation* (OUP 2014) 268.

60 *Aksu* (n 42) paras 53–57.

61 Margarita S Ilieva, 'Behar and Budinova v Bulgaria: The Rights of Others in Cases of Othering – Anti-Victim Bias in ECHR Hate Speech Law?' (*Strasbourg Observers*, 15 April 2021) < https://strasbourgobservers.com/2021/04/15/behar-and-budinova-v-bulgaria-the-rights-of-others-in-cases-of-othering-anti-victim-bias-in-echr-hate-speech-law/ > accessed 10 June 2024.

sparking controversies in academic discussions.[62] Notably, the issue of Holocaust denial, recognized by the Court as a form of anti-Semitism and excluded from the protection of freedom of speech, stands out as unique, lacking similar protection for other forms of denial. The *Perinçek* ruling on the denial of the Armenian Genocide remains a significant example of the Court's distinct approach to genocides other than the Holocaust.

In general, the Court considers all expressions of anti-Semitism to be hateful, and it views extensive restrictions on the freedom of speech for those propagating anti-Semitic hatred speech, imposed at the national level, as legitimate and just measures taken by the state against anti-Semites.[63] As Möschel and Rubio-Marín explain, 'an (unconscious) understanding of racial violence from a Holocaust perspective … triggers a Gestalt shift and, with it, the debunking of the discrimination paradigm by a criminal/genocidal paradigm'.[64] The same seems to apply to racial hatred expressed in words. The prism of the Holocaust strongly influences the Court's perception and thinking about the genocidal and harmful nature of hate speech. However, in the case of the Roma, exactly the same prism and perspective should be applied, given the Holocaust history of the Roma and their annihilation by the Nazi regime.

In this context, a comparison of the *Budinova* case with the *Behar* case provides food for thought. In both cases, the Court found there was a lack of redress in response to discriminatory statements and the violation of the positive obligation to secure respect for the applicants' private lives with respect to persons of Jewish and Roma origin. However, the Court's approach missed the Holocaust aspect in the Roma case. In the *Behar* case, the key point was that the content disseminated by the politician was explicitly anti-Semitic and stigmatizing, as it aimed at arousing extremely negative feelings against Jews. Consequently, the Court classified the statements as tantamount to Holocaust denial and, as such, outside the protection of freedom of expression.[65] In contrast, in the *Budinova* case, the Court omitted any reference to the history of Nazi persecution of Roma, which should have been mentioned, given the nature of the anti-Roma statements, based on the same hateful prejudices as those used against Roma during the Holocaust.

[62] Aleksandra Gliszczyńska-Grabias, '"Never Again" as a Cornerstone of the Strasbourg System: The Reminiscence of the Holocaust in the Jurisprudence of the European Court of Human Rights' in Helmut Ast and Esra Demir (eds), *The European Court of Human Rights: Current Challenges in Historical and Comparative Perspective* (Edward Elgar 2021) 200.

[63] *Garaudy v France* App no 65831/01 (ECtHR, 24 June 2003); *M'Bala M'Bala v France* App no 25239/13 (ECtHR, 10 November 2015); *Williamson v Germany* App no 64496/17 (ECtHR, 31 January 2019).

[64] Ruth Rubio-Marín and Mathias Möschel, 'Anti-Discrimination Exceptionalism: Racist Violence before the ECtHR and the Holocaust Prism' (2015) 26(4) European Journal of International Law 899.

[65] *Budinova* (n 43) para 104.

Notably, the Court avoided references to the Holocaust in Roma cases even when these involved direct anti-Roma propaganda and Nazi-style hate speech. In *Škorjanec v Croatia*,[66] the case involved racist violence accompanied by statements about the need to exterminate all Roma in order to make Croatia a racially pure country again. In *Király and Dömötör v Hungary*, a Nazi-style march in a Roma neighbourhood was accompanied by a 'search' and identification of Roma households. In *Angelova and Iliev v Bulgaria*,[67] there was a racially motivated execution and murder of a Roma. And in *RB*, two right-wing paramilitary groups organized marches in a Roma village neighbourhood, threatening Roma residents that they would build a house there 'out of their blood'.[68]

The only notable exception was the *Vona* case, in which the Court directly highlighted the link between the Hungarian Nazi movement and a paramilitary formation that spread hatred and engaged in hate crimes against Roma. The Arrow Cross had been the backbone of the regime responsible for the mass extermination of Roma in Hungary during the Second World War. The organizational links between this Nazi-like formation and the association that complained about its dissolution allowed the Court to conclude that there was no violation of Article 11 concerning freedom of association in this case.

In cases involving anti-Semitic hatred and Holocaust denial, the Court routinely emphasizes the 'Never Again!' pledge and the suffering of Jews during the Second World War. Very few such reference appears in the Roma cases, yet the hate acts they experience flow directly from the period of their persecution by the Nazis. At the level of language and characterization of hate crimes, these share the same hate DNA that the Roma experienced during the Holocaust. Although the Court in all cases condemns the racial motivation of the crimes committed against Roma, the Court's approach is different in cases against Jews. One may wonder at this point what is the reason for this different treatment of Roma and anti-Semitic cases. Is it due to the way the cases are presented by the complainants themselves and decided at the level of national courts? It can be expected that the Court, not only by its judgments, but also by the way it justifies them, will bring about a change in the way human rights work in practice. Recognizing the link between the Holocaust and Nazism and the continuing attacks on the Roma population this time at the hands of private individuals, as well as extreme organizations, allows the human rights paradigm to shift to a horizontal relationship and thus strengthen its transformative potential.

66 *Škorjanec v Croatia* App no 25536/14 (ECtHR, 28 March 2017) paras 8–11.
67 *Angelova and Iliev v Bulgaria* App no 55523/00 (ECtHR, 26 July 2007).
68 *RB* (n 46) para 10.

## 6. Victim Status in the Cases of Group-Directed Hate Speech

Determining the status of the victim in hate speech cases directed against Roma can have two different dimensions. In the first dimension, the Court evaluates this status when deciding on the admissibility of the application under Article 35 of the Convention. Second, the Court may consider members of a group as 'victims' when assessing the conflict of rights—in this case, freedom of speech and the right to respect for private life. Thus, the determination of victim status depends on the subject matter of the application. If the applicant is an organization alleging a violation of Article 10 in connection with the criminal law measures used at the national level, the Court may consider persons belonging to the group targeted by the speech to be 'victims'. Accordingly, their rights must be taken into account in the substantive analysis of the case at hand. In other words, members of a targeted group can be considered victims under the Convention only in the substantive sense—for the purposes of the Court's weighing of interference with the scope of freedom of expression and the protection of the rights of others as the reason of that interference.

In this context, it is important to note that the Court's determination of the victim status from the perspective of Article 34 of the Convention, ie on procedural grounds, is a rigorous one. This rigour has been particularly evident in cases where the applicants have alleged a violation stemming from a state's failure to apply criminal measures as part of the positive obligation to protect vulnerable groups against stigmatizing speech directed at them. Moreover, the Court's approach to cases filed by Roma applicants was more stringent than for those filed by other vulnerable groups.[69]

However, the Court's approach to Roma cases has evolved in recent years. Initially, the Court refused the admissibility of an application filed by a group of individuals who claimed a violation of their Convention rights on the grounds that criminal measures had not been applied at the national level. While the Court has always stressed that criminal sanctions, including against those responsible for the most serious manifestations of hatred or incitement to violence, can only be used as *ultimum remedium*,[70] it has not generally contested the use

[69] See *Association ACCEPT and others v Romania* App no 19237/16 (ECtHR, 1 June 2021) which concerned a lack of effective protection against hate speech targeting LGBTQ+ persons, including threats of 'death to the homosexuals'. In this judgment, the Court stated that 'while being careful not to hold that each and every utterance of hate speech must, as such, attract criminal prosecution and criminal sanctions, the Court reiterates its finding that comments that amount to hate speech and incitement to violence, and are thus clearly unlawful on the face of things, may in principle require the States to take certain positive measures. It has likewise held that inciting hatred does not necessarily amount to a call for an act of violence or other criminal acts' (para 119). What is missing in the Court's position is a clear indication that threats like the one quoted above oblige the state to use even the most severe free speech limiting tools.

[70] *Beizaras and Levickas v Lithuania* App no 41288/15 (ECtHR, 14 January 2020) para 111. Interestingly, the Court has not invoked the *ultima ratio* measure argument in cases concerning Holocaust denial penalization. The attitude of the Court towards criminal law measures applicable against hate speech is further blurred also in cases concerning other forms of hatred.

of criminal law measures in this area. However, in the Court's initial position, the state's positive obligations arising from Article 8, read in conjunction with Article 14 of the Convention, did not absolutely require the use of criminal law. Consequently, the Court refused to recognize the victim status of applicants who claimed enhanced protection based on the concept of positive obligations and their vulnerable status.

The case at point is an inadmissibility decision in *Panayotova v Bulgaria*.[71] The case concerned anti-Roma speech disseminated in an election brochure of the Siderova Party. A group of Roma applicants filed a complaint before the ECtHR, alleging violations of their right to respect for private life and the prohibition of discrimination with regard to ethnic origin. However, the Court decided that it could not hear *an actio popularis* case, as the applicants had not been sufficiently affected by this hate speech or the refusal of Bulgarian prosecutors to investigate their claims.[72] The decision that the case was inadmissible was further justified by the fact that, at the domestic level, the applicants had requested criminal and not civil measures. Citing the *Aksu* judgment, the Court emphasized that stigmatizing statements about an entire ethnic group required a response from the national authorities primarily under civil law.[73] It also noted that the national authorities could not be required to apply criminal law, as part of their positive obligations under Article 8 of the Convention, in the absence of any evidence about the way in which the brochure affected the applicants.[74]

In light of this assessment, one might get the impression that the Court applies a different standard when assessing victim status in the context of anti-Roma and anti-Semitic hate speech. This may suggest that the Court adopts different criteria for recognizing victim status in these two groups, potentially leading to unequal treatment and undermining the consistency of human rights protection. Indeed, the Court has repeatedly recognized that all Jews living in Germany may have been negatively affected and harmed by a social campaign prepared by an animal welfare organization, depicting prisoners of former Nazi German concentration camps together with suffering animals.[75] Given the real threat of hateful violence against Roma, as well as the severity of the anti-Roma sentiments in Europe, it is difficult to accept this differential approach to the question of who can and cannot be considered 'individually affected' and harmed by various expressions of hate speech. However, in the Court's perspective, there is a significant difference in assessing victim status for the purposes of admissibility of an application and for balancing conflicting rights. The strictness of the former limits human rights protection, while the permissiveness of the latter expands it.

71 *Donka Kamenova Panayotova and Others v Bulgaria* App no 12509/13 (ECtHR, 7 May 2019).
72 ibid.
73 ibid para 61.
74 ibid para 62.
75 *PETA Deutschland v Germany* App no 43481/09 (ECtHR, 8 November 2012).

Therefore, the *Budinova and Chaprazov* judgment is a historic decision as it sets a new standard for assessing the victim status in cases of group-directed hate speech. The applicants alleged that the racist verbal attack was directed against an entire group, and that the state failed to provide Roma with adequate protection against racist hatred. Therefore, one of the questions decided by the ECHR in this case was whether the national courts had fulfilled their positive obligation to provide redress for hate speech that targets a group rather than its individual members. The ECtHR answered this question by identifying criteria for evaluation of group-directed hatred.

The ECtHR referred to:

> (a) the characteristics of the group (its size, its degree of homogeneity, its particular vulnerability or history of stigmatisation, and its position vis-à-vis society as a whole), (b) the precise content of the negative statements regarding the group (in particular, the degree to which they could convey a negative stereotype about the group as a whole, and the specific content of that stereotype), and (c) the form and context in which the statements were made, their reach (which may depend on where and how they have been made), the position and status of their author, and the extent to which they could be considered to have affected a core aspect of the group's identity and dignity.[76]

The Court also made reference to the fact that the social and political climate prevalent at the time when the statements were made is to be taken into consideration, and that all these factors are of importance for the Court to be able to come to the conclusion that in this group-directed hate speech case Article 8 was applicable.

This dictum of the Court should be praised as indicating clearly, for the first time, that victim status in cases concerning verbal hatred directed against an entire group can be granted to all individuals belonging to the group. This is particularly important in states where the judiciary systematically challenges such status, demanding a clear, personal, direct link between hateful words and individually offended vulnerable group member. It is therefore a landmark judgment, but it remains to be seen whether it will be sustainably applied in similar cases, especially filed by Roma applicants, in the future.

## 7. Conclusions

The analysis above underscores the growing need for a critical reflection on the ECtHR's approach to cases involving Roma and, in particular, anti-Roma hate

[76] *Budinova* (n 43) para 63.

speech. The Court's jurisprudence on hate speech targeting Roma is notably fluid and inconsistent, revealing but not enhancing the scope of human rights protection. A particularly troubling example of this inconsistency is the Court's disparate treatment of anti-Semitic and homophobic hate speech in contrast to anti Roma sentiments. While the Court addresses anti-Semitic and homophobic hatred with some rigour, it fails to apply the same standard to hate speech directed against Roma. Given the shared historical context of the Holocaust, it is essential that anti-Semitism and anti-Gypsyism be recognized as twin expressions of racism and prejudice. To effect a 'game-changing' shift, the Court must consistently acknowledge the group victim status of Roma in cases of hate speech, applying the criteria established in the *Budinova* judgment. Furthermore, there is an urgent need for the Court to uniformly invoke Article 17 in cases involving racist statements and Nazi-style propaganda, ensuring that all forms of hate speech are addressed with the seriousness they warrant.

In this context, this chapter reveals the limitations of the current scope of the human rights paradigm in the differential application of the concept of vulnerability. There is no doubt that Roma belong to a vulnerable group. However, the Court's approach to their rights claims, especially in terms of protection against hate speech, is significantly different compared to that applied to cases concerning anti-Semitism or homophobia. We do not find justification for such differential treatment by the top human rights court in Europe. If there is any other example of hate speech that requires the radical approach characteristic of the ECtHR's attitude toward anti-Semitism and homophobia, it is anti-Roma hate speech. And thus the Court, which has rightly pushed the boundaries of human rights for protection against anti-Semitism, and is attempting to push them for LGBTQ+ persons, should do the same for the Roma. The justification for this equal standard paradoxically lies precisely in the memory of the Holocaust and the practices employed by the Nazis against these groups. If the 'Never again' commitment has any relevance and meaning in today's Council of Europe reality, than counteracting Roma-hatred with the tools of law is undoubtedly an obligation that must be taken seriously.

In contrast, the Court's attitude towards the scope of states' positive obligations to protect against hate speech seems more optimistic, expanding the boundaries of human rights protection. The standard articulated in *Budinova* is persuasive and necessary, as it responds to the challenges that are presented by the pressing social need to strengthen the protection of vulnerable groups. In particular, with regard to the situation of Roma, it allows for the proper identification of factors that justify a more demanding approach to what actions should occur on the part of the state in cases of anti-Roma hate speech. The same applies to the recognition of hate speech directed against the whole group as violating the rights of individuals belonging to this group. As the experience in some of the states indicates, domestic courts find it difficult to grant such status when no personal connection between the hateful words and a given individual is notified.[77] Thus, applying the test formulated in *Budinova* will definitely be of guidance and help.

The ECtHR's case law on hate speech and hate crimes against Roma provides a focused look at a number of general issues related to the Court's attitude to hate speech and hate crimes and the concept of vulnerability, but also at the differential treatment of discrimination and hatred against Roma. And while the picture that emerges from this analysis is far from recognizing that the Court's jurisprudence in this area acts as the vanguard of progress toward expanding the boundaries of protection for vulnerable groups, the progress that has been made in recent years in some of the challenging areas, such as recognition of the victim status of the whole group or the expanded interpretation of state positive obligations, allows for moderate optimism.

[77] This is for example the case of Poland. See the judgment of the Regional Court of Warsaw in a civil lawsuit case filled by a group of LGBTQ+ persons who felt offended by an ultra-catholic activist's claims that 'homosexuals are perverts'. The Court stated that as the offended group was 'too broad' and no individually indicated persons were insulted by the remark, the lawsuit had to be dismissed. *The judgment of the District Court of Warsaw* XXV C 2147/18 (28 January 2021).

# 9

# Limits and Opportunities of Desegregation Litigation in View of European Jurisprudence and Related Developments

*Dezideriu Gergely*

## 1. Introduction

Recent developments in jurisprudence and human rights monitoring at the European level paint a vivid picture of the structural problems associated with school segregation affecting Roma children in Central and Southeastern Europe. These developments are emblematic of the extent of systemic change required to mitigate and effectively address the de facto inequalities faced by Roma children in the area of education. A closer examination of desegregation litigation which aims to juxtapose limits and opportunities in a human rights context and to show how 'boundaries of the human rights paradigm' have been pushed, should look at the scope of the judgments, as the immediate outcome of strategic litigation, as well as focusing on the broader implementation context and judicial review in school desegregation litigation.

### 1.1. The context of desegregation litigation

School segregation has been a key issue raised by Roma or pro-Roma civil society organizations in the context of monitoring the state's compliance with Council of Europe standards on racial discrimination or the protection of national minorities. The use of monitoring, mobilization, awareness-raising, and legal advocacy tools in the broader context of Council of Europe treaties or the state's accession to the EU has contributed to the gradual inclusion of the issue on the agenda of European bodies.[1] The development of European anti-discrimination law since mid-2000

[1] European Roma Rights Centre, 'Roma Rights Summer 1998: Roma and the Right to Education' (*ERRC*, 10 September 1998) <https://www.errc.org/roma-rights-journal/roma-rights-summer-1998-roma-and-the-right-to-education> accessed 3 March 2024.James Goldston, 'Lawsuits File by

Dezideriu Gergely, *Limits and Opportunities of Desegregation Litigation in View of European Jurisprudence and Related Developments* In: *The Rights of Roma in European Courts*. Edited by: Kristin Henrard and Lilla Farkas, Oxford University Press. © Dezideriu Gergely 2025. DOI: 10.1093/oso/9780198914358.003.0009

has provided a favourable legal framework for challenging school segregation as a form of discrimination and a political impetus for demanding social inclusion policies.

These processes have helped to highlight the systemic nature and long-term causes of school segregation of Roma children, reflected in the judgments of the European Court of Human Rights (ECtHR), and have contributed to advancing the boundaries of human rights in cases of segregation.

The recommendations of the Committee of Ministers on the education of Roma children, and the positions and recommendations of both the European Commission against Racism and Intolerance and the Advisory Committee of the Framework Convention for the Protection of National Minorities on school segregation have consistently been referred to by applicants, civil society third-party interveners, and, importantly, the ECtHR in the school segregation cases.[2] With the development of the case law of the ECtHR, school segregation has received ever more attention at both international and national levels. Desegregation litigation and legal advocacy supported by civil society organizations have been instrumental in developing international human rights standards in this area, resulting in landmark judgments on school segregation that are a point of reference for policy makers in the area of Roma children's education. Litigation in relation with segregated education before the ECtHR has mostly been driven by NGOs. The Court has so far delivered twelve judgments on segregated education to date, the most recent in February 2025. With two exceptions[3] that were subsequently overturned,

Roma Challenge Racial Segregation in Czech Schools' (*ERRC*, 15 July 1999) <https://www.errc.org/cikk.php?cikk=803> accessed 3 March 2024; Angela Kocze 'Romani Children and the right to education in Central and Eastern Europe' (*ERRC*, 3 October 2000) <https://www.errc.org/cikk.php?cikk=1012> accessed 3 March 2024; European Roma Rights Centre, 'Roma Rights 3-4, 2002: Segregation and Desegregation' (*ERRC*, 7 November 2002), <https://www.errc.org/roma-rights-journal/roma-rights-3-4-2002-segregation-and-desegregation> accessed 3 March 2024; Margarita Ilieva and Daniela Mihaylova, 'Court Action Against Segregated Education in Bulgaria: A Legal Effort to Win Roma Access to Equality' (*ERRC*, 7 February 2004) <https://www.errc.org/cikk.php?cikk=1319> accessed 3 March 2024; European Roma Rights Centre, 'Roma Rights 1, 2008: Roma Education: The Promise of D.H.' (*ERRC*, 3 November 2008) <https://www.errc.org/roma-rights-journal/roma-rights-1-2008-roma-education-the-promise-of-dh> accessed 3 March 2024; European Roma Rights Centre, 'Roma Rights 1, 2010: Implementation of Judgments' (ERRC, 26 July 2010) <https://www.errc.org/roma-rights-journal/roma-rights-1-2010-implementation-of-judgments> accessed 3 March 2024.

[2] The ECtHR referred to ECRI country reports and recommendations in all its judgments on school segregation. With the exception of *Elmazova and Others v North Macedonia* and *Szolcsan v Hungary*, the Court referred in its judgments to the recommendations of the Committee of Ministers on the education of Roma children. The Court also referred to the Advisory Committee's Opinions on the Framework Convention for the Protection of National Minorities in its judgments in *DH and Others v Czech Republic* App no 57325/00 (ECtHR, 7 February 2006); *Sampanis and Others v Greece* App no 32526/05 (ECtHR, 5 June 2008); *Oršuš and Others v Croatia* App no 15766/03, (ECtHR, 17 July 2008); and *Horvath and Kiss v Hungary* App no 11146/11 (ECtHR, 29 January 2013).

[3] *DH and Others v Czech Republic* (n 2); *Oršuš and Others v Croatia* (n 2).

the Court found that segregated schooling for Roma children amounted to discrimination[4] in violation of the European Convention on Human Rights.[5]

## 1.2. Pushing the boundaries of the human rights paradigm in desegregation litigation

The ECtHR has progressively developed the human rights paradigm in cases of segregated schooling for Roma children, shifting its overall approach from examining safeguards against segregation to outlining concrete and specific positive obligations for Member States, placing greater emphasis on inclusive education and, most importantly, on desegregation processes. In contrast to its early jurisprudence, in which the Court did not issue specific orders, the Court has more recently developed prescriptive guidance for states in the context of the implementation of judgments. Under Article 46 of the European Convention on Human Rights the Court has used straightforward language to ensure that national authorities 'put an end to the segregation of Roma pupils'. In one of its most recent judgments, the Court referred not just to measures to end the segregation of Roma children in a particular school, but also to the need to develop a general 'policy against segregation in education and to take steps to eliminate it', a bold step and an unprecedented requirement in the context of implementing judgments on school segregation.[6]

This crucial step is based on the approach developed by the ECtHR in its jurisprudence, which focuses on the harmful effects of segregation on Roma as a vulnerable group, thus going beyond the individual situation of Roma pupils. In this context, the Court has developed its approach to require that de facto inequalities be addressed, not only through safeguards against segregation, but above all through policy desegregation measures. This approach, which implies the application of structural measures to combat school segregation as a facet of systemic discrimination, is

[4] *DH and Others v Czech Republic* App no 57325/00 (ECtHR [GC], 13 November 2007); *Sampanis and Others v Greece* App no 32526/05 (ECtHR, 5 June 2008); *Oršuš and Others v Croatia* App no 15766/03 (ECtHR [GC], 16 March 2010); *Sampani and Others v Greece* App no 59608/09 (ECtHR, 11 December 2012); *Horvath and Kiss v Hungary* App no 11146/11 (ECtHR, 29 January 2013); *Lavida and Others v Greece* App no 7973/10 (ECtHR, 30 May 2013); *X and Others v Albania* App nos 73548/17, 45521/19 (ECtHR, 31 May 2022); *Elmazova and Others v North Macedonia* App nos 11811/20, 13550/20 (ECtHR, 13 December 2022); *Szolcsán v Hungary* App no 24408/16 (ECtHR, 30 March 2023), *Salay v Slovakia* App no 29359/22 (ECtHR, 27 February 2025).

[5] The ECtHR also delivered four decisions, one taking note of a friendly settlement in September 2022, and the rest on inadmissibility, the most recent of which was against Albania in May 2023. See *Horvath and Vadaszi v Hungary* App no 2351/06 (ECtHR, 9 November 2010); *Amanda Kosa v Hungary* App no 53461/15 (ECtHR, 21 November 2017); *Suchy v The Czech Republic* App no 11746/16 (ECtHR, 8 September 2022); *Avdiu and Others v Albania* App no 49516/178 (ECtHR, 23 May 2023).

[6] *Szolcsán v Hungary* (n 4) paras 67–69.

also reflected in the monitoring process of the execution of European Court's judgments.[7] Despite challenges related to the unclear distinction between direct and indirect discrimination in school segregation jurisprudence[8] and questions about the effectiveness of the implementation of the Court's judgments,[9] desegregation litigation at the European level has served as a tool beyond legal advocacy. As indicated by civil society monitoring or subsequent Committee of Ministers assessment of the implementation of European Court judgments, it has played an influential role in triggering policy reform and practice related to the education of Roma children, including changes in legislation on special education, data collection, diagnosis, enrolment of socially disadvantaged pupils, or desegregation policies[10].

The Court's findings of discrimination constitute a diagnosis of the school segregation of Roma children but the paradigm of positive obligations to address inequalities in education can serve as a key avenue at the policy level to address desegregation. The executive bodies of the Council of Europe,[11] and later of the European Union,[12] have called on Member States to take full account of the judgments of the ECtHR beyond individual approaches and to use them as a 'point of reference for the human rights compatibility' of measures to counter segregation in education.

The transposition of the standards developed by the ECtHR at the national level has taken effect through judicial borrowing or transfer,[13] which has become

[7] For example, in *DH and Others v Czech Republic* (n 4) the emphasis was placed on 'the persistence of the problem of overrepresentation of Roma children' against the effectiveness of policy measures to address participation in preschool education, to improve diagnostic tools, school counselling and importantly, of desegregation measures. Similarly, in *Horvath and Kiss* (n 4), the analysis is primarily focused on policy measures aimed at upgrading diagnostic tools, enhancing procedural guarantees against misdiagnosis, and monitoring through comprehensive data collection at national level. This approach was closely followed in the *Salay* judgement. In *Szolcsan* the focus was placed equally on effectiveness of policy-type measures at national level—among others, setting-up anti-segregation working groups, equal opportunities action plans, regular review of school catchment areas, and early school leaving prevention measures. See Ministers' Deputies, 'Notes on the Agenda' CM/Notes/1492/H46-10 (March 2024); Ministers' Deputies, 'Notes on the Agenda' CM/Notes/1492/H46-17 (March 2024).

[8] Lilla Farkas, *Report on Discrimination of Roma Children in Education* (European Union 2014) 24–38.

[9] James A Goldston, 'Challenges in Executing Judgments of the European Court of Human Rights: the Case of the Roma' (*Blog of the European Journal of International Law*, 8 December 2023) <https://www.ejiltalk.org> accessed 10 December 2023.

[10] Open Society Justice Initiative, *Strategic Litigation Impacts: Roma School Desegregation* (Open Society Foundations 2016) paras 36, 40, 44; Ministers' Deputies, 'Decisions' CM/Del/Dec(2024)1492/H46-10 para 3; Ministers' Deputies, 'Decisions' CM/Del/Dec(2024)1492/H46-17 (14 March 2024) para 8.

[11] Council of Europe, 'Recommendation CM/Rec(2009)4 of the Committee of Ministers to Member States on the Education of Roma and Travellers in Europe' (adopted 17 June 2009) para 1b, Appendix I.5-7; Ministers' Deputies, 'The Strasbourg Declaration on Roma' CM(2010)133 paras 15, 24, 33.

[12] Council of the European Union, 'Recommendation on Effective Roma Integration Measures in the Member States' [2013] C 378/01 paras 1.3, 2.1; European Parliament, 'Resolution on the Segregation and Discrimination of Roma Children in Education' P9_TA(2023)0342 paras E, J-L, R, 1, 3, 22.

[13] See eg Alan Watson, *Legal Transplants. An Approach to Comparative Law* (University of Georgia Press 1993); George Mousourakis, *Comparative Law and Legal Traditions. Historical and Contemporary Perspectives* (Springer 2019) 169–94; Rosalind Dixon and David Landau (eds), *Abusive Constitutional Borrowing. Legal Globalization and the Subversion of Liberal Democracy* (Oxford University Press 2020) 40–42. Dixon and Landau emphasize that contemporary comparative scholars use different labels ('transplantation', 'borrowing', 'transfer') to refer to legal borrowing as cross-national

more visible in recent Supreme Court rulings in Slovakia, Czechia, Hungary, and Romania. Supreme courts have progressively addressed the issue of the racial segregation of Roma children by directly transferring the standards set by the case law of the ECtHR. Supreme courts such as those in Czechia and Slovakia have interplayed identical arguments when discussing the legal implications of school segregation in the context of the violations found by the ECtHR. Where the lower courts have failed to apply or have misinterpreted the case law of the ECtHR, the supreme courts have appropriately sanctioned these errors.[14] Compliance by national authorities with positive obligations to desegregate has been assessed against the criteria set by the Strasbourg Court and has been given prominence by supreme courts. In this context, orders addressed to national authorities based on the positive obligations of the state to prevent and remedy racial segregation in equal measure constitute relevant precedents that show how the human rights boundaries pushed by international litigation take concrete form in the rulings of national courts.[15] A similar process has been developed through the work of equality bodies that has emerged in the context of desegregation litigation led by civil society organizations, which is of paramount importance in advancing the fight against segregation. Drawing on the standards set by the Strasbourg Court and national anti-discrimination law, equality bodies have required the relevant authorities to take firm and specific action to tackle school segregation, making explicit the positive obligation to remedy segregation through desegregation measures.[16]

### 1.3. The analysis in the current chapter

In the above context, this chapter takes stock of desegregation litigation that has led to the recognition of various forms of school segregation of Roma children as instances of racial discrimination, more importantly, to the development of positive obligations for states to end school segregation and, ultimately, to adopt desegregation policies. To this end, international litigation is examined chronologically from different perspectives. First, it discusses how the concept of racial segregation in international human rights law has been interpreted in European jurisprudence.

legal influence for Alan Watson's concept of 'legal transplants' as a combination of borrowing and adaptation in the development of legal rules and institutions.

[14] Judgment of the Supreme Court of Czech Republic, no 25Cdo 473/2021 (5 May 2022) paras 26, 52, 57; Judgment of the Supreme Court of Slovak Republic, no 5Cdo/102/2020 (15 December 2022) para 8.

[15] Judgment of the Supreme Court of Slovak Republic no 5Cdo/102/2020 (15 December 2022) para 15.1; Judgment of the Supreme Court of Slovak Republic no 5Cdo/220/2022 (17 July 2023) para 17.1; Judgment of the Supreme Court of Romania, no 1015/2020 (20 February 2020) para II.2.

[16] Albanian Commissioner for Protection from Discrimination in *Avdiu and Others v Albania* (n 5) para 6; National Council for Combating Discrimination in Romania, Decision no 438 (30 August 2023); Commission for Protection against Discrimination in North Macedonia, Opinion no 08-109/1 (18 January 2024).

Secondly, it analyses how the ECtHR has gradually developed more specific obligations and instructions in the context of the implementation of school segregation judgments. Finally, it shows how the standards developed by the European Court have been used by supreme courts in Central Europe to assess national authorities' compliance with non-discrimination requirements in school segregation cases. Through these layers of research, it is argued that for effective change of systemic discrimination faced by Roma children, standard-setting by international jurisprudence needs to be translated into national law and practice. One of the latter avenues is that school desegregation constitutes a legal remedy beyond punitive sanctions in equality law, taking the form of a clear obligation to implement specific and measurable desegregation measures.

## 2. Prohibition of Racial Segregation in Education

A clear prohibition of racial segregation in education as a form of discrimination is not explicitly visible in EU equality law standards or in the Council of Europe treaties.[17] This is relevant in relation to the obligation to prohibit and eliminate all practices of racial segregation as set out in Articles 3 and 5 of the International Convention on the Elimination of all Forms of Racial Discrimination (ICERD),[18] the prohibition of discrimination on the basis of race in relation to the establishment or maintenance of separate educational systems or institutions, and the obligation to formulate policies to promote equal treatment in education, as set out in Articles 1 and 4 of the UNESCO Convention against Discrimination in Education (CADE).[19]

### 2.1. Racial segregation in human rights monitoring and legal advocacy

At the national level, the early litigation cases leading to *DH and Others* and *Orsus and Others* were based on constitutional, civil law, and general education law provisions, while the later cases were essentially narrowed down to the alleged breaches of the equal treatment clause in anti-discrimination and subsequently in education law.[20]

[17] Gergely Dezideriu and Farkas Lilla, *Racial Discrimination in Education and EU Equality Law* (EU Publications Office 2020) 33.

[18] International Convention on the Elimination of All Forms of Racial Discrimination (adopted 21 December 1965, entered into force 4 January 1969) 195 UNTS 660.

[19] UNESCO Convention against Discrimination in Education (adopted 14 December 1960, entered into force 22 May 1962) 243 UNTS 993 art 1 c (discrimination 'includes any distinction, exclusion, limitation, or preference being based on race, colour, ... national or social origin, economic condition, or birth ... impairing equality of treatment in education and in particular: ... establishing or maintaining separate educational systems or institutions for persons or groups of persons').

[20] *Horvath and Kiss v Hungary* (n 4) paras 35, 48; *Lavida and Others v Greece* (n 4) paras 24–27; *Amanda Kosa v Hungary* (n 5) paras 19, 22; *X and Others v Albania* (n 4) paras 4–7, 67; *Elmazova and*

This has been possible due to the development of equality law in Europe since mid-2000, particularly in the EU[21] and gradually also in non-EU Member States. Protocol 12 to the European Convention[22] of November 2000, while extending protection against discrimination beyond the rights provided in the Convention remained virtually unusable because countries where school segregation of Roma children has been litigated have not ratified it.[23] However, desegregation litigation has been brought within the scope of Article 14 and Article 2 of Protocol 1, and the ECtHR has developed its jurisprudence and relevant standards on positive measures and obligations in relation to schooling arrangements for Roma children under the right to education and non-discrimination clause of the European Convention of Human Rights.

The structural nature of racial segregation in the context of widespread discrimination against Roma pupils has been consistently identified by the European Commission against Racism and Intolerance (ECRI), particularly in Bulgaria, Czechia, Hungary, and Slovakia,[24] as well as in other neighbouring countries[25] and to a lesser extent in Western European countries.[26] The serious challenges of school segregation which required a systematic response at national level have also been highlighted by the European Commission in the context of the 2004, 2007, and 2013[27] enlargement rounds and the subsequent accession process.[28]

The systemic nature of discrimination has been central to all cases brought before the ECtHR, whether segregation in special schools, segregated facilities or segregated classes. Apart from certain distinctions made by the Court with regard to the origin of school segregation, for example in *DH and Others, Horvath and Kiss* and *Salay* (national practice) as opposed to *Orsus and Others* (regional practice) or *Elmazova* (local in some respects), the structural nature of school segregation affecting predominantly Roma pupils has played a key

*Others v North Macedonia* (n 4) para 10; *Szolcsán v Hungary* (n 4) paras 12, 18, 19; *Avdiu and Others v Albania* (n 5) paras 5–6, 9; *Salay v Slovakia* (n 4) para 22.

[21] Council Directive 2000/43/EC of 29 June 2000 implementing the principle of equal treatment between persons irrespective of racial or ethnic origin [2000] OJ L180.

[22] Protocol No 12 to the Convention for the Protection of Human Rights and Fundamental Freedoms (adopted 4 November 2000, entered into force 1 April 2005) ETS 177.

[23] Notably Bulgaria, Czech Republic, Greece, Hungary, and Slovak Republic. See Council of Europe, 'Treaty Office Chart of signatures and ratifications of Treaty 177' <https://www.coe.int/en/web/conventions/full-list> accessed 3 March 2024.

[24] ECRI Reports on Bulgaria, Czechia, Hungary, Slovakia <https://hudoc.ecri.coe.int> accessed 3 March 2024.

[25] ECRI Reports on Croatia, Greece, North Macedonia, Poland, Estonia, Lithuania, Latvia, Portugal, Romania, Republic of Moldova, Russian Federation, Serbia, Slovenia, Spain, Ukraine, Albania, Cyprus, Montenegro <https://hudoc.ecri.coe.int> accessed 3 March 2024.

[26] ECRI Reports on Italy, Denmark, Finland, Sweden, Germany <https://hudoc.ecri.coe.int> accessed 3 March 2024.

[27] European Commission Regular Reports on progress towards accession on Czechia, Hungary, Slovakia, Romania, Bulgaria, Croatia <https://op.europa.eu/en/home> accessed 3 March 2024.

[28] European Commission Progress Reports on Albania, North Macedonia, Serbia, <https://european-union.europa.eu/principles-countries-history/eu-enlargement_en> accessed 3 March 2024.

role in the progressive development of the Court's paradigm in cases of racial segregation.[29]

The Council of Europe Committee of Ministers[30] and the UN Committee on the Elimination of Racial Discrimination[31] recommended Member States to prevent and avoid the segregation of Roma pupils. ECRI was one of the first Council of Europe bodies to recommend that Member States include the prohibition of racial segregation as a specific form of discrimination among the key elements of national legislation against racial discrimination.[32] However, in the context of adopting anti-discrimination legislation or aligning with recommendations, few Member States[33] have taken the route of explicitly prohibiting racial segregation, in some cases including ambiguous, unclear, or excessive elements in the relevant definitions.[34]

Notwithstanding the absence of a prohibition of segregation in national law or setbacks caused by judicial interpretation, human rights monitoring and legal advocacy led by civil society organizations in Albania, Bulgaria, Croatia, Czechia, Hungary, North Macedonia, Romania, and Slovakia have been instrumental in advancing the paradigm of desegregation as a human rights obligation on the legal and public agenda at the national and international level.[35] The transposition

[29] *Oršuš and Others v Croatia* [GC] (n 4) paras 151–52. The Court refers by comparison to *DH and Others* (n 4) and *Elmazova and Others v North Macedonia* (n 4) para 75. The Court referred to *Orsus and Others* only in respect to segregation of Roma in separate classes. In *Salay* the Court referred to *Horvath and Kiss* in respect with the history of the inappropriate placement of Roma children in special schools across Europe. *Salay v Slovakia* (n 4) para 97.

[30] Committee of Ministers, 'Education of Roma/Gypsy Children in Europe' CM/Rec(2000)4.

[31] Committee on the Elimination of Racial Discrimination (CERD), 'General Recommendation XXVII on Discrimination against Roma' (2000) A/55/18 Annex V.

[32] ECRI, 'General Policy Recommendation No 7' CRI(2003)8 Rev para 6, Explanatory Memorandum para 16. ECRI recommended that national law should prohibit segregation as a form of discrimination consisting in the act by which a person separates other persons on the basis of race or ethnic origin without an objective and reasonable justification.

[33] Only Bulgaria (2003), Hungary (2003), Croatia (2008), Bosnia-Herzegovina (2009), and the United Kingdom (2010) introduced segregation in their equality laws. In Belgium (2007) incitement to racial segregation was prohibited but segregation per se was not defined. Secondary legislation in education addressed school segregation in Romania (2007), and in primary legislation in Slovakia (2008), in Hungary (2011), and in Bulgaria (2016). Recent amendments to anti-discrimination or education laws relating to segregation were adopted by parliaments in Albania and Northern Macedonia in 2020, and in Romania and Slovakia in 2023. See Gergely Dezideriu and Farkas Lilla, *Racial Discrimination in Education and EU Equality Law* (EU Publications Office 2020) 53–54.

[34] Council of Europe Commissioner for Human Rights, 'Fighting School Segregation in Europe Through Inclusive Education: A Position Paper' (Council of Europe 2017) 19–20.

[35] Challenges relate to the legal interpretation of segregation and elements such as 'compelled separation' in Bulgaria, 'remedies' against segregation in Hungary, 'parental choice' in North Macedonia, 'justifications' in Romania and Slovakia, as well as to national jurisprudence building on the positive obligation to enforce desegregation measures. See Dilyana Giteva, *Country Report Non-discrimination Bulgaria* (EU Publications Office 2023) 38, 40; Andras Kadar, *Country Report Non-discrimination Hungary* (EU Publications Office 2023) 80, 86–87; Biljana Kotevska, *Country Report Non-discrimination North Macedonia* (EU Publications Office 2021) 38–39; Romanita Iordache, *Country Report Non-discrimination Romania* (EU Publications Office 2023) 41–42; Vanda Durbakova, *Country Report Non-discrimination Slovakia* (EU Publications Office 2023) 50–51.

of European racial equality standards[36] at national level, the establishment of equality bodies, legal standing in anti-discrimination proceedings and dialogue with civil society have all provided avenues for NGOs to challenge school segregation before courts or anti-discrimination bodies[37] but also to advocate for desegregation policies with governments and human rights organizations. Indeed, there is a multinational governance dimension that could be questioned and scrutinized when looking at the extent of the development of Roma inclusion policies at the European level,[38] against the findings that policies to combat school segregation still lack a systemic approach.[39] From this perspective, and the paradigm developed by the ECtHR, the question arises as to whether school segregation should be considered as an aggravated form of racial discrimination under national law, triggering a positive obligation for national authorities to implement effective desegregation measures.

## 2.2. Interplay with international standards in litigating specifically 'racial segregation'

Desegregation litigation before the ECtHR has been essentially based on the argument that Roma children have been victims of racial segregation as a result of being placed in separate schooling, receiving a significantly inferior education, and in a general context of prejudice against Roma. In *DH and Others*,[40] *Oršuš and Others*,[41] *Horvath and Vadasi*,[42] and, most recently, *Szolcsán*,[43] the reference to 'racial segregation' was explicitly used by the applicants and constantly referred to in the parties' arguments. In *Horvath and Kiss* as well as in *Salay*, the term was not explicit but was constructed around the systemic impact on Roma children

[36] Uladzislau Belavusau and Kristin Henrard 'The Impact of the 2000 Equality Directives on EU Anti-Discrimination Law Achievements and Pitfalls' in Uladzislau Belavusau and Kristin Henrard (eds), *EU Anti-Discrimination Law Beyond Gender* (Hart Publishing 2019).

[37] Isabelle Chopin, Catharina Germaine, and Judit Tanczos, *Roma and the Enforcement of Anti-Discrimination Law* (EU Publications Office 2017).

[38] See measures addressing education and segregation in the OSCE Action Plan on Improving the situation of Roma and Sinti from 2003, the Decade of Roma Inclusion 2005–14, the EU Framework for National Roma Integration Strategies up to 2020, the Council of Europe Thematic Action Plan on the Inclusion of Roma and Travellers from 2015, the Council of Europe Strategic Action Plan for Roma and Traveller Inclusion from 2020, or the EU Roma Strategic Framework for Equality, Inclusion, and Participation from 2020, and the implementing reports of these pan-European policy initiatives.

[39] Council of Europe, 'Mid-Term Review Report: Strategic Action Plan for Roma and Travellers' ADI-ROM(2022)21; European Commission, 'Assessment Report of the Member States' National Roma Strategic Frameworks' COM(2023) 7 final; OSCE Office for Democratic Institutions and Human Rights, 'Implementation of the Action Plan on Improving the Situation of Roma and Sinti within the OSCE Area' (ODIHR 8 December 2023).

[40] *DH and Others v Czech Republic* (n 3) paras 36, 39.

[41] *Oršuš and Others v Croatia* (n 3) para 36.

[42] *Horvath and Vadaszi v Hungary* (n 5).

[43] *Szolcsán v Hungary* (n 4) paras 36–37.

who are 'uniquely burdened' and particularly disadvantaged.[44] In *Sampanis and Others,* the subsequent *Sampani and Others*, and *Lavida and Others,* even if 'racial segregation' was not used per se, the nature of the claims was fundamentally based on 'racism' as the causal factor of 'segregationist attitudes',[45] the separate school arrangements 'purely based on ethnicity',[46] or the segregationist nature of the school, resulting from the 'opposition to the integration of Roma pupils manifested by the local society'.[47] In the recent case of *Elmazova and Others*, the claims revolved around Roma segregation in the context of 'white flight' as evidence of 'anti-Gypsyism',[48] a specific form of racism,[49] while in the *Szolcsán* case the crux of the complaint was the racially biased refusal to transfer from a racially segregated school to an inclusive school.[50]

The ECtHR did not use the term 'racial segregation' in its *DH and* Others (2006), *Oršuš and Others* (2010) or *Sampani and Others* (2012) judgments and seemed rather reluctant to directly adopt and use the concept of racial segregation or its interpretation as advocated by the Roma applicants. Nonetheless, in its 2013 *Horvath and Kiss* and *Lavida* judgments and recently in *Salay* (2025), the Court not only shared the concern of the Council of Europe bodies of the 'long history throughout Europe' of the misplacement of Roma children and 'segregation',[51] but more importantly it linked the 'history of racial segregation in special schools' and the lack of 'anti-segregation measures'[52] with a violation of Article 14 in conjunction with Article 2 of Protocol 1 of the Convention.

The ECtHR has not always been clear about the extent to which international law standards on racial segregation influenced its interpretation of the ECHR, at least when assessing the merits in desegregation cases. The Court has tended to give primacy to the interpretation mostly of Council of Europe standards and practices. Human rights treaties such as the ICERD or CADE, and the Committee on the Elimination of Racial Discrimination (CERD), were referred to by the Grand Chamber in *DH and Others*[53] and *Oršuš and Others*[54] but without applying tests spelt out in these treaties.[55] Exceptionally, in *DH and Others*, the Grand Chamber cross-referenced the findings of the CERD with those of the Council of

[44] *Horvath and Kiss v Hungary* (n 4) paras 90–93, *Salay v Slovakia* (n 4) paras 69-71.
[45] *Sampanis and Others v Greece* (n 4) para 63.
[46] *Sampani and Others v Greece* (n 4) para 79.
[47] *Lavida and Others v Greece* App (n 4) paras 46, 59.
[48] *Elmazova and Others v North Macedonia* (n 4) para 66.
[49] ECRI, General Policy Recommendation No 13 (CRI(2011)27) Preamble.
[50] *Szolcsán v Hungary* (n 4) paras 36–37.
[51] *Horvath and Kiss v Hungary* (n 4) para 113; *DH and Others v Czech Republic* [GC] (n 4) para 198, *Salay v Slovakia* (n 4), paras 85, 86.
[52] *Horvath and Kiss v Hungary* (n 4) paras 115, 127; *Lavida and Others v Greece* (n 4) para 72, *Salay v Slovakia* (n 4), paras 114- 16.
[53] *DH and Others v Czech Republic* [GC] (n 4) paras 92–102.
[54] *Oršuš and Others v Croatia* [GC] (n 4) paras 87–97.
[55] *DH and Others v Czech Republic* [GC] (n 4) paras 184, 200, 205. *Oršuš and Others v Croatia* [GC] (n 4) paras 154, 159, 174, 176, 180.

Europe bodies on Czechia and considered them as relevant evidence giving rise to a strong presumption of indirect discrimination.[56] This was a step forward in terms of the tests applied in discrimination claims and, in particular, to school segregation cases.

The judgments of the Court Sections in *DH and Others*, *Sampanis and Others*, *Oršuš and Others*, *Sampani and Others*, and most recently, *Elmazova and Others* and *Szolcsán*, did not refer at all to international human rights standards and practice but relied mainly on ECRI standards and findings.[57] In *Salay*, the concerns of UN human rights bodies about school segregation were briefly noted.[58] The exception is in *Lavida and Others*, where the First Section referred to CERD and CADE not only as sources[59] but as relevant standards for the merits the case.[60] The Court emphasized that legal measures must prohibit racial or ethnic segregation and that measures designed to establish or maintain separate education systems or institutions are to be regarded as discriminatory.[61] This approach not only reflects the interplay with the international human rights standards and related jurisprudence on racial segregation but also shows how the Court has pushed forward the boundaries of human rights. In line with previous rulings, the Court has made it clear that Member States must ensure that measures taken by educational authorities do not result in segregation, even in the absence of any intent on their part, but importantly, that authorities must implement desegregation policies, even in the face of opposition from non-state actors[62].

## 3. Pushing Boundaries of the Human Rights Paradigm in Desegregation Litigation

Irrespective of criticism from within the ECtHR of the paradigm used in framing segregation in the context of group disadvantage and indirect discrimination,[63] one of the promising approaches developed by the Grand Chamber of the Court in

[56] *DH and Others v Czech Republic* [GC] (n 4) paras 187, 192, 195.

[57] The ECtHR referenced findings of the European Commission in respect with the situation of school segregation of Roma children in Albania but did not refer to similar findings in respect to Czech Republic, Hungary, Croatia, or North Macedonia.

[58] *Salay v Slovakia* (n 4) paras 62-64.

[59] *Lavida and Others v Greece* (n 4) paras 30–33.

[60] ibid para 71.

[61] ibid.

[62] ibid.

[63] *DH and Others v Czech Republic* [GC] (n 4). The Court's finding was criticized in the dissenting opinions. The approach of the Grand Chamber in applying a social context assessment and a vulnerable group perspective in the case of schooling arrangements for Roma children in special education was considered to be contrary to the role of a judicial body, as it departed from an individual case examination: *Oršuš and Others v Croatia* [GC] (n 4). Dissenting opinions saw the majority's perspective as a means of pushing through the notion of indirect discrimination based on arguments outside the concrete facts of the case, focusing rather on the special position of the Roma population in general.

the early desegregation cases was to obviate the need for individual examination of each applicant's case in school segregation. This approach was essentially based on the adverse impact on Roma as a vulnerable group and implied that Roma pupils should be afforded special protection against discrimination in education.[64] In this context, the Court looked at the broader and structural dimensions of racial segregation that went beyond a particular school or classroom establishment.[65] It gradually emphasized the combination of key factors, such as the role of state policies or practices leading to segregation, and the lack of state response to curb actions of non-state actors, such as overt opposition to the enrolment of Roma children and covert decisions by non-Roma parents having the same effect.[66] More importantly, the Court sanctioned the passive role of the authorities in failing to effectively combat segregation and put increasingly specific instructions as to what is expected from states in fulfilling their positive obligations to remedy discrimination and ensure desegregation actions.[67]

### 3.1. Positive obligations specific to combat school segregation: clarifying content and relevant test

In *DH and Others*, the Grand Chamber did not directly address positive state obligations, but importantly clarified that schooling arrangements for Roma pupils, and the relevant legislation applied in practice, must be accompanied by 'safeguards' which allow their needs to be considered in the light of their disadvantages. This process should aim at the integration into mainstream schools and not have a disproportionately negative effect on Roma pupils.[68] In *Orsus and Others*, the Grand Chamber explicitly required 'positive measures', providing examples such as aiding children to overcome difficulties in following school curriculum, acquiring language skills, including the active and structured involvement of the relevant social services.[69] Further guidance was provided in *Lavida and Others*, where the Court called for anti-segregation measures such as 'sending Roma children in mixed classes ... or proceeding to redistrict the school district map'.[70] More

[64] *DH and Others v Czech Republic* (n 4) para 182; *Sampanis and Others v Greece* (n 4) para 71; *Oršuš and Others v Croatia* (n 4) para 148; *Sampani and Others v Greece* (n 4) para 76; *Horvath and Kiss v Hungary* (n 4) para 102. *Lavida and Others v Greece* (n 4) para 46, 59.

[65] *DH and Others v Czech Republic* (n 4) paras 205–10; *Horvath and Kiss v Hungary* (n 4) paras 109–29; *Szolcsán v Hungary* (n 4) paras 53–59.

[66] *Sampanis and Others v Greece* (n 4) para 81; *Oršuš and Others v Croatia* (n 4) paras 154–55; *Sampani and Others v Greece* (n 4) paras 98, 100; *Lavida and Others v Greece* (n 4) paras 64–73; *X and Others v Albania* (n 4) paras 81–87; *Elmazova and Others v North Macedonia* (n 4) paras 76–77.

[67] *X and Others v Albania* (n 4) paras 81–87; *Elmazova and Others v North Macedonia* (n 4) paras 71–78; *Szolcsán v Hungary* (n 4) paras 57, 69.

[68] *DH and Others v Czech Republic* [GC] (n 4) paras 207–09.

[69] *Oršuš and Others v Croatia* [GC] (n 4) paras 165, 177.

[70] *Lavida and Others v Greece* (n 4) para 72.

explicitly, in *Horvath and Kiss* the Court explicitly established positive state obligations more particularly 'specific positive obligations to avoid the perpetuation of past discrimination of discriminative practices disguised in allegedly neutral tests',[71] implying necessary safeguards against misdiagnoses and school misplacement of Roma children. This approach has practically framed the Court's perspective on the `necessary guarantees [ … ] to undo a history of racial segregation in special schools`, recently reffirmed in the *Salay* case.[72]

The subsequent development of more specific positive obligations in cases of school segregation can best be triangulated in the recent judgments of the ECtHR. In *X and Others,* the Court applied the test of compliance with the state's obligation to avoid 'discrimination that resulted from over-representation in the school'[73] and therefore looked primarily at the practical measures taken to counter segregation.[74] The Court accounted the right to inclusive education enshrined in the national law[75] and the subsequent prohibition of segregation,[76] but importantly gave prominence to the binding decision of the national equality body, the Commissioner against Discrimination. The Commissioner had found that national authorities were under an obligation to take positive measures against discrimination of Roma and Egyptian pupils, on 'account of over-representation'.[77] Against this background, the ECtHR then qualified 'delays' in the application of desegregation measures by the relevant authorities as a failure to comply with the obligation to tackle school segregation.[78] In *Elmazova and Others* the European Court applied a similar test of compliance,[79] focusing essentially on the broader context of the desegregation measures to address over-representation.[80] The Court again considered and confirmed the approach of the national equality body, the Commission for Prevention and Protection against Discrimination and the Ombudsperson. Both national institutions had found that the relevant authorities had to ensure stricter and consistent decisions on school catchment area rules, due to the ethnic segregation of Roma children as a 'systemic problem' in the context of the 'white flight' phenomenon.[81] The lack of concrete official attempts to correct over-representation, to revise the school district map, to redistribute pupils in classes, due to opposition of non-Roma parents, was considered a failure to fulfil

[71] *Horvath and Kiss v Hungary* (n 4) paras 116, 119.
[72] *Horvath and Kiss v Hungary* (n 4) paras 127–28, *Salay v Slovakia* (n 4) paras 114–15.
[73] *X and Others v Albania* (n 4) para 84 referring to *Horvath and Kiss v Hungary* para 116.
[74] *X and Others v Albania* paras 84, 87 referred to *Lavida and Others v Greece* para 71.
[75] ibid paras 19 and 81.
[76] ibid paras 31–32.
[77] ibid paras 6–7.
[78] ibid paras 87–88.
[79] The Court referred to *X and Others* and *Horvath and Kiss*, referenced the importance of inclusive education and noted that segregation was prohibited in national law. See *Elmazova and Others v North Macedonia* (n 4) paras 74, 89, 25.
[80] ibid paras 74–77.
[81] ibid paras 9–10, 36–37, 89.

the state obligation to take positive measures against segregation.[82] This finding is indicative of stronger demands of state action against non-state factors as obstacles to desegregation.[83]

In *Szolcsan,* the issue of segregation arose from a different angle, revolving around the refusal to transfer Roma pupils from a predominantly or so-called Roma-only school to a mainstream school, on the basis of school catchment area rules. Inclusive education was provided for, and segregation was prohibited by national law.[84] Although the case was not brought before the equality body but before administrative courts, it was ruled that the applicant 'belonged to the same school catchment area as other Roma children, which was why the majority of the school's pupils were of Roma origin; [and] that did not constitute segregation'.[85] Following *X and Others* and *Elmazova and Others*, the Court took a firm stance against the position of the national courts, reiterating that the ethnic structure of residents within a school area cannot be sufficient to justify segregation[86] and that 'adequate measures' were required to remedy discrimination resulting from the over-representation of Roma in the school.[87]

### 3.2. Measures articulated in relation to the execution of school segregation judgments

A significant feature of recent European Court rulings on school segregation is the rejection of state justifications based on the ethnic composition of school catchment areas as a means of offsetting the obligation to take positive measures.[88] In *X and Others, Elmazova and Others* and *Szolcsan*, the Court raised the question of lack of anti-segregation interventions aimed at correcting ethnic imbalances of pupils and, in particular, over-representation in schools or classes, redrawing the map of school catchment areas or redistribution into mixed

[82] ibid paras 77–78.

[83] In *DH and Others* the Grand Chamber noted that the authorities faced difficulties in dealing with educational integration, including a degree a hostility on the part of the parents of non-Roma children. In *Sampanis* the Court merely stated that it did not exclude the possibility that the racist incidents organized by some parents of non-Roma students had influenced the authority's decision to segregate Roma. In *Oršuš* the Court strengthened its approach by emphasizing that the state had to show that the practice of segregating Roma children was objectively justified by a legitimate aim, in the context of the opposition from the parents of other children. In the *Sampani* case, the Court noted that municipal and prefectural authorities had refused or failed to act on desegregation measures because of fears of new incidents on the part of parents of non-Roma pupils. See *DH and Others v Czech Republic* [GC] (n 4) para 205; *Sampanis and Others v Greece* (n 4) para 81; *Oršuš and Others v Croatia* [GC] (n 4) paras 154–55; *Sampani and Others v Greece* (n 4) paras 98, 100.

[84] *Szolcsán v Hungary* (n 4) paras 12, 15, 18, 19.

[85] ibid para 16.

[86] ibid para 54.

[87] ibid paras 55, 57–58.

[88] ibid para 74.

classes, irrespective of the lack of intention or obstruction by non-Roma parents. Crucially, the Court placed these measures in the context of its rejection of racial segregation[89] and the emphasis on inclusive education as a means of ensuring non-discrimination.[90]

Other relevant ECtHR guidance as to what measures might be expected of states and what might constitute a remedy in segregation cases could also be extrapolated from *Avdiu and Others*.[91] The Court was satisfied that the national Commissioner against Discrimination had found that Roma children were subject to racial segregation and had ordered authorities to take steps to desegregate. As a result, the segregated school has been 'officially closed', the municipality had provided for the 'transport for the children to a new school' where the quality of education was 'adequate'.[92] The cumulative effect of these measures led the Court to conclude that the authorities had 'complied with their positive obligation to take steps to correct the applicants alleged inequality and to avoid their segregation'.[93] The overall approach to effective positive measures needs to be placed in the context of another relevant step that shows how the human rights paradigm has been further advanced in this line of jurisprudence.

This line of jurisprudence also found its way in the jurisprudence regarding Article 46 of the European Convention on Human Rights concerning the execution of the ECtHR's judgments.[94] In *X and Others*, the Court indicated that the state must implement measures to put an end to discrimination against Roma children,[95] while in *Elmazova and Others* the Court explicitly indicated that measures must ensure an 'end of the segregation of the Roma pupils', an explicit term used for the first time in relation to the implementation of Court judgments.[96] Most importantly, in *Szolcsán*, the Court required not only measures to end segregation of Roma children in school but called on the state to develop a 'policy against segregation in education and take steps to eliminate it'.[97] Arguably, the Court is willing to take this bold step, in a wider context of systemic discrimination.

[89] *X and Others v Albania* (n 4) para 78; *Elmazova and Others v North Macedonia* (n 4) para 89; *Szolcsan v Hungary* (n 4) para 69 referring to *Vona v Hungary* App no 35943/10 (ECHR 9 July 2013) para 57.

[90] *X and Others v Albania* (n 4) para 81; *Elmazova and Others v North Macedonia* (n 4) para 89; *Szolcsan v Hungary* (n 4) para 69 referring to *Çam v Türkiye* App no 51500/08 (ECHR 23 February 2016) para 64.

[91] *Avdiu and Others v Albania* (n 5) paras 13–14.

[92] ibid para 13.

[93] ibid para 14.

[94] Art 46 of the Convention provides that States undertake to comply with the final judgment of the ECtHR and that the Committee of Ministers shall supervise its execution. The Committee examines not only if measures such as payment awarded as just satisfaction has been made but whether other measures have been taken to ensure that the violation has been stopped or preventing the occurrence of similar violations.

[95] *X and Others v Albania* (n 4) para 96.

[96] *Elmazova and Others v North Macedonia* (n 4) para 89.

[97] *Szolcsán v Hungary* (n 4) para 69.

## 4. Judicial Borrowing of Standards Triggering the Positive Obligation to Remedy School Segregation in Recent Practice of Supreme Courts

The Strasbourg Court has rightly been described as having 'challenged the compatibility of segregated education for Roma children with the Convention', not only developing a strong jurisprudence but also changing the way in which the 'Court approaches discrimination cases'.[98] Indeed, the Court has played a prominent role in the development of positive obligations, which is considered 'one of the hallmarks' of its work in interpreting the Convention.[99] National supreme courts, on the other hand, play an equally significant role in interpreting and applying national law, while aligning themselves with the standards set by the European Court.

The judicial borrowing of the Court's standards goes beyond the mere reference to the jurisprudence. It involves a process of adaptation to the specific national context in the application of obligations and requires the provision of practical and clear instructions on how to make positive obligations concrete. This is particularly relevant in cases of school segregation. Civil society-led desegregation litigation in Central and Eastern Europe has been extensive and diverse, given the different circumstances of school segregation at the respective national level, and some of it has not reached the ECtHR, such as litigation in Bulgaria, Romania, or Slovakia.[100]

Much of the national litigation has been affected by difficulties in transposing or interpreting European standards, inconsistencies in the definition of racial segregation in education, lack of compliance with international human rights law, and lack of positive outcomes or distrust of symbolic remedies granted by national courts or equality bodies.[101] Despite an arduous process of interpreting and applying relevant discrimination tests in line with the ECtHR's jurisprudence or EU law, recent practice shows a promising shift in the approach of national supreme courts. This is particularly so when it comes to framing desegregation measures in line with the positive obligation's paradigm of the Strasburg Court in segregation cases.

[98] Claire Fenton-Glynn, *Children and the European Court of Human Rights* (OUP 2021) 153.

[99] Vladislava Stoyanova, 'Framing Positive Obligations under the European Convention on Human Rights Law: Mediating between the Abstract and the Concrete' (2023) 3(23) Human Rights Law Review.

[100] Recently the ECtHR communicated the case of *Adrian Salay v Slovakia*. App no 29359/22 (ECtHR, 9 October 2023). For a broader perspective see Romanița Iordache and Iustina Ionescu, *Effectively Enforcing the Right to Non-Discrimination* (EU Publications Office 2022); Gergely Dezideriu and Farkas Lilla, *Racial Discrimination in Education and EU Equality Law* (EU Publications Office 2020); Isabelle Chopin, Catharina Germaine, and Judit Tanczos, *Roma and the Enforcement of Anti-Discrimination Law* (EU Publications Office 2017).

[101] Isabelle Chopin, Catharina Germaine, and Judit Tanczos, *Roma and the Enforcement of Anti-Discrimination Law* (EU Publications Office 2017); Lilla Farkas, 'Mobilising for Racial Equality in Europe: Roma Rights and Transnational Justice' (PhD thesis, European University Institute, 2020) 193–203.

### 4.1. Overcoming challenges of interpreting and applying standards

Advocates and legal scholars alike have criticized[102] the European Court's findings on indirect discrimination versus direct discrimination in school segregation cases—more particularly, the failure to articulate its own test to distinguish between the two concepts in school segregation cases and the justification test,[103] an approach seen in some circumstances running 'counter to international human rights treaties that categorically prohibit segregation'.[104] Interestingly, equality bodies in EU countries, such as Romania or Hungary,[105] or outside the EU, such as in Albania or North Macedonia,[106] have based their decisions largely on standards set by the jurisprudence of the European Court, finding school segregation of Roma children to be an instance of racial discrimination. Equality bodies ordered relevant authorities to take clear and specific desegregation measures that clearly reflect the positive obligation paradigm.[107] This is a relevant indication of a successful legal transplanting or borrowing process by directly incorporating the Strasbourg Court's standards, through applying relevant tests determining direct and indirect discrimination on the basis of racial or ethnic origin and most importantly in providing practical and clear instructions

[102] William A Schabas, *The European Convention of Human Rights: A commentary* (OUP 2015) 569; Antonia Eliason, 'With No Deliberate Speed: The Segregation of Roma Children in Europe' (2017) 27 Duke Journal of Comparative & International Law 229, 231; Sina Van den Bogaert, *Segregation of Roma Children in Education* (Brill, Nijhoff 2018) 252–53, 271–329.

[103] Sina Van den Bogaert, 'Roma Segregation in Education: direct or indirect discrimination?' (2011) 4(71) ZaöRV 719–53; Farkas Lilla, *Report on Discrimination of Roma Children in Education* (EU Publications Office 2014) 24–38.

[104] ibid 35.

[105] Gergely Dezideriu, 'Segregation of Roma Children in the Romanian Educational System and the Legal Protection Against Discrimination' (2009) 1(5) Noua Revistă de Drepturile Omului 35–56; Lilla Farkas, 'Mobilising for Racial Equality in Europe: Roma Rights and Transnational Justice' (PhD thesis, European University Institute, 2020) 197–98.

[106] *X and Others v Albania* (n 4) paras 6–7; *Avdiu and Others v Albania* (n 5) para 6; *Elmazova and Others v North Macedonia* (n 4) paras 9–10, 36–37, 89.

[107] The Commissioner against Discrimination in Albania ordered educational authorities to take immediate measures to change the ethnic ratio of pupils, the closure of a segregated school, and free transportation to an integrated school. *X and Others v Albania* (n 4) paras 6–7; *Avdiu and Others v Albania* (n 5) para 6. The equality body in North Macedonia issued, among other recommendations, stricter observance of catchment area rules, redistribution of pupils in classes, increased individual support for Roma children, and an increase in teaching assistants in schools. See European Roma Rights Centre, 'North Macedonian Equality Body Finds Discrimination and Segregation of Roma in Prilep School' (ERRC, 01 February 2024) <www.errc.org> accessed 15 February 2024; European Roma Rights Centre, 'Equality Body in North Macedonia Orders Primary School to End Segregation of Roma' (ERRC, 19 August 2022) <www.errc.org> accessed 15 February 2024. The National Council for Combating Discrimination in Romania ruled that segregation in separate classes or facilities of Roma children amounts to direct discrimination, and placement of Roma children in separate classes on the basis of their place of residence amounts to indirect discrimination. NCCD recommended relevant authorities to implement specific measures prescribed in the ministerial decree prohibiting segregation in schools. See Decision no 769 (7 December 2016); no 770 (7 December 2016); no 504 (17 June 2020); and no 438 (30 August 2023) <https://www.cncd.ro/hotarari/> accessed 15 February 2024.

on how to make positive obligations concrete, particularly by desegregation measures.

### 4.2. A further advancement of positive state obligations in school segregation rulings of supreme courts

Recent jurisprudence in the region's highest courts shows important further developments in the articulation of positive state obligations in relation to school segregation. Vertically, high courts have progressively addressed the issue of the racial segregation by directly applying the standards set by the case law of the ECtHR and other international law standards. Horizontally, high courts such as in Czechia and Slovakia have used identical reasoning to outline concrete state obligations to effectively address school segregation faced by Roma children.

The Hungarian Supreme Court upheld[108] lower court rulings that the segregation of Roma pupils in classes on the basis of their ethnicity and the provision of a lower quality of education amounted to racial discrimination.[109] The courts ordered the relevant authorities to put an end to the segregation and to ensure a method of class enrolment that does not result in separation of children by ethnicity.[110] This approach is relevant in view of a previous ruling where the Supreme Court held that courts of law should order specific measures to be taken by relevant authorities to remedy segregation, and not limit themselves to finding a violation of the equal treatment clause.[111] Most importantly, the Supreme Court ruled that in a case of school segregation of Roma children, only monetary compensation could be awarded for non-pecuniary damage, and that there was no legal possibility to award compensation in kind in the form of services such as training.[112] In a similar line of reasoning, the Romanian Supreme Court ruled that in cases of school segregation of Roma children, once the facts of discrimination have been established by the equality body, the public interest is paramount and the best interests of the discriminated child come into play and prevail over other interests, such as reaching an amicable settlement during the judicial review of a decision finding discrimination.[113]

[108] Judgment of the Supreme Court of Hungary (12 May 2020) no Pfv.IV.21.556/2019/22.

[109] In the context of desegregation litigation led by NGOs in Hungary, the Supreme Court outlawed various forms of school segregation, such as school building and class segregation, inter-school segregation, segregation between private and public schools. See judgment of the Supreme Court of Hungary No Pfv.IV.20.936/2008/4; No Kfv.VI.39.084/2011/8; No Pfv.IV. 21.568/2010/5; No Pfv.IV.20.068/2012/3; No Pfv.IV.20.037/2011/7. The Supreme Court found that the choice of religious education justifies ethnic segregation. Judgment of the Supreme Court (22 April 2015) No Pfv.IV.20.241/2015/4.

[110] Previously, the Supreme Court had upheld a lower court's ruling ordering the enforcement of a desegregation measures. Judgment of the Curia (4 October 2017) no Pfv.IV. 20085/2017.

[111] ibid.

[112] Judgment of the Supreme Court of Hungary (12 May 2020) no Pfv.IV.21.556/2019/22 paras 2, 9, 11, 38, 41.

[113] Judgment of the Supreme Court of Romania (2 February 2022) no 580/2022 para 6.

Earlier, the Romanian Supreme Court had ruled for the first time that the segregation of Roma children in separate school buildings and, in particular, the failure to resolve the segregation of Roma children through desegregation measures, constituted a serious form of racial discrimination.[114] The Supreme Court essentially sanctioned the lower court's disregard of international human rights law, in particular ICERD, CERD Recommendation 27 on discrimination against Roma, Article 14 and Protocol 12 of the European Convention, and secondly, the school authorities' failure to implement the ministerial regulations requiring schools to implement desegregation measures.[115] The Supreme Court raised several crucial points for school segregation cases, anticipating similar arguments made by the ECtHR in *X and Others*[116] and *Elmazova and Others*,[117] stating that segregation cannot be justified by school catchment rules and the concentration of Roma in certain geographical areas leading to Roma-only school buildings or classes, and that this is irrelevant in establishing the causal link of segregation even if the ethnicity of pupils is not assumed by way of self-dentification, as long as it is common knowledge that the pupils segregated in separate buildings or classes are of Roma ethnicity, a situation which was not disputed by the education authorities.[118]

In the context of interpreting the conceptual elements of racial segregation as prohibited by national law,[119] the Bulgarian Supreme Court endorsed a regional court interpretation that directly referred to the case law of the Strasbourg Court when applying the criterion of 'compulsory separation' in practice. The Court held that the qualification of 'compulsory separation' should not be interpreted in the strict sense of the word but should be weighed against the perspective of the European Court of Human Rights.[120] The reference to the ECtHR's approach is critical, particularly as in segregation cases the justification arguments based on the 'voluntary' choice of Roma parents to enrol their children in separate schools, classes, or facilities have been rejected and considered contrary to the non-discrimination clause of the European Convention on Human Rights.[121]

[114] Judgment of the Supreme Court of Romania (20 February 2020) no 1015/2020 para II.2.

[115] ibid.

[116] *X and Others v Albania* (n 4) paras 68, 86–87.

[117] *Elmazova and Others v North Macedonia* (n 4) paras 67, 73–74.

[118] Judgment of the Supreme Court of Romania (n 111) para II.2. See by comparison *Elmazova and Others v North Macedonia* (n 4) paras 71–72 and *X and Others v Albania* (n 4) paras 13–14, 85.

[119] Experts view the definition of racial segregation in national law as contrary to European standards, particularly in respect to the requirement for the separation to be forceful or 'compelled', an element that is absent in international law as well as in the Strasbourg jurisprudence. Bulgarian courts interpreted the concept of segregation in a narrow manner, rejecting claims in the absence of a 'compulsory' nature of separation. See Dilyana Giteva, *Country Report Non-discrimination Bulgaria* (EU Publications Office 2023) 39–40; Margarita S Ilieva, *Country Report Non-discrimination Bulgaria* (EU Publications Office 2022) 8, 49–50.

[120] Judgment of the Supreme Court of Bulgaria (14 February 2020) no 80; Judgment of the Pazardzhik Regional Court (25 June 2019) no 233.

[121] *DH and Others v Czech Republic* [GC] (n 4) paras 203–04; *Sampanis and Others v Greece* (n 4) paras 93–94; *Oršuš and Others v Croatia* [GC] (n 4) paras 178–79; *Horvath and Kiss v Hungary* (n 4) para 204.

The Supreme Court referred in general terms to the conditions of free choice but missed the opportunity to refer to any specific judgment or test applied by the ECtHR (informed consent, absence of constraints, waiver of the right to equal treatment) to assess the consequences of consent to segregation.[122]

Just a few months after the Romanian and Bulgarian high court judgments, the Supreme Court of the Czech Republic ruled that, despite the lack of a definition in national legislation, racial segregation in education was illegal, including any separation of members of a particular group on the grounds of race or ethnicity, even if not motivated by racial considerations or provided under the similar educational conditions.[123] The Court highlighted the European standards applicable in cases of racial segregation, drawing a distinction between direct and indirect discrimination and explaining the test of justification and proportionality in light of the ECtHR case law on school segregation. It also clarified that in cases of segregation, the burden of proof shifts when statistical data indicate a disproportionate representation in a particular educational establishment, without referencing a specific percentage,[124] which may be substantiated, inter alia, by the vulnerable position or lower quality of education provided in the case of ethnic minorities, referring again to the case law of the European Court, specifically *DH and Others*, *Sampanis and Others* and *Orsus and Others*.[125]

The Supreme Court of the Slovak Republic adopted an almost identical approach, concluding that segregation is a form of discrimination consisting in the separation of members of a particular group on a prohibited discriminatory ground, even if the concept of segregation is not expressly recognized as a form of discrimination in the law.[126] Like the Czech Supreme Court, it provided a comprehensive review of international human rights law, including the case law of the ECtHR on school segregation[127] but interestingly, unlike its Czech counterpart court, which focused

[122] Judgment of the Supreme Court of Bulgaria (n 120). The Supreme Court has generally held that segregation on the basis of race is unacceptable unless it is the result of the individual's free choice and the conditions for free choice are met. While this position may be correct in certain respects, it may conflict with the position of the ECtHR regarding the free choice of Roma parents as members of a disadvantaged community and the consequences of their consent to the placement of pupils in segregated settings.

[123] Judgment of the Supreme Court of the Czech Republic (5 May 2022) no 25Cdo 473/2021 paras 26, 52, 57. The Supreme Court undertook a comprehensive review of international human rights law, including ICERD, and cross-referenced ECtHR case law with US segregation jurisprudence and doctrine. See paras 29, 32, 38, 41, 47–50, 54–56.

[124] The Supreme Court referred to its decision from 13 December 2013, no 30Cdo/4277/2010 followed by the Constitutional Court ruling from 12 August 2015, no III.US 1136/13 where an aspect of the case revolved around establishing a greater then 50 per cent disproportion for indirect discrimination to be established.

[125] Judgment of the Supreme Court of the Czech Republic (n 123) paras 61–62. In light of the human rights standards applicable in racial segregation cases, the Supreme Court sanctioned the lower court's disregard of the Strasbourg jurisprudence and international law. See ibid para 79.

[126] Judgment of the Supreme Court of Slovak Republic (15 December 2022) no 5Cdo/102/2020 para 8.

[127] ibid paras 8, 11–12. The Supreme Court of Slovak Republic referred to ICERD, CADE and other UN treaties, the European Convention of Human Rights, the EU Race Directive.

on both direct and indirect discrimination, it reflected on the test of justification and proportionality in indirect discrimination, specifically from the perspective of the Strasbourg jurisprudence.[128] However, one essential element is different in the Slovak judgment, namely the fact that the Court ruled that the state and local authorities have a responsibility to take effective measures to prevent the school segregation of Roma children, considering the best interests of the child.[129]

This is a development that could be seen, on the one hand, as mirroring the Hungarian Supreme Court's approach in that it did not limit its assessment to relevant tests finding a violation of equal treatment but also outlined the importance to remedy segregation. On the other hand, it reflects the approach of the Strasbourg Court in that it emphasized the positive obligations for relevant authorities to take preventing measures against segregation. In subsequent judgments, the Slovak Court reaffirmed that segregation on the basis of racial or ethnic origin is a form of racial discrimination but, most importantly, further ruled that measures taken by state authorities to ensure equal access to education must be examined to ensure that they do not disproportionately affect legitimate interests and violate the right to equal treatment of Roma children, in accordance with the criteria against school segregation set out by the ECtHR and the UN Convention against Discrimination in Education.[130] Crucially, the Supreme Court emphasized that state authorities must act and take effective measures to prevent segregation, whether through legislative initiatives, the creation of incentives or the reorganization of school districts and not remain passive[131]. By taking the route of developing specific positive obligations for state authorities to prevent and address racial segregation, the national court is essentially transposing the positive obligations paradigm of the Strasbourg Court, which focuses on the requirements for the state to take steps to redress inequality, to prevent segregation, and to put an end to it.

## 5. Conclusions

The ECtHR has progressively broadened its approach from outlining safeguards against misplacement and discrimination against Roma children to positive measures and, in particular, positive obligations to remedy the inequality of Roma children resulting from systemic school segregation. In the context of the execution

[128] ibid paras 13, 13.1, 13.2.

[129] ibid para 15.1. The Court lists various potential measures, among others: legislative initiatives, creation of incentive conditions, and formation of school districts.

[130] Judgment of the Supreme Court of the Slovak Republic (28 March 2023) no 4Cdo/112/2021 paras 44–46; Judgment of the Supreme Court of the Slovak Republic (12 July 2023) no 5Cdo/220/2022 paras 13–15. The Supreme Court agreed with the litigants and applied its analysis in the context of UNCADE and the ECHR case law.

[131] Judgment of the Supreme Court of the Slovak Republic (12 July 2023) no 5Cdo/220/2022 para 17.1.

of judgments, the Court has further developed its position on preventative and remedial measures withing the framework of the positive obligations approach, which requires Member States to take measures to end discrimination and eliminate segregation, including thorough general policies, as recommended by ECRI and equality bodies.

These outcomes are the result of the desegregation litigation, largely led by NGOs, which played a catalytic role in pushing the Court to look at the root causes of segregation. It could be argued that the need for such specific requirements were triggered by cumulative factors revealing wider dimensions of discrimination, and historical and structural problems related to school segregation of Roma children.

In the context of monitoring state compliance with standards on racial discrimination, ECRI has emerged as a relevant standard-setting actor, particularly in relation to the prohibition of racial segregation and the development of policy recommendations on desegregation in education. Equality bodies have also played a key role in outlawing segregation under national equality law, recognizing the systemic nature of school segregation and imposing positive obligations on education authorities. It is therefore noteworthy that the reasoning of the Court and the imposition of measures to end discrimination and, in particular, school segregation through the adoption of polices to combat segregation, were essentially based on the recommendations of ECRI and equality bodies, which highlighted the structural nature of school segregation.[132]

The jurisprudence of the ECtHR has gradually influenced the decisions of the highest courts in Central and Eastern Europe. Racial segregation has been examined and interpreted in the light of international human rights law. Supreme courts established clear obligations for national authorities to prevent segregation and ensure school desegregation. Civil society and experts acknowledged the impact of desegregation litigation at the national level but stressed the continued need for systemic interventions to achieve real change in tackling school segregation at the grassroots level.[133] This aspect has been emphasized by Council of Europe monitoring bodies or the Committee of Ministers in their supervision of the execution of judgments.[134]

ECRI's General Policy Recommendations have long emphasized the need to adopt key legislative measures, such as the prohibition of racial segregation in

[132] *X and Others v Albania* (n 4) paras 7–8, 43–44, 96; *Elmazova and Others v North Macedonia* (n 4) paras 16, 34, 89; *Szolcsan v Hungary* (n 4) paras 20, 53, 69.

[133] Open Society Justice Initiative, *Strategic Litigation Impacts Roma School Desegregation* (Open Society Foundations 2016) 36, 40, 44; Iulius Rostas (ed), *Ten Years After: A History of Roma School Desegregation in Central and Eastern Europe* (Central European University Press 2012); Iulius Rostas, *A Task for Sisyphus: Why Europe's Roma Policies Fail* (Central European University Press 2020).

[134] ECRI, 'Conclusions on Czech Republic' CRI (2023) 03; ECRI, 'Sixth Report on Hungary' CRI (2023) 02; ECRI, 'Conclusions on Slovak Republic' CRI (2023) 04; ECRI, 'Report on North Macedonia' CRI (2023) 28; Committee of Ministers, 'Decisions' CM/Del/Dec(2024)1492/H46-10; CM/Del/Dec(2024)1492/H46-17.

national law, including obligations on schools to promote equality in education, to ensure equitable enrolment and to prevent over-representation in any school or class.[135] The development of policies on Roma inclusion has proved to be a strong catalyst for further political commitment at the national level including in the area of education of Roma pupils. However, policies to tackle school segregation still lack a systematic approach and impact.[136] From this perspective, and from the view of the paradigm of positive obligations, the fundamental question is whether desegregation should be addressed essentially through individual judicial review and enforcement, or whether it should be considered as a structural, aggravated form of racial discrimination under national law, triggering a positive obligation for national authorities to implement systematic desegregation measures.

The recognition by anti-discrimination bodies and courts of the discrimination faced by Roma children in education does not suffice. Positive measures to remedy the inequality faced by Roma pupils through desegregation actions must be part of the school's obligations to promote equality in education.

Desegregation litigation has led to European Court rulings that have pushed the boundaries of human rights in cases of segregation. Decisions by supreme courts or equality bodies have also established explicit positive obligations at national level based on ECtHR judgments. However, measures at local level to address school segregation of Roma children still need to systematically tackle the problem.[137] Ultimately, it is imperative that policy-makers identify critical actions that can be taken to strengthen political will, overcoming bureaucratic contingencies and the resistance that still perpetuates educational inequalities.[138] As stated in a recent parliamentary resolution, states must ultimately take responsibility for fulfilling their obligations and commitments under international law to ensure that Roma children are protected from racial segregation.[139]

[135] ECRI, 'General Policy Recommendation No 7' CRI (2003) 8 Rev; ECRI, 'General Policy Recommendation No 10' CRI (2007) 6; ECRI, 'General Policy Recommendation No 13' CRI (2011) 27 Rec.

[136] Council of Europe, 'Mid-Term Review Report: Strategic Action Plan for Roma and Travellers' ADI-ROM (2022) 21; European Commission, 'Assessment Report of the Member States' National Roma Strategic Frameworks' COM (2023) 7 final; OSCE Office for Democratic Institutions and Human Rights, *Status Report 2023* (ODIHR 8 December 2023).

[137] ECRI, 'Conclusions on Czech Republic' (n 134); ECRI, 'Sixth Report on Hungary' (n 134); ECRI, 'Conclusions on Slovak Republic' (n 134); Committee of Ministers, 'Resolution on the Implementation of the Framework Convention for the Protection of National Minorities by Albania' CM/ResCMN (2023) 13; Committee of Ministers, 'Resolution on the Implementation of the Framework Convention for the Protection of National Minorities by North Macedonia' CM/ResCMN (2023) 2; Committee of Ministers, 'Resolution on the Implementation of the Framework Convention for the Protection of National Minorities by Romania' CM/ResCMN(2023)11; European Commission, 'Assessment Report of the Member States' National Roma Strategic Frameworks' (Communication) COM(2023) 7 final.

[138] Gergely Dezideriu and Farkas Lilla, *Racial Discrimination in Education and EU Equality Law* (Publications Office of the EU 2020).

[139] European Parliament, 'Resolution on the segregation and discrimination of Roma children in education' P9_TA(2023)0342 Official Journal of the EU C/2024/1180 paras 1, 3, 22.

# 10

# The Right to a Home

## Comparing Juridical Approaches to Systemic Discrimination in the European Court of Human Rights and the European Committee of Social Rights

*Helen O'Nions*

### 1. Introduction

Everyone has a fundamental human right to housing, which ensures access to a safe, secure, habitable, and affordable home.[1] Housing must be culturally adequate, requiring policies that enable 'the expression of cultural identity and diversity of housing'.[2] In their 2005 recommendation, the Council of Europe's Committee of Ministers underlined the need for comprehensive and integrated Roma housing policies, setting out key principles, drawing on General Comment No 4 from the UN Committee on Economic, Social and Cultural Rights.[3] In 2009 the European Fundamental Rights Agency called on EU member states to ensure that Roma and Travellers have 'security of tenure, available services and infrastructure; that their housing is adequate, affordable, habitable and accessible; and that they live in an adequate location and culturally appropriate homes'.[4] The situation was marked as requiring urgent action.[5]

Housing is one of four priority areas for the European Union's Framework for Roma integration, now in its second iteration.[6] Yet it is apparent that across

[1] UN Habitat, 'The Right to Adequate Housing', Factsheet No 21 (Rev 1). <https://unhabitat.org/sites/default/files/documents/2019-05/fact_sheet_21_adequate_housing_final_2010.pdf> accessed 26 March 2024.

[2] UNCESCR General Comment No 4: Art 11 (The Right to Adequate Housing), 6th Session, adopted 13 December 1991, UN Doc E/1992/23.

[3] Committee of Ministers Recommendation Rec(2005) On Improving the Housing Conditions of Roma and Travellers in Europe (Adopted by the Committee of Ministers on 23 February 2005 at the 916th meeting of the Ministers' Deputies Council of Europe 15 June 2005). The Right to Adequate Housing, adopted at the sixth session of the Committee on Economic, Social and Cultural Rights, on 13 December 1991.

[4] Fundamental Rights Agency, *Housing Conditions of Roma and Travellers in the European Union. Comparative Report* (EU Publications Office 2009) 8.

[5] ibid.

[6] For examples see European Commission, Assessment report of the Member States' National Roma Strategic Frameworks COM(2023) 7 final 9 January 2023.

Helen O'Nions, *The Right to a Home* In: *The Rights of Roma in European Courts*. Edited by: Kristin Henrard and Lilla Farkas, Oxford University Press. © Helen O'Nions 2025. DOI: 10.1093/oso/9780198914358.003.0010

Europe a significant number of Gypsy, Roma and Traveller families lack adequate housing.[7] In this chapter housing is defined broadly to reflect the experience of the Roma, Gypsy, and Traveller community, so it includes any place that a person habitually lives in as their home, thus including temporary structures, caravans, and traditional housing. Labelled 'temporary', encampments are typically situated on polluted or otherwise unsafe land, without adequate sanitation, clear water, or basic amenities.[8] Eventually, residents are forcibly evicted and relocated, often to another unsuitable location.[9] In Western Europe, Gypsy and Traveller communities who wish to continue a nomadic lifestyle face criminalization and continual eviction.[10] There are insufficient authorized pitches, forcing many to choose between abandoning their travelling lifestyle or occupying land unlawfully.[11]

In strategic litigation, before the European Court of Human Rights (ECtHR) and the Committee of Social Rights (ECSR), NGOs consistently place the denial of the right to adequate housing within a context of systemic discrimination. 'Anti-Gypsyism' or 'Romaphobia' is a particular type of discrimination which is most visible at a local level where planning decisions for Gypsy sites face organized, vocal opposition; and where forced evictions occur in a climate of open hostility and violence, often with tacit support of police and elected officials.[12]

This chapter will examine the Strasbourg Court's jurisprudence on the right to respect for home life. It will consider both procedural and substantive obstacles, revealing the boundary of a human right to adequate housing, ostensibly a social right, in terms of a convention on civil (and political) rights. In so doing, it undertakes a critical comparison with the jurisprudence of the ECSR through its collective complaints mechanism which has pushed the boundaries of social rights in a way that the Court is constitutionally unable to. The ECSR also acknowledges the importance of the discriminatory nexus in housing cases, whereas the Strasbourg Court has preferred to rely on vulnerability framing to narrow the state's margin of appreciation.

An initial focus on standing considers the different approaches of the European Convention on Human Rights (ECHR) and European Social Charter and asks

[7] Fundamental Rights Agency (n 4); Thomas Hammarberg Commissioner for Human Rights, *Human Rights of Roma and Travellers in Europe* (Council of Europe 2012) 137–56.

[8] Ede Ijjasz-Vasquez, 'Why We Need To Talk About Roma Inclusion' (World Bank Blog, April 14, 2017) < https://blogs.worldbank.org/en/europeandcentralasia/why-we-need-talk-about-roma-inclusion> accessed 25 March 2024; European Commission, *Mid-term Evaluation of the EU Framework for National Roma Integration Strategies up to 2020* (EU Publications Office 2018); Felix B Chang, 'Roma Integration 'all the way down': Lessons from Federalism and Civil Rights' (2018) 1(1) Crit Rom Stud 62. See also Ch 18 in this edited volume on the ECtHR *Hudorivic* case.

[9] *Winterstein and Others v France* App no 27013/07 (ECtHR, 17 October 2013).

[10] Fundamental Rights Agency, *Roma and Travellers in Six Countries* (European Union 2020) <https://fra.europa.eu/en/publication/2021/roma-and-travellers-six-countries-technical-report> accessed 22 March 2024.

[11] Office for National Statistics, *Gypsy and Travellers Lived Experiences, Homes* <https://www.ons.gov.uk/peoplepopulationandcommunity/housing/bulletins/gypsiesandtravellerslivedexperienceshomesenglandandwales/2022> (ONS 2022).

[12] Fundamental Rights Agency, *A Persisting Concern: anti-Gypsyism as a Barrier to Roma Inclusion* (European Union 2018) < http://fra.europa.eu/en/publication/2018/roma-inclusion> accessed 22 March 2024.

which is more suited to strategic litigation. Following this, a focus on the substantive right to housing, considers the material scope of the rights, the different approaches to positive obligations, and the Strasbourg Court's application of a heightened vulnerability frame, rather than a systemic discrimination frame. The final section will ask why, in the two decades since the Committee of Minsters' Recommendation, the housing situation of Gypsies, Travellers, and Roma appears impervious to positive change.

## 2. Opportunities for Strategic Litigation

NGOs are best placed to pursue strategic litigation, having the expertise, resources, and a broad contextual understanding. Restrictions on standing before the Strasbourg Court mean that NGOs will only be able to pursue this avenue in a representative capacity or as third-party interveners. By contrast, the collective complaints mechanism of the European Social Charter offers a different approach, removing the requirement for an individual victim and allowing a more contextual examination.

### 2.1. NGOs before the ECtHR

Under Article 34 of the ECHR the applicant must be a victim of the alleged breach, meaning they must be directly or indirectly affected.[13] To ensure that the rights are practical and effective, the requirement has been lifted in exceptional cases.[14] This exception is very narrowly construed, though.[15] The role of the NGOs is thus limited to representing or otherwise supporting alleged victims, or to making third party *amicus curiae* interventions.

The representative role of NGOs is essential as Roma struggle to access domestic remedies. This is particularly true in Eastern Europe, where Roma face more explicit discrimination and are discouraged from pursuing legal action.[16] Cases can attract widespread media interest, public hostility, and judicial indifference, which can be daunting for individual complainants. This is illustrated by *Paketova*, where the Bulgarian Helsinki Committee represented fifty-five Roma who had been forced from their homes and prevented from returning.[17] The Bulgarian Supreme Court upheld the divisional court's inadmissibility decisions in all cases, and the

[13] *Allianatos and Others v Greece* App nos 29381/09 and 32684/09 (ECtHR, 7 November 2013) para 47.

[14] *Centre For Legal Resources on behalf of Valentin Câmpeanu v Romania* App no 47848/08 (ECtHR, 17 July 2014).

[15] *Bulgarian Helsinki Committee v Bulgaria* App nos 35653/12 and 66172/12 (ECtHR, 28 June 2016).

[16] See for example *LK v Hungary* App no 621/14 (ECtHR, 19 August 2022) where the Court refused to consider the racist motivation of the mayor, as the applicant had been discouraged from pursuing a remedy domestically.

[17] *Paketova and Others v Bulgaria* App nos 17808/19 and 36972/19 (ECtHR, 4 October 2022).

prosecutor refused to pursue criminal investigations concerning the destruction of homes with racist motivations.[18] In a landmark decision, the ECtHR found a violation of the right to a home in Article 8, coupled with the prohibition of discrimination in Article 14.[19] It is difficult to imagine this outcome being reached without the representation, resources, and support of an established NGO.

For most NGOs the *amicus curiae* brief is the route to participation before the ECtHR.[20] The introduction of the Rule 9 procedure also encourages greater participation through interventions and dialogue on the execution of judgments.[21] The European Roma Rights Centre (ERRC)[22] has considerable expertise in providing both representation and briefings which have assisted the Court by situating the specific facts in their broader context.[23] Interventions reference, inter alia, international human rights instruments, EU law, and the OSCE High Commissioner on National Minorities' *Report on Roma and Sinti*.[24] They locate systemic failings in a wider international context, calling for the Court to use its 'evolutive interpretation, in which it treats the Convention as a living instrument' to interpret Articles 8 and 14 'in the light of this clear international consensus about the plight of the Roma and the need for urgent action'.[25] Their intervention in *Paketova* asks that the Court officially recognize the evictions context of anti-Gypsyism, which is rife in Bulgaria.[26] Although the Court did not formally adopt this term, they referred to 'strongly stigmatizing language' which targeted the Roma community in Bulgaria as a whole, finding a violation of both articles.[27]

## 2.2. NGOs before the Committee of Social Rights

The ECSR has facilitated a 'new frontier' in socio-economic rights advocacy,[28] enabled by the collective complaint protocol under the Charter.[29] Although the ECSR does not provide a forum for individual complaints, the mechanism offers

[18] ibid para. 57.
[19] ibid para.168.
[20] Laura Van den Eynde, 'An Empirical Look at the Amicus Curiae Practice of Human Rights NGOs Before the European Court of Human Rights' (2013) 31(3) Neth Q Hum Rights 271, 276.
[21] Rules of the Committee of Ministers for the Supervision of the Execution of Judgments and of the Terms of Friendly Settlements, Committee of Ministers, 10 May 2006 at the 964th Meeting of the Ministers' Deputies [2006] CM/Del/Dec 964.
[22] See also Chapters 4 and 11 by Gledhill and Farkas, respectively, in this edited volume.
[23] Van den Eynde (n 20) 285, writing in 2013 notes that the ERRC had already made interventions in five separate cases.
[24] ERRC, *Amicus Curiae Brief in U.K. Gypsy Housing Case* (ERCC 2000) <http://www.errc.org/roma-rights-journal/errc-amicus-curiae-brief-in-u.k.-gypsy-housing-case> accessed 20 March 2024.
[25] ibid.
[26] *Paketova* (n 17) para 147.
[27] ibid para 161.
[28] For a general discussion of social rights advocacy, see Conor Gearty and Virginia Mantouvalou, *Debating Social Rights* (Hart 2010).
[29] Additional Protocol to the European Social Charter Providing for a System of Collective Complaints [1995] CETS 158.

an opportunity for civil society to pursue strategic goals by exposing the broader context of systemic discrimination which underpins individual housing cases.[30] To date, the ECSR has found violations of the right to housing coupled with non-discrimination in thirteen cases concerning Roma or Travellers, with pending cases against Italy, Czechia, and Belgium.[31]

The collective complaints mechanism was introduced to improve the effectiveness, speed, and impact of the Charter's implementation and has enabled a new European social rights jurisprudence.[32] NGOs are empowered to apply for rulings on possible non-implementation in the countries that have accepted Charter provisions and the complaints procedure. Whilst there is no individual access to the Committee, there is no requirement to exhaust domestic remedies before bringing a complaint, and findings of violations are kept under review, reflecting the progressive nature of the obligations.[33] The ECSR has shown itself willing to develop a quasi-judicial function with very few inadmissibility decisions.[34] It delivers comparatively quick decisions, prioritizing cases of aggravated and egregious allegations, including repeat violations.[35]

Rather than observing from the side, civil society can engage directly with the Committee and challenge national governments in an adversarial procedure. International NGOs must have participatory status with the Council of Europe and then apply to the Charter's Governmental Committee to be included on the list authorized to bring a complaint.[36] It is also possible for governments to recognize a national NGO for this purpose, although only Finland has done so.[37] Smaller NGOs can partner with international organizations to this end.

There are additional advantages for strategic litigation before the Committee as it is quicker, less formal, and less resource-intensive. The absence of the

[30] Helen Duffy, *Strategic Human Rights Litigation: Understanding and Maximising Impact* (Hart 2018).

[31] The respondent states are Italy, France, Bulgaria, Greece, Portugal, and Belgium. *Amnesty International v Italy* 178/2019; *European Federation of National Organisations working with the Homeless (FEANTSA) v Czechia* No 191/2020; *International Federation of Human Rights (FIDH) and International Movement ATD - Fourth World v Belgium* 233/2023.

[32] Council of Europe Collective Complaints procedure <https://www.coe.int/en/web/european-social-charter/collective-complaints-procedure>; Explanatory Report System of Collective Complaints Strasbourg, 9.XI.1995 ETS 158.

[33] Nikolaos A Papadopoulos,'Strategic Litigation Before the European Committee of Social Rights: Fit for Purpose?' (2022) 40 Neth Q Hum Rights 379.

[34] Regis Brillat,'The Supervisory Machinery of the European Social Charter: Recent Developments' in Grainne De Burca and Bruno de Witte (eds), *Social Rights in Europe* (OUP 2005) 34.

[35] For example: *COHRE v Italy* 58/2009 (21 Oct 2010) was determined within six months following the finding of an earlier violation in *ERRC v Italy* 27/2004 (22 April 2006).

[36] Resolution CM/Res (2016)3 Participatory Status for International Non-governmental Organisations with the Council of Europe (adopted by the Committee of Ministers on 6 July 2016 at the 1262nd meeting of the Ministers' Deputies).

[37] Council of Europe Reservations and Declarations for Treaty No 158 Additional Protocol to the European Social Charter Providing for a System of Collective Complaints (ETS No 158), Finland 1 September 1998.

requirement for an individual complainant enables the legal and policy context to be explored, understood, and challenged. It forces national governments to directly engage with the concerns of civil society, and these concerns are placed on the national agenda, something difficult to achieve in the ECHR process. Further, the broader nature of the collective complaint mechanism presents an opportunity for 'advocates to frame the parameters of the dispute, which presents an avenue for novel arguments concerning the indivisibility of human rights'.[38]

An obvious limitation is its comparatively low number of ratifications to the collective complaints procedure (presently sixteen states). It is notable that many states with larger Roma populations, such as Hungary and Romania, have not accepted the complaints mechanism, although scrutiny can still take place through periodic reporting. Additionally, seven states that ratified the original charter have yet to ratify the revised instrument. Although the Committee of Ministers can ask them to report on non-accepted provisions in monitoring,[39] this creates a regrettable lack of uniformity in application. This reporting mechanism allows the ECSR to review implementation against the provisions of the European Social Charter, issuing conclusions. Although the supervisory mechanism typically generates progressive targets, state parties are expected to address non-compliance following a recommendation or resolution from the Committee of Ministers (CoM), and supervision remains open until the necessary action has been taken.[40]

## 3. An ECHR Right to Housing

The ECtHR has developed a rich jurisprudence, identifying positive obligations arising from civil and political rights, although it has stopped short of providing a theoretical underpinning.[41] It has remained cautious in the domain of social rights, implicitly recognizing that its legitimacy will be challenged should it adopt an overly expansionist approach.[42] Nevertheless, the living instrument principle, combining a teleological and dynamic interpretation, and the need for rights to be practical and effective, has resulted in a fragmented extension into the social and economic sphere, with the Court accepting there is no water-tight division.[43] Serious breaches of environmental rights have generated positive obligations

[38] Padraic Kenna and Mark Jordan, 'Housing Rights in Europe. The Council of Europe Leads the Way' in Padraic Kenna (ed), *Contemporary Housing Issues in a Globalized World* (Routledge 2016) 133.

[39] European Social Charter Governmental Committee of the European Social Charter. Abridged report concerning Conclusions XVI-1 (European Social Charter) CM(2002) 182, 183, 184.

[40] (n 29) Art 9.

[41] David J Harris and others, *Law of the European Convention on Human Rights* (Butterworths 1995) 353.

[42] Ingrid Leijten, *Core Socio-Economic Rights and the European Court of Human Rights* (CUP 2018) 25.

[43] *Airey v Ireland* App no 6289/73 (ECtHR, 9 October 1979) para 26.

under the absolute Convention rights.[44] The Court has also accepted that a serious breach of home life contrary to Article 8 will occur if a person is prevented from enjoying the amenities of their home, for example because of excessive noise, emissions, or pollutants.[45] Further, positive obligations may entail 'measures designed to secure respect for private life even in the sphere of the relations of individuals between themselves'.[46]

### 3.1. Balancing rights and interests under Article 8

The absence of a clear demarcation between economic/social and civil/political rights allows the right to home to be construed broadly, but it also presents a challenge for strategic litigation, as the Court's approach can lack consistency.[47] Examples include its rejection of any extension of Article 8 to encompass a particular choice of home in *Chapman*,[48] and the jurisprudence that is currently in flux regarding the extent to which the ECHR provides protection against environmental risks and pollution[49] and against climate change.[50]

The material scope of the right, the legitimate aim, and the proportionality of the interference, are not always neatly compartmentalized, particularly when the actions of private actors are evaluated. The applicant may be identified as a member of a vulnerable minority, but the precise content of any positive obligations this may suggest remains largely within the discretion of the state.

The right to respect for home and possessions engages Article 8 and Article 1 of Protocol 1. Both provisions allow states to justify an interference with the right in the broader public interest and states have historically been afforded a wide margin of appreciation where there are public policy considerations and resource implications.[51] In such cases the Court scrutinizes the existence of domestic procedural guarantees under the proportionality assessment.

44 *Budayeva and Others v Russia* App no 15339/02 (ECtHR, 20 March 2008); *Öneryıldız v Turkey* App no 48939/99 (ECtHR 30 Nov 2004). See also *Moreno Gomez v Spain* App no 4143/02 (ECHR, 16 Nov 2004).

45 *Hatton and Others v UK* App no 36022/97 (ECtHR, 8 July 2003);also *López Ostra v Spain* App no 16798/90 (ECtHR, 9 Dec 1994).

46 *Moreno Gomez* (n 44) para 55.

47 Ingrid Leitjen, 'Defining the Scope of Economic and Social Guarantees in the Caselaw of the ECtHR' in Eva Brems and Janneke Gerards (eds), *Shaping Rights in the ECHR* (CUP 2013) 113.

48 *Chapman v United Kingdom* App no 27238/95 (ECtHR, 18 January 2001) para 99.

49 See especially the extensive list of case law discussed in relation to Art 8 ECHR in the Factsheet on the Environment and the ECHR, <https://www.echr.coe.int/documents/d/echr/fs_environment_eng> accessed 30 October 2024, 9–26.

50 See the Factsheet on Climate Change <https://www.echr.coe.int/documents/d/echr/FS_Climate_change_ENG> accessed 30 October 2024.

51 *Hudorovič and others v Slovenia* App nos 248164/04 and 25140/04 (ECtHR, 10 March 2020) paras 141, 144, 158.

The first home life cases before the Strasbourg Court centred on caravan-dwelling Gypsies who sought to continue a semi-nomadic lifestyle. Whilst some sought security of tenure on public caravan sites, several had purchased their own land but then faced refusals of planning permission. The next group of cases concerned forced evictions, which often occurred in a context of discrimination and police brutality. More recent cases have encompassed arguments over the provision of amenities and utilities. This group presents a direct challenge to the civil and political nature of the Convention, yet it is clear that without such amenities, the ability to enjoy home life is compromised.

### 3.1.1. Gypsy planning cases

In 1992 a Gypsy occupying a caravan home on her own land challenged a refusal of planning permission. Her situation was far from unusual and was exacerbated by a shortage of caravan sites. Without permission the family could be fined and faced eviction, but the planning process was fraught with difficulties, not least the objections from settled residents.[52] The European Commission of Human Rights had found a violation of the applicant's family life under Article 8, emphasizing that 'living in a caravan home is an integral and deeply-felt part of her gypsy life-style'.[53] However, the Court was more cautious, and by a majority of 6-3 found no violation, emphasizing that there was 'a wide margin of appreciation which required only that the decision was fair and afforded due respect to the interests of the individual'.[54] These rudimentary procedural guarantees effectively supported an exclusionary national policy, suggesting that nomadism was a lifestyle that should be controlled for the aesthetic benefit of the wider population.[55]

Only Judge Pettiti showed an understanding of the context in which planning decisions were being made, recognizing that the Court's approach in ignoring the discriminatory nexus effectively nullified the applicant's right to live as a Gypsy:

> the survival of families must come before bucolic or aesthetic concerns ... in this sphere and in situations similar to the Buckley family's, the aspects of discrimination and breach of the right to accommodation and a home, inasmuch as they necessarily have an impact on the right to respect for family life, are indissociable from such respect.[56]

[52] *Buckley v United Kingdom* App no 20348/92 European Commission on Human Rights, para 64 (1997) 23 EHRR 101; *Chapman* (n 48).

[53] ibid para 71.

[54] ibid para 76.

[55] Jérémie Gilbert, 'Still No Place to Go: Nomadic Peoples' Territorial Rights in Europe' (2004) 4 European Yearbook of Minority Issues 141, 152.

[56] *Buckley* (n 52). Dissenting opinion of Judge Pettiti. For further discussion see: Helen O'Nions, 'Buckley v UK. The First in a Series of "Gypsy cases" to Challenge UK Legislation' (1996) 5 Web JCLI. <https://www.bailii.org/uk/other/journals/WebJCLI/1996/issue5/o'nions5.html> accessed 24 March 2024.

Judge Pettiti's opinion was too much of a leap for a conservative Court which showed limited engagement with the prohibition of discrimination or the rights of minorities.[57]

The subject of Gypsy sites in the UK returned to the Court three years later in the seminal case of *Chapman*.[58] The Court again attempted to balance the minority rights of caravan-dwelling Gypsies with broader public interests concerning planning and development. Here they had the benefit of a comprehensive intervention from the European Roma Rights Centre, which drew on numerous regional and international commitments. Echoing the sentiments of the European Commission of Human Rights in *Buckley*, they noted the importance of caravan-dwelling to Gypsy identity and referred to the emergence of an international consensus which justified a positive obligation to 'facilitate the Gypsy way of life'.[59]

However, whilst recognizing this broad positive obligation, the Court stopped short of delineating its requirements, instead emphasizing that it would not stretch to include a 'far-reaching positive obligation of general social policy' to provide sufficient sites.[60]

The boundary of the right to home was gently pushed by the Court's decision in *Connors*,[61] where they narrowed the margin of appreciation and found a breach of Article 8. The case concerned the summary eviction of a Gypsy family from a local authority site. For the first time, the Court recognized a positive obligation to consider the needs and lifestyle of Gypsies in regulatory frameworks.[62] Described by Henrard as 'innovative', the Court noted that a severe intrusion into the personal sphere of the applicant would require particularly weighty public interest reasons, even when there are cost implications for the state.[63]

### 3.1.2. Unlawfully constituted homes and forced evictions

The Court in *Buckley* and *Chapman* recognized that caravans stationed on land without permission could constitute homes under Article 8.[64] To the extent that the applicant can show a proprietary right, such dwellings may constitute 'possessions' under Article 1 of Protocol 1, and their peaceful enjoyment has occasionally been construed to cover situations of lengthy occupation without formal

[57] It is notable that Art 27 of the International Covenant on Civil and Political Rights has no counterpart in the ECHR.

[58] *Chapman* (n 48).

[59] ibid paras 93, 96.

[60] ibid para 98.

[61] *Connors v United Kingdom* App no 66746/01 (ECtHR, 27 May 2004).

[62] ibid para 94.

[63] Kristin Henrard, 'The ECHR and The Protection of Roma' (first published 2004, 2011) 5 European Diversity and Autonomy Papers, 21. <https://papers.ssrn.com/sol3/papers.cfm?abstract_id=1972960> accessed 24 March 2024).

[64] Buckley (n 52) para 54; Chapman (n 48) para 73.

permission.[65] This argument was advanced in *Chapman* but the Court referred to the broad discretion of planning authorities and the principle of fair balance, citing the applicant's illegal occupation and its detrimental impact.[66] In *Connors* the Court preferred to examine the substance of the complaint under Article 8.

*Yordanova* confirms that makeshift homes, occupied for years without permission, may also constitute a home under Article 8, regardless of classification under domestic law.[67] The planned eviction and relocation would have fractured the community of several hundred Roma, thereby affecting private and family life in addition to home life. The Bulgarian government argued that the eviction of Roma families, some of whom had occupied the settlement since the 1960s, pursued a legitimate aim of recovering illegally occupied land and addressing health and safety concerns. The Court accepted this aim but, following *Connors*, narrowed the margin of appreciation and found that the expulsion would not be necessary in a democratic society, stressing alternative, less-intrusive options that the state could take, including legalization of the homes in line with Roma inclusion commitments.[68] Although there is no obligation to provide housing, there is nonetheless an 'obligation to secure shelter to particularly vulnerable individuals' which flowed from Article 8 in 'exceptional cases'.[69] Further, the, 'underprivileged status of the applicants' group must be a weighty factor in considering approaches to dealing with their unlawful settlement and, if their removal is necessary, in deciding on its timing, modalities and, if possible, arrangements for alternative shelter'.[70]

*Yordanova* pushed the boundary of the right to housing and has been described as 'ground-breaking' for its recognition that exceptional circumstances may create an obligation to secure shelter.[71] The autonomous meaning of home was reiterated in *Winterstein*, which concerned twenty-five French travellers and their children.[72] The families had occupied mobile homes on the same tolerated site for years but were summarily evicted without a proportionality assessment or appropriate alternative accommodation. The unanimous finding of an Article 8 violation is significant, showing the impact of sustained litigation (which has been fortified complemented by complaints against France before the ECSR), such that illegal occupation may now

[65] *Hamer v Belgium* App no 21861/03 (ECtHR, 27 Nov 2007) para 76; *Keriman Tekin and Others v Turkey* App no 22035/10 (ECtHR, 15 Nov 2010), para 40–43; European Roma Rights Centre intervention in *Winterstein* (n 9). <http://www.errc.org/uploads/upload_en/file/errc-third-party-intervention-winterstein-and-others-v-france.pdf>, para IV.

[66] Chapman (n 48) para 119.

[67] *Yordanova v Bulgaria* App no 25446/02 (ECtHR, 24 Sept 2012) paras 102–03.

[68] ibid para 125

[69] ibid para 131.

[70] ibid para 133.

[71] Andi Dobrushi and Theodoros Alexandridis, 'International Housing Rights and Domestic Prejudice: The Case of Roma and Travellers' in Malcolm Langford, Cesar Rodriguez-Garavito, and Juliette Rossi (eds), *Social Rights Judgments and the Politics of Compliance: Making it Stick* (CUP 2018) 463.

[72] *Winterstein* (n 9) para 141.

give rights to a home protected under the Convention.[73] This enhanced proportionality review does not preclude all evictions but serves to ensure proper consideration of the impact on particularly vulnerable community members, a position aligned with international obligations such as the UN Convention on the Rights of the Child and the Convention against the Elimination of All Forms of Discrimination.[74]

Much will depend on the context in which evictions are authorized. In *Faulkner and McDonagh v Ireland* a family of Irish Travellers were evicted from a site they had illegally occupied for four years which was situated next to a public road. The site was found to constitute a home for the purpose of Article 8.[75] However, the Court was satisfied that the requirements of proportionality had been met, as the evictions enabled a road development to be carried out, which in turn pursued legitimate aims of public safety and economic development for the community. The Court acknowledged the vulnerability of the Traveller community, which 'could be relevant to how laws had been implemented in relation to this group, and *some* special consideration had to be given to their needs and particular lifestyle'.[76] Since the applicants had not been left homeless and had been granted assistance in obtaining accommodation, the Court considered that sufficient consideration had been given, and held the case manifestly ill-founded and therefore inadmissible.[77]

The length of residence required to constitute a protected home life was addressed in *Hirtu v France*,[78] where the requirement for a sufficient and continuous link was emphasized. The seven applicants represented a group of 141 migrant Roma, including around fifty children, who had been displaced from another camp to a slum on municipal land without basic amenities. All but one of the applicants had a French residence permit and had lived in France for many years, during which time they had been repeatedly evicted and relocated to unsuitable camps. Unlike *Winterstein*, the Roma were not travellers occupying mobile homes, and most expressed a desire to move to social housing, yet the French authorities applied domestic law designed for travellers to authorize evictions. In the event, the Court found a breach of the right to respect for their private and family life as the state had failed in its duty to take into account the needs of the applicants as members of an 'underprivileged *social* group'.[79] The argument that the treatment reached the Article 3 threshold was dismissed.[80]

[73] Dobrushi and Alexandridis (n 71) 456.

[74] Convention on the Rights of the Child (adopted 20 November 1989, entered into force 2 September 1990) UNGA Res 44/25 1577 UNTS 3; International Convention on the Elimination of All Forms of Racial Discrimination (adopted 21 December 1965, entered into force 4 January 1969) UNGA Res 2106 (XX) UNTS 660, 195.

[75] *Faulkner v Ireland, McDonagh v Ireland* App nos 30391/018 and 30416/18 (ECtHR, 8 March 2022) para 91.

[76] ibid para 97.

[77] ibid para 115.

[78] *Hirtu v France* App no 24720/13 (ECtHR, 14 May 2020).

[79] ibid para 70 (emphasis added).

[80] ibid paras 54–56.

Forced evictions are usually pursued with a degree of violence, deploying police and heavy machinery. *Yordanova* and *Winterstein* impose procedural obligations on states and push the boundary of the right to a home by imposing a positive obligation to provide accommodation, albeit 'exceptionally'. At the same time, the Court is clear that the Convention is not a social rights instrument and has consistently stated that there is no general positive duty to accommodate the homeless.[81]

### 3.1.3. Access to amenities

The dire accommodation situation endured by Roma families across Europe is evident from the case law and is highlighted in numerous international reports. In Western Europe, public sites for Gypsies are typically isolated, overcrowded, and in poor condition, whereas necessities such as clean water, electricity, and sanitation, are lacking in many Roma encampments.[82]

First-generation rights are not well suited to challenges concerning the allocation of state resources. The right to life in Article 2 is engaged when the circumstances are so dire as to jeopardize life, and Article 3 may be engaged if the conditions reach the minimum level of severity to constitute inhuman and degrading treatment. Typically, the latter requires 'actual bodily injury or intense physical or mental suffering',[83] but the threshold has also been met by heightened anxiety exacerbated by vulnerability.[84]

The families living in the Seine-Saint-Denis camp in *Hirtu* had no running water, sanitation, or electricity.[85] The ERRC represented the applicants and attempted an analogy with *MSS v Belgium and Greece*[86] in which the Court had found that the treatment of a homeless, destitute asylum-seeker in Greece (and his forced return by Belgium) violated, inter alia, Article 3.[87] Notwithstanding the

[81] *O'Rourke v United Kingdom* App no 39022/97 (ECtHR, 26 June 2001), confirmed in *Hudorovič* (n 51) para 114.

[82] UN Habitat (n 1). More recently see European Roma Grassroots Organisations, 'Roma. Access to Quality and Affordable Housing in Bulgaria, Czech Republic, Hungary, Romania, Slovakia and Spain' (2023) <https://ergonetwork.org/2023/11/research-report-on-roma-access-to-quality-and-affordable-housing/> accessed 29 August 2024.

[83] *Bouyid v Belgium* App no 23380/09 (ECtHR, 28 Sept 2015) para 87; Natasha Mavronicola, 'Bouyid v Belgium: The "minimum level of severity" and Human Dignity's Role in Article 3 ECHR' [2006] Cyprus Human Rights Law Review 7 <https://pureadmin.qub.ac.uk/ws/portalfiles/portal/30410604/Bouyid_Comment_CYHRLR_1_.pdf> accessed 26 March 2024.

[84] The position may be changing as evidenced by the Court's invitation in the climate change litigation case of *Duarte Agostinho and Others v Portugal and Others* App no 39371/20, (ECtHR, 9 April 2024) where the parties were invited to make representations under Art 3. See Corina Heri, 'The ECtHR's Pending Climate Change Case: What's Ill-Treatment Got To Do With It?' (*EJIL: Talk*, 22 December 2020) <https://www.ejiltalk.org/the-ecthrs-pending-climate-change-case-whats-ill-treatment-got-to-do-with-it/> accessed 4 March 2024.

[85] For images of a similar site, see Charlotte Boitiaux, 'French Police Evict Roma from the "Paris Jungle"' *France 24* (3 February 2016) <https://www.france24.com/en/20160203-france-police-evict-roma-slum-paris-jungle-homeless> accessed 24 March 2024.

[86] *MSS v Belgium and Greece* App no 30696/09 (ECtHR, 21 January 2011).

[87] ibid paras 362–68.

submission that one of the families with ten children were forced to sleep in a park following the eviction, the Court found insufficient evidence that the conditions in *Hirtu* reached the degree of severity required by Article 3.[88]

In *Hudorovič and Others v Slovenia*[89] the Court addressed the scope of the state's positive obligation to provide access to utilities, in particular clean water and sanitation. The first Roma applicants, a father and son, were precluded from using the public water supply so collected water from a nearby cemetery or polluted stream. They had been unable to obtain clean water for years. The second applicants were a group of fourteen Roma whose only clean water supply was 1.8 km from their home. Their neighbours had refused to allow them to install a connecting pipe. The applicants argued breaches of Articles 3, 8, and 14, claiming that the lack of clean water and other basic infrastructure had resulted in hygiene problems, frequent diseases, discomfort, embarrassment, and pain.[90] Moreover, for their children, these living conditions and the ensuing stigmatization had compromised their schooling and undermined social integration. Leaving aside the applicants' ethnicity, the facts were comparable to *Dzemyuk v Ukraine*,[91] where the applicant had no option but to drink polluted water from a nearby cemetery. A violation of Article 8 was supported by the specific facts as the authorities had disregarded their own environmental regulations and a judicial decision, but the Court did not engage directly with the right to clean water. The ERRC's intervention framed *Hudorovič* to reflect their campaign for access to clean water, drawing attention to Amnesty International's investigation into clean water for Roma in Slovenia and their own research investigating access to water and sanitation in seven European countries.[92] Alarmingly, in 81 per cent of the sites investigated, Romani neighbourhoods or settlements were not connected to water mains, and in 68 per cent of households there was no tap water or functioning sewerage system.[93]

The Court again rejected the Article 3 arguments for lack of evidence and focused attention on the material scope of Article 8 and its accommodation of fundamental human needs. Here, the ERRC's framing of the case reaffirmed a human rights boundary, with the Court confirming that 'access to safe drinking water is not, as such, a right protected by Article 8'.[94] However, this position was then

[88] *Hirtu* (n 78) para 56.

[89] *Hudorovič* (n 51). See also Ch 18 on the *Hudorovic* case in this edited volume.

[90] *Hudorovič* (n 51) para 107.

[91] *Dzemyuk v Ukraine* App no 42488/02 (ECtHR, 4 September 2014).

[92] Amnesty International, *Slovenia Parallel Lives: Roma Denied Rights to Housing and Water in Slovenia* (2011) <https://www.amnesty.org/en/documents/EUR68/005/2011/en/> accessed 24 March 2024; European Roma Rights Centre, *Thirsting for Justice: Europe's Roma Denied Access to Clean Water and Sanitation* (2017) <http://www.errc.org/uploads/upload_en/file/thirsting-for-justice-march-2017.pdf> accessed 24 March 2024. The states surveyed are: Albania, France, Hungary, Macedonia, Moldova, Montenegro, and Slovakia.

[93] *Hudorovič* (n 51). Third Party Intervention available at: <http://www.errc.org/uploads/upload_en/file/third-party-intervention-slovenia-hudorovic-v-slovenia-&-novak-and-others-v-slovenia-9-october-2015.pdf> para 12.

[94] *Hudorovič* (n 51) para 116.

qualified with the recognition that a 'persistent and long-standing' lack of access to safe water may trigger a positive obligation under Article 8.[95] On the facts, the Court found no violation, highlighting the state's wide discretion in socio-economic matters and the availability of public benefits to the applicants which could have been deployed to remedy their situation. The state was deemed to have discharged its responsibility to take account of the applicants' vulnerability.[96]

The decision is disappointing for several reasons. On Article 3, the applicants had to prove that denial of clean water resulted in sufficiently severe health consequences. This seems unnecessary, given, as *Dzemyuk* suggests, the availability of clean water is 'literally a matter of life and death'.[97] On Article 8, the deference shown to the state is concerning, as is the refusal to explore the discriminatory nexus. By accepting the state's position that people living in informal encampments could be denied access to the public water supply as a matter of policy, the likelihood that Roma would be disproportionately impacted was ignored. The Court accepted that the Roma who lived in these settlements 'face greater obstacles than the majority in accessing basic utilities'[98] but declined to consider these obstacles as prime facie evidence of indirect discrimination. Overall, the judgment shows little understanding of the families' daily struggles and comes close to victim blaming when it suggests that the applicants' limited state benefits should be used to address the water situation.[99]

## 4. A Social Charter Right to Housing

The ECSR monitors compliance with the European Social Charter by periodically reviewing state reports and hearing complaints brought, inter alia, by NGOs under its collective complaints protocol.[100] Unlike the Convention, Charter rights require progressive realization. Whilst the Charter rights must be respected by state parties, they are not directly enforceable in domestic courts. In the original Charter, housing was included indirectly through Article 16 which concerned the right of the family to social, legal, and economic protection. The 1996 revised Charter included a specific right to housing in Article 31 whereby the parties commit to undertake measures designed to: promote access to housing of an adequate standard; prevent and reduce homelessness with a view to its gradual elimination;

95 ibid.
96 ibid para 158.
97 Valeska David, 'The Court's First Ruling on Roma's Access to Safe Water and Sanitation in *Hudorovič* et al. v Slovenia: Reasons for Hope and Worry' (*Strasbourg Observers*, 9 April 2020) <https://strasbourgobservers.com/2020/04/09/the-courts-first-ruling-on-romas-access-to-safe-water-and-sanitation-in-hudorovic-et-al-v-slovenia-reasons-for-hope-and-worry/> accessed 24 March 2024.
98 *Hudorovič* (n 51) para 143.
99 ibid para 158.
100 Council of Europe European Social Charter [1961] CETS 35.

make the price of housing accessible to those without adequate resources.[101] The addition of Article E provides an opportunity to address the discriminatory nexus in much the same way as Article 14 ECHR. Most of the complaints litigated before the ECSR relate to Article E and Articles 31 or 16 regarding housing.[102]

To date, there have been thirteen violations of the Charter right to housing concerning Roma and Travellers.[103] The right to housing is conceived broadly, extending to rented and owner-occupied accommodation, illegal or temporary occupation, and caravan dwellings.[104] Adequacy of housing includes consideration of basic utilities including clean water, sanitation, waste disposal, and electricity, echoing the approach of the CoM recommendation. The Committee has considered structural security, risk of overcrowding, safety from both a sanitary and health perspective, and security of tenure when considering the adequacy of Roma encampments.[105]

Non-ratification of the revised Charter has not precluded the ECSR from investigating violations of rights not included in the original Charter. It adopts a teleological interpretation, recognizing a 'cross article transfer of key concepts',[106] notably extending to the overlap between Article 31 and Article 16 of the original charter. It is clear that Article 16 obligations will be interpreted to cover adequate housing at least for families, including consideration of the standard, size, and protection from eviction/security of tenure.[107] The Committee has regard to housing principles established by the UN Committee on Economic, Social and Cultural Rights, the UN Habitat agenda, and Article 8 jurisprudence, for example re-confirming the position in *Chapman* that there is a 'positive obligation to facilitate the gypsy way of life'.[108] There is an overarching aim to achieve social inclusion which requires that states 'respect difference ensure that social arrangements are not such as would effectively lead to or reinforce social exclusion'.[109]

The broad contextual approach of ECSR can be seen when comparing *International Federation of Human Rights v Belgium* with *Chapman*. Both cases concerned semi-nomadic Gypsy-Travellers but the Strasbourg Court was constrained to address the specific facts of the complaint, ie refusal of planning permission, to which it affords state parties a wide margin of appreciation. By contrast

[101] Council of Europe European Social Charter (Revised) [1996] CETS 163.
[102] Kenna and Jordan (n 38) 122.
[103] Papadopoulos (n 33), also notes that 16 per cent of collective complaints concern Roma, and all were found to constitute violations.
[104] Lukas Karin, *The Revised European Social Charter An Article by Article Commentary* (Elgar Commentaries series, Edward Elgar 2021) 327–38.
[105] ibid; *ERRC v Italy* (n 35) para 35.
[106] Kenna and Jordan (n 38) 133.
[107] *ERRC v Greece* 15/2003 (8 Dec 2004) para 16; *FEANTSA v France*, 39/2006 (5 Dec 2007) para 67.
[108] *Chapman* (n 48) para 96 affirmed in *Connors* (n 61) para 84.
[109] ibid paras 43, 19.

the Committee was able to consider how the right to housing for caravan dwellers was conceptualized in Belgian law and the impact of insufficient stopping places for travellers.[110] Most significantly, the ECSR is willing and ready to explore the discriminatory nexus, which is largely neglected by the Strasbourg court

## 5. The Boundaries of a Right to Housing

Both the ECtHR and the ECSR have recognized some positive obligations in relation to home life, although the Court has tended to approach them through the prism of family and private life. In so doing, both refer to the vulnerability of the Roma and the need for this to be considered when assessing the proportionality of the interference. However, on the question of systemic discrimination, there is a notable divergence of approach.

### 5.1. Positive obligations and vulnerability

Respect for family, private, and home life necessitates some positive obligations in line with Article 1 of the Convention, requiring that states secure Convention rights to all within their jurisdiction.[111] Securing these rights requires the allocation of state resources to ensure that rights are 'practical and effective'.[112] Since *Chapman* the Court has referred to 'a positive obligation to facilitate the *Gypsy* lifestyle' (my emphasis), but this does not appear in the case law concerning sedentary Roma, and the elements of the duty are not articulated. The Court has been clearer on what the duty will not include, as in *Chapman* where they rejected a positive obligation to provide a home.[113] In the Roma settlement cases the positive obligation has been framed differently to emphasize the need to consider the vulnerability of the community, as an 'underprivileged social group' or 'outcast community'.[114] This framing features in the careful balancing required in the proportionality assessment. But the Court will not set out a definitive expectation of minimum standards, such as clean water or sanitation.[115] The interaction of the margin of appreciation with positive obligations empowers states to determine the precise measures needed to address vulnerability. Whilst this reflects the principle of subsidiarity, it is problematic when state institutions persistently fail to address the needs of their Roma communities.

110 *FIDH v Belgium* 62/2010 (21 March 2012) para 59.
111 *Marckx v Belgium* App no 6833/74 (ECtHR, 13 June 1979).
112 *Airey v Ireland* App no 6289/73 (ECtHR, 9 October 1979).
113 *Chapman* (n 48), para 99.
114 *Yordanova* (n 67) para 129
115 *Hirtu* (n 78); *Hudorovic* (n 51).

In *Moldovan (No 2)* the Roma applicants had been violently expelled from their homes by villagers aided by local police. They challenged the destruction of their homes and possessions which had left them living in temporary, extremely overcrowded conditions for years. The Court considered the humiliation and debasement of the applicants and the impact on their dignity, finding it reached the threshold of Article 3.[116] The repeated failure of the authorities to put a stop to breaches of the applicants' rights amounted to a serious and continuing violation of Article 8. On the imposition of specific obligations, the Court noted that the tests of non-interference and positive obligations were broadly similar, requiring simply the application of a fair balance proportionality test.[117]

When positive obligations are identified, they typically centre on family and private life, with the Court avoiding a 'principled jurisprudence of positive obligations on home life'.[118] This may of course be explained by economic and policy considerations, resulting in a particularly wide margin of appreciation. By contrast, the ECSR with its explicit social rights focus has noted that positive obligations are in keeping with the state's obligation to take legal and practical measures to guarantee the right.[119] These measures must be regularly reviewed.[120] There is a distinction between an obligation of means and one of results, however. Whilst the Committee has accepted that Article 31 requires states to adopt suitable measures to secure adequate housing, state parties would frequently argue they were not obliged to achieve particular results. Although this distinction is recognized by the Committee, it has not prevented the application of positive obligations. For the situation to be in conformity with the treaty, state parties must:

a. adopt the necessary legal, financial and operational means of ensuring steady progress towards achieving the goals laid down by the Charter;
b. maintain meaningful statistics on needs, resources and results;
c. undertake regular reviews of the impact of the strategies;
d. establish a timetable and not defer indefinitely the deadline for achieving the objectives of each stage;
e. pay close attention to the impact of the policies on each of the categories of persons concerned, particularly the most vulnerable.[121]

In *ERRC v Italy* the ECSR identified a positive obligation arising from Article 31(3) to adopt appropriate measures for the construction of housing, in particular social

[116] *Moldovan v Romania No 2* App nos 41138/98 and 64320/01 (ECtHR, 12 July 2005).
[117] ibid para 97.
[118] Ellie Palmer, 'Beyond Arbitrary Interference: the Right to a Home? Developing Socio-economic Duties in the European Convention on Human Rights' (2012) 61 NILQ 3, 227, 233.
[119] *ERRC v Bulgaria* 31/2005 (ECSR, 18 Oct 2006).
[120] *FEANTSA* (n 107). See Padraic Kenna and Marc Uhry, 'FEANTSA v France. Collective Complaint on Housing Rights at Council of Europe' (2008) 5 (3) Housing and ESC Rights Law Quarterly 1, 3.
[121] *International Movement ATD Fourth World v France* 33/2006 (5 Dec 2007) para 60.

housing which must be made available equally to disadvantaged groups.[122] A repeat violation was found five years later when special measures were again confirmed as necessary to secure the right to housing for Roma.[123] There is also a positive obligation to ensure adequate stopping places for caravans.[124] Assessments of site suitability require considerations of size and location, but also cultural factors such as the need to meet socially with extended family.[125]

The Committee recommended that integrated and appropriate housing policies should target the needs of travellers in France, having regard to the CoM's 2005 recommendation and previous violations.[126] States are expected to maintain and provide data so that the appropriate policies can be implemented.

The ability to entertain repeat complaints, and relate them to periodic state reporting, has enabled the ECSR to engage with ongoing violations and to maintain scrutiny in a way that is difficult in Strasbourg due to the restrictive procedural requirements. The practical and effective rights doctrine has mitigated the impact of progressive realization, with the Committee expecting progress towards specific deadlines and adherence to other international commitments.[127] Compliance is assessed against a reasonable time frame, measurable progress, and financing that is consistent with maximum available resources.[128]

The ECSR also recognizes the disproportionate impact of institutional shortcomings on groups with heightened vulnerabilities.[129] The identification of the Roma community as vulnerable is in the Committee's statement of interpretation relating to Article 16 of the original Charter, and is repeatedly emphasized in Committee decisions.[130]

Although vulnerability is considered by both Court and Committee, there is a notable difference. For the ECtHR, vulnerability has appeared more as an alternative frame to systemic discrimination. Whilst *Winterstein* and *Yordanova* are welcomed for their recognition that Article 8 may be engaged when a home is illegally constituted, and the confirmation (following *Connors*) that the margin of appreciation should be narrowed to reflect the vulnerability of the community, the question of how this vulnerability is assessed (its origins, causes, and manifestations), and who should be responsible for addressing it (and how), are never elucidated. In its discussion of vulnerability in *Hudorovic* and *Yordanova*, the Court refused to

[122] *ERRC* (n 35) para 45.
[123] *COHRE* (n 35).
[124] *ERRC v France* 51/2008 (19 Oct 2009).
[125] *ERRC v Portugal* 61/2010 (30 June 2011) paras 49–50.
[126] Committee of Ministers Recommendation Rec(2005) (n 3); *ERRC v France* (n 124) para 37; *International Movement* (n 121) para 149.
[127] *FEANTSA* (n 107) paras 62–64.
[128] Kenna and Jordan (n 38) 125.
[129] *International Association Autism-Europe v France* 13/2002 (4 Nov 2003) para 53; *FEANTSA* (n 107) para 56.
[130] European Committee of Social Rights, Conclusions XVI-1 (2002), Statement of interpretation on Article 16.

consider Article 14 directly, but nevertheless applied its case law, recognizing that Roma may need assistance to enjoy equal protection:

> Article 14 … not only does not prohibit a member State from treating groups differently in order to correct 'factual inequalities' between them but, moreover, in certain circumstances a failure to attempt to correct inequality through different treatment may in itself give rise to a breach of Article 14.[131]

To move questions of discrimination into the 'fair balance' assessment reveals a significant boundary for the advancement of housing rights for Roma. Strategic litigation continues to push the Strasbourg Court to recognize that housing rights and systemic discrimination are inextricably linked.[132]

## 5.2. The discriminatory nexus

As *Hudorovič* demonstrates, the state can too easily discharge its obligations by ensuring a cursory examination of proportionality, with a nod to Roma vulnerability. The Court's failure to grapple with systemic discrimination remains a significant obstacle to the realization of rights. It explains the repetition of violations and the 'considerable disparity between court triumphs and the attainment of genuine justice'.[133] By placing the sole responsibility to determine appropriate measures on domestic authorities in the presence of unacknowledged systemic discrimination, the Court gives tacit consent to its continuation.

The discriminatory nexus was first identified by Judge Pettiti's dissent in *Buckley* when he recognized that the justification for interfering with the applicant's right to live in a caravan was founded primarily on the hostile views of the local population. Therefore, the Article 8 interference was intrinsically linked to Article 14.

Eviction cases frequently raise such arguments. The applicants in *Yordanova* argued their evictions were motivated by local hostility and racism, something that the Court considered when applying the proportionality assessment under Article 8 rather than Article 14.[134] Peroni and Timmer describe the Court's failure to explore the link between the group's disadvantaged status and social prejudices as surprising and at odds with the approach in the forced sterilization and educational segregation case law: 'given the particular context of anti-Roma sentiment in which the removal was ordered, the Court should have at least acknowledged the

[131] *Yordanova* (n 67) para 129; *Hudorovič* (n 51) para 142.
[132] *Connors* (n 61) para 82; *Chapman* (n 48) para 119; *Hudorovič* (n 51) para 141.
[133] Senada Sali (General Rapporteur), Execution of Roma and Traveller-related judgments of the European Court 16th Meeting of the Council of Europe Dialogue with Roma and Traveller Civil Society, 6 December 2023 (Strasbourg, Council of Europe).
[134] *Yordanova* (n 67) para. 148.

role played by negative social views against Roma'.[135] The ERRC's intervention in *Hudorovič* also calls for the education approach to be applied to housing cases. At the very least, this would send a powerful message to state parties by reversing the burden of proof when there is prime facie evidence of discrimination.[136]

Evidence of racist motivations on the part of authorities also impacts on the ability of victims to obtain domestic remedies.[137] In *Bagdonavicius and Others*,[138] the homes of forty-three Romani families in an established Romani neighbourhood created by the Russian authorities had been demolished and destroyed by fire, leading to a loss of accommodation, personal property, and access to services. Many Roma families were separated during the relocation, whilst the homes of non-Roma residents were untouched. The Court found a breach of Article 8 but declined to consider Article 14, in what has been described as a missed opportunity 'to provide greater guidance to governments on the steps they must take to ensure that the right to non-discrimination is fully respected'.[139]

There is no principled reason for the ECtHR's reluctance to engage with discrimination complaints. The application of the prohibition of discrimination in Article 14 does not depend on a finding of a substantive right violation.[140] The right instructs states to secure the substantive rights without discrimination, implying an obligation on the state to *fulfil* their obligations (necessitating a positive obligation approach).[141] A negative duties approach to Article 14 would be unlikely to challenge patterns of systemic inequality. In its landmark *Thlimmenos v Greece* judgment, the Court placed a positive obligation on the state, ruling that Article 14 would be violated 'when states without an objective and reasonable justification fail to treat differently persons whose situations are significantly different'.[142] The principle appeared to be quickly forgotten in *Chapman* when the Court found that the applicant could not invoke the Convention to require the respondent state to accord her specific favourable treatment as a Gypsy.[143] It was invoked again in *Yordanova*, but only to feature as part of the fair balance assessment.[144]

[135] Lourdes Peroni and Alexandra Timmer, 'Vulnerable Groups: The Promise of an Emerging Concept in European Human Rights Convention Law' (2013) 11 Int Journal of Constitutional Law 1056, 1066.

[136] *DH v Czech Republic* App 57325/00 (ECtHR, 13 Nov 2007); ERRC Intervention in *Hudorovič* <http://www.errc.org/uploads/upload_en/file/third-party-intervention-slovenia-hudorovic-v-slovenia-&-novak-and-others-v-slovenia-9-october-2015.pdf>.

[137] *LF v Hungary* App no 621/14 (ECtHR, 19 May 2022).

[138] *Bagdonavicius and Others v Russia* App 19841/06 (ECtHR, 11 October 2016).

[139] Minority Rights Group, 'European Court's Decision in Roma Eviction Case a Missed Opportunity Concerning an Urgent Issue, Rights Organizations Say' (*Minority Rights Group*, 11 October 2016) <https://minorityrights.org/2016/10/11/european-courts-decision-roma-eviction-case-missed-opportunity-concerning-urgent-issue-rights-organizations-say/> accessed 24 March 2024.

[140] *Thlimmenos v Greece* App no 34369/97 (ECtHR, 6 April 2000).

[141] Daron Tan, 'Demarcating the Margin: Positive Obligations under Article 14 of the European Convention on Human Rights' [2018] Columbia Journal of European Law.

[142] *Thlimmenos* (n 140) para 44.

[143] *Chapman* (n 48) para 95.

[144] *Yordanova* (n 67) para 148.

It is difficult to understand this reluctance. The vulnerable group paradigm cannot be a substitute for an examination of direct or indirect discrimination. It evokes paternalism and sympathy, something that Roma activists have rightly been keen to distance themselves from.[145] Some judges have recognized this blind spot, calling on the Court to deploy the well-established 'practical and effective' rights doctrine. In their partial dissent in *Hudorovič*, Judges Pavli and Kuris advocated positive obligations cognisant of context and historical fairness, because lack of clear water and sanitation perpetuates 'the stigmatisation and segregation of Roma communities'. They tasked the Court to look beyond formalities and see 'a tale of two communities, one Roma and one belonging to the majority, living a stone's throw from each other – one of them has running water coming out of their taps, and the other has never had it at all for over thirty years'.[146]

Briefings from third party interveners repeatedly reference the broader context of systemic discrimination. The refusal of the Court to grapple with discrimination in housing cases (as distinct from education and police brutality cases) reveals a significant boundary for the realization of rights in Roma housing cases.

By contrast, the ECSR's interpretation of the preamble to the charter and Article E of the revised charter, alongside positive obligations relating to Articles 31 and 16, suggest a nuanced, culturally appropriate approach which secures the Charter's social inclusion objective. Strategic litigation has found that discrimination impacts the realization of housing rights for Roma and Travellers in Italy, Belgium, France, Greece, Portugal, Ireland, and Bulgaria. Decisions have identified discrimination in the availability and conditions of housing, as well as access to utilities, forced evictions and segregated housing.[147] Where the state has not ratified the revised charter, the Committee has applied the non-discrimination principle in the preamble to its interpretation of Article 16.[148]

The tentative approach taken to indirect discrimination in Strasbourg is not followed by the ESCR, which has held that equal treatment requires a ban on all forms of indirect discrimination, which can arise by 'failing to take due and positive account of all relevant differences or by failing to take adequate steps to ensure that the rights and collective advantages that are open to all are genuinely accessible by and to all'.[149] The Committee has developed a positive obligation in respect of access to social housing, and has found Italy in violation due to a failure to adopt differential treatment to address the different situation of Roma, or to introduce measures specifically aimed at improving their housing conditions.[150]

[145] So Yeon Kim 'Les Vulnérables: Evaluating the Vulnerability Criterion in Article 14 cases by the European Court of Human Rights' (2021) 41 Legal Studies 617–32.
[146] *Hudorovič* (n 51), partly dissenting opinion para 17.
[147] *ERRC v Portugal* (n 125).
[148] *ERRC v Greece* (n 107) para 19.
[149] *ERRC v Italy* (n 35) para 20 citing *Autism-Europe* (n 129).
[150] ibid para 46.

In their resolution following *Interrights v Greece*, the CoM confirmed that genuine equality required a nuanced approach which respected human difference: where the 'specific differences of the Roma are not sufficiently taken into account ... they are discriminated against when it comes to the enjoyment of the right to housing under Article 16 of the Charter'.[151] Further, the Committee recognized that formal equality is not sufficient to achieve integration and that positive action is needed.[152]

The ECSR has thus developed the rights in the Charter, underpinning them with substantive equality necessitating appropriate differential treatment to address systemic discrimination. Given the scale of anti-Gypsyism and populist politics across Europe, this approach demands strong supranational oversight, which has to date been lacking in Strasbourg.[153]

## 6. Supervision and Execution of Judgments

Whilst the ECSR's approach to systemic discrimination is welcome, there remains a significant problem in securing state compliance through supervision. None of the violations found in Roma housing cases have been addressed in their entirety, whilst some state representatives have openly criticized the Committee for perceived overreach.[154] Regrettably, the Committee has not been adequately supported by the CoM, which has preferred to issue resolutions rather than specific recommendations, even in cases of repeat violations where there has been persistent non-engagement.[155] The Greek cases show that the authorities were fully aware that over 100,000 Roma were living in substandard housing with serious infrastructure deficiencies and a lack of amenities, yet the CoM declined to issue specific recommendations.[156] Perhaps unsurprisingly, subsequent follow-up monitoring shows little meaningful progress towards compliance.[157]

Repeat complaints against France dating back to 2007 found violations concerning forced evictions, lack of stopping places, and expulsions.[158] The committee noted how core Council of Europe values, notably the rule of law, democracy, and

[151] *INTERRIGHTS v Greece* 49/2008, Resolution CM/ResChS (2011) 8.
[152] *ERRC v Bulgaria* (n 119) para 42.
[153] Fundamental Rights Agency (n 12).
[154] Housing Rights Watch, 'Follow-up to Decisions on the Merits of Collective Complaints: Findings 2021' (*Housing Rights Watch*, 28 March 2022) <https://www.housingrightswatch.org/news/follow-decisions-merits-collective-complaints-findings-2021> accessed 24 March 2024; Dobrushi and Alexandridis (n 71) cite a 'full frontal assault' by the Greek representative.
[155] *INTERIGHTS* (n 151).
[156] ibid.
[157] European Committee of Social Rights Conclusions 2019 Greece, March 2020, 28 < https://rm.coe.int/rapport-grc-en/16809cfda6>; European Committee of Social Rights Follow-up decisions on the Merits of Collective Complaints Findings 2021.
[158] *International Movement* (n 121); *FEANTSA* (n 107); *COHRE v France* 63/2010 (ECSR 28 June 2011).

human rights, were undermined by attempts to expel Roma migrants.[159] Follow-up monitoring in 2014 found that the required assurances were yet to be provided. The European Roma and Travellers Forum then lodged a complaint showing the link between education, housing, and denial of basic utilities (as seen in *Hirtu*).[160] The ECSR found several violations underpinned by discrimination, but again the CoM preferred a resolution to specific recommendations.

Implementation of ECtHR rulings is marginally better. Procedural reforms enable civil society to communicate directly with the Committee of Ministers on the execution of judgments, and the recently agreed Copenhagen Declaration reiterates the importance of this dialogue.[161] Nevertheless, as of January 2022 almost half of all leading cases delivered by the Court are pending implementation.[162] This serves as a reminder that the pursuit of legal remedies for social right violations is part of a wider, complementary advocacy and campaigning role for civil society, and is unlikely to bring about change by itself.[163]

## 7. Conclusion

Social rights are not explicitly guaranteed in the ECHR, and their protection thus remains fragmented.[164] Breaches of Article 8 found in eviction cases are more likely to fall within family and private life, rather than home life.[165] Strategic litigation has had some success in getting the Court to push the boundaries of social rights to recognize a positive obligation to provide housing, as in *Yordanova*, and narrow the margin of appreciation, as in *Connors*.[166] However, the articulation of positive obligations remains muddy, and *Yordanova* has not yet been interpreted as giving rise to a general principle to identify suitable culturally appropriate accommodation.

The right to adequate housing thus remains narrowly construed. The seven principles of adequate housing established by UN Habitat, and approved by the CoM in 2005, commit to ensuring equal access to adequate, safe, and affordable

[159] *COHRE v France* (n 158) para 54.

[160] *European Roma and Travellers Forum v France* 119/2015 resulting in Resolution CM/ResChS (2018) 4.

[161] Committee of Ministers, *Declaration on the Reform of the European Convention on Human Rights System* (Copenhagen, 12 and 13 April 2018) High Level Conference Meeting, paras 33, 34.

[162] European Implementation Network, 'Why Implementation Matters' (*European Implementation Network*, January 2022) <https://www.einnetwork.org/implementation-of-judgments-of-the-european-court-of-human-rights> accessed 24 March 2024.

[163] Aoife Nolan, Conor Gearty, and Virginia Mantouvalou, 'Debating Social Rights' (2012) 75(4) MLR 685.

[164] This fragmentation is discussed in detail by Eva Brems, 'Indirect Protection of Social Rights by the ECHR' in Daphne Barak-Ezez and Aeyal Gross (eds), *Exploring Social Rights: Between Theory and Practice* (Hart 2011).

[165] Dobrushi and Alexandridis (n 71).

[166] *Connors* (n 61) para.86.

housing and basic services. The principles include, inter alia, the availability of services, materials, facilities, and infrastructure; habitability; and cultural adequacy.[167] Cultural adequacy has been mentioned in the Gypsy planning cases but has suffered in the application of a generous margin of appreciation. The question of amenities and facilities, as well as general habitability, are largely overlooked.[168]

Of great concern is the Court's application of vulnerability framing as an alternative to systemic discrimination. This has reduced the effect of strategic litigation and hampered realization of fundamental rights, by placing discrimination as just one factor to consider in the fair balance assessment. The emphasis on subsidiarity pursuant to Protocol 15 means that effective scrutiny is further reduced.[169] In a group of six recent inadmissibility decisions concerning sixty-eight Roma evicted from unauthorized camps in France, a chamber of three judges noted their satisfaction that the domestic courts had applied the principles in the case law, including the vulnerability of the community, to assess the proportionality of evictions. The domestic court limited the positive obligation to provide alternative accommodation to the homeless only in exceptional circumstances, citing *Yordanova*.[170] No reference was made to the repeated Charter violations in France identified by the ESCR.

The Strasbourg Court has the tools to fully examine the discriminatory nexus and is repeatedly asked by interveners to apply the non-discrimination provision in Article 14, to require positive action to take account of material differences.[171] Although the Court has shown willingness to do so in some of the most egregious rights violations against Roma,[172] it is regrettable to find that there is rarely any independent consideration of the discriminatory nexus in which violations of Article 8 occur.

The resistance to change in situations of systemic inequality has historically shown itself to be very strong and this is particularly apparent when the community seeking equality is an unpopular, stigmatized minority.[173] The approach taken to education, where the burden of proof shifts when there is prima facie discrimination, and where any waiver of the right must be unequivocal, has yet to be seriously explored in housing cases. This can be explained to an extent by the

[167] UN Habitat (n 1).

[168] *Hirtu* (n 78); *Hudorovic* (n 51).

[169] Council of Europe Treaty Series No 213, Strasbourg 24.IV.2013.

[170] ECHR, 'The Orders to Vacate Unauthorised Camps did not Interfere Disproportionately with the Right to Respect for Private and Family Life Of the Families Living in them ECHR' (ECHR 384) Press Release 8 December 2022 <https://hudoc.echr.coe.int/eng-press?i=003-7516626-10316882>.

[171] Luke Clements, 'An Emerging Consensus on The Special Needs Of Minorities: The Lessons Of Chapman' (2001, ERRC) < https://www.errc.org/roma-rights-journal/an-emerging-consensus-on-the-special-needs-of-minorities-the-lessons-of-chapman-v.-uk> accessed 25 March 2024; *Hudorovič* (n 51) paras 131–36.

[172] Eg *Moldovan* (n 116); *Nachova and Others v Bulgaria* App nos 43577/98 and 43579/98 (ECtHR, 6 July 2005).

[173] Barbara Cohen, 'Positive Action to Ensure Equality' [2005] 1 Roma Rights Quarterly 6.

proportionality or fair balance principle inherent in the right to property in Article 1 Protocol 1 and home life in Article 8. The comparatively wide margin of appreciation in property cases allows the right to give way to a public or general interest more easily.[174] The right to education in Article 2 of Protocol 1 lacks such caveats and provides a stronger foundation from which to justify adjustments to burden of proof.

By contrast, strategic litigation has had greater success before the ECSR, with the Committee's jurisprudence pursuant to Articles 31 and 16 taking full account of the discriminatory nexus and requiring positive measures to ensure rights are genuine and effective. In several decisions the Committee has confirmed an obligation on state parties to adopt differential treatment to ensure substantive equality for Roma.[175] This should include the provision of culturally appropriate accommodation, including adequate sites for caravan dwellers, and social housing. The quasi-judicial approach of the Committee is a better forum for strategic litigation on housing cases, not just because it is the natural venue to pursue social rights, but also because of its willingness to scrutinize the context in which rights violations continue to take place.

Continual supervision and dialogue with civil society ensures that violations of the Convention and Charter receive ongoing scrutiny, but both Court and Committee judgments face questions as to their impact. Weak implementation and oversight by the Committee of Ministers creates a 'credibility deficit' which has a debilitating effect on the pursuit of systemic goals.[176] There are significant delays in the execution of judgments which remains a significant weakness to the realization of housing rights for Roma, Gypsies, and Travellers under both instruments.[177]

[174] *James v United Kingdom* App 8793/79 (ECtHR, 21 Feb 1986) para 46.
[175] *ERRC v Bulgaria* (n 119); *International Movement* (n 121).
[176] Duffy (n 30) 267.
[177] Senada Sali, 'Execution of Roma and Traveller-related judgements of the European Court of Human Rights' (Strasbourg, Council of Europe, 6 December 2023) 16th Meeting of the Council of Europe Dialogue with Roma and Traveller Civil Society.

# 11

# Addressing Discrimination in Removal of Romani Children from their Families

*Mária Herczog and Zsolt Körtvélyesi*

## 1. Introduction

The over-representation of minority children in the alternative care systems of developed countries is widely documented as concerns indigenous and African American minors, and it also applies to Romani children in Europe.[1] The statistics show a several-fold over-representation of minority children subject to removals. The patterns arguably indicate widespread human rights violations and systemic discrimination. The literature assessing striking disparities in the removal of majority and minority children acknowledges the complexity of causes, while highlighting the strong presumptions of underlying (systemic) discrimination. It is less clear whether direct or indirect discrimination is at hand and to what extent there is a causal link with race/ethnicity and/or socio-economic conditions. Although removal due to poverty is unlawful, this cause still seems to dominate removal decisions in Central and Eastern Europe.[2]

Given the volume and depth of scholarship concerning child removals in the indigenous and African American contexts, important insights from this literature are taken to explore the connection between disproportionality (of removals of Roma children) and discrimination. The chapter does not discuss the case law from outside Europe in depth because the legal context is too distinct to allow meaningful comparison.

The main focus of the chapter is on the grounds, patterns and the effective remedies of structural discrimination suffered by Roma families in relation to child removals. The Roma in Europe are often treated as one group, just like in the case of other diverse non-majority groups, but it is important to note that they are a diverse community,[3]

[1] See section 2 below for data on Roma and other minorities.

[2] Bernard Rorke, 'Blighted Lives: Romani Children in State Care' (European Roma Rights Centre 2021) 7 <http://www.errc.org/uploads/upload_en/file/5284_file1_blighted-lives-romani-children-in-state-care.pdf> accessed 18 June 2023.

[3] For a critical account of administrative and scientific categorizations, see Mihai Surdu, 'Why the "Real" Numbers on Roma Are Fictitious: Revisiting Practices of Ethnic Quantification' (2019) 19 Ethnicities 486.

Mária Herczog and Zsolt Körtvélyesi, *Addressing Discrimination in Removal of Romani Children from their Families* In: *The Rights of Roma in European Courts*. Edited by: Kristin Henrard and Lilla Farkas, Oxford University Press. © Mária Herczog and Zsolt Körtvélyesi 2025.
DOI: 10.1093/oso/9780198914358.003.0011

geographically,[4] linguistically,[5] as well as in terms of their socioeconomic status.[6] Nevertheless, individuals identified as Roma have been more likely to face exclusion on various grounds, as evidenced by surveys,[7] which certainly justifies the use of the overarching label, Roma for our purposes.

Following the Introduction, section 2 explores the debate on disproportionality and statistical data in the United States. section 3 presents the international human rights and equality standards, highlighting that European anti-discrimination law also allows the consideration of socio-economic conditions as a ground of prohibited discrimination. Furthermore, states are under positive obligations to remedy structural discrimination. Section 4 assesses the case law of the European Court of Human Rights (ECtHR) and the European Committee of Social Rights (ECSR), while analysing a Hungarian case to show how strategic litigation can address structural discrimination concerning the removal of children from Roma families. Representative lawsuits or other forms of collective action can facilitate the finding of violations even in cases where direct or indirect discrimination is hard to prove for isolated decisions on removal. We find that law can address structural discrimination in particular where courts work with (a) a strong concept of positive state obligations, including the duty to proactively address the sources of disparities, and (b) evidence on a larger set of administrative decisions that can reveal disparities. This approach and the specificities of European anti-discrimination law can push the boundaries of human rights further by focusing on putting an end to the violations. This chapter concludes that strategic litigation is particularly well-equipped to uncover the facts, identify the wrongdoing and engender effective remedies against the disproportionate removal of Romani children.

While the long history of discriminatory and often violent practices are in themselves not decisive for evaluating current practices and identifying ongoing

[4] Roma and Travellers in Ireland and the United Kingdom, Sinti, Kale, Roma from post-socialist Europe moving to old EU member states.

[5] We find linguistically assimilated groups who speak the majority national language; Romani-speakers, with 'huge dialectical variation' and 'language mixing'. Yaron Matras and Anton Tenser (eds), *The Palgrave Handbook of Romani Language and Linguistics* (Springer International Publishing 2020) 18 <https://link.springer.com/10.1007/978-3-030-28105-2> accessed 2 October 2023. Evangelia Adamou and Kimmo Granqvist, 'Unevenly Mixed Romani Languages' (2015) 19 International Journal of Bilingualism 525. Further there are speakers of other Roma-exclusive languages, like Boyash. Annemarie Sorescu Marinković, Thede Kahl, and Biljana Sikimić (eds), *Boyash Studies: Researching 'Our People'* (Frank & Timme, Verlag für wissenschaftliche Literatur 2021).

[6] For an analysis of the concept of 'super-diversity' in the Roma context, see Annabel Tremlett, 'Making a Difference without Creating a Difference: Super-Diversity as a New Direction for Research on Roma Minorities' (2014) 14 Ethnicities 830.

[7] For a recent account, see European Union Agency for Fundamental Rights, *Roma in 10 European Countries: Main Results: Roma Survey 2021* (EU Publications Office 2023) <https://data.europa.eu/doi/10.2811/221064> accessed 2 October 2023; European Union Agency for Fundamental Rights, *Roma and Travellers in Six Countries: Roma and Travellers Survey* (EU Publications Office 2020) <https://data.europa.eu/doi/10.2811/30472> accessed 2 October 2023.

violations, they provide an important context for the legal assessment.[8] The separation of Roma children from their families is a well-documented practice, going back to the early modern times of European history.[9] The surviving legacy of discrimination prominently includes the tearing apart of families as one of the most egregious forms of oppression, colonialism, and racism, many of which would now constitute genocide. The removal of children from their families has commonly been justified as reducing 'the "negative influence" of Roma culture and language, and to adjust Roma children to "normal" society'.[10] Fear of child welfare services has been present in several European countries during recent decades, not only among the Roma but also among other vulnerable groups, including poor and migrant families.

Reliable and comparable data on current ethnic ratios in child removals is hard to come by. According to estimates, 60–80 per cent of children in out-of-home care in countries with sizeable Roma population are from this minority, which translates to a probability about nine to ten times higher of Roma children, in comparison to majority kids, being separated from their families. The proportion of Romani children in the care system was estimated to be fourteen times more than in the general population in 2014 by a Czech government report on the state of the Romani minority.[11] Based on data collected in some

[8] See eg the argument of the ECtHR: 'The Court notes that as a result of their turbulent history and constant uprooting the Roma have become a specific type of disadvantaged and vulnerable minority. As the Court has noted in previous cases, they therefore require special protection' (citations omitted); *DH and Others v The Czech Republic* App no 57325/00 (ECtHR, 13 November 2007) para 182. See also Council of Europe Commissioner for Human Rights Nils Muižnieks connecting this legacy with ongoing violations: Nils Muižnieks, 'Time to Cure Amnesia about the History of Roma in Europe' (*Commissioner for Human Rights*, 30 July 2015) <https://www.coe.int/hu/web/commissioner/-/time-to-cure-amnesia-about-the-history-of-roma-in-europe> accessed 14 October 2023.

[9] Council of Europe, 'Factsheets on Roma History—Austro-Hungarian Empire' (Education of Roma Children in Europe) <https://rm.coe.int/austro-hungarian-empire-factsheets-on-romani-history/16808b19ed> accessed 14 October 2023; Council of Europe, 'Factsheets on Roma History—Western Europe' (Education of Roma Children in Europe) <https://rm.coe.int/western-europe-factsheets-on-romani-history/16808b19e4> accessed 14 October 2023; Verena Meier, 'Neither Bloody Persecution nor Well Intended Civilizing Missions Changed Their Nature or Their Number' (2018) 1 Critical Romani Studies 86, 95; Marco Hüttenmoser and Kathrin B Zatti, 'Enfants placés', *Dictionnaire historique de la Suisse (DHS)* (ver 28 09 2010, 2010) <https://hls-dhs-dss.ch/articles/016590/2010-09-28/> accessed 21 October 2023; Benoît Collet, 'The Cultural Genocide Committed against the Yenish People in Switzerland Is a Crime That Remains Unpunished' *Equal Times* (27 January 2023) <https://www.equaltimes.org/the-cultural-genocide-committed> accessed 21 October 2023; Jan Selling, 'Sweden – Narrative Essay' (*Roma Civil Rights Movement – RomArchive*) <https://www.romarchive.eu/en/roma-civil-rights-movement/sweden-narrative-essay/> accessed 14 October 2023; Marko Stenroos, 'Roma Civil Rights Movement in Finland' (*Roma Civil Rights Movement – RomArchive*) <https://www.romarchive.eu/de/roma-civil-rights-movement/roma-civil-rights-movement-counter-weight-religiou/> accessed 14 October 2023; Vidar Fagerheim Kalsås, 'Norway – Narrating Essay' (*Roma Civil Rights Movement – RomArchive*) <https://www.romarchive.eu/de/roma-civil-rights-movement/norway-narrating-essay-long/> accessed 14 October 2023.

[10] Kalsås (n 9).

[11] Ryšavý, 'Czech Republic: Proportion of Roma in Children's Homes Increasing' (*Romea.cz*, 3 November 2015) <https://romea.cz/en/czech-republic/czech-republic-proportion-of-roma-in-children-s-homes-increasing/> accessed 14 October 2023.

institutions, the over-representation of Roma children in Bulgaria is estimated to be 60 per cent, in Czechia 40 per cent, in Hungary 75 per cent, in Italy 18 per cent, in Romania 40 per cent, and in Slovakia 90 per cent.[12] In Georgia, Roma children are periodically taken away by authorities and placed in 'children's colonies'; parents must then pay to retrieve their children.[13] According to the official data in 2020, Gypsy, Roma and Traveller children are over-represented in child welfare services in England.[14] In the UK, experts estimate that between 2009 and 2015, there was an increase of 73 per cent in the number of Roma children in foster care.[15]

We find similar patterns in the case of historically discriminated groups outside Europe. A review covering fifty-nine studies published in 2008–18 on out-of-home care in Australia, Canada, and New Zealand found an over-representation of indigenous children compared to national averages.[16] The review also found that these disproportionalities were increasing, sometimes at staggering rates. In Canada, indigenous children are 4.2 more likely to end up in care.[17] In Australia, indigenous children's over-representation in child welfare is eleven-fold and their number is expected to triple by 2037.[18] In this context, Dorothy Roberts notes that 'if you came with no preconceptions about the purpose of the child welfare system, you would have to conclude that it is an institution designed to monitor, regulate, and punish poor families of color.'[19]

The patterns that these statistics reveal hint at the type of widespread discrimination that human rights are meant to protect against, but also show the importance of nuanced analysis on how exactly equality law standards define and recognize forms of discrimination. In the following, we review the applicable international legal standards and revisit the question of discrimination.

[12] Rorke (n 2) 13, 43.

[13] David Szakonyi, 'No Way Out: An Assessment of the Romani Community in Georgia' (European Centre for Minority Issues 2008) ECMI Working Paper No 39 10 <https://www.ecmi.de/fileadmin/redakteure/publications/pdf/working_paper_39.pdf>.

[14] Dan Allen and Victoria Hamnett, 'Gypsy, Roma and Traveller Children in Child Welfare Services in England' (2022) 52 British Journal of Social Work 3904.

[15] Joanna Kostka, 'Social Care: How Gypsy, Roma and Traveller Children Face Discrimination across Europe and the UK' [2022] The Conversation <http://theconversation.com/social-care-how-gypsy-roma-and-traveller-children-face-discrimination-across-europe-and-the-uk-170312> accessed 9 February 2024.

[16] Kathomi Gatwiri and others, 'Indigenous Children and Young People in Residential Care: A Systematic Scoping Review' (2021) 22 Trauma, Violence, & Abuse 829.

[17] ibid 836.

[18] ibid.

[19] Dorothy Roberts, 'Race and Class In The Child Welfare System' *Frontline | PBS* <https://www.pbs.org/wgbh/pages/frontline/shows/fostercare/caseworker/roberts.html> accessed 2 October 2023; cited by Addie Rolnick and Kim Pearson, 'Racial Anxieties in Adoption: Reflections on Adoptive Couple, White Parenthood, and Constitutional Challenges to the ICWA' (2017) 2017 Michigan State Law Review 727, 736.

## 2. Human Rights Standards on Child Removals from Families

This section reviews the relevant international standards and delves into the prohibition of discrimination as a significant issue.

### 2.1. Substantive standards: prohibitions and positive obligations

International human rights standards protect families against undue state intrusion, establish positive obligations to secure compliance with human rights while maintaining the unity of the family wherever possible. They provide equality guarantees against different forms of discrimination suffered by minority families, including on socio-economic grounds.

Since its inception, the post-1945 international human rights framework has acknowledged that special protection is due to family ties. The 1948 Universal Declaration of Human Rights (UDHR) bans arbitrary interference with one's family and recognizes the right to found a family.[20] In addition, socio-economic rights specifically mention the well-being of the family.[21] Similar provisions are enshrined in the 1966 Covenants.[22] The UN Convention on the Rights of the Child (CRC) mentions and protects family ties at several places, under the right to 'be cared for by his or her parents'; 'to preserve his or her ... family relations'; 'not be separated from his or her parents'; 'family reunification'; and freedom from 'arbitrary or unlawful interference with his or her ... family'.[23] The European Convention on Human Rights (ECHR) in Article 8 specifically protects the right to respect for private and family life. As a protection against the most egregious violations, the mass removal of children from families can amount to genocide as defined by the 1948 Convention on the Prevention and Punishment of Genocide.[24] While presumably not applicable today, Roma suffered historically from measures that would fall under this Convention: 'Forcibly transferring children of the group

[20] Arts 12 and 16.

[21] Arts 23 and 25.

[22] Arts 17 and 23, International Covenant on Civil and Political Rights (adopted 16 December 1966, entered into force 23 March 1976) 999 UNTS 171 (ICCPR); Arts 7, 10, and 11, International Covenant on Economic, Social and Cultural Rights (adopted 16 December 1966, entered into force 3 January 1976) 993 UNTS 3 (ICESCR).

[23] Arts 7, 8, 9, 10, 22, and 16.

[24] In 2023, the International Criminal Court issued arrest warrants against President Putin and Commissioner for Children's Rights Lvova-Belova 'for the [alleged] war crime of unlawful deportation of population (children) and that of unlawful transfer of population (children) from occupied areas of Ukraine to the Russian Federation'. International Criminal Court, 'Situation in Ukraine: ICC Judges Issue Arrest Warrants against Vladimir Vladimirovich Putin and Maria Alekseyevna Lvova-Belova' (International Criminal Court, 17 March 2023) <https://www.icc-cpi.int/news/situation-ukraine-icc-judges-issue-arrest-warrants-against-vladimir-vladimirovich-putin-and> accessed 2 October 2023.

to another group' if 'committed with the intent to destroy, in whole or in part, a national, ethnical, racial or religious group'.[25]

Family integrity is not an absolute right and is subject to lawful interference, as long as there is a basis in national law, and the interference is proportionate to the legitimate aim pursued.[26] In terms of the proportionality assessment, removals conform with human rights requirements only if they are 'supported by sufficiently sound and weighty considerations in the interests of the child', taking into account the full context and the specific circumstances of the case. Put differently, it is not enough to show that 'the child would be better off if placed in care'.[27] Article 9 CRC spells out that 'a child shall not be separated from his or her parents against their will, except when competent authorities subject to judicial review determine, in accordance with applicable law and procedures, that such separation is necessary for the best interests of the child'. The latter could be argued for example in the case of abuse, neglect, maltreatment, absence of the parent (detention, exile, deportation, death). Removal from family requires a careful balancing between the right of the children to be protected from abuse and neglect on the one hand and their right to be raised in their families on the other. Removal from the family should be a measure of last resort because state intervention should be primarily aimed at supporting the family to become a safe environment in which to raise children.[28]

In the case law reviewed in section 5 below, the findings of violations turn partly on whether states are able to justify decisions on removal along the necessity and proportionality standard. In line with the principle that removals should be seen as a measure of last resort, they are only lawful under the ECHR if state authorities can be shown to have tried to avoid removal through measures supporting the family and carers, including in areas like housing, education, hygiene, and mental health. This means that states have positive obligations to provide support and assistance.[29] If the lack of adequate support can be seen as contributing to the situation that justifies removal, the removal should still be considered unlawful. Measures are also disproportionate if the state could have avoided removal and could have used a less intrusive option that would have better served the best interests of the children, namely leaving them with their families.

[25] Art II-e, Convention on the Prevention and Punishment of the Crime of Genocide (adopted on 9 December 1948, entered into force 12 January 1951) 78 UNTS 277.

[26] As these types of violations are hardly ever invoked in the context we are considering here, we are not considering them further here. On such a framing, see how the European Roma Rights Centre conceptualizes the (emotional) neglect of children in institutional care as a form of violence, in the context of their call for de-institutionalization. Bernard Rorke, 'Promising Change: Romani Children in State Care in North Macedonia' (European Roma Rights Centre 2023) <https://www.errc.org/uploads/upload_en/file/5539_file1_promising-change-romani-children-in-state-care-in-north-macedonia.pdf> accessed 28 March 2024.

[27] *Olsson v Sweden (No 1)* App no 10465/83 (ECtHR, 24 March 1988) para 72.

[28] Lea Brilmayer and Sonja Starr, 'Family Separation as a Violation of International Law' (2003) 21 Berkeley J Int'l L 213.

[29] See eg *Kutzner v Germany* App no 46544/99 (ECtHR, 26 February 2002) para 58.

## 2.2. Equality guarantees: minority status, material deprivation, and intersectionality

Of particular importance for the debate on the limits of justifiable child removals from minority, including Roma, families is the prohibition of discrimination, which is included in all the human rights instruments.[30] International and European (EU and Council of Europe) law covers the ground of racial or ethnic origin, but also encompasses other grounds that concern socio-economic status. Importantly, the prohibition of discrimination extends not only to direct but also to indirect discrimination.[31] While the latter points to a disproportionate impact of a seemingly neutral provision, the former concerns less favourable treatment on protected grounds. In EU law, direct discrimination is in principle prohibited unless EU law itself provides an explicit exception, whereas indirect discrimination follows the formula that applies in general international law (including under the ECHR), for both direct and indirect discrimination, namely requiring a reasonable and objective justification. A reasonable and objective justification requires not only a legitimate aim for the differentiation, but also a relationship of proportionality between the legitimate aim on the one hand and the differential treatment on the other.

The ECHR now includes two non-discrimination provisions: Article 14 of the Convention and Protocol 12. Article 14 contains an open list for the grounds, prohibiting discrimination in relation to one of the rights protected in the Convention. Article 8 of the Convention protecting private and family life creates a solid ground against the types of violations discussed in this chapter. Article 14 does not constrain the Court from at least considering the complex patterns of racial, ethnic, and socio-economic discrimination that Roma families face because it covers the following grounds: 'sex, race, colour, language, religion, political or other opinion, national or social origin, association with a national minority, property, birth or other status'. The stand-alone non-discrimination clause in Protocol 12 remains limited due to the lack of ratifications. From among the countries with sizable Roma population, neither the Czech Republic, Slovakia, Hungary, Romania, nor Bulgaria have ratified it.

The prohibition to discriminate on socio-economic grounds (property or other status) requires that children should not be removed from their families that live in poverty as long as children from better-off families in comparable situations are not or would not be removed. Crucially, this requirement is also a self-standing

[30] UDHR Art 2, ICCPR Arts 2, 24, and 26, ICESCR Arts 2 and 10, CRC Art 2, ECHR Art 14, and Prot No 12.

[31] This distinction is jurisprudential only in the ECtHR, but in EU law the Equality Directives include definitions of both direct and indirect discrimination, eg in Art 2 of Council Directive 2000/43/EC of 29 June 2000 implementing the principle of equal treatment between persons irrespective of racial or ethnic origin.

safeguard in international human rights law. The UN Guidelines for the Alternative Care of Children, adopted as a resolution of the General Assembly, include a specific prohibition of child removal due to poverty and related hardship:

> Financial and material poverty, or conditions directly and uniquely imputable to such poverty, should never be the only justification for the removal of a child from parental care, for receiving a child into alternative care, or for preventing his/her reintegration, but should be seen as a signal for the need to provide appropriate support to the family.[32]

This prohibition will be important in the analysis below. Furthermore, socio-economic inequalities and minority status can have a combined impact which often enhances disproportionalities in removals. This may constitute intersectional discrimination resulting from the combination of minority status as well as material deprivation. Indirect discrimination refers to practices that appear neutral as concerns racial or ethnic origin and/or socio-economic conditions but have a disproportionate impact on minority and/or impoverished children. This is crucial in the child removal context. The evaluation that leads to the decision to remove children tends to be anchored in majority notions and norms of what constitutes a family and 'the best interests of the child', where abuse and neglect start, what form external support should take and what is expected from families. Majority views tend to devalue minority cultures and practices and treat majority standards as the norm, implicitly resulting in discriminatory outcomes that reveal systemic discrimination. It is essential for adequate protection of the right to family that jurisprudence establishes and maintains clear and effective standards.

In light of the alarming disproportionalities and the historical antecedents, some call for a more minority-conscious standard. International human rights instruments on children's rights also include minority-specific protections.[33] Raven Sinclair argues that racially/ethnically conscious decisions should replace seemingly neutral decisions that often give too much leeway for (majority) bias and ethnocentrism.[34] The more inclusive standards can include special regard for minority cases, especially a recognition that upbringing in a minority heritage requires special measures that are not present in the case of majority children.

[32] UNGA Guidelines for the Alternative Care of Children, UN Doc A/RES/64/142 (2010), para 15.

[33] The CRC in its Art 30 recognizes a minority-specific right for children, mirroring the provision in Art 27 of the ICCPR, and Art 20-3 also includes the obligation to pay 'due regard ... to the child's ethnic, religious, cultural, and linguistic background'.

[34] She cites data from her research on an almost unanimous (98 per cent) view that 'the repatriation to Indigenous heritage was an essential and critical aspect of reconstructing identity as young adults'. Raven Sinclair, 'The Indigenous Child Removal System in Canada: An Examination of Legal Decision-Making and Racial Bias' (2016) 11 First Peoples Child & Family Review 8, 12. He quotes the case *R v Williams* (1998) to the effect that judicial directions to act impartially cannot always be assumed to be effective in countering racial prejudice. Ibid 13.

In addition to positive (affirmative) action that pays special regard to the fact that the decisions concern non-majority children and families, a central aspect of fighting inequalities is mapping the broader context of these decisions. Various international bodies supervising equality guarantees in international human rights law call for recognition of systemic, structural, institutional, or organizational discrimination. The European Commission against Racism and Intolerance (ECRI) defines structural discrimination as:

> rules, norms, routines, patterns of attitudes and behaviour in institutions and other societal structures that, consciously or unconsciously, present obstacles to groups or individuals in accessing the same rights and opportunities as others and that contribute to less favourable outcomes for them than for the majority of the population.[35]

The ECRI calls on national equality bodies to place particular focus on addressing this type of discrimination as it is hard to recognize, and fight against, through individual challenges.[36] In the context of child removals, it is easy to see that this broader perspective is not an extra, but a crucial element of adequate responses. Systemic causes are interrelated, setting in motion a vicious circle that is aptly articulated by Aboriginal and Torres Strait Islander Social Justice Commissioner June Oscar:

> Women have said to me repeatedly that this is another stolen generation. Young people placed in out of home care are 16 times more likely than those who are not to be under youth justice supervision in the same year. It is perhaps most distressing that the Royal Commission into Deaths in custody found a strong relationship between out-of-home care and deaths in custody. Of the 99 deaths investigated in 1991 it was found that almost half had previously been removed from their parents. ... we have to call out these systemic failings, where the over-representation of children in care, driven and compounded by poverty, makes unimaginable crisis all the more likely in our communities.[37]

[35] ECRI General Policy Recommendations No 2: Equality Bodies to Combat Racism and Intolerance at National Level, CRI(2018)06, 7 December 2017, Explanatory Memorandum, para 20 <https://rm.coe.int/ecri-general-policy-/16808b5a23> accessed 28 October 2024. See also the definition of systemic discrimination in UN Committee on Economic, Social, and Cultural Rights, General Comment No 20: Non-discrimination in Economic, Social, and Cultural Rights, Identifying and Preventing Systemic Discrimination at the Local Level E/C.12/GC/20, 2009, para 12.

[36] ECRI General Policy Recommendations No 2: Equality Bodies to Combat Racism and Intolerance at National Level, CRI(2018)06, 7 December 2017, Explanatory Memorandum, para 20, <https://rm.coe.int/ecri-general-policy-/16808b5a23> accessed 28 October 2024.

[37] June Oscar, 'Speech at the AbSec Biennial Conference, Strong Communities, Strong Kids' (*Australian Human Rights Commission*, 20 November 2019) https://humanrights.gov.au/about/news/speeches/strong-communities-strong-kids-absec-biennial-conference accessed 26 February 2023. The Commissioner also cites another way that child placement programmes fail minority children: 'Women have reported to me the failure of the departments they work for in placing children with Indigenous

Indeed, in contravention of the human rights standards, the data reveal systemic discrimination that minorities, including the Roma, face in the context of child removals. We now turn to the debate about the complexities of the underlying factors.

## 3. From Disproportionality to Systemic Discrimination

Whether children are removed from their families in violation of substantive requirements and positive state obligations requires an individual assessment specific to the case. In the case of minorities, and Roma families in particular, we witness systemic discrepancies and disparate effects that point to possible (indirect) discrimination. The legally relevant question is whether the data indicating the over-representation of minority children in removal decisions enables the establishment of a prima facie case of indirect discrimination, after which the burden shifts to the public authorities to provide a reasonable and objective justification. They must demonstrate that the higher rate of removals is justified by reasonable and objective grounds, which in turn requires the showing of a legitimate aim pursued and proportionate means of achieving it, using standards that apply equally to non-minority families.

As is apparent from the case law analysed in the next section, public authorities usually put forward interrelated causes for removal, further complicating the debate on justification. The most pressing reason for removal relates to domestic violence, but even in such cases, authorities should demonstrate that removal is necessary, for example when the child cannot stay with a non-violent parent. Other causes, such as the (special) educational or other needs of the children, are often strongly related to inadequate housing and poverty. Furthermore, different views on how to raise children can be at play. The assessment of these factors can become subjective and problematic especially when there is considerable distance between decision-makers and the families who are subject to their assessment. A Canadian study regarding Aboriginal children found that the factor that best explained the disparity between majority and minority families is alleged 'neglect' and the related inadequacy of the family environment, a concept that arguably conceals culturally loaded reasons for removal.[38]

On the other hand, risk factors, such as 'extreme poverty, serious substance abuse, and single parenting' are disproportionately present in minority families,

carers, even when they recommend a suitable option.' Ibid. She also makes a point on the role of public spending: 'In 2017–18, only 17 of overall child protection funding was invested in support services for children and their families, while 83% was invested in child protection services.' Ibid.

[38] ibid 912–13.

thus a higher level of justified cause for removal might actually be expected.[39] This argument disregards the issue of wealth-based discrimination in implicitly accepting extreme poverty as a valid ground for removal. In this reading, disproportionality remains a problem, but the solution to maltreatment is not simply to decrease removals, which would alarmingly increase exposure to maltreatment, but to address and remove the causes of maltreatment.[40] A closer study of the causes of disparities in child removal cases in the US points to the importance of acknowledging that race may still be the decisive factor in removal decisions: decision-makers' perception of race, not poverty, seems to lead to a 15–20 per cent difference between Black vs White children.[41] This indicates that discrimination is present in child welfare decisions.

In summary, empirical data strongly indicate systemic discrimination in child removals concerning minorities, including Roma children. These statistics are best considered in light of the relevant international human rights standards that are as follows: (1) Decisions cannot be based on minority status as that would constitute direct discrimination. (2) Poverty cannot justify removals because that violates a specific prohibition and goes against the requirement of using removals only as a last resort. (3) Discrimination is present where we can identify considerations that would not apply in a comparable non-minority case and that are more likely to result in removal. (4) More subtle differences can also lead to discrimination, when authorities apply standards that are rooted in majority preconceptions about adequate parenting and that cannot be justified in a culturally inclusive understanding of the best interests of minority children. (5) Such seemingly neutral practices would fail the reasonable and objective justification test.

The effects of systemic discrimination are tangible in child removal decisions, where individual litigation might not be able to capture the nature of the violations. For instance, deprivation and discrimination in other fields like education, work, and housing, can lead to conditions that make it hard or impossible to challenge removals in court, even in the case of disproportionality. In such cases, strategic litigation is a tool to address these broader causes. Where one sees a vicious circle

[39] Elizabeth Bartholet, 'The Racial Disproportionality Movement in Child Welfare: False Facts and Dangerous Directions' (2009) 51 Arizona Law Review 871, 874.

[40] ibid 923. Note that the disproportionality debate goes way beyond child removal. Similar arguments have been made at the intersection of disability and minority, claiming that minority disability children are under-identified, not over-represented in special education in the US. Paul L Morgan and others, 'Replicated Evidence of Racial and Ethnic Disparities in Disability Identification in U.S. Schools' (2017) 46 Educational Researcher 305; Paul L Morgan and others, 'Are Hispanic, Asian, Native American, or Language-Minority Children Overrepresented in Special Education?' (2018) 84 Exceptional Children 261.

[41] Alan J Dettlaff, 'The Evolving Understanding of Racial Disproportionality and Disparities' in Alan J Dettlaff (ed), *Racial Disproportionality and Disparities in the Child Welfare System* (Springer International Publishing 2021) 16–18 <https://doi.org/10.1007/978-3-030-54314-3_2> accessed 11 April 2023.

of removal, criminal behaviour, detention, and death in custody, all links in the chain should be addressed by strategic litigation.

The next section assesses how these standards are used in legal practice and reviews the European jurisprudence on Roma child removal cases.

## 4. European Case Law on Removals of Roma Children

The jurisprudence of the ECtHR and the ECSR on the removal of Roma children is in its infancy but progressive standards on removals already exist. The emphasis is on positive state obligations as an important form of protection against violations, but the analysis of domestic litigation shows that the boundaries of human rights concerning the systemic discrimination in Roma child removals can be further pushed by strategic litigation, particularly by providing adequate remedies. The next section (4.1) reviews ECHR standards on minority child removals, which reveal that minority origin is rarely considered. The subsequent part (4.2) extends the overview to the European Social Charter and national jurisprudence, to assess how the minority origin can become part of addressing systemic violations.

### 4.1. European judicial standards for child removals

The ECtHR has adjudicated complaints about child removal, including cases involving Roma families.[42] The standards include the positive obligations of the state to act, in a timely manner, in line with the relevant legal rules. State authorities should balance three types of interests: those of the child, the parents, and public order, with a heavy emphasis on the child's interests.[43] Removal from the family is considered an extreme form of interference in the right to respect for family life that should be exceptional and that calls for strong justification, placing the burden on the state to prove that the action pursues a legitimate aim and that it is proportionate, ie it is necessary in a democratic society.[44]

The ECtHR has pushed the boundaries of the right to family life by adopting a broad reading of state responsibility: violations can occur even where child removal can be explained by circumstances found in the family if those are a result,

[42] The long list of cases concerning contacts between children and their parents includes disputes between parents, but also claims of discrimination on grounds that include religion, disability, and sexual orientation. For a regularly updated list of cases, see the ECHR Fact Sheet on parental rights <https://www.echr.coe.int/documents/d/echr/FS_Parental_ENG>.

[43] Regarding the procedure, the children who were removed do not always appear as applicants, which does not prevent the Court to assess their best interests, examining, in such cases, the parents' right to family life. This means that the substantive analysis of the Court and the standards applied did not vary along these lines.

[44] See, eg, *Zhou v Italy* App no 33773/11 (ECHR, 21 January 2014) paras 44–48.

at least in part, of the failure of state authorities to provide support and avoid removal. Conversely, the Court has pulled back the boundaries by largely failing to address equality concerns in child removal cases. The judgments focus on individual applicants and do not meaningfully engage with the shocking statistical disparities. Admittedly, the Roma complainants have not raised equality arguments, as discussed below. However, even in a case involving a transgender person and clear direct discrimination in the form of revoking parental rights because the applicant undergoes gender identity change, the Court found it unnecessary to examine the issue of discrimination and was satisfied with finding a violation under Article 8 of the Convention.[45]

Until 2024, the ECtHR has adjudicated three Roma child removal cases. In *Barnea and Caldararu v Italy*, the ECtHR found a violation of the right to family life because the child was removed from the family between 2009 and 2016.[46] The Court stated that removal of a child from the family is an extreme measure that can be justified in the face of immediate danger.[47] The authorities cited a complex set of factors that justified removal, including psychological factors and the affective, educational, and pedagogical incapacity of the parents, while also referring to material deprivation and inadequate living conditions.[48] While the latter were not the sole reason for removal, the Court still found that the circumstances could not justify the exceptional measure of breaking up the family. The judgment stresses that there was never a hint that the child was abused; to the contrary, court documents recurrently cited a strong attachment between the child and the parents,[49] adding that the goal of a better educational environment cannot in itself justify removal.[50] Domestic authorities also cited the passing of time as a factor. However, the Court stressed that this was a result of the inertia of the authorities, and the non-implementation of a 2012 national judgment ordering the return of the child, so that time could not serve as a legitimate ground for denying reunification.[51]

While the obligation not to remove a child seems like a predominantly negative obligation, the Court also stressed the importance of positive obligations with regard to Article 8. Removal can only be justified where the state can demonstrate that there were prompt measures aimed at keeping the family together.[52] The Court noted the vulnerable position of the family (a large family living in a camp) and found that the authorities should have first adopted measures that supported the unity of the family, such as aid and social housing.[53] Only if such measures had

[45] *Savinovskikh and Others v Russia* App no 16206/19 (ECHR, 9 July 2024) para 93.
[46] *Barnea and Caldararu v Italy* App no 37931/15 (ECHR, 22 June 2017) para 89.
[47] ibid para 64.
[48] ibid paras 16 and 29 in particular.
[49] ibid paras 73–77.
[50] ibid para 84.
[51] ibid paras 78 and 88.
[52] ibid paras 63–66.
[53] ibid para 72.

failed and reasons for removal continued to exist despite adequate support could removal be justified, and even then, there should be sustained efforts to allow the return of the child.

The *Barnea and Caldararu* judgment confirms that the Court will only accept arguments for removal: (1) in light of a comprehensive reading of the circumstances that justify this exceptional measure, and (2) where the situation is not the result of the failure of state authorities to do everything in their capacity to keep the family together.[54] While the circumstances of the case reveal the applicants' precarious and minority situation, no equality arguments were raised or considered in the case.

A subsequent case involving a Roma family, *Achim v Romania*,[55] focused on the temporary placement of the family's seven children, after the initial decision on removal and their return after about a year. The Court accepted that the measures were justified and further elaborated the elements of a complex, convention-compliant assessment. The domestic decision-making relied partly on material conditions, including the family home's unsuitability for children, being 'too small and poorly equipped', while concerns were also raised about personal hygiene and diet, and consequently about the children's health.[56] The parents did not let their children go to school or participate in social activities. Parental neglect could be linked to delayed development of language and motor skills, and anxiety-related behaviours. The judgment noted that the parents received psychological and pedagogical support to help them fulfil their parental responsibilities, but their negligent behaviour continued.[57] The Court placed great emphasis on the fact that domestic decisions on appeal considered factors other than material deprivation, such as 'the relationships between the applicants and their children and the applicants' collaboration with the social services'.[58]

The judicial standard on state obligations to return otherwise lawfully removed children is twofold: one based on negative and one based on positive obligations. First, there should be a holistic assessment of the various aspects of the best interests of the children, including factors like hygiene, health, behavioural and skill development, education, social activities, and contact with others. These are negative obligations, in the sense that the state should refrain from interference (child removal) unless exceptional circumstances exist. What seems especially important is that the Court does not stop here but adds positive obligations, pushing the boundaries of human rights law concerning violations that do not result directly from state action, but from complex social phenomena, counteracting which, public authorities could nonetheless prevent family break-up.

[54] ibid paras 86–87.
[55] *Achim v Romania* App no 45959/11 (ECtHR, 24 October 2017).
[56] ibid para 31.
[57] ibid para 32.
[58] ibid para 109 with references omitted.

The standards that emerge from the Court's broad conceptualization of positive obligations are as follows: (a) Removal is only acceptable under the Convention if the state makes all possible steps to maintain the unity of the family. This can cover, as in the concrete case, financial advice, including registration and application for aid (here specifically to repair the roof and install toilets), and other steps to allow the return of the children.[59] The authorities' commitment can be indicated by the fact that removal is temporary and that there is recurrent re-evaluation and a genuine chance of return. (b) Only exceptional circumstances can warrant serious limitations or full deprivation of parental contact, and the authorities should support meetings with the purpose of eventual return. (In this case, the Court underlined the commitment of the authorities in this regard, including providing fuel to make the visits possible.[60]) (c) State authorities have similar positive obligations regarding the circumstances of child placement, which is important because removal can violate the Convention even when it is justifiable. Crucially, family unity remains a guiding principle in that siblings should be allowed to stay together, save for exceptional circumstances.[61] Other conditions of placement can also play a role in the assessment: in the case at hand, the Court was satisfied that the children were closely monitored and that they developed their skills and health during the temporary care.[62]

While the judgment mentions, passingly, the fact that the applicants were of Roma origin,[63] the minority element is not part of the judicial evaluation, probably because there is no indication that the applicants themselves raised the issue of discrimination. Until relatively recently the case law did not provide guidance on state responsibilities regarding non-discrimination in child removal cases, but this partly changed as a result of the judgment to be discussed now.

The minority element was more pronounced in *Jansen v Norway*,[64] where the authorities removed the child from a Roma mother and denied all contact, citing the risk of abduction by a violent maternal grandfather. The domestic authorities considered material elements (the mother living on social security with no other income, losing her earlier home after complaints by neighbours, the risk of losing her home due to non-payment) and a concern for education, complemented by dangers to the child's (physical) security.[65]

The ECtHR acknowledged that the national authorities' examination of the case was holistic[66] but concluded that the interpretation of the domestic courts

[59] ibid paras 121–25.

[60] ibid paras 116–20.

[61] National authorities decided to place the youngest children separately from the other siblings. The Court assessed the justification for this separately and found that these were justified by the special needs due to the child's age. Ibid para 114.

[62] ibid para 115.

[63] ibid para 5.

[64] *Jansen v Norway* App no 2822/16 (ECtHR, 6 September 2018).

[65] ibid para 100.

[66] ibid.

concerning the best interests of the child—which denied the biological mother contact with the child for three years—was not compatible with Article 8. The Court reiterated the state's 'positive duty to take measures to facilitate family reunification as soon as reasonably feasible'.[67] While the judgment acknowledged the difficulties of setting up meetings in a way that protected the whereabouts of the child, the Court found that the efforts made to allow contact were insufficient.[68] The domestic judgment had assigned too much weight to the risk of abduction, creating 'a risk that [the child] could completely lose contact with her mother'.[69] Considering that the mother also was at risk of domestic abuse,[70] providing protection to both the mother and the child would have been a more adequate response by the authorities.

This judgment departs from earlier case law regarding the minority aspect because the national authorities specifically invoked the child's Roma background, the relevant provisions of the CRC and the Framework Convention for the Protection of National Minorities.[71] The court of appeal argued in some detail why the concern for Roma identity did not alter its conclusions:

> Other than the general assumption that it was a good thing for a child to get to know its culture and background, there was little to indicate that contact sessions would be beneficial if they were to take place. Contact would be quite limited and the possibility for the child to get to know her background and Roma culture would thus in any case be significantly reduced. In addition, the foster parents had stated that … the contact sessions had caused her sleep and digestive problems. If contact were to be resumed, [the psychologist] feared that it could cause a significant feeling of insecurity and a reaction against the foster parents for allowing this insecurity, particularly as [the child] had suffered significant neglect in her biological family.[72]

The national court acknowledged here that a concern for maintaining one's cultural identity is part of the assessment. While this element was not central in finding a violation in the case, the Strasbourg Court noted in the judgment that the separation constituted a violation also because it could 'lead to an alienation of [the child] from her Roma identity'.[73]

The question that emerges from this judgment is whether there was really no alternative to removal, one that was less onerous to the child and the family.

67 ibid para 101.
68 ibid para 102.
69 ibid para 103.
70 ibid para 51.
71 ibid paras 17, 25, and 45.
72 ibid para 57.
73 ibid para 103.

What is largely missing is a consideration of the ways in which majority preferences seep into decision-making even in the case of minority families. The non-discrimination framing is only part of the Strasbourg Court's legal assessment in *Jansen v Norway*, but the ECtHR dismissed the claim by giving credence to the allegation 'that many members of the community did not adhere to the Norwegian model for law enforcement and conflict resolution, and the possibility of keeping children away from the Norwegian authorities provided by family ties abroad.'[74]

To illustrate that a discrimination-based legal assessment is possible under European legal standards, we now turn to cases litigated strategically under the European Social Charter (ESC) and Hungarian anti-discrimination law, which transposes the EU Anti-discrimination Directives, including the prohibition of indirect discrimination and the reversal of the burden of proof.[75]

## 4.2. Collective action against discrimination in child removals

As highlighted above, systemic discrimination is considerably easier to prove while using statistical evidence. This aspect has not been addressed in ECtHR judgments that have focused on individual family situations, but litigation in other (international) fora offers insights about the strategic use of this tool in pushing the boundaries further by highlighting the indirect and systemic nature of discrimination through the aggregate review of practices.

The European Roma Rights Centre (ERRC) launched strategic litigation claiming (indirect and) systemic discrimination in child removal practices in relation to Czechia before the ECSR and in relation to a county in Hungarian courts. Under the ESC, the ERRC in collaboration with the Mental Disability Advocacy Centre, launched a collective complaint, while in Hungary the NGO made use of a provision, adopted as part of EU accession compliance, that grants representative standing (*actio popularis*) to NGOs fighting discrimination to litigate in their own name without naming individual victims as plaintiffs.[76]

The use of statistical data revealing ethnic disparities was crucial in both cases. The ECSR did not establish ethnic discrimination due to the lack of sufficient and disaggregated official data. In the Hungarian case, the ethnic data presented by the ERRC was considered sufficient to reverse the burden of proof at trial level and establish indirect ethnic as well as socio-economic discrimination in removal practices. Arguably, the clarity of EU anti-discrimination norms, and the even more

[74] ibid para 47.

[75] European Roma Rights Centre, 'Budapest Court Rules State Removal of Romani Children from Families is Discrimination' (5 October 2021) <http://www.errc.org/press-releases/budapest-court-rules-state-removal-of-romani-children-from-families-is-discrimination> accessed 18 June 2023.

[76] Equal Opportunity Act No CXXV of 2003 (Hungary), Art 18.

beneficial regulation of the burden of proof in Hungarian law, have been crucial in pushing the boundaries of human rights further at the national level.

In *ERRC and MDAC v the Czech Republic,* the ECSR found a violation of Article 17 (the right of mothers and children to social and economic protection) of the ESC because: (1) the application of the legal framework of institutional care and operation of children centres does not ensure appropriate protection and care for children under the age of three; (2) there was a failure to provide alternative services and to progressively de-institutionalize the existing system of early childhood care; and (3) there was a failure to provide appropriate care services for Roma children and children with disabilities under the age of three.[77]

The ECSR did not find discrimination on the grounds of racial or ethnic origin in the case of the Roma children. The ERRC submitted official data showing a steady and robust over-representation of Roma children among institutionalized infants, contrary to a general decrease in the overall numbers.[78] The government denied the official collection of ethnic (and disability) data, which guided the ECSR's assessment as well. The assessment starts with the state's obligation to pay particular attention 'to the situation of disadvantaged and vulnerable groups of children, including children from ethnic minorities and children with disabilities'.[79] The ECSR stressed the state's obligation to collect disaggregated data on vulnerable children, but surprisingly embraced institutional bias and stated that 'it is generally acknowledged that a particular group of children is or could be faced with disproportionate care risks in comparison with the majority of population, as is the case for both Roma children and children with disabilities'.[80] While noting that, 'whatever may be the actual numbers of Roma children and children with disabilities under the age of 3 placed in institutions, there are significant indications that these numbers remain high',[81] the ECSR did not see 'sufficient evidence or elements showing that discrimination against Roma children or children with disabilities is involved'.[82]

Conversely, the Budapest Tribunal ruled that the rights of children removed from their families due to poverty and Roma ethnicity were violated, and established ministerial responsibility for this.[83] Prior to the litigation, the ERRC

[77] *European Roma Rights Centre (ERRC) and Mental Disability Advocacy Centre (MDAC) v The Czech Republic,* Comm No 157/2017 (ECSR, 17 June 2020).

[78] ibid para 67: 'Roma children make up approximately 24% of all children placed in these children centres for children under 3 years of age. Considering that approximately 1.4–2.8% of the population in the Czech Republic is Roma, this represents a disproportionate number of institutionalized Roma children.'

[79] ibid para 171.

[80] ibid para 172.

[81] ibid para 173.

[82] ibid para 175.

[83] Fővárosi Törvényszék [Budapest Tribunal], judgment of 22 September 2021 no 27.P.20.939/2020/44 (Hungary), <https://eakta.birosag.hu/anonimizalt-hatarozatok?azonosito=P.20939/2020/44> accessed 3 October 2023.

commissioned research which found that in Nógrád county, Roma children were significantly over-represented in foster care. While Roma children accounted for 20 per cent of the under-age population there, they constitute 80 per cent of the foster home population.[84] The court found a violation regarding the children who were removed from their families due solely to poverty, because this practice constituted indirect discrimination based on socio-economic conditions (poverty)[85] as well as Roma ethnicity.[86] The judgment concluded that individual expert witnesses who claimed that it was impossible that discrimination could occur in the work of child protection services could not successfully justify the apparently discriminatory practice. Arguably, in the case of poverty, the practice constitutes direct discrimination, but this would not significantly change the outcome of the litigation.

On appeal, the Budapest Court of Appeal agreed with the first instance judgment regarding discrimination based on poverty but found that the witness testimonies had successfully rebutted the claim of ethnic (Roma) discrimination.[87] The Court of Appeal overturned the finding of ethnic discrimination with an argument limited to half a paragraph in a judgment of thirty-nine pages. The trial court's judgment contains sixty-nine pages and describes the facts based on research substantiating the role of poverty and ethnicity in removals, including reports by the ERRC, the ombudsperson, the UN Committee on the Rights of the Child, the Hungarian Central Statistical Office, and the State Audit Office.[88] Conversely, the Court of Appeal agreed with the defendant that 'the witness accounts ... confirm that Roma children were not subject to less favorable treatment due to their ethnic origin'.[89] The relevant half a paragraph seems to indicate that the Court of Appeal only considered direct discrimination specifically targeting individual Roma children. This shortcoming notwithstanding, the case shows how statistical data can provide evidence about the context and systemic shortcomings, pushing the boundaries of human rights.

The importance of strategic litigation that relies on European standards is visible at the domestic level, where lower courts reference judgments arising from such litigation. For instance, in the child removal case the Budapest Tribunal referenced another Hungarian court's judgment concerning discrimination

[84] European Roma Rights Centre, 'Cause of Action: Romani Children in State Care in Nógrád County (Hungary)' (2017) 13 <http://www.errc.org/uploads/upload_en/file/romani-children-in-state-care-in-nograd-county-hungary.pdf> accessed 18 June 2023.

[85] Budapest Tribunal, judgment of 22 September 2021 (n 83), para 99.

[86] ibid para 114.

[87] Fővárosi Ítélőtábla [Budapest Court of Appeal], judgment of 22 March 2022 no 8.Pf.20.817/2021/4/II (Hungary), para 120 <https://eakta.birosag.hu/anonimizalt-hatarozatok?azonosito=Pf.20817/2021/4> accessed 3 October 2023.

[88] Budapest Tribunal, judgment of 22 September 2021 (n 83), paras 3–11.

[89] Budapest Court of Appeal, judgment of 22 March 2022 (n 87), para 120.

against Roma children in education, arguing that courts had already established ministerial responsibility, negligence, and relevant remedies in an analogous case.[90]

## 5. The Potential and Limits of Strategic Litigation in Roma Child Removal Cases before European Courts

This section maps the potentials of Roma rights litigation in fighting discrimination concerning child removal, such as improving legal standards (section 5.1), providing adequate remedies (section 5.2) and tailoring policy responses (section 5.3).

### 5.1. Improving legal standards

Referencing the ECtHR's standards is important in fighting some features of child protection regimes that result in unjustified removals. Strategic litigation can widely 'enforce' the prohibition of removal based on material conditions and the need to justify removals as exceptional measures. The application of the necessity–proportionality test can ensure that states comply with positive obligations under the ECHR, meaning that child removals should only be justifiable in light of a wide range of (alternative) less constraining measures. Removal can only comply with the Convention if it is an ultimate measure because the goal is to safeguard the unity of the family. The Convention also prohibits discrimination, which means that Roma children and families should not be disproportionately affected by decision-making.

The ban on discrimination clearly mandates decisions on removal that are not based on minority status or poverty (property, wealth, socio-economic status), as that would constitute direct discrimination. (Note that this does certainly not preclude regard for the minority element as a cultural factor that can warrant special considerations.) The Convention also prohibits indirect discrimination, of which disproportionality can be a crucial indication. Proper assessment can reveal where majority preconceptions distort the application of seemingly neutral standards. In some cases leading to discrimination based on material deprivation, perceived cultural differences or the combination of these factors, substantiating a claim of intersectional discrimination.

[90] Budapest Tribunal, judgment of 22 September 2021 (n 83), paras 80, 111, and 143. The cited judgment: Debreceni Ítélőtábla [Debrecen Court of Appeal], judgment of 24 September 2020 no Pf.I.20.214/2020/10.

There are broader factors that create material and other conditions that systematically disfavour minority families. There might be cases where the justifications for removal survive the Convention standards, nonetheless the resulting practices fall more heavily on minority members of society. This was flagged in the US debate as disparity without discrimination. Systemic discrimination exists and we see broader forms of inequalities cause circumstances that, if seen in isolation, can pass judicial scrutiny. This should warn activists that some forms of discrimination require broader responses than what can be addressed in a single lawsuit.

Untangling the causes requires a complex assessment in order to identify legitimate policy outcomes. Alan Dettlaff notes that it is a false dichotomy to treat racial bias and disproportionate need as two mutually exclusive reasons for the disproportional number of children from certain minorities. In debating the causes, we should not lose sight of the existing structural and institutional causes, and findings that reduce the role of racism should not, as happened in the US, halt measures that address the racial inequality.[91] The systemic problem is not the racism of child welfare professionals but the societal legacy of racial injustice and the miserable socio-economic conditions that characterize too many Black lives.[92] In other words, while the jury might still be out on how much race *directly* affects the disparity shown in statistics, scholarship unequivocally calls for sustained action that considers the racial background of families.

Luckily for Roma litigants and activists, European legal standards allow for a broader consideration of systemic causes. The ECtHR established standards that require careful and holistic assessments of factors, including the best interests of the child considering the situation in the family and the support provided by child and family welfare services, and child protection. The bottom line is that removal from the family can be only justified in exceptional circumstances. Where omission or neglect on the part of authorities could contribute to the situation where removal can be justified, states cannot escape responsibility: they should have prevented escalation by discharging duties stemming from their positive obligations.

Strategic litigation should be seen as one tool among many to address these broader causes. It might not always be the best or most cost-effective way to bring about the desired changes, but it can go a long way in remedying violations caused by child removal decisions. True, individual cases can easily miss the broader picture and might be less likely to trigger measures effectively remedying systemic issues. Even where courts do a good job in revealing patterns of discrimination, the remedies might not match these findings. We now turn to the question of adequate remedies.

91 Dettlaff (n 41) 10, 19.
92 Bartholet (n 39) 878.

### 5.2. Remedies for unlawful child removals

The ECtHR can find violation and award just satisfaction[93] in the form of monetary compensation; interim measures are for exceptional cases.[94] While compensation can have a deterring effect, especially in the case of a threat of an avalanche of similar claims (the idea behind pilot judgments), the Court specifically focuses on the individual and concrete damage as opposed to punishment or effective deterrence.[95] The monitoring mechanism overseen by the Committee of Ministers is meant to ensure compliance with the judgments.

Domestic courts have more leeway in providing adequate remedies. In the Hungarian case discussed above, the first instance court granted, partially, the request of the plaintiff and ordered that the ministry: (a) conduct a survey, for five years, into the removals of Roma and non-Roma children, (b) conduct a targeted investigation on discrimination in removals based on material conditions and (Roma) origin, (c) adopt an action plan, and publish the resulting documents on its website.[96] The court of appeal only mandated the adoption of methodological guidelines to prevent removals based on material deprivation.[97]

Strategic litigation requires sustained efforts and can be costly, time-consuming, and uncertain. The Hungarian case provides a crucial example for strategic litigation where a US-funded NGO (the most important player in the Roma rights field) collects information, identifies a systemic violation, finds the legal venue for such a claim, litigates, and follows up on the situation on the ground, relitigating, if necessary. This type of strategic litigation is further made possible by representative standing under the Equal Treatment Act adopted as part of EU accession conditionality and an example of over-transposition. Not only did the legislation establish wider grounds for claiming discrimination, but it also provides for public interest litigation by civil society organizations.[98] The Hungarian case demonstrates how special standing rules and a broader take on the social and institutional context can lead to remedies that adequately address systemic violations rather than some of the consequences in a piecemeal fashion.

Courts are often reluctant to overrule experts who have an intimate knowledge of families, their circumstances and the adequate response to crisis situations. An aggregate evaluation, however, can allow courts to make a broader assessment in light of the impact of such practices. In the Hungarian case, the trial court could

[93] ECHR Art 41.

[94] See r 39 of the Rules of Court.

[95] The Practice Direction on just satisfaction claims rejects 'claims for damages with labels such as "punitive", "aggravated" or "exemplary"' as inappropriate. Practice Direction issued by the President of the Court in accordance with r 32 of the Rules of Court on 28 March 2007 and amended on 9 June 2022, Rules of the Court, p 67 <https://www.echr.coe.int/documents/d/echr/Rules_Court_ENG> accessed 23 March 2024.

[96] See the award in Budapest Tribunal, judgment of 22 September 2021 (n 83).

[97] See the award in Budapest Court of Appeal, judgment of 22 March 2022 (n 87).

[98] Equal Opportunity Act No CXXV of 2003 (Hungary), Arts 10 and 20-1-c, respectively.

establish that there is great variation in how professionals define the material causes of risk. Such determination is crucial for the outcome, as removal based on material causes is unlawful and the court found the uncertainty unacceptable—it was proof of ministerial negligence.[99] Establishing responsibility is an important outcome of litigation, as this aspect often remains unresolved on the national level.

The procedural specificities of *actio popularis* also allowed the court to separate the evaluation of individual cases from general patterns revealing systemic discrimination. The court acknowledged the commitment of the professionals while concluding that their individual accounts and the ministry's defence that removal decisions are always based on complex sets of data, never uniquely on material conditions, could not refute the data provided by a more systematic review in the petition.[100] This judicial approach shows the potential of aggregate approaches even if, ultimately, the court of appeal turned this part of the judgment around and evaluated the evidence differently, giving preference to the individual witness accounts over the statistical evidence. Finally, *actio popularis* also allowed the plaintiff organization to avoid the exposure of Roma families to questioning and further victimization despite their extremely vulnerable positions.

*Actio popularis* might not always be available or might not be the most promising option. Enforcing judgments that mandate institutional changes can be challenging. Sometimes financial pressure can be more effective in that it can change the internal calculations of the institutions responsible for discrimination. Especially in cases of systemic discrimination, aggregating claims of the group of victims and litigating for damages can be an appealing alternative.[101] Strategic litigation relying on representative lawsuits, as in the Hungarian case, and collective procedural options—including the much-criticized but essential pilot judgment procedure before the ECtHR—allows for a better match between finding violations and legal remedies.[102]

Class action lawsuits could perhaps better express the gravity of the harm in monetary terms, especially when aggregating claims from all the families wronged by a discriminatory practice.[103] It is not hard to imagine the sense of urgency created by

[99] Budapest Tribunal, judgment of 22 September 2021 (n 83), para 127.

[100] ibid para 131.

[101] The attorney involved in the Hungarian child removal case, Adél Kegye, has successfully litigated school desegregation cases leading to damages. Recently: *Szolcsán v Hungary*, App no 24408/16, Judgment of 30 March 2023. For a 'collective damages' case, see the 'Gyöngyöspata' desegregation damages lawsuit, with the final judgment from 2021: Curia, Judgment of 24 March 2021 no Pfv.IV.20.199/2020/7 (Hungary).

[102] For criticism of the pilot judgment procedure in the minority context, see Dilek Kurban, 'Forsaking Individual Justice: The Implications of the European Court of Human Rights' Pilot Judgment Procedure for Victims of Gross and Systematic Violations' (2016) 16 Human Rights Law Review 731.

[103] In just one county (out of twenty, including the capital) there were hundreds of children in state care. Even assuming a relatively low percentage of unlawful removals from among them—which might not be that low, in fact, given the huge disproportionality—the total number of these types of violations nationally could be high.

the constant threat of mass-scale damages hanging over any institution as opposed to a distant, one-time judgment finding systemic violation in hard-to-change, complex institutional practices. While mass damages might sound like a radical idea, they could breathe life into the normative commitment of compensating for the harm caused. The threat of unprecedented damages could trigger systemic change.[104]

### 5.3. Strategic litigation and broader responses to violations

Strategic litigation also offers benefits that can be instrumental in ending violations. Through the public acknowledgment of violations, the documentation of discriminatory practices, assigning responsibilities and identifying remedies, it can channel public discussion and focus debates, which might then create political momentum for reform. Discrimination in child removals rarely registers on the national political plane, therefore legal intervention has a key role.

Child removals in the minority context are permeated by the legacy and continuing practices of systemic discrimination, which is also the case with Roma children and families. Policy responses must not miss an engagement with this legacy. As a comprehensive overview concludes:

> the best and most effective practice in child welfare that involves Indigenous children and young people should be centered on and grounded in the acknowledgment of the trauma that has been experienced by Indigenous people, as well as the respect and the deep recognition of culture, and Indigenous ways of knowing, being, and doing.[105]

Systemic racial discrimination should be identified and acknowledged in specific ways to enable the reform of complex systems like childcare regimes.[106] Strategic litigation can lead to inquiries, as in the case of the Norwegian child removal scandal,[107] which in turn can trigger policy changes that address hidden biases.

[104] For an argument on how collective procedures could improve equality law and benefit minorities facing systemic discrimination, see Sara Benedi Lahuerta, 'Enforcing EU Equality Law through Collective Redress: Lagging Behind?' (2018) 55 Common Market Law Review; Zsolt Körtvélyesi, 'Transcending the Individual/Collective Minority Rights Divide: A Procedural Solution' (2022) 71 International & Comparative Law Quarterly 73.

[105] Gatwiri and others (n 16) 840.

[106] See the report of the Human Rights Watch and the American Civil Liberties Union which lists the long history of national policies undermining minority family integrity, before moving on to provide recommendations over six pages. Human Rights Watch and American Civil Liberties Union, '"If I Wasn't Poor, I Wouldn't Be Unfit"—The Family Separation Crisis in the US Child Welfare System' (Human Rights Watch/American Civil Liberties Union 2022) 23–31 and 140–45, respectively <https://www.hrw.org/sites/default/files/media_2022/11/us_crd1122web_3.pdf> accessed 26 February 2023.

[107] For a summary, see Tim Whewell, 'Norway's Hidden Scandal' *BBC News* (3 August 2018) <https://www.bbc.co.uk/news/resources/idt-sh/norways_hidden_scandal> accessed 14 January 2024.

Litigation can unearth more data that could help determine whether there is in fact discrimination, and could pave the way to more litigation against discriminatory practices. In the Hungarian case, the trial court made a note about the accessibility of data on removals. It criticized the ministry for preparing its defence based on non-anonymized documents that the plaintiff and the court did not have access to, in violation of the equality of parties. The court also noted that collecting such data by the ministry was unlawful.[108] Conversely, collecting anonymized data, including on Roma ethnicity, would be lawful and necessary, in the assessment of the trial court, to discharge the state obligation to monitor compliance with non-discrimination norms.[109] Respondents bear the burden of proving that the practices do not constitute discrimination, which can push public authorities to reveal data that might otherwise not be made available. Such data can then be used for further challenges of problematic practices.

The full scope of discrimination that minorities face can lead to vicious circles where it is hard to pinpoint what is the root cause of the problem. That is why legal and broader strategies should attack as many sections of the circle as possible. Disproportionality remains a problem, and the solution is not simply to decrease removals, but to address and remove the causes of removals. In addition to providing remedies for the families that were directly impacted by removals, undoing systemic violations requires a broader acknowledgment of the harm caused. An inquiry by the Irish ombudsperson into discriminatory removals in the case of two Roma families suggested that in addition to the real trauma caused to the children and their families, the actions also negatively affected the (small) Roma community in Ireland, which requires remedial measures to (re)build trust in state institutions.[110]

Policies can fail to acknowledge ongoing systemic discrimination and dismiss concerns as something of the past.[111] One key aspect is how majority views, reflected both in media accounts and decision-making, follow a dominant individualistic account of the best interests of the child, while indigenous approaches tend to emphasize the collective, community aspects of child well-being as well, challenging the adequacy of 'colour-blind individualist' approaches.[112]

Strategic litigation can also be instrumental in norm adoption and agenda-setting. States and state institutions often fail even to register the obligations arising from non-binding instruments, including country-specific recommendations.

[108] Budapest Tribunal, judgment of 22 September 2021 (n 83), para 68.

[109] ibid para 112.

[110] Emily Logan, 'Garda Síochána Act 2005 (Section 42) (Special Inquiries Relating to Garda Síochána) Order 2013 Report' (2014) 105–08 <https://www.iasw.ie/download/205/d44782c2-d5b4-4aa7-afb1-50df7337780a.PDF>.

[111] Mikhelle Lynn Ross-Mulkey, '"Baby Veronica" & The Indian Child Welfare Act (ICWA): A Public's Perception' <http://hdl.handle.net/10150/556951>.

[112] Kathryn A Sweeney and Rachel L Pollack, 'Colorblind Individualism, Color Consciousness, and the Indian Child Welfare Act: Representations of Adoptee Best Interest in Newspaper Coverage of the Baby Veronica Case' (2017) 58 The Sociological Quarterly 701.

Strategic litigation can offer a way to 'translate' them into legal obligations unmet by national institutions. Bringing together norms in minority cases also has the potential of transforming existing policy approaches by including the minority element missing from policy recommendations and outputs of international and supranational monitoring. Litigation can call attention to neglected areas and create a sense of urgency—after all, these are not only ongoing and widespread, but also grave violations with lasting impacts on children, families, and communities. The ultimate value of legal decisions lies in improving the situation on the ground.

A cursory view of international recommendations on the topic shows how the role that strategic litigation can play aligns well with desired policy changes. The UN Committee on the Rights of the Child recommends the support of families to provide adequate environments for children in a non-discriminatory manner and interventions for families at risk of separation, with the overall goal that 'all children grow up in safe and nurturing families'.[113] States should prevent separation 'except when separation is in the child's best interest', emphasizing that children should never be removed because of poverty, ethnicity, migration status, or race; states should guarantee the return of children to their families and specific assistance to families to this end. The Committee stresses in particular the obligation to 'combat stigmatizing attitudes and harmful beliefs, which place children at risk of separation from their families'.[114] The Committee calls for creating redress mechanisms to hold states accountable for the caused harm. Special mechanisms should address the 'current, ongoing, recent and historic harm' caused by 'systemic policies of discrimination, structural violence, marginalization and colonization'.[115]

In the case of Hungary,[116] the Committee called for implementing laws prohibiting discrimination,[117] among others, against Roma children, and to strengthen

[113] Committee on the Rights of the Child, 'Children's Rights and Alternative Care—Outcome Report' (United Nations 2022) s II.A.1 https://www.ohchr.org/sites/default/files/2022-06/13Jun2022-DGD-Outcome-report-and-Recommendations.pdf accessed 13 February 2024.

[114] ibid s II.A.2.

[115] ibid s C.1.

[116] Because we covered a Hungarian domestic case above, we also use the recommendation for Hungary for illustration here, but similar recommendations have been addressed to other countries with sizeable Roma population. See eg the recommendations for Czechia, Slovakia, and Romania:Committee on the Rights of the Child, 'Concluding Observations on the Combined Fifth and Sixth Periodic Reports of Czechia' (United Nations 2021)CRC/C/CZE/CO/5-6 <https://www.ohchr.org/en/documents/concluding-observations/crccczeco5-6-concluding-observations-combined-fifth-and-sixth> accessed 13 February 2024;Committee on the Rights of the Child, 'Concluding Observations on the Combined Third to Fifth Periodic Reports of Slovakia' (United Nations 2017)CRC/C/SVK/CO/3-5 <https://undocs.org/CRC/C/SVK/CO/3-5> accessed 14 February 2024;Committee on the Rights of the Child, 'Concluding Observations on the Fifth Periodic Report of Romania' (United Nations 2017) CRC/C/ROU/CO/5 <https://www.ohchr.org/en/documents/concluding-observations/crccrouco5-concluding-observations-fifth-periodic-report-romania> accessed 14 February 2024.

[117] Discrimination-specific recommendations include the strengthening of the work of the Equal Treatment Authority (a body that has since been abolished) and addressing discrimination against 'lesbian, gay, bisexual, transgender and intersex children, and to take measures to educate the public about equality and non-discrimination and to expand its programmes in schools' (information that is now banned).

'measures aimed at eliminating discrimination against Roma children ... with particular focus on education, health, child protection services and housing'.[118] Further, the Committee urged Hungary to 'fully implement the prohibition of the separation of children from their families ... on the basis of the economic situation of those families' and to strengthen support measures, including social housing,[119] with 'particular attention to Roma children and children living in socioeconomically deprived areas'.[120] The Committee's recommendations make it clear that the collection of ethnic data is key to avoid violations.[121]

Strategic litigation focusing on the broader aspects can play a crucial role in identifying and remedying violations, leading to sustained policy reform but this systemic approach is yet to inform Roma child removal litigation on the European level.

## 6. Conclusions

For state institutions to respect basic child protection requirements, including respect for the unity of the family, a ban on child removal due to material deprivation, and non-discrimination, proves to be an ongoing challenge. Roma children continue to be removed routinely in violation of these human rights conditions, similar to other minorities across the globe. While, in light of the available statistical data, it is hard to avoid the conclusion that the biased decision-making violates the best interests of the child and leads to discrimination, some argue that the over-representation of minorities, including Roma children, among those removed does not automatically stem from discrimination. The analysis in this chapter has shown that: (1) whether the often striking disparities also constitute discrimination is an empirical question that can only be assessed on the basis of disaggregated data that is seldom available; (2) even where no direct or indirect discrimination can be found in a particular case, the disparities can be traced back to contextual causes that constitute systemic discrimination, most often patterns of exclusion and deprivation, that seemingly justify child removal. Long-standing systemic discrimination necessitates policy intervention regardless of its ground or form. The difference between direct and indirect discrimination can be decisive in court cases, but the relevant jurisprudence shows that European courts can examine a wide range of practices with discriminatory effects, thus pushing the boundaries of human rights.

[118] Committee on the Rights of the Child, 'Concluding Observations on the Sixth Periodic Report of Hungary' (United Nations 2020) CRC/C/HUN/CO/6 s 16 https://www.undocs.org/en/CRC/C/HUN/CO/6.

[119] ibid 26, 28(a).

[120] ibid 34.

[121] ibid 11, 27, 26(b), 28(c), 34(c), 36(c).

While one should never be too optimistic about the law's potential in changing entrenched institutional practices, moderate confidence is reasonable. The ECtHR case law provides robust protection from unjustified child removals from Roma families, setting the bar high for justifying the break-up of families. The ECtHR standards enforce the unity of the family as part and parcel of Article 8 and include the prohibition of removal for the sole reason of material deprivation. While the European Convention prohibits discrimination in conjunction with the right to family life, the ECtHR is yet to properly examine such violation in cases of child removal from minority families, including the Roma. In this respect, neither the Strasbourg Court nor the European Committee of Social Rights has pushed the boundaries of human rights, but Hungarian courts have. The Hungarian *actio popularis* litigation shows that state institutions may be compelled to provide vital information on internal processes and statistics on removals. This case also shows greater potential for pushing the boundaries of the human rights paradigm and, more specifically, equality law by compelling courts to consider and condemn systemic discrimination.

Systemic problems have to be broken into litigable claims, and strategic litigation has the potential of assembling the pieces of a legal strategy to end systemic discrimination. Strategic litigation of discrimination in child removal can pave the way for further action by revealing patterns of inequalities and, even where unsuccessful, can call attention to underlying systemic causes like exclusion, segregation and material deprivation, that should themselves be addressed through political, policy, and legal reform in housing, education, social, and health services. Given the enormous harm involved in cases of separating families, making states and institutions pay a high price can be an effective and dissuasive remedy, especially where violations reveal systemic discrimination against minorities, such as the Roma. The aggregation of claims in representative or class actions can better hold institutions responsible for a larger part of this systemic harm.

# 12

# Pushing Human Rights Boundaries

## Intersectional Discrimination and Reproductive (In)Justice for Romani Women

*Serena D'Agostino and Tina Magazzini**

### 1. Introduction

Over the past few decades, intersectionality has become an increasingly prominent concept. Scholarship on inequalities and (non-)discrimination in both Europe and the United States[1] has, for instance, steadily recognized structural racism and its intersection with other systems of oppression as key underlying causes of discrimination. Intersectional discrimination asserts that 'mutually constitutive inequalities ... produce an effect which is different from what each of their dimensions would produce separately, and also different from the addition of the separate parts together'.[2] The key tenets in the concept of intersectional discrimination are, as a matter of fact, the interaction among and the inseparability of inequalities. Despite intersectionality becoming more widely used, empirical case studies of complex interconnections between racial and other grounds for discrimination remain under-researched. This can be attributed, at least in part, to a significant mismatch between the existing recognized forms of discrimination in law and the actual forms of discrimination in real life,[3] as well as the difficulties in recognizing the distinctiveness of different sets of inequalities in ways that do not 'equalize' differences.[4]

* This research was supported by the project 'Migration and Us: Mobility, Refugees, and Borders from the Perspective of the Humanities (reg. no. CZ.02.01.01/00/23_025/0008741), co-funded by the European Union (Tina Magazzini). The authors are grateful to the volume's editors and to Ernesto Fiocchetto for their helpful comments on previous versions of this chapter.

[1] Dolores Morondo, Cristina de la Cruz, and Encarnación La Spina, *Desigualdades complejas e Interseccionalidad. Una revisión critica* (Dykinson 2020); Center for Intersectional Justice, 'Intersectional Discrimination in Europe: Relevance, Challenges and Ways Forward' (2020) <https://www.enar-eu.org/wp-content/uploads/intersectionality-report-final-3.pdf> accessed 30 July 2024.

[2] Raphaële Xenidis, 'Intersectionality from Critique to Practice: Towards an Intersectional Discrimination Test in the Context of 'Neutral Dress Codes' [2023] European Equality Law Review 2.

[3] Ashley Terlouw and Kris van der Pas, 'The Battle Against Ethnic Discrimination: Realizing the (Utopian) Promise of Non-Discrimination Law' [2024] Ethnic and Racial Studies.

[4] Mieke Verloo, 'Multiple Inequalities, Intersectionality and the European Union' (2006) 13 European Journal of Women's Studies 211; Tina Magazzini 'Making the Most of Super-Diversity. Notes on the Potential of a New Approach' (2017) 45 Policy & Politics 527.

Serena D'Agostino and Tina Magazzini, *Pushing Human Rights Boundaries* In: *The Rights of Roma in European Courts*. Edited by: Kristin Henrard and Lilla Farkas, Oxford University Press. © Serena D'Agostino and Tina Magazzini 2025. DOI: 10.1093/oso/9780198914358.003.0012

In this chapter, we build on intersectionality and Critical Race Theory to explore the concept of intersectional discrimination and its potential to push the boundaries of human rights in cases where such boundaries have been established and maintained by the European Court of Human Rights (ECtHR). Specifically, we focus on the reproductive injustice faced by Romani[5] women through the practice of involuntary (non-consensual) sterilization[6] in Czechia and Slovakia.[7] We argue that by failing to recognize involuntary sterilization as an intersectional discrimination practice—where Romani women's experiences of sterilization are rooted not only in individual violations but also in systemic and structural racism and sexism, with reproductive injustice and obstetric violence intersecting with racial and ethnic discrimination – courts and policymakers contribute to perpetuating and reinforcing existing systems of subordination, marginalization, and human rights violation. The argument we propose here draws upon and integrates the discussion initiated by Gwendolyn Albert, Eva-Esther Sobotka, and Lilla Farkas in Chapter 16 of this volume. When read in conjunction, these two chapters provide the reader with comprehensive insights into the plight of involuntarily sterilized Romani women in the Czech and Slovak Republics, elucidating on the use of intersectional discrimination in strategic litigation and policy reform, and highlighting its potential to foster social justice and advance the frontiers of human rights.

This chapter is organized as follows. Following this introduction, we set the stage of the case study analysed, namely that of the involuntary sterilization of Roma women. Subsequently, we provide the broader context for Romani women's reproductive rights in Europe, framing the judicial dimension as part of a larger political process. Next, we look at practices of involuntary sterilization as instances of intersectional discrimination. Doing so, we lay the groundwork for unpacking the rationale of the ECtHR in the case law concerning Romani women. Following this, we outline cases that have been brought to the ECtHR, and argue that the ECtHR's interpretation has so far failed to harness the potential of intersectionality in reference to the sterilization of Roma women. Finally, we put forward some

[5] In this chapter, we use the term 'Roma' as both a noun and an adjective, and the word 'Romani' as an adjective only. 'Romnja' stands for Romani women (pl) in Romanes, the Romani language.

[6] We define involuntary, forced, and coercive sterilizations in line with the European Roma Rights Centre (ERRC), 'Coercive and Cruel. Sterilisation and its Consequences for Romani Women in the Czech Republic (1966-2016)' (2016) http://www.errc.org/uploads/upload_en/file/coercive-and-cruel-28-november-2016.pdf accessed 30 July 2024. Namely: 'Involuntary (non-consensual) sterilisation is any sterilisation that happens against the will or without the knowledge of the affected person. Each person who is about to undergo this surgery should be fully aware of its nature, possible consequences and alternative methods of contraception. If these conditions are not present, the sterilisation is involuntary. Forced sterilisation occurs when a person is sterilised after expressly refusing the procedure, without her knowledge or is not given an opportunity to provide consent. Coerced sterilisation occurs in situations when individuals are compelled to undergo the procedure by financial or other incentives, misinformation, or some form of intimidation.' (ibid 12).

[7] We use the terms 'Czech Republic' and 'Czechia', as well as 'Slovak Republic' and 'Slovakia', interchangeably. Czechoslovakia was a federal state of Czechs and Slovaks, which existed from 1918 to 1993. It then dissolved into two separate states: the Czech Republic and Slovak Republic.

recommendations on how courts and policy-makers can contribute to pushing the boundaries of human rights by adopting an intersectional approach to tackle systemic and structural discrimination.

## 2. Reproductive (In)Justice and Romani Women

### 2.1. Involuntary sterilization: general background and case-study context

Throughout the twentieth century, involuntary sterilization, one of the most diffused practices of obstetric violence toward Romani women, has been a recurrent legal practice in several European countries (Sweden, Switzerland, the Czech Republic, Hungary, and Slovakia, among others). Eugenics laws were legitimized under the supremacist notion of 'assisting' the Roma, notably serving the interests of the Roma community by limiting the childbearing of Romani women, in what can be considered a case of 'beneviolence'.[8] In this perspective, Sardelić has referred to the involuntary sterilization of Romani women as the 'biopolitical act'[9] of cleansing citizenry.[10] Although involuntary sterilization has been officially banned, 'it still occurs because of deeply ingrained prejudice against Romani minorities'.[11] Several cases, for instance, have been brought to court by the European Roma Rights Centre (ERRC) against the Czech Republic, Slovakia, and Hungary. However, even when such cases are denounced and investigated, reparatory justice is rarely the outcome.

In its 2016 report *Coercive and Cruel: Sterilisation and its Consequences for Romani Women in the Czech Republic (1966–2016)*, the ERRC defines coercive sterilization as 'one of the most serious human rights violations against women'.[12] Involuntary sterilization of poor and/or racialized minority women, women with disabilities, and intersex people have been programmatically performed for centuries as a means for supporting national policies on population control, across Europe and worldwide.[13] In 2011, Open Society Foundations (OSF) documented

[8] Ana Ivasiuc has put forward this concept as the measures that sustain and legitimize violence against subaltern others under the guise of public benevolence. See https://www.uu.se/en/department/cultural-anthropology-and-ethnology/events/archive/2024-02-28-research-seminar-in-cultural-anthropology-with-ana-ivasiuc.

[9] Huub van Baar, 'Evictability and the Biopolitical Bordering of Europe' (2016) 49(1) Antipode.

[10] Julija Sardelić, *The Fringes of Citizenship: Romani Minorities in Europe and Civic Marginalisation* (Manchester University Press 2021) 47.

[11] ibid 46.

[12] European Roma Rights Centre, 'Coercive and Cruel. Sterilisation and its Consequences for Romani Women in the Czech Republic (1966–2016)' (2016) http://www.errc.org/uploads/upload_en/file/coercive-and-cruel-28-november-2016.pdf accessed 30 July 2024, 7.

[13] In Europe the targets of ethnic-based involuntary sterilization have been mainly Roma women, while in Canada and the United States there is extensive documentation of the involuntary sterilization of Indigenous women. Government Accountability Office, Investigation of Allegations Concerning

cases of forced and coerced sterilization against marginalized women—mainly women living with HIV, women belonging to ethnic and racial minorities, women with disabilities, and poor women—in countries worldwide.[14]

Despite the ethical and moral imperative to condemn this practice, and despite the European Parliament's 2020 resolution denouncing the forced sterilization of Uyghur women in China,[15] involuntary sterilization remains ongoing and widespread also within the EU. According to the European Disability Forum (EDF), as of 2022 Bulgaria, Croatia, Cyprus, Czechia, Denmark, Estonia, Finland, Hungary, Latvia, Lithuania, Malta, Portugal, and Slovakia still allowed for some forms of forced sterilization in their legislation, even though it was not always explicitly framed as such, and only nine EU member states explicitly criminalize forced sterilization as a distinct offence in their criminal code.[16] This (legal) practice contradicts several international human rights treaties, such as the UN Convention on the Elimination of All Forms of Discrimination Against Women (CEDAW)[17] and the CoE Convention on Preventing and Combating Violence Against Women and Domestic Violence (hereinafter Istanbul Convention).[18] Article 39 of the Istanbul Convention expressly condemns forced sterilization and compels all parties to take the necessary legislative or other measures to ensure that 'performing surgery which has the purpose or effect of terminating a woman's capacity to naturally reproduce without her prior and informed consent or understanding of the procedure' is criminalized. Involuntary sterilization is, indeed, an obvious violation of human rights (see also Chapter 16 in this volume).

Indian Health Service (2019) <https://www.gao.gov/assets/hrd-77-3.pdf> accessed 30 July 2024. A comparative discussion of coerced sterilization of Romani women in Europe and Indigenous women in Canada is addressed in Julija Sardelić, *The Fringes of Citizenship: Romani Minorities in Europe and Civic Marginalisation* (Manchester University Press 2021).

[14] Open Society Foundations, 'Against her Will: Forced and Coerced Sterilization of Women Worldwide' (2011) <https://www.opensocietyfoundations.org/publications/against-her-will-forced-and-coerced-sterilization-women-worldwide> accessed 20 March 2024.

[15] European Parliament, Resolution on Forced Labour and the Situation of the Uyghurs in the Xinjiang Uyghur Autonomous Region (Resolution 435/2020) <https://www.europarl.europa.eu/doceo/document/B-9-2020-0435_EN.html> accessed 30 July 2024.

[16] European Disability Forum, 'Forced Sterilisation of Persons with Disabilities in the European Union' (2022) <https://www.edf-feph.org/content/uploads/2022/09/Final-Forced-Sterilisarion-Report-2022-European-Union-copia_compressed.pdf> accessed 20 November 2023. For a broader discussion of cases of involuntary sterilization in Europe, including legislation and compensation schemes, see Christina Zampas and Adriana Lamačková, 'Forced and Coerced Sterilization of Women in Europe' (2011) 114(2) International Journal of Gynecology & Obstetrics 163.

[17] UN Convention on the Elimination of All Forms of Discrimination Against Women (adopted 18 December 1979, entered into force 3 September 1981) 1249(1) UNTS 20378 (CEDAW).

[18] The Istanbul Convention has been signed by all forty-five members of the Council of Europe and by the EU. Only seven CoE members have not yet ratified it: Armenia, Bulgaria, Czechia, Hungary, Latvia, Lithuania, and Slovakia. As for the EU, the Convention entered into force on 1 October 2023. See the Council of Europe Convention on preventing and combating violence against women and domestic violence (CETS No 210).

One interesting development in recognizing it as such can be seen in a 2021 law[19] (hereinafter: compensation law), aimed at compensating thousands of women who were forcibly sterilized in Czechia (and Czechoslovakia) between 1966 and 2012. According to the approved law, survivors are eligible for a compensation of about €12,000 (CZK 300,000). The compensation law has been applauded as a landmark vote and considered a major victory for human rights. For instance, the Council of Europe (CoE) and the Organization for Security and Co-operation in Europe (OSCE), which had pressured the Czech government to investigate involuntary sterilization practices and to establish a compensation mechanism, hailed it as a milestone decision setting an important precedent.[20] Nonetheless, this new legislation has also come under scrutiny by Council of Europe Commissioner for Human Rights Dunja Mijatović[21] and by Romani organizations,[22] both for the amount of the monetary compensation (deemed rather paltry for such a grave violation of fundamental rights) and the obstacles that survivors face in its implementation.

Involuntary sterilization of Romani women in former Czechoslovakia, as elsewhere, has not occurred in isolation. It was part of a broader, and still ongoing, systemic and structural racism that targeted, and targets, Romani individuals and communities. Following the dissolution of Czechoslovakia in 1993, for instance, approximately 150,000 Roma residing in the Czech Republic were forced to (re) apply for citizenship, having been born in Slovakia.[23] Systemic and structural anti-Roma racism manifests in widespread discrimination in access to health, to housing, and to employment, as well as segregated education which, while illegal, not only persists in many EU countries but is on the rise.[24] Within these wider patterns, the involuntary sterilization of Romani women was until recently a normalized, fairly common and legal practice.

[19] *Zákon č. 297/2021 Sb.: Zákon o poskytnutí jednorázové peněžní částky osobám sterilizovaným v rozporu s právem a o změně některých souvisejících zákonů* <https://www.zakonyprolidi.cz/cs/2021-297> accessed 8 December 2023.

[20] Gwendolyn Albert, 'Compensation for Forced Sterilization in the Czech Republic: Reporting the Results of Romani Women's Activism' (2021) 20(1) European Yearbook of Minority Issues 248.

[21] Council of Europe, Commissioner for Human Rights Dunja Mijatović, Report following her visit to the Czech Republic from 20 to 24 February 2023 (Council of Europe 2023) <https://rm.coe.int/report-on-czech-republic-by-dunja-mijatovic-commissioner-for-human-rig/1680ac88cd> accessed 8 December 2023.

[22] Anna Šabatová and Gwendolyn Albert, 'The Czech Compensation Process for Illegally Sterilized Women, Including Romani Women, Has Raised Many Issues' (Romea.cz, 2023) <https://romea.cz/en/opinion/anna-sabatova-the-czech-compensation-process-for-illegally-sterilized-women-including-romani-women-has-raised-many-issues> accessed 8 December 2023.

[23] Celia Donert, *The Rights of the Roma: The Struggle for Citizenship Postwar Czechoslovakia* (CUP 2017).

[24] FRA (European Union Agency for Fundamental Rights), Roma in 10 European Countries: Main Results – Roma Survey 2021 (2021) <https://fra.europa.eu/en/publication/2022/roma-survey-findings> accessed 8 December 2023; FRA (European Union Agency for Fundamental Rights), Fundamental Rights Report 2023 (2023) https://fra.europa.eu/en/publication/2023/fundamental-rights-report-2023 accessed 8 December 2023.

The 1971 Czech Decree on Sterilization[25] legally sanctioned this practice, giving public authorities significant leeway to systematically perform sterilization as a means of birth control on Romani women and on women with disabilities without their full and informed consent. This eugenic[26] state policy was mostly justified by health and poverty-reduction arguments, which begs the question of its racist and classist motives. To control 'the unhealthy nature of the Romani population',[27] Czechoslovakia also introduced a programme that provided financial incentives to encourage sterilization among Romani women in 1979. A report by the České Budějovice District National Committee of the same year states: '[a]fter childbed, women of Gypsy origin receive priority invitations for contraception, which in their case is mostly introduced free of charge ... In some cases women are successfully persuaded to undergo sterilisation.'[28] The Decree on Sterilization was abolished in 1993, after repeated condemnations from international bodies and as part of the broader push for the protection of fundamental rights of individuals belonging to minorities that took place in the early 1990s following the end of the Cold War.[29] Nonetheless, the involuntary sterilization of Romani women and women with disabilities remained common practice in the decades that followed, as highlighted by the cases brought before the ECtHR in the early 2010s.[30]

In this context, the adoption of the compensation law in 2021 was initially seen as a welcome development. Before the adoption of the bill, the CoE's Commissioner for Human Rights had explicitly referred to it as 'a last opportunity to deliver justice to the victims'[31] and called repeatedly on the elected

[25] Ministry of Health of the Czechoslovak Republic, Decree on Sterilization No 01/1972 (passed on 17 December 1971, in Force from 1 January 1972) (Směrnice Ministerstva zdravotnictví ČSR ze dne 17. prosince 1971 o provádění sterilizace) <https://www.epravo.cz/vyhledavani-aspi/?Id=32073&Section=1&IdPara=1&ParaC=2> accessed 6 December 2023.

[26] Public Defender of Rights (VOP), Final Statement of the Public Defender of Rights in the Matter of Sterilisations Performed in Contravention of the Law and Proposed Remedial Measures (23 December 2005). https://www.upr-info.org/sites/default/files/documents/2013-08/pdrczeuprs12008anxmatterofsterilisation.pdf accessed 5 December 2023. At p 69 the document stated that 'the Czech eugenics movement ... dealt with the issue of sterilisation as a practical measure. Czech and Czechoslovak eugenics understood sterilisation as a therapeutic and prophylactic selection method, expecting that when applied, it would bring under *control the sexual life of the inferior* and *define inferiority boundaries*.' (Emphasis added.)

[27] ibid78.

[28] ibid 50–51.

[29] Huub van Baar and Peter Vermeersch, 'The Limits of Operational Representations: Ways of Seeing Roma beyond the Recognition-Redistribution Paradigm' (2013) 3(4) Intersections. EEJSP 120; Tina Magazzini, 'When Ethnicity is "National": Mapping Ethnic Minorities in Europe's Framework Convention for the Protection of National Minorities' (2024) 47(9) Journal of Ethnic and Racial Studies 1812.

[30] For a detailed account of the cases brought before the ECtHR, see Chapter 16 in this volume. See also Elena Ghidoni, 'La Esterilización Forzada en Intersecciones Distintas: Un Enfoque Estructural para el Análisis de las Desigualdades Complejas' (2018) 38 Cuadernos Electrónicos de Filosofía del Derecho 102.

[31] Council of Europe Commissioner for Human Rights, Letter to Mr Radek Vondráček, Speaker of the Chamber of Deputies of the Czech Republic (Ref: CommHR/DM/sf 020-2020) https://rm.coe.int/letter-to-mr-radek-vondracek-speaker-of-the-chamber-of-deputies-of-the/16809fba2e accessed 7 December 2023.

representatives in the Czech Republic to promptly address this 'historic injustice'.[32] Adoption of the compensation law was a long struggle that took more than eighteen years. This lengthy process involved several institutional and political actors (courts, policy-makers, politicians, activists, and civil society) who interacted in different ways and at different political levels (national and supranational/European).

However, the first phase of implementation of the compensation system has been highly criticized by both national (Czech) and international actors.[33] Among the major criticisms raised towards the compensation procedure, which opened for a window of three years to 31 December 2024,[34] are the problematic access to compensation for the victims; the high number of rejected applications justified on claims of insufficient evidence; the lack of clear guidance on the assessment of applications; the excessive lateness of the process; and the lack of cooperation by the Czech Health Ministry (in charge of the implementation of Law 297/2021) with civil society experts.

By the end of May 2022, 261 applications had been submitted and seventy-four had been decided. However, only thirty-five of the decided applications were successful, which is less than half.[35] Paradoxically, what was first celebrated as a human rights victory turned into a vicious circle that put the victims at risk of being further humiliated and traumatized, by having to undergo scrutiny and provide evidence of ill-will on behalf of the medical personnel who had sterilized them.

Throughout this case study, we aim to advance critical reflection on how legal and political actors contribute to pursuing remedies to structural discrimination for intersectionally minoritized communities and groups—or, alternatively, how they fail to do so. We emphasize how uncritical approaches to anti-discrimination measures can, in practice, validate and reinforce certain systems of subordination, oppression, and marginalization.

32 ibid.

33 Gwendolyn Albert, 'Council of Europe Human Rights Commissioner: Roma Continue to be Discriminated in the Czech Republic' and 'Council of Europe's Human Rights Commissioner Appreciates the New Lety Memorial, but Warns Roma are Still Discriminated against, Including Romani Ukrainians Seeking Temporary Protection' (Romea.cz) <https://romea.cz/en/czech-republic/council-of-europe-human-rights-commissioner-roma-continue-to-be-discriminated-in-the-czech-republic-she-criticizes-the-compensation-system-for-the-unlawfully-sterilized-women-and-the-discriminatory> and <https://romea.cz/en/czech-republic/council-of-europes-human-rights-commissioner-appreciates-the-new-lety-memorial-but-warns-roma-are-still-discriminated-against-including-romani-ukrainians-seeking-temporary-protection> accessed 5 December 2023.

34 Section 4.2 of Czech Law 297/2021 states that 'The claim must be submitted to the Ministry no later than three years after the effective date of this Act, otherwise it expires.' All claims can therefore be made only until the end of 2024.

35 'Otevřený dopis – Vyhodnocení efektivity zákona o odškodnění za protiprávní sterilizace' (15 August 2022) <https://llp.cz/blog/otevreny-dopis-vyhodnoceni-efektivity-zakona-o-odskodneni-za-protipravni-sterilizace/> accessed 7 December 2023.

### 2.2. Confronting rights violation through resistance

Romani women’s rights have historically been violated all around Europe. These violations have been normalized, institutionalized, and legitimized by the pervasive conception of the Roma as a ‘non-human other’[36] and bolstered by the legacy of forced child removals, persecutions, and slavery[37]. Structural anti-Roma racism has excluded the Roma from society and denied their basic rights, resulting in segregated maternity wards, child removal (see Chapter 11 on child removal in this volume) and difficult access to justice.[38] In this context of invisibilization and denial of Roma rights, the 2021 Czech compensation law has been considered a major step towards reparation for violence against Romani women, in that its symbolic significance contributes to delegitimizing historical restrictions on Romani women’s rights.

For a comprehensive understanding of this legal shift, it is important to consider the role played by Roma women activists in European politics over the last thirty years. These activists have been key actors in the process of seeking reproductive justice for involuntarily sterilized Romani women. Roma women’s activism arose on the European political scene in the mid-1990s ‘as a force always assisted by and organised around the political agendas of different international organisations’.[39] In the early 2000s, Romani women activists became visible actors on the international political arena. They took part in several international gatherings organized by the UN, such as at the Beijing + 5 meeting in New York (2000) and at the World Conference against Racism in Durban (2001), where they raised forced sterilization as a structural problem.[40] From the mid-2000s to the beginning of the 2010s, several publications on the living conditions and marginalization of Roma women were produced by EU institutions and agencies. Coercive and involuntary

[36] Gabriela Wasileski and Susan Miller, ‘“Bad” Victims? Understanding Social Service Providers’ Responses to Roma Battered Women’ (2014) 38(2) International Journal of Comparative and Applied Criminal Justice 173–89; Margareta Matache, ‘The Deficit of EU Democracies: A New Cycle of Violence Against Roma Population’ (2014) 36(2) Human Rights Quarterly 325.

Ivan Rác, ‘Barriers to Assistance for Women from Marginalised Roma Communities Who Are Experiencing Domestic Violence’ (2020) 22(4) Kontak 25; Shamus McPhee, ‘The Uglier Side of Bonnie Scotland: The Tinker Housing Experiments’ (2021) 3(2) International Journal of Roma Studies 180.

[37] Jaqueline Bhabha, Caroline Elkins, and Margareta Matache (eds), *Time for Reparations: A Global Perspective* (University of Pennsylvania Press 2021).

[38] European Roma Rights Centre, ‘Justice Denied: Roma in the Criminal Justice System of the Czech Republic’ (2023) <http://www.errc.org/uploads/upload_en/file/5451_file1_justice-denied-roma-in-the-criminal-justice-system-of-the-czech-republic-english.pdf> accessed 20 November 2023.

[39] Angela Kócze, ‘Gender, Ethnicity and Class: Romani Women’s Political Activism and Social Struggles’ (PhD Thesis, Central European University 2011) 38; Serena D’Agostino, ‘Intersectional Mobilization and the EU: Which Political Opportunities are there for Romani Women’s Activism? (2018) 15(01) European Yearbook of Minority Issues 23 and ‘(Un) Safe Spaces for Intersectional Activism: Romani Women’s Responses to Transnational Political Opportunities’ (2021) 4(2) European Journal of Politics and Gender 217.

[40] Angela Kócze, ‘The Building Blocks of the Romani Women’s Movement in Europe’ *RomArchive – Digital Archive of the Roma* (2019) <https://www.romarchive.eu/en/roma-civil-rights-movement/building-blocks-romani-womens-movement-europe/> accessed 3 September 2023.

sterilization of Romani women were explicitly mentioned in many of these policy documents.[41] The so-called Romani women's issues, among which involuntary sterilization was key, become thereby visible on the European political arena.

This visibility was contributed to by the presence and engagement of Romani women politicians acting as Members of the European Parliament (MEP)—namely Lívia Járóka and Viktória Mohácsi from Hungary, Soraya Post, a Roma woman activist from Sweden and former President of the International Roma Women Network (IRWN), and Patricia Caro Maya, a Spanish Roma feminist—as well as Roma women activists organizing transnationally and/or working for international organizations, such as the Open Society Institute (until 2010, then OSF). In 2005, for instance, Nicoleta Biţu, one of the major personalities of Romani women's activism in Romania, was invited to present the situation of Roma women in the European Union at a dedicated public hearing organized by the EP Committee on Women's Rights and Gender Equality (FEMM).[42] Biţu reported on cases of involuntary sterilization of Romani women in both the Czech Republic and Slovakia, emphasizing that '[a] strong anti Roma attitude from the medical services [was] one of the main reasons for limited access of Romani women to the health care services. Racial segregation in maternities [had] been signaled recently as well as [coercive] sterilization cases'.[43]

Roma women activists and MEPs have contributed significantly to bringing the concept of intersectional discrimination to the EU level. At the beginning of the 2010s, intersectionality was very marginal in EU equality policy-making. In the few cases where it was mentioned, intersectionality was not embedded in a broader policy framework but was instead driven by individual initiatives from specific political figures, such as Romani women MEPs. A decade ago, in the fields of equality, non-discrimination, and the then-called 'Roma integration', only a handful of policy documents explicitly mentioned the term 'intersectional discrimination'. Interestingly, most of these documents were produced by the EP FEMM and LIBE Committees with regard to the Roma integration strategy and had a Roma woman MEP as a rapporteur.[44]

Even outside of EU politics, Romani women have played a crucial role in highlighting the intersectional nature of discrimination and drawing attention to the issue of involuntary sterilization. In 2016, the conference 'Forced and Coercive

[41] European Parliament, Committee on Women's Rights and Gender Equality, Rapporteur: Lívia Járóka, *Report on the Situation of Roma Women in the European Union and Report on Gender Aspects of the European Framework of National Roma Inclusion Strategies* (2006 and 2013). <http://www.europarl.europa.eu/ sides/getDoc.do?objRefId = 115178&language = EN> and <https://www.europarl.europa.eu/doceo/document/A-6-2006-0148_EN.html> accessed 29 November 2023.

[42] Nicoleta Biţu, 'Romani Women in the European Union: Realities and Challenges' (Presentation for the European Parliament, Committee on Women's Rights and Gender Equality) (2005).

[43] ibid 2.

[44] Serena D'Agostino, 'A Union of Equality: A Promising Step Forward or a Missed Opportunity to be Truly Intersectional?', in C Brière and A Crespy (eds), *Inequality and the European Union. New Frontiers in Political Science and Law* (Routledge 2024).

Sterilization of Roma Women: Justice and Reparations for Victims in the Czech Republic' was organized by the OSCE Office for Democratic Institutions and Human Rights (ODIHR), where Soraya Post was one of the key speakers. In the last twenty years, a number of UN and CoE bodies[45] sent the Czech government recommendations of urgent action to investigate the extent of involuntary sterilization practice and to establish a compensation mechanism. It is within this context that the 2021 compensation law has been conceived and eventually adopted.

## 3. Involuntary Sterilization as an Intersectional Discrimination Practice

The involuntary sterilization of Romani women is presented in this chapter as a specific intersectional discrimination practice, where gender-based, class-based, and other minoritizations intersect with systemic and structural racism against the Roma in a continuous and mutually constitutive manner. The interaction among, and inseparability of, inequalities is an essential aspect of intersectional discrimination: the involuntary sterilization of Romani women belongs to a broader mainstreamed and legitimized[46] 'ideology of oppression'[47] and racism against the Roma historically rooted in Europe and beyond. Against this backdrop, it is therefore unsurprising that the narrative around the sterilization of Roma women has remained one in which this is typically presented as an 'act of kindness'.[48]

This specific intersectional discrimination practice has remained decriminalized and unpunished for centuries in several European countries. As specified by Kóczé, when violations of human rights occur, 'Romani women not only confront more issues quantitatively', but 'their experience is also qualitatively different'[49] from that of both Roma men and non-Roma women. The concept of intersectional discrimination provides us with the necessary means for understanding and addressing the specific kind of discrimination and oppression experienced by Romani women[50]: it is the actual

[45] For a detailed list, see ERRC (n 6) 18.

[46] Huub van Baar, 'The Emergence of a Reasonable Anti-Gypsyism in Europe' in *When Stereotype Meets Prejudice: Antiziganism in European Societies* (Columbia University Press 2014).

[47] Serena D'Agostino, 'Anti-Gypsyism: When a "Specific" Form of Racism is Considered "Reasonable"', in *Migration, Equality and Racism – 44 Opinions* (VUBPRESS 2021) 207.

[48] Jarmila Veselá 69. Sterilizace: problém populační, sociální a kriminální politiky (1938) as quoted in Final Statement of the Public Defender of Rights in the Matter of Sterilisations Performed in Contravention of the Law and Proposed Remedial Measures (23 December 2005).

[49] Kóczé (n 39) 53.

[50] By way of example, according to the European Union Agency for Fundamental Rights (FRA) 'the situation of Roma women in core areas of social life, such as education, employment and health, is worse in comparison to that of Roma men': *Discrimination Against and Living Conditions of Roma Women in 11 EU Member States* (FRA 2014), 3<http://fra.europa.eu/en/publication/2014/discrimination-against-and-living-conditions-roma-women-11-eu-member-states> accessed 22 March 2024.

experiences[51] of Roma women and other marginalized groups that informs an understanding of human rights as indivisible, interrelated, and intersectional.[52] In order to understand instances of discrimination which tend to fall through the cracks of the usual, one-dimensional typologies of discrimination, and to capture the role of the structures, we regard intersectionality and Critical Race Theory[53] as being useful tools 'to quantitatively and qualitatively capturing this subordination of Roma in general and Roma women in particular [and that] [t]his is especially true with regard to Roma women's health and their right to bodily integrity'.[54] It has been argued that bringing Critical Race Theory into European understandings of minority 'integration' could help disentangle some of the intersectional discrimination faced by those who belong, for instance, to both ethnic and racial minorities, as well as dealing with cases such as the Romani minorities in Europe that have long been treated as exceptional and unique.[55]

In the broader current debate on women's reproductive rights—including some serious setbacks in the past decade in both Europe and the United States—racialized women have typically been on the losing end. In this regard, the (lack of) access to reparations for violations of Romani women's reproductive rights is not a matter confined to the past, but is part and parcel of ongoing struggles that are particularly stark in contexts of democratic backsliding. On the one hand, because racialized women (including Romani women in Europe) tend to be overrepresented in populations that live in deprived areas and are at risk of poverty, when access to safe and legal abortion and voluntary reproductive choices and bodily autonomy is curtailed at the national scale.[56] They are at higher risk of being adversely affected by such changes and face the difficulty or impossibility of travelling to access a safe

[51] On the specific intersectional experiences of Romani women, see also Sebijan Fejzula, 'De-Whitening Romani Women's Intersectional Experience' (2023) 44(4) Journal of Women, Politics & Policy 444.

[52] For an analysis of the complexities surrounding the human rights of minority women in general, and Romani women in particular, see Brooke Ackerly, 'Feminist and Activist Approaches to Human Rights' in ME Goodhart (ed), *Human Rights: Politics and Practice* (OUP 2016) 28; and Camilla Ida Ravnbøl, 'The Human Rights of Minority Women: Romani Women's Rights from a Perspective on International Human Rights Law and Politics' (2010) 17(1) International Journal on Minority and Group Rights 1.

[53] By critically engaging law, but with a focus on race, Critical Race Theory acknowledges that race is socially constructed, yet is real through social constructions. See Kimberlé Crenshaw, Neil Gotanda, Gary Peller, and Thomas Kendall (eds), *Critical Race Theory: The Key Writings That Formed the Movement* (Faculty Books 1995).

[54] Alexandra Oprea, 'Toward the Recognition of Critical Race Theory in Human Rights Law: Roma Women's Reproductive Rights' in Jaqueline Bhabha, Alina Mirga, and Margareta Matache (eds), *Realizing Roma Rights* (University of Pennsylvania Press 2017) 40.

[55] Angela Kóczé, 'Racialization, Racial Oppression of Roma', in *The Palgrave Encyclopedia of Imperialism and Anti-Imperialism* (Palgrave Macmillan 2021). See also Tina Magazzini, 'Antidiscrimination Meets Integration Policies: Exploring New Diversity-Related Challenges in Europe' (2024) 10(6) Social Sciences 1.

[56] In October 2020 the Polish Constitutional Tribunal invalidated the constitutionality of the already severely limited access to abortion. In the United States, the US Supreme Court overturned the constitutional right to an abortion in June 2022, undoing decades of legal precedent and allowing each state to set its own limitations regarding reproductive rights.

and legal abortion elsewhere, for instance. On the other hand, because the voices and experiences of racialized women have historically been invisibilized, when violations of their rights take place and they try to fight back, their claims tend to be downplayed, met with disbelief and/or dismissed. In practice, 'anti-discrimination legislation often remains out of reach for racialised precarious [women] workers and anti-racism is too often reduced to the legal framework of anti-discrimination policies, falling short of analysing the structural dynamics that foster racism at multiple levels'.[57]

Despite the attempts of strategic litigation at pushing the current boundaries constructed by the jurisprudence, the failure of courts to recognize involuntary sterilization as a structural intersectional discrimination practice is highly problematic. This lack of recognition validates and reinforces traditional systems of subordination, infantilization and marginalization of Romani women, rooted in widespread and legitimized anti-Roma racism.

In the next section, we discuss some of the cases of involuntary sterilization of Romani women that have been brought in front of the ECtHR to show how the combination of inappropriate procedural hurdles and the statute of limitations make it overly burdensome for victims to obtain redress and the recognition of the violation of their (reproductive) rights. Our analysis demonstrates that by adopting an intersectional approach, courts and policy-makers have the opportunity to reverse this trend, to push the boundaries of human rights, and promote equality and social justice.

## 4. The ECtHR and the Involuntary Sterilization of Romani Women

In the early 2010s, the issue of involuntary sterilization of Romani women in former Czechoslovakia first, and in the Czech and Slovak Republics afterwards, moved beyond the national judicial borders and reached the ECtHR in Strasbourg.[58] Five different cases were decided by the ECtHR in 2011–12: *VC v Slovakia* (2011)[59]; *Ferenčíková v the Czech Republic* (2011)[60]; *NB v Slovakia* (2012)[61]; *IG and Others v Slovakia* (2012)[62]; and *RK v the Czech Republic* (2012).[63] The two Czech cases

[57] Nina Saharaoui, 'From Everyday Racist Incidents at Work to Institutional Racism: Migrant and Minority-Ethnic Workers' Experiences in Older-Age Care' in Sophie Hinger and Reinhard Schweitzer (eds) *Politics of (Dis)Integration* (Springer 2020).

[58] For an extensive analysis of these ECHR cases, see Chapter 16 in this volume by Gwendolyn Albert, and Eva-Esther Sobotka, and Lilla Farkas.

[59] *VC v Slovakia* App no 18968/07 (ECtHR, 8 November 2011).

[60] *Ferenčíková v the Czech Republic* App no 21826/10 (ECtHR, 30 August 2011).

[61] *NB v Slovakia* App no 29518/10 (ECtHR, 12 June 2012).

[62] *IG and Others v Slovakia* App no 15966/04 (ECtHR,13 November 2012).

[63] *RK v the Czech Republic* App no 7883/08 (ECtHR, 27 November 2012).

were both closed with a friendly settlement between the applicants and the Czech Republic, both applicants being awarded €10,000 each.[64] The three Slovak cases were decided upon by the ECtHR. In *VC*[65] the Court found that the applicant, a Romani woman sterilized in 2000, had been the victim of coerced sterilization in violation of Articles 3 (prohibition of torture) and 8 (right for private and family life).[66] In *NB v Slovakia,* the ECtHR unanimously found that the applicant, a minor at the time, had been sterilized in contravention of Articles 8 and 13 (right to an effective remedy). *IG and Others v Slovakia* concerned three Romani women who were sterilized in 2000, 1999, and 2002, respectively. RH died during the legal process, so her case was struck off the list. Concerning IG and MK, both minors when sterilization was performed, they were redressed for violation of their rights under Articles 3 and 8 of the Convention.

The Slovak cases have particularly contributed to making Romani women's involuntary sterilization a visible and recognized violation of human rights at the European supranational level. Yet, in all three cases the ECtHR refused to consider the discriminatory character of involuntary sterilizations of Romani women, claimed under Article 14 of the Convention (prohibition of discrimination). More precisely, '[t]he Court decided that in view of the documents available, it could not be established that the doctors involved acted in bad faith, that the applicants' sterilisations were a part of an organised policy, or that the hospital staff's conduct was intentionally racially motivated'.[67] The consequences of this requirement is that, in the absence of explicit elements showing that the medical personnel acted in bad faith, with the intention of mistreating the plaintiff, it was not possible to prove racial discrimination. Specifically, the fact that direct intentionality on behalf of individual medical personnel was required, and that the burden of proof concerning ethnic discrimination was placed on the victims, rendered the ECtHR incapable of addressing the root cause of the harm. The Strasbourg Court treated each case as an individual violation, rather than expressions of a normalized practice embedded in systemic racism.

In 2021, *Maděrová v Czech Republic*, lodged in 2015, was declared inadmissible by the ECtHR, as was the case of *ZK v Slovakia*, which was lodged first in 2005 before the Prešov District Court and reached the ECtHR in 2014. Both cases were submitted by NGOs as strategic litigation: by ERRC and the League of Human Rights in the case of *Maděrová v Czech Republic*, and by lawyers acting in cooperation with the Centre for Civil and Human Rights, in the case *ZK v Slovakia*. The

64 ERRC (n 6). 19.

65 For a critical discussion on this case, see also Oprea (n 54) 39.

66 While in labour, VC was misled by medical personnel to believe that an eventual future pregnancy would lead to the death of either her or the child. She therefore signed, under conditions of distress and based on false information, a form requesting sterilization. For more details, see Elena Ghidoni, 'La Esterilización Forzada en Intersecciones Distintas: Un Enfoque Estructural para el Análisis de las Desigualdades Complejas' (2018) 38 Cuadernos Electrónicos de Filosofía del Derecho 102.

67 ERRC (n 6) 20.

latter case concerned the sterilization in 1993 of a minor without her knowledge or consent. Because the doctor who had performed the operation had died by the time that the case was brought to court,[68] the government claimed that it was the responsibility of the applicant to prove that she had been sterilized, by undergoing invasive methods of examination entailing possible side-effects and risks to her health. Since the court agreed, and the applicant refused to do so, the case was declared inadmissible nine years after first having been lodged. Similarly, the case of *Maděrová v Czech Republic*, concerning a Romani woman's sterilization in 1982, was rejected for being statute-barred. Even though the case was time-barred, the combination of the fact that it took six years before the ECtHR decided on the inadmissibility of the case, and the reasoning for its dismissal—placing the burden of proof on the victim—are equally problematic.

Analysing the ECtHR's reasoning in these cases helps to understand 'the level of scrutiny adopted by the courts, the interests identified, and the remedies awarded if a violation of the prohibition of discrimination is found'.[69] Furthermore, it helps to assess whether a proper (explicit or implicit) recognition of intersectional discrimination occurs at the judicial level. *IG and Others v Slovakia* was lodged in 2004 and decided upon in 2012. Having found a violation of Articles 3 and 8, the ECtHR eventually ordered the Slovak government to grant compensation to the applicants of €28,500 and €27,000 respectively, while each applicant had claimed €70,000.[70] The reason behind affording a smaller amount to the second applicant compared to the first was that the second applicant had obtained €1,593 as redress in the context of the civil proceedings (which however was not regarded by the ECtHR as financial redress commensurate with the nature of the damage alleged). The ECtHR referred on multiple occasions to *NB v Slovakia*, which had been decided just a few months before. In this case, lodged before the ECtHR in 2010, the Court held that, since it had been proven that there had been a violation under Articles 3 and 8, and considering the early age at which the applicant had been sterilized and the severe effects on the rest of her life, the compensation should amount to €25,000.

In the last two cases, the Court held unanimously that there was no need to examine separately the complaint under Article 14 of the Convention, confirming its general reluctance to address discrimination complaints.[71] In *VC v Slovakia*, in which the majority decided along the same lines, one of the judges had formulated a firm dissent, emphasizing that—

[68] The applicant had meanwhile undergone infertility treatment, until she found out about the sterilization by requesting her medical records.

[69] Kristin Henrard, 'Human Rights, Intersectionality, and Superdiversity' in Fran Meissner, Nando Sigona, and Steven Vertovec (eds), *The Oxford Handbook of Superdiversity* (University of Oxford 2022).

[70] *IG and Others* (n 62).

[71] Kristin Henrard, 'The European Court of Human Rights, Ethnic and Religious Minorities and the Two Dimensions of the Right to Equal Treatment: Jurisprudence at Different Speeds?' (2016) 34(3) Nordic Journal of Human Rights 157–77.

> [the discrimination] complaint was the very essence of this case and should have been dealt with on its merits, with a finding of a violation of Article 14 ... The facts of the case confirm that the applicant had a medical record and that under the 'Medical history' sub-section, the words 'Patient is of Roma origin' appeared ... Finding violations of Articles 3 and 8 alone in my opinion reduces this case to the individual level, whereas it is obvious that there was a general State policy of sterilization of Roma women under the communist regime (governed by the 1972 Sterilisation Regulation), the effects of which continued to be felt up to the time of the facts giving rise to the present case.[72]

Additionally, the dissenting opinion pointed out the Slovak state policy towards the Roma had not really changed since the end of communism, with sterilizations performed on Roma women being not of an accidental nature, but rather relics of systemic discrimination:

> the applicant was 'marked out' and observed as a patient who had to be sterilized just because of her origin, since it was obvious that there were no medically relevant reasons for sterilizing her. In my view, that represents the strongest form of discrimination and should have led to a finding of a violation of Article 14.[73]

This dissenting opinion also correctly stressed how the ECtHR had, in cases that concerned Roma children and education, found a violation of Article 14 without requesting specific proof of bad faith on behalf of the authorities, or of an orchestrated, racially motivated policy aimed at producing discriminatory effects. It is noteworthy that in the Roma education cases the only claim was a violation of the right to education, in conjunction with discrimination. In *DH and Others v Czech Republic*, in particular, the Grand Chamber accepted that the placement of Romani children in special schools had a disproportionately prejudicial effect on the Roma community, and therefore 'the applicants as members of that community had necessarily suffered the same discriminatory treatment'.[74] This was the conclusion, despite acknowledging in the same judgment that 'the Czech authorities' decision to retain the special-school system was motivated by the desire to find a solution for children with special educational needs',[75] ie not by bad faith. While *DH and Others v Czech Republic* dealt with indirect rather than direct discrimination, available statistical evidence regarding school segregation supported the argument that the cases were not isolated instances, but rather the result of structural dynamics and policies at play (see the chapter of Gergely in this volume).

72 Dissenting Opinion of Judge Mijovic in *VC*.
73 ibid.
74 *DH and Others v Czech Republic* App no 57325/00 [GC] (ECtHR 13 November 2007).
75 ibid.

Of course, courts do not adjudicate in a vacuum. The above-described involvement and resistance of Romani women in European politics described in the previous sections is part and parcel of a broader developmentalist 'Europeanization' of Roma representation. This process has translated into a representation of the Roma as a 'European' minority and has implied the launch of development programmes tied to their integration and human rights since the early 2000s.[76] Especially since the late 2000s, the European Union has made a series of declarations and has developed policies and frameworks aimed at advancing the inclusion of the Roma, yet such discursive commitments to human rights have not really translated into effective policy measures and investments needed to empower the most vulnerable groups.[77] In practice, the European 'will to improve' the situation of the Roma, as well as the political and institutional commitment to their 'minority protection' through development programmes, emerged in the 2000s as inherently related to the rise of a post-1989 'institutional developmentalism' that saw the Roma as an 'internal other' not yet 'developed enough'.[78] The approach that emerged towards combating the Roma's marginalization was thus an internalized securitization enmeshed with a developmentalist inclusion, that mirrored the external securitization entangled with a developmentalist approach applied to migrants. Whereas migrants have been conceptualized as Europe's 'external others', the Roma are considered as Europe's 'internal others'.[79]

As institutional framings are never neutral,[80] it can be argued that the different degree of politicization of these various dimensions, and the different degree of difficulty of collecting evidence, have tangible consequences on how different issues are assessed judicially. For instance, since school segregation could be acknowledged as a problem (and even as an instance of racial discrimination), despite it being presented as 'no one's fault' in *DH v Czech Republic,* it was easy to present quantitative hard data and frame it as some kind of 'technical' rather than political issue. Conversely, the credibility of Romani women who demanded autonomy over their bodies continued to be challenged by the same Court.

In the above-mentioned *ZK v Slovakia*, the rationale of the Court was precisely believability. The Court considered that the medical records indicating that ZK had been sterilized were not sufficient, since the doctor accused of performing the operation had died and other medical staff denied having any information. Based

[76] Huub van Baar, 'The European Roma. Minority Representation, Memory, and the Limits of Transnational Governmentality' (PhD Thesis, Universiteit van Amsterdam 2011) <https://pure.uva.nl/ws/files/1164494/98861_thesis.pdf> accessed 23 November 2023.

[77] Eva Sobotka and Peter Vermeersch, 'Governing Human Rights and Roma Inclusion: Can the EU Be a Catalyst for Local Social Change?' (2012) 34(3) Human Rights Quarterly 800.

[78] van Baar (n 76).

[79] Can Yıldız and Nicholas De Genova, 'Un/Free mobility: Roma migrants in the European Union' (2017) 24(4) Social Identities 425.

[80] Carol Bacchi, 'Why Study Problematisations? Making Politics Visible' (2012) 2(1) Open Journal of Political Science 1.

on the considerations that 'medical experts held that an operation would be required in order to establish whether or not the applicant had been sterilised. The applicant preferred not to undergo such a procedure, as she feared that it might jeopardise her health. Thus, during the domestic proceedings, it was impossible to determine with certainty whether the applicant had been subjected to sterilisation', the case was therefore considered inadmissible.

As shown by legal scholars who focus on the cases of involuntary sterilization of Roma women and of women with disabilities before the ECtHR, '[i]nstead of evaluating discriminatory treatment in light of oppressive practices directed at vulnerable women, courts tend to limit themselves to the individual intention of doctors. This on the one hand overshadows the structural aspects of their oppression, and on the other hand minimizes the collective dimension of discrimination.'[81] The choice to focus on the intentionality of individual medical personnel, and to downplay the evidence brought by Roma women compared to the statements of the (non-Roma) medics, is consistent with the definition on the racial oppression of Roma provided by Angela Kóczé. These choices reflect how—

> racialization and racial oppression of Roma are discursive and structural mechanisms that place them in an imaginary hierarchical classificatory system based on phenotypical, cultural, and social markers and render them as 'other'/subhuman. These oppressive discourses became articulated and solidified in concrete social practices, mechanisms, policies, and structures in Roma people's everyday lives.[82]

## 5. Rewriting ECtHR Judgments Intersectionally

The demand for an intersectional approach in the assessment of discrimination cases by courts has been increasingly made in recent years by legal activists in Europe. Particularly interesting, for instance, is the work of Systemic Justice,[83] a Black-led NGO based in Amsterdam that engages in community-driven litigation for racial, social, and economic justice. One of the initiatives launched by Systemic Justice is 'Intersectional Rewrites: European Court of Human Rights Judgments Reimagined', an independent book project where several authors 'reimagine' ECtHR case law from an intersectional perspective. This initiative aims to emphasize the lack of engagement of the ECtHR with intersectionality: 'the Court's

[81] Elena Ghidoni, 'La Esterilización Forzada en Intersecciones Distintas: Un Enfoque Estructural para el Análisis de las Desigualdades Complejas' (2018) 38 Cuadernos Electrónicos de Filosofía del Derecho 119.

[82] Angela Kóczé, 'Racialization, Racial Oppression of Roma', in *The Palgrave Encyclopedia of Imperialism and Anti-Imperialism* (Palgrave 2020).

[83] <https://systemicjustice.ngo> accessed 17 October 2024.

response ... fails to recognise the complexity of compounded harm complainants have experienced as a result of multiple and mutually influencing vectors of oppression, often not recognising that their human rights have been violated at all'.[84]

What emerges from an overview of the ECtHR's decisions and reasoning is a bias that leads it to favour an individualistic perspective when evaluating responsibility for involuntary sterilization, instead of considering the abundant evidence of a systematic practice that is deeply rooted in a history of state policies aimed at controlling the reproductive rights of Romani women. This is true not only for the ECtHR but also concerning the 2021 Law approved by the Czech government, despite obvious differences in their roles and positionality. The burden of proving violations of the ECHR, just as of eligibility for compensation in Czech law, is placed on the victims. Proving that involuntary sterilization has actually been carried out disproportionately burdens the victims when this burden should not have been imposed on them at all. Linked to this, the ECtHR's choice to ignore evidence and dismiss claims of discrimination concerning involuntary sterilizations of Romani women is a testament to the invisibility of racialized women in the broader debate on women's reproductive rights, and how political battles are being carried out over the bodies of women. Additionally, the amounts of compensation afforded by the ECtHR have repeatedly shown that even when a violation is found (usually after a long waiting time, which in itself is highly problematic), Romani women are not worth quite as much as they think they are. The amounts of compensation are systematically and significantly inferior to the claims. While the ECtHR lowers the amount of compensation in other cases as well, the lack of full compensation is likely to have a more profound impact on Roma women, who often face socio-economic deprivation.

If involuntary sterilization judgments could be 'reimagined' and rewritten from an intersectional perspective, one possible action could be to reverse the burden of proof in both legal and policy processes, as has been proposed elsewhere for other groups subjected to structural and intersectional discrimination[85]. This departing point, however, acknowledges involuntary sterilization for what it is: a structural intersectional discriminatory practice deriving from widespread and legitimated anti-Roma racism that requires redress and reparation. Once systemic discrimination is established, the ECtHR could require general measures, such as to abolish the 2024 time limitation for seeking compensation in Czechia. Furthermore, the Strasbourg Court could also impose a positive obligation for medical institutions/hospitals to provide documentation and supporting evidence, rather than making claimants struggle to obtain this.

84 <https://intersectionalrewrites.org/about/> accessed 17 October 2024.

85 Annick Pijnenburg and Kris van der Pas, 'Strategic Litigation against European Migration Control Policies. The Legal Battleground of the Central Mediterranean Migration Route' (2022) 24(3) European Journal of Migration and Law 401.

The failure to comply with this positive obligation could then shift the burden of proof to the medical institutions and hospitals. Recent developments are promising in this regard, as is a judgment issued in July 2024 the Czech Supreme Administrative Court which held that medical institutions must take active steps to verify whether an applicant for compensation had been subjected to unlawful sterilization.[86] At a more fundamental level, whenever institutions engage in reparative actions, it would be crucial to consult the victims, in order to incorporate their needs, views and requests into the proposed legislation, and adapt the implementation of the law accordingly. In the concrete cases analysed in this chapter, such consultations would not only likely increase the amount afforded in reparations, but also require an explicit acknowledgement of wrongdoing and apology on behalf of the state.

## 6. Concluding Remarks

In August 2020, the government of Namibia officially rejected Germany's offer of $12 million as a sum that was supposed to 'heal the wounds' of Germany's 1904–08 colonial war against the Nama and Ovaherero people, which has been described as the twentieth century's first genocide. The reason for the refusal was twofold: on the one hand the sum was considered insulting for the genocide of close to 100,000 people; on the other hand, Germany refused to 'name the reparations as reparations'.[87]

As stated by the author Panashe Chigumadzi:

> You do not say sorry with your mouth. Our historical consciousness of African moral law demands that we ask the Dutch, the French, the British, the Portuguese, the Germans, and all our other enslavers and colonizers—'Nixolisa ngani?' With what are you apologizing? This is the core of our African restorative justice and jurisprudence. As Black people we ask, 'Nixolisa ngani?' (With what are you apologizing?) because it is understood, the material makes manifest the spirit of intent. Reparations enflesh the spirit of atonement in our material world.[88]

[86] Gwendolin Albert, 'Key Court Decision: Czech Health Ministry must change its approach when verifying illegal sterilizations, lack of medical records must not be an obstacle' (*Romea.cz* 2024) <https://romea.cz/en/czech-republic/key-court-decision-czech-health-ministry-must-change-its-approach-when-verifying-illegal-sterilizations-lack-of-medical-records-must-not-be-an-obstacle> accessed 29 July 2024.

[87] Panashe Chigumadzi, 'With What Are You Apologizing?' (2023) https://africasacountry.com/2023/10/with-what-are-you-apologizing accessed 19 October 2023.The Namibian stance eventually forced Germany to acknowledge the genocide and to make an official apology in 2021. While Germany has not yet offered reparations, it ended up offering $1.34 billion in financial aid.

[88] ibid.

The Czech state, while it is unlikely to increase the amount which it is 'apologizing with' through Law 197/2021, could at least start naming the 'benefit according to the regulations on social security' what they actually are: reparations for involuntary sterilization. Civil law compensation and just satisfaction under the ECtHR are based on a finding of violation and entail individual and general measures if indicated by the court. By looking at the case of the Czech Republic and Slovakia, and the kinds of reparations that have been offered or denied to Romani women over recent years for their involuntary sterilization, it remains unclear with what these states apologize to Roma women. In particular, by analysing the Czech and Slovak case studies, the ECtHR's reasoning that failed to engage with the claims of systemic discrimination against Roma women, and by investigating the broader context, the chapter has demonstrated how uncritical approaches to discrimination can actually validate and reinforce certain systems of subordination and oppression.

The analysis shows that so far, the ECtHR has pulled as much as it has pushed the boundaries of human rights, constructing a narrow reading despite strategic litigation for a more inclusive interpretation of the European Convention. Some authors have acknowledged that the current human rights system is incapable of addressing all intersections of discrimination, arguing that people who are 'severally and severely disadvantaged because of their race, religion, gender, age, disability, sexual orientation, class, etc., often find themselves at the margins of human rights; their condition seldom improved and sometimes even worsened by the rights discourse'.[89] An intersectional approach to discrimination is nonetheless essential for pushing the boundaries of human rights toward reparatory justice, which fosters a nuanced understanding of systemic inequalities within the specific historical and social contexts of intersectionally marginalized communities. By adopting this approach, courts and policy-makers would not only acknowledge past harms but also actively work to dismantle the structural barriers that perpetuate inequality.

[89] Shreya Atrey and Peter Dunne, *Intersectionality and Human Rights Law* (Bloomsbury 2020).

# PART IV

# SOCIO-LEGAL ANALYSIS OF STRATEGIC ROMA RIGHTS LITIGATION IN EUROPEAN COURTS

# 13
# The Ontology and Ethics of Roma Rights Jurisprudence

*Lilla Farkas*

## 1. Introduction

This chapter assesses legal mobilization for Roma rights by highlighting distinct legal strategies and framings to further the human rights of a minority labelled 'the Roma'. Legal mobilization has diverse definitions, ranging from simple use of the law by any actor[1] to 'the use of law in an explicit, self-conscious way through the invocation of a formal institutional mechanism'.[2] This 'tighter' definition of legal mobilization encompasses the use of the law by social movements such as the Roma rights movement, and distinguishes between legal strategy and framing.[3] It also directs the spotlight at the law's potential to challenge the status quo and bring about social change by pushing the boundaries of human rights. As Gledhill emphasizes in Chapter 4 of this volume, bringing about social change is also a significant feature of strategic litigation. It pursues distinct legal strategies and framings to achieve this goal as chronicled in this chapter.

Roma rights jurisprudence is a recent but highly visible phenomenon, whose doctrinal analysis is significant, especially concerning the jurisprudence on racial or ethnic discrimination. Since the 1996 *Buckley v United Kingdom* judgment,[4] the number of Roma rights rulings has grown rapidly and today exceeds ninety final rulings in the European Court of Human Rights (ECtHR), a dozen in the European Committee of Social Rights (ECSR), two in the Court of Justice of the European Union (CJEU), and a handful before UN monitoring bodies.[5] A doctrinal analysis would take it for granted that these cases exist and that they revolve

[1] Frances Kahn Zemans, 'Legal Mobilization: The Neglected Role of the Law in the Political System' [1983] 77(3) American Political Science Review 690. Hers is an oft-quoted definition: '[l]aw is mobilized when a desire or want is translated into a demand as an assertion of rights'. Ibid 700.

[2] Emilio Lehoucq and Whitney K Taylor, 'Conceptualizing Legal Mobilization: How Should We Understand the Deployment of Legal Strategies?' (2020) 45 Law & Social Inquiry 169.

[3] ibid.

[4] *Buckley v United Kingdom* App no 20348/92 (ECtHR, 25 September 1996).

[5] European Court of Human Rights Press Unit, 'Roma and Travellers Factsheet' (2024) European Court of Human Rights <https://www.echr.coe.int/documents/d/echr/fs_roma_eng>. The UN monitoring bodies' and the European Committee on Social Rights' websites were accessed separately.

Lilla Farkas, *The Ontology and Ethics of Roma Rights Jurisprudence* In: *The Rights of Roma in European Courts*. Edited by: Kristin Henrard and Lilla Farkas, Oxford University Press. © Lilla Farkas 2025.
DOI: 10.1093/oso/9780198914358.003.0013

around racial violence and speech, segregated education, housing, forced sterilization, and the removal of children.

This chapter however engages in a sociolegal or practice-oriented analysis. This type of analysis asks how these cases come to be, why do we observe more of them before specific international fora, why do they address structural discrimination in certain fields and not others, and what is the role of cause lawyers and legally focused non-governmental organizations (NGOs), so-called 'repeat players' in crafting the Roma rights jurisprudence.[6]

More specifically, the key questions of this chapter are what is litigated, by whom, and how. The key questions necessitate an ontological inquiry that also attends to ethical dilemmas linked to the positionality and agency of different actors in the Roma rights field, their potentially contradicting interests and the ways in which they do things and tell their story. These actors form a transnational advocacy network and include Roma and non-Roma individuals and communities; elected and self-appointed leaders; academics; domestic or international, Traveller and Roma NGOs; public institutions; global funders; and international organizations.[7]

A significant characteristic of Roma communities is widespread social marginalization, a low level of legal consciousness, a gaping lack of minority institutions and the almost non-existent middle classes, which altogether present structural impediments to legal mobilization.[8] Roma rights litigation is relatively expensive because the costs of discovery and client care are high and only a small part can be reclaimed under procedural rules. Many Roma rights claims run counter to majority interests, which makes pro bono representation highly unlikely, for who would want to champion a cause that undermines the interests of paying clients?

As to the question of who litigates, these structural impediments necessarily concentrate Roma rights litigation in legally focused NGOs and invite the participation of cause lawyers, in other words legal practitioners committed to social causes such as minority rights, anti-racism, poverty reduction, or the rule of law.[9] The transnational advocacy network concerned with Roma rights is dominated by a key donor, the Open Society Institute (OSI, renamed as Open Society Foundations in 2012).[10] OSI's own Roma structure has made legal mobilization

6 Marc Galanter, 'Why the "Haves" Come Out Ahead: Speculations on the Limits of Legal Change' (1974) 9(1) Law & Society Review 95.

7 Aidan McGarry, 'Ethnic Group Identity and the Roma Social Movement: Transnational Organizing Structures of Representation.' (2008) 36(3) Nationalities Papers 449.

8 Zoltan Barany, *The East European Gypsies: Regime Change, Marginality, and Ethnopolitics* (CUP 2001); György Csepeli and Antal Örkény, 'Az emancipáció kihívása a mai magyar társadalomban a romák és nem romák viszonyában' (2015) 25(3) Szociológiai Szemle 83.

9 Lilla Farkas, 'Mobilising for Racial Equality in Europe: Roma Rights and Transnational Justice' (2020) <[https://cadmus.eui.eu/handle/1814/66916> accessed 2 August 2024.

10 Margaret E Keck and Kathryn Sikkink, 'Transnational Advocacy Networks in the Movement Society' in David S Meyer and Sidney Tarrow (eds), *A Movement Society: Contentious Politics for a New Century* (Rowman & Littlefield Publishers 1998) 217.

for Roma rights robust, visible, and effective in comparison to other racialized minorities in Europe.[11] Since its establishment in 1995, the European Roma Rights Centre (ERRC) has been the epicentre of this structure.[12]

As to the question of what to litigate, legal mobilization on behalf of the Roma concerns the rights of the Roma, in short Roma rights, which may be defined narrowly, more broadly or even more broadly.[13] An example of the narrow reading is anti-Gypsy violence or hate speech. The broader concept could include a breach of contract, and for the broadest reading a pertinent example would be a systemic issue, such as the general lack of social housing, which nonetheless disproportionately affects the Roma. In this chapter, structural or systemic discrimination is taken to consist of 'both institutional discrimination based upon norms, rules, regulations, procedures and defined positions that determine access to resources, and also a broader cultural discrimination based upon widely shared social paradigms' that devalue vulnerable and stigmatized groups, such as the Roma.[14]

The identity of the Roma as a group is a central question in determining what to litigate. Social scientists posit that the Roma are a heterogeneous group, and some argue that there is a lack of an authentic collective ethnic identity among the Eastern Roma,[15] which means that the Roma are at best a minority 'in a purely negative sense, that is, by common concerns such as poverty, socio-economic exclusion and discrimination'.[16] Legal mobilization for Roma rights has grappled with these issues and experimented with various approaches to legally frame Roma rights claims.

Still concerning the question of what, due to its fragmentation, international human rights law offers incoherent and in many respects weak legal opportunities for making Roma rights claims.[17] In a series of articles, István Pogány shows the shortcomings of specific sets of rights, primarily the minority rights regime.[18]

[11] There is a Factsheet on the Roma rights cases, but no similar ones for Muslims and Blacks in Europe due to the small number of cases. Litigation on the Muslim headscarf is increasing but the volume of rulings is lower than the Roma rights cases, despite the more sizeable Muslim population in Europe.

[12] Farkas (n 9).

[13] Claude Cahn, 'The Names' (2004) Roma Rights Journal <https://www.errc.org/cikk.php?cikk=1843> accessed 20 August 2024.

[14] Tom R Burns, 'Towards a Theory of Structural Discrimination: Cultural, Institutional and Interactional Mechanisms of the "European Dilemma"' in Gerard Delanty, Ruth Wodak, and Paul Jones (eds), *Identity, Belonging and Migration* (Liverpool University Press 2008) 152.

[15] See, for instance, Martin Kovats, 'Problems of Intellectual and Political Accountability in Respect of Emerging European Roma Policy' (2001) 2(1) Journal on Ethnopolitics Minority Issues in Europe.

[16] István Pogány, 'Pariah Peoples: Roma and the Multiple Failures of Law in Central and Eastern Europe' (2012) 21(3) Social & Legal Studies 375.

[17] Chris Hilson, 'New Social Movements: The Role of Legal Opportunity' (2002) 9(2) Journal of European Public Policy 238.

[18] István Pogány, 'Refashioning Rights in Central and Eastern Europe: Some Implications for the Region's Roma' (2004) 10(1) European Public Law 85; István Pogány, 'Minority Rights and the Roma of Central and Eastern Europe' (2006) 6(1) Human Rights Law Review 1.

Compounded by their lack of justiciability,[19] the Roma are less likely to benefit from classic minority rights, being a non-traditional and linguistically as well as culturally diverse minority group in a formative stage, without a kin state and long-standing institutions. Even though robustly justiciable, civil and political rights including equal treatment are also an 'imperfect fit' for the impoverished segments of the Roma community, whose primary need is access to social rights. The Eastern Roma had enjoyed extensive social rights, which they all but lost after 1989.[20] International human rights law covers a broad range of substantive rights, but many states with sizeable Roma populations tend to limit the scope of social rights under the (revised) European Social Charter (ESC).[21]

Now turning to the question of how, it must be noted that many Roma rights issues are structural in nature and could best be challenged through collective legal action. However, raising collective complaints is difficult because many states with sizeable Roma populations limit access to such claims. Procedural rules hamper strategic litigation primarily by blocking the access of collective actors to the ECtHR and failing to address situations when national courts do not refer preliminary questions to the CJEU.[22]

The 'imperfect fit' of international norms and policies shows a failure to respond to the lived experiences of both the culturally different Western Travellers and the marginalized Eastern Roma. It is exacerbated by the shortcomings of domestic law and policy, which persist despite the requirement of compliance with international human rights law.[23] Legal mobilization can address this 'imperfect fit'. The chapter posits that to overcome structural impediments, NGOs and cause lawyers created innovative legal strategies and framing by having recourse to international human rights law.

Following this introduction, section 2 investigates the ways in which strategic litigation has pushed the boundaries of Roma rights as a particular subset of human rights. Section 3 studies the legal master frames and frame innovations. Section 4 briefly assesses jurisprudential developments, to then evaluate critical scholarship about strategic litigation for Roma rights. Section 5 concludes.

[19] Paul Lemmens, Annelies Verstichel, André Alen, and Bruno De Witte (eds), *The Framework Convention for the Protection of National Minorities: a Useful Pan-European instrument?* (Intersentia 2008).

[20] Pogány (n 16).

[21] On the limitations of the ESC, see Nikolaos A Papadopoulos, 'Strategic Litigation before the European Committee of Social Rights: Fit for Purpose?' (2022) 40(4) Netherlands Quarterly of Human Rights 384. See also Farkas (n 9).

[22] Mark Dawson and Elise Muir, 'Individual, Institutional and Collective Vigilance in Protecting Fundamental Rights in the EU: Lessons from the Roma' (2011) 48(3) Common Market Law Review 751.

[23] Elena Marushiakova-Popova and Vesselin Popov, 'European Policies for Social Inclusion of Roma: Catch 22?' (2015) 3(5) Social Inclusion 19.

## 2. Mobilizing the Law: From Legal Strategies to Strategic Litigation

This section situates strategic litigation in the broader concept of legal mobilization and examines the close relationship between the existence of a conscious, potentially politically motivated legal strategy and strategic litigation. There is discord in the literature about three conceptual elements of legal mobilization, which also impact the ontological study of Roma rights jurisprudence. As Lehoucq and Taylor note, the first discord is formulated around the question of whether legal mobilization amounts to litigation only or involves quasi-judicial and other procedures.[24] The second question is essential from the fundamentally state-centred perspective of international human rights law, because it asks whether claims not directed against the state are covered by legal mobilization. The third question problematizes a central component of strategic litigation as highlighted by Gledhill in this volume, namely whether litigation beyond the interests of an individual, in other words impact litigation, is an essential element of legal mobilization, transforming the nature of engagement from legal into a legal as well as political act. The chapter uses legal mobilization in the broader sense of legal actions as defined in the introduction and naturally focuses on claims against the state, which is a characteristic of international human rights law. It does not focus on broader social impact and the political nature of strategic litigation due to lack of space.

Legal mobilization for Roma rights must overcome several hurdles. As chapter after chapter lament the socio-economic deprivation of the Roma communities, it becomes clear that individual Roma clients generally lack the resources to retain lawyers who would not only take their cases through national courts but would also have the professional resources to pursue them before international tribunals. Classic lawyers service a client who chooses to trust them with a private matter, and their duty to pursue a strategy that best serves the individual client's interest in domestic courts is paramount. Conversely, an individual client's interest is only one consideration for a cause lawyer or strategic litigator, who tends to be equally or more concerned with the promotion of political causes, legal and/or policy reform and general or group-specific social change, often using international human rights law.[25] In case the cause lawyers are not ethnic Roma, do not ensure the participation of ethnic Roma, or seem to favour general societal interests or the interests of the entity that foots the bill rather than the interests of the Roma client, ethical issues may arise about which 'master' they serve.[26] Nonetheless, 'Roma participation' does not in and of itself resolve the ethical dilemmas arising from the

[24] Lehoucq and Taylor (n 2) 173.

[25] Austin Sarat and Stuart A Scheingold (eds), *Cause Lawyering: Political Commitments and Professional Responsibilities* (OUP 1998).

[26] Derrick A Bell Jr, 'Serving Two Masters: Integration Ideals and Client Interests in School Desegregation Litigation' (1975) 85 Yale Law Journal 470.

servicing of interests other than the clients' because different Roma individuals and groups may have diverging interests.[27]

Following the end of the Cold War and the political transition in the former Soviet space, structural legal opportunities such as access to international adjudication and funding for litigation, as well as contingent variables such as judicial receptivity,[28] increased the willingness and the prospects to advance Roma rights through litigation.[29] Yet, the broadening opportunities also engendered situations whereby certain clients were solicited to come forward, while others who had already raised complaints were rejected because their grievances did not align with an NGO's definition of Roma rights or its legal strategy. The selection of client, cause, argument—often abbreviated as case selection—as well as the choice of forum are important elements of strategic litigation and thus the present inquiry. This section focuses on case selection and forum shopping, while section 3 deals with legal framing.

## 2.1. Western Travellers

There are temporal and geographic differences in who litigates, what and how, which has profound implications for the directions in which Roma rights are pushed, and the type of structural violations that come before courts. A seemingly unique chapter of legal mobilization centred on Western Travellers after the mid-1980s, when legislation rolled back the protection of the Travellers and English Gypsies' ethnic minority traditions in the United Kingdom and Ireland. It combined political and grassroots activism, legal advocacy, and test case litigation, which targeted the European Convention system because of the lack of political opportunities and the slim chances of legal reform at home, compounded by a lack of access to other treaty mechanisms.[30] The litigation campaign in the UK was a response to the declining legal protection of the Traveller way of life, which the group considers the cornerstone of their ethnic identity.[31] They wanted to restore the status quo, which changed substantially in 1994, when criminal legislation was adopted in response to an increasing number of 'new nomads'.[32]

Luke Clements, a 'left of Labour' solicitor and university lecturer, spearheaded the litigation campaign, about which he wrote widely, and also advised the ERRC

[27] Nidhi Trehan and Angéla Kóczé, 'Racism, (Neo-) Colonialism, and Social Justice: The Struggle for the Soul of the Romani Movement in Post-Socialist Europe' [2009] Racism Postcolonialism Europe 50. The authors investigate 'racialized hierarchies' in the Roma rights movement, not the Roma communities.

[28] This judicial receptivity was uneven though, as highlighted by Sardelic in this volume.

[29] Hilson (n 17).

[30] Farkas (n 9).

[31] Thomas Acton, 'Conflict Resolution and Criminal Justice – Sorting out Trouble' (2005) 37(51) The Journal of Legal Pluralism and Unofficial Law 29.

[32] Luke Clements, 'Human Rights and Gypsy Identity in British Law' in Alessandro Simoni (a cura), *Stato Di Diritto E Identita Ro-M* (L'Harmattan Italia 2005) 99.

that intervened in some cases before the ECtHR in the early 2000s.[33] The *Buckley* case formed part of this litigation campaign, and the applicant's loss turned into a historic victory for the Roma rights movement. It considerably pushed the boundaries of both Roma and Traveller rights, while also revealing an important feature of legal mobilization, namely that even losses can push the boundaries of human rights.[34] In *Buckley*, the Strasbourg Court united the distinct groups of Western Travellers and Eastern Roma and recognized their vulnerable status with reference to cultural traditions, which is analysed in section 3. The dissenting opinions highlighted by Sardelic in this volume reveal the relevance of the geopolitical context. This context explains the 'construction' of the Roma minority by international organizations as described by Majtényi, which in turn lay the ground for the judicial recognition of the minority by the ECtHR.

## 2.2. Eastern Roma and the US transplants of 'who, what, and how'

In transitional Eastern Europe, OSI has 'governed' the Roma rights field, garnering discursive dominance about Roma rights at the international level.[35] OSI chose the Roma rights field to transplant the 'who, what and how' of the US civil rights movement, in which a federal NGO, the National Association for the Advancement of Colored People (NAACP), mobilized the law to dismantle the separate but equal doctrine that prevented the social integration of African Americans.[36] Given the decline of the federal commitment to equality after the Reagan presidency, and its positionality as a US-based progressive philanthropy, OSI set out to globalize this type of legal mobilization and reimport favourable jurisprudential outcomes to push the boundaries of civil rights in the US.[37] This angle is not explored here but scholarship shows that by improving standards in Europe, OSI engendered jurisprudence on racial discrimination[38] that can be borrowed by courts across the globe.[39]

33 <https//errc.org/search?country=&theme=&area=&keyword=Luke+Clements&search_submit=> accessed 20 August 2024.

34 Douglas NeJaime, 'Winning Through Losing' (2010) 96(3) Iowa Law Review 941.

35 Giles Scott-Smith and Moritz Baumgärtel, 'New Paradigms, Old Hierarchies? Problems and Possibilities of US Supremacy in a Networked World' (2011) 48 International Politics 271.

36 Joel F Handler, *Social Movements and the Legal System: A Theory of Law Reform and Social Change* (Academic Press 1978).

37 Scott L Cummings, 'The Internationalization of Public Interest Law' (2008) 57(4) Duke Law Journal 891–1036; Scott L Cummings and Louise G Trubek, 'Globalizing Public Interest Law' (2008) 13(1) UCLA Journal International Law and Foreign Affairs 1–53.

38 See, for instance Bob Hepple, 'The European Legacy of Brown v. Board of Education' [2006] University of Illinois Law Review 605; Martha Minow, 'Brown v. Board in the World: How the Global Turn Matters for School Reform, Human Rights, and Legal Knowledge' (2013) 50 San Diego Law Review.

39 Anne-Marie Slaughter, 'A Typology of Transjudicial Communication' (1994) 29(1) University of Richmond Law Review 99.

### 2.2.1. The questions of who and how

Strategic litigation in the sense of top-down and lawyer-led proactive international human rights litigation seeking structural reform (impact) and the racial discrimination framing of claims are the most visible staples of legal mobilization spearheaded by the ERRC. They are also the most significant transplants from the US civil rights movement.[40] This transatlantic element and the influence of US ways of doing things propelled the Roma rights movement to catch up with the LGBT and other new social movements, which had far more robust endogenous resources and a longer timeframe in which to organize.[41] It also prepared the Roma rights movement to tap into European norms prohibiting racial discrimination after 2000.

The ERRC started to promote strategic litigation against racial discrimination as 'creative human rights litigation' in 1998.[42] Strategic litigation in this sense could take two different forms: in the case of litigation responding to client requests, lawyers and NGOs losing at the domestic level could turn to international courts, whereas in the case of proactive litigation, NGOs selected clients, causes, arguments, and judicial forum with a view to 'going international'. Then-ERRC legal director, James A Goldston's publications span a quarter of a century and show a journey from the second form of strategic litigation, namely proactive top-down lawyer-led litigation to the critique of this type of lawyering.[43]

Importantly, strategic litigation was conceptualized differently by the ERRC and domestic NGOs, because the latter maintained legal aid services and were consequently not as free to select cases or legal forum as the former. The ERRC selected cases from domestic NGOs and lawyers, and importantly, its legal staff specialized in litigation before the Strasbourg Court. This explains differences between the so-called Bulgarian racial violence cases on the one hand and *DH and Others v Czech Republic* on the other.[44] As Coomber shows, racial violence

[40] Farkas (n 9).

[41] cf the ECtHR factsheets on LGBT, women and Roma rights. For a comparison between the LGBT and Roma rights movements, see Loveday Hodson, *NGOs and the Struggle for Human Rights in Europe* (Hart Publishing 2011).

[42] ERRC, 'Roma Rights Autumn 1998: Legal Defence' (1999) 2 Roma Rights Journal <http://www.errc.org/roma-rights-journal/roma-rights-autumn-1998-legal-defence> accessed 6 August 2024.

[43] James A Goldston, 'Race Discrimination Litigation in Europe: Problems and Prospects' [1999] 1 Roma Rights Journal <Race discrimination litigation in Europe: problems and prospects - European Roma Rights Centre> accessed 20 August 2024; James A Goldston, 'Roma Rights, Roma Wrongs' (2002) 81(2) Foreign Affairs 146; James A Goldston, 'Public Interest Litigation in Central and Eastern Europe: Roots, Prospects, and Challenges' (2006) 28(2) Human Rights Quarterly 492; James A Goldston, 'Ending Racial Segregation in Schools: The Promise of D.H.' (2008) 1 Roma Rights Journal <m00000362.pdf> accessed 20 August 2024; James A Goldston, 'The Struggle for Roma Rights: Arguments that Have Worked' (2010) 32(2) Human Rights Quarterly 311; James A Goldston, 'The Unfulfilled Promise of Educational Opportunity in the United States and Eu rope: From Brown v. Board to D.H. and Beyond', in Jacqueline Babha, Andrzej Mirga, and Margareta Matache (eds), *Realizing Roma Rights* (University of Pennsylvania Press 2017) 163.

[44] *DH and Others v the Czech Republic* App no 57325/00 (ECtHR, 7 February 2006), and [GC] (ECtHR 13 November 2007).

could not be challenged in any other way than litigating test cases in a responsive manner in domestic courts, while *DH* could be proactively designed and litigated in international courts.[45] As transpires below, even though structural discrimination is tangible in all the relevant issue areas, proactive collective challenges cannot easily be launched outside the field of education under the ECHR.

Strategic litigation is straightforward and simple under the European Social Charter. INGOs registered under the ESC and challenged forced evictions in conjunction with racial discrimination after 2004, when the collective complaints procedure became operational. The Centre on Housing Rights and Evictions championed this type of strategic litigation, also facilitating the ERRC's involvement with the ESC. The collective complaints are filed without clients or domestic proceedings; this renders the procedure highly prone to proactive top-down lawyering, which requires nothing more than the identification of the relevant Charter provision and researching the facts. Regrettably, even though the number of forced eviction cases has increased steadily, the ESC remains largely inaccessible for the Eastern Roma because many states limit the social rights guaranteed and/or do not permit collective complaints.

Interestingly, responsive litigation more quickly engendered jurisprudence on racial discrimination than proactive strategic litigation. Prior to 2004, when Protocol 12 of the European Convention on human rights and fundamental freedoms (ECHR, Convention) and the EU Racial Equality Directive (RED) became justiciable, litigating racial equality at state level was cumbersome or impossible.[46] Similar to other social movements, which suffered from the non-justiciability of international treaty or constitutional equality provisions, the ERRC and domestic NGOs set out to overcome or at least highlight this shortcoming.[47] Unexpectedly, in *Nachova and Others v Bulgaria*, litigated by the Bulgarian Helsinki Committee's legal director Yonko Grozev, a Chamber of the ECtHR established racial discrimination in relation to the right to life concerning both the substantive and procedural limbs (2004), while the Grand Chamber upheld this finding concerning only the procedural limb (2005).[48] In *DH*, the Chamber did not find discrimination (2005), while the Grand Chamber established ethnic indirect discrimination (2007). Still, *DH* features at the top of the Roma and Traveller Factsheet of the

[45] Andrea Coomber, 'Strategically Litigating Equality – Reflections on a Changing Jurisprudence' (2012) 15(11) European Anti-Discrimination Law Review 11.

[46] Protocol No 12 to the Convention for the Protection of Human Rights and Fundamental Freedoms (adopted 4 November 2000, entered into force 1 April 2005) ETS 177 and Council Directive 2000/43/EC of 29 June 2000 implementing the principle of equal treatment between persons irrespective of racial or ethnic origin [2000] OJ L180.

[47] Lisa Vanhala, 'Legal Opportunity Structures and the Paradox of Legal Mobilization by the Environmental Movement in the UK' (2012) 46(3) Law & Society Review 523.

[48] *Nachova and Others v Bulgaria* App nos 43577/98 and 43579/98 (ECtHR, 24 February 2004) (ECtHR [GC], 6 July 2005).

ECtHR and legal scholarship.[49] This is because the racial discrimination framing became dominant after 2004, especially in the fields covered by the RED, such as education. However, strategic litigation did not engender legal reform because that had already taken place during EU accessions or treaty ratifications in the Council of Europe.

### 2.2.2. The question of what

The consensus in the Eastern Roma rights movement was that structural discrimination prevalent in all social fields must be challenged and the ECHR—the only generally accessible treaty that also covered the whole of Europe when *DH* was launched—safeguarded only one social right: the right to education. Designing a legal strategy that would emulate US desegregation litigation before the Strasbourg Court seemed straightforward, especially because segregated education could only be challenged by invoking the right to education in conjunction with the principle of non-discrimination. In other words, in *DH* and the subsequent Roma education cases the ECtHR could not avoid the examination of racial discrimination. As subsequent litigation shows, with a more inventive legal strategy and framing, forced evictions could have been challenged too, emulating the Traveller cases. However, in the Traveller cases the Strasbourg Court had not established discrimination and it seemed unlikely that in the Roma cases it would. This had already been visible in 2000 due to the Strasbourg Court's negative approach to the Traveller cases, which argued the violation of Article 8 (right to private and family life) alone and in conjunction with Article 14 (non-discrimination).[50] It is highly likely that other than the US civil rights movement's example, the limited legal opportunities were key in choosing segregated education as an example of structural discrimination.

The choice of human rights whose boundaries were pushed was often made by the client, but sometimes by NGOs and cause lawyers, depending on their ideological orientation and the influence of their donors. Differences between—mainly international and domestic—NGOs concerning the question of what to litigate are most visible when it comes to the effective protection of Roma communities from forced eviction and from hate speech. Domestic NGOs situated further from

[49] See, for instance Morag Goodwin, '*D.H. and Others v Czech Republic*: a Major Set-Back for the Development of Non-Discrimination Norms in Europe' (2006) 7(4) German Law Journal 421; Morag Goodwin, 'Taking on Racial Segregation: The European Court of Human Rights at a *Brown v. Board of Education* Moment?' (2009) 170(3) Rechtsgeleerd Magazijn Themis, 114; Helen O'Nions, 'Different and Unequal: The Educational Segregation of Roma Pupils in Europe' (2010) 20(1) Intercultural Education 1; Sina Van den Bogaert, *Segregation of Roma Children in Education* (Brill 2011); Kalina Arabadjieva, 'Challenging the School Segregation of Roma children in Central and Eastern Europe' (2015) 20(1) International Journal of Human Rights 33.

[50] Andi Dobrushi and Theodoros Alexandridis, 'International Housing Rights and Domestic Prejudice: The Case of Roma and Travellers' in Malcolm Langford, Cesar Garavito-Rodriguez, and Julietta Rossi (eds), *Making it Stick: Compliance with Social Rights Judgments in Comparative Perspective* (CUP 2017) 436.

OSI and closer to the minority communities and leftist politics acted differently from the ERRC. The Western Travellers' test case litigation is an exceptional case because not only did it commence before OSI established its own Roma structure, but it responded to a single issue raised by the community itself: the protection of a cultural minority tradition, the Traveller way of life. Unlike the Eastern Roma, the Travellers did not face the dilemma of what issue to prioritize for legal mobilization.

Rather than the ERRC, it was the Bulgarian Helsinki Committee (BHC) and its prodigal legal director, Margarita Ilieva, who designed a winning legal strategy under the ECHR on both forced evictions and hate speech. Proactive anti-eviction strategies could not be designed under the ECHR because of the unforeseeability and urgency of events, but domestic NGOs raised the legal consciousness of communities about the availability of legal remedies. This proved to be a key factor in the first Eastern eviction case, *Yordanova and Others v Bulgaria*, in which Ilieva adapted the Convention arguments from the Traveller cases to the Eastern Roma context by innovatively framing vulnerability, as discussed in the next section.[51] Her strategic innovation created an effective and immediate remedy because even though the case was argued under Article 8, to which the ECtHR had not previously ascribed urgency, she successfully requested interim measures under rule 39 to halt the eviction. *Yordanova* positively influenced complaints filed against forced evictions in the West, such as *Hirtu and Others v France*, in which the ERRC adopted the Bulgarian Helsinki Committee's legal strategy.[52]

The chapter dealing with hate speech reveals that the ERRC never initiated, nor intervened in cases concerning hate speech, which was partly due to the dominance until 2015 of US liberals favouring unmitigated free speech. Conversely, Europeans largely agree on sanctioning hate speech in collaboration with minority activists who also volunteer as clients. The BHC improved the Strasbourg Court's case law, which was seen by activists as setting a particularly negative precedent by not finding a violation in *Aksu v Turkey*, which concerned a publicly funded academic publication riddled with stereotypical and demeaning depictions of the Roma.[53] Following its defeat in *Panayotova v Bulgaria*, the BHC forfeited its legal strategy addressing the shortcomings of the prohibition of hate speech in criminal law and adopted a civil law strategy in *Budinova and Chaprazov v Bulgaria*, merging claims in one petition from different ethnic minorities subjected to hate speech to even out the protection across groups.[54]

51 *Yordanova v Bulgaria* App no 25446/02 (ECtHR, 24 Sept 2012).

52 *Hirtu v France* App no 24720/13 (ECtHR, 14 May 2020).

53 *Aksu v Turkey* App nos 4149/04 and 41029/04 (ECtHR, 27 July 2010) and [GC] (ECtHR, 15 March 2012).

54 Margarita Ilieva, 'Minority Vilification: Redress for Community Members' (2021) Oxford Human Rights Hub <Minority Vilification: Redress for Community Members | OHRH (ox.ac.uk)> accessed 28 August 2024.

Romanian and Hungarian NGOs also challenged Romaphobic hate speech under anti-discrimination law and won before equality bodies or national courts.[55] This explains the lack of international case law from these countries despite robust legal mobilization. This litigation strand shows divergence between liberal US and leftist European cause lawyers, which aligns with the US's refusal and the European states' espousal of prohibiting hate speech under the International Covenant on Civil and Political Rights.[56] Importantly, minorities are critical of the US approach while supportive of the European one.[57] Hate speech litigation demonstrates that the boundaries of human rights may be pushed in domestic proceedings with reference to international human rights law. Conversely, the non-compliance of domestic proceedings to law is a necessary condition for the development of international jurisprudence.

Litigation on forced sterilization clearly shows frictions between the ERRC and domestic NGOs, as a result of which Slovakian cases were litigated separately from Czech ones and knowledge transfer on strategy and framing was scarce. This litigation strand has failed to persuade the Strasbourg Court to acknowledge the structural nature of the rights violations and the underlying racial animus, as noted in Judge Mijović's dissent in *VC v Slovakia*.[58] This is troubling because in analogous cases dealing with racial violence under Article 3 (freedom from torture, inhuman, and degrading treatment) the ECtHR's case law is more progressive, as highlighted below. The chapters on forced sterilization suggest arguments that may persuade the ECtHR to improve its analysis and it seems that strategic litigation on this issue must overcome gender insensitivity among (male) judges.

Litigation concerning the removal of children is in its infancy in the Strasbourg Court, where it seems to be driven by individual Roma applicants with the help of domestic (cause) lawyers.[59] As Henrard and Roberts mention in the chapter on the burden of proof, due to allegedly insufficient statistical data the ECSR rejected the collective complaint concerning the over-representation of Roma children among those removed from families in *ERRC and MDAC v Czechia*.[60] Herczog and Körtvélyesi's chapter describes the reasons why it is particularly complex to design a legal strategy on this issue, which is compounded by the difficulty of soliciting clients. The non-availability of collective complaints under the ESC in several countries with sizeable Roma populations and the difficulty of raising collective claims

[55] Farkas (n 9).

[56] Kristine Ash, 'US Reservations to the International Covenant on Civil and Political Rights: Credibility Maximization and Global Influence' (2005) 3(1) Northwestern Journal of International Human Rights.

[57] Michel Rosenfeld, 'Hate Speech in Constitutional Jurisprudence: A Comparative Analysis' [2003] 24 Benjamin N Cardozo School of Law 1523.

[58] *VC v Slovakia* App no 18968/07 (ECtHR, 8 November 2011).

[59] In *Barnea and Caldararu v Italy* App no 37931/15 (ECtHR 22 June 2017) the applicants were represented by a member of the ASGI, a progressive network of lawyers focusing on migration.

[60] *ERRC and MDAC v the Czech Republic* Complaint No 157/2017 (ECSR, 17 June 2020).

before the Strasbourg Court may explain why strategic litigation is limited to the domestic level, where it takes the form of *actio popularis* claims that are inadmissible under the Convention. Even though the ERRC published a report about the systematic removal of Roma children in Hungary back in 2007,[61] litigation started more than a decade later. Given that collective legal action has not been taken elsewhere, it appears as if NGOs and cause lawyers are not yet responding adequately to community needs on this issue.

In summary, legal mobilization has not been fully successful in persuading the Strasbourg Court to acknowledge the structural nature of violations, especially not on forced sterilization and child removals. Activists have played a significant role in mobilizing the law and steering strategic litigation towards certain structural issues. Pushing the boundaries of Roma rights on racial violence and segregated education were prioritized by both the legal and political branches of the movement, and by international as well as domestic NGOs. Conversely, on hate speech and forced evictions, domestic NGO strategies aligned more closely with activist agendas. The differences stem from the convergence between US liberal and European leftist cause lawyers on the former, and divergence on the latter issues. Litigation on child removal has been driven by individuals, as NGOs are yet to create adequate legal strategies, which necessitates transnational knowledge-exchange.

Starting with the UK Travellers, legal mobilization has been largely responsive to client and activist demands at the domestic level. It has established robust protection in the field of education followed by hate speech, racial violence, and forced evictions. As predicted by Pogány, it has built on negative group identity in the East, responding to racism against the Roma. Conversely, it has only dealt with the preservation of ethnic identity (the Traveller way of life) in the West. Domestic NGOs and leftists cause lawyers have tackled hate speech in defiance of US liberals and the ERRC. It seems that NGOs—especially international vs national NGOs—do not collaborate adequately, and at times compete in the Roma rights field because they prefer full control over litigation.[62] They represent rather than advise clients and do not submit third-party interventions in a coordinated manner. Even though the ERRC has recently increased third-party interventions, collaboration on key issues is not visible and the initial competition negatively affects the efficiency of litigation. Legal strategies seldom travel between the East and the West, across countries or between the international and domestic echelons, which is primarily due to the ERRC's competitiveness and its subsequent unwillingness or

[61] Európai Roma Jogok Központja (European Roma Rights Centre), 'Fenntartott érdektelenség: Roma gyermekek a magyar gyermekvédelmi rendszerben' (2007) <www.errc.org > accessed 20 August 2024.

[62] Sophie Jacquot and Tommaso Vitale, 'Law as Weapon of the Weak? A Comparative Analysis of Legal Mobilization by Roma and Women's Groups at the European Level' (2014) 21(4) Journal of European Public Policy 598.

inability to acknowledge domestic inventions and facilitate transnational knowledge exchange.

## 3. Framing Roma Rights

The previous section has touched upon the master frames of legal mobilization in the Roma rights context, namely ethnic minority rights focusing on cultural traditions in the Western Traveller context and the Eastern Roma master frame of racial discrimination. It has demonstrated that strategic litigation was essential in convincing the Strasbourg Court to adopt these frames. This section delves more deeply into legal framing. After shortly setting out the relevance of this concept in the Roma rights field, the first part of this section studies the master frames and the second part focuses on innovative legal framing.

As part of the wider political or social movement frame, legal framing makes meaning of structural injustices and discrimination that often hides from plain sight.[63] It uses the 'law in an explicit self-conscious way to give meaning to an event',[64] such as the 'use of legal rules, discourses, or symbols' when having recourse to formal legal institutions or referencing 'legal tropes detached from any particular institutional structure'.[65] Framing processes in both politics and the law have been instrumental for the Roma rights movement as they have helped to 'make sense' of pervasive Romaphobia, structural discrimination, and socio-economic deprivation.[66] Vermeersch recalls in Chapter 2 of this volume that in politics, the plight of the Roma is framed in terms of human rights, and special attention is paid to the community's minority rights—primarily to cultural autonomy—as well as to its socio-economic deprivation. In law, the human rights framing is an 'imperfect fit' as discussed above, which may explain differences and similarities between political and legal master frames. The legal master frames include minority rights (mainly in the Traveller context), racial discrimination, and socio-economic deprivation, the latter of which is intrinsically connected to social rights.

For new social movements, such as the Roma rights movement a shared goal, and connected to that a collective identity, are key factors that drive collective action, the success of which is highly dependent on framing.[67] In movement politics, the 'strategic use of the framing process' can build support from the media, the public and authorities, while defining and redefining collective identity and

[63] Lehoucq and Taylor (n 2) 184.
[64] ibid 179–80.
[65] ibid 15
[66] David A Snow, E Burke Rochford Jr, Steven K Worden, and Robert D Benford, 'Frame Alignment Processes, Micromobilization, and Movement Participation' [1986] American Sociological Review 464–81.
[67] Mario Diani, 'The Concept of Social Movement' (1992) 40(1) Sociological Review.

constraining opponents.[68] Vanhala points out that it is not only the resources, political, and legal opportunities that can explain the rise of strategic litigation in Europe, but also the 'identity politics and framing' of social movements.[69]

A collective identity is crucial to political as well as legal framing but the Roma are a heterogeneous minority in terms of identity. Heterogeneity stems from the objective social deprivation of many but not all within the group, the common origin, and racialization of the whole group, as well as from the different ethnic markers such as language, cultural traditions, and religion among the Roma and Traveller subgroups.[70] This heterogeneity fragments rather than unites claim-making for status recognition and redistribution, both of which are necessary for dismantling structural discrimination.[71] Unsurprisingly, questions about Roma identity, claim-making and framing also form the arc of the formidable Roma intellectual, Nicolae Gheorghe's scholarship. He called attention to the belated ethnic identity formation of the Eastern Roma following the political transition, which had undeniably delayed both political and legal mobilization.[72] In the East, this 'ethnogenesis' stood in stark contrast to racialization by the majority. Gheorghe not only distinguished the Eastern sedentary Roma from the Western Travellers but also underlined that it is misguided to apply the Western frame predicated on the Traveller way of life to the Eastern Roma, whose ethnic identity traits are different and who predominantly suffer racial discrimination and social deprivation.[73]

## 3.1. The master frames

The dominant, overarching legal frames are master frames. Three master frames have emerged in the Roma rights context: minority rights, racial discrimination, and socio-economic deprivation. This subsection analyses the emergence of these master frames in a chronological order.

[68] Doug McAdam, 'The Framing Function of Movement Tactics: Strategic Dramaturgy in the American Civil Rights Movement' in Doug McAdam, John D McCarthy, and Mayer N Zald (eds), *Comparative Perspectives on Social Movements: Political Opportunities, Mobilizing Structures, and Cultural Framings* (CUP 1996) 338–56, 340.

[69] Lisa Vanhala, 'Anti-Discrimination Policy Actors and Their Use of Litigation Strategies: The Influence of Identity Politics' (2009) 16(5) Journal of European Public Policy 738.

[70] Antal Örkény and István Vári, 'Szempontok és kérdőjelek a magyarországi roma kisebbség tanulmányozásához' [2009] Fundamentum.

[71] Nancy Fraser and Axel Honneth, *Redistribution or Recognition?: A Political-Philosophical Exchange* (Verso 2003).

[72] Nicolae Gheorghe, 'Roma-Gypsy Ethnicity in Eastern Europe' [1991] Social Research 829–44.

[73] Nicolae Gheorghe and Andrzej Mirga, 'The Roma in the twenty-first century: A policy paper, Project on Ethnic Relations' (2001) <https://eriac.org/wp-content/uploads/2021/01/Mirga-Andrzej_Gheorghe-Nicolae_2001_The-Roma-in-the-Twenty_First-Century_A-Policy-Paper_Eurozine_12th-March.pdf> accessed 2 August 2024.

### 3.1.1. The minority rights master frame

Until 1994, when the Framework Convention on the Rights of National Minorities (FCNM) was adopted, the Traveller complaints based on the minority rights (cultural traditions) master frame met with Western ambivalence to the subject. The ECtHR seemed reluctant to address complaints about discrimination, yet the Travellers' grievances could only be framed under Article 14, which prohibited discrimination based on association with a national minority, among other grounds.

The growing number of ethnic majority 'new nomads' and the subsequent downgrading of the Traveller way of life as a 'lifestyle' instead of a cultural tradition explained the inadmissibility of the complaints before *Buckley*.[74] In this case, the Strasbourg Court obiter dicta recognized the Eastern Roma and Western Travellers as a unified group, holding that the vulnerable position of Gypsies as a minority meant that some special consideration should be given to their needs and their different lifestyle, both in the relevant regulatory planning framework and in deciding particular cases.[75]

It is quite probable that without Eastern accessions to the Council of Europe and the adoption of the FCNM the Travellers would have had to wait longer for recognition or may not have been recognized as an ethnic minority. It is also quite probable that the Strasbourg Court could not have framed violations in terms of minority rights in the case of the Eastern Roma, who have only exceptionally and never solely based their claims on cultural traditions. In *Buckley*, the Court elevated cultural traditions as the core element of the minority rights and also embedded it in the concept of vulnerability. Political consensus facilitated the 'expert construction' of the Roma minority but recognizing its special vulnerability was due to inventive framing by the ECtHR itself.[76] The minority rights framing later broadened to include linguistic traditions, particularly in *Orsus and Others v Croatia* where the applicants spoke the minority language and were segregated as a result.[77]

### 3.1.2. The racial discrimination master frame

Owing to fundamentally different lived experiences, the minority rights master frame adopted in the Traveller cases seemed inadequate in the East, where violent racism spread like wildfire after 1989. Here, the example of the civil rights movement inspired the adoption of the racial discrimination master frame even before the adoption of the RED, which transformed it into the dominant approach

[74] Luke Clements, PA Thomas, and R Thomas, 'The Rights of Minorities A Romany Perspective' (1996) 4(4) ODIHR Bulletin 3–10, 5.

[75] *Buckley* (n 1) paras 76, 80, and 84.

[76] Mihai Surdu and Martin Kovats, 'Roma Identity as an Expert-Political Construction' (2015) 3(5) Social Inclusion.

[77] *Oršuš and Others v Croatia* App no 15766/03 (ECtHR, 17 July 2008), [GC] (ECtHR, 16 March 2010).

in Europe. The racial framing's advance was bolstered by the anti-discrimination conditionality, which required the RED's transposition into national laws of Eastern countries with sizeable Roma populations prior to the EU accessions.[78] This new master frame was taken on by the ECtHR in the anti-Roma violence cases that dominate the case docket.

Subsequently, the Court meshed the two master frames in *DH*, which links racial and ethnic discrimination with reference to Article 1 of the International Covenant on the Elimination of All Forms of Racial Discrimination.[79] This framing dominates the Roma education cases and was also adopted by the CJEU in *CHEZ*, a case concerning access to electricity meters.[80] 'Meshing' enables European apex courts to recognize the Roma's positive ethnic self-identity, while addressing stigma, social stereotypes and assumptions that transform it into a racialized, negative identity.[81]

In the Roma rights context, the racial discrimination framing dominates applications before the Strasbourg Court, which with two exceptions has refused to consistently embrace this master frame. As Gergely's chapter shows, in the Roma education cases, the Court runs a proper analysis of racial (including ethnic) discrimination. As Sardelic shows in her chapter concerning dissents, in the anti-Roma violence cases the Court regularly establishes racial discrimination concerning the procedural limb of Articles 2 (the right to life) or 3 and sporadically finds racial discrimination concerning both the procedural and substantive limbs.[82] When trying to overcome this inconsistency and the Strasbourg Court's failure to establish discrimination in relation to other Convention rights, cause lawyers and NGOs are faced with a dilemma. In case they frame applications only in terms of racial discrimination in conjunction with a Convention right, they risk losing cases, should the Court find no racial discrimination. In case the racial discrimination framing is only secondary, they risk winning without a finding of the violation of a Convention right in conjunction with racial discrimination. This high cost explains why this strategy is not pursued.

Conversely, the ECSR consistently—with very few exceptions—finds discrimination further to a violation of the Roma and Travellers' social rights. The moral wrong prevalent in a racist act is so severe in Europe that it renders the framing of *just* social rights weaker and incomplete. The use of the racial discrimination

[78] Farkas (n 9).

[79] Holly J McCammon and Cathryn Beeson-Lynch, 'Fighting Words: Pro-Choice Cause Lawyering, Legal-Framing Innovations, and Hostile Political-Legal Contexts' (2021) 46(3) Law & Social Inquiry 599–634, 614.

[80] Case C-83/14 *CHEZ Razpredelenie Bulgaria AD v Komisia za zashtita ot diskriminatsia (Nikolova)* (CJEU, 16 July 2015).

[81] Sara Benedi Lahuerta, 'Ethnic Discrimination, Discrimination by Association and the Roma Community: CHEZ' (2016) 53 Common Market Law 797.

[82] Mathias Möschel, 'Is the European Court of Human Rights' Case Law on Anti-Roma Violence "Beyond Reasonable Doubt"?' (2012) 12(3) Human Rights Law Review 479–507.

and socio-economic deprivation frames by the ECSR can adequately capture the racialization of poverty. However, it is potentially pushing the boundaries of Roma rights too far, requiring the provision of housing as well as desegregation. Requiring desegregated housing is a far greater demand than the provision of potentially segregated and lower-quality housing.[83] Unfortunately, in practice, adding the racial discrimination frame to the socio-economic deprivation frame has hampered the national implementation of rulings and policies on housing.[84]

### 3.1.3. The socio-economic deprivation master frame

In *Yordanova*, the applicants threatened by forced eviction successfully utilized the socio-economic deprivation master frame, stating that: 'For people as *desperately poor and outcast* as them the expectation that the inactivity [of the authorities] would last was a basis to build lives on'.[85] The Court engaged with this master frame, stating that: 'such situations, where a whole community and a long period are concerned, [shall] be treated as being entirely different from routine cases of removal of an individual from unlawfully occupied property' and taking issue with the fact that 'persons unlawfully living on municipal land can be removed regardless of any special circumstances, such as decades-old community life, or possible consequences, such as homelessness'.[86] Dismayed by the government's argument that assisting the homeless Roma would amount to privilege and therefore unlawful discrimination, the Court reiterated that 'the applicants' situation as an *outcast* community and one of the *socially disadvantaged groups* must be recognized.[87] The recognition of socio-economic deprivation served as a basis for the Court to carve out a measure of positive 'obligation to secure shelter' for applicants in 'exceptional cases', including when they are 'particularly vulnerable'.[88]

In *Yordanova*, the Court gave credence to the socio-economic master frame as an exceptional case signifying particular vulnerability. This enabled the Court to make the proportionality test between the Roma's right to private and family life and the property rights of public or private proprietors stricter than in the Western Traveller cases concerning cultural traditions. In other words, a higher degree of protection and a lower margin of appreciation seems to be accorded in the case of socio-economic deprivation. This is characteristic of Eastern Roma, who were legally excluded from majority spaces prior to 1945 and practically from privatization after 1989, to then suffer from the CEE states' systemic failure to address homelessness. Notably, however, by subsuming socio-economic status under

[83] Csepeli and Örkény (n 8).
[84] Lilla Farkas and Theodoros Alexandridis, 'The Potential of Positive Obligations against Romaphobic Attitudes and in the Development of "Roma Pride"' (2020) 13 Erasmus Law Review 65.
[85] *Yordanova v Bulgaria* App no 25446/02 (ECtHR, 24 September 2012) para 85 (emphasis added).
[86] ibid paras 121 and 122.
[87] ibid para 129 (emphasis added).
[88] ibid para 130.

vulnerability, the Court throws into doubt whether it would separately examine claims of discrimination based on this or synonymous grounds listed in Article 14. The relevant grounds are social origin, property, and other status, which may include socio-economic status. Under the ESC, this master frame's use has been straightforward.

## 3.2. Innovative legal framing

This section discusses innovative legal framing, which is often employed by cause lawyers to improve litigation outcomes and better reflect the social realities of Roma applicants. Legal framing innovations occur, when 'activists introduc[e] a relatively new ideational frame into the discursive field in which they operate',[89] which 'interjects alternative meanings to articulate their sense of injustice'.[90] Legal framing innovations create discursive opportunities and 'new ways of using legal rationales',[91] which in our context has broadened the meaning of vulnerability and positive obligations and in turn narrowed the states' margin of appreciation.[92] Human rights treaties and EU fundamental rights law provide legal opportunities, set the normative and jurisprudential limitations of strategic litigation, while also granting autonomy to cause lawyers to present new arguments and rationales, in other words, to innovate legal framing.

Until relatively recently, more precisely before the transatlantic transplanting of the Black Lives Matter Movement, the 'European silence about race',[93] the deeply held 'delusion' in Judge Bonello's words that the Old Continent is free of racism, posed impediments for Roma rights litigation.[94] The concomitant aversion towards claims of direct racial discrimination, which are conceived as claims of intentional racism, have diminished the clout of the racial discrimination master frame concerning forced sterilization, anti-Gypsy violence and as mentioned above, until recently concerning anti-Gypsy hate speech. To overcome these impediments, cause lawyers have engaged in constant frame innovation.

There is another thorny issue when it comes to racial discrimination, namely its nexus with discrimination based on socio-economic deprivation. The Court is yet to decide whether the two are neatly separable concepts that, once occurring

[89] McCammon and Beeson-Lynch (n 79) 602.

[90] Mare Steinberg, 'The Talk and Back Talk of Collective Action: A Dialogic Analysis of Repertoires of Discourse among Nineteenth-Century English Cotton Spinners' (1999) 105(3) American Journal of Sociology 736–80, 751

[91] Ruud Koopmans and Paul Statham, 'Ethnic and Civic Conceptions of Nationhood and the Differential Success of the Extreme Right in Germany and Italy' in Marco Giugni, Doug McAdam, and Charles Tilly (eds), *How Social Movements Matter* (University of Minnesota Press 1999) 225–51.

[92] McCammon and Beeson-Lynch (n 79) 602.

[93] Alana Lentin, 'Europe and the Silence about Race' [2008] European Journal of Social theory 11.

[94] *Anguelova v Bulgaria* App no 38361/97 (ECtHR, 13 June 2002), Partly Dissenting Opinion of Judge Bonello, para 2.

simultaneously add up to intersectional discrimination, or as Körtvélyesi and Herczog argue, are historically interlinked in a complex manner. Which one is more dominant in causing less favourable treatment? As transpires from the Eastern forced eviction cases, and particularly from the *Yordanova* judgment cited above, the Court seems to assign a high level of significance to the Roma's socio-economic deprivation, labelling it 'particular vulnerability'. As described in the previous section, even though the applicants made the connection between socio-economic deprivation and racial discrimination and the ECtHR took note of this nexus, it did not analyse it.

The ECHR's scope is too narrow to address the full array of human rights violations against the Eastern Roma, which include socio-economic deprivation in housing, health care, employment, and services available to the public. Cause lawyers and NGOs have made attempts to secure the Roma's right to housing under Article 8 ECHR, but the Strasbourg Court has only dealt with a facet of this right under the procedural limb of Article 8 (due process), which provides limited protection from arbitrary forced evictions. The Convention protects the right to education and the Court has made the positive obligations doctrine more robust, which now in essence requires the provision of substantive equality in the Roma education cases, but only in these cases. As Gergely reminds us in Chapter 9, as a result of a gradual development of this aspect of the case law, today the Court and the Committee of Ministers require states to adopt a wide array of desegregation measures in education.

Various chapters in this book reflect on the actual or potential innovative legal framing of claims concerning forced sterilization, child removal, access to water, begging, and anti-Gypsy violence by paramilitary groups. The innovative frames include structural/long-standing discrimination (in the Roma education and some anti-Roma violence cases), intersectional discrimination concerning the prohibition of begging (*Lăcătuş v Switzerland*[95]), reproductive health (in forced sterilization cases), a combination of precarity and environmental justice concerning access to water (*Hudorović and Others v Slovenia*[96]), and anti-Gypsyism by paramilitary groups (since *Vona v Hungary*, in which the applicant challenged the dissolution of such an association).[97] Judges engage with these legal framing innovations. For instance, in *Lăcătuş*, Ravarani's dissent pointed to the usefulness of the personal autonomy framing concerning begging, which is arguably 'less weak and reductive' than the extreme poverty (precarity) one.

Innovative framings seek to broaden the material scope of Convention rights, increase the level of scrutiny, diminish the state's margin of appreciation, and by expanding positive obligations, increase the effectiveness of sanctions. The emphasis

[95] *Lăcătuş v Switzerland* App no 14065/15 (ECtHR, 19 January 2021).
[96] *Hudorovič v Slovenia* App no 24816/14 and 25140/14 (ECtHR, 10 March 2020).
[97] *Vona v Hungary* App no 35943/10 (ECtHR, 9 July 2013).

on the structural nature and the intersectionality of discrimination shines a light on the inadequacy of the formal equality doctrine and the relevance of treating unalikes unalike. Similarly, while tapping into social science research about the transformation of poverty in a globalized world and leftist social movement frames, the extreme poverty and precarity framings call for a heightened level of protection from economic deprivation and social exclusion.[98] Combined with the environmental justice framing, precarity situates Roma rights claims in more popular, middle-class struggles. Most of these innovative framings have the potential of broadening the meaning of vulnerability, but except for anti-Gypsyism, they have not yet been adopted by the ECtHR.

Framing innovation is a joint effort of actors in the transnational advocacy network on Roma rights that span from local leaders to the international human rights elite, as underlined in the introduction.[99] It often originates from academics or NGOs, travels to monitoring bodies through shadow reporting or consultation with NGOs, to then appear in dissents and finally in judgments. Much of the scholarship referenced or published in this book is concerned with framing innovation, which is presently dominated by anti-Gypsyism and intersectionality but focused previously on the structural nature and racial animus of discrimination against the Roma.[100] The meaning of anti-Gypsyism is not yet unified. Critical Romani Studies (CRS) scholarship[101] understands anti-Gypsyism as the persecution of the Roma to an exceptional degree,[102] which seems to justify a claim on the majority (including allies) 'to examine their own racialized identity', in other words their 'white privileges'.[103] Anti-Gypsyism is defined differently by monitoring bodies, whose work is referenced by the judges, therefore it remains to be seen whether the ECtHR will adopt the CRS-based understanding of anti-Gypsyism, considering that the Roma are only one of many persecuted minorities in Europe.[104]

98 Lorenzo Zamponi and Priska Daphi, 'Breaks and Continuities in and Between Cycles of Protest. Memories and Legacies of the Global Justice Movement in the Context of Anti-Austerity Mobilisations' in Atak, Kivanç, and others (eds), *Spreading Protest: Social Movements in Times of Crisis* (ECPR Press 2014) 193–225.

99 Keck and Sikkink (n 10).

100 The ERRC referred to ECRI General Policy Recommendation No 13, Combating Anti-Gypsyism and Discrimination Against Roma, adopted on 24 June 2011 <hungary-submission-ecthr-12-july-2012.pdf (errc.org)> accessed 20 August 2024.

101 'In Search of a New Deal for Roma: ERRC Interview with Nicolae Gheorghe', *Roma Rights Journal*, 7 November 2001 <In search of a new deal for Roma: ERRC interview with Nicolae Gheorghe - European Roma Rights Centre> accessed 20 August 2024.

102 Huub van Baar, 'The Emergence of a Reasonable Anti-Gypsyism in Europe' in Timofey Agarin (ed), *When Stereotype meets Prejudice: Antiziganism in European Societies* (Ibidem Verlag 2014). He argues that 'The Roma are the last minority in Europe that can be discriminated against without limit—shamelessly, and often without punishment.' Ibid 38.

103 See, eg, Violeta Vajda, 'Towards "Critical Whiteness" in Romani Studies', *Roma Rights Journal* 2/2015, <roma-rights-2-2015-nothing-about-us-without-us.pdf>, accessed 20 August 2024, 48. She writes: 'I contend that until such time that non-Romani people are willing and able to examine their own racialised identity, even those non-Roma who are committed to dismantling the discrimination experienced by Romani communities will be unable to play a powerful role in this process'.

104 ECRI (n 100).

Intersectional discrimination is another framing innovation, and a caveat must be added about its key axis, which in the European leftist academic and activist view is not necessarily race but rather, or equally as importantly, socio-economic status (deprivation).[105] Divergence between the US liberal reading of intersectionality, which focuses on the intersection of race plus gender,[106] and the European leftist concept, which focuses on the racial element within socio-economic deprivation,[107] or the cumulative effect of discrimination based on socio-economic status and other identities[108] is visible when comparing international and domestic developments. International human rights law and policy and the ERRC's approaches are based on race subsuming socio-economic status (deprivation), while domestic law, policy, and NGO practice is often based on socio-economic status (deprivation) and subsuming the racial axis of discrimination.[109]

As transpires from Part III of this volume, legal framings are more diverse than political ones, being pivotal in creating new discursive opportunities.[110] This chapter also reveals the complexity of what political scientists simply label 'the human rights framing' of the Roma issue. The minority rights master frame's usefulness is limited, chiefly to Western Travellers, while the socio-economic master frame has not fully taken root under the ECHR. The racial discrimination master frame has pushed the boundaries of human rights on various issues but the ECtHR has not fully embraced it. To challenge the 'European silence about race', legal framing innovation must address racism to remain legitimate within the movement. Frame transformation is almost inconceivable because anti-Roma racism is real; denying it is what racists do. This is why even though it could bring more tangible results, a shift from the racial discrimination master frame to just a social rights frame is highly unlikely, even if it could facilitate the success of, for instance, Roma housing policies.

## 4. The Debate About Strategic Litigation

As the previous two sections show, legal mobilization for Roma rights has been robust, which has attracted praise as well as criticism. This section first assesses the achievements of legal mobilization (4.1) and then evaluates its critique (4.2).

[105] Andria D Timmer, *Educating the Hungarian Roma: Nongovernmental Organizations and Minority Rights* (Lexington Books 2016) She links Nancy Fraser's and the dominant Eastern social science approaches.

[106] Kimberle Crenshaw, 'Demarginalizing the Intersection of Race and Sex' (1989) 1(8) University of Chicago Legal Forum.

[107] Etienne Balibar and Immanuel Maurice Wallerstein, *Race, Nation, Class: Ambiguous Identities* (Verso 1991)

[108] Mieke Verloo, 'Multiple Inequalities, Intersectionality and the European Union' (2006) 13(3) European Journal of Women's Studies 211.

[109] Timmer (n 105).

[110] McCammon and Beeson-Lynch (n 79) 600.

### 4.1. Boundary-pushing jurisprudence

Cause lawyers have invested tremendous analytical work in Roma rights litigation to develop European jurisprudence on racial discrimination, which has in and of itself pushed the boundaries by undermining the 'European silence about race'.[111] The ECtHR first found racial discrimination in *Nachova*, while in *DH* it found indirect racial (including ethnic) discrimination.[112] The Strasbourg Court followed the jurisprudence of the CJEU on both indirect discrimination and the burden of proof. Two more contributions to the global anti-racist efforts stand out, namely that rather than race *qua* colour, in Europe—and the Roma rights context—ethnicity, socio-economic deprivation, residence (and immigration background) are considered key factors in racial or ethnic discrimination.[113] Secondly, European states are bound by positive obligations to promote equality under both the ECHR and the ESC. Thirdly, chapters in this book identify further issues on which strategic litigation has specifically pushed (racial violence, education, forced evictions, and hate speech) or can push (forced sterilization, child removal, and housing) the boundaries of the human rights of the Roma.

There is, of course, room for improvement. As O'Nions remarks in Chapter 10, the Strasbourg Court's expectations of what constitutes Convention-compliant state policy and action on housing are incoherent. This is not the case on education, though, where ECtHR doctrine is now iron-clad, as Gergely argues in Chapter 9. The difference may be explained by the fact that the right to equal education is fully covered by the Convention while housing is not. Owing to the boundary-pushing nature of collective complaints, which essentially frees adjudication from the assessment of individual circumstances, the ECSR's discrimination doctrine extends to substantive equality and includes a roadmap for legal reform concerning social housing and within that, the housing of the Roma and Travellers. Regrettably, this has not been taken over by the ECtHR, and due to normative limitations is unlikely to be.

Even though strategic litigation can increase the boundary-pushing nature of international jurisprudence, domestic legal mobilization and advocacy both pre- and post-judgment is necessary to increase practical impact. A plethora of actors are invested just in the implementation of *DH*, but in the Eastern Roma context the failure to implement international rulings is endemic.[114] This has inspired NGOs to engage with the execution of judgments and the Committee of Ministers to bolster the role of NGOs. In the West, Traveller rights advocates transformed litigation

[111] Hepple (n 38).
[112] ibid 612–13.
[113] ibid.
[114] Hubert Smekal and Katarína Šipulová, 'DH v Czech Republic Six Years Later: On the Power of an International Human Rights Court to Push Through Systemic Change' (2014) 32:3 Netherlands Quarterly of Human Rights 298–99.

losses into mobilizational tools over the last forty years. As O'Donovan recounts in his chapter, in Ireland it took twenty-six years and a national advocacy campaign to actualize the Convention protection accorded in *Buckley* (1996).

### 4.2. Critical scholarship on Roma rights

As transpires from this ontological inquiry, next to the structural impediments and opportunities, the choices of several actors determine what is litigated in the Roma rights context. The choices that lawyers make may engender legal ethical dilemmas, especially if these choices seem to give preference to the Roma right cause over the interests of the individual client or over the choices of actors who claim higher legitimacy in decision-making. Trehan and Sigona highlight the moral and ethical liability of INGOs for embracing neoliberalism and prioritizing the enforcement of civil rights over social rights.[115] Others point out that if an INGO refuses to fight a cause, domestic NGOs may still champion it, but the discursive dominance of the former may stifle discussion of the latter.[116] Some doubt whether *DH* really pushed the boundaries of Roma rights in the direction where the Roma wanted to go.[117] Critical Romani Studies focuses on grassroots legal empowerment, while US-based Critical Race Theory (CRT) scholars focus on intensifying international human rights litigation.[118]

Criticism is primarily directed at top-down lawyer-led international human rights litigation epitomized by *DH*. Europeans even within the ERRC were cautious about the US model of strategic litigation that was 'mimicked' in this case, including its feasibility and relevance.[119] Goodwin noted the ERRC's devotion to 'the U.S. belief in litigation as the means to achieving a fairer society' and warned that '[l]itigation will not change hearts and minds, quickly if at all. And this should be a warning to those in the Romani civil rights movement that are pursuing *litigation as the dominant approach*.'[120] Coomber also stressed that strategic litigation on its own is not a panacea and that the *DH* litigation is exceptional, including

[115] Nando Sigona and Nidhi Trehan (eds), *Romani Politics in Contemporary Europe. Poverty, Ethnic Mobilization and the Neoliberal Order* (Palgrave Macmillan 2009).

[116] Farkas (n 9).

[117] William New, 'Litigating Exclusion, Inclusion and Separation: Dilemmas of Justice in Roma Education Reform' in Maja Miskovic (ed), *Roma Education In Europe: Practices, Policies and Politics* (Routledge 2013); William S New and Michael S Merry, 'Solving the "Gypsy Problem": D.H. and Others v. the Czech Republic' (2010) 54(3) Comparative Education Review.

[118] Antonia Eliason, 'With No Deliberate Speed: The Segregation of Roma Children in Europe' (2017) 27 Duke Journal of Comparative & International Law 191–241; Felix B Chang and Sunnie T Rucker-Chang, *Roma Rights and Civil Rights: A Transatlantic Comparison* (CUP 2020).

[119] See, eg, Dimitrina Petrova, 'Political and Legal Obstacles to the Development of Public Interest Law' (1996) 5 E Eur Const Rev 62.

[120] Morag Goodwin, 'White Knights On Chargers: Using The US Approach To Promote Roma Rights In Europe?' (2004) 5(12) German Law Journal 1432 (emphasis added).

its costs.[121] Until the mid-2010s *DH* defined the understanding of strategic litigation in the Soros world. Recent critical scholarship comes mainly from this transnational space, which may explain why it has not questioned the focus on international courts.[122] It reiterates Goodwin and Coomber's criticism and demands 'Roma participation', particularly at the grassroots level in the hope that this would fix problems both with legitimacy and efficacy.

### 4.3. Evaluating the critical scholarship

The claim that INGOs have not pushed the boundaries of social rights is debunked by several chapters in this book.[123] The ERRC prioritized desegregation litigation, which revolved around the only social right safeguarded by the ECHR. When it launched *DH,* racial violence and forced evictions dominated its case docket, but the former could only be challenged on a case-by-case basis, while the Strasbourg Court refused to find violations, let alone discrimination in the latter. Therefore, the structural nature and racial motivation of discrimination could in good conscience only be challenged in relation to education under the ECHR, especially because collective complaints had not yet been available under the ESC. Critical scholarship skates over legal mobilization for the housing and minority rights of Western Travellers, and its interlinkages with the Eastern Roma movement. These grassroots efforts led to the judicial recognition of minority status in *Buckley* and protection from forced eviction in subsequent cases that served as inspiration for the *Yordanova* line of cases. Importantly, INGOs raised collective complaints on housing under the ESC, as soon as and wherever they became available after 2004. Clearly, it was not the NGOs but the states that severely curtailed the enforcement of social rights.

Critical scholarship has failed to problematize that *DH* is an exception.[124] As this book shows, domestic NGOs play a pivotal role in Roma rights litigation, and their proximity to clients, communities, advocacy, and bottom-up legal processes

[121] Coomber (n 45).

[122] Bhabha, Mirga, and Matache (n 73); Alphia Abdikeeva, Tamar Ezer, and Alina Covaci, 'Assessing Legal Advocacy to Advance Roma Health in Macedonia, Romania, and Serbia' (2013) 20 European Journal of Health Law 471, 485; <https://brill.com/view/journals/ejhl/20/5/article-p471_3.xml/> accessed 19 August 2024; Tamar Ezer, Alphia Abdikeeva, and Martin McKee, 'Legal Advocacy as a Tool to Advance Roma Health' (2018) 13 Health Economics, Policy, and Law 92; Marek Szilvasi and Maja Saitovic-Jovanovic, 'Social Accountability and Legal Empowerment Initiatives: Improving the Health of Underserved Roma Communities in Eastern Europe' (2023) 25(1) Health and Human Rights Journal 67–80; Filip Sys, 'DH v Czech Republic: Roma Educational Equality and the Vulnerability of Strategic Litigation' (2020) 20(1) Acta Universitatis Carolinae Studia Territorialia 71 <https://www.researchgate.net/publication/347299705_DH_v_Czech_Republic_Roma_Educational_Equality_and_the_Vulnerability_of_Strategic_Litigation)> accessed 19 August 2024.

[123] Sigona and Trehan (n 115).

[124] Farkas (n 9); Dezideriu Gergely and Lilla Farkas, *Racial Discrimination in Education and EU Equality Law* (EU Publications Office 2020).

are antithetical to the ERRC's top-down approach. Critical scholarship is yet to explore litigation before and by equality bodies, such as the Bulgarian Commission for Protection Against Discrimination on access to electricity—which led to the CJEU's *Belov* and *CHEZ* judgments[125]—and the infringement action on account of segregated education in *European Commission v Slovakia*.[126]

There is a lack of analytical rigour in critical scholarship because INGOs are often conflated with non-Roma actors, domestic NGOs with Roma actors, while NGOs may also be treated as a unified category.[127] Distinction should be made between international and domestic, US and European, liberal and leftist, Roma, interracial, or non-Roma, legally focused and other NGOs, while INGOs should not be singled out for analysis. Critical Legal Studies may provide better analytical tools for scholars, turning the limelight on the hegemony of human rights law, the agency and liability of the human rights elite as well as states.[128] NGOs mobilize the law mainly because political tools alone cannot stop rights violations, and also because public bodies either violate or do not effectively protect Roma rights. As Majtényi highlights, states erected normative boundaries to Roma rights litigation, particularly on social and minority rights. In summary, this chapter calls for a focus on all the key actors of international human rights law, including the states, the Roma elite, the political movement and domestic NGOs.

## 5. Conclusions

This chapter has assessed legal mobilization for Roma rights by highlighting distinct legal strategies and framings, assessing jurisprudential developments and evaluating critical scholarship. After 1989, Eastern countries with sizeable Roma populations broadened and deepened their human rights commitments, laws, and institutions. Robust resources and transatlantic transplants have pushed the boundaries of Roma rights further than the rights of racialized minorities in Western Europe. The European Roma Rights Centre has been a key actor, emulating US framing and strategy, and dominated the discourse with a focus on *DH* epitomizing top-down international human rights litigation.

[125] Lilla Farkas, 'NGO and Equality Body Enforcement of EU Anti-discrimination Law: Bulgarian Roma and the Electricity Sector' in Elise Muir, Claire Kilpatrick, Jeffrey Miller, and Bruno De Witte (eds), *How EU Law Shapes Opportunities for Preliminary References on Fundamental Rights: Discrimination, Data Protection and Asylum* [2017] EUI Working Papers 17.

[126] Case C-799/23 *European Commission v Slovak Republic* (22 December 2023) <https://curia.europa.eu/juris/document/document.jsf?text=&docid=282910&pageIndex=0&doclang=EN&mode=req&dir=&occ=first&part=1&cid=72514> accessed 20 August 2024.

[127] See for instance Trehan and Kóczé (n 27).

[128] David Kennedy, *The Dark Sides of Virtue: Reassessing International Humanitarianism* (Princeton University Press 2004).

*DH* is an exception not necessarily because of its jurisprudential gains but because litigation is generally bottom-up, commencing and concluding in national courts or quasi-judicial bodies, often with reference to international human rights law and jurisprudence. Consequently, perhaps the most important avenue of pushing the boundaries of human rights is vertical judicial dialogue. Strategic litigation, in the sense of both domestic legal action invoking international human rights law and jurisprudence, and international human rights litigation, promote this judicial dialogue, indicating that domestic cause lawyers and NGOs using international human rights law are indispensable for impactful legal mobilization in Europe.

Legal mobilization is necessary to overcome political gridlock at the national level and it has been more effective than just ethno-political mobilization. The crippling limitations of domestic political processes meant that litigation and advocacy had to be Europeanized. And here lies a crucial characteristic of boundary-pushing human rights litigation: it is based on international human rights law from the start, even if the final forum is not an international judicial body. International human rights law has been vital for pushing the boundaries of Roma rights, which justifies the ERRC's approach, even if it does not justify every facet of its operations.

Legal mobilization has faced challenges due to the belated 'ethnogenesis', the lack of endogenous resources and legal consciousness, the 'imperfect fit' of international human rights law, and a high level of animosity against the Roma. A broad definition of Roma rights, innovative legal strategies and framings have contributed to its successes. Strategic litigation and the racial discrimination master frame enabled the Roma rights movement to catch up with more advanced social movements. The key components of strategic litigation have been the selection of causes, framings and international legal forum, with an overwhelming emphasis on the European Court of Human Rights, which has been directly accessible for the longest period of time.

The inherently responsive claim-making against racial violence, housing, hate speech, forced sterilization, and child removal limit the potential of strategic litigation. Even though structural discrimination is tangible in all fields, due to the unavailability of collective complaints under the European Convention, proactive legal strategies are hard to design outside the field of education. The limitations on social rights—in terms of their scope and access to collective complaints—are also normative and stem from states' resistance to international human rights law, which substantially pulls back the boundaries of Roma rights.

Innovative legal framings have overcome some normative limitations by broadening the scope of the Convention rights to private and family life and to equal treatment, and by expanding the positive obligations doctrine and the concept of vulnerability, while narrowing states' margin of appreciation. However, the ECtHR's doctrinal analysis of Convention rights is not as coherent as that of the ECSR, therefore it pulls back the boundaries of the right to housing and its practical implementation. More needs to be done to fully dismantle the 'European silence about race' and to address discrimination based on socio-economic conditions and issues in the private sphere.

This chapter complements existing scholarship on the ontology and ethics of Roma rights jurisprudence by highlighting the role of domestic NGOs in framing and litigating landmark cases in all the key fields of Roma rights and divergence between liberal and leftist cause lawyers on hate speech and forced evictions. Domestic litigation has been highly responsive to community and activist demands. Future scholarship needs to be analytically more rigorous and evenly focused on all the actors who mobilize the law for Roma rights or hamper the boundary-pushing potential of international human rights law.

# 14
# The Contribution of Equality Bodies to Countering Discrimination Against Roma in the EU

*Tamás Kádár and István Haller*

## 1. Equality Bodies Enforcing EU Equality Law

Despite numerous political commitments at European and national level, the scale of and the systemic nature of Roma discrimination, and the widely known precarious situation of Roma, persist.

Against this background, there is a surprisingly low number of cases both at the national level and before the Court of Justice of the EU.

Although in certain countries and in certain fields the number of Roma discrimination cases is significant, it remains questionable whether all the relevant types of Roma discrimination are properly addressed through litigation and case law. For instance, the casework of a particular equality body may demonstrate a heavy focus on examples of hate speech, with no or very few cases in healthcare, education, or social protection.[1]

The promise of equality bodies has been that as expert institutions, they can effectively support enforcement of the legislation and policies, promote equality in practice, and facilitate access to justice for those discriminated against, including those most deprived and subject to systemic and structural forms of discrimination. Strategic litigation and quasi-judicial decision-making are key powers in the toolbox of equality bodies to further this goal, but they also hold important potential to achieve societal change through their powers concerning research and data collection, communication and awareness-raising, and policy advice and promotion of good equality practices.

This chapter will first look at the legal framework determining the work of equality bodies and the recent changes with the adoption of EU directives on standards for equality bodies. This will be followed by a discussion of the potential of equality bodies as low-threshold complaints bodies, using also their 'soft

[1] Margarita S Ilieva, *Country Report Non-Discrimination, Bulgaria* (European Union 2022) 95.

Tamás Kádár and István Haller, *The Contribution of Equality Bodies to Countering Discrimination Against Roma in the EU* In: *The Rights of Roma in European Courts*. Edited by: Kristin Henrard and Lilla Farkas, Oxford University Press.  DOI: 10.1093/oso/9780198914358.003.0014

powers'. Thirdly, we look at practical examples of the work of equality bodies in fields of particular relevance for Roma discrimination, followed by a discussion of some key obstacles to this work. The fourth and last section provides a more in-depth analysis through a case study of the work of the Romanian equality body in the field.

### 1.1. The legal framework

The EU has a robust, albeit not comprehensive, legal framework protecting equal treatment.[2] However, adopting and transposing strong substantive legislation may not be sufficient to achieve the objectives of equality and non-discrimination. There is a need for strong institutions, including specialized public bodies that promote equality and enforce the legislation. It is this realization that led to the emergence of equality bodies and their eventual codification into EU law.

Originally, the idea of equality bodies was 'not a European phenomenon. Their introduction in the EU is fairly recent and can be seen as the result of a chain of legal transplants that started in the US and was brought into Europe via the UK'.[3] Importantly, the codification of equality bodies in EU law is also the result of a successful campaign in the 1990s by the so-called Starting Line Group of NGOs.[4]

Driven by EU legislation, equality bodies are now present in all EU member states, in all EFTA countries, as well as in the UK and in EU candidate countries.[5] Below, we will focus primarily on the Racial Equality Directive as the first, most comprehensive and, for Roma equality, most relevant source. Similar provisions can be found in the gender equality directives but not in the Employment Equality Directive (EED).[6] This is also a manifestation of the often discussed 'hierarchy of discrimination grounds' within the EU legislative framework.

By virtue of Article 13(1) of the RED, all EU member states shall designate an equality body covering the grounds of racial or ethnic origin. The directive does not establish detailed standards for these bodies, but it stipulates in Article 13(2) that their functions must include 'providing independent assistance to victims of discrimination in pursuing their complaints about discrimination', 'conducting

[2] See eg <https://equineteurope.org/equality-in-europe/eu-legislative-framework/> accessed 31 August 2024.

[3] Sara Benedi Lahuerta, 'Equality Bodies in the EU: Origins, Challenges and Future Prospects' (2022) 4(5) UCD Working Papers in Law, Criminology & Socio-Legal Studies; Tamás Kádár, 'Equality bodies: A European Phenomenon' (2018) 18(144) International Journal of Discrimination and the Law.

[4] Isabelle Chopin, 'The Starting Line Group: A Harmonised Approach to Fight Racism and to Promote Equal Treatment' (1999) 1 European Journal of Migration and Law 111.

[5] For a list of equality bodies, see Equinet's Directory of Equality Bodies, <https://equineteurope.org/european-directory-of-equality-bodies/> accessed 31 August 2024.

[6] Council Directive 2000/78/EC establishing a general framework for equal treatment in employment and occupation [2000] OJ L303.

independent surveys concerning discrimination', and 'publishing independent reports and making recommendations on any issue relating to such discrimination'. Given the topic of this book, our chapter will focus on the first compulsory function, providing independent assistance to victims of discrimination.

While this provision has been interpreted differently by different member states, it has resulted in many equality bodies being granted strong enforcement powers, from legal standing before the courts to own decision-making and sanctioning powers as quasi-judicial bodies. A useful typology for the possible roles in court cases of equality bodies differentiates: 1) representing victims of discrimination before the courts, 2) bringing proceedings in their own name, 3) intervening in support of a party, 4) filing an *amicus curiae* brief or similar, and 5) defending legally binding decisions before the courts (binding decisions by equality bodies on the merits of the complaints they receive and investigate are always subject to judicial review).[7] In the absence of clear provisions in the EU directives, some member states interpreted assistance to victims restrictively, granting their equality bodies neither legal standing, nor decision-making powers, arguably significantly curbing their potential to effectively assist victims of discrimination.[8] A relevant aspect of EU equality law, and in particular the RED, underpinning the legal powers of equality bodies is that associations, organizations, or other legal entities, which have a legitimate interest in combatting discrimination 'may engage, either on behalf or in support of the complainant, with his or her approval, in any judicial and/or administrative procedure provided for the enforcement of obligations under this Directive'.[9] Equality bodies are not explicitly named in this provision, but some of their powers listed above can be seen as anchored in this provision.

The fields of application of the RED, under which Roma are protected from discrimination, include a wide range of legal relations, ranging from employment to education, goods and services, and social protection,[10] even if serious gaps remain, notably actions by law enforcement, a prime field for structural and systemic discrimination against Roma.[11] Despite these gaps, the RED remains the most comprehensive piece of EU non-discrimination law, covering a large number of potentially discriminatory situations, including in the field of economic and social rights. The importance of this is underlined by the fact that economic and social rights are in themselves not necessarily easily justiciable, given the principle of

[7] Tamás Kádár, 'The legal Standing of Equality Bodies' [2019] European Equality Law Review 1.

[8] This is the case, for instance, in Germany's *Antidiskriminierungsstelle des Bundes* <https://www.antidiskriminierungsstelle.de/DE/startseite/startseite-node.html> accessed 31 August 2024.

[9] Council Directive 2000/43/EC implementing the principle of equal treatment between persons irrespective of racial or ethnic origin (RED) [2000] OJ L180, Art 7(2).

[10] ibid Art 3(1).

[11] 'Study to support the preparation of an EU initiative to address possible gaps in the legal protection against discrimination on grounds of racial or ethnic origin, Final Report' (European Commission 2022).

'progressive realization',[12] but discrimination in the enjoyment of social rights is prohibited in all cases.

The gender equality acquis has a more restricted field of application, yet one that is still more extensive than for the grounds of age, disability, religion or belief, and sexual orientation protection, as the Employment Equality Directive (EED) only applies to the field of employment and occupation.[13] Arguably, the fragmented and hierarchical nature of EU anti-discrimination law also renders it more difficult to introduce and apply the concept of intersectional discrimination, as demonstrated by the CJEU's *Parris* judgment.[14] This hierarchy of grounds was, until the adoption of the directives on standards for equality bodies in May 2024, also reflected in provisions relating to equality bodies, whereby the EED, in contrast with the RED and the Gender Equality Directives, did not require member states to designate an equality body. This resulted in a lower level of effective protection to persons suffering discrimination.

This seemingly theoretical hierarchy of discrimination grounds could have very real consequences when discrimination on certain grounds or in certain fields is not covered by EU legislation.

Nevertheless, we note that the majority of member states have extended their national legislation and the competences of their equality bodies to cover all six grounds in all fields.[15] This so-called gold-plating by member states, resulting in the majority of equality bodies possessing a comprehensive mandate, may contribute to an improved ability to address intersectional discrimination, such as that experienced by Roma women, for instance.[16]

### 1.2. Towards further standards for equality bodies

Observing the vulnerability of equality bodies to political attacks[17] and the differences in mandates and powers, including a lack of litigation and decision-making

[12] See eg International Covenant on Economic, Social and Cultural Rights (adopted 16 December 1966, entered into force 3 January 1976) 999 UNTS 171 (ICESCR), Art 2.

[13] Note that despite this hierarchy of protection, and perhaps contrary to expectations, case law before the Court of Justice of the EU on racial or ethnic origin is scarce, while case law on age or sex discrimination is notably richer.

[14] Case C-443/15 *David L Parris v Trinity College Dublin et al* (CJEU, 24 November 2016).

[15] Isabelle Chopin and Catharina Germaine, *A Comparative Analysis of Non-Discrimination Law in Europe 2023* (European Union 2023), in particular ch 1 and ch 2.2.2. Sara Benedi Lahuerta mentions that such equality bodies with competence on all grounds and in all EU law fields have a valuable capacity to take a comprehensive and non-hierarchical approach to equality and non-discrimination, particularly where they cover an open list of grounds. On the other hand, they may face challenges to secure sufficient visibility for and action relevant to each ground covered: Lahuerta (n 3).

[16] Niall Crowley, *Innovating at the Intersections. Equality Bodies Tackling Intersectional Discrimination* (Equinet 2016).

[17] See for instance political attacks against the Romanian equality body in 2018, calling for it to be closed down <https://www.equalitylaw.eu/downloads/4710-romania-attacks-against-the-romanian-equality-body-nccd-pdf-193-kb> accessed 31 August 2024.

powers resulting in a low number of established cases of discrimination, led to calls for further guidance for member states on equality bodies. As a result, two sets of recommendations were published in 2018, at both the Council of Europe and the EU level, followed by two EU directives adopted in 2024.

The European Commission Against Racism and Intolerance (ECRI) identifies and underscores the importance of three core functions for equality bodies, namely promotion and prevention, support, and litigation and decision-making.[18] These recommendations also address questions relating to the establishment of equality bodies, institutional architecture, powers to obtain evidence and information, independence and effectiveness (including resources), accessibility (to those whose rights they are established to protect), and monitoring of the recommendations by ECRI.

The European Commission's Recommendation on standards for equality bodies, adopted six months later and making reference to ECRI's standards, also provides guidance on the grounds, scope, and functions to be covered by the equality bodies' mandate (including strategic litigation to address structural and systematic discrimination[19]), independence (including equality bodies' place in the overall administrative structure and procedures for appointing and dismissing staff), and resources (including human, technical and financial resources, premises, and infrastructure), among others.

In its 2021 report on the RED and EED, the European Commission found 'a limited and unequal level of implementation of the Recommendation'.[20] As a result, it committed in several EU equality strategies, including the EU Roma strategic framework for equality, inclusion, and participation for 2020–30,[21] to strengthen the role and independence of equality bodies. To do so, in December 2022, the Commission proposed two Directives on standards for equality bodies, one based on Article 157 of the TFEU and one based on Article 19 of the TFEU.

[18] European Commission against Racism and Intolerance, General Policy Recommendation no 2: Equality Bodies to Combat Racism and Intolerance at National Level (Council of Europe 2018) para 10.

[19] Commission Recommendation (EU) 2018/951 of 22 June 2018 on standards for equality bodies [2018] OJ L167. See 1.1.2 (2): 'independent assistance to victims can include granting equality bodies the possibility to engage or assist in litigation, in order to address structural and systematic discrimination in cases selected by the bodies themselves because of their abundance, their seriousness or their need for legal clarification'.

[20] Report from the Commission to the European Parliament and the Council on the application of Council Directive 2000/43/EC implementing the principle of equal treatment between persons irrespective of racial or ethnic origin ('the Racial Equality Directive') and of Council Directive 2000/78/EC establishing a general framework for equal treatment in employment and occupation ('the Employment Equality Directive') COM(2021)139 (European Union 2021).

[21] EU Roma strategic framework for equality, inclusion, and participation for 2020–30, COM(2020) 620 final (European Union 2020), 12. See also, for instance: A Union of Equality: EU anti-racism action plan 2020–25, COM(2020) 565 final (European Union 2020), 6. The wording in these equality strategies committed to strengthen the role and independence of equality bodies.

These Directives, adopted on 7 May 2024,[22] introduce the obligation on EU member states to designate equality bodies that cover also the grounds of discrimination of the EED. This fills a gap in EU-level legal protection, even if equality bodies in most member states already cover these grounds. Importantly, the directives also provide a guarantee against backsliding in this field. They furthermore provide the first ever comprehensive, legally binding set of standards for equality bodies, covering for instance their mandate, independence, resources, decision-making, and litigation powers. These standards are designed to enable equality bodies to effectively fulfil all their functions and, ultimately, better assist individuals and groups at risk of discrimination, such as Roma. It is noteworthy that the directives also define intersectional discrimination, albeit in the provisions on awareness-raising, prevention, and promotion.[23] This, however, may also catalyse discussions and case law on intersectional discrimination. The requirement of introducing litigation powers for all equality bodies is particularly important from the perspective of our chapter.

## 2. The Potential of Equality Bodies

Equality bodies have the potential to contribute to equality and non-discrimination at multiple levels and using their multiple functions and powers, including litigation and decision-making. Beyond such litigation and enforcement powers, equality bodies also hold significant 'soft powers', including making policy and legislative recommendations, promoting good equality practices by duty bearers (including equality impact assessments, equality duties, and equality planning), research and survey work, or awareness-raising and communication work.[24]

The potential of equality bodies ranges from contributing to social change (a societal valuing of equality), organizational change (achieving institutional policies, plans, and cultures that further and prize equality), to individual change (assisting victims of discrimination).[25] They can do so typically on more than one ground, distinguishing them from grounds-based NGOs or government structures and making them particularly well suited to address multiple and intersectional

[22] Council Directive (EU) 2024/1499 on standards for equality bodies in the field of equal treatment between persons irrespective of their racial or ethnic origin, equal treatment in matters of employment and occupation between persons irrespective of their religion or belief, disability, age or sexual orientation, equal treatment between women and men in matters of social security and in the access to and supply of goods and services, and amending Directives 2000/43/EC and 2004/113/EC [2024] OJ L2024/1499 and Directive (EU) 2024/1500 of the European Parliament and of the Council on standards for equality bodies in the field of equal treatment and equal opportunities between women and men in matters of employment and occupation, and amending Directives 2006/54/EC and 2010/41/EU [2024] OJ L2024/1500.

[23] ibid art 5.

[24] Kádár (n 3).

[25] ibid.

discrimination. This could be especially valuable when faced with intersectional discrimination of Roma women and girls, Roma living in poverty, or Roma migrants, for instance, given that they often face discrimination that takes place on the basis of several personal grounds or characteristics/identities, which operate and interact with each other at the same time in such a way as to be inseparable.

Equality bodies provide a low threshold and accelerated complaints mechanism for victims of discrimination, with a low level of formalities and costs involved. Indeed, equality bodies provide their services free of charge in practice and this is an explicit requirement under Article 12(3) of the new EU directives on standards for equality bodies. The notion of independent assistance has been interpreted in different ways by member states, having clear implications for the emphasis in the work of the respective national equality bodies. Using the typology of the ECRI GPR No 2, 'independent assistance' can take the form of a focus on support and litigation or on decision-making in their own quasi-judicial procedures. ECRI considers the first as a necessary function for all equality bodies, while the second one is optional.[26] The new EU directives on standards for equality bodies require all member states to grant decision-making powers to their equality bodies, although leaving it to states' discretion whether this should mean legally non-binding opinions or binding decisions.[27]

In practice, some equality bodies, especially in Central and Eastern Europe, have a clear and quasi-exclusive focus on their quasi-judicial function, even if they have litigation powers. Importantly, in both cases, the directives foresee the possibility of including 'specific measures to remedy any breach of the principle of equal treatment found and to prevent further occurrences' and require appropriate mechanisms for follow-up.[28] This is particularly important given that today, even where the equality body can apply sanctions, these are rarely truly effective, proportionate, and dissuasive. This was identified as a difficulty by the European Commission, as well as scholarly literature.[29]

There are potential challenges and tensions where, as in some of the member states with the largest proportion of Roma, the equality body is accorded a decision-making function along with the promotion and prevention function and the support and litigation function. The decision-making function requires an impartiality that runs counter to the approach required under the other two functions. According to ECRI, combining these functions limits the nature and quality of the assistance provided to the victim of discrimination. For ECRI, the best practice evidently is to locate the decision-making function in another equality body.[30]

[26] ECRI (n 18) para 10.
[27] See Art 9 of Directive 2024/1499/EU and Directive 2024/1500/EU.
[28] ibid.
[29] See Vincenzo Tudisco and Emma Lantschner, *Preventing and Reacting to Discrimination through Sanctions and Remedies* (Equinet 2022) 14–15.
[30] ECRI (n 18) para 45.

If the equality body holds both functions, each should be implemented by a different unit or by different staff, and this should be clearly visible to the public.[31]

Equality bodies can contribute to the development of equality law through their case work (including litigation representing or supporting the victim or in the equality body's own name, *amicus curiae* briefs, and decision-making in their own procedures). They are also using their specialist expertise to engage in litigation at the European level, encouraging national courts to refer preliminary questions to the Court of Justice of the EU (CJEU)[32] and participating in cases in front of the European Court of Human Rights (ECtHR).[33]

Triggering and intervening in landmark cases before these regional courts sheds light on various important substantive and procedural questions, for instance the limits of legality of internal (neutrality) rules of a private undertaking prohibiting the visible wearing of any political, philosophical, or religious sign in the workplace[34]; the possibility to challenge public discriminatory statements in court even in the absence of a complainant[35]; that public statements may be sufficient to shift the burden of proof to the defendant[36]; that a non-Roma can complain about racial discrimination against Roma by way of association[37]; or that victims of discrimination have the right to have their case examined by a court even if the defendant agrees to pay the compensation claimed, without however recognizing that discrimination took place.[38]

Naturally, even if the equality body is involved in a case at the national level, the decision to refer the case to the CJEU rests with the national courts, limiting the former's control over the litigation process. A further limitation in Roma cases is that the equality bodies of member states with the largest Roma populations, due to the tensions between litigation and decision-making functions discussed above, tend to focus on their quasi-judicial decision-making function rather than litigation before courts. While some of them (Bulgaria, Hungary, Romania) have strong decision-making and sanctioning powers and do act as quasi-courts, when

[31] ibid para 46.

[32] See eg the Swedish equality body's role in Case C-236/98 *Jämställdhetsombudsmannen v Örebro läns Landsting* (CJEU, 30 March 2000); the Belgian equality body's role in Case C-54/07 *Centrum voor gelijkheid van kansen en voor racismebestrijding v Firma Feryn NV* (CJEU, 10 July 2008) and in Case C-157/15 *Samira Achbita and Centrum voor gelijkheid van kansen en voor racismebestrijding v G4S Secure Solutions NV* (CJEU, 14 March 2017); the Bulgarian equality body's role in Case C-83/14 *'CHEZ Razpredelenie Bulgaria' AD v Komisia za zashtita ot diskriminatsia* (CJEU, 16 July 2015); and the Romanian equality body's role in Case C-673/16 *Relu Adrian Coman, Robert Clabourn Hamilton, Asociația Accept v Inspectoratul General pentru Imigrări, Ministerul Afacerilor Interne, Consiliul Național pentru Combaterea Discriminării* (CJEU, 5 June 2018).

[33] See eg the British Equality and Human Rights Commission's intervention in *Eweida and Others v the United Kingdom* App nos 48420/10, 59842/10, 51671/10, and 36516/10 (ECHR, 15 January 2013).

[34] *Eweida* (n 33) and *Samira Achbita* (n 32).

[35] *Feryn* (n 32).

[36] ibid.

[37] *CHEZ* (n 32).

[38] Case C-30/19 *Diskrimineringsombudsmannen v Braathens Regional Aviation AB* (CJEU, 15 April 2021).

the Bulgarian equality body claimed the status of 'court or tribunal' under the EU Treaties and referred a Roma discrimination case to the CJEU, the case was found to be inadmissible, effectively closing this avenue for strategic litigation.[39] Nonetheless, the legal issue in this case (discriminatory placement of electricity meters at extreme heights in districts predominantly inhabited by Roma) is also illustrative of the complementary nature of strategic litigation by equality bodies and by NGOs, since subsequent domestic litigation supported by the NGOs led to the successful *CHEZ* case.

An undeniable challenge to the potential of equality bodies lies in the high levels of under-reporting to and low levels of awareness about equality bodies. Several FRA surveys show that equality bodies have a long way to go in ensuring sufficient awareness of their existence and of the range of services that they provide. The 2021 Roma survey of the FRA found that, on average, 50 per cent of Roma respondents had heard of at least one equality body, national human rights institution, or ombudsperson's office in their country.[40] Awareness of equality bodies and their functions has increased significantly since 2016 and is above the average for people of African descent,[41] but well below the average for LGBTI persons.[42] On the other hand, this increased awareness does not seem to lead to higher levels of reporting to equality bodies (or any public authority), as only 5 per cent of all Roma victims of discrimination reported or made a complaint about the last incident of discrimination.[43] This reporting rate should be seen as a major concern and further analysed, as it remains well below the already low rates for people of African descent and LGBTI persons (9 and 11 per cent, respectively).

## 3. Equality Bodies Working on Roma Discrimination

The following sections put forward some concrete examples of important issues affecting Roma taken up by equality bodies (without being able to provide a comprehensive picture), followed by some general observations concerning this work, with a specific focus on the obstacles that can be identified. The chapter will be followed by a closer look at the practice of one of the leading equality bodies in the field, Romania's National Council for Combating Discrimination, to provide a more detailed (albeit still not comprehensive) case study.

[39] Case C-394/11 *Valeri Hariev Belov v CHEZ Elektro Balgaria AD and Others* (CJEU, 31 January 2013).

[40] European Union Agency for Fundamental Rights, *Roma Survey—Main results* (FRA 2021) 31.

[41] European Union Agency for Fundamental Rights, *Being Black in the EU—Experiences of People of African Descent* (FRA 2023) 50.

[42] European Union Agency for Fundamental Rights, *A Long Way to Go for LGBTI Equality* (FRA 2020) 35.

[43] FRA (n 40) 30.

## 3.1. Equality bodies working on issues of key importance for Roma

This section provides examples and a brief analysis of the work of equality bodies on Roma discrimination in the fields of education, the provision of personal documents, goods and services, and housing.

### 3.1.1. Education

The field of education, and in particular the segregation of Roma pupils, seems to take centre-stage, when it comes to the depth of case law and action against Roma discrimination. It is a field where we can observe the use of a breadth of powers of equality bodies, ranging from quasi-judicial decision-making, interventions in court cases, assisting victims in litigation, monitoring, and cooperation with other public bodies.

For instance, in Hungary, the Equal Treatment Authority (ETA) intervened in only one case during its entire history. The intervention concerned segregation, where the municipal council of Jászladány had rented out one half of the local school building to a private foundation (where families had to pay a tuition fee, which prevented most of the local Roma children from attending the school), thus contributing to the segregation of local Roma and non-Roma children. The ETA intervened on the side of the Office of Public Administration against the municipal council, but the claim was rejected and thus the ETA's intervention was ultimately unsuccessful. However, underlining the importance of synergies between strategic litigation by equality bodies and by NGOs, the same practice was found by the Supreme Court to constitute segregation in a lawsuit brought by the NGO Chance for Children Foundation.[44]

In the Czech Republic and Slovakia, equality bodies have been active both in launching ex officio investigations and responding to individual and collective complaints, while cooperation between the equality bodies and school inspectorates seems to have bolstered the fight against school segregation.[45] The Slovak National Centre for Human Rights, similarly to the practice developed by the Czech Public Defender, has a strategic cooperation with the State School Inspectorate and the Government Plenipotentiary for Roma in order to provide assistance in the preparation of action plans to address segregation and to ensure its monitoring.[46] The School Inspectorate informs the Centre when it identifies any segregation practices of Roma pupils in classrooms/schools/school facilities.

[44] András Kádár, Country Report Non-Discrimination, Hungary (European Union 2022) 112.

[45] Lilla Farkas and Dezideriu Gergely, *Racial Discrimination in Education and EU Equality Law* (European Union 2020) 10.

[46] Slovak National Centre for Human Rights: *Report on the Observance of Human Rights Including the Principle of Equal Treatment in the Slovak Republic for the Year 2022 (Slovak National Centre for Human Rights 2023).*

These findings are mostly based on the over-representation of Roma pupils in classrooms/schools/school facilities.

This practice indicates a lack of capacity on the side of the equality body to effectively and comprehensively monitor and investigate alleged or suspected discrimination. However, it may also be seen as a resourceful solution for this issue, by relying on the field presence of a sectoral regulator public body. Of the seven cases reported in 2022, four were launched following a warning from the School Inspectorate. Several recent cases, some of which the equality body was involved in, contributed to the appropriate interpretation of the reversal of the burden of proof, to the use of data and statistics on over-representation of Roma pupils, and to no longer automatically accepting parental consent as sufficient justification for segregation. This seems to confirm the finding of Farkas and Gergely that field-specific agencies such as school inspectorates, in constructive cooperation with equality bodies, can effectively act as agents of EU (equality) law.[47]

Overall, Farkas and Gergely found significant differences in enforcement of equality law in education across the member states. In Ireland, Sweden, and France—and previously in the Netherlands—the equality bodies have investigated complaints and/or assisted victims of racial discrimination in education. Elsewhere in the West and more particularly in Southern Europe, individual litigation and collective legal action (for instance in Greece) has been the major avenue of enforcement,[48] often without any significant contribution by equality bodies to such enforcement. They found that, albeit often dealing only with a low number of cases, quasi-judicial agencies in Eastern Europe played a significant role with, for example, the Romanian equality body developing robust standards for protection against ethnic segregation or the Bulgarian equality body instructing the Minister of Education to take measures to cease the admission of non-disabled Roma children in special schools.[49] The last example also underlines the importance of enabling effective, proportionate, and dissuasive sanctions, including a way to require proactive steps and prevent future discrimination. Such proactive and preventive steps could include for instance the development of an equality plan, the provision of training to employees, or the use of equality impact assessments.

Another important, more recent example is the *X and Others v Albania* case, where the ECtHR found segregation due to the over-representation of Roma and Egyptian pupils in the Naim Frashëri elementary school in Korça. It is noteworthy that the domestic case concluded with the decision of the equality body (Commissioner for the Protection from Discrimination), as that wasn't challenged before the courts and thus the ECtHR accepted that domestic remedies had been exhausted.[50] Importantly, this case also represents another example of equality

47 Farkas and Gergely (n 45) 10.
48 ibid 10.
49 ibid 64.
50 *X and Others v Albania* App nos 73548/17 and 45521/19 (ECtHR, 31 May 2022) para 62.

body–NGO cooperation, given that the domestic complaint before the equality body was launched by the European Roma Rights Centre.

### 3.1.2. Personal documents

In a number of European countries Roma continue to face difficulties having adequate identity documents issued by the state. This, in turn, leads to various challenges in accessing basic goods and services (such as a bank account) and significantly increases the chances of experiencing discrimination.

In this respect a good practice example can be identified in the work of the French equality body (Defender of Rights), whose two opinions on draft legislation contributed to the repeal and replacement of an Act from 1969, which laid down provisions relating to travel documents (special travel documents and travel books) and the commune of residence, which constituted a considerable obstacle to free movement and led to discrimination against Travellers.[51] Historically, all French citizens who pursue a travelling way of life (including Roma and non-Roma) have had a specific legal and administrative status. Roma Travellers constitute 80 per cent of this administrative category. The predecessor of the Defender of Rights, the HALDE, had recommended in 2007 a reform of the status of Travelling people in order to eliminate all specific identity papers and all measures resulting in increased police checks. The Defender of Rights reiterated the need for a legislative reform in a decision in 2014.

The Law of 27 January 2017 in article 195 repealed the Act of 3 January 1969, thereby putting an end to the derogatory status of Travellers which limited their right to choose a town of elective residence, required them to carry special interior passports and to report regularly to local authorities.[52] It is noteworthy that instead of the litigation or decision-making powers observed in many other fields, here, the French equality body primarily used its powers to make recommendations to the legislator, and did so to good effect.

### 3.1.3. Goods and services

There are several well-known and well-documented examples, including cases taken by equality bodies, of Roma being refused certain services, ranging from overt prohibition to enter premises or rejection of being served, to more covert examples of refusing entry with reference to a 'closed/private event' or the need for a 'membership card'.[53] The focus in this field appears to be on quasi-judicial decision-making by equality bodies.

[51] Niall Crowley, *Roma and Traveller Inclusion: Towards a New EU Framework Learning from the Work of Equality Bodies* (Equinet 2020) 18.

[52] Sophie Latraverse, *Country Report Non-Discrimination, France* (European Union 2018) 131.

[53] Isabelle Rorive, *Proving Discrimination Cases. The Role of Situation Testing* (Centre for Equal Rights and Migration Policy Group 2009).

Bulgaria provided a leading example of strategic litigation in a line of cases concerning the placement of electricity meters at extreme heights in Roma districts.[54] The Bulgarian Supreme Administrative Court (SAC) did not find this practice unlawful, in the absence of ethnic homogeneity in the Roma districts and an explicit racial motive, and arguing that a lack of access to electricity meters did not adversely affect a right or legitimate interest.[55] In the controversial *Belov* case, an inhabitant of a Roma district complained to the Commission for Protection against Discrimination (CPD), the Bulgarian equality body that referred a set of questions to the CJEU, partly in order to counterbalance this restrictive interpretation of the Bulgarian SAC. In 2013, the *Belov* reference was dismissed by the CJEU, refusing to accept the judicial character of the CPD, despite support for such interpretation by the European Commission, Bulgaria, and Advocate General Kokott. This finding of inadmissibility may also have resulted in a chilling effect on future CJEU references by quasi-judicial equality bodies.[56] The subsequent *CHEZ* case,[57] where on identical facts the CJEU found elements of both direct and indirect discrimination, followed an administrative decision by the CPD.

These two cases were part of a test case strategy and large-scale litigation campaign, including by the NGOs Romani Baht Foundation and the Bulgarian Helsinki Committee.[58]

### 3.1.4. Housing

Equality bodies are also active in the field of housing, and the examples below illustrate the use of quasi-judicial powers that we have seen above, but also others, such as submitting *amicus curiae* briefs and conducting ex officio investigations resulting in reports by the equality body. For instance, in 2020, the Cypriot equality body prepared an ex officio report regarding the living conditions of the Roma community. In this report, the equality body noted that the housing of Roma in unsuitable premises/houses, in conjunction with difficulties in accessing adequate health services, exacerbated social marginalization and widened the gap between Roma and the rest of the society.[59]

[54] Lilla Farkas, 'NGO and Equality Body Enforcement of EU Anti-Discrimination Law: Bulgarian Roma and the Electricity Sector', in E Muir and others (eds), *How EU Law Shapes Opportunities for Preliminary References on Fundamental Rights: Discrimination, Data Protection and Asylum*, EUI Working Paper Law 2017/17.

[55] ibid.

[56] Tamás Kádár, 'The Standing of National Equality Bodies before the European Union Court of Justice: the Implications of the Belov Judgment' (2013) 11 Equal Rights Review.

[57] *CHEZ* (n 32).

[58] Farkas (n 54).

[59] <https://equineteurope.org/cyprus-ex-officio-report-regarding-the-living-conditions-of-the-roma-community/> accessed 31 August 2024.

The French Defender of Rights acted as *amicus curiae* in a case on eviction before the European Court of Human Rights, *Hirtu and Others v France*. In its judgment, the Court ruled against France, finding that owing to the short time between the issuing of the prefect's order and its implementation, no account had been taken of the repercussions of the eviction or the applicants' particular circumstances; the remedy provided for by domestic law had come into play after the decision had been taken by the administrative authorities and had been ineffective; and there was a failure to take account of the particular needs of the applicants as belonging to an under-privileged group, which breached their right to respect for their private and family life.[60]

In Hungary, in an *actio popularis* claim by the Hungarian Civil Liberties Union, the Equal Treatment Authority found that a mayor committed harassment when calling on local residents not to sell real estate to Roma people.[61] In another landmark case, the Hungarian Equal Treatment Authority established in its quasi-judicial procedure that the municipality of Miskolc subjected the residents of a segregated, mostly Roma neighbourhood ('Numbered streets') to the threat of homelessness or having to move to other segregated areas through a series of highly controversial measures and that this represented multiple discrimination on the basis of their social status, financial situation, and Roma origin.[62] Notably, in addition to an administrative fine, the Authority obliged the municipality to develop an action plan detailing where it could provide the tenants with adequate housing and the resources it would use. The Authority also obliged the municipality to prepare another action plan detailing how it would provide housing to those who had already become homeless or faced a direct threat of becoming so due to the municipality's discriminatory practices. Importantly, when the decision of the Authority was challenged before the national courts, it was upheld in every aspect, including the obligation to prepare action plans. The court pointed out that the statutory possibility of obliging the discriminator to terminate the injurious situation would be devoid of meaning when the violation is an omission if the Authority could not oblige the violator to take specific action.[63] This strategic case and decision represents a major step forward, as it pushed the boundaries of a traditionally reactive anti-discrimination law by opening up new avenues to apply proactive, preventative sanctions.

[60] Niall Crowley (n 51) 12. See also *Hirtu and Others v France* App no 24720/13 (ECtHR, 14 May 2020).

[61] <https://www.equalitylaw.eu/downloads/4005-hungary-mayor-found-to-have-committed-harassment-when-calling-on-local-residents-not-to-sell-real-estates-to-roma-people-pdf-136-kb> accessed 31 August 2024.

[62] Kádár (n 44) 113.

[63] ibid 98 and 113–14.

### 3.2. Key obstacles to effecting change

This section attempts to shine a light on some of the key obstacles limiting the effectiveness of equality bodies' work on Roma discrimination. Going beyond the issues mentioned above about lack of awareness and under-reporting and ineffective sanctions, these include a lack of prioritization, a lack of visibility and statistical data, a relatively low number of cases, the under-use of litigation and ex officio investigation powers by equality bodies, as well as political and institutional challenges.

#### 3.2.1. A lack of prioritization

In contrast with the strong policy focus at EU level, there are some questions concerning the lack of prioritization by equality bodies of Roma discrimination issues. While equality bodies are handling important cases of Roma discrimination, the overall number and scale of these actions does not seem to reach a critical mass. Furthermore, in some countries they seem to be concentrated in only a few relevant fields, despite Roma discrimination being pervasive in practically all areas of life. Equal treatment legislation seems to have succeeded to some extent in rooting out, or at least calling serious political and societal attention to, the most explicit and overt cases of discrimination and inequality faced by Roma. Unfortunately, some of these actions and practices have apparently only been transformed into more covert and less obvious, legally challengeable forms, for instance with employers having learnt that job ads explicitly excluding Roma are indefensible.

Against this backdrop, a report by the European network of legal experts in gender equality and non-discrimination in 2017 found that Roma and their specific issues are not explicitly treated by equality bodies as a priority issue in eighteen member states and that this causes concerns regarding the enforcement of their anti-discrimination rights.[64] This is despite the fact that in some of the countries in question discrimination of Roma takes up a significant part of their work. In comparison, Equinet's 2020 perspective found that thirteen equality bodies gave their work with Roma and Travellers high priority, while only three of them gave it medium priority and two of them low priority.[65] However, prioritization by the equality body does not necessarily translate into casework. In the Czech Republic, the equality body identified access of the Roma to education as one of three areas of potential concern,[66] but in 2022 race or ethnic origin represented a relatively low proportion of all complaints, less than disability, age, nationality, gender, and EU

[64] Isabelle Chopin, Catharina Germaine, and Judit Tanczos, *Roma and the Enforcement of Anti-Discrimination Law* (European Union 2017) 8.
[65] Crowley (n 51) 10.
[66] Jakub Tomšej, *Country Report Non-Discrimination, Czechia* (European Union 2023) 71.

citizenship and only superseding complaints on religion or belief and on sexual orientation[67].

The picture appears to be similarly bleak when it comes to addressing structural forms of discrimination against Roma. Crowley found an uneven engagement by equality bodies across the member states with the issue of structural discrimination on the ground of racial or ethnic discrimination, with some equality bodies noted as having little or no engagement with such issues. This could reflect barriers, such as limited resources, and inadequate mandate and powers, but also a reluctance within the leadership of the equality body to taking up what can be a controversial issue.[68] Indeed, in principle equality bodies with their broad mandate to promote equality and combat discrimination, are well placed to play a role in driving policy action to dismantle structural discrimination on the ground of racial or ethnic origin, using their different powers, from research and policy advice to promotion of good equality practices, litigation, and quasi-judicial decision-making. In any case, the absence of sufficient prioritization can be interpreted as lacking ambition and it leads to the perpetuation of an individual model of redress against discrimination, rarely capable of effecting structural change.

### 3.2.2. Lack of visibility and statistical data

It may prove surprisingly difficult to find reliable and comprehensive statistical information on Roma and discrimination against them due to a general lack of visibility of Roma and Roma-related cases in equality body, as well as overall national, statistics. For instance, Equinet found that in a number of instances, equality bodies do not gather data on the specific ethnic identity of complainants, and thus do not have detailed data on Roma complainants.[69] This is also a crucial issue given the importance of statistical data in strategic litigation cases. Furthermore, ensuring such visibility would be arguably all the more important in response to the context of under-reporting to and low awareness about equality bodies, mentioned in previous chapters.

### 3.2.3. Relatively low number of cases

While the number of racial discrimination cases before the CJEU is in itself relatively low, we can observe a severe shortage of references to the CJEU in cases of discrimination against Roma. In fact the only two such cases both originate from Bulgaria, relate to the same issue and in both cases the equality body was involved in the case.[70] This stands in contrast both with the widespread discrimination

[67] ibid 74.
[68] Niall Crowley, *To Name and Address the Underlying Problem: Structural Discrimination on the Ground of Rracial or Ethnic Origin* (European Union 2022) 79.
[69] Crowley (n 51) 15 and 19.
[70] *CHEZ* (n 39).

experienced by Roma, and the relatively more developed national and European Court of Human Rights case law.[71]

### 3.2.4. Under-use of litigation powers by equality bodies

Many equality bodies have a relatively strong legal standing, but the use of their powers in front of the courts seems to remain limited in the majority of cases. Litigation powers of equality bodies present a complex picture, from representing victims before the courts, bringing proceedings in their own name, to intervening in support of a party and filing an *amicus curiae* brief or similar. Furthermore, some quasi-judicial equality bodies are vested with the power of adopting legally binding and enforceable decisions, which may only be challenged before the courts[72]. Where the quasi-judicial equality body can start proceedings ex officio, such as in Hungary or Romania, the use of this power can also be understood as similar or in some ways even equivalent to strategic litigation.

However, despite the breadth of these powers and the well-documented discrimination against Roma, the use of these powers by equality bodies in general and in Roma cases in particular remains overall limited.

While the French Defender of Rights and the Czech Public Defender of Rights (Ombudsperson) only has the power to intervene (and in the Czech Republic even this is restricted to proceedings before the Constitutional Courts), others, such as the Slovak National Centre for Human Rights have the power to bring complaints to the court themselves, alongside the power to intervene. Yet, in 2021, the Centre was involved in only four court proceedings, with none of them being *actio popularis* cases[73]. On the other hand, over the years, the French Defender of Rights has presented observations in discrimination cases in an average of 100 cases per year and has substantially contributed to the development of jurisprudence in France[74].

### 3.2.5. Under-use of ex officio powers

Many equality bodies, such as the Czech, French, and Slovak ones mentioned here, also have the power to investigate cases in a quasi-judicial function and close them with a decision, but the number of Roma discrimination cases so investigated also remains low and, in any case, these equality bodies' decisions are not legally binding.

As discussed above, some of the equality bodies with a strong decision-making function, such as in Bulgaria, Hungary, or Romania, also have a comprehensive legal standing to bring cases to the courts and to intervene. Nevertheless, they don't

[71] See eg the European Court of Human Rights' Factsheet on Roma and Travellers: <https://www.echr.coe.int/documents/d/echr/fs_roma_eng> accessed 31 August 2024.

[72] Tamás Kádár (n 7).

[73] Vanda Durbáková, *Country Report Non-Discrimination, Slovakia* (European Union 2022) 100.

[74] Sophie Latraverse, *Country Report Non-Discrimination, France* (European Union 2023) 109.

use the latter powers, or just very sparingly in general and in Roma discrimination cases in particular, largely due to considerations about the necessary neutrality for the quasi-judicial function.[75]

Evidence also shows a strong reliance by equality bodies on individual complaints (brought by the victims of discrimination themselves or an NGO representing them) and on collective complaints by NGOs, as equality bodies take relatively few ex officio cases, with the notable exception of the equality body in Romania, further discussed below. While this remains a general trend and a major problem of the enforcement model of European anti-discrimination law, arguably, this is particularly problematic in addressing Roma discrimination, where the majority of the main issues relate to structural and institutional discrimination and thus strategic litigation, including by equality bodies would be highly necessary.

### 3.2.6. Political and institutional challenges

Alongside individual discrimination, equality bodies also report high levels of institutional discrimination, reflecting that public institutions not only fail to protect Roma from discrimination, but they are also sometimes the cause of the problem[76]. A good example of this may be brought from Hungary, whose Prime Minister has been heavily involved in stirring up anti-Roma sentiment.[77] This provides a particularly challenging environment for equality bodies to work for Roma equality and, without strong EU standards for independence, may well lead to self-censorship, failing to take up Roma cases as being too politically sensitive.

Institutional changes and challenges, or political interventions, may also limit the equality body's ability to engage in strategic litigation in general and in Roma cases in particular. Examples of these may include political attacks on the equality body and its leadership or the merger of the equality body with another institution, decreasing the resources for and attention to equality and non-discrimination[78].

## 4. Case Study on the Work of the Romanian Equality Body, Including the Use of Ex Officio Investigation Powers

The following case study represents an interesting example of how an equality body, even if mostly focused on decision-making, can contribute significantly to developing the jurisprudence on non-discrimination law and defending the rights

[75] Expert opinions by the Romanian equality body represent an important and positive exception here.

[76] Niall Crowley and Tamás Kádár, 'Equality for Roma and Travellers: Time to Deliver' (Equineteurope.org, 28 July 2020) <https://equineteurope.org/equality-for-roma-and-travellers-time-to-deliver/> accessed 31 May 2024.

[77] András Kádár (n 44) 104.

[78] ibid.

of Roma people. This section, based on the Romanian equality body's case law, analyses the possibility to fight against Roma discrimination not only by solving individual complaints, but also through the strategic litigation of NGOs and the ex officio actions of the equality body. Despite the possibilities provided by the law, the results are not encouraging.

The Romanian equality body, the National Council for Combating Discrimination (NCCD), is a quasi-judicial, multi-mandate, and multi-ground body (covering an open list of grounds). Persons considering themselves to be victims of discrimination can petition the NCCD or directly the civil court. The NCCD also accepts petitions formulated by NGOs and various institutions, such as the National Agency for Roma.[79] After hearing the parties and investigating[80] the facts, the NCCD resolves the petition by a vote of the Steering Board. If it finds discrimination, it can apply a fine (up to approximately €20,000), it can oblige the perpetrator to publish a summary of the decision in the press, and respectively it can make recommendations.[81] Reporting to the NCCD has a number of advantages: the resolution is faster,[82] it does not involve costs similar to court fees, and, if there is not enough evidence, the NCCD can carry out independent investigations. There is also a disadvantage: very often the NCCD applies only a warning, which does not provide real moral satisfaction for the victims. Those who go directly to the court mainly seek to obtain damages; for them, proceedings before the NCCD do not provide a comprehensive solution.

Victims seeking to obtain damages must go to court, and they can do so using the NCCD's decision in their favour, but without any assistance from the NCCD. If the person directly addresses the court, according to the law, the court has the obligation to summon the NCCD. While in practice, the representative of the NCCD typically does not appear at the trial, but only send an expert point of view to the court, this mandatory expert position provides an opportunity for the NCCD to follow all discrimination cases in the country and to influence the jurisprudence through the expert opinions.

For our topic it is of particular relevance that members of the Steering Board of the NCCD can initiate ex officio actions, which are analysed like petitions. Even if the Council cannot litigate on behalf of individual victims, through ex officio

[79] The Constitutional Court of Romania stated that: 'non-governmental organizations do not participate in the process as representatives of the parties, but by virtue of their own active procedural quality that the law attributes to them' (Decision no 285/2004) <https://legislatie.just.ro/public/DetaliiDocument/54196> accessed 31 August 2024.

[80] If the petitioner does not know the identity of the person who committed the discrimination or indicates evidence that they cannot obtain, an investigation can be triggered, during which a team of two lawyers from the NCCD conducts research and prepares an investigative report.

[81] The decisions of the NCCD can be challenged in administrative court. Sometimes the petition is sent back to the Council to modify the decision; rarely, the court annuls the Council's decision and resolves the petition.

[82] The law provides a term of three months for the resolution of petitions, but in practice it can take more than two years. Nonetheless, this remains shorter than court proceedings.

actions it can promote equality in key areas, such as school segregation.[83] But there is also a disadvantage: if the NCCD does not find discrimination, the decision cannot be subject to the control of the courts (there being no interested person to challenge the decision in court).

In employment, the first cases were analysed following an ex officio action against seven newspapers that published discriminatory advertisements, and the perpetrators were warned.[84] The purpose of this action was to make the media aware of the discriminatory nature of this practice. The first fines were applied for two companies for the following advertisements: 'I am hiring experienced car mechanics, age 30–40 (excluding Roma)' and 'dressmakers, tailors, excluding Roma'. The fine for the employer was approximately €500, the fine for the company that published the advertisement was approximately €100 (Decision no 97/2005). There have also been attempts by some far-right organizations to use, or rather abuse, the legal provisions against the Roma. A petitioner considered that the organization of a job fair for Roma represents discrimination against non-Roma. The NCCD decided that this represents an affirmative measure, not discrimination (Decision no 158/2005).

In Romania, before 2000, more than 60 per cent of job advertisements contained discriminatory elements based on gender, age, or ethnicity.[85] As a consequence of law enforcement, including by the NCCD, such advertisements appear extremely rarely now. However, employers use other methods to exclude Roma from the labour market. Even if the NCCD is trying to identify these means, but only through individual cases, it is not possible to hope for a change for the better in equality for Roma in employment.

The NCCD issued a decision in approximately two dozen cases of segregated education, seven of them initiated ex officio.[86] In four cases the ex officio action was based on false newspaper articles, so it was established that segregation did not exist. In one of the cases it was found that a school had classes predominantly with Roma students and classes without Roma students, and the NCCD applied a warning (Decision no 75/2006). One ex officio action was launched against six schools and kindergartens, establishing segregation in four cases. The

[83] The Constitutional Court of Romania established: 'the possibility to carry out judicial activity ex officio is based on the active role that the NCCD must fulfil, as an authority whose objectives and tasks were exclusively oriented towards the field of discrimination, a role exercised in order to find out the truth and prevent and combat all acts of discrimination ... Although the jurisdictional activity is also triggered ex officio, its subsequent development is left at the disposal of the injured person, who may or may not appropriate the referral to the NCCD regarding the acts or acts of discrimination by which he is directly affected' (Decision no 1096/2008, <https://legislatie.just.ro/Public/DetaliiDocumentAfis/99652> accessed 31 August 2024.

[84] Decisions nos 188/2003, 189/2003, 190/2003, 191/2003, 192/2003, 193/2003, 194/2003. All the decisions are available in Romanian at <https://www.cncd.ro/hotarari/?_sft_anul_publicarii=2022&sort_order=date+asc> accessed 31 August 2024.

[85] István Haller, 'Discriminarea—între teorie și practică' [2001] Info Pro Europa 9–10.

[86] Farkas and Gergely (n 45).

decision formulated a proposal to the school inspectorate to eliminate segregation (Decision no 306/2009). In one case the school fixed the problem as soon as it received the petition (Decision no 540/2009).

Similarly to the example in employment mentioned above, the NCCD also dealt with cases that can be classified as abuse of rights to the detriment of Roma and the effective protection of Roma rights. In one case, a teacher considered the obligation to teach in a class with many Roma students to be discriminatory. The petition was considered to have been introduced outside the legal terms (Decision no 153/2015). In another case, there were attempts to use the legislation against the affirmative measures created by the Romanian state by offering special places in high schools and universities for Roma, but the NCCD dismissed the case (Decision no 344/2010).

As a result of action by the NCCD and other actors, there are no more reported cases in recent years of physical segregation in different schools, classes, except residential segregation, Roma children being enrolled in segregated schools due to the fact that the school is located in the Roma community or they live in the vicinity of the school. Moreover, the local authorities build schools in Roma communities, claiming that in this way they support the education of the Roma, when in fact they promote segregation. This practice has not yet been sanctioned by the NCCD.

The eviction of Roma from homes where they have a semi-legal status was a practice in many Romanian localities after the 1990s. The first finding in this field refers to the forced relocation of Roma from the central area of the Miercurea Ciuc municipality to the city's sewage treatment plant (Decision no 366/2005). Ex officio actions were initiated in five cases, four based on newspaper articles, and closed due to the lack of information necessary for the decision. In one case it was found that the Roma were relocated in newly constructed buildings from improper living conditions, so the act does not represent discrimination (Decision no 18/2005).

The decisions of local councils that made it difficult for Roma to obtain social housing were brought to the NCCD's attention (in seven cases it established discrimination). The respective municipal decisions were changed following the activity of the NCCD, but there is no data to show that Roma obtain social housing more easily. The sanctions applied by the NCCD for the forced relocation of Roma, such as to the garbage dump at Pata Rât, did not have the effect of solving the housing situation of the victims. After the fines were paid by the local authorities, the Roma tried in vain to obtain a remedy through the courts.

The Romanian legal system interprets hate speech as representing a violation of the right to personal dignity.[87] The Council's case law in this field is extremely vast,

[87] István Haller, Romanita Iordache, and András Kádár, 'Using Anti-Discrimination Remedies For Discriminatory Speech—The Hungarian and Romanian Experiences' [2006] European Equality Law Review 2.

diverse, and sometimes contradictory. Some statements that accused the Roma of criminal behaviour were considered to be within the limits of freedom of expression, if they were expressed in a more academic way. Some more serious cases (incitement to violence and hatred, the promotion of extremist ideologies), were sent to criminal investigation bodies (Decision no 141/2003). Among the persons and bodies sanctioned by the NCCD were politicians, newspapers, journalists, sports clubs (being responsible for their supporters), bloggers, the Romanian Academy, civil servants, priests, teachers, restaurants, or even neighbours of those to whom the statements referred. The sanctioned statements included generalizations regarding Roma criminality, affirmations that claim that Roma have antisocial behaviour, are dirty, without education, use racist terms (for example 'crows'). Fifty-two ex officio actions were started in this field, twenty-four concluding with a finding of discrimination. The NCCD applied a warning in three cases, fines in the other twenty-one cases (between €120 and €2,000). In some of the remaining cases, the statements were considered to be protected by the freedom of expression, in others there was insufficient evidence, sanctions were applied by other institutions, or the cases were sent for penal prosecution. Ex officio actions were formulated against the media (newspapers and journalists, fourteen cases), sports clubs (for their supporters, eleven cases), other legal entities (one case), natural persons (public persons, such as politicians, university professors, athletes, twenty-six cases). Even if most of the petitions and, consequently, findings and fines of the NCCD were in the field of the right to dignity, the use of hate speech against Roma is a daily phenomenon: for example, banners with the text 'death to the Roma' still appear at football matches.

In the statistics of the NCCD the term ethnic discrimination is used for discrimination against Roma (racial discrimination refers to discrimination against people of African or Asian origin, discrimination based on nationality against ethnic minorities in Romania, excluding Roma). In the first period of activity (2003–06), 42.2 per cent of the petitions received by the NCCD relating to discrimination of Roma originated from individuals, 33.3 per cent from NGOs, and 24.5 per cent of the actions were initiated ex officio. In the last period (2021–22) the percentage of petitions from individuals increased (60.4 per cent, partly due to the pandemic), the percentage of petitions from NGOs remained similar (33.0 per cent), while ex officio actions decreased to 6.6 per cent. The effectiveness of the Council and its role and ability pushing the boundaries of non-discrimination law is arguably negatively affected by the decrease of strategic ex officio actions. There are multiple reasons why the number of ex officio actions decreased: the change in the composition of the Board, the increasing number of cases (due to the pandemic, hundreds of complaints had to be solved concerning the measures taken by the government) combined with the accumulation of unresolved files (with delays of more than two years compared to the legal deadline of six months). The number of these actions will decrease even more since, according to the new procedure from 2024, an ex officio action cannot be started without being voted by the Board. This change in the official procedural rule is also in contradiction with the equality directives' non-regression clause.

On average, less than 10 per cent of the petitions refer to discrimination against Roma, the maximum percentage recorded was in 2003 (25.4 per cent), the lowest in 2021 (4.7 per cent). The number of Roma cases decreased, on the one hand, because the number of individual Roma complaints, which were actually supported by Roma NGOs, decreased. The decrease in proportion can also be explained by the fact that the number of other types of cases has increased. Most of the petitions refer to the right to personal dignity (more than 60 per cent).[88] While initially ex officio actions focused mainly on discrimination in the field of employment, school segregation or access to public services (including housing), in the last period their object was most often the right to personal dignity. As a consequence, many cases have a symbolic object and not a practical one aimed at increasing the quality of life for Roma.

Until 2012, more warnings than fines were applied, afterwards the number of fines increased (relative to warnings), and from 2018 the number of fines has been approximately equal to the number of warnings. The number of recommendations is generally less than the number of warnings, although the legislation stipulates the obligation to formulate these recommendations if a fine is not applied. The effectiveness of the Council is affected, on the one hand, by the application of overly lenient fines, on the other hand, by the decisions of the courts that consider that there is no need to remedy.

It can be stated that at the beginning of the Council's existence it solved several cases that brought positive changes, but recently there are no actions focused on promoting non-discrimination of Roma according to the potential offered by the legislation. In addition, important Roma NGOs (such as Romani Criss) have become inactive, so the hybridity of enforcement has come to an end and the Council does not feel the pressure from these organizations to continue firmly the action of preventing and sanctioning discrimination against Roma. As the European Union's pressure on Romania decreased, so did the political will to improve the situation of the Roma. Showcase actions are prioritized instead of concrete actions (eg there are two Roma on the Council's board of directors, but without a majority vote they cannot start proceedings ex officio).

[88] Personal dignity refers first of all to hate speech, but also when discrimination seriously affects the dignity of the person, for example, when a Roma schoolchild is not allowed on the bus in front of his classmates.

## 5. Conclusions

Equality bodies can play a crucial role in combating discrimination against Roma, including the strategic use of their litigation and decision-making powers to address and call attention to structural and systemic forms of discrimination. These institutions are the cornerstones of an effective equality infrastructure, and they live in a symbiosis with anti-discrimination NGOs, well complementing each other's powers and strengths. The recent adoption of EU directives on standards for equality bodies may further strengthen their role in certain EU member states, by ensuring that all equality bodies are granted adequate investigation, litigation and decision-making powers. The directives will also enhance equality bodies' independence and resources, in principle allowing them to overcome some of the obstacles detailed above, relating to prioritization of work on Roma discrimination or political considerations.

Equality bodies will also need to overcome barriers related to the lack of data and under-reporting of discrimination cases by Roma. They could usefully ensure a proactive focus in their work on strategic litigation in Roma cases, with special attention to cases revealing systemic and structural forms of discrimination.

Numerous examples illustrate the importance of using such powers in close and strategic cooperation with NGOs, demonstrating a working model of 'hybrid enforcement'. This relies on the complementary strengths of equality bodies and NGOs and can manifest in several ways. NGOs can file complaints to the quasi-judicial equality bodies, essentially representing a short-cut for access to justice, with shorter time-limits, dedicated equality expertise and significantly lower costs. Equality bodies can also launch ex officio proceedings or litigation based on signals from NGOs, and they can intervene on the side of NGOs in strategic cases. In either of these cases, it seems necessary to ensure a professional dialogue between equality bodies and NGOs engaging in strategic litigation, to identify and tackle pressing structural examples of discrimination against Roma.

At the end of the day, we return to the finding that equality bodies are public institutions with a great potential to enhance access to justice, help Roma victims of discrimination, and prevent Roma discrimination from happening in the first place. This potential is further enhanced by the recent adoption of EU directives on standards for equality bodies, allowing equality bodies to act with more independence, resources, and powers. Nevertheless, it remains to be seen how equality bodies will use this potential in practice, as further efforts in prioritizing effective work on Roma discrimination is required.

# 15

# Pushing the Boundaries of Human Rights Through Dissent

## An Analysis of ECtHR Dissenting Opinions on the Rights of Romani Minorities

*Julija Sardelić*

### 1. Introduction: Why Dissenting Opinions?

This chapter explores how dissenting opinions in the cases on the rights of Roma at the European Court of Human Rights (ECtHR, 'the Court') identify and push the boundaries of human rights. ECtHR dissenting opinions have seldom attracted the spotlight in an academic inquiry separate from the analysis of cases. Similarly, the analysis of dissenting opinions at other international courts is still in its infancy.[1] Yet the available analysis[2] has shown that dissenting opinions[3] could shed a different light on human rights violations and possibly also set paths for new interpretations on human rights, thus pushing the boundaries of the human rights paradigm. Dissenting opinions can have an important contribution to the ongoing development of human rights jurisprudence, especially when it comes to non-dominant or minority groups, as scholars have shown using the example of religious minorities.[4]

Up until now, there has been no systematic review on dissenting opinions in the ECtHR cases related to the rights of Roma and Travellers. However, several legal scholars[5] have highlighted the significance of dissenting opinion in these cases, especially where they expose the Court's reluctance to pinpoint systemic racism towards Roma as the basis of the human rights violations. This chapter investigates

[1] Ke Song and Xuechan Ma, 'Individual Opinions as an Agent of International Legal Development?' (2022) 13(1) Journal of International Dispute Settlement 54.

[2] Robin CA White and Iris Boussiakou, 'Separate Opinions in the European Court of Human Rights' (2009) 9(1) Human Rights Law Review 37.

[3] Ruth Bader Ginsburg, 'The Role of Dissenting Opinions' (2010) 95(1) Minnesota Law Review 1.

[4] Sophie van Bijsterveld, 'A Typology of Dissent in Religion Cases in the Grand Chamber of the European Court of Human Rights' (2017) 12(2–3) Religion and Human Rights 223.

[5] Matthias Möschel, 'Is the European Court of Human Rights' Case Law on Anti-Roma Violence "Beyond Reasonable Doubt"?' (2012) 12(3) Human Rights Law Review 479; Claude Cahn, 'Triple Helix: The Jurisprudence of the European Court of Human Rights, Roma and Racial Discrimination' in Claude Cahn (ed), *Human Rights, State Sovereignty and Medical Ethics* (Brill 2014) 106–48.

Julija Sardelić, *Pushing the Boundaries of Human Rights Through Dissent* In: *The Rights of Roma in European Courts*. Edited by: Kristin Henrard and Lilla Farkas, Oxford University Press. © Julija Sardelić 2025.
DOI: 10.1093/oso/9780198914358.003.0015

whether and to what extent a systematic review of all available dissenting opinions in the cases related to the rights of Roma and Travellers would reveal that dissents push the boundaries of human rights, inter alia: (1) by flagging the context of structural racial discrimination not recognized in the judgments, and exploring its implications for the Court's reasoning; (2) by a broad interpretation of the scope of application of particular fundamental rights; (3) by identifying the vulnerability of the Roma and Travellers as a minority; (4) by (calling for) a restrictive approach to the margin of appreciation; and (5) by an extensive reading of positive state obligation aimed at the effective protection of Romani rights.

There have been dissenting opinions questioning the Court's approach to possible human rights violations against the Roma since the first judgment in the 1990s. This 1996 case of the ECtHR on the rights of Romani minorities[6] in Europe,[7] *Buckley v United Kingdom*,[8] reveals several of the above-mentioned themes typical of dissenting opinions in Roma cases. It is indeed striking that one of the dissenters, Judge Pettiti, considered the *Buckley* case a missed opportunity for properly addressing structural racial discrimination against Roma, which is a theme revisited in subsequent cases and dissenting opinions.

This chapter offers a socio-legal analysis (a perspective on law in context usually using methods from social sciences[9]) to investigate the extent to which ECtHR dissenting opinions in cases on the rights of Roma can be seen as advancing the boundaries of human rights, particularly when the majority of the judges are hesitant to do so. As academic analysis has rarely focused solely on ECtHR dissenting opinions,[10] and especially not in the cases concerning the human rights of Romani minorities in Europe, the chapter aims to provide a meaningful contribution to both the Roma-related and the human rights literature.

Based on the review of 110 judgments delivered between 1996 and 2022 directly on the human rights violations against Romani minorities and listed in an ECtHR's Factsheet on Roma and Travellers,[11] this chapter identifies thirty-four

[6] I am using the term Romani minorities to highlight heterogeneity and non-dominant position of people who self-identify as Roma but to also include people who might be externally categorized as Roma but themselves prefer another identification (Sinti, Manouche, Travellers, Gitano, among others). My usage of the term minority indicates the fact Roma are always in a subordinated minority position, but it is also informed by recent research that questions whether the current conceptualization of minority rights can in fact address such subordination (for more see Mohammad Shahabuddin, 'Decolonising Minority Rights Discourse' (2023) 30(5) International Journal of Minority and Group Rights 931).

[7] Nikolai Gughinski, 'The European Court of Human Rights Turns Down the First Case Involving a Gypsy Applicant' (European Roma Rights Centre 1996) <http://www.errc.org/roma-rights-journal/the-european-court-of-human-rights-turns-down-the-first-case> accessed 14 August 2023.

[8] *Buckley v United Kingdom* App no 20348/92 (ECtHR, 25 September 1996).

[9] Sally Wheeler, 'Socio-Legal Studies in 2020' (2020) 47(2) Journal of Law and Society 209.

[10] Erik Voeten, 'The Impartiality of International Judges: Evidence from the European Court of Human Rights' (2008) 102(4) American Political Science Review 417.

[11] European Court of Human Rights Press Unit, 'Roma and Travellers' (European Court of Human Rights, December 2022) < https://www.echr.coe.int/documents/d/echr/fs_roma_eng> accessed 15 August 2023.

judgments with sixty-five (partly) dissenting opinions. The section after the introduction highlights what scholarship has so far revealed about ECtHR dissenting opinions on the rights of Roma. In the third section, starting with a closer analysis of *Buckley*, the chapter offers a systematic review of all the dissenting opinions identified in judgments relating to the rights of Romani minorities. The judgments are primarily grouped thematically and secondarily by chronological order. In the fourth section, the chapter discusses common patterns in dissenting opinions and what approaches they use to push the boundaries of human rights especially when highlighting structural racial discrimination. The chapter concludes with the recommendation that differing perspectives brought by dissenting opinions should be highlighted by the Court reports on judgments and in case law guides, to better alert academia, civil society, and the ECtHR itself about alternative interpretations.

## 2. The Role of Dissenting Opinions for the Development of Jurisprudence

Based on the literature review (and to the best of my knowledge) there has been no systematic review on dissenting opinions on the ECtHR cases concerning the human rights of Roma. Admittedly, several scholarly papers have highlighted the role of individual dissenting opinions on the development of the Court's jurisprudence, pushing the boundaries of human rights protection. For example, while analysing the 'distinct way of life' and the cases that followed *Buckley*, Henrard argued that a significant dissent (by several judges) could announce a change in the future reasoning in ECtHR judgments: 'the considerable dissent does carry potential for alterations in the jurisprudence in the not too distant future'.[12] Möschel, focusing particularly on anti-Roma violence and the role of racism, commented that the opinion of Judge Bonello in *Anguelova v Bulgaria* expressed a strong dissent on the failure of a 'racially-blind' ECtHR in recognizing institutional racism under Article 14 and also gave suggestions on how to overcome this shortcoming.[13] In analysing the subsequent ECtHR judgments up to 2015, Claude Cahn claimed that Bonello's dissenting opinion significantly upscaled the discussion on racial discrimination against Romani minorities:

> since Judge Bonello's dissent in Anguelova, the ban on racial discrimination has moved from the margins of the Court's preoccupations to its normative core. In the period of less than a decade and a half, since the Court's first tentative steps in

[12] Kristin Henrard, 'The European Convention on Human Rights and the Protection of the Roma as a Controversial Case of Cultural Diversity' (2004) 5 European Diversity and Autonomy Papers 17.
[13] Möschel (n 5).

> Buckley, the Court has developed a substantial jurisprudence concerning Roma/Gypsies on the one hand, and the ban on racial discrimination on the other.[14]

At the same time, Cahn showed that not all dissenting opinions questioned the inability of the court to address racial discrimination, and that there were also judges 'defending' their own countries in the cases where the ECtHR established racial or ethnic discrimination.[15]

Most of the current scholarship highlights dissenting opinions in relation to particular cases or the overarching theme of the failure to acknowledge racial discrimination.[16] This chapter takes a different approach and first analyses the content of dissenting opinions to then highlight how dissenting opinions push the boundaries of human rights concerning the Romani minorities. The next section will offer an analysis of all the dissenting opinions identified in the sample of 110 judgments on the rights of Roma. The next sections discuss the ways in which these opinions reveal and/or push the boundaries of human rights.

## 3. A Systematic Analysis of Dissenting Opinions in Cases on the Rights of Roma

The following discussion is organized thematically, and within each theme per judgment, in order to provide the best possible insights into the range of dissents. The next section will then lift the analysis to a more overarching perspective.

### 3.1. Starting point: cases involving questions on housing

The ECtHR judges themselves identified *Buckley*[17] as the first case where the applicant belonged to the Romani minorities. The judgment in this case is important not only simply because it was the first, but also because the three dissenting opinions identified Romani minorities as vulnerable and called for a stricter scrutiny by the Court. Second, they questioned whether the European Convention on Human Rights (ECHR) can protect the rights of minorities without taking into account cultural diversity. And third, the dissenting opinion of Judge Pettiti[18] was critical of the Court's failure to identify racial discrimination and to recognize Romani minorities' vulnerability.

[14] Cahn (n 5) 144.
[15] ibid.
[16] Möschel, Cahn (n 5).
[17] *Buckley* (n 8).
[18] ibid.

In *Buckley*, the ECtHR examined whether the UK had violated Article 8 and Article 14 in conjunction with Article 8 of the ECHR. The applicant in this case was identified as belonging to the English Gypsy community. She wanted to station a caravan on the land that she legally owned. The local authorities prevented her from doing so. The government put forward the legitimate aim of preventing interference with highway safety, environment preservation and public health.[19] While the European Commission on Human Rights concluded that the UK had violated her rights, the ECtHR's conclusion was the opposite: the UK had acted within its margin of appreciation hence, the Court decided the UK had not violated Ms Buckley's human rights.[20]

Three judges wrote (partly) dissenting opinions disagreeing with the majority. The dissenting opinions highlighted the vulnerable status of Travellers in the UK, but also considered the future cases of human rights violations against the more sizeable Romani communities in Central and Eastern European states. For example, in his dissenting opinion, Judge Repik expressed his disagreement with the finding of non-violation of Article 8, urging the Court to review the case more strictly:

> it must be borne in mind that this *is the first case before the Court concerning the right of a member of the Gypsy minority*; … especially a minority as vulnerable as the Gypsies, the Court has an obligation to subject any such interference to particularly close scrutiny. In my opinion, the Court has not fully performed its duty as it has not taken into account all the relevant matters adduced by the Commission and was too hasty in invoking the margin of appreciation left to the State.[21]

Judge Lõhmus argued that the judgment in question failed to protect the members of the vulnerable minority and that special minority rights are required by 'equality in fact'. He emphasized that: 'It may not be enough to prevent discrimination so that members of minority groups receive equal treatment under the law. In order to establish equality in fact, different treatment may be necessary to preserve their special cultural heritage.'[22]

The strongest dissent in the *Buckley* judgment was presented by Judge Pettiti. In his view the members of Romani minorities were discriminated against on the basis of their specific group membership: 'If the Buckley case were transposed to a family of ecologists or adherents of a religion instead of Gypsies, the harassment

19 ibid para 62.
20 ibid paras 85–89.
21 Dissenting Opinion of Judge Repik in *Buckley* (emphasis added).
22 Partly Dissenting Opinion of Judge Lõhmus in *Buckley*.

to which Mrs Buckley was subjected would not have occurred'[23]. Pettiti concluded his dissenting opinion in the following manner:

> the European Court had, in the Buckley case, an opportunity to produce, in the spirit of the European Convention, a critique of national law and practice with regard to Gypsies and travellers in the United Kingdom that would have been transposable to the rest of Europe, and thereby partly compensate for the injustices they suffer.[24]

Common to the three dissenting opinions in this case is the call for a stricter scrutiny[25] and thus a more narrow margin of appreciation, given that the applicants were particularly vulnerable to human rights violations because of their belonging to Romani minorities.

Similar dissenting opinions occurred in the following five cases at the Grand Chamber level: *Chapman v UK, Coster v UK, Beard v UK, Lee v UK* and *Jane Smith v UK*.[26] All the cases above were examining Article 8 concerning a distinct was of life (parking caravans, living in caravans, etc). In these cases, the ECtHR ruled that there was no violation due to the state's 'wide margin of appreciation'. However, as Henrard argued, 'the fact that there was a significant dissent (seven of the seventeen judges of the Grand Chamber), concluding to a violation of Article 8, criticizing the majority to be too careful and reserved, indicates a clear potential for further, more positive developments pro minority protection generally'.[27] The five cases received their judgments on the same day (18 January 2001), and dissenting opinions also referred to those made in the *Chapman* case. In all five cases, seven judges (Pastor Ridruejo, Bonello, Tulkens, Strážnická, Lorenzen, Fischback, and Casadewall) wrote a joint dissenting opinion, to which Judge Bonello also added his additional dissenting opinion. The dissenters in *Chapman* and other cases argued that given the vulnerability of Romani minorities, the Court should not follow the reasoning of the *Buckley* judgment[28] and should rather identify positive state obligations to recognize the specific lifestyle of Romani minorities under Article 8.[29] The dissenters urged the ECtHR to consider the broader social context, especially considering the vulnerability of Travellers, because of their subordinated

[23] Partly Dissenting Opinion of Judge Pettiti in *Buckley*.
[24] ibid.
[25] Lilla Farkas, 'Mobilising for Racial Equality in Europe: Roma Rights and Transnational Justice' (2020) <https://cadmus.eui.eu/handle/1814/66916> accessed 18 August 2024.
[26] *Chapman v United Kingdom* App no 27238/95 (ECtHR, 18 January 2001); *Coster v United Kingdom* App no 24876/94 (ECtHR, 18 January 2001); *Beard v United Kingdom* App no 24882/94 (ECtHR, 18 January 2001); *Lee v United Kingdom* App no 25289/94 (ECtHR, 18 January 2001); *Jane Smith v United Kingdom* App no 25154/94 (ECtHR, 18 January 2001).
[27] Henrard (n 12) 19.
[28] Joint Dissenting Opinion of Judges Pastor Ridruejo, Bonello, Tulkens, Strážnická, Lorenzen, Fischback, and Casadewall in *Chapman*, para 1.
[29] ibid para 2.

position in the UK. While these cases might have been about particular rights of Romani minorities in the UK (and minorities who continue to follow a nomadic lifestyle), Luke Clements, who was involved in litigation, argued that these questions have implications for all Roma in the Council of Europe space.[30]

In the case *Winterstein and Others v France*[31] the ECtHR examined similar challenges as in the *Buckley* and *Chapman* cases in regards to minority culture and the right to a specific way of life. However, here dissenting opinion presents an important shift that such cases are not simply a matter of the right to private life but also need to discuss the question of racial discrimination. Judge Power-Forde highlighted her dissatisfaction that the Court only examined Article 8 but not Article 14: 'Where unacceptable treatment of a vulnerable minority is known to State authorities ... a heightened vigilance is required of such authorities to investigate ... discrimination'.[32] The judge based her dissent on a positive obligation of the state to address racial discrimination.

The case of *Bagdonavicius and Others v Russia*[33] concerned the forced eviction of a Romani community and the destruction of their village. The majority found a violation of Article 8 but did not examine Article 14 ECHR. Judge Keller dissented:

> From a strictly quantitative point of view, it appears that, during the demolition, only two dwellings were spared and that these belonged, it seems, to Russian families. Consequently, all of the Roma dwellings have been destroyed, despite the regularization of some of them ... The differentiated and clearly discriminatory treatment, implied by the origin of the applicants, is beyond doubt in the present case ... Once again, the authorities have demonstrated a subjectivity that borders on racism[34].

In the cases examining the right to private life, and especially when it comes to places where Romani communities (be it semi-nomadic in the UK and France or sedentary in Eastern Europe), most dissenting opinions highlighted the vulnerability of a minority group and positive obligations of the state. Notwithstanding Pettiti's initial dissenting opinion, following dissents often did not look at the racial discriminatory dimension separately until the dissent in *Winterstein.* The dissenting opinion in *Bagdonavicius* in 2016, however, mentions institutional racism as the context for forced evictions.

[30] Luke Clements, 'An Emerging Consensus on the Special Needs of Minorities: The Lessons of Chapman v UK (European Roma Rights Centre 2001) <http://www.errc.org/roma-rights-journal/an-emerging-consensus-on-the-special-needs-of-minorities-the-lessons-of-chapman-v-uk> accessed 15 August 2023.

[31] *Winterstein and Others v France* App no 27013/07 (ECtHR, 17 October 2013).

[32] Partly Dissenting Opinion of Judge Power-Forde in *Winterstein and Others v France* (2013).

[33] *Bagdonavicius and Others v Russia* App no 19841/06 (ECtHR, 11 October 2016).

[34] Dissenting Opinion of Judge Keller in *Bagdonavicius.*

## 3.2. Cases involving violence or degrading treatment against Roma

The next case with a dissenting opinion arguably had the highest impact on subsequent ECtHR judgments and was also extensively discussed in the academic literature[35]: the dissenting opinion of Judge Bonello in the case of *Anguelova v Bulgaria*.[36] The case concerned a Romani man who died in police custody. The applicant (the victim's mother) claimed that her son died because of the treatment by the police, which spanned from being beaten while being unlawfully detained to not being given appropriate medical assistance. In addition, the applicant complained that the authorities failed to properly investigate the case. As an underlying cause for such treatment and flawed investigation, the applicant highlighted structural racial discrimination of Roma in Bulgaria.[37]

While the ECtHR found violations of Articles 2, 3, 5, and 13, they did not find proof 'beyond reasonable doubt'[38] of a racially motivated violent attack by the police. Judge Bonello wrote a strong dissent, arguing that it was problematic that the Court had never found racial motivations for such attacks:

> [A]n uninformed observer would be justified to conclude that, for over fifty years democratic Europe has been exempted from any suspicion of racism, intolerance or xenophobia. The Europe projected by the Court's case-law is that of an exemplary haven of ethnic fraternity, in which peoples of the most diverse origin coalesce without distress, prejudice or recrimination. The present case energises that delusion.[39]

Judge Bonello was particularly appalled that judgments give the impression that individuals belonging to vulnerable minorities (he also mentioned Kurds, Muslims, and people of colour) are being deprived of life or are subjected to the most degrading treatment by chance rather than by design. The dissenting opinion in the *Anguelova* judgment can be considered as a call to push beyond the existing human rights boundaries in situations of structural racial discrimination, if the Court is to live up to its mission. Bonello offered not only criticism but also practical solutions for future judgments: shifting the burden of proof and identifying a procedural violation of the prohibition of discrimination.

Bonello's recommendations were followed in the Chamber judgment in *Nachova and Others v Bulgaria*,[40] a case where the military police had killed two

[35] Möschel; Cahn (n 5).
[36] *Anguelova v Bulgaria* App no 38361/97 (ECtHR, 13 June 2002) para 5.
[37] ibid para 5.
[38] Partly Dissenting Opinion of Judge Bonello in *Anguelova v Bulgaria* (2002) para 2.
[39] ibid.
[40] *Nachova and Others v Bulgaria* App nos 43577/98 and 43579/98 (ECtHR, 24 February 2004).

Romani individuals. Here, noting the indications of possible racist motivation and the lack of proper investigations into this motivation, the Court shifted the burden of proof to the government and found a procedural as well as a substantive violation of Article 14 in conjunction with Article 2. Bonello wrote a concurring opinion where he expressed satisfaction that in this case his previous remarks had been followed. Unfortunately, following an appeal by Bulgaria, the Grand Chamber[41] no longer shifted the burden of proof, but maintained the distinction between substantive and procedural violation of Article 14. The Grand Chamber withheld unanimously racial discrimination concerning the procedural violation, but decided by eleven against six that there had been no substantive violation of Articles 2 and 14, because it had not been proven that racism had motivated the police killing. Judges Casadewall, Hedigan, Mularoni, Fura-Sandström, Gyulyuman, and Spielman wrote a joint dissenting opinion, noting that, ironically, the distinction between the substantive and procedural limbs of Article 14 led the majority of judges to decide the (limited available) evidence was not strong enough in favour of a substantive violation.[42]

The next case in 2005 with dissenting opinions was *Moldovan (No 2) and Others v Romania*,[43] a case that involved a pogrom against the Romani community and the murder of three Romani individuals in the village of Hădăreni in Romania, with racial motivation being clearly documented. Because the ECHR was not yet into force at the time of these events, the Court could only consider the subsequent proceedings and follow-up by the Romanian authorities. In this case, the judges reached a unanimous agreement that there had been violations of Article 3 and 8 as regards the living conditions to which the Roma were subjected following the burning of their houses, and the racial discrimination they were subjected to publicly in the way their grievances were dealt with.[44] The Court also established a violation of Article 6 as far as the length of proceedings was concerned. The judges furthermore unanimously ruled that there had been a violation of Article 14 in conjunction with Articles 6 and 8, without making a distinction between procedural and substantive aspects, because the applicants' Roma ethnicity was decisive for the length and the result of the domestic proceedings.[45] However, the Court did not find a violation of Article 6 for lack of access to Court due to the fact that the applicants had not been able to submit a claim for damages against the police officers involved. The Court opined that they had had access to Court because they had been able to file claims for damages against the

[41] *Nachova and Others v Bulgaria* App no 43577/98 and 43579/98 [GC] (ECtHR, 6 July 2005).

[42] Joint Partly Dissenting Opinion of Judges Casadewall, Hedigan, Mularoni, Fura-Sandström, Gyulyuman, and Spielman in *Nachova* [GC] para 7.

[43] *Moldovan and Others v Romania (No 2)* App nos 41138/98 and 64320/01 (ECtHR, 12 July 2005) paras 15–19.

[44] ibid paras 109 and 112 respectively.

[45] ibid paras 139–40.

civilians implicated.[46] The latter finding elicited the following dissent by Judge Thomassen and Loucaides:

> In my view, it would be unfortunate if the finding of the majority ... could be understood as implying any acceptance that, where State agents allegedly violate human rights, they could escape their responsibility as soon as a private person is held liable for the impugned acts. To me, such a result would flout the rule of law[47].

The dissenting opinion suggested that the Court should have adopted a higher level of scrutiny than it had when it comes to racially motivated hate crimes.

In the following case, *Carabulea v Romania*[48] the ECtHR once again examined police killing of a Romani individual. It concluded that there had been both substantive and procedural violations of Articles 2 and 3, but the majority did not think it necessary to examine Article 14. Three judges, Gyulumyan, Power, and Ziemele,[49] dissented and argued that Article 14 should have been examined given the context of racial discrimination against Romani individuals, making them much more likely to suffer extreme police violence. As Ziemele pointed out:

> I believe that the Court has been very clear about the special duty to unmask racist motives behind the actions of State agents. In the Nachova case it explained very clearly that it was a duty apart and that failing to comply with it or treating racist violence on an equal footing with other violence would be turning a blind eye to the particularly destructive character of racism.[50]

The dissenters criticized the Court of once again failing to recognize racism despite its previous judgments already pushing the boundaries of human rights on racial discrimination.

Another Romani individual was killed by the police in the *Mižigárová v Slovakia*[51] but the Court did not establish a racist motive behind it. Yet in this case too, a dissenting opinion by Judge Thór Björgvinsson found such a conclusion disturbing, especially considering the backdrop of numerous reports of racist violence against Roma.[52] Similar disagreement on Article 14 arose in the 2011 case *Soare and others v Romania*.[53] While one judge (Myer) dissented[54] because of

[46] ibid paras 120–22.
[47] Partly Dissenting Opinion of Judge Thomasen, joined by judge Loucaides in *Moldovan and Others (No 2)*.
[48] *Carabulea v Romania* App no 45661/99 (ECtHR, 13 July 2010), para 168.
[49] Partly Joint Dissenting Opinion of Judges Gyulumyan and Power (Joint), and Ziemele in *Carabulea*, para 5.
[50] ibid.
[51] *Mižigárová v Slovakia* App no 74832/01(ECtHR, 14 December 2010).
[52] Partly Dissenting Opinion of Judge David Thór Björgvinsson in *Mižigárová*.
[53] *Soare and Others v Romania* App no 24329/02 (ECtHR, 22 February 2011).
[54] Partly Concurring and Partly Dissenting Opinion of Judge Myer in *Soare*.

the different view on non-pecuniary damages and the amount awarded on this basis, Judge Power[55] (joined by Judge Zupančič) wrote a similar dissent as in the *Carabulea* case, referring explicitly to it. In these cases the dissenting judges disagreed with the Court that no racial motivation could be found in the violent attacks. Similarly, in *Adam v Slovakia*,[56] Judge Serghides[57] dissented as he found a violation of Article 3 substantiated too but he did not comment on Article 14. In the case of *Király and Dömötör v Hungary* Judge Kūris[58] dissented as he considered the case inadmissible due to the failure to exhaust domestic remedies. Judge Keller and Judge Serghides dissented because the Court did not examine Article 14 in *AP v Slovakia*, another case of police violence against a Romani individual:

> In the context of racial discrimination against Roma, the Grand Chamber has called for 'special vigilance and a vigorous reaction' on the part of domestic authorities ... Confronted with the degrading treatment of a Roma boy by police against a background of racial tension, the Court ought to have demonstrated similar attentiveness by examining the merits of the complaint under Article 14.[59]

The dissents in the cases on violence against Roma were dissatisfied that the Court did not find the most severe violence against Roma to have been racially motivated.

Another complex case highlighting intersectional discrimination (see section 3.5) was the case of *Centre for Legal Resources on Behalf of Valentin Câmpeanu v Romania*.[60] The case dealt with, among other things, the degrading treatment and death of a Romani man with severe mental disabilities and HIV diagnosis in state care. Three judges, Spielmann, Bianku and Nußberger,[61] dissented as the Court did not examine Article 3 alone or in conjunction with Article 13. Two judges, Bianku and Ziemele,[62] dissented because the Court did not examine Article 14 in conjunction with Article 2 and did not consider the fact that Câmpeanu was mentally disabled and a Roma.

Additional dissenting opinion on Article 14 was written by Judge Kjølbro in *Balázs v Hungary*.[63] However, in this case the dissenting judge disagreed with the majority that there had been a violation of Article 14 and disagreed that the violence in this case had racial motivation:

55 Partly Dissenting Opinion of Judge Power Joined by Judge Zupančič in *Soare*.

56 *Adam v Slovakia* App no 68066/12 (ECtHR, 26 July 2016).

57 Partly Dissenting Opinion of Judge Sergidhes in *Adam*.

58 Dissenting Opinion of Judge Kūris in *Király and Dömötör*.

59 Joint Partly Dissenting Opinion of Judges Keller and Serghides in *AP v Slovakia* App no 10465/17 (EtCHR, 28 January 2020).

60 *Centre for Legal Resources on Behalf of Valentin Câmpeanu v Romania* App no 47848/08 (ECtHR, 17 July 2014).

61 ibid, Joint Partly Dissenting Opinion of Judges Spielmann, Bianku, and Nußberger.

62 ibid, Joint Partly Dissenting Opinion of Judges Bianku and Ziemele.

63 *Balázs v Hungary* App no 15529/12 (ECtHR, 20 October 2015).

> my colleagues fail to recognize the difference between violence against a person who is of Roma origin, and violence against a person because of the person's Roma origin. In the first situation the ethnic origin of the victim is a statement of fact, in the other it is the cause of the violence.[64]

The dissenting judge in this case argued for a narrower application of law without assumption of racial discrimination. However, in *RB v Hungary*,[65] Judge Wojtyczek[66] dissented because the Court did not examine Article 3 and Article 14 in a case that questioned whether the police responded adequately to anti-Roma rallies that caused distress to the applicant who was a Roma. As mentioned above, similarly in the case *Adam v Slovakia*, Judge Serghides from Cyprus dissented as he also found a substantive violation of Article 3 was not only procedural but did not comment on Article 14. *Király and Dömötör v Hungary* Judge Kūris dissented as he saw the case inadmissible due to his view that domestic remedies had not been exhausted. In another case, *JI v Croatia*,[67] the national Judge Derenčinović from Croatia[68] partly dissented in regards to violation of Article 3 and he found that the police had not effectively investigated the claims of a young Romani woman raped by her father (hence he did not side with the government's arguments).

### 3.3. Dissents highlighting stereotyping of Roma

The 2010 *Aksu v Turkey*[69] case was arguably about the stereotypical portrayal of Roma in a government-funded publication. The Chamber decided there was no violation of Article 14 in conjunction with Article 8, while three judges, Tulkens, Tsotsoria, and Pardalos, dissented: 'In our view this is a particularly sensitive question as, in respect of a minority and highly vulnerable social group, prejudice is the breeding-ground of discrimination and exclusion.'[70] When the case was referred to the Grand Chamber in 2012, the judges reached a similar conclusion, with one dissenting opinion by Judge Gyulumyan who argued that there had been a violation of Article 14 in conjunction with Article 8 and called for a more narrow margin of appreciation: 'The continued stereotyping of the Roma must come to an end. It would be highly unfortunate for this Court to be seen to condone incitement to discrimination of the kind contained in the books in question.'[71]

64 ibid, Dissenting Opinion of Judge Kjølbro, para 4.
65 *RB v Hungary* App no 64602/12 (ECtHR, 12 April 2016).
66 ibid, Dissenting Opinion of Judge Wojtyczek.
67 *JI v Croatia* App no 35898/16 (ECtHR, 8 September 2022).
68 ibid, Partly Dissenting Opinion of Judge Derenčinović.
69 *Aksu v Turkey* App nos 4149/04 and 41029/04 (ECtHR, 27 July 2010).
70 Joint Dissenting Opinion of Judges Tulkens, Tsotroria, and Pardalos in *Aksu*, para 1.
71 Dissenting Opinion of Judge Gyulumyan in *Aksu v Turkey* App no 4149/04 and 41029/04 [GC] (ECtHR 15 March 2012), para 10.

## 3.4. Cases on the right to education

In 2006, an ECtHR Chamber ruled in *DH and Others v Czech Republic*[72] that there had been no violation of Article 14 in conjunction with Article 2 of Protocol 1. In this case Romani children had much higher chances of being unjustifiably placed in schools for children with learning impairment. Goodwin commented:

> The decision of the Strasbourg Court to ignore the evidence of indirect racial discrimination by a 6-1 majority represents not only a setback for those working for the improvement of the situation of the Roma – widely acknowledged as the most disadvantaged, discriminated and marginalised group in Europe – but also for the crystallisation of non-discrimination norms in Europe.[73]

In his dissenting opinion, Judge Barreto from Portugal noted that: 'in "specialised schools" Romany pupils made up between 80% and 90% of the total number of pupils … this constitutes an express acknowledgement by the Czech State of the discriminatory practices complained of by the applicants.'[74]

*DH* became a landmark case when it was referred to the Grand Chamber,[75] which in 2007 made a judgment that there was a violation of Article 14 in conjunction with Article 2 of Protocol 1, meaning that the Czech Republic racially and ethnically discriminated against Roma children in education. The case is often dubbed as the 'European *Brown*'[76] and is possibly the most high-profile case relating to Roma rights in Europe. The Grand Chamber judgment has been discussed at great length in the academic literature,[77] which also included reflections on the four dissenting opinions. While the Chamber judgment included only one dissenting opinion protesting that no violation had been found, the Grand Chamber dissenting opinion painted a different picture: 'The verdict provoked a heated debate in the Strasbourg Court and four judges presented unusually harsh dissenting opinions which reinforced each other.'[78]

[72] *DH and Others v Czech Republic* App no 57325/00 (ECtHR, 7 February 2006).

[73] Morag Goodwin, '*D.H. and Others v Czech Republic*: a Major Set-Back for the Development of Non-Discrimination Norms in Europe' (2006) 7(4) German Law Journal 421.

[74] Dissenting opinion of Judge Barreto in *DH and others v Czech Republic* App no 57325/00 (ECtHR, 7 February 2006).

[75] *DH and Others v Czech Republic* App no 57325/00 [GC] (ECtHR, 13 November 2007).

[76] Morag Goodwin, 'Taking on Racial Segregation: the European Court of Human Rights at a *Brown v. Board of Education* moment?' (2009) 170(3) Rechtsgeleerd Magazijn Themis 114.

[77] Helen O'Nions, 'Different and Unequal: The Educational Segregation of Roma Pupils in Europe' (2010) 21(1) Intercultural Education 1; Sina Van den Bogaert, *Segregation of Roma Children in Education* (Brill 2011); Kalina Arabadjieva, 'Challenging the School Segregation of Roma Children in Central and Eastern Europe' (2015) 20(1) The International Journal of Human Rights 33; Noam Peleg, 'Marginalisation by the Court: The Case of Roma Children and the European Court of Human Rights' (2018) 18(1) Human Rights Law Review 111.

[78] Hubert Smekal and Katarína Šipulová, '*DH v Czech Republic* Six Years Later: On the Power of an International Human Rights Court to Push Through Systemic Change' (2014) 32(3) Netherlands Quarterly of Human Rights 298–99.

*DH* was a ground-breaking case on racial discrimination, and it was a case that also provoked strong friction among judges visible in the dissenting opinions. Three out of four dissenting opinions were written by judges from post-socialist states, interestingly all to a certain extent arguing the importance of context, and especially showing discontent that Central and East European post-socialist countries are held to different standards than Western Europe. The first dissenting opinion was by Judge Zupančič:

> the Czech Republic is the only Contracting State which has in fact tackled the special-educational troubles of Roma children. It then borders on the absurd to find the Czech Republic in violation of anti-discrimination principles. In other words, this 'violation' would never have happened had the respondent State approached the problem with benign neglect. No amount of politically charged argumentation can hide the obvious fact that the *Court in this case has been brought into play for ulterior purposes*, which have little to do with the special education of Roma children in the Czech Republic. The future will show what specific purpose this precedent will serve.[79]

Zupančič also stated that he fully supported the dissenting opinion of the national Judge Jungwiert, who wrote a particularly strong dissent.

Similarly to Župančič, but more elaborately and based on context and figures from other countries, Jungwiert argued that the Czech Republic was the only country that worked on the inclusion of Romani children within the education system. It did so in an unequal manner, while many 'old' EU Member States never even attempted including Romani children in their education systems:

> difficulties exist in the education of Roma children not just in the Czech Republic but in other European States as well. To describe the total absence of a school education for half of Roma children ... in a number of States as 'difficulties' is an extraordinary euphemism. To explain this illogical approach, the majority note with satisfaction that, unlike some countries, the Czech Republic has chosen to tackle the problem.[80]

Another strong dissent was expressed by Judge Borrego Borrego, who referred to Bonello's dissent in *Anguelova*:

> While I agree with Judge Bonello's criticism that the absence, five years ago, of a single case of racial discrimination concerning the core Convention rights was disturbing, the judgment in the present case has now got the Court off to a flying

[79] Dissenting opinion of Judge Zupančič in *DH and Others v Czech Republic* [GC] (emphasis added).
[80] Dissenting opinion of Judge Jungwiert in *DH* [GC] para 14.

> start. The Grand Chamber has in this judgment behaved like a Formula One car, hurtling at high speed into the new and difficult terrain of education and, in so doing, has inevitably strayed far from the line normally followed by the Court.[81]

He asserted that in this case the ECtHR had started becoming a new European Commission against Racism and Intolerance (ECRI). In the last dissent, Judge Šikuta[82] argued that a broader geopolitical and historical background needed to be taken into account when it comes to the education of Roma in the post-socialist context.

While diametrically opposed to each other, the Chamber dissenting opinion had one thing in common with the four dissenting opinions from the Grand Chamber: they all called for taking broader contexts beyond the fact presented at Court into account, but very different contexts. In the Chamber judgment, Barreto noted that the Court was disregarding structural discrimination of Roma. In the Grand Chamber one, the post-socialist judges argued that the Court was creating double standards, and was not scrutinizing Western European states to the same extent. Yet while these opinions were regressively pushing back on the boundaries of human rights, they raised a valid question as to whether the Court was recognizing racial discrimination towards Roma to the same extent in the West as well as the Eest.

The Grand Chamber judgment in *Oršuš and Others v Croatia*[83] examined the existence of Roma-only classes in mainstream schools as a form of discrimination. Nine judges found that there was a violation of Article 14 in conjunction with Article 2 of Protocol 1, while eight judges wrote a dissenting opinion. Thus, this was among the most divisive cases with dissents from Judges Jungwiert, Vajić, Kovler, Gyulumyan, Jaeger, Myjer, Berro-Lefèvre, and Vučinić.[84] They argued in their joint dissenting opinion that this case was about what the schools in question were doing in practice, rather than the position of Romani minorities, which called for a wider margin of appreciation. They put forward a view that if the schools were taking a different practice there would be discrimination against majority children and also that the Grand Chamber overruled the Chamber judgment, which was according to their view more reasonable: 'That argument should not have been set aside without balancing also the interests of the Croatian-speaking children: the importance for Croatian-speaking pupils of being able to progress properly at school is not mentioned at all in the judgment.'[85] Noam Peleg found such reasoning inappropriate:

[81] Dissenting opinion of Judge Borrego Borrego in *DH* [GC] para 15.
[82] Dissenting opinion of Judge Šikuta in *DH* [GC].
[83] *Oršuš and Others v Croatia* App no 15766/03 [GC] (ECtHR, 16 March 2010).
[84] Joint Partly Dissenting Opinion by Judges Jungwiert, Vajić, Kovler, Gyulumyan, Jaeger, Myjer, Berro-Lefèvre, and Vučinić in *Oršuš and Others* [GC] para 9.
[85] ibid.

> On the conceptual level, prioritising the right to education of the privileged group (in terms of their opportunities, structure and access to public goods in comparison to Roma children), over the rights to education and non-discrimination of children who are members of a disadvantaged and systematically discriminated group, is morally wrong.[86]

In stark opposition to cases related to police violence, the dissenting opinions in the cases related to education disagreed with the Court's judgment that there had been a violation of Article 14, and argued for more scrutiny of the context and a wider margin of appreciation on how states address the disadvantage of the Roma.

### 3.5. Cases highlighting multiple vulnerabilities and intersectional discrimination, including forced sterilization

*Petropoulou-Tsakiris v Greece*[87] was the first case with a dissenting opinion in relation to the reproductive rights of Romani women, examining intersectional discrimination on an individual level. This was a case in which a Romani woman suffered a miscarriage after a violent attack by a police officer. The ECtHR found a procedural violation of Article 14 in conjunction with Article 3, but not a substantive violation, which followed a pattern similar to *Nachova and Others v Bulgaria* (Grand Chamber judgment). The dissenting Judge Loucaides questioned why the majority diminished the complaint:

> The applicant stated her complaint in a coherent and convincing manner. She explained that she had been kicked on her back and as a result had felt an intense pain in the abdominal area and started bleeding. There followed a miscarriage. She could not identify the police officer who had kicked her. That is understandable. What I cannot understand is why the majority did not believe her story, without even finding a concrete well-founded reason why she must have lied. In fact the evidence does not disclose any such reason.[88]

In 2008, the ECtHR decided on the first case regarding forced sterilization[89] of Romani women: *KH and Others v Slovakia*.[90] The case did not have a ruling on racial discrimination because the main complaint concerned access to medical records and the procedure itself. The Court decided there had been a violation of

[86] Peleg (n 77) 125.
[87] *Petropoulou-Tsakiris v Greece* App no 44803/04 (ECtHR, 6 December 2007).
[88] ibid, Partly Dissenting opinion of Judge Loucaides.
[89] For more on intersectionality and gender, see Chapter 12 by D'Agostino and Magazzini in this volume.
[90] *KH and Others v Slovakia* App no 32881/04 (ECtHR, 28 April 2009).

Article 8 and Article 6 ECHR. National Judge Šikuta wrote a dissenting opinion, as in his view the applicants did not have such a limited access to the records as to have inhibited their access to the national court.[91] *VC v Slovakia*[92] dealt with forced sterilization more explicitly than *KH*. The Chamber unanimously agreed there had been a substantive and procedural violation of Article 3 as well as Article 8 but did not find a need to examine Article 14. Judge Mijović dissented, arguing that the reason why the medical practitioners had performed sterilization was Romani ethnicity:

> To my mind, the applicant was 'marked out' and observed as a patient who had to be sterilised just because of her origin, since it was obvious that there were no medically relevant reasons for sterilising her. In my view, that represents the strongest form of discrimination and should have led to a finding of a violation of Article 14 in connection with the violations found of Articles 3 and 8 of the Convention.[93]

It is in regard to forced sterilization cases and non-recognition of racial discrimination that Angéla Kóczé[94] argued that law can be both an 'ally' but in many aspects also an 'enemy', if it undermines racial discrimination as an important factor that contributed to forced sterilization and with it violation of reproductive rights.

*Muñoz Diaz v Spain*[95] was another case centred around the rights of Romani women. The case concerned a Romani woman who applied for a survivor pension after her late husband, but was denied it because their marriage had been conducted according to Roma traditions, rather than in a civil ceremony. While the ECtHR did not recognize the marriage per se, it did conclude that the applicant had the right to the pension as she had a good faith marriage, that had been recognized by the Spanish authorities themselves. Denying her the pension amounted to discrimination because of her Romani origin. Judge Myer dissented[96] as in her view, among other things, the case reflected a broader position of Romani minorities in Spain rather than the individual case and should have examined structural and intersectional discrimination as well as multiple vulnerabilities in a broader context (in which the alternative marriages occur).

*M and Others v Italy and Bulgaria*[97] was a complex case revolving around the question of human trafficking and intersecting the vulnerable position of Roma

[91] ibid, Partly Dissenting Opinion of Judge Šikuta.
[92] *VC v Slovakia* App no 18968/07 (ECtHR, 8 November 2011).
[93] ibid, Dissenting Opinion of Judge Mijović.
[94] Angéla Kóczé, '"Ally" or "enemy"? Law and the Forced and Coerced Sterilization of Romani Women' (2021) 4 Juridikum 539.
[95] *Muñoz Diaz v Spain* App no 49151/07 (ECtHR, 8 December 2009) para 81.
[96] ibid, Dissenting Opinion of Judge Myer.
[97] *M and Others v Italy and Bulgaria* App no 40020/03 (ECtHR, 31 July 2012).

women. The state authorities failed to investigate the case in detail due to their own conception of 'Romani culture', even blaming the victim. The decision in this case was that the steps Italian authorities took were sufficient, but not in terms of investigating how the applicants had been mistreated by private individuals. Judge Kalaydjieva wrote a dissenting opinion as she saw a violation of Article 6 where the explanation of Romani applicants had not been taken seriously:

> This explanation appears to be more reasonable than that offered to the Court, namely, that the 'Italian authorities opined that the circumstances of the present case fell within the context of a Roma marriage'. Even if correct (and I would venture to doubt it), such an 'opinion' could not reasonably explain the manner in which the authorities dealt with the applicants' complaints of ill-treatment, non-consensual sex, forced participation in criminal activities, etc., unless it is seen as an understanding that a Roma marriage constituted an agreement of the parents to sell a bride 'for all purposes'.[98]

In the last two cases, the dissenting judges claimed that the majority failed to take into account intersectional discrimination that Romani women are faced with. The dissenting opinions discussed in this section have been mostly written by women judges and raised suspicions as to why the judgments downplayed both racial and gender discrimination in these cases. They particularly highlighted a need for more expansive state obligations to protect the rights of Romani women.

## 3.6. Cases highlighting the future boundaries of human rights

A case that could be considered as widening the scope of application of human rights was *Hudorović and Others v Slovenia*.[99] It opened a question previously not examined by the Court: is access to clean drinking water and sanitation a human right under the ECHR? The case was specifically focused on two villages in Slovenia, but in fact portrayed the reality that many Roma face in Europe. While most citizens in Europe take drinking water and sanitation for granted, the *Hudorović* case showed that even in Europe there is not universal access to them. The case of Slovenia is particularly telling as access to water is safeguarded in the Constitution.[100] Despite contemplating that access to clean water and sanitation could be considered a human right, the ECtHR decided that Slovenia had not violated Article 8 and Article 14. Judge Pavli (joined by Judge Kūris) wrote a dissenting opinion in which they both argued that every human being needs water

[98] ibid, Dissenting Opinion of Judge Kalaydjieva.
[99] *Hudorovičand Others v Slovenia* App nos 24816/14 and 25140/14 (ECtHR, 10 March 2020).
[100] See Chapter 18 by Matiaško and Szilvasi in this volume.

to live, and also that the Roma are discriminated against because of unequal access to water: 'The finding of no violation by the majority in this novel and important case will contribute little, I fear, to alleviating the plight of inequality and disadvantage that many European Roma continue to face. "Separate but equal" access to water is, simply, not good enough.'[101] The dissenting opinions highlighted the role of structural racial discrimination as an underlying factor in the Roma's lack of access to drinking water. While the right to drinking water is not part of the ECHR, the dissenting opinions argued that the interpretation of Article 8 should be broadened to include it as a human right.

The case *Lăcătuş v Switzerland*[102] could be considered as another significant and future-oriented case, as it looked at how poverty and human rights violations fuel each other. The case concerns a young Romani women from Romania who was begging on the streets of Geneva as she had no other means of survival. Swiss domestic courts ruled that poverty is not a protected ground of discrimination, and that the applicant had not been targeted because she was a Roma. The ECtHR ruled that there had been a violation of Article 8, but it did not examine Articles 10 and 14. Judge Keller dissented because of Article 10 and Judge Lemmens and Judge Ravarani both dissented because Articles 10 and 14 had not been examined. The European Roma Rights Centre provided a third-party intervention, arguing that Swiss laws on begging were based on anti-Roma racism. Again, the dissenting opinions expressed dissatisfaction that the Court omitted the examination of structural racial (and poverty-based) discrimination to broaden the contextual scope in which human rights violation occur.

The two cases show possible future directions for pushing the boundaries of how we understand human rights.

## 4. By Way of Conclusion: Dissenting Opinions Pushing Human Rights Boundaries, Especially Regarding Structural Racial Discrimination

This section discusses what common patterns can be observed in dissenting opinions concerning Convention rights and principles. Starting with *Buckley*, the dissenting opinions on housing and the way of life initially highlighted vulnerability of Romani minorities and argued for a stricter margin of appreciation (*Buckley*) compounded by a broader scope of the actual Convention right and positive state obligations. While dissents in *Buckley* mentioned Article 14, it was not until dissents in *Winterstein* that the dissenting judges fully connected vulnerability and structural racial discrimination with positive state obligations. The

[101] Partly Dissenting Opinion of Judge Palvi joined by Judge Kūris in *Hudorovič and Others*.
[102] *Lăcătuş v Switzerland* App no 14065/15 (ECtHR, 19 January 2021).

dissenting opinion in *Bagdonavicius* argued that racial discrimination was the reason for forced evictions and the demolition of a Romani settlement.

In the cases of racist violence against Roma especially by the police the dissenting opinions have overwhelmingly argued that the Court had too readily refused to examine or find violations of Article 14, and with it avoided identifying structural racial discrimination as an underlying cause. Even when the Court became less reluctant to examine Article 14—especially after Bonello's dissent in *Anguelova*—the dissents in many cases noted reluctance from the Court to find substantive violations rather than only procedural ones. This could be observed especially, but not exclusively, in the cases of racially motivated violence against the Roma, as previously noted by Möschel. In *Aksu*, the dissenting judges initially highlighted positive state obligations and also argued for a narrower margin of appreciation in cases that consider racial discrimination.

Overall, dissenting opinions show that the judges are not unanimous when it comes to the question of racial prejudice infusing human rights violations against Roma. Interestingly, strong dissents were issued against the *DH* and *Oršuš* rulings of the Grand Chamber, in which the majority found racial or ethnic discrimination in education. In *DH* four judges dissented with unusually strong language, among them three judges from post-socialist states. Although these dissenting opinions could be seen as regressive, they justifiably question whether the Court has double-standards in how it treats countries in Western Europe in comparison to the post-socialist countries. In the dissenting opinion in *Oršuš* the judges argued that states should be given a wide margin of appreciations on how to address the disadvantages of Romani children in education.

A number of dissenting opinions in cases on multiple vulnerabilities and structural racial discrimination concerning social rights (right to water, protection against poverty) will show in the future whether the boundaries of human rights can be pushed even further. The cases where human rights violations against Romani women have been examined were the ones where women judges have dissented because they have found the Court insensitive to the multiple vulnerabilities that Romani women face. In cases on forced sterilization, the dissenting opinions also highlighted the Court's reluctance to discuss structural racial discrimination. The dissenting opinions in the two latest cases, *Hudorović* and *Lăcătuş*, have been particularly revolutionary when it comes to pushing the boundaries of human rights, being future oriented and arguing for the broadening of the examinable scope of Convention rights. The question remains whether in the future we might be able to witness the discussions about the effect of anti-Roma racism on the socio-economic human rights of Romani minorities in the Council of Europe region.

In conclusion, the chapter found that most dissenting opinions aim to push the boundaries of human rights in cases related to the rights of Roma, especially challenging the failure to recognize structural racism as a foundation of human rights violations against Roma. Dissents have also pushed the boundaries of human rights: (1) by flagging the context of structural racial discrimination and exploring its implications for the Court's reasoning; (2) by a broad interpretation of the scope of application of particular fundamental rights; (3) by identifying the vulnerability of the Roma and Travellers as a minority; (4) by (calling for) a restrictive approach to the margin of appreciation; and (5) by extensive reading of positive state obligation aimed at the effective protection of Romani rights.

The Court's reluctance to recognize systemic racism towards Roma as the basis of the human rights violations remains significant in the ECtHR's case law, which is not consistent when it comes to finding racial or ethnic discrimination against the Roma. This is also the key issue on which dissenting opinions sometimes pull the boundaries of human rights, when judges argue that the ECtHR has gone too far or become too political. Regardless of the direction of the dissents, it is a task for the relevant Council of Europe bodies to bring public attention to dissents and for future scholarship to trace the direct effect of these dissenting opinions on future judgment.

# 16

# Seeking Justice for Forcibly Sterilized Romani Women in Czechia and Slovakia

*Gwendolyn Albert, Eva-Esther Sobotka, and Lilla Farkas*

## 1. Introduction

This chapter focuses on the agency of Romani women in uncovering and strategically advocating/litigating against forced and coerced sterilization in the former Czechoslovakia and its successor states, Czechia and Slovakia.[1] It pays particular attention to their access to justice and adequate remedies. It connects the dots between the human rights framing of this practice towards the end of the 1970s, the human rights field research conducted after 1989, and the subsequent advocacy as well as litigation before European and national courts, finally assessing the policy change.

The chapter tells a chronological story of a difficult and lengthy road to justice, while also offering insight into the case law of the European Court of Human Rights (ECtHR), including its failure to recognize the structural nature of the violation and the discriminatory treatment of the Romani women. It discusses the opportunities and limitations of social change tools, such as research, advocacy, and litigation, and raises questions about how the boundaries of international human rights law are retracted through adjudication and policy-making at both the international and national levels. Following this introduction, in the global context of sterilization campaigns, section 2 recounts the Czechoslovak initiative to promote sterilization launched in the 1960s, which in the 1970s–80s was transformed into coerced and forced sterilization through financial incentives, intimidation, or existential threats. Section 3 summarizes human rights field research and advocacy efforts, first at the national, then at the international level. Section 4 investigates strategic litigation, focusing on the legal framing of forced sterilization and the subsequent jurisprudence, especially its shortcomings. Section 5 evaluates policy change and sheds light on interruptions in the trajectory of seeking justice and points out the shortcomings of the implementation of the Czech compensation scheme. Section 6 presents conclusions.

[1] To Vlasta H (in memoriam), Elena G, Iveta C, and all the women still fighting for redress, with deep respect.

Gwendolyn Albert, Eva-Esther Sobotka, and Lilla Farkas, *Seeking Justice for Forcibly Sterilized Romani Women in Czechia and Slovakia* In: *The Rights of Roma in European Courts*. Edited by: Kristin Henrard and Lilla Farkas, Oxford University Press. © Gwendolyn Albert, Eva-Esther Sobotka, and Lilla Farkas 2025.
DOI: 10.1093/oso/9780198914358.003.0016

## 2. Czechia and Slovakia within the Global Context of Forced Sterilization

Forced sterilization occurs when a person is sterilized after either expressly refusing the procedure, or is sterilized without her knowledge, or is never given an opportunity to provide consent. Coerced sterilization occurs when financial or other incentives, misinformation, or intimidation tactics are used to compel an individual to undergo the procedure.[2]

Forced sterilization has been a global phenomenon since the early twentieth century, prompted by ableism (fear of people being born with disabilities or of those living with disabilities reproducing), racism (fear of stigmatized ethnic groups reproducing, including indigenous people), and targeting the poor, the unhoused, the unmarried, women seeking abortion, HIV+ persons, intersex persons, persons struggling with substance abuse and mental illness, and transgender persons.[3] In some circumstances, men have also been targeted. Historically, the instrumentalization of the medical profession and, in many cases, of the social work profession to undertake coerced and forced sterilization has been prevalent worldwide under varied regimes or political settings.[4]

The scientific development of human contraceptive methods during the early twentieth century was, from its inception, intertwined with the eugenics movement's attempt to 'breed' human beings in order to eliminate undesirable traits and promote desirable ones.[5] Especially in the aftermath of the population losses sustained during the First World War, many European governments became concerned about repopulation and the 'quality' of their future citizens (and soldiers). At this time, some provinces in Canada and some states in the USA ran programmes that forcibly sterilized thousands of people selected through eugenic criteria, including indigenous people. After the Second World War, family planning accelerated even as eugenics fell out of favour after the Nazi genocide against the Jews and Roma in Europe (which also featured forced sterilizations), and advances in the understanding of heredity revealed how simplistic it was for certain traits to have once been considered genetically transmitted. However, the proscription on eugenic rhetoric did not change the idea that misery and poverty could be alleviated just by preventing the birth of more poor people, including in the Global South.

[2] Human Rights Watch, 'Sterilization of Women and Girls with Disabilities, a Briefing Paper,' 10 November 2011, <https://www.hrw.org/news/2011/11/10/sterilization-women-and-girls-disabilities> accessed 28 October 2024.

[3] Stephanie Hyatt, 'A Shared History of Shame: Sweden's Four-Decade Policy of Forced Sterilization and the Eugenics Movement in the United States' (1998) 8(2) Indiana Int Comp Law Rev 475.

[4] Gwendolyn Albert, 'Forced Sterilization of the Marginalized: A Global Issue' (Soft Spots 2022), <https://www.tranzit.org/en/publications/0/publication/soft-spots-mekka-mista> accessed 29 October 2024.

[5] Matthew Connelly, *Fatal Misconception* (Harvard University Press 2010)

The first eugenically motivated forced sterilizations were openly undertaken in the USA, and representatives of Nazi Germany drew from their example. The people initially targeted were allegedly 'mentally defective'. The first state to propose and adopt such legislation was Indiana in 1907.[6] The 1927 US Supreme Court decision *Buck v Bell* upheld the forced sterilization of intellectually disabled patients in Virginia.[7] As recently as 2020, illegal hysterectomies were performed in the state of Georgia on migrants detained in a particular US Immigration and Customs Enforcement (ICE) centre.[8]

In Europe, Sweden permitted forced sterilizations between 1934 and 1976. Compensation was paid to some victims in the 1990s, including some Romani women. Intellectually disabled people were sterilized in England and Wales during the twentieth century, and in Spain in the twenty-first century. Denmark has recently admitted to causing sterility in indigenous Inuit women by intra-uterine contraceptive devices in the 1960s.[9] Several European countries have provided special remedies for forced sterilization victims.[10]

Forced sterilization of women living with HIV has been reported from Brazil, Chile, Namibia, and South Africa, while the forced sterilization of women living with disabilities has been reported from Argentina, Australia, Kiribati, the Solomon Islands, and Tonga. In Uzbekistan, almost all women are automatically sterilized once they have a certain number of children by a certain age.[11] Forced sterilization also occurs in Latin America and Asia, the most notorious example being China.[12] In the Xinjiang Uyghur Autonomous Region, mass forced sterilization was reported in 2019 and 2020 as part of the genocide of Uyghurs.[13] The sterilization of Rohingya refugees from Myanmar is said to be underway in Bangladesh

[6] 1907 Indiana Eugenics Law, 377 <https://www.in.gov/history/state-historical-markers/find-a-marker/1907-indiana-eugenics-law/> accessed 28 October 2024.

[7] *Buck v Bell*, 274 US 200 (1926).

[8] Miranda Bryant, 'Allegations of Unwanted Ice Hysterectomies Recall Grim Time in US History' *The Guardian* (21 September 2020) <https://www.theguardian.com/us-news/2020/sep/21/unwanted-hysterectomy-allegations-ice-georgia-immigration> accessed 29 October 2024.

[9] '67 Greenlandic Inuit Women Seek Compensation from Denmark in Forced Contraception Scandal' *Nationalia* (11 October 2023) <https://www.nationalia.info/brief/11562/67-greenlandic-inuit-women-demand-compensation-from-denmark-in-forced-contraception-scanda#:~:text=The%20Danish%20state%20imposed%20an,intrauterine%20devices% 20(IUDs)%20inserted> accessed 29 October 2024.

[10] Dan Balz, 'Sweden Sterilized Dozens of "Useless" Citizens For Decades' *The Washington Post* (29 August 1997) <https://www.washingtonpost.com/archive/politics/1997/08/29/sweden-sterilized-thousands-of-useless-citizens-for-decades/3b9abaac-c2a6-4be9-9b77-a147f5dc841b/> accessed 29 October.

[11] ibid.

[12] Åse Johanne Roti Dahl, *Changing the Public Narrative: The Case of Forced Sterilizations in Peru* (Chr. Michelsen Institute 2019) <https://www.cmi.no/publications/6827-changing-the-public-narrative-the-case-of-forced-sterilizations-in-peru> accessed 18 October 2024.

[13] 'China cuts Uighur births with IUDs, abortion, sterilization' Associated Press (29 June 2020) <https://apnews.com/article/ap-top-news-international-news-weekend-reads-china-health-269b3de1af34e17c1941a514f78d764c> accessed 29 October 2024.

today.[14] India has long forcibly sterilized both men and women.[15] During the Gandhi regime, 6.2 million Indian men were forcibly sterilized in one year alone, with thousands dying from botched operations. Today, impoverished women in rural areas continue to be targeted: 4.6 million such women were forcibly sterilized in 2012.

Czechoslovakia and its successor states, therefore, are far from isolated examples when it comes to targeting the marginalized, especially racialized minorities, for sterilization. Paradoxically, however, forced sterilization there was initiated despite the fact that during the late 1960s, the communist authorities became increasingly concerned about their country's declining population rates, as were most communist governments in the Eastern bloc at the time. The fertility rate in Czechoslovakia fell from 2.20 between 1960–65 to 2.07 in 1968, according to UN data.[16] Government incentives—mainly cash payments and improved entitlements from the socialist state—caused the fertility rate to peak at 2.51 in 1977. At that very same time, however, the authorities believed the birth rate among the Czechoslovak Roma population was 'too high' compared to the general population. The stigma of Romani identity in Czechoslovak society played a large role in that belief and its policy consequences.

In 1969, the Czech and Slovak Socialist Republics became legislatively independent of each other. The Czech Socialist Republic adopted Directive No 01/1971 in order to regulate tubal ligation for what were called 'non-medical' (ie, contraceptive) or 'social' reasons.[17] Also in 1972, the Czechoslovak Federal Ministry of Labour and Social Affairs published a report titled 'Care for Socially Unadjusted Citizens'. Because 'material inequalities' had allegedly been eliminated by socialism and the country's population was reportedly ethnically 'homogenous', the report argued that any 'social pathology' remaining from the old capitalist regime was now only being spread by the 'culturally substandard'.[18] The communist authorities found themselves unable to explain the chronic deprivation still suffered by Romani communities into the 1970s as the result of their social inequality, which socialism was supposed to have eradicated, and so they sought another

[14] 'Bangladesh to Offer Sterilisation to Rohingya in Refugee Camps' *The Guardian* (28 October 2017) <https://www.theguardian.com/world/2017/oct/28/bangladesh-to-offer-sterilisation-to-rohingya-in-refugee-camps> accessed 29 October 2024.

[15] Ramya Jawahar Kudekallu, 'India's Forced Sterilization Practices Under International Human Rights Law' *Völkerrechtsblog* (10 March 2022).

[16] 'Partnership and Reproductive Behavior in Low-Fertility Countries', May 2003, Population Division, Department of Economic and Social Affairs, United Nations Secretariat, <https://www.un.org/en/development/desa/population/publications/pdf/fertility/reproduction.pdf>accessed 29 October 2024.

[17] Sp. zn.: 3099/2004/VOP/PM a násl., Závěrečné stanovisko veřejného ochránce práv ve věci sterilizací prováděných v rozporu s právem a návrhy opatření k nápravě, p 73. Veřejný ochránce práv, Brno, 23 December 2005.

[18] Vera Sokolova, *Cultural Politics of Ethnicity: Discourses on Roma in Communist Czechoslovakia* (ibidem-Verlag 2008) 224.

explanation: Romani 'culture' was to blame for their plight. For the government, Roma were therefore 'culturally substandard' or inferior, because communism could not be at fault.

In 1973, the provision of one-time grants for undergoing surgical sterilization was set forth in an internal act of the Czech Socialist Republic's Labour and Social Affairs Ministry.[19] Social workers proceeded to target Romani women (among other vulnerable groups such as persons living with disabilities) to encourage them to undergo this surgery, sometimes misleading them as to the reversibility of the procedure. This widespread practice is argued to have been a prime example of the impact of antigypsyism on the practice of medicine and social work in the former Czechoslovakia and its successor states.[20]

The issue caught the attention of the anti-communist dissidents of Charter 77, who released their twenty-third samizdat campaign document, 'On the Position of our Romani Fellow-Citizens', on 14 December 1978. They argued that consent from Romani women for sterilization was being obtained by 'suspicious' means. 'Czechoslovak institutions will soon have to answer charges that they are committing genocide', it stated.[21] In sum, during communism, not long after the party launched its forced sterilization initiative, dissidents had already framed the issue as a human rights violation.

However, the government did not budge. In fact, in 1979—

> the government upgraded its program of financial incentives for sterilization as a way 'to control the highly unhealthy Roma population through family planning and contraception'. Those incentives, combined with the provision of incomplete or misleading information about what sterilization even is, resulted in many Romani women undergoing these procedures without understanding that their fertility would be irreversibly curtailed by them.[22]

Class and racial criteria provided the broader context for these policies that 'extensively permeated' Czechoslovak socialist society, and were clearly 'driven by discriminatory attitudes against [Roma]', which continued into the twenty-first

[19] Claude Cahn, *Human Rights, State Sovereignty and Medical Ethics: Examining Struggles around Coercive Sterilisation of Romani Women* (Nijhoff 2014) 40.

[20] Gwendolyn Albert, 'Nucené sterilizace jako projev anticikanismu: Příklad Československa a České/Slovenské republiky' (2019) 26(2) Romano Džaniben 21 <1f510daf48bfdff5c370d51d0af59d82.pdf (dzaniben.cz)> accessed 29 October 2024.

[21] Sarah Marks, 'The Romani Minority, Coercive Sterilization, and Languages of Denial in the Czech Lands' (2017) 84 History Workshop Journal 128 <https://doi.org/10.1093/hwj/dbx033>; Final Statement of the Public Defender of Rights in the Matter of Sterilizations Performed in Contravention of the Law and Proposed Remedial Measures, 23 December 2005, <http://www.ochrance.cz/filead min/user_upload/ENGLISH/Sterilisation.pdf>, accessed 29 October 2024.

[22] Jan Rakosnik and R Sustrova, 'State Socialist Biopolitics' in B Klich-Klucewska and others (eds), *Biopolitics in Central and Eastern Europe in the 20th Century: Fearing for the Nation* (Routledge 2023) 197.

century.[23] Human rights field research in 2003–04 revealed that many of these women were misinformed by their physicians (after the fact) that their sterilizations had been 'lifesaving' and thus necessary.

## 3. Human Rights Field Research and Advocacy in Czechia and Slovakia

Charter 77 dissidents condemned the forced sterilization policies in 1978 as eugenic, racialized incentive programmes that were contrary to international human rights law.[24] However, the situation did not receive the full attention of the domestic and international human rights movements before the early years of the democratic transition following the fall of communism in 1989.[25] The issue first gained traction in domestic law and politics due to the efforts of the emerging human rights organizations (NGOs), as assessed in section 3.1. Shortly afterwards, it became an issue at the United Nations and later at the Council of Europe and European Union level, as described in section 3.2. Czechoslovakia had already been a member of the UN by the time of the political transition and therefore that advocacy forum had been accessible. The focus shifted to Europe later because the partition of Czechoslovakia somewhat stalled accession to the Council of Europe, while the EU only adopted fundamental rights norms and procedures in 2000, when the accession process for post-communist countries also accelerated.

### 3.1. Domestic advocacy efforts for recognition

Public authorities became the first port of call for victims and human rights activists after 1989. Non-governmental organizations (NGOs) also issued their own reports to make sense of the situation in a way that could boost their advocacy efforts aimed at recognition and redress at the national and international level. This subsection first lists investigations by public authorities spurred by advocacy, and

[23] Council of Europe Commissioner for Human Rights: 'Letter to the Prime Minister of the Slovak Republic and the Minister of Justice of the Slovak Republic', 12 July 2021, <https://rm.coe.int/letter-to-mr-eduard-heger-prime-minister-of-the-slovak-republic-and-ms/1680a332a3> accessed 29 October 2024; Gwendolyn Albert and Marek Szilvasi, 'Intersectional Discrimination of Romani Women Forcibly Sterilized in the Former Czechoslovakia and Czech Republic' (2017) 19(2) Health and Human Rights Journal 25.

[24] Public Defender of Rights (Ombudsman) of the Czech Republic, Final Statement of the Public Defender of Rights in the Matter of Sterilizations Performed in Contravention of the Law and Proposed Remedial Measures, Brno, 23 December 2005 <http://www.ochrance.cz/fileadmin/user_upload/ENGLISH/Sterilisation.pdf> accessed 29 October 2024.

[25] See the contributions to the special issue of Romano Džaniben (2019/2) dedicated to this history <https://www.dzaniben.cz/publication.html?m=002b666e42d85f921a8ee0ee4a290105&t=201902> accessed 29 October 2024.

second, independent NGO reporting based on field research, which was necessitated by the inadequacy of official investigations and responses.

### 3.1.1. Investigation by public bodies

In response to the advocacy efforts of emerging civil society organizations, the Czechoslovak General Prosecutor's Office launched an inquiry in 1990 to investigate the allegations that Romani women were being sterilized without their informed consent.[26] The incentivizing of sterilizations under communist rule had proceeded in Slovakia much as it had in the Czech lands,[27] but the impact is likely to have been much more extensive there, as the Romani population of Slovakia has always been much larger and their state of marginalization has always been much more intense.[28] In 1990, the Czech General Prosecutor's Office and the Slovak General Prosecutor's Office separately investigated on their territories and reported their results to the federal level.[29]

The Czech Prosecutor offered no legal opinion of its own, but merely conveyed the Czech Ministry of Health and Social Affairs' claim that the measures adopted in the 1970s had been 'pro-population', in that they aimed to promote the birth of '*healthy* children ... in such families as can provide them with everything for an overall *healthy bodily and mental development* and proper social inclusion'.[30] The Czech ministry also explicitly rejected the charge that the measures were intended to reduce the Romani population, claiming they had instead intended to 'influence giving birth to such numbers of children as the parents are capable of caring for and bringing up'.[31] The high amounts of benefits for sterilizations paid in Roma settlements were said by the Czech ministry to be due to the number of Romani families in destitution there.[32] The Czech ministry also rejected characterizing these benefits as 'incentives', claiming the choice of sterilization was 'entirely voluntary'; the latter has since proven to be a gross overstatement.[33]

It was not until 2005 that the Public Defender of Rights (the Ombudsperson) published a report on its own investigation into the allegations that Romani women had been and were still being illegally sterilized in the Czech Republic. That report found, inter alia, that from the 1970s until 1990, the Czechoslovak government had sterilized Romani women programmatically as part of policies aimed at reducing their allegedly high, unhealthy birth rate.[34] It also found that

[26] Public Defender of Rights (Ombudsman) of the Czech Republic (n 24) 28.
[27] Czechia and Slovakia became independent countries on 1 January 1993.
[28] Country Fiche, Slovakia, Roma Civil Monitor, https://cps.ceu.edu/sites/cps.ceu.edu/files/attachment/basicpage/3172/c1-slovakia.pdf>, accessed 29 October 2024
[29] Public Defender of Rights (Ombudsman) of the Czech Republic (n 24) 29.
[30] ibid (emphasis added).
[31] ibid 30.
[32] ibid.
[33] ibid.
[34] ibid 78.

sterilizations were performed illegally after 1993 in the Czech Republic and that forced sterilizations were carried out differently after the incentive programme stopped. The report also noted that even during the 1970s and 1980s, legal measures were in place for patients to provide informed consent to sterilization. The nature of the cases investigated by the Ombudsperson ranged from 'minor to very flagrant', but they were all breaches of law and therefore human rights violations nonetheless, and the Final Statement (unlike the previous investigation of the issue by the Czechoslovak State Prosecutor in the early 1990s) was the first official statement of this fact.

By contrast, in 1990 the General Prosecutor's Office of the Slovak Republic gave its own legal characterization of the benefits for sterilization as 'incorrect, and in contravention of the principles of social policy, the reason being that the legislator makes social assistance under the said provision conditional on performing a medical treatment that [prevents] further fertility of the person concerned'.[35] However, the Slovak prosecutor also disagreed that the disproportionate payment of such benefits to Romani women constituted an incentive targeting them on the basis of their ethnicity. The prosecutor did convey that the Slovak Ministry of Health and Social Affairs considered sterilization to be 'an important means of improving population quality, dealing with the undesirable birth rate of feeble-minded and otherwise mentally backward children'.[36] In summary, the public institutions investigating forced sterilization established the illegality of the practice and therefore a violation of fundamental human rights, but none admitted to the racially discriminatory or genocidal nature of the practice, nor did they prosecute the lawbreakers.

The Czech and Slovak prosecutors' different approaches characterize the distinct 'national' styles that would continue to prevail with regard to this issue in the following decades: silence at the international level followed by limited action at home on the Czech side and refusal to take responsibility followed by international condemnation on the Slovak side. In 1990, the Czech authorities stayed silent on the human rights issues, while the Slovak authorities admitted the facts but refused to accept responsibility. The Czech authorities used the seemingly neutral (but actually eugenically loaded) term 'healthy' to describe the aim of the benefits, while the Slovak authorities openly stated that preventing the birth of children with disabilities was in their view an unproblematic objective of the programme. Later, the Czech state would silently settle with an applicant in Strasbourg to avoid a judgment finding a violation, while the Slovak state would fight tooth and nail, which would result in the ECtHR establishing its liability.

Cross-border contact and collaboration, exchange of knowledge and ideas, and networking among advocates and ombudspersons proved useful for strengthening

[35] ibid 30.
[36] ibid 31.

advocacy efforts in Czechia. Here, the Slovak case was included in the 2005 'Final Statement' of the Czech Public Defender of Rights (the Ombudsperson) which reached very different conclusions to those produced by the extensive, rapid reaction of the authorities in Slovakia. The Czech Ombudsperson concluded that his review of the almost ninety cases occurring both before and after 1990 found that they involved the absence of fully free and informed consent in the 'human rights sense'. This directly contradicted the findings of the Czech Health Ministry, which viewed the procedures under review as having been unlawful in just a handful of cases. The Ombudsperson recommended the law be amended to institute greater safeguards, that the victims sterilized prior to 1990 be compensated by the state, and that those sterilized after the incentive programme was no longer in effect should sue in the civil courts.[37]

### 3.1.2. Field research by human rights NGOs

The first batch of information about forced sterilizations was disseminated by Charter 77 as mentioned above. Following the political transition, former political dissidents collaborated with the US-based Helsinki/Human Rights Watch on its first comprehensive report about the violations of Roma rights. Forced sterilizations featured as the second most important issue in the report *Struggling for Ethnic Identity: Czechoslovakia's Endangered Gypsies*, which for the first time presented the violation of Roma rights as a matter of racial or ethnic discrimination.[38] Subsequently, international NGOs published several reports about forced sterilization, predominantly presenting it as an issue of racial discrimination.

An important change in reporting occurred in 2003, when the Centre for Reproductive Rights (CRR), an international NGO fighting gender discrimination, in collaboration with the Slovak Centre for Civil and Human Rights (Poradňa) conducted the first post-1990 human rights field research and published the 'Body and Soul' report on forced sterilizations and other obstetric violence in Slovakia.[39] Given the CRR's primary focus, it reframed the issue as not just racial, but also or primarily as one of gender discrimination. While the CRR became involved on the initiative of domestic activists, its status as an INGO bolstered advocacy efforts and redirected them at the international level. As a result of the heightened attention generated by the report and the facts uncovered, a formal investigation was launched in the wake of the Slovak government's Human Rights and Minorities Section's criminal complaint against

[37] ibid 77–79.

[38] Rachel Tritt, *Struggling for Ethnic Identity: Czechoslovakia's Endangered Gypsies* (Helsinki Watch 1992) <czech928full.pdf> accessed 30 October 2024.

[39] Center for Reproductive Rights and Counselling Centre for Citizenship and Human Rights, *Body and Soul: Forced Sterilization and Other Assaults on Reproductive Freedom* (CRR 2003) <https://reproductiverights.org/body-and-soul-forced-sterilization-and-other-assaults-on-roma-reproductive-freedom/> accessed 29 October 2024.

an 'unidentified perpetrator' on suspicion of bodily harm.[40] The Košice Regional Police initiated prosecutions.[41] An expert inspection of the maternity wards implicated in the report was conducted and concluded there were no grounds to suspect genocide; while some administrative steps required by the directive on sterilization had not been followed, ethnicity was reportedly not a motivating factor in those errors.[42]

The authors of *Body and Soul* refused to disclose the identity of the women whom they had interviewed; therefore, the Slovak authorities appealed for Romani women to contact police if they believed they had been illegally sterilized. Dozens of health care personnel were interviewed, all of whom said they believed the sterilizations at issue had been conducted lawfully.[43] The Slovak Health Minister also extensively criticized the authors of *Body and Soul* for not sharing information with investigators and speculated that the report would negatively affect Slovakia's upcoming EU accession.[44] The authors responded with a critique of the criminal investigation as inconsistent with the rule of law and respect for victims' rights.[45] A criminal complaint was filed against the authors, which they said constituted harassment and intimidation.[46]

Ultimately, despite the ministry in Slovakia finding no violations of law, its Central Ethics Commission drafted legislation to raise the minimum age for sterilization to twenty-five years; reduce medical personnel's role in decision-making about sterilizations; require application forms for sterilization to clearly explain the implications of such surgery; discontinue the definition of a 'medical indication' for sterilization, clarifying that it is not the kind of surgery to undertake in response to a 'life-threatening situation'; and ended coverage for sterilizations under public health insurance.[47]

Given that the CRR was based in New York and published an English version of the report there, in 2005 the Slovak government closed its inquiry and issued a statement to the effect that, inter alia, the *Body and Soul* report had been published 'abroad' without informing the Slovak authorities in advance of its findings. The government considered this 'unacceptable', and reiterated that the revision of healthcare legislation to bring it in line with EU law and Slovakia's international commitments had begun.[48] The Health Minister was tasked with ensuring—

40 Joint NGO Statement on the Issue of Illegal Sterilization of Romani Women in Slovakia' (Human Rights Watch, 21 July 2003) <https://www.hrw.org/news/2003/07/21/joint-ngo-statement-issue-illegal-sterilization-romani-women-slovakia> accessed 29 October 2024.

41 Public Defender of Rights (Ombudsman) of the Czech Republic (n 24) 38.

42 ibid.

43 ibid.

44 ibid 39.

45 ibid.

46 ibid 40.

47 ibid 41.

48 ibid.

> treatment respecting the rights of patients, the adoption of legal provisions concerning the right to equal access to healthcare including a prohibition of both direct and indirect racial segregation, all other forms of racial discrimination including verbal and physical abuse in medical facilities as well as of effective sanctions against individuals and facilities.[49]

### 3.2. International human rights advocacy for recognition and redress

International advocacy unfolded roughly a decade after the decisions of the Czech and Slovak prosecutors' offices were released in 1990. It was undertaken primarily within the framework of the UN and the Council of Europe and involved monitoring and specialized bodies, such as the Office of the Commissioner for Human Rights (OCHR), the European Commission against Racism and Intolerance (ECRI), the Advisory Committee of the Framework Convention on the Rights of National Minorities (FCNM AC), as well as the Contact Point for Roma and Sinti at the Organization for Security and Cooperation in Europe (OSCE-ODIHR).

Advocacy first targeted the UN. Elena Gorolová, a forced sterilization survivor who was informally elected as the spokesperson for the Romani women who had come together in Ostrava (Czechia) to complain to the Ombudsperson in 2004, gave a detailed record of her experience and began advocating for compensation for all victims. After the *Body and Soul* report reframed forced sterilizations as a violation of women's reproductive rights and brought renewed attention to the victims, joined by Gwendolyn Albert, she took the Ombudsperson's 2005 recommendations regarding redress to the UN Committee for the Elimination of Discrimination against Women (CEDAW) in 2006.[50] During that intervention, Romani women were protesting outside of the hospital in Ostrava where many of them had been sterilized without their informed consent. This marked the first of many such advocacy efforts conducted both nationally and at international human rights venues.[51] The Committee reinforced the voice of the Romani women in its communication with the Czech government.

In 2014, six agencies of the United Nations, led by the Office of the High Commissioner for Human Rights, issued their interagency statement addressed to all interested parties on 'Eliminating forced, coercive and otherwise involuntary

[49] ibid 42.

[50] UN Committee on the Elimination of Discrimination Against Women (CEDAW 25 August 2006) Concluding Comments, Czech Republic <https://www.refworld.org/policy/polrec/cedaw/2006/en/35483> accessed 29 October 2024.

[51] 'We have succeeded by speaking out' (Amnesty International 21 March 2013) <https://www.amnesty.org/en/latest/campaigns/2013/03/we-have-succeeded-by-speaking-out/> accessed 29 October 2024.

sterilization'. The Czechoslovak, Czech and Slovak sterilizations of Romani women were specifically referenced there.[52]

Different human rights monitoring bodies of the Council of Europe have devoted systematic attention to this subject since 2006. Responding to input from civil society and human rights defenders, the Council of Europe's Commissioner for Human Rights has periodically urged both Czechia and Slovakia to compensate the victims of these abuses and institute measures to prevent their recurrence.[53] In 2011, the European Commission Against Racism and Intolerance (ECRI) called for policies which would specifically prohibit the forced sterilization of Roma.[54]

Since 2015, the FCNM AC has repeatedly addressed forced sterilization in several opinions on Czechia and Slovakia, finding that Romani women suffer discrimination in reproductive and maternal healthcare and that nothing had been done yet to compensate those who have undergone forced sterilization.[55] The FCNM AC noted in 2016 that positive steps had been taken by the Norwegian government since its Third Opinion in 2011, taking responsibility for the past policy of assimilation towards the Tater/Romani minority.[56] This important turning point in Norwegian policy and the role played by the international human rights monitoring mechanism was beneficial to the further advocacy efforts in Czechia. Through a meeting organized by the Contact Point for Roma and Sinti Issues of the OSCE/ODIHR in 2016 in Prague, Romani survivors of forced sterilization, activists, and representatives of the Czech authorities learned about the Norwegian example, including the compensation mechanism.[57]

A bill on compensation for illegally sterilized persons had been pending in the Czech Chamber of Deputies since 2019. In 2021, the FCNM AC stated that the forced sterilization of Roma women for over four decades in Czechia,[58] and the

52 OHCHR and others, *Eliminating Forced, Coercive and Otherwise Involuntary Sterilization. An Interagency Statement* (2014) <https://www.unaids.org/sites/default/files/media_asset/201405_sterilization_en.pdf> accessed 29 October 2024.

53 Commissioner for Human Rights of the Council of Europe (2023) <https://rm.coe.int/report-on-czech-republic-by-dunja-mijatovic-commissioner-for-human-rig/1680ac88cd> accessed 29 October 2024.

54 ECRI, General Policy Recommendation No 13 On Combating Anti-Gypsyism and Discrimination against the Roma <16808b5aee> accessed 29 October 2024.

55 Advisory Committee on the Framework Convention for the Protection of National Minorities, Fifth Opinion on the Slovak Republic, 2 February 2022 <https://rm.coe.int/5th-op-slovak-republic-en/1680a6e4ee> accessed 29 October 2024; FCNM AC, Fifth Opinion on the Czech Republic, 31 May 2021 <https://rm.coe.int/5th-op-czech-republic-en-restricted/1680a2b3d6> accessed 29 October 2024; FCNM AC, Fourth Opinion on Sweden, 22 June 2017 <https://rm.coe.int/fourth-opinion-on-sweden-adopted-on-22-june-2017/168075fbab> accessed 29 October 2024; FCNM AC, Fourth Opinion on Norway, 13 October 2016 <https://rm.coe.int/168070741d> accessed 29 October 2024.

56 FCNM AC, Fourth Opinion on Norway, 13 October 2016 <https://rm.coe.int/168070741d> accessed 29 October 2024.

57 Justice and Reparations for Victims in the Czech Republic (OSCE/ODIHR Contact Point for Roma and Sinti Issues, 1 June 2016) <https://www.osce.org/files/f/documents/3/b/288606.pdf> accessed 29 October 2024.

58 FCNM AC, Fifth Opinion on the Czech Republic, 31 May 2021 https://rm.coe.int/5th-op-czech-republic-en-restricted/1680a2b3d6 accessed 29 October 2024.

issue of their compensation, had been a matter of deep concern for over a decade.[59] It noted with regret that the new draft legislation on compensating Roma women who were victims of forced sterilization had so far not been considered by the Czech parliament. The law was adopted in 2021 and provided one-time compensation to women who were the victims of forced sterilization in the period from 1 July 1966 to 31 March 2012.[60] In 2022, the FCNM AC also recommended to Slovakia that a joint Working Group of the ministries of justice and of health of the two countries should be established to 'explore a response to possible sterilizations, especially in the communist past'.[61]

The fight against forced sterilization also fed into standard-setting at the European level. The Convention for the Protection of Human Rights and Dignity of the Human Being with regard to the Application of Biology and Medicine was opened for signature by the member states of the Council of Europe in 1997. The Convention on Preventing and Combating Violence against Women and Domestic Violence (CETS No 210), the Istanbul Convention, was opened for signature in 2011 and entered into force in 2014. Forced sterilization is specifically criminalized in this treaty, which was also ratified by the European Union in 2023 and now indirectly, in matters under Union competence applies in both Czechia and Slovakia despite the fact that neither country ratified it on their own.

## 4. Strategic Litigation

Forced sterilization has also been challenged in the framework of strategic litigation and bolstered advocacy efforts while also delivering justice to Roma women. Section 4.1 looks at the difficulties of framing forced sterilization under international human rights law and section 4.2 briefly assesses the relevant jurisprudence.

### 4.1. Legal framing

Claude Cahn provides an in-depth study of 'how the harm of coercive sterilisation of [Roma] women has been articulated in human rights law', which serves as the basis of the analysis here, highlighting the difficulty of making a case under

[59] ibid.

[60] Zákon č. 297/2021 Sb., Zákon o poskytnutí jednorázové peněžní částky osobám sterilizovaným v rozporu s právem a o změně některých souvisejících zákonů <https://www.zakonyprolidi.cz/cs/2021-297#:~:text=Z%C3%A1kon%20%C4%8D.,a%20o%20zm%C4%9Bn%C4%9B%20n%C4%9Bkter%C3%BDch%20souvisej%C3%ADc%C3%ADch%20z%C3%A1kon%C5%AF> accessed 29 October 2024.

[61] FCNM AC, Fifth Opinion on the Slovak Republic, 2 February 2022, <https://rm.coe.int/5th-op-slovak-republic-en/1680a6e4ee> accessed 29 October 2024.

international human rights law.[62] It seems that what Cahn identifies as 'contested' articulations of harm do in fact amount to diverse political, and more importantly, legal framings of the coercive sterilization of Roma women.[63] The legal framings include what Cahn identifies roughly as: (1) genocide; (2) women's rights, including the prohibition of violence against women and reproductive rights; (3) free and informed consent as an element of the right to health; and (4) the violation of civil and political rights. The latter frame can be utilized under the ECHR in relation to degrading treatment under Article 3, the right to private and family life under Article 8, the right to marry and found a family under Article 12, and the right to an effective remedy under Article 13.

Racial discrimination is an overarching concern that permeates each and every potential framing of coercive sterilization, while also providing a viable argument in and of itself. The fact that it has been vehemently contested by both states is a testament to its salience in the eyes of Roma women victims and the context of human rights advocacy. Gender discrimination functions in an analogous manner, especially if the emphasis is on the sex of the direct victims of forced sterilization and their agency in strategic litigation. There is a difference between simple legal framing—such as civil rights—and the use of master frames, such as racial and/or gender discrimination, which dominate explanations of and arguments about forced sterilizations. Once the victims of human rights violations are identified as a racialized group, such as the Roma, and if the violation stems from their racialization, activists rightly employ the racial discrimination master frame under Article 14 ECHR or similar provisions of international human rights law. The same applies to gender discrimination once the victims are identified as women.

What happens when the victims are both Roma and women? In Chapter 12 of this volume, D'Agostino and Magazzini problematize the framing of forced sterilization as specifically targeting Roma women and posit that the most adequate framing is intersectional rather than just racial or just gender discrimination, because the intersectional frame addresses both the racialized and gendered nature of the wrongdoing, and highlights its systemic nature. The advocacy efforts presented in this chapter show that activists initially used only the racial discrimination master frame, while the Centre for Reproductive Rights and, in its wake, mainly (Roma) women activists specifically promoted the gender equality master frame. The benefit of the intersectional framing is that it creates a bridge between the anti-racist/Roma and women's movements and doubles the advocacy efforts against the forced sterilization of Roma women. It also fully captures the identity of the victims, which is why Gorolová, who testified before the CEDAW Committee, naturally adopted this framing. This is in line with Crenshaw's thesis about the

[62] Cahn (n 19) 149.

[63] Emilio Lehoucq and Whitney K Taylor, 'Conceptualizing Legal Mobilization: How Should We Understand the Deployment of Legal Strategies?' (2020) 45 Law & Social Inquiry 166, 184.

strength of intersectional mobilization and the central role that racialized women should/do play in it.[64] Its legal relevance is that it magnifies the harm suffered, as visible from *AS v Hungary*, a decision discussed below.[65]

Below the surface, however, questions remain on whether the forced sterilization of Roma women is a gender + or a race + issue, in the sense of one ground playing a more significant role, or whether both protected grounds play an equally significant role. Different intersectional framings recognize the victimhood of different groups to different degrees. In the first case, Roma women are targeted and the impact on the community is less relevant.[66] In the second case, the group targeted by racial discrimination is the whole Roma community, whereas Roma women suffer a particular harm.[67] In the third case, the severity of the harm inflicted on both Roma men and women is seen as roughly equal.

Puzzles about the cause and the severity of the harm are not limited to the different axes of discrimination. Cahn notices a difference in the severity of the harm inherent in the diverse legal framings, finding genocide to be the most severe.[68] He recalls that this frame did not gain traction in either law or politics because of its 'intolerability'. In other words, the public discourse rejected the claim that forced sterilization amounted to genocide, even though it did qualify as one of its less brutal forms, namely 'intended to prevent births within the group'.[69]

The rejection of (or intolerance toward) the claim of genocide is not specific to the Roma because it stems from a structural issue, namely the 'European silence about race' that following the Holocaust has generally perceived the Old Continent as inherently anti-racist, a point so eloquently made by Judge Bonello in his dissent in *Anguelova*.[70] It is important to recall that the denial of genocide also rejects the original framing of forced sterilization by the Czechoslovak dissident movement, which was the first to frame the issue in human rights terms, using both the genocide and informed consent frames as discussed above in relation to Charter 77.

Rubio-Marin and Möschel explain the failure to use the genocide frame by pointing to the so-called Holocaust prism.[71] They posit that in Europe, including in the ECtHR, the Holocaust is considered the ultimate evil. If a harm is not akin or

[64] Kimberlé Crenshaw, 'Demarginalizing the Intersection of Race and Sex: A Black Feminist Critique of Antidiscrimination Doctrine, Feminist Theory and Antiracist Politics' [1989] U Chi Legal F.

[65] *AS v Hungary* Communication No 4/2004 (CEDAW/C/36/D/4/2004).

[66] Kristina Koldinská, 'EU Non-Discrimination Law and Policies in Reaction to Intersectional Discrimination Against Roma Women in Central and Eastern Europe' in Dagmar Schiek and Anna Lawson (eds), *European Union Non-Discrimination Law and Intersectionality* (Routledge 2016).

[67] Angela Kóczé and Raluca Maria Popa, *Missing Intersectionality: Race/Ethnicity, Gender, and Class in Current Research and Policies on Romani Women in Europe* (CEU Press 2009).

[68] Cahn (n 19) 150.

[69] United Nations, Convention on the Prevention and Punishment of the Crime of Genocide (adopted on 9 December 1948, entered into force 12 January 1951) 78 UNTS 277, Art II d).

[70] *Anguelova v Bulgaria* App no 38361/97 (ECHR, 13 June 2002), Partly Dissenting Opinion of Judge Bonello, para. 2.

[71] Ruth Rubio-Marín and Mathias Möschel, 'Anti-Discrimination Exceptionalism: Racist Violence Before the ECtHR and the Holocaust Prism' (2015) 26(4) European Journal of International Law 881.

at least analogous to that caused by the Holocaust, its severity is perceived as lower, which applies to the forced sterilization of Roma women, too. Indeed, one could cynically argue that the known number of sterilized Roma women is much below the number of Roma lives lost when the Nazis exterminated approximately 90 per cent of the Czech Roma population, which in turn is much lower than the number of Jewish lives taken during the Holocaust.[72] The question still remains: how many lives must be taken or abused to put an end to the 'European silence about race'?

Intent rather than the result is at issue when it comes to the qualification of the wrongdoing as genocide, which is particularly difficult to establish in a Europe that prides itself on being free of intentional racism. As to the result, the wrongdoing is massive, because even though the Roma community constituted less than 2 per cent of the entire population, Roma women accounted for 36 per cent of all sterilizations carried out between 1972 and the 1990s.[73] The discriminatory practice was institutionalized because the communist government adopted legislation in the run-up to a robust sterilization campaign and local administrations as well as healthcare workers specifically targeted the Roma women under their 'authority'.[74] In order to justify this racial targeting, the Czechoslovak Federal Ministry of Labour and Social Affairs demonized the Roma as 'socially pathological' in the 1972 publication *Care for Socially Unadjusted Citizens*.[75] Forced sterilization was not simply an institutional practice; the underlying cultural norms and widespread stigmatization reveal structural discrimination, an issue with which litigators must grapple.

## 4.2. Jurisprudence and its shortcomings: recognition and redress

The following is a list of the court cases brought by Romani plaintiffs in these matters in Central Europe and an examination of their ramifications.

Even though the practice of forced sterilization was, as far as is known, most robust in Czechoslovakia and its successor states, the first successful challenge to it under international human rights law was made in Hungary, following a lengthy and unsuccessful civil procedure seeking compensation for forced sterilization. *AS v Hungary* was brought to the CEDAW Committee under the Optional Protocol by the Legal Defence Bureau for National and Ethnic Minorities in collaboration with

[72] Helena Sadílková and Milada Závodská, 'Asserting a Presence in the Public Sphere: Autobiographies by Two Romani Holocaust Survivors in Communist Czechoslovakia' in Celia Donert and Eve Rosenhaft (eds), *The Legacies of the Romani Genocide in Europe since 1945* (Routledge 2021) 185.

[73] Vera Sokolova, *Cultural Politics of Ethnicity: Discourses on Roma in Communist Czechoslovakia* (ibidem-Verlag 2008)

[74] Sadilkova (n 72).

[75] Albert and Szilvasi (n 23).

the European Roma Rights Centre (ERRC). This 2006 decision had a direct and significant impact on advocacy because it marked the first time an international human rights body held a state accountable for failing to provide the necessary information to a woman to enable her to give informed consent to a reproductive health-related medical procedure.[76] It also stipulated that women have a right to make autonomous, informed decisions about their reproductive health and that states are responsible for providing the information and advice that will enable women to make such informed decisions.

Ms AS, a Hungarian Roma woman, was twenty-seven and a mother of three when she was sterilized without her informed consent.[77] The Committee found three violations of CEDAW in this case. First, a violation of Article 10(h), requiring States Parties to provide 'access to specific educational information to help to ensure the health and well-being of families, including information and advice on family planning' was established, taking note of the stressful, inappropriate conditions under which AS was given information about the sterilization procedure.[78] Secondly, the Committee concluded to a violation of Article 12, on women's right to equality in the field of health care because of her lack of informed consent to the sterilization.[79] Thirdly, the Committee held that Article 16(e) on equality in the family, was violated because this requires that women have the same rights as men to decide freely and responsibly on the number and spacing of their children and to have access to the information, education, and means to enable them to exercise those rights.[80] The Committee also referred to General Recommendation No 19 on violence against women, where compulsory sterilization is identified as having an adverse effect on women's physical and mental health.[81]

This decision is particularly important because it affirms that the right to health includes the right to information about health, and that health-related information is critical to the enjoyment of the rights to life, to autonomy in decision making, and to all the other reproductive rights of women and girls. The Committee also called on Hungary to amend its legislation, compensate the applicant and to take comprehensive measures to ensure that all medical staff are trained on the UN standards, including those issued by the World Health Organization, and to monitor health centres which carry out sterilizations. Importantly, the CEDAW Committee made no findings about racial or intersectional discrimination, because these issues had not been raised by the applicant.

In 2005, a Czech court ruled that Helena Ferenčiková, a Roma plaintiff, had been sterilized in 2001 without her informed consent, ordering the hospital to

[76] *AS* (n 65) para 11.1–11.6.
[77] ibid.
[78] ibid para 11.2.
[79] ibid para 11.3.
[80] ibid para 11.4.
[81] ibid.

apologize in writing, but not awarding damages. Both sides appealed, the verdict was upheld, and the hospital apologized in 2007. Ferenčiková appealed for compensation and the ECtHR declared her case admissible in 2010. She settled in 2011; the Czech government informed the ECtHR it would pay her €10,000 to cover court costs and damages.[82] In 2007, a Czech court awarded €18,200 in damages to Iveta Červeňáková, who had been forcibly sterilized but not informed of that fact at the time; she did not come to understand the kind of procedure that had been performed on her and its implications for her reproductive future until seven years after the operation.[83] That ruling was overturned; she was told the statute of limitations applied from the time she had been sterilized, not the time she had become aware of her sterilization. The hospital was instructed to apologize. In 2011, the Supreme Court upheld the original ruling and returned the case to the High Court. It was declared admissible before the ECtHR in 2012 but was not pursued; she later settled with the hospital for €20,340 in damages and €2,457 for court costs.

The case of *RK v the Czech Republic* also ended with a friendly settlement in November 2012 after four years pending before the ECtHR. First and second-instance rulings had established the rights violation and ordered financial compensation.[84] The parties agreed to a financial award of €10,000. The government admitted the case had been an 'exceptional' failure by the state but denied any systemic practice. As mentioned above, the Czech state's openness to friendly settlements prevented strategic litigation from securing a string of judgments from the ECtHR on forced sterilization.

In Slovakia, the Counselling Centre for Civil and Human Rights went on to litigate forced sterilization after the publication of the *Body and Soul* report; because of the highly dismissive attitude of the Slovak state, these cases reached judgment in the ECtHR. These judgments are all framed around the civil rights listed by Cahn and protected under the ECHR. Importantly, in cases putting forward such claims the Strasbourg Court established violations of Article 3 on account of the severity of inhuman treatment inherent in forced sterilization and also of Article 8 on account of the violation of private and family life. In this regard, the ECtHR noted that Slovakia had failed to comply with its positive obligation under Article 8 to sufficiently protect the applicant from the wrongdoing, an issue discussed below.

The first such case, *KH and Others v Slovakia*, was decided on 28 April 2009.[85] Eight women of Roma origin found themselves unable to conceive after C-sections were performed on them; the case did not concern the surgery itself, but access to their medical records by the patients and their legal representatives. The Court

[82] *Ferenčíková v the Czech Republic* App no 21826/10 (ECtHR, 30 August 2011).

[83] 'Hospital ordered to compensate Romani woman for sterilisation' (Radio Prague International, 10 December 2007) <https://english.radio.cz/hospital-ordered-compensate-romany-woman-sterilisation-8460867> accessed 29 October 2024

[84] *RK v the Czech Republic* App no 7883/08 (ECtHR, 27 November 2012).

[85] *KH and Others v Slovakia* App no 32881/04 (ECtHR, 28 April 2009).

ruled that there had been a failure to fulfil the positive obligation to ensure effective respect for the applicants' private and family lives in breach of Article 8. The Court also established a violation of Article 6(1) (right to a fair trial), even though the victims never complained to a national court, agreeing with their argument that the lack of access to their medical records rendered an approach to the national courts moot.[86]

Despite the fact that three more cases were brought by Romani women complaining of forced sterilization, all of which were decided against Slovakia—*VC v Slovakia*,[87] *NB v Slovakia*[88] and *IG and others v Slovakia*[89]—none of the judgments found it necessary to examine whether ethnic discrimination had occurred, nor examined intersectional discrimination, which was not raised by the complainants.[90] The Court's approach to these cases was as follows: in *VC*, the Court unanimously held that Article 3 had been substantively violated because of how the sterilization was handled. A violation of Article 8 was also found, but Articles 12, 13, and 14 were not found to have been violated. The Strasbourg Court noted that the materials indicated that the practice 'affected vulnerable individuals from various ethnic backgrounds' but that they were insufficient to establish the doctors' liability or that the wrongdoing was 'part of an organised policy' which was 'intentionally racially motivated'.[91] The ECtHR's strict approach, which required the establishment of intent even under Article 8 taken in conjunction with Article 14 resulted in its failure to establish direct systemic racial discrimination but it did not stop the Court from recognizing that the legislative and practical 'shortcomings were liable to particularly affect members of the Roma community, who were severely disadvantaged in most areas of life'.[92] The problem with this approach is that it fails to recognize the difference between direct and indirect discrimination, and that even in the case of direct discrimination it places the bar too high, requiring direct intent for establishing discrimination based on race as concerns the right to private and family life. This undifferentiated view blurs the lines between Article 3 and Article 8 on the one hand and organized policy or structural discrimination on the other, even though the latter may occur when intent is missing.

86 Cahn (n 19) 58–59.

87 *VC v Slovakia* App no 18968/07 (ECtHR, 8 November 2011).

88 *NB v Slovakia* App no 29518/10 (ECtHR, 12 June 2012).

89 *IG and Others v Slovakia* App no 15966/04 (ECtHR,13 November 2012).

90 Judit Gellér, 'Coercive Sterilisation of Romani Women: Inhuman and Degrading Treatment But Not Discrimination According to the ECHR' (ERRC 25 November 2011) <http://www.errc.org/blog/coercive-sterilisation-of-romani-women-inhuman-and-degrading-treatment-but-not-discrimination-according-to-the-echr/39> accessed 29 October 2024; Judit Gellér, Adam Weiss, and Bernard Rorke, 'Strasbourg Delivers a Blow to Reproductive Rights, Women Rights, and Roma Rights in One Go' *Rightsviews* (22 March 2016) http://blogs.cuit.columbia.edu/rightsviews/2016/03/22/strasbourg-delivers-a-blow-to-reproductive-rights-womens-rights-and-roma-rights-in-one-go/ accessed 29 October 2024.

91 *VC* (n 86) para 177.

92 ibid para 178.

The ECtHR remedied these flaws in the analysis and argument somewhat by finding that Slovakia—

> failed to comply with its positive obligation under Article 8 of the Convention to secure to the applicant a sufficient measure of protection enabling her, as a member of the vulnerable Roma community, to effectively enjoy her right to respect for her private and family life in the context of her sterilisation.[93]

Curiously, this finding was made in relation to Article 14 and the Strasbourg Court seemed to require protection by the state even in the case of unintentional or indirect discrimination. This argument seems inconsistent with finding no discrimination in the context of Article 8 and the conclusion that because this issue had been deliberated elsewhere, it is not necessary to separately examine the claim of racial discrimination under Article 14.[94] If this is the case, the judgment contains no argument as to why Slovakia should protect the applicant in view of her being an ethnic Roma. *VC* seems to have become the template for subsequent rulings, such as *NB* and *IG*.[95]

Given that both the Czech and Slovak domestic courts initially dismissed lawsuits seeking compensation, forced sterilization was brought before the European Court of Human Rights. Inspired by monitoring bodies' reports, the ECtHR noted racially disproportionate trends but did not go as far as to establish structural discrimination. All of the Czech cases brought to Strasbourg have been settled out of court.[96] The question arises as to whether the strategy involved in bringing them was not simply to achieve friendly compensation awards; indeed, the NGO behind much of this litigation ran a project called 'Fair Hospital' that explicitly publicized itself as endeavouring to achieve out-of-court settlements of healthcare disputes.[97] Recently, domestic courts have also awarded compensation in forced sterilization cases, which put an end to litigation in Strasbourg.[98] Neither the domestic courts nor the ECtHR establish discrimination as a factor in these sterilization procedures, although the latter does engage with this claim to a certain degree.[99] Importantly, the applicants have not so far framed their claims as intersectional discrimination, nor have courts introduced this framing on their own accord.

[93] ibid para 179.
[94] ibid para 180.
[95] Cahn (n 19) 167.
[96] Albert (n 20).
[97] Sarah Borufka, Court confirms – and increases - historic first compensation for sterilization victims, Radio Prague International, 1 August 2010, available at <https://english.radio.cz/court-confirms-and-increases-historic-first-compensation-sterilization-victims-8577665>, accessed 18 March 2025.
[98] Poradňa pre občianske a ľudské práva [Counselling Centre for Citizenship and Human Rights], 'Our NGO calls on the Slovak Parliament to Address the Shortcomings of the Currently Negotiated Draft Law on Compensation for Illegally Sterilized Women' (20 June 2023) <https://www.poradna-prava.sk/en/news/the-slovak-court-awards-compensation-to-another-forcibly-sterilised-roma-woman/> accessed 18 March 2025.
[99] Gellér and others (n 90).

## 5. Policy Change and its Shortcomings

This section describes how law and policy have changed since the advocacy started. Developments will be briefly summarized and then assessed in terms of their shortcomings in terms of effective remedy.

Bolstered by its strategic litigation victories, the Counselling Centre for Citizenship and Human Rights (Poradňa) in Slovakia has recommended that the Slovak authorities adopt a law on compensation including the rebuttable presumption of the illegality of all sterilizations, in order to reverse the burden of proof from the applicants to the state. The decision-making body involved can prove otherwise, thus rebutting the presumption. This was proposed because many women may not have access to the medical records concerning sterilization, given the considerable amount of time that may have passed since the procedure was performed. Poradňa also recommended that the timeframe for applying for financial compensation be set at five years as opposed to the proposed two years, because most applicants come from marginalized communities with scarce access to information and because the two-year timeframe is less than the three-year statute of limitations on bringing a lawsuit.[100]

In Czechia, the option to sue for compensation in civil court was made impossible for the vast majority of the women who had been unlawfully sterilized when, in 2008, the Czech judiciary issued a finding that a three-year statute of limitations applies to a plaintiff's eligibility to sue in civil court for compensation concerning the violation of personality rights.[101] The vast majority of forced sterilizations had not occurred within the last three years, leaving the victims no avenue of redress. The amount of compensation awarded had been increasing for those victims who managed to bring their suits; for instance in 2012, two women were given awards by the High Court in Prague, in a CZK 200,000 (€8,000) award correcting a lower-instance judgment awarding just CZK 50,000 (€2,000), and another award of CZK 150,000 (€6,000), doubling the amount awarded by the lower court. Another Romani woman was awarded CZK 500,000 (€20,000) by the regional court in Ostrava.[102]

In 2009, the Czech government followed the Ombudsperson's lead and issued an expression of 'regret' over forced sterilizations. As the Czech Government

[100] Comments by the Slovak National Centre for Human Rights to LP/2023/64 Legislative intent of the law on financial compensation for women sterilized in violation of the law, 5 June 2023, available at <Pripomienky-MVO-Poradna-pre-obcianske-a-ludske-prava-na-doplnenie-navrhu-zakona-o-jednorazovom-financnom-odskodneni-osob-sterilizovanych-v-rozpore-s-pravom.pdf>, accessed 18 March 2025.

[101] Czech Helsinki Committee, 'Návrh věcného záměru a paragrafového znění zákona o odškodnění osob sterilizovaných v rozporu s právem na území České republiky' (2013) <http://www.helcom.cz/dokumenty/chv/sterilizace/Navrh_zakona_v_rozporu.pdf> accessed 26 July 2023.

[102] 'Hospital Ordered to Compensate Romany Woman for Sterilisation' *Radio Prague International* (10 December 2007) <https://english.radio.cz/hospital-ordered-compensate-romany-woman-sterilisation-8460867> accessed 18 March 2025.

Human Rights Commissioner emphasized at the time, the statement was worded in such a way as to communicate that the wrongs were 'individual' (in other words, isolated) cases, downplaying their systemic nature.[103]

In November 2011 the Czech parliament adopted a new Act on Specific Medical Services, which entered into force in April 2012 and included control mechanisms with regard to consent that are more strict.[104] Procedures must ensure that the medical personnel provide detailed information to the person requesting sterilization about what it entails and its irreversibility; a waiting period of anywhere between seven and fourteen days before the surgery was required, depending on whether the sterilization is medically indicated or purely elective for contraceptive purposes.

In 2015, a bill on compensation for victims of forced sterilization was drafted by the Czech Minister for Human Rights and Equal Opportunities, but in October of that year the government decided not to establish this special compensation mechanism, opining that 'court action remained the way to the award of damages for the victims of illegal sterilizations' and that 'an out-of-court mechanism would in all probability not be an effective complement to the existing means of redress for the individual failures in the performance of sterilizations which occurred in the past'.[105] The Council of Europe Commissioner for Human Rights publicly regretted this decision and underlined that the majority of the victims 'have been left without an effective national remedy to obtain compensation for the harm they have suffered'.[106]

In 2019, a compensation bill was finally submitted to the Czech legislature. In 2021, Czechia joined the small list of the world's countries with legislation offering not just apologies, but also one-time compensation equivalent to €12,000[107] available to anybody forcibly sterilized between 1966 (when it was still part of Czechoslovakia) and 2012. The process ran from 1 January 2022 to 31 December 2024 and as of this writing, legislation to extend it for another two years has been submitted for adoption.

In November 2021, reversing its previous findings, the government of Slovakia apologized for the forced sterilizations, acknowledging that Romani women

[103] 'Vláda: Litujeme nezákonných sterilizací romských žen', Lidové noviny (23 November 2009) <https://www.lidovky.cz/domov/vlada-litujeme-nezakonnych-sterilizaci-romskych-zen.A091123_165045_ln_domov_mtr> accessed 26 July 2023

[104] Act on Specific Health Services, 6 November 2011 <https://www.zakonyprolidi.cz/cs/2011-373> accessed 26 July 2023.

[105] FCNM AC, Fifth Opinion on the Czech Republic, 31 May 2021 https://rm.coe.int/5th-op-czech-republic-en-restricted/1680a2b3d6 accessed 29 October 2024.

[106] ibid.

[107] Zákon č. 297/2021 Sb., Zákon o poskytnutí jednorázové peněžní částky osobám sterilizovaným v rozporu s právem a o změně některých souvisejících zákonů, <https://www.zakonyprolidi.cz/cs/2021-297#:~:text=Z%C3%A1kon%20%C4%8D.,a%20o%20zm%C4%9Bn%C4%9B%20n%C4%9Bkter%C3%BDch%20souvisej%C3%ADc%C3%ADch%20z%C3%A1kon%C5%AF> accessed 29 October 2024.

in particular had been harmed, and adopting its 'Apology of the Government of the Slovak Republic for sterilization of women in violation of the law'.[108] Slovakia apologized for cases of sterilizations and human rights violations, mostly against Romani women from 1966 to 2004.[109]

In March 2023, the Justice Ministry of Slovakia submitted its 'Legislative intent of the law on financial compensation for women sterilized in violation of the law'[110] to the inter-ministerial commentary procedure. The bill proposed a one-off compensation of €5,000 to 'physical persons who underwent sterilization in violation of the law in the period from 1 July 1966 to 31 December 2004 in a medical facility on the territory of the Slovak Republic'.[111]

While welcoming the bill, the Slovak Ombudsperson raised several issues, including a recommendation to increase the amount of the financial compensation, to introduce the right to submit such requests in the languages of national minorities, and to propose that the Justice Ministry be the decision-making authority in the proceedings instead of the Health Ministry. The Ombudsperson also recommended incorporating a support system for victims who may face stigmatization or various forms of abuse and to minimalize potential administrative, financial, and language barriers for victims, which could indirectly affect their ability to avail themselves of the opportunity to seek compensation, as well as that the legislation include at least a partial reference to the substantive information that should be included in the request for compensation.[112] At the time of writing, this bill has yet to be adopted.

## 5.1. Evaluation

There are serious gaps in the Czech compensation scheme. On 1 January 2022, Act 297/2021, Coll., 'on the provision of a one-time sum of money to persons sterilized in violation of the law' came into effect,[113] awarding victims of illegal sterilizations

[108] Zdeněk Ryšavý, 'Slovak Government Apologizes for Illegal Sterilizations, Lawyer and Plenipotentiary for the Romani Community Say Compensation Must Follow' *ROMEA* (26 November 2021) <http://www.romea.cz/en/news/world/slovak-government-apologizes-for-illegal-sterilizations-lawyer-and-plenipotentiary-for-the-romani-community-say> accessed 29 October 2024.

[109] Resolution of the Government of the Slovak Republic No 674 on Apology of the Government of the Slovak Republic for sterilization of women in violation of the law, 22 November 2021 <https://rokovania.gov.sk/RVL/Material/26642/1> accessed 29 October 2024.

[110] Ministry of Justice of the Slovak Republic: 'LP/2023/64 Legislative intent of the law on one-time financial compensation for women sterilized in violation of the law' <https://www.slovlex.sk/legislativne-procesy/SK/LP/2023/64> accessed 29 October 2024.

[111] ibid para 2.1.1.

[112] ibid.

[113] Zákon č. 297/2021 Sb., Zákon o poskytnutí jednorázové peněžní částky osobám sterilizovaným v rozporu s právem a o změně některých souvisejících zákonů, <https://www.zakonyprolidi.cz/cs/2021-297#:~:text=Z%C3%A1kon%20%C4%8D.,a%20o%20zm%C4%9Bn%C4%9B%20n%C4%9Bkter%C3%BDch%20souvisej%C3%ADc%C3%ADch%20z%C3%A1kon%C5%AF> accessed 29 October 2024.

a one-off sum of CZK 300,000 [EUR 12,000]. The League of Human Rights, which undertook domestic litigation of such cases in the 2000s, is currently helping victims of illegal sterilizations with the submission of applications, as are other NGOs. Legislators expected approximately 400 women to be compensated.

The first gaps in the application of the law soon became apparent. Civil society had advised the Health Ministry that compensation requests should first be assessed by a committee including experts who have been dealing with the topic of illegal sterilizations for a long time and who are able to assess the requests in the context of this human rights issue. Unfortunately, the decision-making ultimately fell to the Legal Department at the Health Ministry and no such expert commission was established. So far, only roughly half of the requests have been successful, largely because no means of proof other than the original medical records are being accepted by that department, despite the fact that the explanatory memorandum to the law states that affidavits could be submitted in cases where the original medical records no longer exist (many records have been shredded, including before the expiration of the lawful deadline for maintaining them). This reasoning has since been explicitly rejected by the Supreme Administrative Court.[114]

As of this writing, the compensation procedure for forced sterilization victims has closed. It has been managed such that many of those who were sterilized longest ago and who have suffered the longest from this abuse were rejected because their original medical records no longer exist (by law such records only have to be kept for forty years). One of these victims was Vlasta Holubová, the Romani woman who helped launch the human rights research into this issue in Czechia in 2003. She passed away before that highest national instance could rule on her case, which it ultimately did, awarding her compensation. Many applicants from that era have been rejected because their original medical records no longer exist in the hospitals where the sterilizations happened (if the facilities even still exist).

Victims whose medical records were shredded were therefore de facto not considered eligible for compensation, despite a 2024 Supreme Administrative Court ruling that explicitly states that a lack of original records is not an argument for rejecting an applicant. The ministry also does not even consider in its decisions whether the shredding was done legally or illegally. The ministry has automatically rejected applications from those sterilized before 1982, even though the law was written with the intention of compensating all who were sterilized in violation of the law between 1966 and 2012.

[114] Gwendolyn Albert, 'Key Court Decision: Czech Health Ministry Must Change its Approach When Verifying Illegal Sterilizations, Lack of Medical Records Must not be an Obstacle' (ROMEA 8 July 2024) <https://romea.cz/en/czech-republic/key-court-decision-czech-health-ministry-must-change-its-approach-when-verifying-illegal-sterilizations-lack-of-medical-records-must-not-be-an-obstacle> accessed 29 October 2024.

Lastly, in some rejections, the ministry has ignored documented violations of the procedure for sterilizations. In several cases, the written authorizations of the sterilization required under § 11 of the directive on sterilization were missing from the medical records, but the ministry ignored that fact and rejected the applicants anyway. Such rejections can then be litigated at no cost to the plaintiff. So far, the first-instance court, in its rulings, has instructed the ministry that the state itself is supposed to be actively attempting to correct its own wrongdoing through this compensation procedure. Both the administrative code and the law itself make it possible to use evidence other than the original medical records, and the burden of proof cannot lie entirely on the applicant, especially in a situation where records are no longer available. According to both the lower courts and the Supreme Administrative Court, the ministry must acknowledge that it was the state that failed in the past and this compensation must be an effective means of redress. However, the ministry has persisted in appealing to the higher instance, which has rejected its appeals in 100 per cent of the cases ruled on as of this writing.

The law requires the ministry to make a first decision within sixty days of the submission of the application and expressly allows other means of proof than medical documentation. However, the ministry has delayed the communication of its decisions by more than a year in many cases. Civil society has already drawn attention to this problem in an open letter.[115] The average turnaround for these compensation requests is 154 days.

The draft bill for compensation in Slovakia may avoid these pitfalls if it manages to reverse the burden of proof from the outset, but its adoption is pending.

## 6. Conclusion

While Czechia and Slovakia have made progress toward the recognition of forced sterilizations which were perpetrated during communism and well into the democratic transition, what remains sufficiently unacknowledged is that the campaign to incentivize sterilization in Czechoslovakia strongly drew on racist stereotypes and specifically targeted Romani women. The way domestic authorities and courts have handled the recognition of human rights violations and their redress clearly shows that racism, anti-Romani prejudice, and antigypsyism are not features of the past. It is equally important to acknowledge that the practice stemmed from structural, including institutional, racial discrimination. While it was the communist regime that introduced the state sponsored sterilization policy, it was healthcare

[115] League of Human Rights, 'An Open Letter—Evaluating the Effectiveness of the Law on Compensation for Wrongful Sterilizations' <https://llp.cz/blog/otevreny-dopis-vyhodnoceni-efektivity-zakona-o-odskodneni-za-protipravni-sterilizace/> accessed 29 October 2024.

professionals, local administrations and social services who targeted Romani women, often pro-actively.

The quest for justice by the Romani women who have been subjected to forced sterilization has been a 'Groundhog Day' scenario for the last twenty years. The human rights field research, the subsequent advocacy, litigation and policy-makers' responses have taken far too long to provide effective remedy to the victims. In addition, domestic and ECtHR rulings, and even the compensation process in Czechia, have all failed to fully address the issue of the discriminatory treatment of the Romani women subjected to forced sterilization.

Human rights research, advocacy, and strategic litigation engaging international tribunals have been necessary to create political opportunities at state level for the recognition of the wrongdoing, the issuing of apologies, and the institution of a compensation scheme. Notable in this context, has been the positive contribution of the Czech Public Defender of Rights and systematic reporting by the Slovak National Human Rights Institution. However, domestic legislators, courts and policy-makers have delayed on delivering the legal and policy reforms required under international human rights law, and this has necessitated the repetition of advocacy and litigation efforts. In Czechia, access to compensation was not instituted for more than three decades after the political transition, which further victimized Romani women or simply denied justice to those who passed away while waiting for redress.

Caution is called for when considering the direct causality between human rights advocacy efforts, the influence of human rights standards, and eventual policy changes. In order to fully remedy the situation, what may be needed, is an overall awareness raising campaign and systematic human rights education efforts of policy makers, and medical and social care fields.

# 17

# Strategic Litigation and Roma Housing Rights in Europe

## The Complexities of Unlocking Change

*Darren O'Donovan*

### 1. Introduction: Confronting the Roma Housing Rights Challenge

This chapter explores how to effectively challenge the prevailing systemic barriers to accessing secure and stable housing solutions for Roma in Europe. It commences by interrogating why European human rights institutions have been slow to frame Roma housing rights in terms of racism and structural discrimination. While human rights litigation has provided a foothold to fight against punitive campaigns of eviction, it has not generated sufficient local or national movement towards tackling housing exclusion and related poverty. This chapter seeks to reset the failure—national and international—to adopt a 'housing first' emphasis upon substantive equality in human rights development. It argues for stronger legal and policy actions targeting structural discrimination against Roma in social housing and rental markets.

To achieve this, it puts forward three key streams of future litigation. Firstly, advocates should use existing protections restraining evictions or enforcement to promote a more holistic responsibility for changed outcomes on the ground. The growing emphasis upon procedural protections such as needs assessment in European Court of Human Rights (ECtHR) jurisprudence finally allows advocates to connect threatened eviction with the broader policy failure that has led to that point. This offers an avenue to promote a more holistic national government responsibility for housing, beyond narrow, reactive supervision of a single enforcement event.

The second stream involves broadening existing litigation strategies to promote greater emphasis upon priority issues for Eastern European Roma. The chapter argues for more sustained invocation and enforcement of European Union discrimination law in housing contexts. It highlights how European Union structural funding rules offer increasing opportunities to mainstream human rights

Darren O'Donovan, *Strategic Litigation and Roma Housing Rights in Europe* In: *The Rights of Roma in European Courts*. Edited by: Kristin Henrard and Lilla Farkas, Oxford University Press. © Darren O'Donovan 2025.
DOI: 10.1093/oso/9780198914358.003.0017

conditionality into housing projects. This offers a distinct legal avenue for 'designing in' increased housing provision and improved on-the-ground conditions for Roma communities.

The chapter concludes by reflecting upon the importance of using litigation to challenge prevailing social discourses. Discriminatory narratives—which deny culture and history—are practical enablers of housing exclusion. Future housing litigation needs to emphasize tackling discriminatory narratives and enhancing the representation and participation of Roma in society. International human rights fora can be used to promote Roma agency in decision-making and to undercut discriminatory narratives.

As an introduction, it is first necessary to take stock of the prevailing dynamics shaping Roma housing rights litigation in international fora and the widespread absence of state compliance with international human rights norms. The term 'Roma' is adopted as an umbrella term in the manner of the European Union Roma Strategic Framework for Equality, Inclusion and Participation 2020–30.[1] It is important to note that Roma housing needs are diverse, with some Roma living in and with community in urban or rural settings, others in deeply segregated and discriminatory settings, or others seeking accommodation suited to traditional nomadic or semi-nomadic living patterns. The housing rights challenge extends to the homelessness of migrant Roma and the marked discrimination of European private rental markets. Across all contexts, however, the scale of the challenge is clear. The 2020 EU Roma Strategic Framework outlines a stark gap in the rates of housing deprivation. Sixty-one per cent of Roma communities will experience deprivation, compared with 17.9 per cent of the general population.[2]

A lack of adequate housing often results in a cascade of further rights violations. The 2021 EU Council recommendation emphasizes that effective housing interventions must be accompanied by:

> measures to ensure access to essential services—such as tap water, safe and clean drinking water, adequate sanitation, waste collection and management services, environmental services, electricity, gas, transport, financial services and digital communications—and physical infrastructure, by safeguarding continuity of basic utility services, both under normal conditions and during pandemics, ecological catastrophes and other crises.

[1] EU Commission, Communication from the Commission to the European Parliament and the Council—A Union of Equality: EU Roma Strategic Framework for Equality, Inclusion and Participation (COM(2020) 620 final, 7.10.2020). The Strategy adopts the following approach, centred on recognizing specificity of all individuals: 'The reference to 'Roma', as an umbrella term, encompasses a wide range of different people of Romani origin such as: Roma, Sinti, Kale, Romanichels and Boyash/Rudari. It also encompasses groups such as Ashkali, Egyptians, Yenish, Dom, Lom, Rom and Abdal, as well as traveller populations, including ethnic Travellers or those designated under the administrative term gens du voyage and people who identify as Gypsies, Tsiganes or Tziganes, without denying their specificities.'

[2] ibid 5.

Thus, as the ERGO Network of Roma grassroots organizations have argued, for many Roma communities a 'rights-based, housing first' approach is key to their enjoyment of other fundamental rights.[3] Yet, the bounded norms and enforcement mechanisms of European human rights law do not reflect this. Anti-Gypsyism, environmental racism, and state inaction combine to result in what Pontradolfo has described as 'bare citizenship', where unstable living conditions hinder or prevent, both formally and substantially, access to citizens' rights.[4] The case studies analysed in this chapter interrogate the consistent dynamics of state non-compliance with international human rights law on Europe's historically nomadic minorities.

## 2. The Current Context: Consistent Rights Violation and State Inaction

Before outlining how litigation can support accelerated reform, it is necessary to confront squarely the failure of existing efforts to interrupt the realities of exclusion on the ground. In relation to Roma housing rights, the prevailing human rights paradigm suffers from a number of key outcome-limiting boundaries which this section will explore. These are:

(i) The failure of key European human rights institutions to drive an enforceable and justiciable vision for Roma housing firmly centred upon substantive equality, minority, and cultural rights.
(ii) The lack of state willingness to grant justiciable housing rights at national and international level.
(iii) A halting evolution towards a focus on minority rights, Roma participation, and coordinated policy-making structures in housing decision-making.

The first boundary is particularly prevalent under the European Convention on Human Rights (ECHR). Article 8 of the ECHR—the right to family and private life—offers only a narrow frame for the advancement of housing rights in Europe. The text of Article 8 reflects a formal conception of civil and political rights and is focused on restraining state interference with one's home.[5] While the Court has

[3] European Roma Grassroots Organisations Network, *Roma Access to Quality and Affordable Housing in Bulgaria, Czech Republic, Hungary, Romania, Slovakia and Spain*, Report of November 2023 <Research report on Roma access to quality and affordable housing – ERGO Network> accessed 30 June 2024.

[4] Stefania Pontrandolfo, 'Roma "Acts of Citizenship": Negotiating Categories and Housing' (2018) 22(1) Nomadic Peoples 83–103.

[5] For a general discussion on privacy and restraint on the state as the motive force for the article see Thomas De la Mare and Brian Kennelly, 'Article 8: Right to Respect for Private and Family Life, Home and Correspondence' in Anthony Lester and David Pannick (eds), *Human Rights Law and Practice* (2nd edn, Lexis Nexis 2004) 261.

recognized that the article places an obligation on states to facilitate a Traveller way of life,[6] this offers only heavily circumscribed possibilities for the positive provision of accommodation in cases of severe deprivation.[7] The ECtHR has consistently underlined that 'a right to respect for home has been held to be an entirely different concept to a right to a home'.[8] At national level, it has often been stressed that Article 8 cannot mandate 'social engineering in the housing field'.[9] A traditional human rights paradigm which stresses the programmatic and polycentric nature of socio-economic rights restricts the Convention in this area. Despite the findings of rights violations by other European human rights institutions discussed in this chapter, there remains no directly justiciable duty to provide appropriate housing accommodation before the ECtHR or European Court of Justice (ECJ).

Efforts to capitalize upon the limited obligation to facilitate have encountered setbacks. Strategic litigation on Roma housing has been adversely affected by the large margin of appreciation afforded to Member States in areas of general social policy.[10] In the majority of planning and allocation decisions, the obligation to facilitate a Traveller way of life is only a factor for local authorities to weigh in balance against considerations such as planning control imperatives and environmental protection.[11] The precise weight which should be attached to the obligation to facilitate remains unclear outside of the particular circumstances of the case, and the obligation is often discharged upon the mere mention of it by planning decision-makers. Even successful litigation yields judgments which are highly contextual and fact-specific, rather than systemic in their framing.

Strategic litigation in housing thus frequently takes the form of efforts to moderate immediate negative outcomes in the hopes of creating pressure beyond the courtroom. Absent procedural errors or particularly severe intrusions, the Article 8 obligation often does not have sufficient substantive strength to overrule European and national courts' reluctance to interfere with planning determinations by initial decision-makers.

The limited nature of rights afforded by the ECHR is underscored by the recurrent findings of violation in other human rights fora. The European Committee of Social Rights (ECSR) has consistently found violations across Europe of the housing rights of Roma communities under Article 31(2) of the Revised Social

[6] *Chapman v The United* Kingdom, App no 27238/95 (ECtHR, 18 January 2001) para 90.

[7] A number of Irish and UK cases have ordered the provision of accommodation in specific instances of severe rights deprivation. These limited and rare examples are discussed in Darren O'Donovan, 'Breaking the Cycle of Discrimination? Traveller/Roma Housing Exclusion and the European Convention on Human Rights' (2016) 16(1) International Journal of Discrimination and the Law 5–23.

[8] *Harrow London Borough Council v Qazi* [2004] 1 AC 983 [69] (Bingham LJ).

[9] ibid [123].

[10] States tend to get a broad margin of appreciation in relation to 'general policy decisions', which is particularly the case when housing matters touch on social policy. See, inter alia, *Buckley v United Kingdom* App no 20348/92 (ECtHR, 29 September 1996) [80].

[11] See eg *Connors v United Kingdom* App no 66746/01 (ECtHR, 27 August 2004) [82] and [84].

Charter.[12] Yet these findings have struggled to generate much progress on the ground, as states fail to drive either local implementation or grant stronger, justiciable legal protection at national or international levels. The Committee of Ministers supervision mechanism in relation to the collective complaints often stymied efforts to hold national government to account, by rarely addressing recommendations to states due to the two-thirds majority requirement for doing so. Instead, the Committee adopted resolutions which 'noted' the findings without prescribing firm measures for reform.[13] The result has been a cycle of non-compliance that sees repetitive findings made against multiple countries. Since July 2020, the Committee of Ministers has increasingly made specific recommendations outlining steps required to implement ESCR rulings.[14] Nevertheless, the absence of effective enforcement continues to haunt efforts to litigate violations.

Consider, for instance, the latest collective complaint to the ECSR, against France.[15] This asserts that expediting procedures for the imposition of fixed fines on Travellers in France for 'illegal halting in order to set up a home even temporarily' is discrimination and a violation of fundamental human rights. After referencing the previous findings against France by international human rights bodies, the complainants argue this fresh measure amounts to 'completing the legislative arsenal that contributes to the systemic discrimination of Travellers'.[16] In relation to Italy, the ECSR itself recently noted that despite fifteen years of recommendations with regards to 'nomad camps' and forced evictions, many Roma continue to live 'in deplorable conditions, in spite of court rulings confirming that assigning housing in prefabricated containers surrounded by fencing constitutes discrimination'.[17] It found that forced evictions remain a 'current practice' which the government has admitted, and that Italy has failed to adopt a legal framework to ensure

[12] Most recently, as discussed below, in *Amnesty International v Italy* Complaint No 178/2019 (European Committee of Social Rights, 13 May 2024). Art 31(2) of the Charter provides for the right to housing:

'With a view to ensuring the effective exercise of the right to housing, the Parties undertake to take measures designed:

(i) to promote access to housing of an adequate standard;
(ii) to prevent and reduce homelessness with a view to its gradual elimination;
(iii) to make the price of housing accessible to those without adequate resources.'

[13] For a detailed analysis see: Holly Cullen, 'The Collective Complaints System of the European Social Charter; Interpretative Methods of the European Committee of Social Rights' [2022] 1 Human Rights Law Review 65–66; Guiseppe Palmisano, *Collective Complaints as a Means for Protecting Social Rights in Europe* (Anthem Press 2022) 42.

[14] Prior to this, as Palmisano notes, the Committee of Ministers had only made a recommendation prescribing measures for implementation in a single instance. Palmisano (n 13) 42. States must now also submit a report on their follow-up actions two years after these recommendations are received. See Ministers' Deputies, 'Implementation of the Report on Improving the European Social Charter System', CM(2022)114-final, 27 September 2022.

[15] *European Roma Rights Centre (ERRC) v France* Complaint No 230/2023 (ECSR, 20 March 2024).

[16] ibid *Case Document No 1 - Complaint*, 21.

[17] European Committee of Social Rights, 'Follow-up to Decisions on the Merits of Collective Complaints' December 2018, para 497.

remedies when they occur.[18] The Committee also emphasized that 'in practice segregation of Roma, Sinti, and Caminanti communities continues to exist'.[19]

This latter point moves us to another key flaw in the prevailing human rights paradigm towards Roma housing rights. International human rights courts have consistently failed to adopt a vision which is centred upon substantive equality and minority culture. This reflects the slow evolution of human rights law's equality protections from their original emphasis upon direct, de jure discrimination, towards tackling indirect and de facto discrimination. The failure of the ECtHR to frame Roma housing rights cases in terms of the prohibition of discrimination is well canvassed. Hopes that the landmark education rights case of *DH v Czech Republic*[20] would alter this have not yet eventuated, despite the Court's affirmation of the abiding relevance of the Article 14 ECHR non-discrimination guarantee in the case of *Yordanova*.[21] The *DH* case ultimately reflected the higher status accorded to rights to education under the Convention. Efforts to rely on unreasonable discrimination in the housing sphere are also complicated by the presence of the right to private property under the Convention. The case of *Winterstein v France* did at least strengthen the Court's position on the *nature* of the interests at stake in housing cases.[22] It affirmed that Roma Article 8 cases involve rights of central importance to the individual's identity, self-determination, physical, and moral integrity, maintenance of relationships with others and a settled secure place in the community.[23]

The European Union's Roma rights initiatives have also been slow to directly label the nature of interests at stake in Roma housing in terms of racism, culture, and equality. As Cittadini has argued, the first decade of Union policy-making was instead framed around concepts of 'integration' and exclusion.[24] She argues that the framework risked the 'ethnicization of poverty', positioning the community as requiring intervention or integration, rather than self-determination and agency.[25]

The current 2020–30 Strategic Framework, together with the recent Council conclusions on Roma rights, seek to reset this. The Strategic Framework introduced measurable objectives for four dimensions including housing. The 2023 EU Council Conclusions on Roma Housing highlighted the acute lack of housing provision, policy measures or financial investment in Roma housing which is driving existing dynamics of discrimination and segregation.[26] The 2020–30 strategy also

18 *Amnesty International v Italy* Complaint No 178/2019 (ECSR, 13 May 2024) para 75.

19 ibid para 98.

20 *DH and others v Czech Republic* App no 57325/00 [GC] (ECtHR, 13 November 2007).

21 *Yordanova v Bulgaria* App no 25446/06 (ECtHR, 24 April 2012) para 129.

22 *Winterstein v France* App no 27013/07 (ECtHR, 17 October 2013) para 90.

23 ibid para. 70.

24 Silvia Cittadini, 'Roma, Adequate Housing, and the Home: Construction and Impact of a Narrative in EU Policy Documents' (2019) 1(2) Critical Romani Studies 40–56.

25 ibid 52.

26 Council of the European Union, Council Conclusions, Measures to Ensure Equal Access for Roma to Adequate and Desegregated Housing, and to Address Segregated Settlements, 9 October 2023

introduced the key horizontal concepts of fighting anti-Gypsyism[27] and ensuring participation for the first time. These concepts also have measurable targets, and represent an effort to tackle the local and national dynamics which frustrate compliance and perpetuate rights violation. As Brinks has argued, it is only rarely that states invoke purely financial reasons for a failure to adequately implement Roma housing rights.[28] Instead, the real operative reason behind this persistent failure remains deeply entrenched prejudice against the Roma and Travellers across Council of Europe states. Deeper change will only emerge through a renewed focus on naming and tackling this overarching dynamic.

The remainder of this chapter proposes three streams of strategic litigation which can be used to push back against key normative and enforcement boundaries.

Section 3 explores the potential benefits of ECHR litigation which looks to connect eviction and other planning enforcement events to the broader lifecycle of housing policy failure at national and local levels. The case of *Winterstein* contains important signs that that the ECtHR is willing to interrogate the degree to which eviction decisions result from broader failures of needs assessments, planning and engagement with Roma communities. Strategic litigation in this area can promote a more coordinated and consultative housing policy, centred upon engagement with local and national Roma communities. It can help ensure national governments do not turn a blind eye to local government inaction, but take more holistic responsibility for changed outcomes on the ground.

Fundamentally, however, procedural protection or needs assessment must ultimately yield substantive results. Section 4 of this chapter therefore calls for more diverse forms of Roma housing rights litigation, particularly in addressing priority issues for Roma in Eastern Europe. It is time for a renewed focus on interrogating exclusion and discrimination in rental markets and social housing. Strategic litigation in such areas could place greater reliance on Directive 2000/43, which prohibits discrimination in access to goods and services available to the public. This is particularly the case where the above-mentioned 2023 EU Council Conclusions attribute housing exclusion not simply to the absence of government provision but

2023/C 13517/2. See also Council of European Union, Recommendation of 12 March 2021 on Roma Equality, Inclusion and Participation 2021/C 93/01.

[27] EU Roma Strategic Framework for Equality, Inclusion and Participation (n 1) 1. The Framework documents notes that some debate may be generated by centring this term: 'Antigypsyism (a form of racism against Roma) is a historically rooted structural phenomenon that appears at institutional, social and interpersonal levels. It has its origins in how the majority views and treats those considered "gypsies". It is rooted in a process of "othering" that builds on negative as well as positive, exoticising stereotypes. While there is consensus about the understanding of antigypsyism among proponents of the need to reinforce the fight against it, there has been a debate about the term.'

[28] Daniel Brinks, 'Solving the Problem of (non)Compliance in Social and Economic Rights Litigation' in Malcolm Langford, Cesar Garavito-Rodriguez, and Julietta Rossi (eds), *Making it Stick: Compliance with Social Rights Judgments in Comparative Perspective* (CUP 2017).

also to neoliberal gentrification and private rental market discrimination.[29] The concept of environmental racism also provides opportunities for highlighting the living conditions of Roma and fostering their visibility within the broader human rights and climate justice movements.

There are also opportunities to promote the mainstreaming of human rights within European Union funding rules. There are increasing legal obligations on states and the EU Commission to ensure EU development project spending is compatible with fundamental human rights norms. As is discussed later, the latest programme rules tie structural funding approvals and disbursements to concrete actions on Roma inclusion. Complaints in this developing forum could potentially broaden the focus of litigation efforts towards 'designing out' exclusion in Eastern Europe. It would also transcend existing boundaries by finally offering a legal forum where structural discrimination and the actual provision of social housing could be centred and debated.

Finally, section 5 argues that future housing rights litigation needs to enhance the visibility of Roma in society and tackle the public discourse and attitudes that shape the spatial politics driving Roma housing deprivation. The 2023 European Commission EuroBarometer evaluation found 43 per cent of Roma are discriminated against when trying to buy or rent housing.[30] Only 64 per cent of Europeans stated they would feel comfortable having daily contact with a Roma colleague, with only 20 per cent reporting having Roma friends or acquaintances. Sixty-one per cent of Europeans believed that discrimination against Roma was widespread in their country. In this context, human rights litigation needs to aim at greater visibility and improved representation of Roma communities. The Traveller ethnicity campaign from Ireland is used as an example of a successful strategic human rights litigation strategy centred on countering discriminatory narratives.

## 3. Challenging the Bureaucratic Lifecycle of Roma Housing Exclusion

The first area of proposed strategic litigation builds off the existing obligation to facilitate a Traveller/Roma way of life jurisprudence. The last major ECtHR eviction case, *Winterstein v France*—in which an eviction was successfully challenged—contained a number of important threads which can still be productively exploited.[31] While there is little doubt the ECHR offers only limited prospects for the

[29] Council of the European Union (n 26).

[30] European Commission, Directorate-General for Communication 'Eurobarometer SP535 Report: Discrimination in the European Union' (December 2023) <https://europa.eu/eurobarometer/surveys/detail/2972> accessed 30 September 2024.

[31] *Winterstein* (n 22).

actual provision of housing, it can be used to stimulate improved housing policy at local and national levels.

*Winterstein*, in effect, conditions the exercise of enforcement powers against Roma communities upon coordinated needs assessment. When evicting Roma families, state parties are obliged to assess the impacts upon their health, education, and other needs, and to consider what housing solutions are available for them. While this may seem like a marginal procedural protection, crucially the ECtHR has firmly connected the eviction event to a broader policy lifecycle. Advocates may have an increased ability to draw out the relationship between enforcement and housing provision, and stop the false isolation of evictions from broader dynamics of discrimination.

This is important, as a key distinguishing feature of Traveller/Roma housing rights disputes is often their multifinal nature. This term was first coined by Zygmunt Bauman in his study of modernity and bureaucracy.[32] A key feature of housing rights violation is often the fragmentation of responsibility—both ethical and legal—between actors. Accountability, or even visibility of wrongdoing, can be defrayed through the segmentation of decisions between actors. Housing rights are particularly vulnerable to this dynamic, given governance in the area is often shaped by local and national actors—and often reflects the interaction of public servants and elected officials. Bureaucratic divisions of labour between the local or regional authority and the national government often result in both parties nominating the other as responsible for the absence of provision. Domestic legal frameworks compound this by presenting eviction and related criminalization as separate, discrete decisions from previous steps to secure accommodation for the individual.

The result can be a bureaucratic landscape where the public is told national government is working progressively towards solutions while also pursuing (or being betrayed by) regressive local measures. In Ireland this has often been physically embodied by the action of members of parliament, who in their national role would support Traveller housing projects, yet vote against local projects. As Arendt warned:

> In every bureaucratic system the shifting of responsibilities is a matter of daily routine, and if one wishes to define bureaucracy in terms of political science, that is, as a form of government—the rule of offices, as contrasted to the rule of men, of one man, or of the few, or of the many—bureaucracy unhappily is the rule of nobody and for this very reason perhaps the least human and most cruel form of rulership.[33]

[32] Zygmunt Bauman, *Modernity and the Holocaust* (Cornell University Press 1989) 101.

[33] Hannah Arendt, *Responsibility and Judgement* (Random House 2003) 31.

Another Irish example of this dynamic was the bureaucratic coinage of the category of the 'local Traveller'. This meant that the local authority was responsible only for those Travellers residing in their functional area. In justifying the failure to provide culturally appropriate accommodation, local authorities cited the potential magnet effect whereby Travellers would cross administrative boundaries in search of greater security.[34] Authorities could assert good intentions while arguing that providing accommodation would subject them to first mover disadvantage. This bureaucratic defraying of responsibility has resulted in decades of low provision of temporary accommodation sites to facilitate Travellers' nomadic identity. It has functioned as a rhetorical cover for a process of constructive assimilation whereby the best available outcome presented to Traveller families was to request permanent housing accommodation without the ability to undertake traditional travel.

International fora, whether judicial or expert, require the state to present the full picture, and adopt a rights-centred account. The ECtHR ruling in *Winterstein v France* is best understood as requiring holistic engagement which prevents any fragmentation of responsibility.[35] The Court prohibited the use of eviction powers where inadequate consideration has been given to alternative accommodation options. The failure of state parties to assess families' housing, health, education, or other needs accurately, or to avoid unjustifiable delay, can also represent violations of Article 8. Politicians and bureaucrats can no longer isolate an eviction event from the broader context of accommodation provision. Strategic litigation on behalf of Travellers/Roma in this area is an opportunity to affirm a holistic legal and ethical responsibility of the national states that has been clouded historically. A key normative boundary—the legal fiction that the only state action involved is enforcement—can be transcended. States are, at a minimum, forced to account for and explain how the situation arose in a deeper way.

The recent landmark Irish Supreme Court case of *Clare County Council v McDonagh*[36] is a good example of how the calculus of eviction has been broadened by *Winterstein*. This case overturned orders which required the appellants to remove their caravans and property from council-owned land without delay. After a fire destroyed the Traveller accommodation site where they had lived in 2014, the families had cycled between private rented and council lands without a sustainable solution. A lower court had initially found that as the caravans had not been in their specific location long enough to satisfy the requirement for 'close and continuous links' laid out in the *Winterstein* judgment.[37] This finding was overturned

[34] Sinead Ni Shuinear: 'Why do Gaujos hate Gypsies so much, anyway? A Case Study in Gypsy Politics and Traveller Identity' in Thomas Acton (ed), *Gypsy Politics and Traveller Identity* (University of Hertfordshire Press 1997) 4.

[35] *Winterstein* (n 22).

[36] *Clare County Council v McDonagh* [2022] IESC 2.

[37] *Winterstein* (n 22) para 70.

by the Supreme Court which emphasized that the location of the caravans and mobile homes was only about 1 km away from their long-standing, though now destroyed, accommodation site.

In that context, Article 8 protection was a live issue but the court proceeded to focus upon the Irish constitutional protection of one's 'dwelling'.[38] It construed the Irish constitutional provisions in a manner informed by *Winterstein*, assessing whether domestic laws could be seen as compatible with it. Justice Hogan found that in the specific circumstances of the case, an order to immediately vacate the land was not proportionate. He placed emphasis on the fact that Travellers were a vulnerable minority group who have struggled for recognition of their cultural identity, particularly in the housing sphere.[39] He stressed that it was at least arguable that the local authority was in breach of its statutory duty in failing to provide the family with Traveller-specific accommodation suitable to their needs and addressing the medical needs within the family. This was also an instance where occupation did not impact on third party rights, with the land being owned by the local authority.

Like *Winterstein*, *McDonagh* will not frustrate or restrain the possible future use of eviction powers. Indeed, the Court specifically noted there was a presumption in favour of eviction, given the lawful interest of public authorities in their land. The situation would shift immediately if the council was able to cite any immediate threat to the amenities of others, public safety, or any other compelling public interest ground. What *McDonagh* has achieved however, is to ensure that eviction does not occur in isolation: inaction in the sphere of accommodation provision can rebound on the local authority.

Lawyers who undertake future eviction cases will increasingly be mobilizing what Elster calls the 'civilising force of hypocrisy'.[40] The state is now forced to speak to how it arrived at an eviction event, and it cannot exclude the needs of Traveller/Roma from its reasoning. This is a good example of how human rights law can push past convenient bureaucratic or governance divisions to maintain a focus on the outcome the state, as a whole, has underwritten.[41]

A similar dynamic has marked recent strategic litigation in the United Kingdom. The 'persons unknown' cases—which involve challenges to expansive, preventative banning orders on the parking of caravans across the country—have made visible the blunt reality of forcible assimilation. These injunctions are granted without prior notice, against persons unidentified at time of grant and who have

[38] The Irish judiciary take a 'Constitution first' approach in cases regarding housing rights: the issue is assessed under the Irish constitutional protections first, and if these prove insufficient, we progress to the legislation incorporating the ECHR into Irish law.

[39] *McDonagh* (n 36) paras 96 and 113.

[40] Jon Elster, 'Deliberation and Constitution Making', in Elster (ed), *Deliberative Democracy* (CUP 1998) 111.

[41] Sidney Tarrow, *Power in Movement: Social Movements and Contentious Politics* (2nd edn, CUP 1998) 7.

not yet, or not even threatened to, encamp in the areas listed. These cases leverage *Winterstein*, highlighting the absence of consideration for minority identity or the individual. In *The Mayor and Burgesses of the London Borough of Bromley v Persons Unknown*,[42] the Court of Appeal delivered a forceful decision reaffirming the reality of Traveller nomadic identity, and highlighting the interconnection between systemic exclusion and planning enforcement:

> there is an inescapable tension between the article 8 rights of the Gypsy and Traveller Community ... and the common law of trespass. The obvious solution is the provision of more designated transit sites for the Gypsy and Traveller community ... The reality is that, without such sites, unauthorised encampments will continue and attempts to prevent them may very well put the local authorities concerned in breach of the Convention.[43]

The Court emphasized that expansive invocation of planning enforcement frameworks is a serious threat to the cultural identity of the Romani and Traveller community, with the former having been in Britain since at least the 1500s and Irish Travellers since the 1800s. It affirmed that 'the Gypsy and Traveller community have an enshrined freedom not to stay in one place but to move from one place to another'.[44] Lord Coulson stressed that local authorities must carry out welfare assessments, engage in dialogue to avoid the need for injunctions. Local authorities must demonstrate understanding and respect for a community's culture in their forward planning for accommodation. Where an injunction is sought, the court should be provided with evidence of suitable alternative housing or sites which are reasonably available to those being moved. Such accommodation not being available would weigh heavily against the granting of an injunction.

Core elements of the Bromley approach have recently been reaffirmed by the Supreme Court in *Wolverhampton City Council and others v London Gypsies and Travellers and others*.[45] The Court stressed that it could not sanction injunctions of indeterminate length over wide geographical areas. In an important comment it linked such an approach to the forcible assimilation of Traveller/Gypsy identity:

> We have considerable doubt as to whether it could ever be justifiable to grant a Gypsy or Traveller injunction which is directed to persons unknown, including newcomers, and extends over the whole borough or for significantly more than a year.

[42] *The Mayor and Burgesses of the London Borough of Bromley v Persons Unknown* [2020] EWCA Civ 12.
[43] ibid [100].
[44] ibid [53].
[45] Pontrandolfo (n 4).

> It is to be remembered that this is an exceptional remedy, and it must be a proportionate response to the unlawful activity to which it is directed. Further we consider that an injunction which extends borough-wide is likely to leave the Gypsy and Traveller communities with little or no room for manoeuvre.[46]

Traveller advocates have now moved to challenge the criminalization of trespass in the Police, Crime, Sentencing and Courts Act 2022. The Advisory Committee on the Framework Convention for the Protection of National Minorities condemned this legislation as a structural threat to the cultural identity of Gypsies and Travellers in England:

> This Act appears to the minority as a criminalisation of the option of last resort ... and it is difficult for the minority itself to discern the difference between that and forced assimilation. The fear this act has sparked among the minority is profound.[47]

Beyond the formal outcomes, strategic litigation against these regressive enforcement powers also offer redress for what Fricker terms 'testimonial injustice'.[48] By opening space for stories to be told, and by rendering more visible 'harder to see' violence and consequences, litigation can address the 'ethical loneliness' of victims.[49] Without such court processes the prevailing dynamics of forcible assimilation could go unmarked. Strategic litigation before the ECtHR has succeeded in making clear that eviction is not an isolated event experienced by individuals, but a marker of systemic discrimination.

## 4. Broadening Strategic Litigation on Roma Housing Rights

This narrative of slow progress around evictions, however, merely brings us to the point of confronting the overarching structural discrimination and housing exclusion which Roma face, especially in Eastern Europe. While human rights litigation has provided a foothold to fight against punitive campaigns of evictions, it has not generated sufficient local or national movement towards tackling housing exclusion and related poverty. The traditional concepts and emphases of European institutions—human rights ones included—have consistently failed to drive

[46] *Bromley* (n 42) [225].

[47] Advisory Committee on the Framework Convention on the Rights of National Minorities, Fifth Opinion on the United Kingdom, adopted 8 December 2022, ACFC/OP/V(2022)003 para 4.

[48] Miranda Fricker, *Epistemic Injustice: Power and the Ethics of Knowing* (OUP 2007) 9.

[49] Cath Roper and Piers Gooding, 'This is Not a Story: From Ethical Loneliness to Respect for Diverse Ways of Knowing, Thinking and Being' in Eilionóir Flynn and others (eds), *Global Perspectives on Legal Capacity Reform* (Routledge 2018) 154–64, 155.

meaningful change in Eastern European states. More than half (52 per cent) of the EU Roma population face housing deprivation—defined as including absent indoor plumbing, leaking roof, rot or damp, or a dwelling that is too dark or humid.[50] Housing deprivation affects 32 per cent of Roma living in the mainstream population. In neighbourhoods where all or the majority of inhabitants are Roma, the proportion rises to 61 per cent. Eighty-two per cent of Roma live in overcrowded households compared to 18 per cent in the general population. Even the full implementation of current European Strategy by 2030 would only see a bare majority (51 per cent) of European Roma no longer face deprivation of overcrowding.

This section will interrogate why European human rights institutions have been slow to frame these issues in terms of racism and structural discrimination. This failure is attributable to two key boundaries on change outlined in the opening section of this chapter. Firstly, there is the failure of national and international institutions to adopt a 'housing first', substantive equality emphasis on the ground. Secondly, there is a need for stronger tools to root out the structural discrimination against Roma in social housing and rental markets, and the actors who author it. How can strategic litigation be used to generate progress on these issues?

This section of the chapter identifies two areas as particularly ripe for litigation. Firstly, advocates should aim to increase the number of discrimination law actions targeting the private rental and social housing allocation spheres. Secondly, efforts should be made to enforce the newly strengthened human rights mainstreaming regulations applicable to EU-funded projects. Both avenues sidestep existing boundaries, allowing housing rights advocates to target a broader range of actors, and focus us on tackling the reality of inadequate housing provision.

While de facto equality and discrimination lie at the heart of Roma housing deprivation, legal norms of anti-discrimination have often been eclipsed or subordinated to the separate legal provisions related to housing. In the ECHR context, this reflected the marginalization of the Article 14 non-discrimination guarantee due to initial uncertainty in defining its scope of application. The evolution of the article was initially marked by judicial confusion as to when and why to examine cases under the article, and the tendency of the ECtHR to refrain from a non-discrimination analysis where a violation of another article has already been found. The seminal *Belgian Linguistics*[51] case emphasized the accessory nature of Article 14, while also stating that there can be findings of violation of this article in conjunction with other articles. While the application of Article 14 does not presuppose a breach of other Convention articles, however, the subject matter of the facts at hand must be such as to fall within the ambit of the Convention articles.[52]

[50] EU Fundamental Rights Agency, Roma Survey 2021 https://fra.europa.eu/sites/default/files/fra_uploads/fra-2022-roma-survey-2021-main-results2_en.pdf

[51] *Belgian Linguistics Case (No 2)*, App nos 1474/62, 1677/62, 1691/62, 1769/63, 1994/63, 2126/64 (ECtHR, 23 July 1968).

[52] *Thlimmenos v Greece* App no 34369/97 (ECtHR, 6 April 2020) para 40.

United Kingdom Human Rights Act cases concerning Roma/Travellers also fostered restrictive interpretations of Article 14. In the case of *Clarke v Secretary of State for the Environment*, the court held that 'Article 14 . . . does not provide a self-standing right . . . to the citizen . . . what Article 14 does is inform, strengthen and expand other rights'.[53] The result of this conservative approach has been that litigants have 'become so accustomed to criticising Article 14 for its limitations that they are unable to see its possibilities'.[54]

The matter is compounded by the slow rate of ratification of Additional Protocol 12 of the ECHR—an additional discrimination protection. At the time of writing there have been only twenty ratifications of this additional discrimination protection out of thirty-eight signatory states parties. This has particular importance to Roma, as Protocol 12 was, at one time, cited as a basis for suspending work on adding minority rights protection under the Convention.[55] Article 1(1) of the Protocol provides that 'the enjoyment of any right set forth by law shall be secured without discrimination on any of the specified grounds'. This is supplemented by Article 1(2), which requires that 'no one shall be discriminated against by any public authority on one of the specified grounds'. This protection may be inferred from a duty imposed upon a public authority, and not simply from a legal right which is specifically granted. This means that local authorities cannot exercise their discretionary powers in a discriminatory manner.[56] Nevertheless, even Protocol 12 eschews the language of differential equality or cultural identity, with the Explanatory Report noting that while 'positive obligations cannot be excluded altogether, the prime objective of Article 1 is to embody a negative obligation for the Parties'.[57] The duty under Article 1(1) 'might entail positive obligations' though these are 'likely to be limited'.[58]

There were hopes that the right to education judgment of *DH v Czech Republic*[59] would catalyse more of a focus on leveraging discrimination law norms in the housing sphere. While the right to education is a Convention right, where housing is not, there were legitimate hopes that equality would become a touchstone for evaluating local authority decision-making on Roma issues. A potential area for action would be where local authorities consistently fail to designate any areas for private halting sites within their development plans. Or where planning laws make no provision to assess or take Roma inclusion into account in developments.

53 *Clarke v Secretary of State for Environment, Transport and the Regions and another* [2002] EWCA Civ 819 [5].

54 ibid [246].

55 In 2002, The Committee of Ministers of the Council of Europe argued that the adoption of Protocol 12 rendered the appeal for an additional protocol 'somewhat premature'. See Committee of Ministers, 'On the rights of national minorities', Adopted at the 799th Meeting of the Ministers Deputies (12 June 2002).

56 See in particular Sandra Fredman, *Discrimination Law* (OUP 2002) 86.

57 Committee of Ministers (n 55) para 24.

58 ibid para 26.

59 *DH* (n 20)

It seemed that indirect discrimination was well placed to supply a systemic lens for Convention case law on basic services and respect for family and home life.

Unfortunately, however, high-profile indirect discrimination claims relating to Roma housing have not yet eventuated under the ECHR or the European Union discrimination frameworks. The May 2024 findings of the ECSR in relation to Italy should encourage reflection on future litigation possibilities. In the decision, the ECSR stressed that three wide-ranging violations it had identified were of Article E of the Revised Social Charter, read together with Article 31 (on housing). Article E represents a fundamental, cross-cutting guarantee provided to all EU citizens:

> The enjoyment of the rights set forth in this Charter shall be secured without discrimination on any ground such as race, colour, sex, language, religion, political or other opinion, national extraction or social origin, health, association with a national minority, birth or other status.

At paragraph 68 the Committee emphasized that Article E 'establishes an obligation to ensure that, in the absence of objective and reasonable justifications, any individual or groups with particular characteristics benefit in practice from the rights in the Charter'. It embraces a guarantee against indirect discrimination, including 'failing to take due and positive account of all relevant differences or by failing to take adequate steps to ensure that the rights and collective advantages that are open to all are genuinely accessible by and to all'.[60] The Committee proceeded to find a violation of Article E of the Charter read in conjunction with Article 31(2) in respect of forced evictions, sub-standard housing and lack of equal access to social housing.

The findings point strongly towards the need to push for stronger, formal enforcement of EU anti-discrimination frameworks in the area of Roma housing. The Committee's decisions contrast sharply with the European Commission's inaction. In 2019, it closed its investigation into a complaint made by the European Roma Rights Centre against Italy.[61] The European Roma Rights Centre had requested that it take enforcement action against Italy for insufficient compliance with EU anti-discrimination law, on the basis of inadequate access to social housing and the diversion of Roma into substandard camps. The Commission found that insufficient evidence existed to pursue the matter, citing pragmatic barriers to framing cases in the area:

[60] Citing *Autism-Europe v France* Complaint No 13/2002 (ECSR, 4 November 2003) para 52 and *ERRC v Bulgaria* Complaint No 31/2005 (ECSR, 18 October 2006) para 40.

[61] The basis for this decision is available at <https://www.errc.org/uploads/upload_en/file/5311_file1_a-letter-from-the-commission-discrimination-in-housing-of-roma-people-in-italy.pdf> accessed 30 September 2024.

> To prove the existence of a consistent administrative practice, a relatively small number of individual cases is not sufficient, even if the infringements are sufficiently established in each case, if together they do not represent a substantially adequate percentage of the overall number of possible occurrences of the challenged administrative practice. This means that a single or a small number of possibly isolated cases of incorrect application of a national provision in contravention with EU law are not sufficient for the Commission to initiate an infringement procedure.

Citing a 'change in the situation on the ground', the Commission found it had 'insufficient evidence of a consistent administrative practice of criteria for access to social housing designed in particular to exclude Roma people'. In relation to eviction, the Commission stressed that Directive 2000/43 prohibits discrimination in access to goods and services available to the public, including housing. It found that 'access to goods and services available to the public' seems to refer to goods and services offered on the market or by the public sector, not to one's own house or one's residence in an unofficial camp, neither of which is 'available to the public'.

The Commission's vision of its competences here, ironically, illustrates the potential benefits of a focus on rental markets, gentrification, and related government policies. The Fundamental Rights Agency 2021 survey found 31 per cent of respondents were prevented from renting a private apartment/house because of their Roma background. In a growing pattern of gentrification, 21 per cent were prevented from buying an apartment/house. A 2023 study of real estate agents and landlords in Hungary found that discrimination against Roma in the rental housing market was 'understood to be a widespread and socially acceptable practice'. Discrimination was driven by stereotypes and 'justified by social norms, relying on the expectations of local residents, neighbours and owners of the homes'.[62]

A renewed focus on such strategic litigation under Directive 2000/43 would diversify the jurisprudence relating to Roma housing rights. The ruling of the Czech Constitutional Court in the 'benefit free zones' case is an example of the types of dynamic that EU discrimination law should be well placed to tackle.[63] In that case, national legislation enabled municipalities to designate whole territorial areas as ineligible for certain forms of housing support. The declared justification was to combat the exploitation of poor people by the owners of residential hotels charging

[62] Luka Váradi, Blanka Szilasi B, Anna Kende, Jeremy Braverman, Gabor Simonovits, and Bori Simonovits (2023) 'Personally, I feel sorry, but professionally, I don't have a choice.': Understanding the drivers of anti-Roma discrimination on the rental housing market (2023) 8 Front Sociol.

[63] Constitutional Court of the Czech Republic <Aktuálně | Ústavní soud (usoud.cz)> accessed 30 September 2024. European Roma Rights Centre (ERRC), 'Czech Constitutional Court bans "benefit free zones"' (1 September 2021) <Czech Constitutional Court bans 'benefit free zones' - European Roma Rights Centre (errc.org)> accessed 30 September 2024.

exorbitant rents. The municipalities which instituted such bans were, however, found to have acted with the discriminatory intent of excluding from their areas the poor and mostly Romani people who drew housing benefits.

Fresh litigation conducted within European Union anti-discrimination frameworks has also challenged Roma exclusion within the *private* rental market. The 2015 CJEU ruling in *CHEZ Razpredelenie Bulgaria AD v Komisia za zashtita ot diskriminatsia, Anelia Nikolova*[64] represents a model of well-selected litigation which targeted privatized forms of anti-Roma discrimination. In that matter, Ms Nikolova took action against the company which supplied electricity to her shop in a mainly Roma district of Dupnitsa, Bulgaria. The company had a policy of placing electricity meters out of easy reach of local householders, on tall poles—which prevented Ms Nikolova tracking her electricity usage. The Court of Justice ruled this practice was based on race or ethnic origin, as the practice was targeted at the district due to its predominantly Roma character. The court did not accept that it was a neutral practice tied to problems of interference with meters. It stressed that the practice had 'offensive and stigmatizing' effects. The case points to the abiding potential of EU discrimination law as a potential avenue of litigation—particularly to challenge general practices in the environmental or planning sphere. Relative to the scale of societal challenge recognized by European institutions, it is striking how few preliminary references concerning anti-Roma discrimination have been referred to the Court of Justice. This is an undoubted area for future improvement.[65]

Separately, another litigation strategy to promote increased provision would be to seek greater enforcement of human rights mainstreaming requirements within EU funding structures. The European Union's Cohesion Policy for 2021–27, by Regulation, includes a 'National Roma Inclusion Strategic Policy Framework' as a thematic enabling condition for funding.[66] The Regulation expressly notes that the intention is to implement Principle 20 of the European Pillar of Social Rights—to ensure equal treatment of Roma people in access to adequate, non-segregated housing and essential services. The Regulation sets four criteria for the fulfilment of the condition in the context of funding and overseeing projects using European Union funds:

[64] Case C-83/14 *CHEZ Razpredelenie Bulgaria AD v Komisia za zashtita ot diskriminatsia, and Anelia Nikolava, and Darzhavna Komisia za energiyno i vodno regulirane* (CJEU, 16 July 2015).

[65] For reflection on the need to expand the emphasis and enforcement of EU discrimination law into a more diverse range of actors see: Uladzislau Belavusau and Kristin Henrard, *EU Anti-Discrimination Law beyond Gender* (Hart Publishing 2018).

[66] Regulation (EU) 2021/1060 of the European Parliament and of the Council of 24 June 2021 laying down common provisions on the European Regional Development Fund, the European Social Fund Plus, the Cohesion Fund, the Just Transition Fund and the European Maritime, Fisheries and Aquaculture Fund and financial rules for those and for the Asylum, Migration and Integration Fund, the Internal Security Fund and the Instrument for Financial Support for Border Management and Visa Policy ([2021] OJ L231/159).

1. measures to accelerate Roma integration and prevent and eliminate segregation, taking into account the gender dimension and situation of young Roma. Arrangements and approvals for projects should include baseline and measurable milestones and targets set in relation to this.
2. Arrangements to monitor, evaluate and review the Roma integration measures prescribed within projects.
3. Arrangements to mainstream Roma inclusion at regional and local levels.
4. Arrangements to ensure that its design, implementation, monitoring and review are conducted in a close cooperation with the Roma civil society and all other relevant stakeholders, including at regional and local levels.

Significantly, while, in the past, these conditions were assessed ex ante, the 2021–27 programme will see them assessed on a rolling basis. Article 15 of the Regulation states that if enabling conditions are not fulfilled, the Commission will not reimburse expenditure declared by the Member State for the purposes of support from a CPR-funded programme until compliance is evidenced. Article 69(7) of the CPR 21–27 requires Member States to make arrangements to ensure the effective examination of complaints concerning the award and oversight of funds and projects, including those concerning fundamental rights. Complaints may cover any dispute between potential and selected beneficiaries regarding the proposed or selected operation and any disputes with third parties on the implementation of the programme or operations. It is possible for rights organizations to object to the funding of operations that violate key enabling conditions.

Strategic litigation through this mechanism offers an avenue to challenge some traditional boundaries. Advocacy groups would escape from the traditional pleas of limited competence and challenge EU institutions and member states to genuinely mainstream Roma housing into economic development programmes. Litigation to ensure compliance with the requirements is an opportunity to finally have a first principles conversation about the need to drive housing provision, especially in Eastern Europe.

## 5. Strategic Litigation as a Counter to Discriminatory Narratives

This final section will consider how strategic litigation in housing rights can promote a broader interruptive agency for Travellers and Roma in the public sphere. As Cittadini has argued, understanding and challenging the construction and representation of groups in public discourse is key to the delivery of housing policy. For Travellers, Gypsies, and Roma in Europe, the ability of the majority to suppress their distinct history and culture has underwritten discrimination against them in the housing sphere. As Taylor and Hinks note, enforced historical narratives continue to structure relations between minority and majority:

> an attitude which insists on positioning Gypsies and Travellers in an idealised historical past—one of bow-topped caravans, horses and fairs—when their presence was 'fine', and simultaneously, through denying them the possibility of change over time, placing them outside of history. And in a society where written histories and a publicly acknowledged heritage goes hand-in-hand with wider social acceptance, to be marginalised from the historical record is to be denied not only historical agency but the very right to claim a history.[67]

This section highlights how strategic litigation before international human rights bodies can be used to promote Roma participation in decisions and undercut discriminatory narratives.

Irish Travellers' successful campaign for recognition as an ethnic minority represents an important example of advocacy and litigation efforts geared at reclaiming history and gaining recognition in the public sphere. Since its formation, the Irish state had continually attempted to represent Travellers' identity as a 'culture of poverty', with their distinctive existence to be ascribed solely to economic deprivation. The earliest formal policy in relation to Travellers began by asking 'Who are today's travellers?'—deliberately creating a disjuncture between 'traditional' Travellers and modern realities.[68] It combined the social imperatives of law and order with the traditional exclusionary discourses surrounding Travellers. Travellers were presented as victims of poverty—excluding their culture and history enabled the state to propose a civilizing project of settlement into mainstream housing.

Discriminatory narratives—which deny culture and history—are practical enablers of housing exclusion. Roma are presented as 'newcomers' or outsiders. Discriminatory stereotypes about Travellers, Roma, and Gypsies are ultimately majoritarian efforts to avoid challenges to historical self-understanding at national and European level. As Bhabha argues, excluded minorities are always first made subject to a metaphor of inclusion—that where they present themselves in a particular way, subordinate nomadism, or remain in their traditional areas—they would be included.[69] The discriminatory narrative then shifts into metonymical or contextual elements: for instance, claims that the 'local' Travellers or Roma communities of the past have become disruptive outsiders or 'foreign' Roma.[70]

[67] Becky Taylor and Jim Hinks, 'What field? Where? Bringing Gypsy, Roma and Traveller History into View' 18(5) Cultural and Social History 2021 630.

[68] *Report of the Commission on Itinerancy* (Stationery Office 1963) 4.

[69] Homi K Bhabha, *The Location of Culture* (Routledge 1994) 63.

[70] ibid 74.

The history of Traveller/Roma housing rights in Europe is underwritten by renunciations of histories of discrimination and minority resistance. In Ireland for instance, the 1963 Commission on Itinerancy at once sought a civilizing mission, but also acknowledged the need to force Travellers to settle. Exclusion was presented as a reality that could not be overcome, and, if it impelled Travellers to change, it was sanctioned as a measure of social integration. This was most forcefully seen in the recommendation by the Commission that:

> If the assumption that the life span of itinerants is, on average, so much shorter than that of the settled population is correct, the fact should be publicised amongst them to encourage them to abandon the itinerant life.[71]

Discrimination combines the 'metaphor' of inclusion—which allows majority narratives of rule of law and equality to go unquestioned—with metonyms of exclusion—where the minority is associated with disadvantage, poor choices, and disruption.

The decades-long struggle to secure recognition as an ethnic group by the Irish Travelling Community is a leading example of how litigation can challenge majority narratives. For Irish Travellers, their housing exclusion had a clear departure point—the renunciation of culture and ethnic identity written into government policy in 1963:

> Itinerants (or Travellers as they prefer themselves to be called) do not constitute a single homogenous group, tribe or community within the nation although the settled population are inclined to regard them as such. Neither do they constitute a separate ethnic group.[72]

Conducted mainly through United Nations and European treaty bodies, Traveller representatives successfully undercut narratives of exclusion and secured a recognition of their history and related exclusion. They highlighted how the Irish state was attempting to present anti-Travellerism as residual to international understandings of discrimination and race. In the Equal Status Act 2000, the Irish state had created a legislative definition of Traveller, which included all the elements of Traveller ethnic status already recognized by the United Kingdom and Northern Ireland courts:

> Traveller community means the community of people who are commonly called Travellers and who are identified (both by themselves and others) as people with

[71] Stationery Office (n 68).
[72] ibid 37.

> a shared history, culture and traditions including, historically, a nomadic way of life on the island of Ireland.[73]

Despite this definition, the government refused to recognize Traveller ethnicity before the United Nations Committee for the Elimination of Racial Discrimination in March 2005. It stated that, while respecting the right of Travellers to a cultural identity, its view was 'that Travellers do not constitute a distinct group from the population as a whole in terms of race, colour, descent or national or ethnic origin'.[74]

With support from the Irish Human Rights Commission and Ireland's Equality Authority, Ireland's Travelling Community worked to overturn this position. The refusal to recognize ethnicity attracted early criticism from the Committee on the Convention on the Elimination of Racial Discrimination (CERD)[75] and the Advisory Committee on the Framework Convention on National Minorities.[76] Traveller advocates successfully framed the ethnicity issue as a question of power. They argued that it 'ought not to be decided by a Government. It ought to be decided by people working in the area, through objective criteria'.[77] The campaign mobilized around the need to stop Traveller culture and history being put up for debate, and to finally disavow the core 'culture of poverty' stereotype propagated by the Irish state since its foundation. This eventually led to particularly strong criticism from the United Nations Human Rights Committee in their Concluding Observations during Ireland's reporting cycle. It stated that it was 'concerned' at the current state position—framing it as a question of power. They stressed the principle that the primacy of self-identification lay at the heart of minority recognition in international law. It recommended that the state 'should take steps to recognise Travellers as an ethnic minority group'.[78]

On 1 March 2017, the then Prime Minister of Ireland, An Taoiseach Enda Kenny, made a short parliamentary statement in which he recognized Traveller ethnicity.[79] The statement was deliberately framed by the government as 'symbolic'—without direct legal effect. It was presented solely as an act of recognition,

[73] Equal Status Act 2000 s 2(1)

[74] Ireland's First and Second Reports under the Convention for the Elimination of Racial Discrimination Un Doc CERD/C/460/Add 1 at 90.

[75] Committee on the Elimination of Racial Discrimination Comments on the Initial and Second Report of the Irish Government under the Convention on the Elimination of Racial Discrimination CERD/C/IRL/CO/2 para 20.

[76] Advisory Committee Opinion on Ireland's Second Report under the Framework Convention on the Protection of National Minorities ACFC/OP/II(2006)007 para 29.

[77] Irish Traveller Movement, 'Shadow Report and Commentary on the First National Report by Ireland to the CERD Committee' 4.

[78] ibid.

[79] Department of the Taoiseach, 'Statement by An Taoiseach Enda Kenny TD on the recognition of Travellers as an ethnic group, Dáil Éireann' (2017) <https://www.gov.ie/ga/oraid/d29014-statement-by-an-taoiseach-enda-kenny-td-on-the-recognition-of-travel/> accessed 30 September 2024.

but one which clearly renounced past discourses which had seen Travellers denied their place in community. Nevertheless as McVeigh has argued, recognition at last places the Irish Travelling Community 'in the correct paradigm', underlining that addressing inequalities must 'start from the right place,' and be informed by international law.[80] Traveller representative body Pavee Point underlined that the campaign for recognition reflected the reality that inclusion and equality could not be secured without a change in the 'assimilationist mindset' on the part of the state.[81]

As Haynes, Joyce, and Schweppe argue, recognition now needs to be used as a launching pad to target local councils who continue past assimilationist approaches.[82] They cite the work of advocates such as Rosaleen McDonagh, who has effectively targeted the inconsistency between symbolic, national actions and local violations:

> Now is the moment to make things fair and equal ... Metaphors and euphemisms are vacuous without practical evidence in the area of social policy.[83]

While strategic litigation aimed at recognition or interrupting discriminatory discourse might seem 'symbolic', it can produce a visible dissonance in government action. The recognition of ethnicity, and the related disavowal of past discourses, has at a minimum, forced national government to separate itself from local practices of exclusion. In 2024, Traveller advocates continue to invoke national–local disjuncture in advocating for that an oversight body, such as the National Traveller Accommodation Authority, to be tasked with driving delivery where local authorities fail to provide appropriate accommodation.

Even in circumstances where human rights litigation—such as current European Court of Human Rights jurisprudence—has a clear ceiling, it can secure greater agency of Travellers/Roma in policy about them. The process of legal complaints itself provides access to a public forum in which minorities can 'make visible the ways they are affected by relations of domination, albeit fragmentarily and in line with juridical form'.[84] In the context of the European Social Charter, the expansion from monitoring national reports to collective complaints was aimed at

[80] Houses of the Oireachtas, Joint Committee on Justice and Equality: Report on the Recognition of Traveller Ethnicity 2017 32/JAE/03 <https://data.oireachtas.ie/ie/oireachtas/committee/dail/32/joint_committee_on_justice_and_equality/reports/2017/2017-01-26_report-on-the-recognition-of-traveller-ethnicity-january-2017_en.pdf> accessed 15 September 2024.

[81] ibid.

[82] Amanda Haynes, Sindy Joyce, and Jennifer Schweppe, 'The Significance of the Declaration of Ethnic Minority Status for Irish Travellers' (2021) 49(2) Nationalities Papers 270.

[83] Rosaleen McDonagh, 'When Will There Be an Official Apology to the Traveller Community? A State Apology for the Discrimination, Abuse and Hurt Inflicted On Our People Is Long Overdue' *The Irish Times* (25 September 2018).

[84] Sonja Buckel, Maximilian Pichl, and Carolina A Vestena, 'Legal Struggles: A Social Theory Perspective on Strategic Litigation and Legal Mobilisation' (2024) 33(1) Social & Legal Studies 23, citing Carolina A Vestena, *Das Recht in Bewegung. Kollektive Mobilisierung des Rechts in Zeiten der Austeritätspolitik* 34.

such transparency and democratic participation—deliberately bringing a broader range of voices into policy design and implementation. The initial use of legal process becomes a tactic within the framework of a broader mobilization process. While incremental, the ultimate goal must be to 'strengthen the public resonance of the collectively articulated demands'.[85]

In Ireland, the Housing (Traveller Accommodation) Act 1998 is the primary mechanism through which the state seeks to ensure compliance with decisions such as *Chapman*,[86] *Connors*[87] and *Winterstein*. In a visible instance of domestic norm internalization, it places great emphasis on Traveller participation in policy and implementation. The 1998 Act created a duty to provide Traveller-specific accommodation in the form of group housing, as well as permanent and temporary halting sites. It requires local authorities to adopt a Traveller Accommodation Programme (TAP), specifying the accommodation needs of Travellers and accommodation projects required to address these needs.[88] It must also include measures for implementation, specific to each category of accommodation required.[89]

While the limited reach of the legislation's obligation to take 'reasonable steps' to implement accommodation plans can be critiqued, the framework does represent an effort in rights socialization.[90] Each local council is required to consult with Traveller representatives and bodies through the formation of the Local Traveller Accommodation Consultation Committee (LTACC). The role of the LTACC is to provide a forum whereby Traveller accommodation issues can be addressed in a timely and coordinated manner and where decisions are reached as far as possible on the basis of mutual consensus. Importantly, the emergence of such communities of practice offers a different form of minority agency than victimhood or passive objects of regulation. It also provides an accessible site for the translation of international human rights principles into local housing policies. Where litigation triggers increased minority participation and recognition in the public sphere, it has the potential to reframe the political framing and standing of those being represented.

## 6. Conclusion

This chapter has endeavoured to preserve some optimism about strategic litigation in a context where Travellers/Roma are regularly confronted with systemic

[85] ibid citing Cecilia McDowell Santos, 'Mobilizing Women's Human Rights: What/Whose Knowledge Counts for Transnational Legal Mobilization?' 10 Journal of Human Rights Practice 2018 191–211.
[86] *Chapman* (n 6).
[87] *Connors* (n 11).
[88] Housing (Traveller Accommodation) Act 1998 s 7.
[89] ibid s 10(e)(i).
[90] O'Donovan (n 7).

discrimination and widespread housing deprivation. Strategic litigation in such a context is necessarily slow and painful work, rather than a 'big bang' moment. The history of Roma housing litigation suggests that it can contribute to greater political influence and cultural visibility for on-the-ground advocates. At a minimum, litigation creates an agency beyond depersonalized victimhood. As O'Brien concludes: 'so long as a gap exists between rights promised and rights delivered, there is always room for rightful resistance to emerge'.[91]

Fully capitalizing on the progress made in ECtHR cases like *Winterstein* can secure a vital foothold of consultation and assessment for communities long marginalized from local policy processes. The impact of the eviction stream of case law may ultimately lie downstream of the court: in the policy processes which must now be created to ensure proportionality and right compliance. The implementation of human rights requires, in the words of Van Bueren, the 'development of a culture of co-operative effort between the judiciary, the government and the people to fulfil the entitlements of citizens'.[92]

But a change in the emphasis of litigation undertaken is also required, particularly given the prevalence of structural discrimination across Eastern European societies. Targeting discrimination within housing and utilities market through EU laws potentially offers more direct impact on key outcomes: housing equality, access to basic services and energy poverty. Attempting to enforce greater conditionality and inclusion in EU structural funding could finally promote the needed 'rights-based, housing-first approach' towards social housing, which has been urged by Roma representative bodies.

The arc of securing respect, protection and fulfilment of the housing rights of the Roma/Travellers will be long, but we should not lose faith in the ability of strategic litigation to contribute to the reshaping of relationships. Alongside the formal outcome, Traveller/Roma housing rights litigation should be seen as important narrative acts which moderate and highlight cycles of exclusion. The goal is for litigation to stimulate a broader process of transformation, for as Marc Galanter counsels:

> Just as health is not found primarily in hospitals or knowledge in schools, so justice is not primarily to be found in official justice-dispensing institutions. Ultimately, access to justice is not just a matter of bringing cases to a font of official justice, but of enhancing the justice quality of the relations and transactions in which people are engaged.[93]

[91] Kevin J O'Brien, 'Rightful Resistance' (1996) 49 World Politics 55.

[92] Geraldine Van Bueren, 'Including the Excluded: The Case for an Economic, Social and Cultural Human Rights Act' [2002] Public Law 456.

[93] Marc Galanter, 'Justice in Many Rooms: Courts, Private Ordering, and Indigenous Law' (1981) 13 The Journal of Legal Pluralism and Unofficial Law 17.

# 18

# Facing Reification of Vulnerability

## Roma, Environmental Justice and the Failed Potential of the *Hudorovič* Case

*Maroš Matiaško and Marek Szilvasi*

### 1. Introduction

In her exploration of positive vulnerability in the book *Ethics of Vulnerability*, Erinn Gilson employs the example of access to water to underscore the disparity in how political communities assess the worth of various groups' lives.[1] There is likely no better description of the phenomenon when political society treats some lives as less valuable than pointing to a situation where access to fundamental resources, such as water, is limited. According to Gilson, living in areas with limited access to clean and safe water significantly heightens the precariousness of life, and water scarcity can occur due to the different valuations of lives in society. For some, lack of access to water is hardly imaginable; for others, such as Roma in many states across Europe, it is a daily reality.[2]

According to Gilson, the reason for the disparate understanding of the value of lives lies in the frame through which we view them. The framing of the situation is crucial, notes Gilson, because it amplifies the vulnerability experienced by rural, impoverished, non-white communities. How lives are perceived influences the material support they receive, yet this material reality also shapes whether and how lives are perceived. 'Framing', Gilson writes, 'is not just a matter of how people are regarded or overlooked, but of the practices that coincide with, support, and perpetuate that way of regarding them, linking material conditions to the differential ways of regarding lives'.[3]

Considering this, we can ask, first, whether framing through a human rights lens has the potential to transform the structures that either enable or reinforce systemic inequality, and second, if the answer to this is affirmative,[4] how this

1 Erinn Gilson, *Ethics of Vulnerability. A Feminist Analysis of Social Life and Practice* (Routledge 2014) 45.

2 See Ch 3.

3 Gilson (n 1).

4 See the discussion on the transformative aspect of the right to remedy in Rodrigo Uprimny Yepes, 'Transformative Reparations of Massive Gross Human Rights Violations: Between Corrective and Distributive Justice' (2009) 27(4) Netherlands Quarterly of Human Rights 625–47; Brianne McGonigle

Maroš Matiaško and Marek Szilvasi, *Facing Reification of Vulnerability* In: *The Rights of Roma in European Courts*. Edited by: Kristin Henrard and Lilla Farkas, Oxford University Press.
 DOI: 10.1093/oso/9780198914358.003.0018

transformative potential is realized in practice or, conversely, how it may be obscured or enclosed. In this chapter, we do not problematize the first concern but presume that despite voices against the human rights paradigm which has emerged since the Universal Declaration of Human Rights,[5] this still allows us to respond efficiently to systemic inequality. What interests us, however, is the present-day boundary of this paradigm that reveals not only a horizon, as currently seen, but also brings prospects to cross it.

At the moment, nothing better describes the idea of border space for Roma rights than issues related to environmental justice. Well-known themes and topics, such as access to water and sanitation, have recently taken a different meaning in Europe. Indeed, the right to water and sanitation was expressly recognized in 2003 by the UN Committee on Economic, Social and Cultural Rights in its General Comment no 15 on the right to water,[6] and later in 2010 by the UN General Assembly.[7] Yet, only in 2020, the European Court of Human Rights (ECtHR, the Court) had a chance to address these rights for the very first time in its *Hudorovič and Others v Slovenia* judgment.[8]

Two Romani families brought the application after decades of petitioning the local authorities to provide their households with drinking water and functioning sanitation. They claimed violation of Articles 3 and 8 of the Convention because their homes did not have access to essential public utilities, and further submitted that they had been subjected to a negative and discriminatory attitude by the local authorities, who had refused to address their disadvantaged situation in any meaningful manner. The outcome of this litigation was twofold. The Court recognized that the right to water and sanitation falls within Article 8 of the Convention, which is certainly a step in the right direction, yet still rejected the substantive claims of the applicants.

Reading the judgment, what stands out is how the majority of judges justified the rejection, relying at the same time on the vulnerability of Roma. The concept of vulnerability in Roma rights cases has a long history. It dates back to 1996 when Judge Repík used the term in his dissenting opinion in *Buckley v the United Kingdom*. Later, the Court referred to the vulnerability of Roma in 2001, defining vulnerability as something that is rooted in different Roma culture. For the Court,

Leyh and Julie Fraser, 'Transformative Reparations: Changing the Game or More of The Same?' (2019) 8 Cambridge International Law Journal 39.

[5] See Roberto Esposito's powerful philosophical critique of the current paradigm in his book *Third Person Politics of Life and Philosophy of the Impersonal* (Polity Press 2012).

[6] See E/C 12/2002/11.

[7] The terminology sometimes differs. The UN documents refer either to the right to water and sanitation (see eg A/HRC/12/24, para 35), or to 'the right to safe and clean drinking water and sanitation' (see eg A/RES/64/292; A/RES/70/169). In this article, we will refer simply to the right to water and sanitation, considering that UN bodies use both expressions interchangeably (compare A/RES/64/292, 2).

[8] *Hudorovič and Others v Slovenia* App nos 24816/14 and 25140/14 (ECtHR, 10 March 2020).

concerning Roma, vulnerability has inherently cultural grounds, as it is based on a different or traditional lifestyle.[9] Subsequently, this rationale was supplemented by referencing the unique experience of the 'turbulent history' of Roma and their 'constant uprooting'.[10]

As Timmer noted, the concept of vulnerability revolutionized human rights adjudication at the Court.[11] The introduction of the concept redefined the potential of the human rights paradigm in addressing systemic discrimination but also brought concerns of essentialism, stigmatization, and paternalism,[12] reifying the boundaries of human rights adjudication instead of making it more adaptable to the gravity of the issues at hand. We will argue that precisely this happened in the *Hudorovič* judgment, in which most judges relied on a narrow reading of vulnerability. In this chapter, we juxtapose two readings of vulnerability: narrow and extensive or closed and open. The narrow or closed reading of vulnerability seems typical for the current Court's adjudication. In contrast, in political philosophy, vulnerability has been thematized to overcome the aforementioned fears while preserving its transformative potential. Gilson also argued this, developing the already-mentioned concept of positive vulnerability.[13]

Focusing on vulnerability and its potential by closely reading the *Hudorovič* judgment, we try to achieve two aims. First, identify the boundaries of the human rights paradigm by analysing how a Court's approach to vulnerability operates in cases that reveal historic systemic discrimination requiring a transformative remedy. Second, to show that vulnerability can be a proper instrument to address complex historical injustices, thus pushing the existing boundaries, but only if reconceptualized along the ideas introduced in the work of critical philosophers.

[9] For how the Court failed to take into account the culture, see Sal Buckler, 'Same Old Story? Gypsy Understandings of the Injustices of Non-Gypsy Justice' in Marie Dembour and Tobias Kelly (eds), *Paths to International Justice* (CUP 2007) 243.

[10] In 1996, in *Buckley v the United Kingdom* App no 20348/92 (ECtHR, 29 September 1996), Judge Repík, in his partly dissenting opinion, labelled Roma as vulnerable, calling for a 'particularly close scrutiny' of an interference. Later, in *Chapman v the United Kingdom*, Roma were considered, for the first time, as having 'a vulnerable position', due to their 'traditional lifestyle different from that of the majority' (App no 27238/95 (ECtHR, 18 January 200) para 96). In 2007, the Court in *DH and Others v Czech Republic* App no 57325/00 (ECtHR, 13 November 2007) para 182 referred to the 'turbulent history' and 'constant uprooting' of Roma. The vulnerability of Roma has developed into a general principle that the Court applies in certain contexts as a frame. However, the Court's approach is not consistent. In some cases, vulnerability is recognized expressly as a general principle, which was also the case in *Hudorovič* (n 8) para 142; in some cases, the Court refers to 'main principles', including vulnerability, see *DH* para 181. Sometimes, the Court does not list general principles independently but refers to vulnerability as a principle from the outset of its reasoning. This is the example from *Szolcsán v Hungary* App no 24408/16 (ECtHR, 30 March 2023) para 47.

[11] Alexandra Timmer, 'A Quiet Revolution: Vulnerability in the European Court of Human Rights' in Martha Fineman and Anna Grear (eds), *Vulnerability: Reflections on a New Ethical Foundation for Law and Politics* (Ashgate 2013).

[12] Among lawyers, these concerns were identified by Peroni and Timmer, see Lourdes Peroni and Alexandra Timmer, 'Vulnerable Groups: The Promise of an Emerging Concept in European Human Rights Convention Law' (2013) 11 International Journal of Constitutional Law 1056d. In political philosophy, detailed discussion offers Gilson (n 1) 34–35.

[13] Gilson (n 1).

The *Hudorovič* case fits well with the critical analysis we developed here for several reasons. First, vulnerability was the applicants' argument,[14] third-party intervener,[15] the government,[16] the Court,[17] and the dissenting judges.[18] Second, not only did everyone agree that Roma are specifically vulnerable, but their vulnerability was used to justify adopting special measures to address the lack of access to water and transform their precarious environmental situation.[19] In other words, the vulnerability was thematized not only as a frame through which we should acknowledge the situation of Roma but as a reason for altering what we perceive. Thus, besides the epistemic element, there was also a normative element. And finally, the case revealed the dialectic between these two elements. It is not without significance for the human rights assessment why we understand that Roma are vulnerable, whether it is because of their culture or because they have been historically experiencing environmental injustice. The rationale behind vulnerability has consequences for legal arguments.

The chapter is structured into three sections. While the background of our discussion is the right to water and sanitation, or in a broader sense, environmental justice, vulnerability is the frame that defines the practical milieu in which Roma rights have been adjudicated by the Court. We, therefore, start with the discussion of vulnerability. The discussion is rather theoretical, yet it aspires to offer a practical framework. By introducing relevant philosophical discourse, we try to translate it into an analytical tool and offer a reconceptualized idea of vulnerability. The analytical tool we propose is based on the idea of reification and will be used to read the *Hudorovič* judgment.[20] The suggested reconceptualization reflects the concept of positive vulnerability introduced by Gilson. It will also be further discussed in the third part of this chapter, in which we read in detail the *Hudorovič* judgment, trying to pinpoint those moments when the Court could have pushed the boundaries of Roma rights, but failed to do so. The whole analysis is preceded by a discussion of what environmental justice means and what is the situation of Roma in Europe, zooming in, especially on the access to water and sanitation. This context serves as a background, allowing us eventually to explain and interpret Roma's vulnerable situation in a reframed manner, emphasizing two interconnected circumstances that should have been, in our opinion, crucial in framing vulnerability, namely time and space.

[14] *Hudorovič and Others* (n 8) para 120.
[15] ibid para 134.
[16] ibid para 147.
[17] ibid paras 142, 156, and 158.
[18] ibid para 13.
[19] The Human Rights Centre of the University of Ghent, which submitted a third-party intervention, argued that vulnerability should justify the violation of Article 14 of the Convention, which would eventually impact domestic water policies and planning. See *Hudorovič and Others* (n 8) para 134.
[20] One of the authors developed this analytical tool: Maroš Matiaško, *The Right to Remedy and Reparations for Human Rights Violations* (UPOL 2024).

## 2. Vulnerability Reconceptualized: Positive Vulnerability, Situational Vulnerabilities and Vulnerability as a Heuristic Tool

Environmental justice recognizes that specific populations are at greater risk of structural injustice and face specific vulnerable situations.[21] The question is, however, whether vulnerability, an already well-established human rights concept, offers, under the present interpretation by the Court, a viable tool for addressing those challenges or, instead, is a stigmatizing concept that should be abandoned by lawyers pushing the boundaries of the human rights paradigm through strategic litigation.

On the one hand, vulnerability is a concept with a long tradition in jurisprudence and especially in political philosophy, at least since Hobbes. It has been used across various disciplines besides human rights law, bioethics,[22] and development studies.[23] On the other hand, it provokes controversy because it can lead to unintended consequences, such as stigmatization of the vulnerable or paternalism.[24] These risks are not ignored in political philosophy and human rights discourse. Various authors have tried to counter them by juxtaposing what we can call *closed* and *open* conceptions of vulnerability.[25] Both positions are usually discussed against a so-called negative understanding of vulnerability, meaning an understanding of vulnerability as mere weakness, helplessness, or incapacity. A more complex reading would then emphasize the ambivalence of the concept metaphorically portrayed as opening, also underlining the positive aspects of vulnerability in terms of abilities or dispositions.[26]

Undeniably, vulnerability often appears in philosophy alongside images of violence, fear, incompetence, or need.[27] Suppose only the negative aspects define vulnerability. Such a perspective would define vulnerability as a closed concept, only as 'susceptibility to injury, weakness, addiction, powerlessness, incompetence, inadequacy, and passivity'.[28] And such a perspective is reductive, as argued by Gilson,

[21] See section 3 for more details.

[22] The literature is vast. We refer to two studies: Henk ten Have, *Vulnerability: Challenging Bioethics* (Routledge 2016) and Florencia Luna, 'Elucidating the Concept of Vulnerability: Layers Not Labels' (2009) 2 International Journal of Feminist Approaches to Bioethics 121.

[23] Greg Bankoff and others, *Mapping Vulnerability. Disasters, Development and People* (Routledge 2004).

[24] Gilson (n 1) 34–35.

[25] Peroni and Timmer suggested that the Court should 'always make sure that it does not apply vulnerability as simply a "label" (a label easily turns into a stigma), but as a "layered" concept' (see Peroni and Timmer (n 12). They borrowed the term from Florencia Luna, who is a bioethicist and proposed layering of vulnerability (see Luna (n 22) 121). The layering of vulnerability is also a typical theme for political philosophers, see Maroš Matiaško, 'Access to Justice through Lenses of Vulnerability and Equality: A Dialogue Between Philosophy and Law' (2021) 22 ERA Forum 717.

[26] Gilson (n 1).

[27] Ann Murphy, *Violence and the Philosophical Imaginary* (State University of New York Press 2012) 65–66.

[28] Gilson (n 1) 5.

who noted that it refers only to one aspect of vulnerability: those negative qualities that should be repudiated or controlled.[29]

A reductive understanding of vulnerability leads to several interrelated problematic consequences that we propose to explain on the background of reification.[30] The first consequence can be described as *alienation*. The alienation of vulnerability refers to the result where a closed understanding of vulnerability creates a binary category: vulnerable x non-vulnerable. At its core, the problem concerns the fact that a restricted and negative reading of vulnerability allows the constitution of the vulnerable and the non-vulnerable subjects to stand opposite each other. The second we call *fixation*. Fixation refers to a situation wherein vulnerability leads to understanding another's circumstances as a persistent state of being. It relates to how the category of vulnerability is formed and what criterion becomes central. There is a difference in whether the vulnerability is understood principally as a feature of relations and situations, or exclusively concerning a given characteristic, typically ethnicity, gender, sexual orientation, or disability. The vulnerability would be dynamic in the former case since relations and situations change, while in the latter case it is somewhat fixed. The third criticism of the negative and closed understanding of vulnerability concerns *paternalism*. Paternalism is usually when the state restricts others to protect them from perceived harm. Specifically, those identified as vulnerable are perceived to be at risk of harm, and this risk is subsequently controlled.[31] In other words, it is no longer a matter of contesting that we are all vulnerable, or denying that artificial categories of vulnerability are being constructed that fail to take account of complex situations and lead to stigmatization. Instead, it is a critique of social control's extent that explicitly targets those identified as vulnerable.

On the other hand, if vulnerability is associated with openness rather than closure, it can prevent problematic consequences and become a human rights concept that can efficiently address structural problems.[32] The idea of openness can be well described by a reference to etymology. In *Inclinations*, Cavarero explains that vulnerability has two etymological meanings.[33] The common meaning is derived from the Latin word *vulnus*, which means wound. Our bodies are open to wounding, and the 'vulnus' is the result of a violent blow inflicted from the outside by a sharp instrument and with blunt force, tearing and gashing the skin.[34] The imaginary is violence, and the figure is a warrior. However, as Cavarero noted, there is yet another possible etymological conjecture. The meaning of *vulnus*, through its root *vel*, may also indicate 'above all skin that is smooth, hairless, and naked—skin

[29] ibid.
[30] Matiaško (n 20).
[31] Gilson (n 1) 33.
[32] Matiaško (n 20).
[33] Adriana Cavarero, *Inclinations: A Critique of Rectitude* (Stanford University Press 2016) 158–59.
[34] ibid.

that is, in other words, exposed to the highest degree'.[35] This reading concerns a body 'in its absolute nakedness, without hair, covering, or protection', a defenceless body. The image is not about violence, writes Cavarero, because the perception has changed as violence 'slips to the background and allows for the emergence of a tender and defenceless skin that inspires caresses'.[36] The figure is a newborn, naked and unveiled, and enters the world with 'paradigmatic nudity of the defenceless' that emphasizes an ethical responsibility of positive relationality.[37]

What combines these two readings is the idea of opening and contact with the other. In other words, vulnerability is relational and inter-subjective on the level that precedes any valuation; it is ambivalent, as noted by Estelle Ferrarese,[38] who explained that three dominant ideas cut across contemporary philosophical theories of vulnerability. These ideas are: (i) there is a prior or universal vulnerability that is inherent in human embodied nature, (ii) vulnerability is multi-dimensional because it depends on our universal characteristics as embodied beings but also on situations we find ourselves in, and (iii) vulnerability is an instrument with epistemological and normative significance.[39]

In other words, the starting point is that vulnerability does not express only a negative ontology in that vulnerabilities should be prevented or somehow remedied. Neither does it explain a strictly positive understanding that situations of vulnerability should be fostered or reproduced. Instead, it is a disposition to take on both negative and positive modalities. Simply put, there is a universal bodily vulnerability in the sense of the ability to be affected by others, or in other words, *openness* or disclosure.

Another typical feature of vulnerability is layering. For example, Ferrarese described this aspect as a picture within a picture when, usually, two levels are distinguished.[40] The universal one, which relates to mortality as a universal human experience, is followed by a particularistic dimension. The latter expresses the experience of a particular individual in the plurality of relationships and situations in which she finds herself during her life. Interdependence comes to the fore in the relationships that we necessarily enter, where the intertwining of negative and positive duties is shown by the fact that we and others refrain from something, tolerate something, or do something. At this, one might say derivative level, the flexibility of situations of vulnerability that are transforming, naturally or artificially, is pointed out.

This is a crucial point that means that vulnerability is situational. In *Frames of War*, Judith Butler distinguishes between two intersecting levels of embodied

[35] ibid.
[36] ibid.
[37] ibid.
[38] Estelle Ferrarese, *Vulnerability and Critical Theory* (Brill 2018).
[39] ibid.
[40] ibid 29.

vulnerability: precariousness and precarity.[41] Precariousness is defined as a shared condition of life, and it refers to life's destructibility, either by chance or will.[42] On the other hand, some circumstances affect this insecurity, increasing or decreasing it. According to Butler, the ones that increase insecurity are called states of precarity and are politically induced. In other words, precarity means politically induced circumstances in which insecurity is maximized, for example, when the distribution of resources or goods in society affects some, such as Roma. It can be said that precarity is exacerbated by an allocation of both common vulnerability and resources and concerns a situation when some people are 'differently exposed to injury, violence, and death', when they are 'at heightened risk of disease, poverty, starvation, displacement, and of exposure to violence without protection'.[43]

Gilson conceptualizes vulnerability similarly, though she emphasizes openness as a fundamental motive. According to Gilson, universal vulnerability—ontological vulnerability—is a condition that all share, and it should be distinguished from constituted patterns of vulnerability—situational vulnerabilities.[44] The ontological vulnerability is thematized as unavoidable openness that points to our bodily ability to affect and be affected.[45] It cannot be controlled or predicted because we cannot fully know what 'we are open to and how it will affect us'.[46] Yet, this actual state of openness makes the other conditions possible. It is a condition of potential and thus without any negative connotations. Situational vulnerabilities designate factual situations of concrete individuals or groups that can acquire both modalities, exclusionary and inclusionary. Among these situational vulnerabilities, she included, inter alia, 'psychological/emotional, corporeal, economic, political, and legal vulnerabilities, which can overlap, interacting and reinforcing one another'. Significantly, these situational vulnerabilities are 'inflected by the most salient social differences like race, class, gender and sexuality, disability, nationality, and so on',[47] yet these markers do not substitute them.

Situations of vulnerability, whether we think of them as politically induced circumstances or as situations, have two things in common. They are complex and multi-dimensional. Considering this, a new perspective emerges. The vulnerability no longer depends on the dominant identity, such as ethnicity. Still, it refers to the complexity of situations, such as historical unfairness represented, for example, by coercing Roma into a polluted, hazardous environment without access to safe drinking water and sanitation, or maintaining segregated areas without

41 Judith Butler, *Frames of War: When is Life Grievable?* (Verso 2009) 25–26.
42 ibid 25.
43 ibid 26.
44 Gilson (n 1) 137.
45 ibid 37.
46 ibid 127.
47 ibid 37.

access to water and sanitation, the situation of poverty and the rationale of choices Roma families have to make with the resources at their disposal, etc.

The dynamic aspect of situational vulnerabilities is followed by the third characteristic of vulnerability, which expresses its functional nature. Namely, vulnerability can be recognized as an *instrument* in two senses. First, vulnerability can be considered a guiding principle for the design of social institutions. In this case, the vulnerability would become a reference point for designing or transforming institutions[48] that can also address systemic discrimination in general and concerning access to water and sanitation in particular through laws, policies and practices. Second, vulnerability can also be recognized as a heuristic[49] or critical[50] instrument to determine what is unjust and what remedy to choose when the facts reveal a situation of systemic discrimination.

This instrumental nature of vulnerability allows us, in the first place, to recognize institutional responses to universal and situational vulnerabilities, including specific situational vulnerabilities of Roma. As we propose, this can be understood as the *epistemic* character of vulnerability in human rights adjudication and litigation. Moreover, the normative element serves as a tool not only for arguing cases from the perspective of vulnerability—focusing on the failure of institutions to react to situational vulnerabilities—but also to assess and criticize a judicial response to situational vulnerabilities. In other words, vulnerability can also be understood as a tool with transformative potential by disclosing harmful structures and naming those responsible for remedying identified precarity, including a long-lasting lack of access to drinking water and sanitation.

## 3. Roma, Environmental Justice, and Access to Water

European environmental programmes did not traditionally take an interest in studying the impact of systemic discrimination and socio-economic stratification processes.[51] However, there have been changes in the last decade in this respect and more attention is now paid to the fact that environmental problems of industrial societies are often on the shoulders of those who find themselves in the most vulnerable situation, and race, ethnicity, and class play a part in who has to live

[48] This position is typical for Joan Tronto, *Moral Boundaries. A Political Argument for an Ethic of Care* (Routledge 1993) 168.

[49] Martha Fineman, 'The Vulnerable Subject and the Responsive State' (2010) 60(2) Emory Law Journal 266. Martha Fineman argued within the human rights discourse that institutions should ensure resilience against vulnerabilities. Her position was criticized for not solving structural issues (see Ferrarese (n 38) 36). In our lexicon, resilience is not a solution to systemic discrimination, but a radical transformation is needed.

[50] Robert Goodin, *Protecting the Vulnerable: A Re-analysis of Our Social Responsibilities* (University of Chicago Press 1985) 191.

[51] David Harvey, *Justice, Nature and the Geography of Difference* (Blackwell 1996).

near toxic waste and flooding zones, or who has access to clean drinking water.[52] Environmental justice approaches looking at the distribution of harmful exposures and systematic discrimination by the institutions regulating the environment are gaining more traction. Highlighting the entropic, conflictual, and extractive aspects of the relationship between economy, people, and nature, the field of environmental justice integrates environmental, racial and social justice movements, it becomes a response to the development of societies producing and maintaining intensified situations of vulnerability and harms due to environmental degradation and limited access to public utilities.[53]

The environmental justice movement, first developed in the US in the 1970s and 1980s, was systematically conceptualized by Robert Bullard in his Houston Black Community Study on solid waste sites,[54] and the term environmental racism was coined by Benjamin Chavis in the Warren County, North Carolina suit in 1982.[55] It combines approaches aimed at protecting the survival of endangered species, national parks, and unique landscapes with the challenges of rural and urban poverty, racial and ethnic discrimination, exploitation of public resources, and quality of public spaces. Sometimes referred to as the environmentalism of the poor because people in specifically vulnerable situations, such as the poor, minorities, and indigenous groups, are often the main actors defending the environment, it concentrates on neglected urban spaces, environmental processes incorporated into social life, and responses to urbanization and industrialization.[56] The environmental justice context is invoked by the premise that a clean and healthy environment and fundamental public infrastructure need to be available, accessible, and affordable to all people regardless of their race, ethnicity, gender, and socio-economic status.[57] This, however, remains an aspirational horizon as there are many legal and institutional structures in place limiting some, typically members of minority groups such as Roma in benefitting equally and without discrimination in the development, implementation, and enforcement of environmental normative and policy frameworks.[58] As we argue later, one such structure can be demonstrated by how the Court approaches the concept of vulnerability of Roma, failing to recognize that what matters is especially

[52] Ghassan Hage, *Is Racism an Environmental Threat?* (Polity Press 2017).

[53] Joan Martínez-Alier, *Land, Water, Air and Freedom: The Making of World Movements for Environmental Justice* (Edward Elgar Publishing 2023).

[54] Robert Bullard, 'Solid Waste Sites and the Black Houston Community' (1983) 53(2–3) Sociological Inquiry 273–88.

[55] Benjamin Chavis, 'Foreword' in *Toxic Wastes and Race in the United States* (Commission for Racial Justice/United Church of Christ 1987).

[56] Joan Martínez-Alier, *The Environmentalism of the Poor. A Study of Ecological Conflicts and Valuation* (Edward Elgar Publishing 2002).

[57] David N Pellow, 'Toward a Critical Environmental Justice Studies' (2016) 13(2) Du Bois Review Social Science Research on Race 221–36.

[58] Eloi Laurent, 'Issues in Environmental Justice within the European Union' (2011) 70 Ecological Economics 1846–53.

the temporal character of systemic discrimination, deeply rooted for decades in many societies in Europe.

The phenomenon of systemic discrimination revealed in the background of the environmental justice context in recent decades has both spatial and temporal aspects. Eastern European countries top the charts for industrial pollution in Europe from coal plants,[59] and people have higher chances of dying as a result of pollution than those in the Western part of the continent, with Bosnia and Herzegovina, Albania, and Romania having the highest rates of pollution-related deaths.[60] In these countries, it is Roma who often live in residentially segregated communities in proximity to industrial zones.[61] Therefore, there is no surprise, as the European Environment Agency acknowledged, that environmental inequalities in Europe are linked to ethnicity, pointing out that 'Roma communities in Central and Eastern Europe are often excluded from basic services and exposed to environmental pollution, with serious health consequences'.[62]

Existing research demonstrates that across Europe, Roma are more likely to receive fewer environmental and public health benefits, while they are exposed to more of the harms.[63] How do Roma face environmental racism? On a symbolic level, Roma have traditionally been associated with trash and pollution through concepts of racial impurity and social disorder. They face a variety of environmental risks such as: (i) exposure to hazardous waste and chemicals through residency and/or work at contaminated sites; (ii) environmental costs of industrial development such as land, water, and air pollution; (iii) vulnerability to floods and other natural hazards; (iv) limited access to drinking water and sanitation; and (v) negligence in waste management practices.[64] Their disproportionate exposure to environmental harms and the lack of fundamental public infrastructure have direct health effects.[65] One of the main factors affecting Roma's health is the poor quality of urban space and public infrastructure in their neighbourhoods. Segregated, unstable, insecure (due to frequent evictions), densely populated, and inaccessible housing, lacking in access to electricity, piped drinking and utility

59 Health and Environment Alliance, *Health Impacts of Coal Fired Power Stations in the Western Balkans* (Heal 2016).

60 European Environment Agency, *Healthy Environment, Healthy Lives: How the Environment Influences Health and Well-being in Europe* (EEA 2019) 26.

61 Roman Matousek and Ludek Sykora, 'Environmental Justice and Residential Segregation in Czechia: The Case of Roma Resettlement in the Town of Vsetín' (2011) 46(2) AUC Geographica 81–94.

62 European Environment Agency (n 60) 16.

63 European Environmental Bureau, *Pushed to The Wastelands: Environmental Racism against Roma communities in Central and Eastern Europe* (EBB 2020).

64 Tamara Steger and Richard Filčák, 'Articulating the Basis for Promoting Environmental Justice in Central and Eastern Europe' (2008) 1(1) Environmental Justice 49–53; Kirsten Harper, Tamara Steger, and Richard Filčák, 'Environmental Justice and Roma Communities in Central and Eastern Europe' (2019) 19 Environmental Policy and Governance 251–68.

65 Daniela E Miranda, *Developing A Multi-Level Advocacy Framework for Roma Health at the Local Level* (University of Seville 2021).

water supplies and sanitation facilities, and neglected waste collection.[66] Forced to reside in spatially segregated and environmentally hazardous land of former industrial zones, agricultural farms, mines, and land endangered by floods (the worst-quality land that nobody else would claim), Roma are also disproportionately exposed to water, land, and air pollution.

Furthermore, indoor air pollution by open fire heating and the use of solid fuels for cooking remains high as Roma use coal and wood for heating and/or cooking significantly more frequently than majority populations in all countries.[67] The share of Romani households using wood for heating and cooking ranges from 62 per cent in Albania to 96 per cent in Montenegro. Hence, most of the Roma population is exposed to health risks stemming from carbon monoxide, benzene, particulate matter, and formaldehyde pollution. Romani women and children are particularly exposed to these health risks, causing respiratory diseases, as they spend more time within their homes.[68] Spatial segregation, social exclusion, and exposure to environmental harms, pollution, and noise annoyance can also produce serious mental distress. In the Czech Republic, a country leading the EU anti-Gypsyism statistics,[69] Roma consistently report a significantly higher prevalence of chronic headaches, stress, anxieties, depression, and addictions.[70]

These are some examples of how systemic discrimination against Roma is interwoven in the exposure and distribution of environmental harms that have serious impacts on their health, well-being, and economic performance. Indeed, there is a long history of Roma being coerced into an environment that has been polluted, hazardous, and without access to safe drinking water and sanitation, like those in Pata Rat in Romania, who were forced to live on toxic wastelands, heavily polluted areas, and river floodplains. Electromagnetic, radiation-producing high voltage electricity pylons surround Roma neighbourhoods in Tvarditsa in Bulgaria, and Tirana, Albania,[71] and one of the largest Roma neighbourhoods, the Luník IX Košice, Slovakia, was built near a large landfill site.[72]

Of all the examples of environmental harm, one stands out: the precarious situation of Roma in accessing drinking water and sanitation. European Roma

[66] Andrej Ivanov and others, *Integrated Household Surveys Among Roma Populations: One Possible Approach to Sampling used in the UNDP-World Bank-EC Regional Roma Survey 2011* (UNDP 2012) 30.

[67] ibid 27.

[68] ibid 28.

[69] European Union Agency for Fundamental Rights, *A Persisting Concern: Anti-Gypsyism as a Barrier to Roma Inclusion* (FRA 2018) 16–18.

[70] National Health Institute, *Health Support Programs in Excluded Neighbourhoods—Decreasing Health Inequalities* (NHI 2015).

[71] European Environmental Bureau (n 63); Rosalina Babourkova, 'The Environmental Justice Implications of Utility Privatization: The Case of the Electricity Supply in Bulgaria's Roma Settlement' (2010) 2/1 International Journal of Urban Sustainable Development 24–44.

[72] Richard Filčák and Ondřej Ficeri, 'Making the Ghetto at Luník IX in Slovakia: People, Landfill, and the Myth of the Urban Green Space' (2021) 57(3) Sociologický časopis/Czech Sociological Review 293–313.

are being left to live in unsafe environments, detrimental to their health and well-being, suffering disproportionately from the failures of public authorities to secure access to water and sanitation.[73] According to FRA, Roma have been facing 'severe deprivation' of access to safe drinking water.[74] For example, it was reported that one out of five Roma households (22 per cent) were without access to tap water inside their dwelling during the COVID-19 pandemic in 2021.[75] While this shows some improvement since FRA started collecting the data in 2016, when 30 per cent of Roma households were without water, it also demonstrates extremely slow development as the UNDP Roma household report in 2012 found that 'improved water sources, defined as having piped water inside the dwelling, are not available to almost one-third of Roma households surveyed throughout the (European) region'.[76]

In 2017, the European Roma Rights Centre (ERRC) reported that in two-thirds of visited Roma neighbourhoods in seven research countries, they were able to establish a prima facie case of ethnic discrimination in access to water.[77] There was either clear evidence that Roma experienced less favourable conditions for accessing water, or the less favourable conditions which they disproportionately experienced (compared to non-Roma communities) could not be objectively justified (indirect discrimination).[78] Similarly, detailed research in Slovakia in 2020 revealed that as many as 202 segregated Roma neighbourhoods were entirely without access to water; seventy Roma concentrations in mixed villages did not have access to water, although the majority did; 109 settlements used private wells as their only water source; in forty-seven settlements, the only water source used was from a public place; and in twenty-four settlements, people were entirely dependent on a non-running water source, such as a forest stream. The research estimates that tens of thousands of people might be affected by this situation.[79] Frequently, the nearest water source was more than 100 metres away, and in some places, Roma had to walk several kilometres. Distant water resources result in a high risk to public health from insufficient sanitation.

Surprisingly, international human rights catalogues do not list the right to water. One can find references to food, living conditions, housing, or health, but not water expressly. It was recognized by the UN Committee on Economic, Social and

[73] Marek Szilvasi, *A Thirst for Justice: Europe's Roma Denied Access to Clean Water and Sanitation* (ERRC 2017). See also: Richard Filčák, Marek Szilvasi, and Daniel Škobla, 'No Water for the Poor: The Roma Ethnic Minority and Local Governance in Slovakia' (2018) 41(7) Ethnic and Racial Studies 1390–407.

[74] FRA (n 69) 42–43, 47–49.

[75] European Union Agency for Fundamental Rights, *Roma in 10 European Countries* (EU Publications Office 2023).

[76] Ivanov and others (n 66).

[77] Szilvasi (n 73).

[78] ibid.

[79] Dušana Dokupilová, Richard Filčák, and Daniel Škobla, *Ensuring Access to Sanitation Infrastructure. Roma Settlements and Structural Inequalities in Slovakia* (CSPV 2020).

Cultural Rights in 2002[80] and later in 2010 by the UN General Assembly, following almost forty years of high-level negotiations. This period, marked by emerging human rights discourse on the right to water, translated into concrete actions. Roma communities in several countries started to mobilize, petition public authorities, and get involved in strategic litigation demanding clean water, waste removal, and better sanitation.

In 2016, Romani women who had been evicted unlawfully in Skopje appealed to the UN CEDAW, which condemned the eviction order and specifically urged the authorities to restore their access to water, electricity, and sanitation.[81] In 2018, a Romani community in the Albanian town of Fushe Kruje in 2018 won a case to get access to clean drinking water.[82] The Roma community from the Balzoni Camp in Bosnia and Herzegovina also won a case in which they had been denied access to drinking water in 2018.[83] In 2022, a district court in Slovakia ordered the municipality of Veľký Krtíš to provide access to water for Romani settlement.[84] While relying on claims framed by the right to water, these cases demonstrate trends in unequal access to drinking water for Roma and indicate lasting systemic discrimination due to ethnicity.

The *Hudorovič* case, initiated by two Roma families in 2014, was one of the first major litigation initiatives. It aimed to reshape the Court's approach to the question of whether there is a right to water under the European Convention—the Convention does not recognize a stand-alone right to water or a healthy environment—and what it means concerning Roma, who have been labelled as a particularly vulnerable group. In other words, in this case, two specific questions emerged. The recognition of a right to water, and its meaning concerning Roma. More specifically, whether the vulnerability of Roma, as perceived by the Court, justifies pushing the boundaries of Roma rights into the domain of environmental justice, necessitating not only universal recognition of the right to water but especially clearly defined responsibility for historic systemic discrimination. As we will

[80] The history goes back to 1977, when the United Nations Water Conference was held in Mar del Plata, Argentina. The conference's conclusion that people have the right to water was confirmed by the 1992 Agenda 21, adopted at the United Nations Conference on Environment and Development. Later, in 1996, the United Nations Conference on Human Settlements (Habitat II) recognized water and sanitation as part of the right to an adequate standard of living.

[81] UN CEDAW, Views adopted by the Committee under article 7(3) of the Optional Protocol, concerning communication No 107/2016.

[82] European Roma Rights Centre, 'Albanian Authorities Ordered to Supply Clean Water for Roma after Discrimination Case' (*ERRC* 12 December 2018) <http://www.errc.org/press-releases/albanian-authorities-ordered-to-supply-clean-water-for-roma-after-discrimination-case> accessed 26 September 2023.

[83] European Roma Rights Centre, 'Banzoli Roma Camp, Bosnia: Put up a Fence and this Would be a Real Concentration Camp' (*ERRC* 21 August 2018) <http://www.errc.org/news/banlozi-roma-camp-bosnia-put-up-a-fence-and-this-would-be-a-real-concentration-camp> accessed 26 September 2023.

[84] European Roma Rights Centre, 'Court Orders Access to Water for Romani Tenants in Velky Krtis, Slovakia' (*ERRC* 6 December 2022) <http://www.errc.org/news/court-orders-access-to-water-for-romani-tenants-in-velky-krtis-slovakia> accessed 26 September 2023.

try to show in the following analysis, the answer is negative, begging the question of whether the vulnerability of Roma, as a human rights principle, should not be approached from an entirely different perspective.

## 4. Close Reading of the *Hudorovič* Judgment

The critique of the Court's reasoning in the *Hudorovič* judgment can be broken down into three arguments against the backdrop of one concept associated with a negative reading of vulnerability. That concept is *reification*. Reification became part of the critical vocabulary, thanks to Marx.[85] Later, the idea was considerably developed by György Lukács[86] and thematized further by many others, including Jean-Paul Sartre,[87] Iris Marion Young,[88] and more recently Axel Honneth.[89] The concept is relevant for this chapter because it points to the mechanism of closure instead of openness, illuminating how a simplistic and limited reading of vulnerability instrumentalizes Roma and reinforces social exclusion.

When we discuss reification, we mean a process of forgetting that vulnerability is not an exclusive category or, equally, mistaking it for natural, even if it is artificial. We apply reification as an instrument for critique, relying on its three different modalities, as have been discussed by critical scholars. The first modality of reification, through which we can approach the application of vulnerability, is *alienation*. The idea of alienation can be connected to reification as thematized by Honneth in his book *Reification: A New Look at an Old Idea*. According to Honneth, reification can be read as 'forgetting' of having recognized the other.[90] He argues that the reification cannot be equated with the general process of objectification of social relationships, but instead with disregarding the primal recognition that two individuals accord each other. In a nutshell, the reification of others results from a mechanism when others are treated like things because the original recognition is suspended. As Christian Lazzeri puts it, by 'deactivation of any identification with others and thus of any capacity for affective participation'.[91] The emphasis on deactivation of intersubjective recognition can explain that reification that alienates the other requires an effort and a vehicle. In human rights law, vulnerability can be such a medium if understood as a closed concept and based on typical negative reading, promoting the myth of the invulnerable subject. At the core, the argument

[85] See the short introduction in Iris Marion Young, *Responsibility for Justice* (OUP 2011) 155.
[86] Georg Lukács, 'Reification and the Consciousness of the Proletariat' in Georg Lukács (ed), *History and Class Consciousness: Studies in Marxist Dialectics* (MIT Press 1968).
[87] Jean-Paul Sartre, *Critique of Dialectical Reason* (New Left Books 1976) 176.
[88] Young (n 85) 154–57.
[89] Axel Honneth, *Reification: A New Look at an Old Idea* (OUP 2008).
[90] ibid 56.
[91] Christian Lazeri, 'Réification et reconnaissance. Une discussion avec Axel Honneth' (2011) 38(2) Revue du MAUSS 259–85.

is that if some are labelled by law as exclusively vulnerable, others are deemed invulnerable. Then, the law forgets what the invulnerable inherently shares with all others. This derecognition creates an artificial distance that can grow, paradoxically, by its recognition in human rights adjudication.

The alienation of a group labelled as vulnerable refers to the consequence where a closed understanding of vulnerability creates a binary category: vulnerable versus non-vulnerable. Principally, the problem concerns the fact that a restricted and negative reading of vulnerability allows the constitution of the vulnerable and the non-vulnerable subjects to stand opposite each other. The perspective of how we read vulnerability shapes the imagination about the subject and her identity. People tend to see themselves in categories and with an identity, and their self-perspective can be reinforced differently. If others are labelled as vulnerable based on a characteristic that is unique in a certain way, it can quickly become an exclusive label. Distance arises because the constitutive characteristic of the subject is not her vulnerability connecting her to others. Instead, vulnerability becomes a mode of demarcation and separation.

Turning to the *Hudorovič* judgment, the alienation is revealed with an emphasis on the idea of choice. Reading the judgment, it appears the Court rejected Roma families' complaints on two grounds: the applicants chose not to use their social benefits and invest them to improve their access to public infrastructure, and, at the same time, the state had adopted a plan to improve living conditions in the settlements, sufficiently reflecting their vulnerability. The starting point of legal reasoning was the applicants' precarious situation; however, it was gradually relativized on the grounds of hypothetical autonomy. The Court noted, at the outset, that 'the domestic and international materials referred to by the parties show that a considerable part of the Roma population in Slovenia, who live in illegally built settlements that are often removed from the densely populated areas with a public water-distribution system, face greater obstacles than the majority in accessing basic utilities'.[92] Yet, this factual situation did not justify the allocation of specific positive obligations on the grounds of vulnerability,[93] because the judges decided to shift the burden of the effects of segregation and extreme poverty onto the applicants.

The argument of choice was raised in two circumstances. The first concerns the place where Roma families lived and the availability of social housing. The Court was unsure 'whether the applicants had a realistic possibility of relocating to settlements with better … or obtaining alternative accommodation, such as public housing units at a subsidised rent rate', yet most judges concluded that '[n]evertheless, irrespective of whether public housing was available, the Court can only conclude that the applicants remained in their respective settlements by

[92] *Hudorovič and Others* (n 8) para 143.
[93] ibid para 142.

choice.'[94] The second circumstance in which the choice was emphasized concerns the use of social benefits. According to the Court, 'the applicants were not prevented from making use of their social benefits, allowing them to provide for their essential needs', and 'while it falls upon the State to address the inequalities in the provision of access to safe drinking water which disadvantage Roma settlements, this cannot be interpreted as including an obligation to bear the entire burden of providing running water to the applicants' homes'.[95]

The choice argument is based on the presumption of its rationality, not the availability of options. However, the assessment of rationality is influenced by the social, economic, and cultural conditions of those who define it. The other adapts or remains unintelligible and alien. The vulnerability of the Roma presupposed this alienness, so the irrational choice corresponded to the assumption of vulnerability and reinforced their otherness and the associated imagination of the Roma as a group for whom access to drinking water and sanitation is not as significant an issue as it is for the rational—invulnerable—majority. The practical consequence is the emphasis on emergency and limited solutions. Two circumstances demonstrate this. First, when the Court was open to adopting an exceptional position on access to public infrastructure by over-emphasizing Roma's specific needs and different lifestyle. In concrete terms, it was when the Court distinguished between interim and permanent solutions, but then it was satisfied with proof of interim solutions for short-lived water tanks.[96] Under the framing of the nomadic Roma lifestyle in the Court's case law, the options of distant water sources became acceptable for the applicants, notwithstanding their living a sedentary lifestyle like the majority of Roma in Slovenia.[97]

At the same time, the vulnerability justified a general requirement to improve Roma's living conditions, but only in the physical area delimited by their alterity. As the Court expressly stated, Slovenian authorities were not completely inactive, when referring to vulnerability. The domestic authorities recognized the vulnerability of the Roma community and acknowledged the need for positive measures aimed at improving their precarious living conditions.[98] That activity, which was sufficient for the judges, consisted of adopting a plan to settle the property rights to the land on which the Roma settlements stood and legalize their dwellings and provide essential public services to those places.[99] In other words, the vulnerability of Roma could have necessitated the adoption of positive measures by the state but only in areas defined by the horizon of existing segregation. The desegregation of settlements and inclusive social housing was not on the table. Roma's historical and

94 ibid para 148.
95 ibid para 156.
96 ibid para 149.
97 ibid para 120.
98 ibid para 147.
99 ibid.

unjust exclusion for ethnic reasons from those localities where the majority lived, and the absence of legal possibilities to connect their homes to water and sanitation networks, were reified by ostensibly socially just policies based on the alienation of their vulnerability.

The whole argument about rationality and choice could be interpreted differently. The choices of Romani families seem irrational to most. However, given their vulnerability, we cannot judge their rationality because it would be the dominant rationality of the majority. However, without reconceptualizing vulnerability as a whole, such a reformulation could lead to another problem, namely the fixation of a particular characteristic, eg irrationality, as dominant for a specific group of people. And this would be the problem of so-called fixation, which is the second mode of reification characterized by the denial of responsibility, as observed by Jean-Paul Sartre and especially Iris Marion Young in *Responsibility for Justice*. According to Sartre, as quoted by Young, reification points to 'the necessity imposed by the structures of society on members of a social group, that they should live the fact that they belong to the group and, thereby, to society as a whole, as a molecular statute'.[100] Within this perspective, reification becomes a process when actors treat 'products of human action in particular social relations as though they are things or natural forces'.[101] The eventual avoidance of responsibility seems to combine these two positions. From the viewpoint of vulnerability, one is typically vulnerable because one shares specific characteristics with a particular group, and one is invulnerable if standing outside. Once the vulnerability is attributed to a group or an individual, it leads to a simplistic perception of their problems. It does not consider the intertwined situations and the different levels of the issue at stake, which is open to its full extent. And if a group already faces stigma, it leads to its reinforcement. The label of vulnerability becomes a representation of a particular characteristic or quality. It reifies not only the situation of those who are vulnerable but also problematic structures that remain unchallenged. In such a constellation, responsibility is flattened.

Fixation refers to a situation wherein vulnerability leads to understanding another's circumstances as a persistent state of being. It relates to how the category of vulnerability is formed and what criterion becomes central. There is a difference in whether the vulnerability is understood principally as a feature of relations and situations, or exclusively concerning a given characteristic, typically skin colour, gender, sexual orientation, or disability. The vulnerability would be dynamic in the former case, since relations and situations change, while in the latter case, it is somewhat fixed.

When the Court thematizes vulnerability exclusively on the grounds of a particular characteristic, that characteristic becomes dominant and overrides

100 Young (n 85) 156.
101 ibid 154.

everything else. As a result, the problems of those identified as vulnerable are seemingly simple, even when complex. In other words, fixed vulnerability allows blindness to other circumstances, eg historical injustice and inaction of authorities. This happened precisely in the *Hudorovič* case. All parties relied on vulnerability with its fixed characteristic, namely the different lifestyle of Roma,[102] which overshadowed other relevant circumstances. The wording of 'different lifestyle' can be traced back to *Buckley v the United Kingdom* and *Chapman v the United Kingdom,* two decisions that concerned the refusal of planning permission to enable the Roma family to live in caravans on land they owned. In both cases, Roma women were recognized as vulnerable because of their ethnicity, and their vulnerability was expressly linked to their otherness—their alleged nomadic lifestyle. As one can read in *Chapman*, 'the vulnerable position of Gypsies as a minority means that some special consideration' should be given not only to their 'specific needs' but also to 'their different lifestyle'.[103] The Court emphasized culture and defined vulnerability in a manner that disregarded the fact that the applicants were mothers in a particular social and economic situation. The crux of the whole issue was safe housing for families with children. Judge Repík described this omission in his dissenting opinion in *Buckley.* He noted that there 'was never any mention of the applicant's right to respect for her home or of the importance of that right to her given her financial and family situation. Nor was any account taken of the possible consequences for the applicant and her children if she was evicted from her land.'

Repík's insight is also significant for our discussion. His reading of the *Buckley* case suggests a more complex, multi-layered, and dynamic understanding of vulnerability, one that goes beyond a simple and fixed construction of the concept that may contribute to the stigmatization of Roma. Repíks suggests that vulnerability is a situational phenomenon. The economic and family situation can be just as critical as cultural aspects. In other words, the emphasis on situational perspective means that various, possibly equally important circumstances must be considered. Thus, the idea of a unique culture, however relevant it may be, is only a sole circumstance that should not override other circumstances. Each case can reveal specific circumstances, some more relevant than others. It is primarily the judges' job to identify those circumstances that are revealed in the particular situation of applicants and consider them, taking into account that different circumstances create an embossment metaphorically, be it, for example, poverty or historical injustice represented by coerced living in a place affected by environmental burden.

This situational understanding of vulnerability, transparently explained in the judgment, can, in our opinion, prevent alienation and fixation, as well as paternalism, the third mode of reification, by revealing what exact circumstances

[102] *Hudorovič and Others* (n 8) paras 120, 134, and 142.
[103] *Chapman v the United Kingdom* App no 27238/95 (ECtHR, 18 January 2001) para 96.

have been reflected as crucial and especially why precisely those have prevailed. Paternalism can be described as 'the interference with a person's liberty of action justified by reasons referring exclusively to the welfare, good, happiness, needs and interests or values of the person being coerced'.[104] It is often invoked as a problematic consequence of a closed understanding of vulnerability, and it is inherently linked to alienation and fixation. As Butler observes in her essay 'Rethinking Vulnerability and Resistance', if group vulnerability is reified within 'human rights discourse or legal regimes', the group is 'fixed in a political position of powerlessness and lack of agency'.[105] In other words, it is when alienated and fixed vulnerability 'fortifies a paternalistic form of power'.[106] In this view, paternalism represents a unique realization of reification directed against those alienated and fixed as vulnerable.

Considering paternalism, we make a distinction between particularistic paternalism, a situation when the state acts virtuously, in the best interests of the vulnerable, and may even violate norms for the benefit of others who are powerless and universal paternalism, a situation when formal rules are universally enforced, to fulfil the public interest and the role of public authorities as just *pater patriae*, regardless of unique circumstances. Turning to the *Hudorovič* judgment, we perceive the dynamics of both these seemingly contradictory paternalistic strategies.

The first strategy is apparent in a subtle manner in how the Court accepted the government's position about their inaction concerning solving the illegal status of Roma settlements. Localities without access to water where the applicant's family lived were, in one instance, marshy agricultural land that was categorized 'as the best category of agricultural land, where construction of residential buildings is not allowed', and in the second instance, the settlement was 'located outside of settlement areas under high-voltage power lines where construction is not allowed owing to electromagnetic radiation'.[107] In the judgment, we read the government's argument that the illegal status of Roma settlements had not been tolerated, and inhabitants of both Roma settlements had been ordered to remove illegally constructed buildings and restore the land to its previous state. Yet, '[a]lthough those decisions had been enforceable, they had not subsequently been enforced, since many of the buildings had housed families with children who would have had to be provided with alternative accommodation in the event of demolition.'[108]

The argument that the government did not act in the case of eviction and demolition orders because of the presence of Roma children was primarily aimed at

[104] Gerald Dworkin, 'Paternalism' in Richard Wasserstrom (ed), *Morality and the Law* (Wadsworth 1971) 108.

[105] Judith Butler, 'Rethinking Vulnerability and Resistance' in Judith Butler, Zeynep Gambetti, and Leticia Sabsay (eds), *Vulnerability in Resistance* (Duke University Press 2016) 25.

[106] Judith Butler, *The Force of Non-Violence. An Ethico-Political Bind* (Verso 2020) 71.

[107] *Hudorovič and Others* (n 8) para 9.

[108] ibid para 128.

presenting the authorities' inaction as a virtue. At the same time, there was obvious national authorities' insistence on the illegal status of settlements when refusing to provide an effective drinking water access solution. As a result, Roma families have found themselves in a cycle of legal powerlessness. The acknowledged vulnerability, because of its construction on a cultural background, did not challenge this powerlessness but rather justified it because of alienation and fixation. Indeed, the judges did not dismiss the government's argument concerning the eviction orders and did not underline the state's responsibility to ensure that the legal status of Roma settlements did not impede the enjoyment of the right to water. This was criticized by Judge Pavli, who—relying also on vulnerability—argued that 'in the specific context of Roma communities, other vulnerable groups (including children) or even the general population in some respects, the legality argument has been repeatedly rejected by this Court as not constituting sufficient justification, on its own, for serious interferences with Article 8 rights'.[109]

Further, the over-emphasis on formal arguments was also evident in the government's strategy to argue procedural obstacles before the Court: false identity application, expired mother's power of attorney, and incorrect residency,[110] which the Court rightly rejected as they did not prevent the identification of the applicants. However, emphasis on formal rules remains a particular challenge for judges. It should be treated carefully because it not only overshadows the core of the human rights issue—in other words, it overshadows centres of interest in the embossment of vulnerability -but also traps applicants in an impasse. The consequence of such overshadowing can be demonstrated in the Court's decision on health impact. The Court concluded that only proof of serious health risk would 'justify imposing a burden on the State to take any steps with regard to the applicants' respective situations'.[111] The applicants did not provide such proof, and as a consequence, the Court could conclude that the 'measures adopted by the State in order to ensure access to safe drinking water and sanitation for the applicants took account of the applicants' vulnerable position'.[112] However, as Jjudge Pavli noted, the '[l]ack of access to a clean water supply and basic sanitation for extended periods of time is, by *definition* [emphasis added], a predicament that adversely affects core private life interests and basic human dignity'.[113]

Another paternalistic tendency was also in place when the Court requested the applicants to quantify what would constitute a meaningful alternative to adequate access to water.[114] As Pavli notes, it is 'after all, very hard to accept that noise

109 ibid dissenting opinion of Judge Pavli para 13.
110 ibid paras 78–79.
111 ibid para 157.
112 ibid paras 110 and 158.
113 ibid Dissenting Opinion of Judge Pavli para 7.
114 ibid paras 122 and 154.

pollution or unpleasant smells can be significant enough nuisances to interfere with a person's personal and home life, but that living without safe water for decades is somehow not as significant'.[115]

Considering this critique, the question arises of how the Court should have construed its reasoning. First, the Court should have delved into the evolving and politically conditioned nature of precarity experienced by Roma. As we argue, vulnerability is not a monolithic concept but a multi-layered phenomenon requiring nuanced understanding. In this regard, the Court ought to have identified specific circumstances that exacerbated the precarious situation of the Roma community in the case at hand. It appears to us that the interconnected central circumstances were time and space. The *Hudorovič* case, first and foremost, concerned the environmental injustice towards Roma as a historical phenomenon, distinguishable from culture and economy. This circumstance can be called the historicity of systemic discrimination against Roma. Moreover, the prolonged inaction of authorities over thirty years further compounded the vulnerable situation of Roma communities. This glaring neglect perpetuated their marginalization and signalled a systemic failure in addressing their precarious situation.

Furthermore, the territorial segregation experienced by Roma communities, stemming from historical decisions made by authorities, highlights the limited agency and actual choices available to them concerning a place to live. As Judge Pavli noted, 'Roma communities, including those in the present case, may not have had a genuine choice in settling in certain informal locations in the past'.[116] And finally, the problem of access to water and sanitation exceeds national boundaries, shedding light on a pervasive pattern of structural discrimination against Roma across Europe. Treating it as an isolated situation in Slovenia overlooks the transnational nature of the issue and the interconnectedness of Roma communities' struggles. The scale of the problem cannot be understated, as it affects a significant number of people throughout Europe. This accentuates the gravity of the situation and the urgent need for comprehensive action to address systemic inequalities.

In conclusion, a holistic approach to understanding the vulnerable situation of Roma communities would necessitate, in our opinion, considerations of historical environmental injustice, governmental inaction, transnational dynamics, the scale of the issue, and the impact of territorial segregation. Against this background, the radically reconceptualized vulnerability would have the potential to frame a more accurate picture of systemic discrimination faced by Roma across Europe in its complexity, pushing the boundaries of human rights into a new, more attentive landscape.

[115] ibid Dissenting Opinion of Judge Pavli para 6.
[116] ibid para 14.

## 5. Conclusion

In her famous discussion with Axel Honneth, Nancy Fraser explores the nuances between affirming existing rights, statuses, and identities in social struggles versus engaging in their transformative deconstruction.[117] Fraser argues that while strategies centred around affirmation may have their utility in specific contexts, they also carry the risk of solidifying existing power structures by essentializing rights and identities. By employing fixed—or in our lexicon closed—frames by lawyers arguing human rights cases and judges deciding them, there's a danger of entrenching forms of subordination already existing within society.

Conversely, although inherently riskier, transformative argumentative strategies possess the potential to challenge and dismantle these fixed categories. By nature, they work towards de-reifying or breaking down these rigid constructs, allowing for more fluid and inclusive understandings of rights and identities. This approach aims to disrupt existing power dynamics rather than perpetuate them. In essence, Fraser advocates for a critical examination of the strategies employed in social struggles, weighing the benefits of affirmation against the potential pitfalls of reification while also acknowledging the transformative potential of strategies that seek to deconstruct established norms and identities, such as the ones that have been associated with Roma, whose identity, as it seems, concern primarily, as the Court repeats relentlessly, in their 'different lifestyle'.

In our opinion, approaches determining legal arguments in cases with the potential to push the boundaries of the human rights paradigm, such as the *Hudorovič* case, should involve utilizing reasoning to bring about positive changes in social and legal structures, in Fraser's words, should be transformative rather than affirmative. These strategies should aim at de-reification, which entails breaking down rigid and historical structures and challenging fixed identities and rights that may contribute to reinforcing existing situations of systemic discrimination. By targeting concepts that contribute to reification, such as vulnerability, as we tried to show in this particular context, and endeavouring to break their caging aspect, strategic litigation can actively work towards demystifying abstract notions and their hidden potential of subordination to others.

The intricate interplay between vulnerability and historical fairness in the legal arena underscores the complexities of human rights litigation if it seeks the transformation of precarity. The judgment in the *Hudorovič* case, which diverged from the conclusions drawn by expert bodies such as the Council of Europe's ECRI and the Slovenian Ombudsman, reflects the independent and sometimes contentious nature of judicial interpretation. In this case, the Court served dual roles. On the one hand, it actively established whether there was an interference with

[117] Nancy Fraser and Axel Honneth, *Redistribution or Recognition? A Philosophical - Political Exchange* (Verso 2003) 76–77.

the Convention's rights, which required a meticulous examination of the facts and the applicable legal framework. The conclusion that access to water and sanitation falls within Article 8 of the Convention is an improvement. However, it is hardly surprising or ground-breaking. The second less sympathetic role is a failure to adopt an adequate perspective to long-lasting precarity.

We tried to demonstrate that the vehicle allowing the Court to address the facts of the case from the outset differently could have been vulnerability, a concept well-established in the Court's jurisprudence; however, under the condition that it is understood from the situational perspective. Situational vulnerability would express an objective description of the situation of a social group in its historical dimension. This situation would need to be understood as a precarious situation, and the role of institutions further examined accordingly. Second, vulnerability can turn the attention to the architecture of how the state copes with the objectively existing precarious situation of certain groups. More emphasis would be placed on institutions and their competence and efficiency in addressing circumstances that produce vulnerable situations and far less on the applicants and their perceived actions or inactions. Third, the question of historical environmental injustice and the allocation of positive obligations to transform the situation of the Roma would likely come to the centre of consideration. The vulnerability would serve as a practical concept justifying concrete and targeted actions to correct those circumstances, considering its systemic nature, regardless of how seemingly challenging that would be for state institutions. Precisely, this systemic nature justifies a stronger emphasis on targeted steps that the state must take to remedy the situation of systemic discrimination faced by Roma living in territories burdened by environmental problems.

# Index

*For the benefit of digital users, indexed terms that span two pages (e.g., 52–53) may, on occasion, appear on only one of those pages.*